ENGLISH PLACE-NAME SOCIETY

VOLUME LXXVII FOR 1999–2000

GENERAL EDITOR

VICTOR WATTS

THE PLACE-NAMES OF LINCOLNSHIRE

PART VI

THE SURVEY OF ENGLISH PLACE-NAMES
UNDERTAKEN WITH THE APPROVAL AND SUPPORT OF
THE BRITISH ACADEMY

THE PLACE-NAMES OF
LINCOLNSHIRE

BY

KENNETH CAMERON

in collaboration with

JOHN FIELD and JOHN INSLEY

PART SIX

THE WAPENTAKES
OF MANLEY AND ASLACOE

NOTTINGHAM
ENGLISH PLACE-NAME SOCIETY
2001

Published by the English Place-Name Society

Registered Charity No. 257891

© English Place-Name Society 2001

ISBN 0 904889 62 9

Typeset by Paul Cavill & Printed in Great Britain
by Woolnough Bookbinding, Irthlingborough, Northants.

This volume is dedicated to the memory of

John Field

who worked with me on all six volumes of

The Place-Names of Lincolnshire

Sadly Professor Cameron did not live to see the publication of this volume. He died suddenly at Tealby, his base for the study of Lincolnshire place-names, on March 10th, aged 78. He had, however, read the proofs and completed the index, and had begun the preparation of volume seven. His loss to the Society and to place-name study will be irreparable. A full appreciation of the man and his work will be published elsewhere.

Victor Watts
General Editor

CONTENTS

PREFACE

The sixth part of *The Place-Names of Lincolnshire* covers two Wapentakes in the West Riding of Lindsey, those of Manley and of Aslacoe. The area is bounded on the north by the Humber, on the east in part by the Ancholme, on the west again in part by the Trent and on the south by Saxilby, Burton by Lincoln, Riseholme, Nettleham and then the R. Witham.

Once more I have to thank my friends in the Lincolnshire Archive Office for their constant help during the many years I have been collecting material there. In particular my special thanks must go to Mr Nigel Colley, but unfortunately this is the last time I shall have cause to pay my respects to him in this way. Changes in the staff of the Archives Office have resulted in Mr Colley having moved elsewhere. I have remarked on previous occasions that the text of the volume itself indicates how many of the Archives' Collections have been searched and the time and energy spent by members of the staff to place them at my disposal.

My wife led me on our numerous "practical place-name trips" around the area looking at the topography of individual places and fields. In addition she has checked the text and also prepared the index. My debt of gratitude to her is considerable, not least, as I have said before, for her constant support and encouragement whilst literally living with Lincoln-shire place-names over the years. Once again, my friends Mr John Field and Dr John Insley have helped so considerably in the preparation of this volume that their names appear as collaborators on the title-page. Mr Field prepared the draft of the field-names of each parish and made many suggestions of etymology, most of which have been silently incorporated into the text. Only he will know his contributions to this book. Dr Insley has read all the text and with his expertise in the field of personal names and in philology generally he has made a considerable contribution which enhances the scholarship of the book.

At this point, I heard of the sudden death of Mr Field. He had completed checking the final parish and had sent me his notes only six days before his death. I have decided in view of his considerable contribution to the published volumes of the Lincolnshire Survey to dedicate this volume to his memory. Only he knows how much he has contributed to the text and perhaps that is how it should be. I have lost a firm and loyal friend.

My grateful thanks go to Mrs Anne Tarver who once again has drawn the detailed map of the parishes of the wapentake. It is, of course, a very great pleasure to thank Mrs Janet Rudkin and Dr Paul Cavill for all their help. Mrs Rudkin copied the text as it was being prepared so many times that she must have almost known it by heart. Dr Cavill guided the text of the volume through the press. His patience, skill and attention to detail are remarkable. Nothing has been too much trouble to them both and they have earned my very special thanks. All errors are of course entirely my own.

University of Nottingham   Kenneth Cameron

ADDITIONS to the ABBREVIATIONS and BIBLIOGRAPHY printed in THE PLACE-NAMES OF LINCOLSHIRE PARTS 1–4

BH	Documents in the Brown, Hudson and Hudson Collection in LAO
Elwes	Documents in the Elwes Collection in LAO
Healey	Hilary Healey, *A Fenland Landscape Glossary for Lincolnshire*, Lincolnshire County Council, 1997
LRA	Documents in the Lincolnshire River Authority Collection in LAO
MaltCart	The Cartulary of Malton Priory, BM. MS Cotton Claudius D. xi (c1250), forms supplied by the late Mr J.T. Fowler
Red	Documents in the Redbourne Collection in LAO
Shef	Documents in the Sheffield Collectiom in LAO
TGH	Documents in the Taylor, Glover and Hill Collection in LAO
VEPN	*The Vocabulary of English Place-Names*, CENS Nottingham, in progress
WinteringhamPD	Winteringham Parish Documents in LAO
WintertonPD	Winterton Parish Documents in LAO

NOTES ON ARRANGEMENT

(1) Following the names West Riding, R. Ancholme, R. Humber, R. Trent and Manley Wapentake, the parishes in the Wapentake are set out in alphabetical order.

(2) Each of the parish names is printed in bold type as a heading. Within each parish the names are arranged as follows: (i) the parish name; (ii) other major names (i.e. names of sizeable settlements and names of primary historical or linguistic interest), each treated separately in alphabetical order; (iii) all minor names (i.e. the remaining names recorded on the 1906 edition of the O.S. 6" map, as well as some names that are "lost" or "local", *v. infra*, again treated in alphabetical order but in a single paragraph; (iv) field-names (which include other unidentified minor names) in small type, (a) modern field-names, normally those recorded after 1750, with any older spellings of these names in brackets and printed in italics, (b) medieval and early modern field-names, i.e. those recorded before about 1750, printed in italics, the name in each group being arranged alphabetically.

(3) Place-names no longer current, i.e. those not recorded on the editions of the 1" and 6" maps are marked "lost". This does not mean that the site to which the name refers is unknown. Such names are normally printed in italics when referred to elsewhere.

(4) Place-names marked "local" are those not recorded on the 1" and 6" O.S. maps but which are still current locally.

(5) The local and standard pronunciation of a name, when of interest and not readily suggested by the modern spelling, are given in phonetic symbols in square brackets after the name.

(6) The early spellings of each name are presented in the order "spelling, date, source". When, however, the head-form of a name is followed only by a "date and source", e.g. COUNTESS CLOSE, 1768 *EnclA*, 1828 Bry, the spelling in 1768 *EnclA* and in 1828 Bry is the same as that of the head-form.

(7) In explaining the various place-names and field-names, summary reference is frequently made, by printing the elements in bold type, to the analysis of elements which will appear in the final volume of the

Lincolnshire County Survey, and more particularly to *English Place-Name Elements* (EPNS 25, 26), to *Addenda and Corrigenda* to these volumes in *English Place-Name Society Journal* 1 and to *The Vocabulary of English Place-Names* (CENS, in progress). In many of the minor names and field-names, the meaning is so obvious as to need no comment or so uncertain as not to warrant it. For personal names which are cited without authority, reference should be made for Old English names to Redin, Searle and Feilitzen, for Old (Continental) German to Förstemann PN and Forssner, and for English surnames to Bardsley and Reaney (for details of these sources, *v*. Abbreviations and Bibliography in *The Place-Names of Lincolnshire*, Part 1 (EPNS 58).

(8) Unprinted sources of the early spellings of place-names are indicated by printing the abbreviation for the source in italics. The abbreviation for a printed source is printed in roman type. The exact page, folio or membrane is only given where the precise identification of an entry is of special importance, e.g. *AddReg i*, f.71.

(9) Where two dates are given for a spelling e.g. Hy2 (m13), 1190 (Ed1), the first is the date at which the document purports to have been composed and the second the date of the copy that has come down to us (in many cases the latter is a cartulary, ecclesiastic or lay). Sources whose dates cannot be fixed to a particular year are dated by century, e.g. 11, 12, 13, 14 etc. (often more specifically e13, m13, l13 etc., early, mid and late 13th century respectively), by regnal date, e.g. Ed1, Eliz, Jas1 etc., or to a range of years, e.g. 1150–60, 1401–2 etc.

(10) The sign (p) after the source indicates that the particular spelling given appears in the source as a person's surname, not primarily as a reference to a place.

(11) When a letter or letters (sometimes words or phrases) in an early place-name are enclosed in brackets, it means that spellings with and without the enclosed letter(s), words or phrases occur. When only one part of a place-name spelling is given as a variant, preceded or followed by a hyphen or ~, it means that the particular spelling only differs in respect of the cited part from the preceding or following spelling. Occasional spellings given in inverted commas are usually editorial translations or modernisations, and whilst they have no authority linguistically they have chronologically.

(12) Cross-references to other names are given with *supra* or *infra*, the former referring to a name already dealt with, the latter to a name dealt with later in the text.

(13) Putative forms of personal names and place-name elements which will appear asterisked in the concluding volume of this Survey are not always asterisked in the text, although the discussion will often make it clear which are on independent record and which are inferred.

(14) In order to save space in presenting the early spellings of a name, *et passim* and *et freq* are sometimes used to indicate that the preceding form(s) occur respectively from time to time or frequently from the date of the last quoted source to that of the following one, or to the present day.

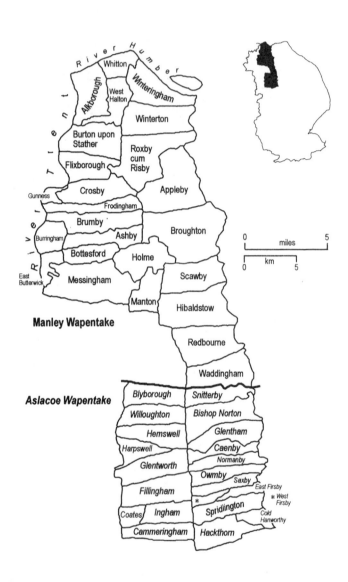

THE WAPENTAKES OF MANLEY AND ASLACOE
Based upon the 1963 Ordnance Survey four miles to one inch map,
with permission of Her Majesty's Stationery Office.
© Crown Copyright.

West Riding

West Treding 1086 DB, *Westreeding* (5x) 1086 ib, *West Triding* c1115 LS, *Westrithing* c1160, 1183–89 RA iv, 1219 Cur, 1311 Ipm, *West Trithing'* 1275 RH, *Westtrithing* 1276 ib, 1287 *Ass*, 1319 Pat, *Westriding* 1190 RA ix, 1201 Cur, *Westeredinge* c1213 Gir, *Westrething'* 1276 RH.

The division of Lindsey, like the county of Yorkshire, was into three parts — North, South and West Riding. Riding is derived from ON **þriðjungr**, late OE **þriðing** 'a third part'; initial *þ*- has become *t*-through AN influence, cf. North Riding, PN L **2**, 7, and was absorbed by the final *-t* of **west** to give *Riding*.

River-Names

ANCHOLME, R.

neah þare éa þe is genemnod Oncel c1000 Saints

Ancolnam 1150–60 Dane, c1160 RA iv, *Ancolna* 1150–60 Dane,
  Hy2 (1319) Dugd vi, *Ancolnie* eHy2 Dane, *Ancolnia* Hy2 (l13)
  Stix, *Ancolne* 1160–66 Dane, Hy2 (e14) Selby, 112 Dane, c1275
  LNQ vii, 1288 IpmR, 1290, 1294, 1312, 1362 Pat, 1684 *Yarb,*
  Ancoln R1 (1318) Ch, 1316 *KR,* 1330 *Foster,* 1345 *FF,* 1349 Pat,
  1369 Ipm, 1598 *Nelthorpe, old Ancoln* 1668, 1674 *Terrier,* 1702
  Nelthorpe

Ancolm 1256 FF, 1275 RH, 1329, 1331, 1345 Pat, 1353 *Cor,* 1356,
  1391 Pat, *Ancolm flu.* 1536–39 Leland, *Ancolme* 1577 Harrison,
  1638 SP, *old Ancolme* 1690 *Terrier*

Ancholm e13 *LandsCh,* 1275 RH, 1287, 1289 Ipm, 1292 RSu, *-holme*
  1288 Inqaqd, *old Ancholme* 1656 *Red,* 1788 *Terrier, Anchom*
  1457 WillsPCC, *Ankholm* 1285, 1334 Ipm, 1365 Pat, 1374 Ipm,
  1374, 1375 Works, 1411 Pat, *-holme* 1422, 1482 Pat, 1544 LP ii,
  1640 Imb, *Ankeholme* 1510 *BP,* 1536–39 Leland, 1538 *AOMB
  211,* 1550, 1554 Pat

Ankam flu: 1576 Saxton, 1610 Speed, *~ fluv.* 1675 Ogilby

the drayne or new Cutt called newe Anckholme 1657 *Yarb, old
  Anckholme* 1680 *ib*

Ancholme is a pre-English r.n., the etymology of which is uncertain.
The later development to *-holme* is presumably due to popular
etymology associating the original ending with the common L *holme.*

HUMBER, R.

Forms in L documents include: *usque Humbrae fluminis, ad terminum
Humbrae, ad meridianam Humbre fluminis ripam* 731 Bede, *be suþan
Humbre* s.a. 827 (c900) ASC A, *ofer Humbre muþan* s.a. 867 (c900) ib,

oð gemæro Humbre streames c890 (10) OEBede, of Humbre, on Humbre 971 (12) BCS 1270 (S 782), Humbra éa s.a. 942 (c955) ASC A, to Humbran muðe s.a. 993 (1121) ASC E, in to Humbran muðan s.a. 1013 (1121) ib, into Humbran s.a. 1066 (1121) ib, innan Humbran s.a. 1069 (1121) ib, in to Humbran s.a. 1070 (1121) ib, transitum Humbrie 1115 (14) Bard, in flumine humbrie eHy2 (m13) NCot, in Humbria 1143–47 Dane, ad Humbriam 1241 HarlCh, inter Humbriam 1263 HarlCh, ad flumen quod dicitur Humbre p1131 (e13) LibEl, in Humbre 1155–60, 1160–66 Dane, Humbre 1240 FF et freq to 1411 Pat, in Humbra c1141 HarlCh, c1155 Dane, p1167 (l13) Stix, Humber Hy3 (e14) Selby, l13 (e14) Havelock, 1319 YearBk 1329 Pat et freq, Humbir 1442 ib, Humer 1536 LP xi, Hummer 1654 FMB.

Humber is a pre-English r.n., found also in two lost names in O (PN O 15), Humber Brook (PN Gl 1, 8), Humbrel's Fm (PN Hu 227–28), and Humberholme (PN Db 490). Indeed, Humber may well be pre-Celtic, since no convincing Celtic etymology can be suggested, v. Jackson 510. If so, it would belong to the group of r.ns. referred to as Old European, cf. Swallow PN L 5, 144–46.

TRENT, R.
Forms in L documents include: be Trentan s.a. 679 (1121) ASC E, iuxta fluuium Treanta 731 Bede, mid Treontan streame c890 OEBede, andlang Trentan s.a. 1013 (m11) ASC C, betwyx ... ꝼ Trentan s.a. 1069 (1121) ib E, ad Trentam 1139 RA i, in Trente m12 (c1331) Spald i, iuxta ripam trente 1163 And, Trente 1172 P, Hy2 (1409) Gilb, 1242 (13) Alv et passim to le Trente 1541 PetTD, Trentam c1184 (15) Templar, 112 RA iv, c1200 (1409) Gilb, Trenta c1189 (e14) Selby, 1198 (1328) Ch, 1199 P, 1230 And, Trent c1184 (15) Templar, 1236 Cl, 1275 AD iv, 1275 RH, 1296 Ipm et freq.

Trent is from Brit **Trisantonā**, PrW *Trıhanton, a r.n. of doubtful meaning, but which has been translated as 'strongly flooding' which would be appropriate enough for the R. Trent.

Manley Wapentake

Manelinde 1086 DB, *Maneli* c1115 LS, *Maneslei* 1130 P, *-lea* 1176
ib, *Manneslai* 1169 ib, *-lea* 1175 ib, *Manelea* 1167 ib, *Mannelai*
1168 ib, *Manlea* 1166, 1180 *et passim* to 1193 ib, *Manle* 1171,
1183 *et passim* to 1431 FA, *Manlei* 1202 SelectPleas, 1202 Ass,
Manlet 1185 RotDom, *Manled* e13 (1333) Ch, *Manley* 1265
Misc, 1360 Peace, 1409 Cl *et passim*.

The forms are preceded or followed by some form of Latin
wapentacium. The second el. of Manley appears to be OE **lēah** 'a wood,
a glade, a clearing'. It has been suggested, however, the some early
spellings point rather to ON **hlíð** 'a slope'. The first el. may then be the
ODan pers.n. *Manni,* as in Manby a village in this wapentake. The site
of the meeting-place of the wapentake (ON **vápnatak,** late OE
wæpengetæc 'a subdivision of a shire') is not known, but, if the
connection between the wapentake name and the village name Manby
is correct, it was probably on the slopes west of Manby. The name of the
deanery is Manlake (not Manley), cf. *Manlack* 1254 ValNor, *-lak* 1291
Tax, 1292 RSu, 1304 *DCAcct*, 1347 Pat, the reason for this change being
completely obscure.

Alkborough

Alchebarge (2x) 1086 DB, *-barua* c1115 LS, c1128 (12) ChronPetro,
   -barue 12 HC, *Halcbarge* 1212 Fees
Aucebarge 1154–58 (1300) Ch, *-barg'* 1199 (1300) Ch, 1200 ChR
Alkebarwe m12 (c1331) *Spald i*, 1219 Ass, 1231 *PetLN*, 1235 Cl,
   1272 *Ass*, 1286 Misc, 1287 Cl *et freq* to 1411 Cl, *-barwa* 1190
   (1301) Dugd vi, *-barewe* 1305 Cl, *-barowe* 1311 ChancW,

1313–15 *MinAcct*, 1323 Cl, 1327 *SR*, 1328 Pat *et freq* to 1431 FA, *-barow* 1312 RA ix, 1349 Ipm, *-barou* 1349 Ipm, 1349 Cl, *-baru* 1328 Ch, *-barough* 1323 Cl, *-bargh* 1402 FA, 1424 IBL, 1451–53 *MinAcct*, 1510 LP

Alkeberwe 1321 Cl, *-berugh* 1327 ib, *-bergh* 1335 Pat, 1402 FA

Alkbarowe 1389 Pat, 1407 RRep, 1535 VE iv, *-barow* 1517 ECB, 1530 Wills iii

Aukebargh 1472 Pat, *-barowe* 1504 ib, 1504 Cl

Alkeborowe 1517 ECB, *-burrowe* 1603 *BT*, *Alkborowe* 1579 *Monson*

Aulkebarghe 1562 *Surv*

Awkbarow 1514 LNQ v, *Aukbarrow* 1576 Saxton

Auckborowe 1576 LER, *-brough* 1666, 1681 *ib*, *-borough* 1724 Stukeley, *Aukborough* 1592 SP ii, *-borow* 1644 *BT*, *Awkborrowe* 1624 *LCS*, *-borow* 1644 *BT*

Awkbarrow 1612, 1615, 1618, 1621 *BT*

Awkeburgh 1649 *MiscDep*, 1662 *Yarb*, 1685 *Dudd*

Aulkbrough 1649, 1663, 1694 *BT*

Alkborough 1707 *BT*, 1780 *LD et passim*

Hautebarge m12, Hy2, R1, 1200 (c1331) *Spald i*, 1201 Cur *et passim* to 1322 Cl, *-barg(')* 1206 Ass, 1259 RRGr, 1265 Misc, 1266 *AD*, 1276 RH

Altebarge 1170 P, *Haltebarge* 1171 ib, a1223 RA ii, 1265 Misc, e14 *PetWB*

Autebarge lHy2 Dane, 1294 *Ass*

Haultebarge 1209–35 LAHW, p1220 WellesLA, c1221 Welles

Alta Barga 1242–43 Fees, 1428 FA

Halteburg' (altered from *-barg'*) 1206 P

Hauteburg' 1236 Cl

Hauteberge 1204 FF, 1219 Ass, 1253 Cl, *-berg(')* 1219 Ass, 1232 Cl, 1233 Ch, 1254 ValNor, 1257 Ch, 1261 Cl, 1291 Tax, *Hauteberg* 1428 FA

Dr Insley suggests that this is 'Al(u)ca's hill', early forms in *-barge*, *-barg(h)* showing that we are concerned with OE **beorg** (Angl **berg**) 'a hill', topographically appropriate, rather than OE **bearu** 'a grove', as has been previously been proposed. He points out that the diphthong /eo/ which would have been the normal result of breaking has undergone early interchange with /ea/, cf. K. Brunner, *Altenglische Grammatik*, 3rd ed., Tubingen 1965, para 35 Anm. 1. Subsequent smoothing here must have resulted in /a/ (< /æ/) rather than /e/. Forms in *-we* show the vocalisation of the medial guttural spirant -*g*- after liquids in inflected forms, cf. J. Wright, *An Elementary Middle English Grammar*, 2nd ed., Oxford 1928, 84. The first el. is the OE pers.n. *Al(u)ca*, which is attested independently in the form *Hroðolf Alca sune* e12 Exeter Book (D), for which *v.* J. Insley, *Namn och Bygd* 70 (1982), 84. There are a number of 13th century spellings in *Altebarge, Haltebarge, Hautebarge*, etc. due initially to scribal confusion between -*c*- and -*t*- and then to popular etymology, associating the first el. with OFr *haut* 'high'. In two forms the name has been latinised to *Alta Barga*.

WALCOT

> *Walcote* 1067 (12) RRAN, 1093–98 ib, m12 (c1331) *Spald i*, 1284–85 FA, (*iuxta Humbram*) 1296 *Ass*, 1299 Ipm, 1316 FA, 1327, 1332 *SR*, 1347 Pat, 1351 Ipm, 1400 Cl, 1428 FA, 1523–34 *MinAcct*, 1536 PetLD, 1541 PetTD, 1608–9 *MinAcct*, -*kote* 1212 Fees, 1290–1312, 1316, 1333 (m14) CNat, 1346 FA, -*cot* 1303 ib, 1304 Ipm, 1346 FA, (*super Humb'*) WB, 1576 Saxton, 1610 Speed *et freq*, *Walcott* 1546 PetLD, *Waucott* 1531 Wills iii
> *Walecote* 1067–69 (c1150) HC, (5x) 1086 DB, c1128 (12) ChronPetro, m12 (c1331) *Spald i*, (*super Humbria*) 1189 (1332) Ch, 112 (1409) Gilb, 1200 *Spald i*, 1208 FF, 1219 Ass *et freq* to 1297 CoramR, -*cota* (3x) c1115 LS, 1154–58 (1330) Ch, *Ualecot'* c1115 LS, *Walecot* Hy2 (c1331) *Spald i*, 1199 (1330), 1227 Ch, (*in Lindsey*) 1251 ib, -*cot'* 1200 ChR, 1202 Ass, 1204 Cur, 1220 ib (p), (*sup' Humbram*) 1231 *PetLN*, 1235, 1236 Cl, 1297 *PetWB* (p)
> *Wallecote* 1276 RH, 1307 *FF*, *Wallcott* 1690 *BRA 1171*
> *Waldcote* 1451–3, 1496–98 *MinAcct*

Forms in *Wale*- by far outnumber those in *Wal*- so this must be 'the cottage, hut, shelter of the Welshmen', *v.* **walh** (gen.pl. **wala**), **cot**, identical with Walcot near Folkingham and Walcott near Billinghay, both in Kesteven. If the names are early, they must represent isolated groups of Welshmen identifiable as such in Anglo-Saxon England, perhaps as late as the late 7th century. For a full discussion, *v.* Kenneth Cameron, "The meaning and significance of Old English *walh* in English place-names", *JEPN* 12 (1980), 1–53.

ALKBOROUGH FLATS, THE FLATS, *The Flatts* 1765, 1822 *Terrier, Flats* 1835 *BH (Plan)*, self-explanatory, the name of the low-lying land by the R. Trent. THE CLIFF, *the cliffe, the cliffe edge* 1577 *Terrier, Cliffehill* 1601 *ib, the Cliffes* 1624 *LCS, Cliff End* 1824 O, cf. *clifgate* Hy3 (c1331) *Spald ii*, self-explanatory, *v*. **clif, gata**. COLEBY WOOD, 1824 O, named from Coleby in the neighbouring parish of West Halton. COLLEGE FM, named from Magdalene College Cambridge. COUNTESS CLOSE, 1768 *EnclA*, 1828 Bry, *Countess close, Lady pitt, or Countess pitt* 1697 Pryme, *countess close* 1724 Stukeley, perhaps cf. *Counteshous* eHy3 (c1331) *Spald ii*. This is the name of an earthwork, traditionally associated with a Countess of Warwick who gave the manor to Magdalene College Cambridge, but there is no evidence to support the claim. COW CLOSE HOLT. FIR BED PLANTATION. HILL SIDE PLANTATION. HILL TOP PLANTATION, cf. *The Hill Topp* 1662, *the Hill topp* 1686, ~ *hill Topp* 1697, ~ *top* 1709 all *Terrier*, cf. *In collo* Hy3 (c1331) *Spald ii*. JERUSALEM COTTAGES. JULIAN'S BOWER, 1718 *BRA 1416*, 1768 *EnclA*, ~ *bower* 1724 Stukeley, *Gillian's bore* (sic) 1697 Pryme, the name of a maze cut in the turf, sometimes alternatively known as Troy Town. KELL WELL, 1697 Pryme, 1642 White, *Keld Well* 1768 *EnclA*. If the 1768 form is to be taken at face value the first el. is ON **kelda** 'a spring' to which was added *well*. MANOR HO, *Manor house or Cheife Mansion house* 1624 *LCS, manor of Aukborough Hall Garth* 1768 *EnclA, v*. **hall, garðr** 'an enclosure', cf. *atte Halyatte* 1327 *SR, ad portam aule* 1332 *ib* both (p), *v*. **hall, geat** 'a gate'. THE MILL (lost), 1828 Bry. MOUNT PLEASANT, no doubt a complimentary nickname. SOUTHDALE FM, cf. *the South dale* 1609 *DuLaMB 119, South dales* 1709 *Terrier, v*. **sūð, deill** 'a share, a portion of land'. STICK HOLT. STRATE BOTTOM PLANTATION. SWISS COTTAGE. TRENT FALLS, *Trent-falle* 1511 LP i, *Trent-fall* 1677 Pryme, where the Trent joins the Humber. TRENT NESS (lost), 1828 Bry. VICARAGE, *the vicaredge of Alkebarrowe* 1601, *the Viccaridge* 1606, *The vicarage house is dilapidated all the materials wherof it was built removed* 1709, *A house commonly called the parsonage* 1709, cf. *the Vicarage yard* 1762 all *Terrier*. WALCOT HALL, 1824 O. WALCOT LANE, 1768 *EnclA*, cf. *in la Lane* 1316 (14) CNat, *in Le Lane de Walkote* 1322 (14) ib, *in the lane* 1327, 1332 *SR, in ye lane de Walkote* 1333 (14) CNat, *in the Lane* 1343 NI all (p). WALKER DYKE CLOUGH, named from the family of William *Walker* 1842 White. WALKS END, cf. *Walk wood* 1709 *Terrier, Walks* 1841 *TA, Walks End Road* 1841 *TAMap, v*. **walk** denoting land used for the pasture of animals, especially sheep, hence the common *Sheepwalk*. WINDMILL, *vni' molendinum ad ventum* 1231 *PetLN*.

FIELD-NAMES

Forms dated m12 (c1331); Hy3 (c1331), lHy3 (c1331), Ed1 (c1331), 1320–21 (c1331) are *Spald ii*; 1231 *PetLN*; 1257 Ch; 1271–2 *Ass*; 1286 Misc; 1287 Cl; 1290–1312 (14), 1299 *PetWB*; 1312 (c1331), 1325 (c1331) *Spald i*; 1313–15, 1327–29, 1382–85, 1421–23, 1451–53, 1496–98; 1523–24, 1608–9 *MinAcct*, 1562 *Surv*, 1316 (14), 1325 (14), 1333 (14) CNat, 1577, 1601, 1606, 1662, 1674, 1686, 1690, 1693, 1697[1], 1700, 1706. 1709, 1762, 1822 *Terrier*; 1609 *DuLaMB*; 1624 *LCS*; 1630 Wills iii; 1690 *BRA 1171*; 1697[2] Pryme; 1768 *EnclA*; 1770, 1772 LNQ xviii; 1780, 1789 *LindDep 109*; 1835 *BH (Plan)*; 1841 *TA*; 1850 *TAMap*.

(a) Aukborough Fd 1768, Alkborough ~ 1789 (*campo de Alkbarwe* (sic) Hy3 (c1331), *campo de Hauteb'* Ed1 (c1331), *v.* **feld**); Bell Cls 1768; Bonding 1768 (*Bondhing* Hy3 (c1331), *bondings meadowe* 1609 (the first el. is probably the surn. *Bonde*, cf. Richard *Bonde* Hy3 (c1331), the second is **eng** 'meadow, pasture', as elsewhere in this parish); Bridle Road from Burton 1850 (referring to Burton upon Stather); the Broad Lane 1789; Buts cl 1772 (*v.* **butte** 'a strip of land abutting on a boundary, etc.); Church Yd 1850; Coleby Cl(s), Coleby Lane (from Coleby a neighbouring village, cf. *Coalby beck* 1607[1], *v.* **bekkr**); (the) Common 1768, 1772; Cow Lane Rd 1850; Fitties 1835 (*v.* **fitty**; a common name in north L coastal parishes meaning 'the outer marsh', *v.* further PN L **2**, 153); Garth 1841 (*v.* **garðr** 'an enclosure, as elsewhere in this parish); Glebe Land 1850; Haughton Road 1768 (*halton(e)gate* Hy3 (c1331), 'the road to West Halton (a neighbouring parish)', *v.* **gata** and cf. *Halton feild* 1601, *halton mor'* Hy3 (c1331)); Haverdale 1822 (*Hauerdale* 1333 (14), 'the share of land where oats are grown, *v.* **hafri** (ME **haver**) 'oats' and **deill** 'a share, a portion of land', as elsewhere in this parish); Holmfleets Cls 1768 (no doubt to be associated with *holflete* m12 (c1331), *Holfled* eHy3 (c1331), *-flet* c1340 (14), *-flete* 1382–85, *Halflet* (sic) 1421–23, *Halleflete* (sic) 1451–53, 'the stream, inlet flowing in the hollow', *v.* **hol**, **flēot**; forms from *MinAcct* are notoriously unreliable); Humber Bank 1835; Ings 1768, 1772, the Inggs 1789 (*Inges* 1624), (the) Ings Rd 1768 (*v.* **eng**); Jackson Dales 1841 (from the surn. *Jackson* and the pl. of **deill**); (Little) Lawns 1841; long-lose Cow (sic) 1762 (*a fourlonge callid Lonnge Nosco* (sic) 1577, *Lonnge Loscoe* 1601, *longe Loscoe* 1606, *Longe Loscowe* 1662, *Long Losco* 1674, *Longloscow* 1686, 1693, *long loss kow* 1690, ~ *loscow* 1709, cf. *estloskhow* eHy3 (c1331), *shorte nosco* 1577), Loskow Hill 1772, Loscow slack Cls 1789 (cf. *loskehoudale* eHy3 (c1331), *Loscowe daile* 1606, *Loscow Slacke* 1662, *Long Loscow slacke* 1686 (*v.* **slakki** 'a small shallow valley', an OWScand word, rare in the East Midlands, cf. PN L **2**, 27, 132. The forms are late but Loskow etc. is perhaps derived from ON **loft**, ON **skógr** 'the wood with a lofthouse', cf. Loscoe, PN Db 434, where earlier forms of this name-type are recorded); Long Pingle 1768 (*v.* **pingel** 'a small enclosure'); two low Cls 1768; Nordy Croft 1768, 1841 (*Noddy crofte* (sic) 1601, *v.* **croft**); the North Dales 1768 (*North dale* 1609, *v.* **norð, deill** and cf. Southdale Fm *supra*); North field 1772 (*North feild* 1609, *the north Feilde* 1690, *ye North field* 1693, *the north Feild* 1697, *ye North Feild* 1700, *The ~ ~* 1706, *the North field* 1709, *v.* **norð, feld**, one of the open fields of the village); Occupation Rd 1850; Old May Cl 1835 (alluding to an unidentified woman); Pale Cl 1768 (Robert *Pale* is mentioned in the same document); the garden in the Paradis 1770, Parridise 1772 (a complimentary nickname, *v.* **paradis**); the Pingels (sic) 1768 (cf. *Pigtelle* (sic) 1299, *v.* **pightel** 'a small enclosure', rare in north L, the nasalised variant **pingel** is the normal form); Plantation(s) 1841; Sandfield 1762, 1768, Sand fd 1772 (*ye sand Feild* 1706, cf. *pastures called the Sands* 1624, self-explanatory); Scom lings (partially illegible) 1768, Scamblings 1841 (presumably to be identified with *skamlandes* 1601, *the Scamlandes* 1606, *v.* ON **skammr** 'short', **land** 'a selion' in the pl.); Scotchman Cl (sic) 1835 (this is Scotchburn Cl on 1835 *Plan* and is from the surn. *Scotchburn*, cf. William *Scotchburn* 1789); the Smithy Marsh 1768; Steward's ~, Stewards Cl 1768, 1850 (from the surn. *Steward* or from the occupational name); Sunken Dale 1768; the Town Garths 1768 (*v.* **garðr**); The Town Street 1768; Walcot Cls 1768, 1841, Walcott ~ 1768 (cf. *camp' de Walcot* lHy3 (c1331), *campo de Walcote* 1312 (c1331), 1320–21 (c1331), *campis de Walkote* 1316 (14),1322 (14), *campo de ~* 1333 (14), *wawcote felde* 1577, *v.* **feld**); the Wells on the Westside of the town of Aukborough 1768 (*v.* **wella**); West Croft 1841 (*v.* **croft**); West Dykes 1768, ~ Dikes 1835, West Dykes Rd 1768 (*westdic* Hy3 (c1331), c1340 (14), *-dich* 1257, c1340 (14), *v.* **west, dīc, dík**); Wheat Cl 1841; Whins and Plantation 1841 (*v.* **hvin** 'whin, gorse'); Whitton Gate 1762 (*Witengate* Hy3 (c1331), *v.* **gata** 'a road'), Whitton Road 1768 (*the high way to Whitton* 1709. self-explanatory, cf. *witenmare* Hy3 (c1331), 'the boundary with Whitton (an adjacent parish)'; Wigalsworth land 1772 (from the surn. *Wigglesworth*, cf. Charles *Wigglesworth* 1768); Willow Holt 1841 (*v.* **holt**); the Wood Cl 1762 (cf. *super siluam, desuper boscum* Hy3 (c1331), *Bosco de Hauteb'* lHy3 (c1331), *v.* **wudu**); Wybeckes 1822 (*v.* **bekkr**).

(b) *the Acres* 1624 (*v.* **æcer**); *acrisdikscarth* lHy3 (c1331) (*v.* **æcer, dīc** or **dík** with **skarð** 'an opening, a gap'; *acerdik* is a fairly common minor name in L, the exact sense of which is uncertain, *v.* PN L **2**, 13 and VEPN 27); *alkebardaile* Hy3 (c1331) (from the parish name and **deill**); *ye Argh'* 1333 (14) (*v.* **ærghi** 'a shieling, a summer-pasture', an el. chiefly found in north-west England and noted here for the first time in the L survey); *atelacpites* Hy3 (c1331) (*v.* **pytt**; the first el. is obscure, but may perhaps be the OE pers.n. *Ēadlāc*; for the formation, cf. *ategategreinis infra*); *bekeniltre, bekenildetre* Hy3 (c1331) (*v.* **trēow**; Dr Insley suggests that the first el. is a variant of ME *beggild* 'a beggar'); *Borwdaile* 1325 (c1331) (*v.* **deill**); *del Boure* 1286, *de Boure* 1287, *La Bour'* 1327, *La Boure* 1332 all (p) (*v.* **būr** 'a cottage, a dwelling'); *Brontland* Hy3 (c1331) (*v.* **land**); *herbag' de Brous* 1421–23, *herbagio de ~* 1451–53; *super Bule* Hy3 (c1331); *Burgesbek* 1290–1312 (14), *-beke* 1322 (14), *Boresbek* 1316 (14), *Burresbek* 1333 (14) (presumably 'the stream of the *Burgh*', *v.* **bekkr** and cf. *super Burgh'* Hy3 (c1331), *v.* **burh** 'a fortified place', the significance of which is not clear, unless it refers to the earthwork at Countess Close); *cod furlange* Hy3 (c1331) (the first el. is uncertain); *le Croft* Hy3 (c1331) (*v.* **croft** 'a small enclosed field'); *dikewell'* eHy3 (c1331), *dicwelle* lHy3 (c1331) (*v*. **dīc** or **dík**, **wella**, denoting a spring from which a drainage ditch rises); *dilfeld* Hy3 (c1331) (*v*. **dile** 'dill', **feld**); *the east Feild* 1609, *The East Feild* 1690 (one of the open fields of the village, *v*. **ēast, feld**); *Elisheuidland* Hy3 (c1331) (from the ME pers.n. *Elis, Elias* and **hēafod-land** 'the head of a strip of land left for turning the plough'); *Ennyngetu'* (sic) 1299 (obscure); *the Furclose* 1662, *~ fureclose* 1674, *~ Fur close* 1686, *~ Firr-close* 1690, *~ furz close* 1709 (*v*. **fyrs, clos(e)**); *a le* (i.e. **lea** 'meadow, pasture') *callid the furrowes* (sic) 1577 (*v*. **furh**); *furtwelgate* Ed1 (c1331) (*v*. **wella, gata**; the first el. is obscure); *ategategreinis* Hy3 (c1331) ('at the road-forks', *v*. **gata, grein**, preceded by **atte(n)**); *gigger houcke* 1577, *Jagger Hooke* 1686 (from **hōc** 'a hook, an angle of land', presumably with the surn. *Jagger*); *super graft* Hy3 (c1331) (*v*. **graft** 'a ditch', cf. *the Grafte* PN L **4**, 91); *la Grene* lHy3 (c1331), 1271–2 both (p) (*v*. **grēne** 'a village green, a grassy spot'); *hazland* Hy3 (c1331) (perhaps 'land where hazels grow', *v*. **hæsel, land**); *Haregraue* 1299 ('the grey, hoar copse, grove' *v*. **hār, grāf**); *Haythebigarthes* 1333 (14) (named from the lost *Hairby* in West Halton *infra* and **garðr**); *henrideilis fil' Regin' de Walcote* (sic) lHy3 (c1331) ('Henry son of Reginald of Walcot's shares of land', *v*. **deill**; an unusual formation but cf. *terram filii Andreæ* PN L **2**, 175); *hilte landes, hiltelands, -landes, Hildland, hildlandes* Hy3 (c1331) (the first el. is obscure, the second is **land** 'a selion' chiefly in the pl.); *super houe* Hy3 (c1331) (*v*. **haugr** 'a mound'); *the hye meare* 1577, *~ heighe Meare* 1606, *~ High Meare* 1662, *yᵉ high meare* 1686, *the high Mear* 1697 (*v*. **hēah, (ge)mǣre** 'a boundary, land on or forming a boundary'); *houstondic* Hy3 (c1331); *Iron hyll* 1577, *-hill* 1601, *the Ieron hill* 1606, *Iron Hill* 1662, 1674, *the ~ ~* 1686, *yᵉ Iron hil* 1593, *the Iron hill* 1700, *~ iron hill* 1709 (apparently from OE **īsern** 'iron' and **hyll**, in what sense is not clear); *le kirkedeile* Hy3 (c1331) (*v*. **kirkja, deill**); *meddowe . . . naumed Kirkmore* 1562 (*v*. **kirkja, mōr**; *langlandes* Ed1 (c1331), *Lange-* 1290–1312 (14), *-londes, Langeslondes* 1316 (14) ('the long selions', *v*. **lang, land** in the pl.); *Litligaile slacke* (sic) 1577, *littldall ~* 1601, *the little daile slacke* 1606, *Little Dale Slacke* 1674, 1693, *little dale Slacke* 1690 (*v*. **lȳtel, deill** and **slakki** 'a small shallow valley', an OWScand word rare in the East Midlands, cf. *Potterdale slacke* PN L **2**, 27); *littelthorp* 1290 (*v*. **lȳtel, þorp** 'an outlying settlement'); *le male* Hy3 (c1331) (perhaps from OE **malu** 'a gravel ridge'; unfortunately the site is not known so that the topography cannot be checked); *marfer* 1601 (*v*. **marfur** 'a boundary furrow'); *le Marrays* 1313–15, *~ marreys* 1327–19, *Marys* c1340 (14), *in marisco Burgo sancti Petri* (*v*. **mareis** 'a marsh'; Peterborough Abbey held land in Alkborough); *Middeleng* c1340 (14), *Medeleng dich, Medelengdic* c1340 (14), *methelingdic* 1320–21 (c1331), *Medlin Hurne abutting uppon the River of Trent* 1624 ('the middle meadow, pasture', *v*. **meðal, eng**, a Scand compound, with **dīc** and **hyrne** 'an angle, a corner of land', *ad medietatem prati* c1340 (14) presumably alludes to the same piece of land); *yᵉ midle field* 1683, *~ Middle Feild* 1697, 1700, 1706 (one of the open fields of the village); *the mylne feilde* 1601 (*v*. **myln, feld**); *nictisfurlang* Hy3 (c1331) (perhaps from **cniht** 'a youth, a servant' and **furlang**); *Norbecke Close* 1690 (*v*. **norð, bekkr**; *North metelholm* Hy3 (c1331), *~ metilholm* lHy3 (c1331) ('the middle piece of raised land in marsh', *v*. **meðal, holmr**, a Scand compound, prefixed by **norð**, cf. *suthmedilholm infra*); *ostcroft* lHy3 (c1331) (no doubt a miswriting or misreading of *estcroft*, *v*. **ēast, croft**); *Oustdic* eHy3 (c1331) (*v*. **austr** 'east', **dík**, a Scand compound); *peseland* Hy3 (c1331), *langpeselandes* eHy3 (c1331) ('the selion(s) where pease grows', *v.* **pise**, **land** in the pl. prefixed by **lang** in the second form); *portermeteholm* (sic) Hy3 (c1331) (*meteholm* is perhaps 'the mean, poor raised land in marsh' from OE **mǣte** 'mean, poor, bad' and **holmr**, but **mǣte** is very rare in p.ns. and f.ns.; to this was prefixed the ME surn. *Porter*); *The Rideings* 1690 (apparently OE **ryding** 'a clearing', a rare el. in north L); *yᵉ slack* 1706 (*v.* **slakki**, as in *Litlidaile slacke supra*); *Robyneson hows* 1630 (from the surn. *Robinson*); *South feild* 1609 (one of the open fields of the village, cf. *The East Feild supra*); *Sutheby* 1231, *Suthebi de Walcot* 1312, *Southiby* 1332, *Suthiby* c1340 (14) all (p), *pratum Walteri de Suthiby* c1340 (14) ('(place) south in the village', *v.* **sūð, í, bȳ**, a common formation in L, denoting a person who lives in the south of the village); *Stainhil* Hy3 (c1331), *stainland* Hy3 (c1331) (*v.* **steinn, hyll, land**); *le stainpittes* Hy3 (c1331) (*v.* **steinn, pytt**); *super stegras* eHy3 (c1331) (obscure); *Stert* Hy3 (c1331) (*v.* **steort** 'a tail or tongue of land, a projecting piece of land'); *le Stiche* Hy3 (c1331) (probably from **stycce** 'a small plot or strip of land'); *the Stigh* 1662 (*v.* **stīg**. **stígr** 'a path'); *Stikelyng flete, Stikeleng flet* c1340 (14) (perhaps 'the steep meadow', *v.* **sticol** 'steep', **eng**, with **flēot** 'an inlet; a stream'); *sutherneholme* Hy3 (c1331) (*v.* **sūðerne** 'southern, southerly', **holmr**); *apud stechetas* (sic) Hy3 (c1331) (obscure); *stocwelle gate* (*v.* **gata**), ~ *heuedland* Hy3 (c1331) (*v.* **hēafod-land**), *stoke welle* eHy3 (c1331) (*v.* **stocc, wella**, probably denoting a spring marked by a standing tree-stump); *suthmedilholm* Hy3 (c1331) (cf. *North metelholm supra*); *suthwell'* Hy3 (c1331) (*v.* **sūð, wella**); *swertforis* (sic) Hy3 (c1331), *sweteforwis* Ed1 (c1331) (uncertain); *terram Symonis de le Pyt* 1316 (14) (*v.* **pytt**); *terram Templariorum* 1290–1312 (14), ~ *que quondam fuit Templariorum* 1333 (14) ('the Templars' land'); *Talyor hows* (sic) 1630 (from the surn. *Taylor*); *Til* c1340 (14) (p); *thuerfores, þuerfores, þuerfures, tuerfores* Hy3 (c1331) ('the transverse furrows' from ON **þverr** 'athwart, lying across' and **furh** 'a furrow' in the pl.); *the town head* 1630 (self-explanatory); *Walecotebekke* eHy3 (c1331) (*v.* **bekkr**), *Walcotedyk'* 1313–15, *Walkotdyk'* 1327–29, *Walcotdik'* 1381–85, *-dyk'* 1421–13, *Walcotedyke* 1523–24, *-dike* 1609 (*v.* **dík**), *Walecotehirne* eHy3 (c1331) (*v.* **hyrne**) (all three are named from Walcot *supra*); *Warr far heads* (sic) 1662; *Wellehil* eHy3 (c1331) (*v.* **wella, hyll**); *Westeredall hows* 1630 (named from the surn. *Westerdale*, cf. Henry *Westeredall* 1630); *Westlang* Hy3 (c1331) (*v.* **west, lang** 'a long piece of land'); *wettdic* Hy3 (c1331) (self-explanatory, *v.* **wēt, dík**); *Wibdale Lease* 1690 (*v.* **lǣs** 'pasture, meadow-land'; the first el. may well be a surn.)); *Witebeche* Hy3 (c1331) (*v.* **hwīt** 'white', **bēce** 'a stream', no doubt a reference to the bed of the stream); *Wrongland* Hy3 (c1331) ('the crooked selion', *v.* **vrangr, land**).

Appleby

APPLEBY

    Aplebi (3x) 1086 DB, c1115 LS, 1130 P (p), c1128 (12th) ChronPetro, 1150–60 YCh iii, *-beia* 1088 (l13) Blyth, *Apleby* 1537 *AOMB 211*, 1564 Pat

Apelbi a1175 Hy2 Goke (p), 1202 FF, *-by* Hy2 (14) Dugd iii, 1202 FF, 1250, 1254 Ipm

Appelbiea 1086–88 (l13) Blyth, *-bia* 1102, John (l13) ib, *-by* 1114–23 (l13) ib, 1154–55 RBE, 1208 FF (p), 1229 Pat, 1242–43 Fees, 1246 Ipm, 1254 ValNor, 1261 Pat *et freq* to 1429 Fine, *-bi* 1156–57 (14) YVh i, c1160 Semp (p), 1166, 1167, 1176, 1182 *et freq* in P, 1185 Templar, 1202 Ass, 1212 Fees, 1325 Cl

Applebeia 112 (l13) Blyth, *-by* 1555 Pat *et passim*, *-bye alias Appulbye* 1563 Pat, *-bye* 1576 Saxton, 1610 Speed *-bie* 1576 LER, *-be* 1690 *Inv*

Appilby 1294 *Ass*, 1382 Ipm, 1388 Fine, 1398 Pat, 1429, 1432 Fine, 1433 Pat, 1433 YD x, 1438 Cl, 1539 *AD*, *Appylby* 1428 FA, 1433 YD x

Appulby 1407 RRep, 1430 Fine, 1431 FA, 1442 Fine, 1451, 1466 Cl, 1476 AD *et passim* to 1558 InstBen, *-bye* 1563 Pat

Appelby 1434 Pat, 1434 Cl

'The farmstead, village where apples grow', *v.* **æppel**, **bȳ**, a hybrid Anglo-Danish compound. It is highly likely, from the situation of the village, that this was originally an English p.n. Appleton in which the second el. **tūn** 'a farmstead, village, estate' was later replaced by ODan **bȳ**.

SANTON, SANTON, HIGH & LOW

Sanctone (2x) 1086 DB, 1535 VE iv, 1576 Saxton, 1607 Camden, 1610 Speed

Santone 1086 DB, *-tuna* (3x) c1115 LS, *-tun* a1175 Goke, 1212 Fees, *-ton'* 1176 P (p), 1196 ChancR, 1197 P, 1202 FF, 1206 Ass, 1206 Cur, c1263 RA ii, *-ton* 1246 Ipm, 1275 RH, 1295 *Ass*, 1312 Ch, 1318 Fine, 1319 Orig, 1322 Ipm, 1332 Cl *et freq*

Saunton' 1242–43 Fees, 1298 Ass (p), 1314 Selby, 1332 *SR*, *-ton* 1279 Ch, 1288 Cl, 1292 Ipm (p), 1298 ib *et passim* to 1404 *Yarb*, *-tone* 1272 *Ass*

Sandton 1280 Pat

Saundton 1296 Ipm (p)

Sampton 1276 RH (p), 1346 Orig, 1346 Pat

Saynton' 1508 *Yarb*, *Sainton* 1612 WillsStow, *Seynton* 1549 Pat

"Great" *Santon* 1564 *Pat*, *Upper* ~ 1606 *Terrier*, 1649 *Yarb*, 1831 *Terrier*, *High* ~ 1810 *Yarb*, 1824 O, 1828 Bry, *East Santon otherwise Upper Santon* 1833 *EnclA*, *South Santon* 1686 *Terrier*

Nether Santon 1592–86 WillsStow, 1649 *Yarb*, *Neither Santon* 1606 *Terrier, Low* ~ 1707, 1745 *ib*, 1824 O, 1828 Bry

'The farmstead village on sandy ground', *v.* **sand, tūn**. This is identical with Sancton, PN YE 227, where forms in -*ct*- are recorded from the 12th century and persist to the present day. They have been explained as due to popular association with OE, ME **sanct**, ME **saint**, though this does not sound altogether convincing. Whatever the explanation they are hardly to be taken into consideration from an etymological point of view. Spellings in -*au*-, found from the 13th to 15th centuries here, persist in Saunton, PN D 33, also identical with Santon. They are due to Norman influence and may be compared with Staunton by the side of the common Stanton. The name is now also distinguished as High Santon and Low Santon.

THORNHOLME PRIORY

> *Tornholm* 1157–63 Dane, 1206 FF, 1207 , 1208 P, 1212 Fees, 1233 WellesW, -*holm'* 1194 CurP, 1200 P, 1202 Ass, 1204 Cur, 1208 FF, 1219 Ass
> *Torneholm* a1175 Goke, c1190 RA ii, c1213 Gir, -*holm'* 112 (e14) YCh xi
> *Thornholm* eHy2 (1409) Gilb, 1200 Abbr, c1200 BS, 1202 FF, 1205 ChancR, 1206, 1209 P, 1210, 1220 Cur, a1223 Goke *et freq* to 1745 *Terrier,* -*holm'* c1210 RA ii, 1212 Cur, 1218 Ass, 1223 RA ii, 1225, 1228 Cur, 1232 Pat *et passim* to 1430 *AD*
> *Thornholme* c1186 RA ix, 1203 Abbr, 1248 Ch, 1262 RRGr, 1285, 1347 Pat, 1366 Ipm *et passim*
> *Thorneholm* 1202 (15) Bridl, 1218 (m14) CNat, -*holm'* 1238–43 Fees, -*holme* 1352 Blyth, 1374, 1433 Pat *et passim* to 1652 *Yarb,* ~ *alias Thornam* 1536 *AOMB 232,* ~ *als Thornham* 1652 *Yarb*
> *Thorenholm* 1229 Cur, 1242 FF
> *Thyrnholm* 1450 LLD, *Thyrneholme* 1553 Anc, *Thirneholme* 1564 Pat
> *Thornham* 1729 *BT, Old Thornham* 1794 *MiscDep* 77

'The higher ground amidst the marshes where thorn-trees grow', *v.* **þorn, holmr**, a hybrid OE-ODan compound.

APPLEBY CARRS, 1824 O, *Carr* 1788 *Elwes*, 1784 *MiscDep 77*, cf. *litle carr* 1668, *Little carr* 1674, ~ *Carre* 1703, ~ *Carr* 1706, 1745 all *Terrier, Low Carr* 1767 *Stubbs, v.* **kjarr** 'a marsh, especially one

overgrown with brushwood', as elsewhere in the parish. APPLEBY
HALL, *The Hall* 1828 Bry, cf. *Northaleng* 1316 Ipm, *Northalle Eng*
1388 Misc, *the Halling* 1625 *Terrier*, ~ *Hallings* 1652 *Yarb*, *Halinge*
1662, *Hallings* 1674, 1686, 1706, 1745, *Hallingsbecke* 1625, *Halling
beck* 1662, *the Hall Ings Becke* 1674, ~ ~ ~ *beck* 1706, 1745 all *Terrier*,
and *Hall Paddock* 1794 *MiscDep 77*, *v*. **hall**, **eng** 'meadow, pasture' as
elsewhere in this parish, **bekkr** 'a stream'. APPLEBY INGS, 1824 O, *le
ynge de Appulbye* 1535–46 *MinAcct*, *the Inges* 1602, ~ *Ings* 1625, 1668,
1674, 1686, 1706 all *Terrier*, *v*. **eng**. APPLEBY WARREN (lost), 1824 O,
1828 Bry, *Warren* 1794 *MiscDep 77*. APPLEBY WOOD, *Wood* 1784
MiscDep 77, 1823 *Yarb*, *Appleby W^d* 1828 Bry, *bosco de Appelbi* 1202
Ass, 1203 Abbr. BIRDHOUSE CLOUGH, cf. *Birds House* 1768 (1815)
LRA. BROOM HILL, cf. *Broom Close* 1794 *MiscDep 77*, *v*, **brōm**
'broom'. BURNT SLIP. CARR SIDE, *Appleby Carr side* 1824 *Terrier*, ~
Carrside 1824 O, ~ *Car Side* 1828 Bry, *Appleby-Car-Side Farm* 1848
TA MAP, *v*. **kjarr**. CHURCH LANE, *the king's street called the Church
Lane* 1625, *the king's street called The Church lane* 1662, *the kings
street called the church lane* 1674, *the kings street called the church
Laine* 1686, *the Church lane* 1697 all *Terrier*. COMMON PLANTATION,
cf. *the Common* 1625, 1697, 1706, *ye Coman* 1703, *the Comon* 1745 all
Terrier, *Common* 1794 *MiscDep 77*. CORONATION WOOD. CROSS.
FISH POND, FISHPOND PLANTATION. THE FOLLIES, *Folies* 1794 *Misc
Dep 77*, *Follies* 1824 O, *Follys W^d* 1828 Bry. GOOSEHOLE PUMPIMG
STATION. HAVERHOLME HO. JULIAN BOWER (lost), "Near the Roman
road was a *Julian Bower*, of which there were distinct traces till the
middle of the last century" 1842 White. Cf. Julian's Bower in
Alkborough parish *supra*. KEB WOOD, 1794 *MiscDep 77*, 1824 O, *Kib
W^d* 1828 Bry, cf. *Kebb Home Field* 1850 *TA*, no doubt named from the
surn. *Keb(b)*, cf. Nicholas *Kebbe* 1332 *SR*. LOW WOOD. MARE WALK,
1794 *MiscDep 77*, 1824 O, 1828 Bry, *v*. **walk** 'a stretch of grass used for
pasturing animals', hence the common L *sheepwalk* (*v*. **shepe-walk**), but
here for a *mare*. This is the first reference to a **mare-walk** so far noted
in this survey. MAUD HOLE, 1794 *MiscDep 77*. MICKLEHOLME, 1625,
1686, 1706, 1745 *Terrier*, 1794 *MiscDep 77*, 1824 O, *Mickalholme*
1662, *Mickle holme* 1674 both *Terrier*, 'the big raised land amidst the
marshes', *v*. **míkill**, **holmr**, a Scand compound. It is described as "a
sandy Hill" in 1794. MILL FM, cf. *Appleby Mill* 1824 O, *The Mills* 1828
Bry, *Water Corn Mill* 1652 *Yarb*, *ye mylndyke* 1577 (*v*. **dík**), *Milnefield*
1625, *far miln feild* 1668, *Mill field* 1674, *the mill field* 1686, ~ *Mill
field* 1706, 1745 all *Terrier* (*v*. **feld**). MORTAL ASH HILL. NEW

ENCLOSED BROOM, cf. Broom Hill *supra*. NORTH SIDE PLANTATION.
OAK TREE PLANTATION. OLD BROOM COVERT, cf. Broom Hill *supra*.
PADMOOR PLANTATION, cf. *Padmore* 1622 *Elwes*, 1652 *Yarb*, 'the
marshy land where toads are found', *v*. **padde** 'a toad', **mōr**, here
presumably in the sense 'marsh, marshy ground'. PASTURE LANE. PAUL
LANE. THE PITS (lost), 1828 Bry. REDDINGS WOOD (lost, adjoined west
of Top Wood), 1824 O, *Riddings Wood* 1794 *MiscDep 77*, *Rydyngs*
1387 Peace, *Readings* 1606 *Terrier*, ~ *Farme* 1652 *Yarb*, *Reddings* 1652
ib, 1788 *Terrier*, *the Hamlet of Readings* 1833 *EnclA*; probably 'the
clearings' from the pl. of **ryding**, though this is a rare el. in north L p.ns.
THE ROW. ROWLAND PLANTATION, 1824 O, 1828 Bry, presumably
from the forename or surn. *Rowland*. SAND HO, 1728 *Inv*, *Sandhouse*
1824 O. It is *Sand Hall* 1697 Pryme. SANTON COMMON (lost), 1824 O.
SANTON COTTAGES, 1824 O, 1828 Bry. SANTON GRANGE (lost), 1843
TA (Brumby), apparently a late example of **grange**, common in L, for
which *v*. EDD s.v. 2 'a homestead, a small mansion or farm-house, esp.
one standing by itself remote from others', a sense quoted from L.
SANTON HILL. SANTON WARREN (lost), 1810 *Yarb*, 1824 O, 1828 Bry.
SANTON WOOD, *boscum Santonie* a1175 YCh vi, *Santon W^d* 1828 Bry.
SCAB HILL. SIR ROWLAND WINN'S DRAIN, 1772 *EnclA* (Winterton),
1768 (1791) *LindDep Plans*, 1824 O. SOKE NOOK PLANTATION.
SPRING WOOD, 1824 O, ~ *W^d* 1828 Bry. STONE PIT PLANTATION.
STONEWALL PLANTATION. SWEETING THORNS. THORNHOLME MOOR
(local), *Thornholm more* 1695 Pryme, ~ *moor* 1697 ib. THORNHOLME
PLANTATION. TOP LARCHES. TOP WOOD. VICARAGE, *the Vicaredge
house* 1606, *Vicaridge* ~ 1625, *the vicarage* ~ 1662, 1686, ~ *vicaridge*
~ 1668, ~ *Vicarige* ~ 1697, ~ *Vicarridge* ~ 1706, ~ *Vicarage* ~ 1745, ~
House 1788, 1822, 1831, 1864 all *Terrier*. WEST DRAIN.
YARBOROUGH WOOD, named from the Earls of *Yarborough* who held
land in the parish. YOULL CLOSE, 1824 O, *Yowle close* 1662 *Terrier*,
Youle Close 1767 *Stubbs*, *Youls Close* 1769 *LindDep Plans*, cf. *Youle
close dyke* 1625, *youle close dicke* 1674, *youl close dicke* 1686 all
Terrier, named from the family of Christopher *Youle* 1606 *BT*.

FIELD-NAMES

The undated forms in (a) are 1794 *MiscDep 77*; those dated 1202[1] are
FF; 1202[2] Ass; 1203 Abbr; 1272, 1294, 1329 *Ass*; 1327, 1332 *SR*; 1343
NI; 1382, 1434 Cl; 1388 Misc; 1390 Works; 1535–46 *MinAcct*; 1573
AS; 1577, 1602, 1606, 1619, 1625, 1647, 1662, 1668, 1674, 1686, 1697,

1703, 1706, 1745, 1788², 1822, 1831, 1864 *Terrier*; 1583, 1698 *Asw*; 1622, 1657, 1788¹ *Elwes*; 1652, 1810, 1823, 1850, 1851 *Yarb*; 1660 (c1900) *LindDep 78*; 1661 *Featley*; 1695, 1697 Pryme; 1724, 1728 *Inv*; 1740 *Foster*; 1767 *Stubbs*; 1833 *EnclA*; 1848¹ *TA*; 1848² *TA Map*.

(a) Bank 1788¹, 1794, 1850, 1851; Beggers Bush 1848¹ (a common derogatory name for a piece of rough ground); Bell Beck (*Bellbecke* 1625, 1674, ~ *becke* 1625. *-becks* 1662, *belbeck* 1668, *Bell Becke* 1686, *Bell-beck* 1697, *Belbeck* 1706, 1745; the first el. is perhaps the surn. *Bell*, the second is **bekkr** 'a stream', as elsewhere in the parish); Boroughs; Broom Cl (*v.* **brōm** 'broom'); Burnt Carr (self-explanatory, *v.* **kjarr** 'a marsh' as elsewhere in this parish); Calf Cl 1848¹; Carr Eaves 1794 (*v.* **kjarr, efes** 'eaves; an edge or border' and cf. Appleby Carrs *supra*); Clarkes Carr (probably from the surn. *Clarke* and **kjarr**); Cottager Cl (or Carr) 1767, Cottager Carr, Cottagers Cl; Cow Cl 1794, 1848¹, ~ ~ Pasture 1848¹; Coxes ~, Cox's Carr 1767 (from the surn. *Cox* and **kjarr**); Criftins (*Criftings* 1662, 1668, *Criftinge, the Criftins* 1686, *Crifteings, Criftings* 1697, *the Criftings* 1703, 1706, 1745, *v.* **crifting** 'a small croft'); Croft (*v.* **croft**); Davids Cl 1848¹ (from the pers.n. or surn. *David*); East Carr 1850 (*v.* **kjarr**); the East Moor 1833; Eight Acre Fd; Eighteen Acre Fd 1810; Far Carr 1794, 1850 (*v.* **kjarr**); Far, Near Fd 1794, Far fd, Far far fd (sic), Near Far Fd 1848¹ (cf. *campis de Appelby* 1272, *the Fyldes of Appelby* 1583, *Appleby feild* 1647, *v.* **feld**); Firman's Cl 1767, Furman Cl (from the surn. *Firman* or *Furman*); Fish Carr 1767, 1794 (*v.* **kjarr**; *Fish* may well be a surn. here); Great Fitts (from **fit** 'grassland on the bank of a river', found in coastal parishes of L); Foal Cl; Gads (from ME **gadd(e)** defined in NED s.v. *gad* 6b as 'a division of an open pasture, in Lincolnshire usually 6 and a half feet wide', but note *2 gades of meadow at 9 foote the gad* 1606 *Terrier* (Scawby)); Gale Croft; Garings (from dial. *gairing* (EDD s.v. *gair*) 'a triangular piece of land which cannot be ploughed with the rest of the field' recorded only from L; it is a derivative of ON **geiri**, cf. PN L **3**, 62 and 108); Garth (*v.* **garðr** 'an enclosure', as elsewhere in the parish; this is adjacent to a house); Gokewell Fd 1810 (probably from the surn. *Gokewell*); Hawdy Fd 1794, Hawdys ~ 1848¹; Hemp Garth 1794, the hemp-garths 1822, ~ Hemp-garths 1831 (*v.* **hænep** 'hemp', **garðr**); Highfield; Home Cl; Home Fd 1848²; Horse Carr 1848¹ (*v.* **kjarr**); Ings Bank (cf. Appleby Ings *supra*); Kiphouse Cl 1767, Kippars Carr; Lane end Fd 1848¹; Lill Ing 1767 (*Lill Ings* 1603, 1657, *lill Inges* 1622, *Lill Ings* 1657, *the lill ings* 1671 (*v.* **eng**)), Lill Fd 1788², ~ Fds 1822, Lill-fields 1831, Lill-fields 1864 (*Lilfeild* 1552, *the lill fields* 1671, *Lillfields* 1745, *the new lill Feilds* 1603, 1619, *le newe lill feild* 1622, *New Lill feildes* 1654, *the old Lill Feildes* 1603, *le ould lillfeildes* 1622, *the old Lill feildes* 1657, cf. *Lill Garthes* 1603, *lill garthes* 1622, *Lill garthes* 1657, and *Middle Lyll Inges* 1667, *the lill ings close* 1626 and *Lyllemilledam* 1388 (*v.* **myln**, ME **damme** (ON **dammr**), probably named from the ME surn. *Lille*); Low Carr 1794 (*v.* **kjarr**); Low Warren 1810 (*v.* **wareine**); Middle Bank; Middle Carr 1850 (*v.* **kjarr**); Milnes Carr (from the surn. *Milne(s)* and **kjarr**); Miry Woodfield; Moor, Moor Cl; New Cl 1810; Nine Acres 1848¹; Nooking (from dial. *nooking* 'a nook of land', *v.* **nōk** and cf. *The Nookings* PN L **3**, 144); Old Saintfoins Cl 1810 (*v.* **sainfoin**); Pimperton Carr 1767, 1794 (named from the *Pimperton* family, cf. Nicholas *Pimperton* 1642 LPR, with **kjarr**); Pingle (*the Pingle* 1652, *v.* **pingel** 'a small enclosure'); Pond Cl 1810; Pry Ings (v. **eng**; *Pry* is probably from ME **prey**, **pre** 'a meadow'); Rush Carr 1848[1] (v. **risc**, **kjarr**); Rye Garth (v. **ryge**, **garðr**); Sandhills; Santon Odd Tree (a picture of one tree is shown on the plan), Santon Cl 1810, Santon Ings 1794, 1810, 1823 (v. **eng**, each named from Santon *supra*); Scawby Gates (from Scawby and the pl. of **gata**); Sear(s)by Carr (probably from a surn. *Sear(s)by* and **kjarr**); Second Fd; Sheep Dike Cl 1848[1] (adjoining a dike); Shift Carr (v. **kjarr**; the sense of *shift* is uncertain, as in previous references, cf. PN L **2**, 60, 116 and **4**, 40); South Fd (*the littiel* (sic) *Southe feild* 1602, ~ *litle south field* 1625, ~ ~ *southfeild* 1662, ~ ~ *south feild* 1668, ~ *Little South field* 1674, 1686, ~ *little South field* 1690, ~ *Little South-field* 1706, ~ *little southfield* 1745, one of the open fields of the village, v. **sūð**, **feld**); Spinner Cl, Little ~ ~; Stothard Dale (from the surn. *Stothard* and **deill** 'a share of land'); Thatch Carr 1767, Thack Carr 1767, 1794 (v. **þæcc** 'thatching material', Scandinavianised in two examples, and **kjarr**); Thornham Hills (cf. *bosco de Thorn'holm* 1329, from Thornholme *supra*); Tithe Pce; Top Fd; Townend Cl; Twelve Acres 1848[1]; West Carr 1850 (v. **kjarr**); Westidge or Home Cl (*Westead Close* 1652, *Westhead* 1724, v. **west**, **hēafod** 'a headland in the common field'); Yadmir(e) Ings (sic) (v. **eng**).

(b) *the Abbey Land* 1606; *Appleby dike end* 1573 (v. **dík**); *Appleby Grange* 1740 (apparently a late use of **grange**, for details of which v. *Santon Grange supra*); *the Awlners or Awners Close* 1652 ('an enclosure assigned to the *alnager* or inspector of cloth', v. NED s.v. *alner, aulner*); *battholme* (sic) 1577, *battyl holme* 1602, *Batlet holme* (sic) 1606, *Battleholme* 1625, 1674, 1686, 1674, 1745, *Batletholme* 1668, *Batleholme* 1674, *Battle holme* 1690, ~ *home* (sic) 1696 (perhaps from **bataille** in the sense 'a legal battle, a juridical battle' and **holmr** 'raised land amidst marsh'); *the Beck-half Spenny* (sic) 1745; *Blind Laine* (v. *long horne lane infra*); *a comon way called Bownam* 1598; *Bratton-grave-hill* 1697; *the Canon land* 1606 ('the land assigned to a community of canons', v. **canoun**); *the Church land* 1660 (c1900), 1697; *Coltbecke lane* 1625, *Colt beck* ~ 1662, *Cols beck* ~ 1668, *Colltbecke (Laine)*, *Coltbecke Laine* 1674, *Coult becke* ~ 1686, *Cole beck lane* 1697, *Colebeck-lane* 1706 (probably 'the stream where colts are found', v. **colt**, **bekkr**, with **lane**); *Cottwalle* 1535–46; *Cranes wood* 1652 (named from the *Crane* family, cf. William *Crane* 1642 LPR); *Dians ground* 1668; *doue coat lane* 1625, *the lane called Douecoat* 1662, *Dovecoat lane* 1668, *Douecoat Laine* 1674, *douecoat* ~ 1686, *Doves Court lane* 1697, *Dove Coate-Laine* 1706 (self-explanatory, v. **douve-cote**); *the Dry Ings* 1745 (v. **drȳge**, **eng** 'meadow, pasture'); *the East heads* 1625, 1668, 1697, 1745, *the east* ~ 1674, *yᵉ East Head* 1703 (v. **ēast**, **hēafod** and cf. Westidge in f.ns. (a) *supra*); *Estwode* 1382 ('the wood to the east', v. **ēast**, **wudu**); *the Firthes* 1652 (v. **fyhrð** 'a wood'); *Gallows hills* 1697 (self-explanatory, v. **galga**, **hyll**); *griswell* 1625, *Griswell* 1674, *Grasill* 1703, *Greswell becke* 1697, -*beck* 1662, *greswll beck* 1668, *Greswell Becke* 1674, *Greaswell beck* 1706, *Griswell* ~ 1745 (*griswell* may be 'the spring where young pigs are found', v. **gríss** (ME **grise**), **wella**, but the forms are too varied for certainty); *Hoops Lane* 1661; *the horseclose* 1652; *Howdicke gate* 1624, *How dicks* ~ 1662, *Howdick* ~ 1668, *How-dike* ~1697, *How dick* ~ 1745, *North Howdicks* 1625, 1662, *North How dicks* 1668, *north how* ~ 1674, *North Howdicke* 1686, ~ *Howdick* 1703, 1706 (*How* is uncertain here, but may be **haugr** 'a hill, a mound'; the name is perhaps to be identified with Hawdy Fd in f.ns. (a) *supra*); *Kemps Wood*

1652, *Kemp Wood Hous* (sic) 1728 (no doubt from the surn. *Kemp* with **wudu**); *the knowle* 1625, *The Knowle* 1662, 1668, 1706, 1745, *the knowles* 1674, ~ *Knowls* 1686, ~ *Knolls* 1697, *y* *knoule* 1703, *the knowles* 1745 (*v.* **cnoll** 'a hillock'); *Atte Kylne* 1327 (p) (*v.* **kyln**); *Linholme staines* 1625, *line Holme stains* 1662, ~ *holme stanes* 1668, *Linholme Staines* 1674 ('the raised land amidst the marsh where flax grows', *v.* **līn** or **lín** and **holmr** with the pl. of **steinn** 'a stone', in what sense is not clear); *Longholme* 1625 (*v.* **lang**, **holmr**); *blind lane or long horne lane* 1625, ~ ~ *or longhorne lane* 1662, *Blind Laine or Longhorne Laine* 1674, *Long horne Laine* 1686, *long-horn-lane* 1697, *Longhorn-lane* 1706 ('the long horn-shaped piece of land', *v* **lang**, **horn** with **lane**; a *blind lane* is a cul-de-sac); *the Lords dayle Marfer* 1625, ~ *lords dayle Marfer* 1662, ~ *lords-Dail marfer* 1668, ~ *Lords dayle marfer* 1674, ~ ~ *daile marfer* 1686, *y* *Lords dale Marfar* 1703, *the Lords-dale-marfer* 1706, ~ *Lordsdale Marfar* 1745 ('the lord's share, portion of land', *v.* **deill**, with **marfur** 'a boundary furrow'); *Micheles acras* 1202[1] (from the ME pers.n. *Michel* and **æcer**); *Maut Hills* 1697; *Northyby* 1327, *Northiby* 1332, 1343 all (p) (literally '(place) north in the village', *v.* **norð**, **í**, **bȳ** and cf. *Westiby infra*); *the North-way* 1706, ~ *north way* 1745; *parco . . . de Appelby* 1271 (*v.* **parke**); *Rosiman* 1625, 1662, 1674, *Roseiman* 1686, *Rosemain* 1745 (obscure); *le Santon' Bek* 1390 (*v.* **bekkr**), *Santon gate* 1625, 1668, 1697, 1745, (*South*) *Santon gate* 1662, *Santon gat(e)* 1674, 1686, ~ *Gate* 1703 ('the road to Santon', *v.* **gata**); *Segcroft* 1388 (*v.* **secg** 'sedge', in a Scandinavianised form, **croft**); *lez Shepegarthes* 1535–46 (*v.* **scēap**, **garðr**); *le Shepegattes* 1535–46 (*v.* **shep-gate** 'pasturage or right of pasturage for sheep', cf. Sheep Gates PN L **2**, 244); *Southegate* 1706 (*v.* **sūð**, **gata**); *atte strete* 1294 (p) (*v.* **strǣt** 'a Roman road', no doubt a reference to Ermine Street); *Stridge more* 1625, 1668, *Strig more* 1674, *String more* (sic) 1686, *Strigmore* 1703, 1706, 1745 (obscure); *Swinheard horne* 1625, 1652, *Swin heard horne* 1668, *Swinerd Horne* 1674, ~ *horne* 1686, *Swine heard Horne* 1703, *Swineheard horn Lane* 1745 (from the occupational name *Swinherd* or the derived surn. and **horn** 'a horn-shaped piece of land', cf. *long horne lane supra*); *the Threescore Gadd* 1652 (*v.* **gadd(e)** and also Gads in f.ns. (a) *supra*); *Wallynge place* 1434 (from the ME surn. *Walling* and **place** 'a plot of ground, a residence'); *Waymersch* 1388, *wamarsh becke* 1625, *way marsh beck* 1662, *wa marsh Beck*, *way marsh beck* 1668, *wamarsh Becke* 1674, *Wamarsh becke* 1686, *Waymarsh beck* 1697, *wamarch beck* (sic) 1703, *Wamarsh Beck* 1706, ~ *beck* 1745 (*v.* **bekkr**; the first el. of *Weymersch* is obscure, the second is **mersc** 'marsh'); *Westiby* 1327, *Westyby* 1332 both (p) (literally '(place) west in the village', *v.* **west**, **í**, **bȳ** and cf. *Northyby supra*); *the Williamsons wood* 1562 (named from the family of Michael *Williamson* 1642 LPR).

Ashby

ASHBY

    Aschebi (4x) 1086 DB, c1115 LS

    Asebi c1115 LS, *-by* 1305 *KR*, ~ *als Ashby* 1671 *BRA* 787

    Esseby c1090 (1402) Dugd iv, *-bi* 1136–40 (1464) Pat

Eschebi John (p1263) YCh iii

Askebi 1178 P, Hy2 (1464) Pat, 1194 CurP, 1212 Fees, 1219 FF, *-by*
Hy2 (e14) Selby, 1196 ChancR. 1204 ChR, 1223, 1240–43 RA ii,
1271 Ch, 1281 QW, 1282 *FF et freq* to 1522 CA, *-bye* 1573 Hall,
Ascebi 1214 Cur

Askby 1393 Peace, 1402 FA, 1535 VE iv, *Ascby alias Ashby* 1671
Red

Asby 1451 Cl, 1488 *FF*, *-bie* 1584 Hall

Assheby 1481 Pat, 1550 Pat, *Asheby* 1556 AASR xxxvii, 1566 Pat,
-bie 1589 NCWills i

Asschby 1548 ChantCert, *Ashby* 1599 *DCLB et passim*, *-bee* 1606
Terrier, *-bie* 1637 *Foster*

There are six p.ns. Ashby in L. The forms of each are similar and
they are probably Danish compounds meaning 'the farmstead, village
where ash-trees grow', *v.* **askr, bȳ**. It is possible, however, that the first
el. is the ON, ODan pers.n. *Aski* found occasionally in independent
sources in L, cf. Ashby, PN Nf **2**, 41. *v.* also the discussion of Ashby, PN
L **4**, 48–49.

ASHBY DECOY, 1824 O, 1828 Bry. ASHBY DECOY FM, *Decoy Ho* 1828
ib, *there is still a large Decoy (9 miles W. of Brigg,) abounding in wild
ducks and other aquatic birds and having near it a handsome mansion,
called Decoy Cottage, built in 1841, by its owner and occupier, Hy.
Healey, Esq.* 1842 White. ASHBY NORTH & SOUTH GRANGE, cf. *Ashby
Grange* 1824 O, 1828 Bry, *v.* **grange** and for the significance *v. Santon
Grange supra.* BRAT HILL. COMMON PLANTATION, cf. *ashby Comans*
1724 *Terrier* (Bottesford), *Ashby Common* 1787 *MiscDep* 77, 1797
EnclA (Bottesford). EMANUEL BRIDGE, 1824 O. GREEN LANE, 1828
Bry, forming part of the boundary with Brumby. LOWER HO, 1828 ib.
MANOR FM. MILL FM, cf. *Ashby Mill* 1828 ib, *molendinum de Eschebi*
John YCh iii, *uno molendino in campis de Ashbi* 1573 *TLE, mill furlong*
1668 *Terrier*, *-furlong* 1750 *FLMisc*, self-explanatory. PRIORY LANE,
Prior Lane 1809 *EnclA*. SCOTTER RD, 1797 *ib* (Bottesford). SCREEDS,
cf. *Back Screed* 1750 *FLMisc*, *West Cliffe North Screed, ~ ~ South ~*
1772 *ib*, from dial. *screed* 'a small narrow piece of land'. SLATE HOUSE
PIT, 1828 Bry. STANIWELL HILL. WEST END FM. WOODHOUSE.

FIELD-NAMES

Forms dated John are YCh iii; e13, e14 *AD*; c1263 RA ii; 1282 *FF*; 1298 Ass; 1301, 1302, 1303, 1306, 1307, 1311, 1314 *KR*; 1327 *SR*, 1388 Cl; 1416 *LCCA*;, 1551 Pat; 1573 *TLE*; 1606, 1668, 1679, 1700, 1706, 1724, 1745, 1749, 1755 *Terrier* (Bottesford); 1616, 1784, 1787 *MiscDep 77*; 1750, 1772 *FLMisc*; 1797 *EnclA* (Bottesford); 1802 *Td'E*; 1809 *EnclA*.

(a) Ashby East Moor (*East More* 1616, self-explanatory); Ashby fd 1755, 1797 (1697, 1700, 1749, *in campo de Askeby* 1306, *in campis de Askebi* 1314, *in campis* 1616, *Ashby-field*, *Ashby field mere* 1706 (*v.* (**ge**)**mære** 'a boundary') (*v.* **feld**, referring to the open fields of the village); Ashby Scammons 1755, Scum holms 1750, Scum holms 1784 (*Ashby Scumans* 1706, ~ *Scammans* 1745, obscure); Ashby South Fd 1797 (one of the open fields of the village); Ashby Moor 1787 (cf. Ashby East Moor *supra*); Beanlands Flg 1750, 1772 (*v.* **bēan**, **land** 'a selion' in the pl.); Between Closes Flg 1750, 1772; Boarden Bridge 1809 ('the bridge made of boards, planks', from ME **borden** and **brycg**; it adjoined Brumby); Bramers Flg 1750, Brames ~, Upper Breams ~ 1772); Bransdale Flg 1750, Brooms Dale ~1772; Brigg Rd 1809 (the road leading to Glanford Brigg); Bull Piece Flg 1750, ~ piece Flg 1772; Brumby Cl 1750,1772 (from Brumby an adjoining parish); Burringham Rd 1809 (the road to Burringham, a neighbouring parish); Burton Rd 1809 (the road to Burton upon Stather); the Catchwater Drain 1809; Low Cawthorn Flg 1750, Low Cawkithorn Flg (sic) 1772; Chapel Cl 1772 (cf. *le Chappell Garthe* 1551, *v.* **garðr** 'an enclosure'); Chapple Lane Cl 1750; Upper Cock Mores Flg 1750; Collton Pasture 1809 (named from the *Colton* family, cf. David *Colton*, David *Coulton* (the same person) 1819); Coney hows Flg 1750, 1772 (*v.* **coni** 'a rabbit', **haugr** 'a mound, a hill'); Upper Crofts Flg, Crofts Close Flg 1750 (*v.* **croft**); Cross Drain 1809; Curwells Flg 1772 (perhaps from the surn. *Curwell*); the East Common 1784, 1802, 1809, ~ Commons 1809; East fd 1750, ~ Fd 1784, 1809 (*Ashby Eastfield* 1679, ~ *East fied* (sic) 1706, one of the open fields of the village); Gainsborough Rd 1809 (the road to Gainsborough, some 25 miles to the south); Low Heller trees Flg 1750, Low Heller Trees 1772, Short Heller trees Flg 1750, 1772, Long ~ ~ ~ 1772 (*v.* **elri** 'an alder-tree'); Hemps Crofts Flg 1750, Hemp Croft 1772 (*v.* **hænep**, **croft**); Hey Gates Flg 1750; Hills Flg 1750 (John *Hill* is named in the document); Home Cl 1750, 1772; Houlsikes Flg (*v.* **hol**[1] 'a hollow', **sík**); Huntson Mares Flg 1750, 1772 (probably from the surn. *Huntson* and (**ge**)**mære** 'a boundary, land forming a boundary'); one othe (sic) private Drain to be called the Impropriators 1809; Inglow Flg 1750, 1772 (probably from the surn. *Inglow*); Inner Delf Drain, the Inner Delve Drain 1809 (*v.* (**ge**)**delf**, here 'a trench, a channel'); Kirk Briggs Flg 1750 (*v.* **kirkja**, **brycg** the latter in the pl. and in a Scandinavianised form); Lane End Flg 1750; Leayses Cl 1772 (*v.* **lǣs** 'pasture, meadow-land' in the pl.); Lightfoot House (from the surn. *Lightfoot*, cf. Thomas *Lightfoott* 1611 *BT* (Bottesford)); Longworths Flg 1750, 1772 (from the surn. *Longworth*); Manby gates Flg 1750, 1772 (*v.* **gata** 'a road' and Manby in Broughton parish); Manwell Bridge 1809; Low, Upper Market Stile Flg 1750, Low, Upper Markit Steel Flg 1772 (*v.* **market**, **stigel** 'a stile'); Marsh 1750, 1772, 1809,

Marsh Ends 1750, 1772, the Marsh Gate 1809 (v. **gata**), Marsh Side flg 1750 (self-explanatory); Messingam Gates Flg 1750, 1772 (the road to Messingham a few miles to the south); Middle Dales Flg 1750 (v. **middel, deill** 'a share, a portion of land'); Milforms Meer 1784 (v. **(ge)mǣre**); the Mill Mear 1784 (v. **myln, (ge)mǣre**); the Moors 1809; New Close Flg 1750; North Fd 1750, 1772, 1784, 1809 (one of the open fields of the village); North Lane 1809; North leares Flg 1750, ~ Leayers 1772 (perhaps from **leirr** 'clay'); Patrick Dale Flg 1750, ~ Dales Flg 1772, Paterick Dales Stinting 1784 (from the surn. *Patrick* and **deill**, with **stinting** 'an individual share of the common meadow' and cf. *Stintinge* PN L **3**, 63); Pease hows Flg 1750, the Pease Hows 1784 (v. **pise** 'pease', **haugr** 'a mound, a hill'); Ranhows Flg 1750, Ranhow House Corner 1784; Riding Heads Flg, Low ridings Platt 1750, ~ riding platt 1772 (v. **plat** 'a plot, a small piece of ground'), Middle ridings Flg 1750, 1772, the Reddings 1784 (probably from **ryding** 'a clearing'); the Sand Hills 1809; the Sand Pitt 1809; Scotter Rd 1809 (the road to Scotter, south of Ashby); Short Butts Flg 1750, Short butts 1772 (v. **sc(e)ort, butte** 'a strip of land abutting on a boundary', 'a short strip at right angles to others'); (Long, Short) Sound Wells Flg 1750; South Fd 1750, 1772, 1809 (cf. (the) East Fd *supra*); South East Fd 1809; South Lane 1809; the Stone Pit 1809; Streets Flg 1750, 1772; Swarthacres Flg 1750 (the first el. may be OE **sweart** or ON **svartr** 'dark, black' with **æcer**); Swikes Flg 1750 (the first el. may well be OE **swice** 'a trap, a snare'); Low Tanhous Flg 1750, ~ Tanhows Flg, Upper Tanhows ~ 1750, 1772 (from ME **tan-hous** 'a tannery'); Short Tharms Flg (sic) 1750; Low, Upper thrushpit flg 1750, Low Thrush pits 1772 ('the pit haunted by a giant, a demon', v. **þurs, pytt**, cf. *Thurspits* in Bottesford f.ns. (b)); Town End Drain 1809; (Upper) Tumblestangs Flg 1750, 1772 (*low Thimble stonge, upper thimble stonges* 1668, the second el. is **stǫng** 'a pole, a stave' used as a standard of measure 'a pole'; the first is doubtful); Wait land 1772; Wastelands Flg 1750 (self-explanatory); West Cliff Cl 1750 (cf. Screeds *supra*); West Commons 1809; (the) West Fd 1784, 1809 (cf. (the) East Fd *supra*); Low, upper Windham(s) Flg 1772 (presumably from the surn. *Windham*); Upper Windings Flg 1750, Low, Middle, Upper Windings Flg 1772 (apparently literally 'the winding place' in some topographical sense and unrecorded in dictionaries, from OE **(ge)wind**[2] and OE **ing**[1], and cf. PN L **2**, 173).

(b) *Asbee Becke* 1606 (v. **bekkr** 'a stream'); *Asbee Rundell* 1606 (v. **rynel** 'a small stream, a runnel'); *Bersewic* e13 (from the ON pers.n. *Bersi* and OE **wīc** probably the sense 'berewick, outlying farm'); *Callum* (sic) 1668, *Columland* 1679 (obscure); *flates* 1668 (v. **flat** 'a piece of level ground', dial. 'a division of the common field'); *aulam de Askeby* c1263, 1298, *aula de* ~ e14, *atte Halle* 1388, *atte Hall' de Askby* 1396, *atte Halle de Askeby* 1416 all (p) ('the hall', v. **hall**); *atte Kirkeyate de Askeby* 1301, *attekirkyat* ~ ~ 1314 both (p) (v. **kirkja, geat** 'a gate'); *Trentinges* 1573 (from the R. Trent and **eng** 'meadow, pasture'); *attewell'* 1311, *ad Fontem* 1332 both (p) (v. **wella** 'a spring'); *attewesthall'* 1282 (p) (v. **west, hall** and cf. *aulam de Askeby supra*); *Westyby* 1302, *Westiby* 1307, 1332 all (p) ('(place) west in the village', v. **vestr, west, í, bȳ**, denoting X who lived in the west of the village, a common formation in L); *West more* 1616 (cf. Ashby East Moor in f.ns. (a) *supra*).

Bottesford

BOTTESFORD

Budlesforde 1086 DB
Bulesforde (sic) 1086 DB
Botlesforda c1115 LS, *-forde* c1128 (12) ChronPetro, c1265 RA ii,
  -ford(') 1196 ChancR, 1202, 1203 Ass, 1223 RA ii, 1240 FF *et
  passim* to 1379 Cl, *Botelesford('*) 1220 Cur, 1226 FF, 1230 Cur,
  1230 FF *et passim* to 1376 Cl, *Botellesford* 1332 ib, *Bothelesford*
  1236–47 YCh x, *Bottlisford'* 1242–43 Fees
Botleford' 1254 ValNor, *Botelforde* c1265 RA ii, *Botilford* 1346 FA,
  -forth 1428 ib
Botenesford(') 1189 (e14) Selby, c1210 RA ii, 1220 Cur, 1282 Fine,
  1290 RA ii, 112 *AD*, 1300 Ipm *et freq* to 1446 *DCAcct*, *-fordia*
  c1190 RA ii, *-forde iuxta Messingham* 1305 ib, *Botensford* 1297
  AD, Bottensfort 1275 RH, *Bottenesford* 1443, 1479 *DCAcct*, 1526
  Sub, *-forth* 1519 DV, 1566 Pat
Botnesford(') 1204 ChR, 1271 Ch, (*in Lyndeseye*) 1272 FF, 1305,
  1306 RA ii, 1338 Hosp, 1522 CA, 1535 VE iv, *Bottnesford* 1601,
  1606 *Terrier, -forth otherwise Bottsford* 1760 *DCLB*
Botenforde c1263 RA ii, *-ford* 1276 RH, 1314 *KR*
Botisford c1189 (e14) Selby, *Botesford* 1212 Fees, 1375 Pat, 1393
  Pap, 1409 RRep, *-forth* 1637 Foster, *Botysford* 1428 FA
Bottesford(') 1220 Cur, 1220 Welles, 1398 Pap, 1445 Pat, 1526 Sub
  et passim, -forth 1548 ChantCert, *-forthe* 1548 PrState, *Bottesford
  alias Bottnesforth* 1590, 1599 *DCLB, Botesforde als Bottesforth*
  1607 *ib, Bottisford* 1535 VE iv, 1576 LER, 1679 *Terrier, -forth
  alias Bottnesforth* 1584 *ib, -ford als Bottisforth* 1664 *DCLB*
Botsford 1638 *Foster*
Bottesworthe 1558–79 ChancP, 1576 Saxton, 1614 Hall, *Bottsworthe*
  1586 ib, *Bottsworth* 1696 Pryme

'The ford belonging to the building, house', *v.* **botl** (in the gen.sg.),
ford, identical with Bottesford Lei. It was presumably a ford over
Bottesford Beck. The interchange of the consonants *l* and *n* is due to AN
influence. The replacement of *-ford* by *-worth* in some 16th and 17th
centuries spellings is noteworthy.

YADDLETHORPE

Iadulftorp (2x) 1086 DB
Iadulfestorp 1086 DB
Edoltorp 1100–15 (1397) Pat (p), *-thorp* 1219 Ass
Edoluestorp c1115 LS, *Eduluestorp* 1196 ChancR
Hiadeltorp 1212 Fees
Yadiltorp e13 *AD*, *Yadeltorp* e13 *ib*, *-thorp*(*e*) m13 *ib*, *-thorp*(') 1281
    QW, (*iuxta Boteneford'*) 1282 *FF*, 113 *AD*, 1300 Ipm, 1301 *KR*,
    e14 *AD*, 1307 *KR*, 1316 FA, *-thrope* 1558–79 ChancP
Yatelthorp(') 1272 *Ass*, 1304 Pat, 1327, 1332 *SR*, *Yatilthorp* 1382
    Misc
Yedlethorpe 1599, 1607, 1664 *DCLB*
Yadlethorpe 1616 *MiscDep 177*, 1637 *Foster*, *-thorp* 1666 *ib*, 1689
    WillsStow, *Yaddlethorpe* 1643 Hall *et passim*

The first el. is a Scandinavianised form of *Iadulf*, cf. the OE pers.n
Ēadwulf. The normal English development is represented in forms in
Edolt(*h*)*orp*, *Edoluestorp*, *Eduluestorp*. Forms in *Iadulf*(*es*)*torp*,
Hiadeltorp, *Yadiltorp*, etc., have been Scandinavianised, as Dr Insley
points out. He further notes that in these forms the OE diphthong /ēa/
has undergone a shift of stress to /jā/, which must have happened before
the late OE monophthongisation of /ēa/ and which must have also
existed side by side with the native form which was continued in the ME
forms in *Edol-*, *Edolu-*, *Edulu-*. The second el. is **þorp**, hence 'Iadulf's
secondary settlement, dependent outlying farmstead or village (of
Bottesford)'.

BOTTESFORD BECK, 1797 *EnclA*, 1824 O, 1828 Bry, *yᵉ botsford beck*
1583 *MiscDon 344*, *Bottnesford Becke* 1606 *Terrier*, *the Becke* 1601, ~
Beck 1679, 1697, 1706, 1724, *yᵉ Beck* 1745 all *Terrier*, v. **bekkr** 'a
stream' as elsewhere in the parish. BOTTESFORD MOOR, 1797 *EnclA*,
"the moor of" *Botsworthe* (sic) 1585 Hall, self-explanatory. BRANK
WELL, 1887 *TAMap*, ~ *well* 1797 *EnclA*, v. **wella** 'a spring', topograph-
ically appropriate; the first el. is perhaps *brank* 'buckwheat', v. NED s.v.
brank, sb¹. HILLS FM (lost), *Hills Fᵐ* 1828 ib, probably named from the
Hill family, cf. John *Hill* 1603 *BT*. IVY COTTAGES, 1887 *TAMap*. LEYS
FM, 1887 *ib*. MANOR HO, *Manor Farm* 1887 *ib*, cf. *it seemeth that the*
Pryor of Newsted, had certaine landes vnder the name of a Manor in
Bottesforde, and vpon the disslucion of the pryorye, that lande

comminge to the handes of the Kinge the kinge graunted the same in fee vnto one Charles Sutton 1616 *MiscDep 77.* MOOR WELL FM. NEWDOWN, 1887 *TAMap.* PEACOCKS & HALLS DRAIN (lost), 1828 Bry; named from the families of E.S. *Peacock* 1842 White, lord of the manor, and Thomas *Hall* 1669 *BT.* SNAKE PLANTATION, 1887 *TAMap.* SOUTHFIELD FM. TEMPLAR'S BATH, cf. *Templewood* 1545 LP xxii, commemorating lands formerly held by the Knights Templar. THE THISTLES, 1797 *EnclA,* 1887 *TAMap.* VICARAGE (lost), *the Vicaredge* 1601, ~ *Vicaredge howse* 1606, ~ *vicaridge house* 1697, *The Mansion or vicaridge howse* 1724, *The Vicarage house was many years ago burnt down; about 12 years ago* y^e *late Bishop gave leave to* y^e *present* Vic^r *to take all* y^e *remains of Stone & Timber and use them towards* y^e *rebuilding* y^e *Vicarage house at Messingham to which Bottesford is united, so* y^t *now there are no remains of* ye s^d *old house* 1745, *Plot of Ground where the Vicarage formerly stood* 1755 all *Terrier.* WARP FM, *Warp* F^m 1828 Bry, from *warp,* v. NED sb.[1], 6.a. 'alluvial sediment deposited by water; silt'. WARPING CLOSE FM (lost), *Warping Close* F^m 1828 Bry, for *warping v.* NED s.v. 'the process of flooding low-lying land . . . so that the muddy alluvium may be deposited when the water is withdrawn'. WATER MILL FM, y^e *water myln* 1583 *MiscDon 344,* cf. *Mildam hole* 1601, *mildam* ~ 1606, *milllane* 1668, *the Milne Lane* 1697, *milne lane* 1700, *the Milne-lane* 1706, y^e *milnlane* 1724, ~ *Miln Lane* 1755 all *Terrier.* YADDLETHORPE GRANGE.

FIELD-NAMES

Forms dated 1219, c1310 are RA ii; e13, m13 *AD;* 1306 *KR;* 1327, 1332 *SR;* 1343 NI; 1583 *MiscDon 344;* 1595 *Brace;* 1616 *MiscDep 177;* 1601, 1606, 1668, 1679, 1697, 1706, 1724, 1745, 1755 *Terrier;* 1797 *EnclA;* 1887 *TAMap;* 1904 *TA.*

(a) Ashby field Mear 1755 (~ ~ *meer* 1679, 1696, ~ ~ *mere* 1706, ~ ~ *meare* 1745, 'the boundary with Ashby Field', *v.* (**ge**)**mǣre** and cf. Ashby fd in Ashby f.ns. (a)); Ashby Rd 1797 (*the Kings heighe waie going to Asbee* 1606, self-explanatory); Bean Cl 1755 (y^e *Beane Close* 1679, *Bean Close* 1697, 1745, *Bean-Close* 1706, self-explanatory); Black Land Fd 1904; Bleach Yd 1887; Bottesford Fd (1745, *Bottisford field* 1706, *Botsford field* 1724, *v.* **feld,** referring to the open field of the village); Broom Cl 1755 (*Broom close* 1706, ~ *Close* 1724, 1745, *v.* **brōm** 'broom', **clos(e)**); ye Butt Cl 1755 (*the but Close* 1668, *Butclose* 1679, 1696, *the But-close* 1706, y^e *But Closse* 1724, *Butts Close* 1745, cf. *the furlong called Butte furlong* 1601, *Butt furlonge* 1606, *v.* **butte** 'a short strip or ridge at right angles to other ridges, etc.'); Butt close Pingle 1755 (*Butt Close pingle* 1724, *Butts Close* ~ 1745, *v.* **pingel** 'a small enclosure'); Clay Pit fd 1904; Common 1755 (y^e *Common* 1679, 1745), Bottesford Common 1797 (*the Commons of yadlethorpe and Bottesford* 1616); the Common Lane, the Common Rd 1797; ye Conygarth 1755 (*Le Coninger* c1310, *Cony garths* 1595, (*the*) *Conigarth* 1679, 1697, y^e ~ 1706, ~ *Conygarth* 1745, *Conie garth Closse* 1601, *Cunnigarth* 1668, 'the rabbit-warren', *v.* **coninger**, apparently replaced by **coni**, **garðr** with the same meaning); Cow Cl 1755 ((*the*) *Cow Close* 1679, 1724, 1745, *Cow-Close* 1697, *Cow close* 1706); Croakom Cl 1755 (*Crukam Close* 1697, *Crookam* ~ 1706, *Crookem* ~ 1724, *Crookham* ~ 1745, probably as Dr. Insley suggests 'the piece of dry land in a marsh, etc., at a curve or bend', a Scand compound, *v.* **krókr**, **holmr**; (*h*)*am* etc. is a frequent reflex of **holmr** in L); Cross Lane 1797; Eight Acres 1904; Floodgate Cl 1755 (1745, *fludyeatt Closse* 1601, *Fluddyeatt* ~ 1606, *Floudgat Close* 1668, *floodgate close* 1679, 1724, *Floodgate* ~ 1697, 1706, self-explanatory); Part 14 Acres 1904; Gravel Pit 1795, the Gravel pitts in Hiller Stubbs, Gravel Pit Rd 1797 (*v.* Hiller Stubbs *infra*); Green How Hill 1797; ye headland 1755 (1679, *the* ~ 1697, 1724, *Headland* 1745, *v.* **hēafod-land** 'the head of a strip of land left for turning the plough'); Hill Side 1904; Hiller Stubbs 1797 (*Hillerstob* c1310, *Ellerscrubs* (sic) 1679, *Heller stubs* 1697, *v.* **elri** 'an alder-tree', **stubb** 'a tree-stump'); Kitlingdale 1755 (*Kiteledail* m13, *Kitleindale Close* 1679, 1706, *Kitleindale-close* 1697, *Kitlindale Close* 1745; the first el. is probably a ME pers.n. *Kiteling* with **deill** 'a share, a portion of land'); Great, little Langhows 1755 (*langhou* c1310, *a furlong called long howes* 1601, *the long howes* 1606, *litle* ~ ~ 1668, *Little-longhowe* 1679, ~ *Longhowe* 1687, *great*, *Litle Langhows* 1706, y^e *great Longhowes*, *litt* (sic) *Long howes* 1724, *great*, *little Langhows* 1745, *v.* **lang**, **haugr** 'a hill, a (burial) mound'); Letter Box Fd 1904 (presumably a reference to the shape of the field); Low Cl 1904; ye low Dale 1755 (*the low dale* 1706, y^e *Low Dail* 1724, *v.* **deill**); Great Miln fd, ye little Milnfield 1755 (*the great mill fild*, *the littel millfild* 1668, *the milnefield* 1679, *the great-milne field*, ~ *litle mil-fild* 1697, *Great*, *litle miln(e)field* 1706, y^e *great Millfield*, ~ *little Mill-field* 1745, self-explanatory); ye New Cl 1755 (*the new closse* 1601, 1606, ~ ~ *Close* 1668, 1679, ~ ~ *close* 1697, *nue Close* 1724, *new Close* 1745); ye Oak Cl 1755 (*the oke closse hedge* 1601, *Oke closse* 1606, *the Oak Close* 1679, ~ *Oak-close* 1697, 1745, y^e *Oak Close* 1745); Pan-field 1755 ((*the*) *Panfield* 1679, y^e *panfield* 1724, *the Pan pce* 1606, *pan pees* 1668, *Panpiece* 1697, 1745, *panpiece* 1706, *Midow caled painpies* (sic) 1724, probably from **panne** 'a pan' in p.ns. used topographically of something thought to resemble a pan in shape, with **feld** and **pece**); ye Prince of Wales's lands 1755; Rate pit Cl 1755 (*the nether Ratepyttes*, *the upper Rate pyttes* 1601, *the nether*, *the Uppermost Ratte pyttes* 1601, ~ *Rat Pit Close* 1668, *Ratepit* ~ 1679, 1706, *Rait pit Close* 1724, perhaps 'the rat holes', *v.* **ræt**, **pytt**); the Redhouse Garth 1755 (*the Red-house garth* 1697, y^e *Red howse garth* 1724, ~ *Read house garth* 1745, *v.* **garðr**); the old Sand Cl 1797; Sand Pit 1797; Shepherds Barn 1904 (probably named from the family of Thomas *Sheperd* 1614 *BT*. The surn. goes back at least to the 14th century in the parish, note William *Shephird* 1332); Short Butt Cl 1755 (*Le Schortbuttes* c1310, *the shortt Buttes* 1601, ~ ~ *Butt* 1606, *short buttes* 1679, *Short butts* 1706, y^e *Short but Close* 1668, *Short but close* 1679, *Shortbut-close* 1697, *short Butt-Close* 1745, *v.* **sceort**, **butte** and cf. ye Butt Cl *supra*); a piece of meadow called Shoulder of Mutton 1755 (*a close called Shoulder of Mutton* 1679, ~ ~ *called the Shoulder of mutton* 1697, *a Close Called shoulder of Mutton* 1706, *a parcell of Meadow called Shoulder of Mutton* 1745, a common fanciful name for a piece of land so shaped); the Spring in the Common 1797; Stone Cl 1755 (*Stone close side* 1679, *Stone Close* 1697, 1706, 1724, 1745, self-explanatory); the Street 1755 (*ye Street* 1724, 1745); Stripes Cl and Orchard 1904; Ten Acres 1904; ye way to Yaddlethorpe 1755 (*ye way to Yadle thorp* 1724); Whimmam Busk 1755 (*Whin um buske* (sic) 1668, *Whinam Busk* 1679, 1745, *~ Bush* 1724, obscure); Whitacre Lees 1755 (*Whitakers leas* 1679, *Whitacre Lees* 1697, *~ lees* 1706, *Whiteker Leeas* (sic) 1724, *Whitacre lees* 1745, *v.* **lea** (OE **lēah**) 'grassland, pasture' in the pl.; *Whitacre* is probably a surn. here); ye Wood 1755 (*the wood* 1601, 1679, 1706, *Bottnesford wood* 1606, and cf. *ex suth' parte bosci* c1300); Yaddlethorpe Beck fd 1797 (*v.* **bekkr**); Yaddlethorpe Channel fd 1797; Yaddlethorpe Common, *~* Common lane end 1797; Yaddlethorpe Ferrand Fd 1797 (Thomas Gerrard *Ferrand* is named in the document); Yaddlethorpe fd 1755, *~* Fd 1797 (*Yaddellthorpp feeldes* 1601, *Yadlethorp field* 1679, *yadlethorp ~* 1706); Yaddlethorpe Lane, *~* Moor, *~* North fd, *~* old street Cl, *~* Sand fd, *~* Town Street all 1797 (named from Yaddlethorpe *supra*).

(b) *a furlong called the Acars* 1601, *ye Acckers* 1745 (*v.* **acer** in the pl.); *Basnit dalle* 1668, *One Dale called Basnet-Dale containing 27 lands* 1679 (*v.* **deill** 'a share, a portion of land'; *Basnet* is presumably a surn.); *Beck-bridge* 1679 (named from Bottesford Beck *supra*); *Bottnesford north feeld* 1601, *in campo boriali* 1616 (one of the open fields of the village); *Bottnesford woodfeeld* 1601, *the neither, the upper wood feeld* 1606 (*v.* **wudu**, **feld** and cf. ye Wood in f.ns. (a) *supra*); *le Brill(e)* c1310 (obscure); *the Carre dicthe* (sic) 1601, *the Carr* 1679 (*v.* **kjarr, dīc**); *dikdales* 1668 (*v.* **dík, deill**); *Nether-, Ouerdedemanacre* c1310 (from **dēad-mann** 'a deadman' and **æcer** 'a plot of cultivated land', presumably a reference to a medieval tragedy); *thest feeld* 1601, *in campo orientali* 1616 (*v.* **east, feld**, one of the open fields of the village); *Le Foulesik'* (*v.* **fūl** 'foul, dirty', **sík** 'a ditch, a trench'); *the Nether, the upper Frinstangs* 1679 (*v.* **stǫng** 'a pole'; the sense of *Frin-* is not clear); *Galighov, Galghoufurlanges* e13 (*v.* **galga** ' a gallows', **haugr** ' hill, a mound', with **furlang**); *ye gray inges* 1583 (*v.* **græg** 'grey' in what sense is not clear, **eng** 'meadow, pasture'); *atte Grene* 1332 (p) (*v.* **grēne** 'a village green, a grassy spot'); *atte Hall* 1343 (p) (self-explanatory); *hogges headland* 1601, *hogge ~* 1606 (*v.* **hēafod-land**; *Hogg* may well be a surn. here); *clausi de Langeneia* 1219 (perhaps 'at the long piece of dry land in marsh', *v.* **lang** (dat.sg. *langan*) and **ēg**, cf. *Langleys* PN L **3**, 123–24); *Dr Lincolne Acres* 1697 (from a *Dr Lincoln* named in the document); *long Akares* 1668 (self-explanatory); *ye Common Merfer* 1679 (*v.* **marfur** 'a boundary furrow'); *Mikelhou* c1310 ('the great, big mound, hill', *v.* **mikill, haugr**, a Scand compound); *midge holes* 1601 (presumably self-explanatory, *v.* **micg, hol** 'a hollow'); *motton medow(e)* 1601, *~ medowe* 1606; *prato commune vocato Mott mere* 1616 (*v.* **gemōt** 'a meeting-place', **(ge)mære** 'a boundary'); *Northwode* e13 (self-explanatory); *Nortons Closse* 1601, *norton close* 1606 (no doubt from the surn. *Norton*); *ye parsonage lane* 1706; *Peashows* 1679 (*v.* **pise** 'pease', **haugr**); *Rameschou* m13 (probably 'the raven wood', *v.* **hrafn, skógr**, a Scand compound); *Ramsey Close* 1679 (from the surn. *Ramsey*, cf. John *Ramsey* 1642 LPR); *the Road land* 1697; *the Seauen Nobles Close* 1668, *seaven nobles Close* 1679, *7 nobles close* 1697, *seven nobles Close* 1706 (a reference to a rent or purchase price, a *noble* was a coin worth one-third of a pound sterling); *Sidland gat Close* 1668 (probably 'the broad selion', *v.* **sīd, land,** with **gata** and **clos(e)**); *the nether, the upper Skowes* 1601, *the neither, the upper skowes* 1606 (perhaps 'the woods', *v.* ON **skógr**); *in campo australi* 1616 (one of the open fields of the village); *the stack close* 1668; *Steynberyge* e13, *stainberge* m13 ('the stony hill', *v.* **steinn, berg,** a Scand compound); *ye staking,* ~ *Steyking,* ~ *stay king* 1583; *the stonne pyttes* 1601, *y^e* ~ ~ 1706; *Tesacre* c1310 (the first el. may be OE **tǣse** 'useful', but additional forms are needed); *Thurspits* 1679 ('the pits, hollows haunted by demons, giants', *v.* **þurs** 'giant', **pytt**, and cf. Low, Upper thrushpit flg in Ashby f.ns. (a)); *Le toftis* c1310 (*v.* **toft** 'a messuage, a curtilage' in the pl.); *the twenti Shilling Close* 1668 (probably an allusion to rent, cf. *the Seaven Nobles Close supra*); *the upper furlong* 1601; *2 Oxganges of Land called warneot* 1616 (for a discussion of *Wardnoth, v.* PN L **2,** 104 and for additional references PN L **3,** 57–58 and ib **4,** 72); *Westiby* 1332 (p) ('(place) west in the village', *v.* **vestr, í, bȳ,** a common formation in L, denoting X who lives in the west of the village); *ye willow beck* 1583; *the furlong called windell signe furlong* (the reading is doubtful); *Le Wodecroft* c1310 (self-explanatory, cf. ye Wood in f.ns. (a) *supra*); *Wodhus* 1306, *Wodhous* 1327, 1332 all (p), 'the house in the wood', *v.* **wudu, hūs**); *the wood furlong* 1668; *Wryith miers* (sic) 1601; *Wybaldwelles* e13, *Wybaldeswellles* m13 ('Wibald's springs', from the ContGerm pers.n. *Wi(g)bald* and **wella**).

Broughton

BROUGHTON

> *Bertone* (2x) 1086 DB, 1100–08 YCh vi, 1197, 1108 P, -*ton('*) 1166–79 YCh vi, 1187 *et passim* in P to 1199, 1185 RotDom, a1223 Goke, 1224 Cur, 1254 ValNor, 1491 Ipm, -*tona* 1090–1110 YCh vi, 1135–40 ib, 1136–40 1136–40 (1464) Pat, 112 CollTop, -*thona* 1100–08 YCh vi, -*tuna* c1115 LS, -*tun* a1175, 1175, 1205–23 Goke
>
> *Berchtun* c1128 ChronPetro, -*ton'* 1185 Templar, *Berehtun* 1154 BMFacs (p), -*ton* Hy2 (1464), *Bercton* 1223 Pat
>
> *Bergtun* 1212 Fees, -*ton* 1224, 1225, 1226 FF, -*tone* 1277 RRGr, -*ton'* 1305 RA ii *Berghetun'* 1224 Cur, 1327 *SR, Berghton* 1242–43 Fees, 1291 Tax, 1294 Abbr, 1303 FA, 1305 Ch, 1309 *FF,* ("by" *Scalleby*) 1311 Pat, 1316 FA, 1318 Pat, 1328 Banco *et freq* to 1428 FA, 1531 *Yarb*
>
> *Braghton* 1425 IBL, 1511 LP i, 1512 *Yarb,* 1526 Sub, 1573 *AS,* 1574 *Yarb, Braughton* 1434, 1470 *ib,* 1502 Ipm *et passim* to 1700 *Terrier*
>
> *Broghton* 1460 Pat, - *als Browghton* 1574 *Yarb, Broughton* 1494, 1501 Ipm, 1521 *Yarb,* 1535 VE iv, 1542 *AS,* 1547 *Yarb et freq,*

Broughton is as much as to say Burrow town from the vast plenty conney borrows that are round about it 1695 Pryme

'The farmstead, village, estate on the hill', *v.* **berg, tūn**. The village is situated on the slope rising from the R. Ancholme to the ridge along which Ermine Street runs.

CASTLETHORPE

Castorp 1086 DB
Cheistorp (2x) c1115 LS
Kaistorp 1224 FF, c1270 RA ii (p), *Keistorp* Hy3 (1311) Ch,
 Keysthorp 1531 *Yarb*, *Kaystorp* 1275 RH, *-thorp* 1271 FF, 1460
 Pat, *Kaystthorp'* 1290 RSu (p), *Kayesthorpe* 1347 Pat, *Kaysthorp'*
 als Casthorp' 1533 *Yarb*
Caysthorp(') 1281 Ass, 1316 FA, 1321 RA ii (p), 1332 *SR*, 1352 Pat,
 1362 Ipm, 1374, 1460 Pat, 1504–15 ECP xxix, *Caisthorpe* 1317
 ib, 1373, 1376 Peace, ~ *als Castlethorpe* 1705, 1716, 1769, 1784
 Yarb, *-thorp* 1365 Pat, 1529, 1626 WillsStow, ~ *als Castlethorpe*
 1716 *Yarb*
Casthorp(') e14 *Asw* (p), 1381 Peace, 1431 FA, 1464, 1470, 1488,
 1510, 1512, 1531 *Yarb*, 1576 Saxton, 1607 Camden, *-thorpe* 1487
 Yarb, 1506 Pat, 1509 *Yarb*, 1610 Speed, ~ *alias Castlethrop* 1659
 Yarb, ~ *als Castlethorpe* 1697 *ib*
Casthrope 1506 Ipm, *Casthrop* 1510 LP i, 1512 *Yarb*, *-trop* 1532,
 1538, 1747 *ib*, ~ *als Castlethorp* 1599 *ib*, 1685 WillsStow, *-trope*
 1535 VE iv, 1536 LP xi, 1575 *Shef*, *-tropp* 1574, 1614 *DCLB*, ~
 als Castlethorpe 1689 *Yarb*
Caistrop 1536–37 Dugd vi, 1680 WillsStow, 1704 FMB, 1712 *Yarb*,
 Caystroppe 1576, 1625 *Yarb*, *-tropp als Castlethorpp* 1602 *ib*,
 Caistroppe 1657, 1724 *ib*, *Caisthrop als Castlethorp* 1693 *ib*,
 -trope otherwise Castlethorpe 1745 *Foster*
Castilthorpe als Castlethorpe 1680 *Yarb*, *Castlethorp* 1685
 WillsStow, *-thorpe* 1695 *Yarb et passim*, ~ *otherwise Caisthorpe*
 1734 *ib*, ~ *otherwise Castrop* 1762 *ib*

The second el. is **þorp** 'a secondary settlement, a dependent, outlying farmstead or hamlet', no doubt of Broughton. The first el. is difficult, but Dr Insley suggests it may be a Scand byname, either ON *Keikr*, from ON *keikr* 'crook-backed' or ON *Keiss* from Nynorsk *keis* 'a bend, a curve' or the adj. *keis* 'difficult to manage, prevail upon'. The change to Castlethorpe has not been noted before the late 16th century and presumably was due to popular etymology of the kind inferred from Pryme (1696). He wrongly believed that *Castrop* [was] *formerly call'd Castlethorp* and he explains the latter as being named *from a great castle that was there in King John's days, the ruins of which are now scarce to be seen, onely the place where it stood is called Castle Hill to this day.*

GOKEWELL PRIORY FM

Gaukeuell' 1185 Templar, -*well* 1382 Wills i, *Gawkewell* 1526 Sub
Goucuella 112 CollTop, -*well* 1257 Ch, *Goucewelle* 1269 (m13) NCot
Goukewell e13 YCh vi (p), 1314 Ch, 1343 NI, -*well'* 1212 Fees, 1270 (m13) *NCot*, 1270 Cl, 1321, 1329 RA ii, 1359 Wills i, -*welle* 1445 Visit, *Goukwelle* 1270 *NCot*, 1334 Misc, 1335 Inqaqd, -*well'* 1279 RRGr, -*well* 1328 Banco, 1382 Misc, 1397 Pap
Goukeswelle 1311, 1315 Pat, -*well* 1318, 1374 ib, 1410 Inqaqd, 1411 Pat
Gokewell' 1395 Peace, *Gokewelle alias vocat' le aschedale* 1487 Yarb, -*well* 1552 PrState, 1576 Saxton, 1610 Speed *et passim*
Goykwell 1530 Wills iii, 1535 VE iv, 1537 *AOMB 209*, 1538 LP xiii, 1561 Pat, *Goikewell* 1546 LP xxi, *Goikwell* 1563 Pat
Gookewell 1526 Sub, *Gookwel als Gooquell* 1517 *Yarb*

'The spring frequented by cuckoos', *v.* **gaukr, wella**, a hybrid Anglo-Scandinavian name. The site of the Priory here was called *eskadal'* a1175 Goke, *Eskadal'* Hy2 ib, *le aschedale* 1487 *Yarb*, 'the valley where ash-trees grow', *v.* **eski, dalr**, a Scand compound.

MANBY

Mannebi 1086 DB, a1175, 1175 Goke, 1191, 1192 P (p), 1205–23 Goke, 1209 P (p), a1223 Goke, -*b'* Stephen CollTop, -*by* c1216 (m14) CNat, 1257 Ch, 1310 YearBk, 1316 FA, 1532 *Yarb*, ~ *iuxta Bergh'ton* 1329 *Ass*, ~ *iuxta Caisthorp'* 1370 *Yarb*
Manebi 1181 P (p)
Manby 1340 Pat, 1344 *Yarb*, 1383, 1383 Fine, 1387, 1388 Cl *et freq*, ~ *iuxta Raventhorpe* 1487 *Yarb*, *Manbye* 1610 Speed

'Manni's farmstead, village', *v*. **bȳ**. The first el. is the ODan pers.n. *Manni*. The place is described as being near Broughton, Castlethorpe and Raventhorpe, the name surviving in Manby Hall *infra*. *v*. also Manley Wapentake *supra*.

BARROW HILL (local), 1824 O, ~ *Hills* 1828 Bry, 1828 *Survey*, the name of a mound at approx SE 957 088. BECKINGHAM SHAW, 1824 O, 1828 *Survey*, *woode called Beckingham Shawe* 1578 *Yarb*, named from a long-established family in the parish, cf. Thomas *de Bekyngham* 1386 Fine, and *v*. **sceaga** 'a small wood, a copse'. BLEACHING HO (lost), 1824 O. BLOWTHORNE SITWATE, cf. *Blowthorns* 1828 *Survey*, 1841 *TA*, obscure. BRACKEN HILL, 1824 O, 1846 *Nelthorpe*, cf. *Bracken hill closes* 1672 *Yarb*, ~ *hill Closes* 1700 *Dixon*, self-explanatory. BRICKHILLS FM, *Brick Hills Farm House* 1823 *Yarb*, *Brick Kiln F^m* 1828 Bry, cf. *Brickhill close* 1659, ~ *Close* 1667, 1697, *Brickhill* 1676, *Brickkiln Close* 1810 all *Yarb*; *Brickhill(s)* is frequently for *Brickiln(s)*. BRIDGE FM, *Bridge House* 1852 *Padley*, named from Broughton Bridge *infra*. BROADHAM COVER (lost), 1828 Bry, perhaps 'the broad raised piece of land in the marsh', *v*. **brād**, **holmr** as elsewhere in this parish. BROOMFIELD PLANTATION. BROUGHTON BRIDGE, 1824 O. BROUGHTON CARRS, 1768 *Stubbs*, *Braughton Carres* 1632 *Yarb*, cf. *Broughton Carr Side* 1824 O, 1828 Bry, *v*. **kjarr** 'brushwood', 'a marsh, a bog, especially one overgrown with brushwood', as very frequently in this parish. BROUGHTON COMMON, 1768 (1791) *LindDep Plans*, 1824 O, 1828 Bry, *the common* 1601 *Terrier*, *Browton Common* 1799 *Yarb*. BROUGHTON DECOY FM, DECOY HO, *Decoy* 1824 O, *Decoy Ho.*, *The Decoy* (now OLD DECOY) 1828 Bry, cf. *Decoy Carr* 1768 *Stubbs*, 1828 *Survey*, ~ *Car* 1841 *TA*. BROUGHTON GRANGE, built in 1848 and for the significance of **grange** here, *v*. *Santon Grange* in Appleby parish *supra*. BROUGHTON SCHOOL HOUSES, *School House* 1824 O, cf. *School-house Field* 1841 *TA*. BROUGHTON VALE. BROUGHTON WOOD (lost), 1696 Pryme, 1828 Bry, "wood of" *Berghton* 1358 Ch, *the wood of Broughton* 1531 *Yarb*, *Braughton Woodes* 1542 *AS*. CASTLETHORPE BRIDGE, 1799 *Yarb*, 1824 O, *Castleton Draw Bridge* (sic) 1828 Bry. CASTLETHORPE COVERT, ~ *Cover* 1824 O. CASTLETHORPE HALL, *Casthorpe als Castlethorpe Hall* 1683 *Nelthorpe*, *This hall was built about the year 1600 (as appears from a stone over the gate)* 1696 Pryme, cf. *le Hallfeld* 1538 SP xiii. CASTLETHORPE MILL (lost), *Mill* 1828 Bry, cf. "the mill-pond of" *Caysthorp* 1362 Ipm. COAL DYKE END, *v*. PN L **2**, 118. CRESSEY WOOD (local), 1841 *TA*, cf. *Cressey*

Close 1810 *Yarb*, named from the family of Michael *Creshey* 1659, Ralph *Cressey* 1696 both *Yarb*. CROW COVERT. DENT WOOD, *Dents Wood* 1846 *Nelthorpe*, cf. *Dents Carr* 1680, 1697 *Yarb*, named from a long-established Broughton family, cf. Robert *Dent* 1541 WillsStow, with **kjarr**. DIAMOND LEYS WOOD, cf. *Diamond Leys* 1810 *Yarb*, 1828 *Survey*, 1841 *TA*; names in *Diamond* usually have reference to shape, but the wood today forms a square; for *Leys, v.* lea (OE **lēah**) 'meadow, pasture' in the pl. EAST WOOD, 1824 O, 1828 Bry. EMANUEL WOOD. FAR WOOD, 1824 O, 1841 *TA*. FIRST WOOD, 1841 *ib*, ~ ~ *E. of Roman Road* 1846 *Nelthorpe*. GADBURY WOOD, 1823 *Yarb*, ~ *wood* 1810 *ib*, presumably from the surn. *Gadbury*. GOKEWELL STRIP, a narrow strip of woodland. GYP WELL (local), *Gipwell* 1695 Pryme, *Gyp or Gil-well* 1697 ib, described by Pryme as *a low sunken place*. HERON HOLT. ICEHOUSE STRIP. LUNDIMORE WOOD. MALTKILN COTTAGE (local), dated 1715 P&H, and cf. Malt Kiln in f.ns. (a) *infra*. MANBY COMMON, 1828, ~ *Com*[n]. MANBY HALL, 1828 Bry, *the maner plac' of Manby* 1513 *Yarb*, and cf. *the Hallgarth* 1507 *ib, v.* **garðr** 'an enclosure' as elsewhere in this parish. MANBY WOOD. MILLFIELD PLANTATION, cf. *in maragio de Bertun unum molendinum* 1175 Goke, *molendini mei in Bertona* 112 CollTop, *in marisco de Bertun vnum molendinum* 1205–23 Goke, *Mill field* 1810 *Yarb*, *Mill* 1828 Bry. OLD DECOY, *v*. Broughton Decoy Ho *supra*. THE OAKS (lost), 1828 Bry. OWSTONE NEW HO (lost), 1828 Bry, presumably from the surn. *Owston*. PARSONAGE (lost), 1547 *Yarb*, *the parsonage of Braughton als Browton* 1602 *Nelthorpe, the parsonage house* 1662, *A parsonage house* 1668, *The* ~ ~ 1686, 1700, *the Parsonage House* 1822 all *Terrier*. PLANKER DIKE, 1768 (1791) *LindDep Plans*, ~ *Dyke* 1824 O. POND HEAD WOOD, cf. *Fish Ponds* 1842 *TA*. RECTORY FM. RED LION, 1842 White, the "Red Lion" Public House 1845 *Padley*. SINNEY HILLS PLANTATION. SKIN HOUSE (lost), 1828 Bry. SODWALL PLANTATION. SPRING DIKE. SPRINGFIELD PLANTATION, *Spring Field Cover* 1824 O, *Springfield* ~ 1828 Bry, cf. *Spring field* 1810 *Yarb*. STEAM BONE MILL (lost), 1828 Bry. TOP HEDGE. TOWER MILL (local), *Tower Wind Mill* 1845 Padley, perhaps cf. *Goykwell' Molendin' ventrit'* 1540–41 Dugd v. It was built in 1804 P&H. WATERMILL PLACE. WEIR DIKE. WEST WOOD, 1841 *TA*. WRESSELL HO, *Wressle Houses* 1824 O, cf. *one Close . . . commonly called . . . Wressel* 1761 *Yarb*, *Wressel Closes* 1799 *ib*, named from the family of John *Wressell* 1680 *ib*. YARBOROUGH PLACE, named from the Earls of *Yarborough* lords of the manor.

FIELD-NAMES

Undated forms in (a) are 1841 *TA*. Those dated a1175, 1175, 1205–23
are Goke; 1257 Ch; 1310 YearBk; 1327, 1332 *SR*; 1362 Misc; 1383,
1397 Peace; 1487, 1507, 1603, 1616, 1633, 1649, 1655, 1659, 1667,
1676, 1680, 1687, 1689, 1695, 1697, 1716, 1722, 1724, 1734, 1761,
1762, 1769, 1784, 1799, 1800, 1810, 1815, 1818, 1823 *Yarb*; 1540–1
Dugd v; 1541, 1573 *AS*; 1601, 1662, 1668, 1679, 1688, 1693, 1700,
1745, 1794, 1800, 1806, 1867 *Terrier*; 1602, 1611, 1683, 1710, 1792,
1846 *Nelthorpe*; 1600 (c1900) *LindDep 78*; 1696, 1697 Pryme; 1719,
1764 *Dixon*; 1768 *Stubbs*; 1828 *Survey* (ex. Mr N. Lyons of Scawby);
1839 *TGH*; 1845, 1852 *Padley*.

(a) Acre. Pce 1815; Almsdale Stone Pit 1852; Ancholme Bank 1810, 1823;
Appleby Car (from Appleby, a neighbouring parish, with **kjarr**; Carr(s) occurs
regularly in the parishes bordering the R. Ancholme and is particularly common in
the f.ns. of Broughton); Ash Cl 1810, Ash Garth 1815 (cf. *Atte Esc'* 1327, *atte Essh'*
1332 both (p), *v.* **æsc, garðr**); Ass Paddock 1828, 1841; Back; Back Cl 1846; Back
Yd; Badger Cl 1828, 1841, 1845; Bainton Cl, ~ Yd 1810, Banton Hill 1828, ~ Hills
1841 (named from the *Bainton* family, cf. Richard *Bainton* 1586 *PR*); Baldwin Carr
1810 (named from the *Baldwin* family, cf. Robert *Baldwin* 1629 *PR*); Bank; Barleys
Cl 1828, Barley's ~ 1841 (Thomas *Barley* is named in the document and *v.* Dunkirk
infra); Barn and Field, Barn Car, ~ Cl; Beck Cl 1846 (*v.* **bekkr** 'a stream' as
elsewhere in this parish); Bedlam Fd 1810 (a common derogatory f.n., alluding to the
Hospital of St Mary of Bethlem in London, for difficult land that only a madman
would attempt to cultivate); Bennett Cl 1810 (named from the *Bennett* family, cf.
Gregory *Bennytte* 1559 *PR*); Bottany Bay 1828, Botany ~ 1841 (referring to the penal
settlement in New South Wales, used in many parts of England of land that was
remote or needing much hard labour); Bottom Carr 1828, ~ Car 1841; Bramble
Nooking 1828 (from dial. *nooking* 'a nook', a derivative of **nōk** 'a nook', and for
early examples *v.* PN L **2**, 144); Brickyard Car 1846; Broad Cl 1810; Broad Lands
1810, ~ lands 1828, 1841 (*Broadlane* (sic) 1667, ~ *Lane* (sic) 1676, ~ *lands* 1680,
1697, *the Broad Lands* 1683, *v.* **land** 'a selion'); Brook Fd 1841, 1846; Broughton
Cl 1846 (*v.* Ox cl *infra*); Broughton Fd 1828, 1841, 1846; Bun Fd 1810; Burial Grd;
Burny Carr 1828, ~ Car 1841 (perhaps alluding to the burning of turf below the
surface); Butt Garth 1815 (perhaps *v.* **butt** 'an archery butt', **garðr**); Cabbage Yd;
Calf Cl 1819, 1841, 1846; Cainey Cl 1828; Cano Cl; Low Capar Hills 1828; Caped
Carr 1831; Carr Heads 1810, the Carr heads 1831 (*v.* **hēafod** in what sense is
uncertain); Carrot Garth (*v.* **garðr**); Low, Top Casson Hill; Castlethorpe Carrs 1768,
1810 (*the Carrs of Caistroppe* 1687, *v.* **kjarr**); Castlethorpe Causeway 1831 (*the
Cawsey* 1680, *v.* **caucie**); Castlethorpe Lane and Field 1810; Cat Garth 1828 (*v.*
garðr); Causeway Carr 1828, ~ Car (**caucie**); Causway Brig (sic) (*v.* **brycg**, in a
Scandinavianised form); Corseway Corner (sic) 1828; Chafor's Car (named from the
family of John *Chafor*, an occupier); Chery Tree Fd 1828, 1841; Church Cl 1815, ~

Twenty Acre (sic) 1815; Clammers 1828, Clamors; Clunterton Beck, ~ Btm 1828, ~ Walk 1845 (*Clunterton* is presumably a surn., so far untraced in the documents searched); Cold Harbour Fm (a common name for a sheltered place in an exposed situation); Comthornham (sic) (obscure); Cook Fd 1810 (named from the *Cook* family, cf. Ralf *Cooke* 1540 *PR*); Cottager's Cl 1841, 1845, Cottagers Common 1846; Cow Cl 1810, 1841 (*Cow Closes* 1710), Cow Garth 1810 (*v.* **garðr**); Cow House 1818; (Bottom, First, Second, Third) Coy Carr 1828 (cf. *Coy Causey* 1660 (c1900); *Coy* is short for *Decoy*, cf. Broughton Decoy Fm *supra*); Crow Garth 1828, 1841, ~ Yard 1841 (*close called Crawgarth* 1683, *v.* **crāwe, garðr, geard**); Damsels (Cl) 1810 (*damsealls* 1603, obscure); Dawson Cl 1810 (named from the *Dawson* family, cf. Robert *Dawson* 1556 *PR*); Dove Cote Cl 1799, ~ cote Cl 1800, Dove Cote Garth 1810 (*v.* **garðr**); the late Erected Malt Kiln comonly called . . . Dunkirk and formerly by the name of Moorhouse and of Old by the name of Barley House 1768, that late erected Maltkiln comonly called . . . Dunkirk and formerly by the name of Moorhouse and of Old by the name of Barley House 1784, a Maltkiln . . . formerly known by the name of Moorhouse and of old by the name of Barley house 1809, that Maltkiln with the yard or Toft . . . commonly called or known by the name of Dunkirk formerly by the name of Moor House and of old by the name of Barley House 1831 (*that Cottage house now partly demolished . . . called by the name of Moor house* 1694, *that Cottage house . . . of late called by the name of moore house of olde by the name of Barley house* 1695, *that Cottage . . . called by the name of Dunkirk and some time of late called by the name of Moore house and of old by the name of Barley house* 1722, *New Errected Malt Kiln . . . comonly called . . . Dunkirk and formerly by the Name of Moor house and of Old by the Name of Barley house* 1734. The sense of *Dunkirk* in p.ns. and f.ns. is usually derogatory, indicating a place of hardship or disaster); Gt, Lt Dunnanlees 1828, Dunmowe Leys (obscure); East Cl 1846; East Fd 1815, 1841; Eastland Carr 1828, ~ Car 1841 (*v.* **land**); Eight Acres 1810, 1841; Eighteen Acres; Eleven Acres; Engineer Carr; Euston or Ellson Carr 1828, Euston Car; Far Carr 1828, ~ Car, ~ ~ Lane Cl 1841; Far Cl 1799, 1841, 1845; Far Fd 1841, 1846; Far Twenty Acres; Feeding Cl; Fen 1815; the fifteen Acres 1799, Fifteen ~ 1815; First Car; Five Acres 1815; Five Stong 1815 ('five roods of land', *v.* **stǫng**); Fools Cl 1810, ~ cl 1831 (*a furlonge called foules* 1601, *Fowles close* 1683, obscure); Forty Acres 1810; Fourteen Acres; Fox Carr, Fox Cover 1810; Freehold Fd 1828, 1841; Furs Fd 1828, Furze ~ 1841, 1846; Galloway Cl 1810, 1823, ~ Garth 1810 (named from the *Galloway* family, cf. Francis *Galloway* 1725 *PR*, with **clos(e)** and **garðr**); Garden; Garth 1810 (*pastura vocat le Garthe* 1542, *v.* **garðr**); The George and dragon 1818, the George and Dragon Inn 1823; Gokewell Beck 1810 (*v.* **bekkr**), ~ Fd 1810; Gosling Hurn 1815 (perhaps from the surn. *Gosling* with **hyrne** 'an angle, a corner of land'); Gowsell Beck (sic) 1828, Goswell ~ (*Goose hill* 1680, *v.* **gōs, hyll**, with **bekkr**); Great Cl 1815 (*the great close* 1683); Green Cl 1846; Green Marsh 1828, 1841; Grey Yds 1828; Haggerthorn ~, Higgerthorne Btm (sic) 1810, Hagthorn Cl (*Haggathorne* 1680, 1689, 1716, *Hagathorne Close* 1683 (the first el. of Haggerthorn is obscure); Hannah Parish Cl; Heding Carr 1828, Heading Car (for the possible meaning of *Heading*, *v.* PN L **2**, 14, ib **3**, 69, ib **4**, 91; it is suggested that it may well have a similar sense to *Headland* denoting a place at the end of a ploughed field where the plough is turned); High Wood 1841, 1846; Hill side (Cl) 1810, 1841, Hillside Cl 1828; Lower, Upper Holmes 1810 (*v.* **holmr**); Holt

Fd 1810, Little Holt Hill (v. **holt**); Home Car 1846 (v. **kjarr**); Home Cl 1815, 1845, 1846, Home Cl (and Buildings) 1841, Home Fd 1810, 1841, 1846; Hopples 1828, 1841, Bracken Hopple, Broken ~ 1841(obscure); Hop Yd 1828; Hopyard Cl 1841, Hopyards 1810; Horse Back (sic); Horse Cl; Horse Pasture; Howes 1815; Hungry Leys 1815 (v. **hungrig** 'hungry, poor', **lea** (OE **lēah**) in the pl.; this name denotes infertile land, needing much manure); Hunt Fd 1810, 1828, the ~ ~ 1831, Far, Near Hunt Fd (named from the *Hunt* family, cf. Charles *Hunt* 1621 *PR*); Hunter's Car (named from the *Hunter* family, cf. John *Hunter* 1731 and John *Hunter*, an occupier, 1841); Huntsmans Moor 1846; the Ings 1761, 1762, 1799 (1689, 1747), The ~ 1841, Ings Carr 1810, 1828, 1841 (cf. *Ings Close* 1655, v. **eng** 'meadow, pasture'); Intake 1852 (v. **inntak** 'a piece of land taken in or enclosed'); Isaac Street Cl 1846; Island Carr 1818; Jewel Fd; Kannell Paddock (sic) 1810; Kilns Yd 1810; Far Knowls Cl 1828, ~ Knowles, Knowles Cl 1841 (v. **cnoll** 'a knoll, a hillock'); Labourers Cl; Lime Kiln Fd 1828, 1842; Lawn 1846 (probably v. **launde**); Little Car (*little Carre* 1660 (c1900)); Little cl 1810, 1846; Little Leys 1828 (v. **lea** (OE **lēah**) in the pl.); long Cl 1782, Long Cl 1794, 1806, 1841, 1846 (*the long close* 1688); Low Car 1841, 1867; Low Cl 1815, 1841, 1845; Low Fd; Malt Rooms Cl; Manby Common 1810, Manby Cl, ~ Plains (v. **plain** 'a piece of flat meadow-land'; cf. *campis de Manby* 1383); Markham's Cl 1828, 1841 (named from the *Markham* family, cf. Robert *Markham* 1642 *PR*); Marsh Cl 1810 (*marisco de Bertun* 1205–23); Martin Carr 1810 (presumably from the surn. *Martin*); Mawmill Cl 1810; Maumer Cl; Meadow Car, ~ Ings (v. **kjarr**, **eng** in the pl.); Middle Car; Middle Cl 1799, 1841; Middle Fd, ~ ~ Pce; Mill and Newhills (v. New Hills *infra*); Mill Carr 1828, ~ Car (*the Mill Carr* 1680, 1724 and cf. Millfields Plantation *supra*); Mole Car(r) 1826, 1841; Momas Cl 1828; Moor Cl 1846 (cf. "the moor" 1257); Moor Ling Wood 1846 (v. **mōr**, **lyng** 'heather'); Morley Car 1799 (named from the *Morley* family, cf. *Jessias Morley* 1676 *PR*); Nanpie Wood (for *nanpie*, v. EDD s.v *nantpie* sb. 'the magpie'); Narrow Cl; Narrow Strope; Nats Cl; Near Car Lane Cl; Ned Cl 1799, Neds Cl 1810, Ned's Cl; Nelson's Carr 1828, ~ Car (named from the *Nelson* family, cf. Thomas *Nelson* 1615 *PR*); Nelthorpe Arms Inn 1846; Nettleship Cl 1810 (presumably from the surn. *Nettleship*); New pce 1810; New Hills 1810, Newhills Cl 1828, Newhills 1841 (*the neweill close* 1603, *the Great North, South Newells* 1683); Nine Acre Carr 1810; Nine Acres 1810, 1841; First, Second, Third Nineteen Acres; North Cl 1810, 1841; Oathills 1828; Old Bank 1828, 1841; Old Cl; "old man Car" (sic) 1841, Old Man Car 1867; Old Sainfoin Pce 1810 (v. **sainfoin**); Old Street Platt 1828, 1841, ~ ~ Cl 1846 (v. **strǣt**, with reference to Ermine Street on which the village is situated; v. **plat**); Old Wife's Garth 1828. Old Wives ~ (v. **garðr**); the Onset 1815 ('premises; house, yard, outbuildings etc.'); Orchard 1828; Ox cl 1810 (*Ox Closes or Broughton Closes* 1710); Ozier Bed 1846; Pad Cl 1828, 1841 (*padd Close* 1660 (c1900), the first el. is probably **padde** 'a toad'); the Paddock (adjoining Malt Kiln) 1799, Paddock 1819, 1867; Parish Fd 1828, 1841; Peacock Cl 1810 (named from the *Peacock* family, cf. Richard *Peacocke* 1645 *PR*); Pinfold Cl 1810, 1841 (v. **pynd-fald**); Pingle 1815, 1841, ~ N[th] of Nook 1848 (v. **pingel** 'a small enclosure'); Plantation 1841, Plantation Fd 1841, 1846; Far Plough Car; Plump Car 1828, 1841; Popple Island 1810, Popple's Car (from the surn. *Popple*, cf. James *Popple*, an occupier in 1841); Potatoe Cl; Pump Fd; Rape Car 1828, 1841 (referring to oil-seed rape); River Car, Road Car (v. **kjarr**); Rope Walk 1818; Rough Cl, ~ Hills 1828, 1841; Roughs; Round Plantn; Sain

foin Cl 1810, Sangfoil Cl (sic), Sainfoin Cl 1841 (*v.* **sainfoin** and cf. Old Sainfoin
Pce *supra*); Sand Cl 1841, 1867, Sand Fd 1810, 1841, 1852, 1867, Sand Walk 1841,
1845 (*v.* **sand**, **walk**, cf. *a furlong caled the sandes* 1601); Sandersson Ness 1815
(named from the *Sanderson* family, cf. Edward *Saunderson* 1638 *PR*, and **nes**); Saw
Fd 1818; Scawby Gate Fd 1828, 1841 (cf. *Scaubie gate* 1601 'the road to Scawby (an
adjoining parish)', *v.* **gata**, cf. also *Scawby close* 1659, ~ *close* 1667, ~ *Closse* 1680,
Scalby close 1683 and *Scawby feild* 1680); Second Fd 1810, 1841, Seconds Fds
1831; Seed Walk 1828, 1841 (*v.* **walk**); Seven Acres 1815, 1841; Shaw 1810 (*v.*
sceaga); Sheep Walks 1792 (*the sheep walke* 1680, ~ *sheepe walke* 1683, *v.* **shepe-
walk**); Gt, Lt Silly Hills 1828, Silly Hills; Six Acres; Small Cl 1846; Spire Fd 1810
(probably from dial. *spire* 'reeds, rushes' *v.* **spīr**); Spring Cl 1810, 1828, ~ Fd 1810,
1845; Stack Yard Cl; Stainton Cl 1810 (named from the *Stainton* family, cf. Robert
Staynton 1538 *PR*); that newly erected Steam Corn Mill 1831, Steam Mill and Steam
Engine 1839; Stone Hills 1846; Stone Pit Cl 1828, 1846, Stonepit Cl; Stoney Dales
1810, Stony ~ 1828, 1841; Stripe Car (*v.* **strīp** 'a narrow tract of land'); Swannock
Cl 1846; Tan Yard Cl; Tape Cl 1815; Taylors Fen 1815 (named from the *Taylor*
family, cf. William *Taylor* 1604 *PR*); the ten Acres 1799, Ten ~ 1815, 1841; thirteen
Acres 1799, Thirteen ~ 1810; Thirty Acres (*Thirty Acres* 1676); Timothy Carr 1828,
~ Car 1841 (an allusion to catstail grass, *Phleum pratense*, the cultivation of which
was advocated by *Timothy* Hanson in the early eighteenth century, as Mr John Field
points out); Toad Pike Carr 1828, ~ ~ Car 1841(referring, under its popular name,
toadpike, to field horsetail, *equisetum arvense*, a weed of damp meadows, *v.* **kjarr**);
Tom Carr 1828; Top Car; Top Cl; Top Garden; Top Paddock Plantn 1810, Top
Paddock; Top Yd 1841, 1845; Tower Wind Mill 1845 (perhaps cf. *Goykwell'
Molend' ventrit'* 1540–41); the Town Carrs 1823, "The Town Car" (sic) 1841, Town
Car 1828, 1867 (presumably part of the Carrs belonging to the village); Town Fen
1815 (cf. the previous f.n.); Triangular Pce 1846; Turkey Carr 1810, Tucky ~ 1828,
~ Car, ~ Fd; Turf Pits 1810; Twelve Acres 1810, 1841, 1845, Twelve Acre Fen 1815;
Twenty Acres; Twenty one Acres; Twenty three Acres 1815; Twenty two Acres; Two
Acres; Upper Mill Carr 1810; Walk Fd 1810; (Low, Middle, Top) Walks 1810,
Walks 1831, Walk 1841 1845 (*the Walke or Warren* 1716, probably a sheep-walk,
v. **walk**); Ward Fd 1828, 1841 (named from the *Ward* family, cf. John *Ward* 1712
PR); Water Mdw 1852; West Fd 1815 (*the west feild* 1601, one of the great fields of
the village); Westland Carr 1828, ~ Car 1841); Wharf House & Bldgs 1852; the
White Hart 1818, The White Hart Public House 1823; Whitening Bldgs 1818; White
Walk 1828, Middle Whitewalk 1841 (*v.* **walk**); Wood (~ Cl, ~ Fd), Wood Eleven
Acres, Wood End Cl 1828, road towards Burringham Ferry sometimes called Wood
Lane 1792 (cf. *Broughton Wood supra*); Wood's Car (named from the *Wood* family,
cf. William *Wood*, an occupier in 1841); Wussle Fd 1810.

(b) *Applebies dike ende iuxta Braghton* 1573 (presumably named from Appleby,
an adjacent parish with **dík**, **ende**); *Berrie knole hill* 1602, *Berri knoll* ~ 1611 (*v.*
beorg, **cnoll**); *Blackmyles* 1601 (*v.* **blæc**, **mylde** 'soil, earth'); *the furlong called
B.wlandes* 1601 (the document is illegible in parts, but the reading of the last word
is probably *Bowlandes*, *v.* **boga** 'bow', referring to some topographical feature that
is curved, **land**); *Bromby Carrs*, ~ *close* 1680 (from Brumby a neighbouring parish);
Broughton Beck 1649 (*v.* **bekkr**); *a high way called Brother Stigh* 1612, *Brotherstigh*

leading to Glanford Brigges 1611 (*v.* **stīg, stígr** 'a path, a narrow road'; the sense of *Brother* here is uncertain); *Calwehulles* 1362 ('the bare hills', *v.* **calu, hyll**); *the Carre dyke causey* 1660 (c1900) (*v.* **kjarr, dík, caucie**); *Carr Eaves* 1680 (*v.* **kjarr, efes** 'an edge'); *Cockell dale* 1680, *South Cockle Dale* 1683 (perhaps referring to corn cockle, *Lychnis githago*, a weed of cornfields, with **deill** 'a share, a portion of land'); *Colsworth closes* 1683 (in the tenure of Christopher *Colsworth*); *Coule dike Carr, Couldike* ~1688 (the first element is uncertain, *v.* **dík, kjarr**); *Crauthorn* a1175 (probably 'the thorn bush frequented by crows', *v.* **crāwe, þorn**); *a dextro angulo ubi crux sita est* a1175 ("from the right corner where the cross is located"); *the Draughtes* (sic) 1660 (c1900); *the Eastlong close* 1683; *Estyby* 1327 (p) ('(place) east in the village', *v.* **ēast, í, bȳ**, a common formation in L, denoting X who lives in the east of the village); *the fourscore acres* 1689, *fourscoreacres* 1695; *the Frith Hill* 1603, *Frith Hill Carr* 1683 (perhaps from **fyrhð** 'a wood, woodland, wooded country', in some later sense such as recorded in MED s.v. *firth* (2) 'a park, a woodland meadow', 'an enclosure' and in EDD s.v. *firth* 'a wood, plantation, coppice', 'unused pastureland'. Unfortunately the site of the field is not known); *le Grene atte Touneshende* 1310, *the Common Greene* 1649 (*v.* **grēne** 'a village green'); *Gookwell more* 1633 (*v.* **mōr**); *the furlong called grene croftes* 1601 (*v.* **grēne** 'green', **croft** in the pl.); *Grime cloas* 1697 (presumably *Grime* is a surn. here, but it has not been noted in the material searched); *Halcroftes* 1601 (*v.* **hall, croft**); *Harrison Ings* 1680, 1697 (named from the *Harrison* family, cf. Richard *Harrison* 1548 PR, with **eng**); *the Hay-carr* 1603 (*v.* **hēg, kjarr**); *le haylawnds* 1487 (*v.* **hēg** 'hay', **launde** 'an open space in woodland, woodland pasture'); *Horsefleetdale* 1683 (*v.* **hors, flēot** 'a stream', **deill**); *John Hides Carr* 1680 (*v.* **kjarr**); *Howards close* 1683 (Thomas *Howard* is named in the document); *the hygh streite, the Hygh Street, the high streete* 1602 (*v.* **strǣt**, the reference being to Ermine Street); *the hygh moore* 1616 (*v.* **mōr**); *Inholmes* 1538 SP xiii (probably from **innām** 'a piece of land taken in or enclosed', with a common interchange of *-am* and *holme*); *Kerman Carr* 1680 (presumably from the surn. *Kerman* with **kjarr**); *atte Kirkgarth' de Gokewell'* 1395 (p) (*v.* **kirkja, garðr**); *Lamcoates* 1601 (*v.* **lamb, cot** 'a shed' in the pl.); *the Land dike* 1680; *Langhousiic* (sic) a1175, *Langhouse* (sic) 1257 ('the long mound', *v.* **lang, haugr**; the 1257 form presumably denotes the pl.); *high waie Leedinge from Linco'n to Brawghton als Broughton* 1602 (presumably this refers to Ermine Street); *the Lodghill Carr* 1616 (*v.* **kjarr**); *long, short cratenes* 1601 (obscure); *Long Lands* 1659, *Longlands* 1667, 1680 (*v.* **lang, land** 'a selion' in the pl.); *Mainhoues* 1257 (*v.* **haugr**; the first el. is uncertain); *the far, the hither Mealings* 1616; *the new causey* 1660 (c1900), ~ ~ *Cawsway* 1676, *the new Cartway* (sic) 1680, 1697 (*v.* **caucie**); *the new close* 1603; *the north feilde* 1601 (one of the great fields of the village); *Northyby* 1327, *Northiby* 1332 both (p) ('(place) north in the village', *v.* **norð, í, bȳ**, cf. *Estyby supra*); *Nun's well* 1696 (named from the nuns of Gokewell Priory); *Oaketree Carr* 1683; *close called Oves* 1683; *oxlauwnds* 1487 (*v.* **oxa, launde** and cf. *le haylawnds supra*); *the parsons long Close* 1662, ~ *Parsons long close* 1679, ~ *Parson's long close* 1688, ~ *Parsons long Close* 1693, 1745; *the Parsonage Cow Close* 1700; *a cartayne waye called peasdayle gate* 1601 (from **pise, deill**, with **gata** 'a road'); *Old plaine syde Close* 1660 (c1900) (*v.* **plain** 'a piece of flat meadow-land'); *Pole* 1327, 1332 both (p) (*v*. **pōl** 'a pool'); *Reddhall close* 1683; *a certayne pece of grounds called the Scrubbes* (*v*. **scrubb** 'brushwood'); *the Sleight Carr* 1680, *Sleigh Carr* (sic) 1697 (named from the *Sleight* family, cf. Robert *Slyght* 1602 *Yarb*); *the South Carr* 1616 (*v*. **kjarr**); *the South feild of Castthrop, the Southfield* 1667, ~ *South feild* 1676, 1680, 1683 (one of the great fields of Castlethorpe); *Stannas Close* 1602, *Stannass closes* 1611; *the Starre Carre* 1660 (c1900) (*v*. **storr** 'sedge', **kjarr**, a Scand compound); *Stoope Carr* 1680, *Stoop* ~ 1683 ('the marsh marked with a post or posts', *v*. **stolpi, kjarr**, also a Scand compound); *Stove Acres* 1680, *Stoveacres* 1683 (the first el. is perhaps **stofn** 'a tree stump' with **æcer**); *Touneshende* 1310 (self-explanatory, *v*. **tūn, ende**); *Welle de Manby* 1383 (p) (*v*. **wella**); *close called Westdale* 1683 (*v*. **deill**); *Westholmes* 1310 (*v*. **west, holmr**); *the West House* 1558–79 ChancP; *Westiby* 1327, *Westyby* 1332 both (p) ('(place) west in the village', *v*. **west, vestr, í, bȳ**, cf. *Estyby* and *Northyby supra*. This is a common formation in L, denoting X who lives in the west of the village); *the westlong closes* 1683; *William close* 1603 (held by *William* Gilliat); *in the Wraa* 1327 (p) (*v*. **vrá** 'a nook, a corner', in dial. 'a nook, a secluded spot, a cattle shelter'.

Brumby

BRUMBY

> *Brunebi* 1086 DB, a1175 Goke (p), 1196 ChancR, -*b'* Hy2 Goke (p), -*by* 1334 (e14) Selby (p), 1395 Pat, *Brunby* 1316 FA, 1327 *SR*, 1331 Ch, 1370 *Cor*, 1382 Misc, 1388 Peace, 1436 SR
> *Brunneby* 1271 Ch, 1272 FF, 1281 QW, 1296 RSu (p), 1298 Ass, 1302 *KR et passim* to 1360 QW
> *Bronneby* 1271 *Ass*, 1301, 1305 *KR*
> *Bromeby* 1300 Ipm, 1517 ECB, *Bromby* 1360 Inqaqd, 1635 SP, 1644 LAAS ii, 1648 *Foster*, 1824 O
> *Broumby* 1402 FA, 1569 Pat
> *Brumby* 1388 Cl, 1424 Hall, 1499 Cl, Eliz ChanP, 1616 *MiscDep 77 et passim*
> *Burneby* 1301 *KR*, 1481 Pat, -*bye* 1545–47 *MinAcct*

'Brúni's farmstead, village', *v*. **bȳ**. The first el. is the ON pers.n. *Brúni*, ODan *Bruni*, a name recorded independently in DB in Yorkshire.

BRUMBY COMMON EAST & WEST, *Brumby West Common* 1828 Bry, *East*, *West Common* 1843 *TA*. BRUMBY GRANGE, for the significance of **grange**, *v. Santon Grange* in Appleby parish *supra*. BRUMBY GROVE. BRUMBY HALL, *aula super edific'* 1311 *KR*, *Bromby Hall* 1799 *Stubbs*.

BRUMBY LANE (lost), 1828 Bry. BRUMBY WARREN (lost), 1828 Bry, *Brombye Conye Warren* 1638 *Goulding, Bromby Warren* 1787 *MiscDep 77*, 1799 *Stubbs*, cf. *the Coney Warren* 1787 *MiscDep 77* and *a warren of Cunyes in Brumby* 1616 *ib, the hills and Coney Boroughes* 1710 *TGH, the Warren of Coneys . . . Commonly called Brumby East Warren* 1740 *LD 70, v.* **coni, wareine**. BRUMBY WOOD, *Brumbye Woode* 1616 *MiscDep 77, Bromby Wood* 1635 SP, 1787 *MiscDep 77, -wood* 1700 *MiscDep 147*, cf. *Bromby Wood Hall* 1799 *Stubbs*. BURGESS HALL is *Boggard Hall* 1824 O, presumably a building thought to be haunted by a goblin or the like; see *boggard*[1] NED 1 'a spectre, a goblin, or bogy', still common in Northern and North Midland dial. The modern form is no doubt from a surn. GOOSEHOLE. LODGE, *Bromby Lodge* 1799 *Stubbs*. NEW BRUMBY. ROWMILLS PLANTATION. SANDHOUSE, 1740 *LD 70*, 1824 O. WARPING DRAIN, cf. *Warping Close Fm supra* in Bottesford parish. WORTLEY HO, presumably from the surn. *Wortley*.

FIELD-NAMES

The principal forms in (a) are 1843 *TA*. Spellings dated 1302, 1306, 1307, 1311, 1312 are *KR*; 1356 BPR; 1545–47 *MinAcct*; 1568 Pat, 1583 *MiscDon 344*; 1589 *Cragg*; 1616, 1787 *MiscDep 77*; 1638 *Goulding*; 1647 *Foster*; 1671, 1701, 1740 *LD 70*; 1680 *Yarb*; 1699, 1710 *TGH*; 1700 *MiscDep 147*; 1743, 1754 *Shef*; 1799 *Stubbs*; 1809 *EnclA* (Ashby).

(a) Asholt (*v.* **æsc, holt** 'a holt, a wood'); Banks; Barn cl; Bracken, Low, Middle, Rough, Top Becks (*Brachin Becks* 1740, *v.* **brakni, bekkr** 'a stream'); Far Bracken (*v.* **brakni**); Calf Garth (*v.* **garðr** 'an enclosure' as elsewhere in the parish); Campbell cl (from the surn. *Campbell*); Car (*heretofore called . . . Bromby Carrs . . . and now by the several names of the Mill Carr the six acres Goosehill and Bromby Closes* 1680, *v.* **kjarr**); Castle Garth (*clausum vocatum Castle garth* 1616, *Castlegarth Close* 1743, *v.* **garðr**); Clarks cl (named from the *Clark(e)* family, cf. Alice *Clarke* 1591 *Inv*); Cliff, Low Cliff, Cliff cl, ~ Top (*v.* **clif**); Cocks cl (from the surn. *Cock*); Colum cl (probably from the surn. *Colum*); Cow cl; Dalby Green (probably from the surn. *Dalby* with **grēne** 'a village green, a grassy place'); Duck Ponds; East cl; the East Moors; Fish pond, Great, Little, Top; Fourteen acres; Front cl; Garth (*v.* **garðr**); Gipy Ings (*v.* **eng** 'meadow, pasture'; *Gipy* is presumably an error for *Gipsy*, which may be from **gip(s)** 'a gap, an opening', dial. *gipsey* 'an intermittent spring'); Great cl; Holland Garth (probably from the surn. *Holland* with **garðr**); Home cl; Home Garth; Homestead & Garth; Hop Garth (*v.* **hoppe** 'a hop plant', **garðr**); Horse cl; Houghton cl (probably from the surn. *Houghton*); Ings (*brumby Inges* 1583, *les Inges, Brumby Inges* 1616, 1671, 1701 (*v.* **eng** 'meadow, pasture'); Lacy cl (probably from the surn. *Lacy*); East Lane cl; Lankrams (sic) (cf. *Lantrom* 1740); Linghams (*v.* **lyng** 'ling, heather', **holmr**; the interchange between *holme* and *ham* is common in L); Long cl; Low Car (*v.* **kjarr**); Low cl; Low, Top Manmers (perhaps 'the common boundaries', *v.* **(ge)mǣne** 'common', **(ge)mǣre** 'a boundary'); Messuage & Garth; Middle cl; Mildram; Mill cl, ~ fd; The Moors, the East Moors 1787, Brumby Moors and Commons 1809, Brumby Moor 1839, Moor 1843 (*mora de Bronneby* 1306, *le More* 1616, *Moore, More* 1647, *the more of Brumby* 1699 (*v.* **mōr**); Pinfold (*v.* **pynd-fald**); Plats (*v.* **plat** 'a plot, a small piece of ground'); Princes Wood 1799 (the wood belonged to the Duchy of Cornwall); Prior cl; Pudding poke (a fanciful name for land with soft, sticky soil); Riddings (*Riding'* 1306, *les Suth redingges* 1302, *Suthridinges* 1303, *v.* **ryding** 'a clearing'); Ringlands (*v.* **hring, land** 'a selion'); First Road cl, Second road cl; Roam hill (*Rome hills* 1740); Sand Garden, Sand Garth (cf. *Sand field* 1740); Screed (*v.* **screed** 'a narrow strip of land'); Seeds cl; Little, Long south fd; Square cl; Stone pit cl; Summer pasture ('pasture used only in summer', *v.* **sumor**); Middle Top; Top cl; Townend cl; Towns House & Garden (perhaps from the surn. *Town*); Traffords cl (named from the *Trafford* family, cf. *James Trafford*, who was an occupier in 1843); Trent bank and Forshore (adjoining the R. Trent); Twelve acres; Two acres; Upper Car (*v.* **kjarr**); Walks (*v.* **walk** 'a sheep-walk'); Warp cl (for *warp, v.* Warp Fm *supra* in Bottesford parish); West croft; West lane cl; Whatham(s); Wilks cl (no doubt from the surn. *Wilks*); Wod End Cl (sic) 1799, Wood end, ~ side 1843 (cf. Brumby Wood *supra*).

(b) *attekyrkelan'* 1311 (p) (*v.* **kirkja, lane**); *Brombimershe* 1568, *Brombymarshe* 1589 (*v.* **mersc**); *Bagghole* 1740; *brumby Causey,* ~ *Caulsey* 1583 (*v.* **caucie**); *brumby sure head* 1583 ('Brumby sewer head', from ME **sewere**); *campis de Brunby* 1312, ~ ~ *Brumby* 1616 (referring to the open field of the village); *Clay pits* 1616; *Foldingmarshe* 1589 ('the marsh on which sheep are folded', *v.* **falding, mersc**); *Goosehill* (self-explanatory, *v.* Car in f.ns. (a)); *Grime ~, Gryme dale* 1616 (named from the surn. *Grime, Gryme,* cf. Richard *Gryme de Bromeby* 1517 ECB, with **deill** 'a share of land'); *half oxgang* 1311 (*v.* **oxgang** 'a measure of land' of 10–30 acres, an eighth of a ploughland); *messuagium . . . canabarium* 1616 (alluding to the growing of hemp, *Canabis sativa*); *Lower, Upper Mill Becks* 1740 (*v.* **bekkr**); *Mill Carr* 1680 (self-explanatory; *v.* Car in f.ns. (a) *supra*); *Morton Meadow* 1740 (presumably from the surn. *Morton*); *unum capitale messuagium pomarium* 1616 ('the apple orchard'); *Shepherd Close* 1740 (presumably from the surn. *Shepherd*); *the six acres* 1740 (*v.* Car in f.ns. (a) *supra*); *Spite wod(')* 1307, *Spitewod* 1308, *Spittewode* 1356, *Spytewood'* 1545–47, *Spitewoode* 1616 (the first el. is difficult, but may well be, as Dr Insley suggests, ME *spit(e)* from OE *spitu* 'a spit for roasting meat, fish', hence 'the wood where spits were obtained'. In 1616 it is said to be part of Brumby Wood).

Burringham

BURRINGHAM

Buringeham 1218 Ass, 1223 RA ii
Burengham 1196 ChancR
Burringham 1199 P, 1272 *Ass* (p), 1554 Pat, 1576–7 *AD et passim*
Burningham 1214 Cur, 1218, 1219 Ass, 1271 Ch
Buringham 1219 Ass, 1610 Speed, *Buryngham* 1340 Cl, 1535 VE iv
Boringham 1300 Ipm, 1301 *KR*, 1316 FA, 1329 *Ass*, 1382 Misc,
  Boryngham 1327 *SR*, 1329 *Ass*, 1332 *SR*, 1373, 1375 Peace, 1402
  FA, 1409 *DCAcct*, 1412 Pat, 1421 *DCAcct et passim* to 1574 Hall

This is a difficult name, but Dr Insley suggests that it is perhaps 'the homestead, the estate of the Burgrēdingas or Burgrīcingas', *v.* **hām**. The first el. would then be the gen.pl. *Burgrēdinga* or *Burgrīcinga* of the OE group-names *Burgrēdingas* or *Burgrīcingas*, 'the family, the dependents of *Burgrēd* or *Burgrīc*'. Burringham is an example of an OE p.n. formation confidently believed to belong to an early period of Anglo-Saxon settlement in the area in which it occurs.

BURRINGHAM COMMON (lost), 1828 Bry. BURRINGHAM FERRY (lost), 1787 *EnclA* (Bottesford), 1824 O, cf. *Ferry House* 1823 *TGH*. BURRINGHAM MOORS (lost), 1809 *EnclA* (Ashby), 1624 O, *Moores* 1841 *TA*, cf. *More Dike* 1596 Hall. BURRINGHAM NORTH & SOUTH GRANGE, for the sigificance of **grange**, *v. Santon Grange* in Appleby parish *supra*. CARR DYKE RD, cf. *the Carr dike* 1755 *BM*, ~ ~ *Dike ib*, 1824 O, *v.* **kjarr** 'a marsh (overgrown with brushwood)', as elsewhere in the parish, **dík**. FERRY BOAT INN, 1842 White. HALL, *Atte halle* 1317 *SR*, *atte Halle de Boringham* 1329 *Ass*, *ad aulam* 1332 *SR*, "at Hall of" *Boryngham* 1424 Hall all (p), *the New, the Old Hall* 1661 *Foster, Old Hall* 1823 *TGH*, cf. *Hall Flatt* 1661 *Foster, Hall Close* 1841 *TA*. MIDMOOR DRAIN, cf. *le Mydd More* 1584, *myd more* 1585, *Midmore* 1586, *le Middmore* 1627 all Hall, *le midmore* 1647 *Foster, Midmoor* 1755 *BM, Middle moor* 1756 *ib*, ~ *Moor* 1800 *ib*, *Mid Noor* 1842 *TAMap*, probably '(the place) amidst the marshland', *v.* **mid** 'among, amidst', **mōr**, rather than 'the middle marshland'.

FIELD-NAMES

Principal forms in (a) are 1841 *TA*. Spellings dated 1301 are *KR*; 1327, 1332 *SR*; 1329 *Ass*; 1424, 1429, 1574, 1584, 1596, 1627, 1629 Hall; 1583 *MiscDon 344*; 1589 *Cragg*; 1661 *Foster*; 1755, 1756, 1769, 1800, 1822, 1839 *BM*; 1724, 1823 *TGH*; 1809 *EnclA* (Ashby); 1854 *Padley*.

(a) All Moor (perhaps for *Hall Moor*, cf. Hall Moors *infra*); Arnold Lane 1823 (presumably from the surn. *Arnold*); Bank & foreshore; Betty Fox Tree 1823 (the tree is shown on the 1823 Plan); Bottom fd; Bowles Cl 1823, 1841 (*Bowles Closes* 1724, named from the *Bowles* family, cf. *Elling Bowles* 1687 *Inv*); Brick Holes 1823; Brick-kiln Cl 1823, Brick kiln ~ 1841; Brick Pond 1823; Brick Yard (Cl); Brock Cl, ~ Moore, Brocks (cf. *brocke dyke* 1583); (Upper) Brooks; Brown Lawn Hill 1823; Butterwick or Bradley Cl 1823, Bradley Cl 1841 (named from East Butterwick *infra*, and from the *Bradley* family, cf. *Mr Bradley* 1791 *BM*); Butterwick Cl 1823 (cf. prec.); Butterwick Moor 1823 (cf. *ye butterweek laine suer* 1583, self-explanatory and *v.* above); Calf Cl 1823, 1841; Car, Carr 1841, Carrs 1823 (*v.* **kjarr**); Carr Side Bank 1822; Coggan Cl 1823, Coggon ~ 1841 (named from the *Coggan* family, cf. Robert *Coggan* a landowner in 1841); North, South Common Piece 1823; Cow Cl 1823; Croft Land 1823, Crofts 1841 (cf. *the Crofts* 1661, *v.* **croft**); Dent Carr 1841, Dent Carr Cl, Dent Moors 1823 (from the surn. *Dent* with **kjarr** and **mōr**); Drain, ~ side Cl; Duffield Bank & foreshore (named from the *Duffield* family, cf. John *Doofield* 1642 LPR); Farmhouse Homestead etc.; (Low) Field Carr 1823 (*v.* **kjarr**); (Bottom, Middle, Top, Second, Third) Field Cl 1823, (2nd, 3rd) Field Cl 1841; Fields Cl 1823; Goat Dike 1841 *TAMap* (*v.* **gotu** 'a sluice'); Green's Cl 1823, 1841, ~ Close Moors 1823 (named from the *Green* family, cf. John *Green* 1841, perhaps a descendant of *Will' fil Will' de la Grene* 1301); Groves 1823; Half Acre 1823; Hall Moors 1823 (cf. All Moor *supra*); Haystack Cl 1823, Hay Stack Cl 1841; Home Cl, ~ croft 1841 (*v.* **croft**); Hop Cl 1823, 1841, ~ Yd 1823, ~ Garth 1841 (*v.* **hoppe** 'a hop plant', **garðr** 'an enclosure'); Horse Cl 1823, 1841; Hudson's Cl 1823, Hudson(s) Cl 1841 (from the surn. *Hudson*, cf. John *Hudson* 1743 *TGH*, John *Hudson*, an occupier in 1841); Kirkland (Moors), Kirklands 1823, Kirk Lands 1841 (probably from the *Kirk* family, cf. Elizabeth *Kirke* 1664 *Inv*, with **land**); Land-side Cl 1823; Lane Side Cl, ~ ~ Cl(s), Laneside Cl (cf. *atte Lane* 1327, *atte Lane* both (p)); Lockwood's Moors 1823 (named from the *Lockwood* family, cf. Thomas *Lockwood* 1841 *TA*); Maltkin Yard Messuage; the Mare cls 1755, ~ ~ Cls 1800, 1822, 1839, Mare Cl 1823 (*le Far Mare Close* 1629, self-explanatory); Mare Hole, Marehole foreshore 1854; the Common Marfur 1854 (*v.* **marfur** 'a boundary furrow'); May rose Bank and foreshore; the Common Meer 1769 (*v.* **(ge)mǣre** 'a boundary, land on a boundary'); Mill Cl 1823; Mill Hill 1823 (it was situated beside the R. Trent); Ming Piece 1823, 1841 (from dial. *ming* denoting land belonging to different proprietors lying mixed); Moor Cl 1823; Narrow Cl (Moors) 1823; Newdike Gate, ~ Hills 1823 (cf. *buringham new Dikke* 1593, *v.* **dík**); North Carr (Moors) 1823, ~ ~ Moor 1841 (*v.* **kjarr**, **mōr**); North

Croft(s), Northcrofts 1841, the North Crofts 1854, Marfur in North Crofts (*v*. **norð, croft, marfur**, and cf. the South Croft *infra*); North Lane 1841 *TAMap* (cf. South Lane *infra*); North Pce; a place called Nuffield 1756, 1800, Low, Top Nuffields 1823, Heigh, Hugh, Law, Low Nuffields, Nuffield Bank & foreshore 1841; Parkinson Carrs 1823, Parkinsons Carr, Parkinson's Cars 1841 (named from the *Parkinson* family, cf. Anne *Parkinson* 1663 *Inv*, Joshua *Parkinson* 1743 *TGH*); Pinfold 1823 (*v*. **pyndfald**); Popple's Carr 1823, Popple Carr 1841, Popple's Moors 1823 (named from the *Popple* family, cf. *Annis Popple* 1600 *Inv*; George *Popple* was the holder in 1823); Pyeclose 1769, Pie Cl 1823, Pye Cl 1841; Rand Dike 1841 *TAMap*; Roberts Land, Roberts' Lane 1823 (presumably from the surn. *Roberts*); Rodney (sic); Rush Carr 1823 (*v*. **risc, kjarr**), Low, Top Rush Cl 1823; the Sand Fd 1854; Sandhills 1823, Sandhill 1841; Sand Way 1841 *TAMap*; (Little) Seedlands 1823; Sewer Bank, ~ Cl 1841; Sewer Drain 1841 *TAMap*; Sewer Side Cl 1823, Sewerside ~ 1841; First, Second, Third Six Acres 1823, 1841 (cf. *the Six acre Close* 1724); Smith Moors 1823, ~ Cl (named from the *Smith* family, cf. Edward *Smith* 1687 *Inv*, William *Smith* 1823); South Common; the South croft 1755, South Crofts 1823 (*v*. **sūð, croft**, cf. North Croft(s) *supra*); South Lane 1841 *TAMap* (cf. North Lane *supra*); the South Moor 1755, 1800; Stile Croft 1823, Style ~ 1841 (*v*. **stigel** 'a stile', but probably also used topographically for a steep ascent); Taproom & Garden; Ten Acres 1823, 1841 (area 6a.2r.30p); Thirty Six Acres 1823; Thorn Knowles 1823, 1841 (cf. *Middle Thorn Knowle Close, the broad upper Thorn Knowle Close* 1724, *v*. **cnoll** 'a knoll, a hillock'); Thorn Moors 1823, Thorn Old Moor 1841 (*v*. **þorn, mōr**); Tinker Cl 1823 (*v*. **tink(l)ere** 'a tinker'); Tofthow (Hills) 1823, Toft Old Cl 1841 (*v*. **toft** 'a messuage, a curtilage', **haugr** 'a hill, a mound'); Top fd, ~ Fd Close; Trent Bank & foreshore; Warp Carr 1841, Warp Cl 1823, 1841 (for *warp*, *v*. Warp Fm *supra* in Bottesford parish); Warping Drain 1823, 1841 *TAMap*, ~ Bank 1841 (for *warping*, *v*. Warping Close Fm *supra* in Bottesford parish); Whiteridges 1823, White ridge 1841 (*lee Whitrigge, Whytrygges*, 1574, *Whittrigge* 1584, *Whiterigge* 1596, 1627, *v*. **hwīt, hryggr**, but perhaps having a significance different from its literal meaning, cf. the appellative expression *3 Whiteridges* 1823 *TGH*); Willow Holt 1813, 1841 (*v*. **holt** 'a holt, a thicket'); Lower, Upper Willows 1823, 1841 (*v*. **wilig**); Wood & Smiths Cl (*v*. **wudu** and Smith Cl *supra*).

(b) "the acre" 1574 (*v*. **æcer**); *Burringham wyndmyll* 1589; *the Chappel garth* 1661 (*v*. **garðr**); *the Grass garth* 1661 (*v*. **garðr**); *hempecroft* 1661 (self-explanatory, *v*. **hænep, croft**); *Hille* 1332 (p) (*v*. **hyll**); *at Hykkes* 1429 (p) (a type of p.n. rare in L denoting X who lives at Hykkes, *Hykkes* being from the surn. *Hicks*, itself a derivative of the ME pers.n. *Hikke*, a hypocoristic form of *Richard*); *the Low Close* 1661; *the Middle Close* 1661; *Rowell Land* 1627 (probably from the surn. *Rowell*); *Middle and Low South broad Thorn* 1724 (*v*. **brād, þorn**); "south fields" *of Boryngham* 1424, *the south field* 1627 (one of the open fields of the village); *the upper Close* 1661; *yᵉ banckes cauled willow beck banckes* 1583 (*v*. **wilig, bekkr, banke**).

Burton upon Stather

BURTON UPON STATHER

Burtone 1086 DB, *-ton('*) 1199, 1201 P, 1202, 1218 Ass, 1202
Welles, 1254 ValNor *et passim* to 1610 Speed
Borton' 1383 Peace
Burtonestathel 1201 Ass, *Burtonstathel* 1348 Pat
Burtonestatheher (sic) 1208 FF
Burtonstather 1275 RH, 1316 *FF*, 1318 Ipm, 1319 Misc, 1327, 1332
   SR, 1327 Banco *et passim* to 1431 FA, *-stathir* 1271 RRGr, 1371
   Ipm, 1416 Cl, *-stathyr* 1437 Fine, ~ *Stather* 1300 ChancW, 1313
   Pat, 1314 Ch, 1315 *DuLaCh*, 1316 Ipm, 1323 Cl, 1329, 1334 Pat,
   1342 Cl *et passim* to 1758 *Td'E*, ~ *alias Burton upon Stather*
   1613 *Yarb*, *Burton Stathere* 1347 Pat, ~ *Stathre* 1316 FA, 1318
   Cl, ~ *Stadire* 1397 Pap
Burtonstathe 1316 FA, 1326 Pat, *Burtonestath'* 1326 Ipm
Burton cum Stather 1343 NI, 1575 *Shef*
Burton super Stather 1384 Peace, 1601 *Terrier*, 1613 *Yarb*, 1640
   Foster, 1680 FMB
Burton iuxta Stather 1554 InstBen, 1579 *Yarb*, 1580 *Shef*, 1609 *Yarb*
Burton apon Stather 1588, 1655 *Yarb*, ~ ~ ~ *alias Burton withe*
   Stather alias Burton iuxta Stather 1580 *Shef*
Market Burton 1403 Inqaqd, 1405 Pat

'The farmstead, village at or belonging to a fortified place', *v.* **burh**,
tūn. The site of the fortification is not known. The earliest forms for the
affix, *stathel*, are presumably derived from OE **staðol** 'a foundation,
base, support', in p.ns. also 'a platform'. Forms in *-stathe* are from ON
stǫð 'a landing-place, a jetty', while the rest are derived from **stǫðvar**,
the pl. of **stǫð**. *Stather* is found in other parishes bounding on the R.
Trent, cf. Flixborough Stather. The landing-places were presumably at
Burton Stather on the river a little north-west of the village itslf. The
market is referred to in *mercatum de Burton'* 1329 *Ass*. In the
neighbourhood of Burton are *Northstather* 1502, 1503 Ipm and *South
Stachre* (*-c-* for *-t-*) 1317 Ipm, *Southstathere* 1347 Pat, *-stather* 1503
Ipm; unfortunately the sites cannot be identified.

DARBY

Derbi 1086 DB, 1210 P (p), 1212 Fees, *-by* 1275 RH, 1305 Pat (p),
   1327 *SR*, ("by" *Burtonstather*), 1328 Banco, 1332 *SR*, 1335 *Shef
   et passim* to 1591 *ib*
Derebi 1199, 1200, 1201 P, 1202 Ass (p)
Dorby 1210–12 RBE, 1316 FA (both *-o-* for *-e-*)
Darby 1530 Wills iii, 1566 WillsStow, 1613 *Yarb et passim*, *-bye*
   1576 *Shef*, 1610 Yarb

Literally 'the farmstead, village of the animals, deer', *v*. ODan **diūr**,
gen.pl. **diūra, bȳ**, identical with Derby (PN Db 446), denoting a place
where animals were kept or deer were found.

NORMANBY

Normanebi (4x) 1086 DB, c1115 LS, c1128 (12) ChronPetro
Nordmanab[i] c1115 LS
Normanneby 1206 Ass
Normanby 1212 Fees, 1215–20 RA iv, 1231 *PetLN*, 1242–43 Fees,
   c1263 RA ii, 1275 RH, 1287 Ipm, (~ *iuxta Burton'stather*) 1288
   Ass, 1304 Ipm, 1316 FA *et passim*, (~ *next Burton*) 1559 *Shef*, (~
   iuxta Burton Stather) 1580 *ib*, *-bye* 1549 Pat, 1579 *Shef*, *-bie*
   1549 Pat, *-bee* 1575 *Shef*
Northmanby 1295 *Ass*

'The farmstead, village of the Norwegians', *v*. **Norðmann**, gen.pl.
Norðmanna, bȳ, a reference to an isolated settlement of Norwegian
Vikings. The name occurs also in L as Normanby le Wold, PN L **3**,
71–72, and as Normanby by Spital and Normanby by Stow in LWR.

THEALBY

Tedulfbi (3x) 1086 DB, *Tedulbi* (sic) 1086 ib
Tedolfbi c1115 LS
Tedelbi 1202 Ass
Teuilby 1287 Ipm, *Teuelby* 1316 FA, 1322 *FF*, 1382 Fine, *Tevelby*
   1308 Cl, 1339 ib
Theleby 1289 *FF*, 1402 Pat, 1403 Inqaqd, 1405 Pat, 1405 Cl, 1471
   LCCA

Theuylby 1295 *Ass*, *Theuelby* 1298 Ass, 1304 Ipm, 1305 *FF*, 1305
RA ii, 1322 YD iv, 1327 *SR et passim* to 1448 Pat, *Thevelby* 1305
Pat, *Thewelby iuxta Burton'stather* 1329 *Ass*
Thelby 1376, 1678 FMB, 1706 *Terrier*, *Thelleby* 1397 *Shef*
Theylby 1504 Pat, ~ als *Tevylby* 1558 *Shef, Theilby* 1504 Cl, 1535
VE iv, 1580 *Shef, -bye* 1549 Pat, 1576 *Shef, Theilbie iuxta Burton*
1575 *ib*
Thealby 1591 *Shef*, 1613 *Yarb*, 1710 *Shef et passim, -bye* 1610 *Yarb*,
-bie 1645 *ib*, *Theilbye* 1686 *Terrier*

'Þjóðulf's farmstead, village', *v.* **bȳ**. The first el. is the ON pers.n.
Þjóðulfr, ODan *Thythulf*. Forms in *Tedul(f)-, Tedolf-, Tedel-* show
contamination by the cognate ContGerm pers.n. *Theodulf*.

ALCOCK HOLT, named from the family of William *Alcock* 1842 White.
BAGMOOR FM, *Bagmore* 1681 WillsStow, *-moor* 1806 *EnclA*, perhaps
'the moor where badgers are found', *v.* **bagga, mōr**. BARKER'S HOLT,
named from the family of Henry *Barker* 1842 White, but note the *Barker*
family is recorded here as early as John *Barker de Burton* 1381 Peace.
BULLWOOD HOLT. BURTON HILL (lost), 1798 *Terrier*, 1828 Bry.
BURTON STATHER, *v.* Burton upon Stather *supra*. BURTON WOOD,
1824 O, cf. *ye woode side* 1583 *MiscDon 344, the woddclose hedge*
1601, *the wood-close-hedge* 1668, *ye wood-Close Hedge* 1693 all
Terrier, Wood Close 1722 *Shef*. THE CLIFF (local), 1798 *Shef, del Clyf
de Burton* 1290–1312 (m14) (p), *Burton Clyffe* 1601, ~ *cliffe* 1668, ~
Cliffe 1679, 1693, 1700 all *Terrier*, self-explanatory. DARBY GRANGE,
for the significance of **grange** here, *v. Santon Grange* in Appleby parish
supra. EAST HOLME. FERRY HOUSE INN, cf. *Ferry House* 1842 White;
there are references to *Burton Feria* from 1314 Ch. NORMANBY
GRANGE, cf. Darby Grange *supra*. NORMANBY HALL, 1780, 1802 *Shef*;
Pryme 1697 comments *a very fine well built hall or pallace there ... It
is of modern building*. NORMANBY PARK, 1828 Bry. SAND PIT. SWEEP
HOLT. THEALBY HALL. THEALBY LANE, *the way to Thealbie* 1601,
1668, ~ ~ *to Thealby* 1679, *ye Way to* ~ 1700, ~ ~ *to Thelby* 1706 all
Terrier. THE VICARAGE (lost), *the vicaredge* c1577, 1601, ~ *vicaridge
house* 1668, ~ *Vicaridge house* 1679, *ye Vicarage house* 1693, ~ ~
House 1706, *the Vicarage House* 1788 all *Terrier*, ~ ~ *Homestead* 1806
EnclA, *Pars^e* 1828 Bry.

FIELD-NAMES

Forms dated 1275 are RH; 1285, 1329 *Ass*; 1314 Ch, 1327, 1332 *SR*; 1343 NI; 1383 Peace; 1548 ChancCert; 1552 Pat; c1577, 1601, 1668, 1679, 1693, 1700, 1706, 1788 *Terrier*; 1583 *MiscDon 344*; 1605, 1611, 1613, 1614, 1615, 1628, 1636, 1646, 1648, 1650, 1662 *Yarb*; 1697 Pryme; 1805–16 *MiscDon 248*; 1806 *EnclA*; 1840 *TA*. The rest are *Shef*.

(a) Alkborough Rd 1805–16, 1806; R. Bakin's Wood Cl 19; Bellwoods and Lyons Cottages (named from two families, cf. Thomas *Bellwood* 1645 *PR* and Thomas *Lyon* 1642 LPR); Bennington's Lands 1771 (John *Bennington* is named in the document); Buckles Cl 1805–16, 1806 (named from the *Buckle(s)* family, cf. Francis *Buckle* 1650 *PR*, William *Buckles* 1728 *Inv*); Burringham Rd 1805–16, 1806; Burton Ings 1752, 1798, ~ or Stather Ings 1771, the Ings 1798, 1806, the Ings Clough (*v.* **clōh**), Ings Rd, the Ings of Burton 1806 (*burton Stather Ings* 1583, *Burton Inges* 1605, ~ ~ *vel Stather Ings* 1603, *the Inges* 1614, *le Ingges* 1625, *the Inges of Burton Stather* 1628, *Burton Inges or Stather Inges* 1636, *Burton Darby & Stather Inges* 1646, *Burton Darbie & Thealbie Ings* 1650, *v.* **eng** 'meadow, pasture' as elsewhere in the parish); Burton Mill 1821; Burton Tofton fd (sic) 1798; Calf Cl 1840; the Carr Cl 1821, Carrs Cls 1806, Car Close North, ~ ~ South 1840 (cf. *la Ker'* 1332 (p), *Carr* 1722, *the Carr Closes* 1734; *v.* **kjarr** 'a marsh overgrown with brushwood', as elsewhere in the parish); Car Rd 1806; Catherine Cl 1758; Lower, Upper Cogdale 1840; Coleby Rd 1806; the Cottager's cl 1788 (*yᵉ Cottagers Close* 1679, 1700, 1706); Coverley Course E, ~ ~ NW, ~ ~ SW 1840 (named from the *Coverley* family, cf. Edward *Caverley* 1642 LPR, Edward *Cawvarly* 1659 *PR*); the Cow Cl 1796; Dally Meare (sic) 1776 (*the dalley Meare* 1625 (*v.* (**ge**)**mǣre** 'a boundary, land forming a boundary'); Dallyson fd late Dallysons 1775 (named from the surn. *Dallyson*); Darby Lane 1830; Dovecoat Deal 1758 (*v.* **deill** 'a share, a portion of land'); East Fd 1840 (*the East feild* 1625, ~ ~ *Field of Thealbie* 1648, one of the open fields of the village); Far Cl 1806; Far Fd 1805–16; For Fd (sic) 1806 (probably the same as the prec.); the Furr Cl 1780, 1787 (*the Firr-close* 1668, ~ *Firr Close* 1679, *yᵉ Firr close* 1693, ~ ~ *Close* 1700, ~ *Fir-close* 1706 (*v.* **fyrs** 'furze'); Greenhill Furlongs 1803; the half Cl 1790, 1787; Hall Garth 1772 (*v.* **hall**, **garðr**); Haverdale 1806 (*v.* **hafri** 'oats', **deill**); Hewitson Cl, Hewitson's ~ 1806 (named from the *Hewitson* family, cf. Samuel *Hewitson* 1648 *PR*); the Hill 1780, 1787 (*atte Hille* 1332 (p), *the Hill* 1662, cf. *Hill furlong* 1611); Home Cl 1803; Horse and Cow Pasture 1840; Houghton Rd 1806 (named from the *Houghton* family, cf. James *Houghton* named in the same document); Jacksons Cottage 1780, 1787 (named from the *Jackson* family, cf. John *Jackeson* 1600 *PR*); little Croft 1752 (*v.* **croft**); Long Cl 1806; Mast Hill 1806 (probably to be identified with *the Mastalls, loco . . . vocat le Mastalls* 1625, *Close . . . called Mastills* 1662; this is presumably to be compared to *Mill Mastall butts*, a f.n. in Goxhill PN L **2**, 133, and *le Marstal*, a f.n. in Killingholme PN L **2**, 209, derived from OE ***mær(e)stall*** with some such meaning as 'a pool, a pool of stagnant water'); cottage . . . called the Meeting House 1771, cottage in Thealby called Meeting House 1788, cottage called the Meeting House 1821 (*that Cottage . . .*

commonly called or known by the name of the Meeting house 1742); Metcalfs ~, Metcalfe Cl 1806 (named from the *Metcalf* family, cf. Anne *Metcalfe* 1604 *PR*); the Middle Briggs 1788 (*Middlebrigges* 1615, *the Little Middlebrigs* 1679, y^e *litle Midle briggs* 1693, ~ ~ *Middlebriggs* 1700, ~ ~ *Middle-Briggs* 1706, v. **middel, brycg,** the latter in a Scandinavianised form); Middle Fd 1840; a certain Mill 1797 (*the Mill* 1722), East, West Mill Fd 1840; Miln Butts 1803 (v. **butte** 'a strip of land abutting on a boundary', 'a short strip or ridge at right angles to other ridges, etc.'); New Cl 1803, 1836; Normanby Fds (*the feilde of Nort Normanbee* c1577, *Normanbe feild* 1601); Normanby Rd 1806; the North Beck, North Beck Drain 1806 (*the North becke* 1601, ~ *North beck* 1679, y^e *North-Beck* 1706, v. **norð, bekkr**); The Great, Little North Cl 1801; the Oate Cl 1802; a certain ancient Inclosure called Old Coleby 1806 (cf. Coleby in West Halton parish *infra*); Parson Car, ~ Cl 1840 (v. **kjarr**); Peterborough Ings 1780, 1787 (leased by *the Cathedral Church of Peterborough*); One other Deale or Oxgang called pond Deale otherwise north Deale 1758 (v. **deill**); Roundhill Cl 1840; Roxby Cliff Cl acres 1806 (alluding to Roxby, a neighbouring village); East, West Sainfoin Cl 1806 (v. **sainfoin**); Sand Field Rd 1806 (*the Sand Field of Thealbie* 1648); S. Sewell's Cottagers Cl 19; Sixteen Acres 1840; the South Beck Cl 1803 (*sowthe becke* 1601, *Southbeck* 1625, *the south beck* 1679, y^e *South Beck* 1693, 1700, 1706, cf. the North Beck *supra*); the South Cl 1796; Square Seeds 1840; Stather Cl 1758, 1798, Stather Common 1806, Stather Rd 1806 (all named from Burton Stather *supra*); Surbeck Cl 1806 (v. **sūr** 'sour', **bekkr**); Thealby Carr 1806 (v. **kjarr**); Thealby Fd 1802 (cf. *the feildes of Burton, Darbee and Thealbee* 1577); Thirty Acres 1840; the Town Street 1771, The Town Street of Thealby 1806; the Trent Furlong 1780, 1787 (cf. *Trent Close* 1722, land by the R. Trent); Triangle 1840; Turkey Garth 1800 (v. **garðr**); Twenty Acres 1806 (area 12a.1r.37p.); Twenty-eight Acres 1840; the Vicarage cl 1788 (cf. *Vicarage supra*); West Fd 1840; Willough Beck or Hop Cl 1803 (v. **wilig, bekkr,** and **hoppe** 'a hop plant'); close ... called Willow Holt 1823 (v. **holt**); Willow Row 1758, 1806, ~ Cl 1814 (*de salicis plantac' super viam regiam* 1275, *Burton Willoraw* (sic), ~ *Willorow* 1601, *Burton Willow-row* 1668, ~ *Willow row* 1679, ~ *Willowe-row* 1693, y^e *Willow-Row* 1700, ~ *Willow Row* 1706, v. **wilig, rāw** 'a row'); Wilson's Cl 1806 (named from the *Wilson* family, cf. William *Willson* 1600 *PR*); Winterton Gate 1776, ~ Rd 1806 ('the road to Winterton (an adjacent parish)', v. **gata**); (Low) Wybeck Cl 1806.

   (b) *Anderson Close* 1722 (named from the *Anderson* family, cf. John *Anderson* 1600 *PR*); *the bean crofte* 1601, ~ *Beane Crofts* 1668, 1679, y^e *Bean Crifts* (sic) 1693, ~ ~ *Crofts* 1700, 1706 (v. **bēan, croft**); *Atte Beke* 1327 (p), *the becke* 1601, ~ *Beck(e)* 1668, ~ *beck* 1697, y^e *Beck* 1693, 1700, 1706 (v. **bekkr**); *John Beltone Dovecoate* 1668, ~ *Belton Douecoat* 1679, ~ *Belton's Dovecoat* 1693, *Belton's Dove Coat* 1700, *John Belton's Dove Coat-dale* 1706 (v. **deill**); y^e *bridge*, y^e *sd. Sure bridge* (i.e. 'sewer bridge'), *burtton bridge, burton bridges* all 1583; *campis de Burton stather* 1335, *campis de Borton'* 1383, *the feildes of Burton, Darbee and Thealbee* 1577, *Campis ... de Burton* 1625, *Burton feildes* 1601, *the feildes ... of Burton* 1625, *Burton-Feild* 1668, *Burton field* 1679, ~ *Field* 1693, 1706 (v. **feld,** a reference to the open fields of the village); *Burton Hempe garthes* 1601, *Burton-hemp-garths* 1668, *Burton hempgarths* 1679, ~ *Hemp Garths* 1693, 1700, y^e ~ ~ (self-explanatory, v. **hænep, garðr**); *the chapel of Stather* 1548, *Chappell Yarde*

1549; *a messuage called le Chauntriehouse* 1549 (for Burton Chauntrie, *v.* ChancCert 36, 261); *Coleby Carr* 1734 (*v.* **kjarr**), *Colbie meare* 1601, *Colby meare* 1668, *~ meer*(*e*) 1679, *Coleby-Mear* 1693, *~ Mears* 1700, *Coleby Mear* 1706 ('the boundary with Coleby (in West Halton *infra*)', *v.* **(ge)mǣre**); *campis de darby* 1611 (cf. *campis de Burton stather supra*); *le Duckhoole* 1620, 1650 (*v.* **dūce, hol**[1] 'a hole'); *Empson Close* 1722 (named from the *Empson* family, cf. John *Emson* 1600 *PR*); *Fogg Close* 1722 (*v.* **fogga, fogge** 'aftermath, long grass left standing during the winter'); *yᵉ banck called yᵉ fore daile banck* 1583 (*v.* **fore** 'in front', **deill**); *medowe . . . called four swaythes* 1620 (*v.* **swæð** 'a strip of grassland'); "the" *Gara* 1314 (*v.* **gara** 'a gore, a triangular plot of land'); *the gayte inges* 1601, *~ Gateings* 1668, 1679, *yᵉ ~* 1693, 1700 (*v.* **gata, eng**); *the hygh way to Lyncolne* 1601, *~ highway to Lincolne* 1668, *the high way ~ ~* 1679, *yᵉ ~ ~ ~ ~* 1693, 1700, *~ ~ ~ to Lincoln* 1706; *one Dale called Hobthrust Dale* 1698 (from *hob-thrush, hob-thrust* 'a goblin', *v.* NED s.v. hob-thrush, a compound of ME *hob*(*be*) 'a hobgoblin' and ME *thurs*(*e*) 'a devil, evil spirit' < OE **þyrs**, ON **þurs** 'a giant, a troll', here the latter. This is a reference to a share of land (*v.* **deill**) thought to be haunted by a goblin); *le Ing Dyke* 1620, *~ Ingg dike* 1646, *~ inge dike* 1650 (*v.* **eng, dík**); *Kirkedike* 1552 (*v.* **kirkja, dík**); *the mylne close Dyke* 1601, *~ Mill-Dike* 1668, *~ Milldike* 1679, *yᵉ Mill Dyke* 1693, *~ Mill-Dike* 1700, *~ Mill dyke* 1706 (*v.* **myln, dík**); *Netherwyke* 1327, *-wyk* 1332, 1343 (all (p) ('the lower farm', *v.* **neoðera, wīc**, but this may not be a local surname); *campos de Normanby* 1551 (*v.* **feld**); *Normanbie meare* 1601, *Normanby-Meares now called Millclose hedge* 1668, *Normanby Meare now called Millclose hedg* 1697, *Normanby-Meare now called Mill-close hedge* 1706 (*v.* **(ge)mǣre**); *Normanby sure head* 1583 ('Normanby sewer heading', *v.* **hēafod**); *the Northe feild of Burton Thealbie and Darbie* 1601, *the North-Fielde of Burton Thealbie and Darbie* 1668, *the North Fieldes of Burton Thealby & Darby* 1679, *yᵉ North-Field of Burton . . . Thealby & Darby* 1693 (*v.* **norð, feld**); *Oat Close* 1722; *the parsonage close* 1601, 1668, *~ Parsonage Close* 1679, *yᵉ ~ ~* 1693 (cf. the Vicarage cl *supra*); *loco . . . voc the Reedes* 1620, 1650 (*v.* **hrēod** in the pl.); *Rod Inges* 1722 (*v.* **eng**); *the L. Sheffeilde his dove-coat* 1601; *Six Swaythes* 1650 (cf. *four swaythes supra*); *the southe feilde of Burton* 1601, *~ South-Field* 1668, *~ south field* 1679, *yᵉ South field* 1693, *~ Field* 1700, 1706 (one of the open fields of the village, *v.* **sūð, feld**); *Southiby* 1327, 1332 both (p) ('(place) south in the village', *v.* **sūð, í, bȳ**, a common formation in L denoting a person living in the south of the village); *Spillo hills* 1697 (no doubt from **spell** 'speech' and **hōh** 'a heel, a spur of land' or **haugr** 'a hill, a mound', denoting a meeting-place); *Three Swaythes* 1650 (cf. *four swaythes supra*); *Vpeflet'* 1327 (p) (*v.* **upp** 'up, higher up', **flēot** 'a rivulet, a stream'); *Westeby* 1295 (p) ('(place) west in the village', *v.* **west, vestr, í, bȳ**, and cf. *Southiby supra*); *Westmynster staythe* 1583 (named from Westminster Abbey, cf. *be repared by the deayne & Chapter of Westmynster* 1583, with **stæð** 'a landing place'); *Molendinum ventriticum* 1551, *one parcel of grounde with a wynde mylne hereupon buylded, wynde mylne* 1579; *the wraa* 1327, 1332 both (p) ('the nook, the corner of land', *v.* **vrá**).

EAST BUTTERWICK

> *Butrewic* 1086 DB, Hy2 (1409) Gilb, 1208 ChancR, *-wyk* 1293 *FF*,
> 1303 Pat, *Buterewich'* 1186, 1188, 1190 P
> *Buterwic* (*super Trentam*) 1204 ChR, 1219 Ass, 1221 Cur, 1266 Pat,
> e14 AD ii, *-wik* (*super Trentam*) 1272 *Ass*, 1279 Orig, *-wyk* 1278
> Cl, 1298 *Ass*, 1309, 1314 Pat *et passim* to 1389 Misc, *Buttrewyck*
> (*super Trentam*) c1189 (e14) Selby, 1297 Ipm, *-wyk* 1301, 1317
> Cl, 1345 Pat
> *Butterwyck'* (*super Trentam*) c1189 (e14) Selby, 1314 Ipm, *-wyk*(')
> e13 (e14) Selby, 1271 Ch, 1276 RH, 1281 QW *et passim* to 1430
> *AD*, *-wych* c1200 (1409) Gilb, *-wic'* 1223 RA ii, *-wik*(') 1266 Pat,
> 1279 Fine, 1314 Selby, *-wyke* 1327 *SR*, 1404 Cl, 1429 Hall, 1526
> Sub, 1535 VE iv, *-wick* 1551, 1560 Pat
> *Boterwyk* 1189 (e14) Selby, 1296 Ipm, 1312 Fine, 1322 Pat, 1328
> Banco, 1348, 1364 Pat, 1402 FA, *-wyke* 1293 Abbr, 1312 Ipm,
> 1399 Cl, *-wyc* John *AddCh*, *-wike* 1275 RH, *-wik* 1316 FA, 1392
> *Rental*
> *Botrewycke* (*super Trent*) 1204 (e14) Selby, *-wich* 1208 P, *-wic* 1265
> Misc, *-wyk* 1342 Cl
> *Estbuterwyk*(') 1282 *FF*, 1288 *Ass*, 1415 Pat
> *Estbutterwike* 1295 ChronPetro, *-wyk* 1360 Peace, 1502, 1503 Ipm,
> *-wyke* 1547 Pat, *Est Butterwyke* 1536–37 Dugd vi, 1544 LP ii, *Est*
> *Butterwike* 1563 Pat, *Eastbutterwyke* 1573 Hall, *E. Butterwick*
> 1576 Saxton
> *Est Boterwyk* 1296 Ipm, *-boterwyke* 1416 Cl

For convenience forms without an affix are assembled together since
for the most part there is no evidence to indicate whether they refer to
East or West Butterwick.

'The farmstead well-known for butter', 'butter farm', *v*. **butere, wīc**.
It is **East** in relation to **West Butterwick** on the opposite bank of the R.
Trent in Axholme.

BUTTERWICK COMMON, *the Common* 1703, 1716 *TGH, The* ~.
BUTTERWICK HALE, 1797 *Stubbs*, 1824, *The Hale* 1842 *TAMap*, *v*. **halh**
(dat.sg. **hale**) 'a nook, a corner of land'. BUTTERWICK HALL, *The Hall*
1842 *TA*. CHAPEL LANE. GREEN LANE. INGS FM, cf. *Butterwekyngis*

1527–39 LDRH, *Butterweeke Ings* 1629 *Foster*, cf. ~ *South Inges* 1602
Cragg, *v.* **eng** 'meadow, pasture', as elsewhere in the parish. SAND
HILL. SHIPYARD COTTAGES. WARPING DRAIN, for Warping, *v.*
Warping Close Fm in Bottesford *supra*.

FIELD-NAMES

Forms dated 1573, 1574, 1585, 1698, 1616, 1622, 1624 are Hall; 17,
1605, 1703[1] *Terrier*; 1602 *Cragg*; 1654 LNQ xxii; 1669 *Foster*; 1703[2],
1716, 1724 *TGH*, 1756, 1776 *Deeds*; 1842 *TA*.

(a) Butterwick Moors 1842 (cf. *the more dyke* 1585, *the Moor Close* 1724); Carr
Dike Bank 1842 (*v.* **kjarr, dík, banke**); Croft 1842; Dolley Ley 1842 (*Dolley* is
probably a surn. with **ley** (OE **lēah**) 'a meadow, pasture')); Fanny Cl 1842; Five Lands
1842 (*v.* Twelve Lands *infra*); Foreshore 1842; Four Lands 1842 (*thee foure Lands*
1669, cf. Twelve Lands *infra*); Green's Cl 1842 (from the surn. *Green*); Grove or
Foreshore (for *grove*, *v.* Trent groves in Gunness parish *infra*); the Hemp Croft 1756
(1703[2], *the Hempcroft* 1716, *v.* **croft**); Hempland Cl 1776 (cf. *one Hempelond* 1774,
v. **hænep, land** and prec.); (Low) Home Cl 1842 (there are no buildings in this field);
Low Croft 1842; Mid Moor 1842 *TAMap*; Moors Land 1842; Parsonage Land 1842;
Rand Dike 1842 *TAMap* (*Rand* is presumably a surn. here, though it could formally
be from OE **rand** 'an edge, a border' with **dīc, dík**); (Low) Six Lands 1842 (*the Six
Lands* 1654, *v.* Twelve Lands *infra*); Stather Crofts Moor 1756 (cf. *Stather Crofts
Moor* 1716, cf. *the Stather Crofts* 1654, *the Stather Croft Close* 1724; for *Stather v.*
Burton upon Stather *supra*); the Stocks Close 1776 (self-explanatory); Toft Croft
1842 (*v.* **toft** 'a curtilage, a messuage'); Townend Cl 1842; Twelve Lands 1842 (*the
several mores commonly called Twelve landes, Five lands and Six lands* 1654, *v.*
land 'a selion'); Warping Drain 1842 (for *warping*, *v.* Warping Close Fm in
Bottesford parish *supra*).

(b) *the barly Close* 1669 (self-explanatory); *le beckebancke* 1624 (*v.* **bekkr** 'a
stream', **banke**); *The Beets* 17; *the Bobbards* 1654; *the Boornes* (sic); *An angle
called Boysun* 1703[1]; *the Calfe Close* 1669; *Carr Close* 1724 (*v.* **kjarr**); *Common
Ings* 17 (*v.* **eng**); *le common pasture* 1624; *Crom Acre* 1605; *the Farr(e) field* 1654,
~ *farre feild* 1669; *ye feilde dyke* 1585 (self-explanatory); *one fishery called a
fishgarthe* 1598 (*v.* **fisc, garðr**); *the Flatts* 1669 (*v.* **flat** 'a flat piece of land', later
with reference to 'a larger division of the common field')); *Gold Garth* 1669, *Gould
Garth* 1684 (*v.* **garðr**; the first el. may be **golde** with reference to a gold plant, or
perhaps the surn. *Go(u)ld); the Great Cloase* 1654, ~ *great Close* 1669; *Holme* 1605
(*v.* **holmr** 'a raised piece of land amidst marsh'); *the house Close* 1669; *Lanster Butts*
17; *Lea Field* 1703[1] (*v.* **lea** (OE **lēah**) 'meadow, pasture'); *Longlands* 17 (*v.* **lang,
land**); *Newdyck* 17 (*v.* **dík**); *North Field* 17; *le nue close* 1598, *twenty-three Gadds
of meadow lying in le Newclose* 1616, *le Newe Close* 1622 (self-explanatory); *le
Pighell* (sic) 1602 (*v.* **pightel** 'a small enclosure, a croft', a comparatively rare word
in L, the usual form is **pingel** a nasalised form of **pightel**); *Sea Field* 17; *One fishery
of sex Rowmes* 1573, *Sex Rowmes of one Fysshenge in ye water of Trent* 1574; *the

south field 1598 (one of the open fields of the village); *Susworth Meare* 17 ('the boundary with Susworth', *v.* (**ge**)**mǣre**); *the Tenn Lands* 1654, *the hither ten Lands, the Farre ~ ~* 1669 (cf. Twelve Lands *supra*); *Wateringstead Land* 1654 (a watering place, *v.* **stede**, a compound not recorded in Sandred).

Crosby

CROSBY

Cropesbi (2x) 1086 DB
C[*r*]*oc*[*hes*]*bi* c1115 LS (a conjectured form, partly illegible)
Crosseby 1206 Ass, 1206 Cur, 1227 ib (p), 1238–45 RA ii (p), 1272
    Ass, 1275, 1276 RH, 1291 Ipm, c1300 *Shef*, 1316 FA *et freq* to
    1546 LP xxi, *-bi* 1207 Cur, 1210 P (p), 1214 ib, 1219 FF, 1219
    Ass, 1219–29 *Shef*
Crosceby 1294 *Ass*
Crosby 1327 *SR*, 1350 Ch, 1445, 1504 Cl, 1525 *Shef*, 1535 VE iv,
    1576 Saxton *et passim*, *-bye* 1591 *Shef*, *-bie* 1612 *Foster*
Croxby 1303, 1346, 1428 FA, 1347 Pat

According to Ekwall, DEPN s.n., Crosby is identical in etymology with Croxby, PN L **3**, 26–27. This seems unlikely for the only spellings supporting such a suggestion are one partially illegible and those from the 13th–14th century. These are too late to be significant etymologically. Other early spellings which have been identified with Crosby, like *Crochesbi* 1130 P (p), belong to Croxby itself.

If the DB spelling is correct then Crosby was probably 'Kropp's farmstead, village' from the OScand pers.n. *Kroppr* and ODan **bȳ**. In that case medial *-ps-* has been early assimilated to *-ss-*. However, it is quite possible that the DB spelling is simply an error, unsupported as it is by later forms, and that the name means 'the farmstead, village marked by crosses', from the gen.pl. of ON **kross**, late OE **cros** 'a cross', and ODan **bȳ**.

CONESBY, NORTH & SOUTH

Cunesbi (2x) 1086 DB, *-bi* 1290 Cl
Cuningesbi c1115 LS, 1199 P, 1219 Ass (p), *Cunyngesbia* Hy2
    (1437) Pat, *Cunigesbi* c1115 LS, *Cunningesby* 1243 Pat,
    Cunnygesby lHy2 (1409) Gilb, *Connygesby* lHy2 (1409) ib

Coningesby 1242–43 Fees, 1317 *SR*, 1351 Ipm, 1405 Pat, 1274
RRGr, *Coninggesby* 1271 *Ass*, *Conyngesby* 1294 *ib*, 1298 Ass,
1303 FA, (~ "by" *Burton Stathe*) 1328 Banco, 1332 *SR*, 1346 FA,
1371 *FF*, 1428 FA, 1431 LNQ xii, 1445 Cl, *Conynggesby* c1300
Shef, *Conyngsby* 1428 FA, *Conighesby* 1245 FF
Cuningebi 1205 P, 1214 Cur, *Cuninghebi* 1205 ChancR, *Cunhingby*
1275 RH
Coningeby 1206 Cur
Conysby 1432 LNQ xii, 1481, 1504 Pat, 1504 Cl, 1535 VE iv,
1536–37 Dugd vi, *-bye* 1591 *Shef*, *Conisby* 1616–18 WillsStow,
1718 *Foster*, *Conesby* 1785 *Shef*
Nortkuningesby 1219 Welles, *-cuningesby* 1280 *Alv*
North Conyngesby 1445–48 Inqaqd, 1452 Cl, ~ *conynesby*
"otherwise Little" *Conyngesby* 1449 Cl, *Northconyngesby* 1502
Ipm
parua Cuningesby 1260 *Alv*, *Parva Cunhingsby* 1275 RH
Parva Conyngesby 1316 FA, 1350 *FF*, 1431 FA, *Lytle Conyngesby*
1452 Cl
Suthcuningesbi a1229 *Shef*
Southconynygesby 1449 Cl, 1485 Pat, 1502 Ipm, 1503 AASR xxiii,
South Conyngesby "otherwise Great" Conyngesby 1445 Cl
Magna Conyngeby 1316 FA, 1328 Banco
Conesby Farm 1825 *Shef*

'The king's farmstead, village', *v.* **kunung, bȳ**, identical with
Coningsby (LSR). Little is known of the early history of the Conesbys,
nor when they were in the king's hands (unlike Coningsby, *v.* DB 1, 96).
North Conesby is depopulated and South Conesby represented by
Conesby Fm.

AMERICA PLANTATION. CLIFF PLANTATION, *the Cliff*, ~ *Cliff Hill* 1812
EnclA, *Cliff Common* 1823 *Shef*, *v.* **clif**. CONESBY BOTTOM (lost), 1824
O, cf. *Bottoms* 1825 *Shef*, *v.* **botm**. CONESBY GRANGE (lost), 1876 *Shef*,
Grangiam . . . de Cunigesby c1240 (13), *Grangiam de Cuninghesby*
1245 (13), *Grangiam quam habetis in villa de Connisgeby* (sic) a1251
(13), *Grangiam de Cuninghesby* 1254–61 (13), *firma grangie nost' de
north conyngesby* 1486 all *Alv*; it was a **grange** of Alvingham Priory.
CONESBY WARREN (lost), *warannum in Parva Cunhingsby* 1275 RH,
warennam apud parva Cunhingby 1276 ib, *Warren* 1768 *Shef*, *the
Warren in Conesby* 1812 *EnclA*, *Conesby Warren* 1828 *Shef*, *v.*

wareine. CROSBY LE MOOR FM, cf. *Crosby Moores* 1706 *Shef, the Moor* 1828 *ib.* CROSBY WARREN, 1826 *Shef*, cf. *the Warren Gate* 1812 *EnclA, East Common or Warren* 1823 *Shef.* FOXHILLS PLANTATION, cf. *Thorn Wood or Fox Hills* 1838 *TA* (West Halton). HEMPDYKES, *Hemp Dikes* 1823 *Shef,* cf. *le Hempyeard* 1615 *Shef,* self-explanatory. HORNSBY'S HOLT, no doubt from the surn. *Hornsby.* LOCKWOOD PLANTATION, from the surn. *Lockwood,* cf. Jonathan *Lockwood* 1842 White. OLD PARK FM, 1838 *TA* (West Halton), *the Old Park* 1768 *Shef, del Parke* 14 *Alv* (p), *Conisby Parke* 1574, *Conysbye parke* 1591, *Conisbye parke* 1598 all *Shef, Connisbe Park* 1663 *Inv, Conesby Park* 1690 *Terrier* (Flixborough), *Conisby Park* 1746 *Foster, v.* **park**. SKIPPINGDALE PLANTATION, cf. *High, Low, New Skippingdale* 1838 *TA* (West Halton), perhaps from **scypen** 'a shippen', in a Scandinavianised form, and **deill** 'a portion, a share of land', cf. *Skippingdale* in Manton f.ns. (b). TRACINGS PLANTATION. WINTERTON RD, 1812 *EnclA*, self-explanatory.

FIELD-NAMES

Forms dated Hy2, eHy3, c1240, 1242, a1251, 1269, Hy3 all (13), 14 are Alv; 1271–73, 1294 *Ass*; 1298 Ass; 1306 *KR*; 1327, 1332 *SR*; 1416 Fine; 1431 LNQ xii; 1583 *MiscDon 344*; 1620, 1706, 1746, 1750, 1753, 1754, 1768, 1770, 1773, 1785, 1803, 1805, 1810, 1823, 1826, 1828, 1831, 1839, 1844, 1876 *Shef*; 1718 *Foster*; 1812 *EnclA*; 1838 *TA* (West Halton detached).

(a) John Baildon Dailes 1750, ~ Baildon's Dales 1754, ~ Bailden's Dales 1839 (*John Baildon dales* 1620, *v.* **deill** 'a share, a portion of land' as elsewhere in the parish); Beltons Garth 1823 (from the surn. *Belton* with **garðr** 'an enclosure' as elsewhere in the parish); Berry Cl 1823; Blackburn Dyke Bank 1826 (from the *Blackburn* family, cf. Jonathon *Blackburn* 1842 White, with **dík** and **banke**); Buckle's Cl 1825 (from the surn. *Buckle*); Burnthouse Garth 1823 (*v.* **garðr**); the Burton Rd 1812, 1844 (*viam de Burtun, Burtungate* eHy3, 'the road to Burton upon Stather', *v.* **gata**); Calf Cl 1838; the open Carrs 1754, the Carrs 1768, Car 1823, Carr(s) 1828, Carr 1838 (*le Ker* 1242, *the Open Carrs of Crosby* 1620, *v.* **kjarr** 'brushwood', 'marsh overgrown with brushwood' as elsewhere in the parish); Chapman Trace Hills 1823 (named from the *Chapman* family, cf. W. *Chapman* 1828 *Shef*); Chapel Fd 1825; Clap Brigg 1838 (perhaps referring to a *clapper* bridge, i.e. one built of timber or rough stones); Colonel Carr 1828 (*v.* **kjarr**); Clay Fd 1823; Clerkpiece 1823; Common 1828; Cottagers Mdw, ~ Pasture 1823; Cow Cl, ~ Dales 1823 (*v.* **deill**), ~ Pasture 1825, ~ Slack Hill 1838 (*v.* **slakki**); Crabby Cl 1823 (*v.* **crabbe, -ig**); Crabtree Cl 1823 (perhaps from the surn. *Crabtree*); Cutler Ings 1823 (probably from the surn. *Cutler* with **eng**); the Dales Fd 1812, North, South Dales

1823 (v. **deill**); Dendrige Cl 1812, Dendridge ~ 1823 (from the surn. *Dendridge*); the East Common 1812; Featherbed Lane 1812, 1844 (*Featherbed* is used of soft, unresisting soil); the Ferry Road 1812, 1824, 1825, 1844; Fifteen Acres 1838; Fish Pond Cl 1825, Fishpond ~ 1838; Furzy Piece 1823, ~ Btm 1838 (v. **fyrs** 'furze'); Grange Beck Cl, ~ ~ Mdw 1825 (v. **grange, bekkr**); Great Cl 1823; Green Garth 1823 (v. **grēne, garðr**); the North Greens 1839 (v. **grēne** 'a village green, a grassy spot'); Gunhouse Lane 1812 (the lane leading to Gunness); Eliza Hacks Cottage 1823; Half Guinea Cl 1823 (alluding to a rent or other payment of 10s.6d); Hell Hole 1823 (a derogatory name for an unpleasant place); Hill Cl 1823; Hilly Car 1838 (v. **kjarr**); Hobson Car 1838 (from the surn. *Hobson* with **kjarr**); Holt 1823 (v. **holt**); Home Cl 1823, 1838, ~ Garth 1838 (v. **garðr**); House Cl 1823; Ings 1823, 1828 (*Crosby Inges* 1683, *yᵉ Ings* 1718, v. **eng**); Jonathan Dales 1823 (v. **deill**; *Jonathan* is a pers.n., perhaps referring to *Jonathan* Blackburn or *Jonathan* Lockwood both 1842 White); Gt, Lt Jyst Cl 1838 (from ME *agist* 'a right of pasture'); Gt Lawn 1838; Little Dale 1823; Long Btm 1838 (v. **botm**); Long Cl 1823; the Meadow btms 1768 (cf. *in prato de Cuningesby* 1241 (13), v. **mǣd, botm**); Middle Cl 1823; Narrow Cl 1876; Neap House Lane 1812 (leading to Neap Ho in Flixborough parish); Nine Lands 1823 (v. **land** 'a selion'); the North Fd 1812, 1823 (*le nort Campo* Hys (13), one of the great fields of the village); the North and South Sand Fds 1812, North Sand Fd 1812, 1823 (cf. South Sand Fd *infra*); Oate Cl 1823; the open Ings 1812 (v. **eng**); the Oxgangs (sic) 1750, the Outgangs 1754, Great, Little Out Gangs 1823, the Outganges 1839 (*The Outgangs* 1620, 1706, v. **ūtgang** 'an exit, a way out' for cattle etc.; the 1750 form appears to be an error); the Park btms 1768 (cf. *yᵉ parke Inges* 1583, v. **eng**); Peacock Lane 1770, 1803, 1805 (probably from the surn. *Peacock*); Peat Moor 1754, ~ Moors 1839 (*Peat Moor* 1620, the *Peate Moores* 1706, self-explanatory); Potatoe Garth 1823 (v. **garðr**); Sainfoin Pce 1823 (v. **sainfoin**, the leguminous plant, *Onobrychis viciifolia*); Sand Cl 1825; the South Sand Fd 1773 (1746), South Sand Fd 1812, 1823; Sandfield Rd 1812; Sand Hill 1823; Scroggy Pce 1823 (v. **scrogge** 'brushwood'); Scunthorpe Ings 1753 (v. **eng**); Seeds Cl 1825; Sheep Cl 1838; Gt Sheep Walk 1823, Sheep Walk 1823 (v. **shepe-walk**); Sheve Acres 1823; Sike Cl 1823 (v. **sík**); Slater's Trent Cl 1825 (from the surn. *Slater* and the R. Trent); the Soak Mear 1750, ~ ~ Meer 1773, 1812 (1746), Soak Meer or Road 1823, The Soak Mere 1839 (the *Soak Mear* 1620, the *Soake Mear* 1706, ~ *Soke Meer* 1746, v. **soc** 'a drain', **(ge)mǣre** 'a boundary'); The South Field Cl 1785, Crosby South fd 1750, Crosby Southfield 1754, ~ South Fd 1839 (*Crosby south field* 1620, ~ *South Field* 1706, one of the open fields of the village); Spiny Holt 1823 (v. **holt**); Spring Wood 1838 (v. **spring**); Standing Lands 1823; The Town Street 1812, 1831; Trace hill 1812, Trace Hill Cl, Tracehill Wood 1823, Meadow, North, South Trace Hill 1823 (cf. Chapman Trace Hills *supra*); Two Lands 1823 (v. **land** 'a selion'); Underwood 1823; the Upper Ings 1750, 1754, 1839 (v. **eng**); the Vicarage 1812; Wadd Fd 1825 (perhaps the first el. is OE **wād** 'woad'); Waitland Cl 1825 (v. **hwǣte** 'wheat', **land**); Warping Drain 1826, Warp Cl, ~ Lane 1838 (for *warp* and *warping*, v. Warp Fm and Warping Close Fm both in Bottesford parish *supra*); Waterlands Cl 1823 (named from the *Waterland* family, cf. Thomas *Waterland* 1788 *Shef*); Water Lane 1812; the West Common 1773, 1810, 1825 (1746), West Common 1823, the late West Common 1825, West Common Rd 1812; Philip Williamson's Dale 1750,

1764, 1839 (~ ~ *dale* 1620, *v.* **deill**); Wilson Car (named from the *Wilson* family, cf. Thomas *Wilson* 1716 *Inv*, *v.* **kjarr**); Wybeck Lane 1812, Wyebeck Cl 1823, Gt, Lt Wybeck 1825 (*v.* **bekkr**; early forms are needed to explain the first el.).

(b) *aquam que dicitur Bec* eHy3 (13) (*v.* **bekkr**); *del Broyl* 1271–73 (p) (from OFr **broile** 'a park, an enclosed park for deer or other game'); *ad Brueriam* Hy2 (13), *uersus Brueriam* eHy3 (13) (*v.* **bruiere** 'heath, heathland'); *Criftinge, Criftin* eHy3 (13), c1240 (13), *crifting* Hy3 (13) (*v.* **cryfting** 'a small croft'); *dayla que uocatur elleuestange* eHy3 (13) ('a share of land which is called eleven poles', *v.* **deill**, **en(d)leofan, stǫng**); *Flikesburcmare* eHy3 (13) ('the boundary of Flixborough', *v.* (**ge)mǣre**); *Haldanscroft* 1269 (13) ('Hal(f)dan's croft' from the ODan pers.n. *Hal(f)dan* and **croft**); *Atte halle de Crosceby* 1294, *atte Halle "of" Crosseby* 1416, both (p) (*v.* **hall**); *haltunsti* eHy3 (13) ('the path to West Halton', *v.* **stīg**); *Haselwode de Crosseby* 1306, *Haselwod'* 1327, 1332 all (p) (*v.* **hæsel** 'a hazel', **wudu**; this may not be a local surn.); *Kerdich* 1242 (13) (*v.* **kjarr, dīc**); *Kirgarthe* 1431 (*v.* **kirkja, garðr**); *Linland* lHy3 (13) ('the selion where flax grows', *v.* **līn, land**); *Lyncolnsland* 1431 (*v.* **land**; perhaps alluding to ownership by the chapter of Lincoln Cathedral); *maregate* eHy3 (13), *le maregate que diuidit inter campos eiusd' uille & Normanby* Hy3 (13) (*v.* (**ge)mǣre** 'a boundary', **gata** 'a road'; alluding to the road forming the boundary between the open fields of Crosby and the neighbouring hamlet of Normanby); *del more* 14 (p) (*v.* **mōr**); *Nortdaile* eHy3 (13), 1242 (13), *Nortdayll* 14 (*v.* **norð, deill**, cf. *Suthdaile infra*); *Northgate* eHy3 (13) (*v.* **norð, gata**); *the Oatmeal mill and Malt house* 1718; *Pepilstather* 1431 (*v.* **popel** 'a pebble', **stǫð (stǫðvar** nom.pl.) 'a landing place'); *le Sloght called Pewedykslowte, le Slought* 1431(*v.* **slōh** 'a slough, a mire'; *Pewe-* is obscure); *pynsondayll* 14 (*v.* **deill**; the first el. alludes to *Ric' Pynson*, named in the document); *Quab, quabethorn* eHy3 (13), *Quab* c1240 (13), *ad aque ductum que uocatur Quabbebech* Hy3 (13) (from **cwabba** 'a marsh, a bog' with **þorn** 'a thorn-bush' and **bæce, bece** 'a stream' or perhaps **bekkr**); *Reddam, de Rededm* (sic) *usque ad viam que uadit de salecliue ad flikesburc* Hy3 (13) ('from *Rededm* as far as the road which leads from Sawcliffe (in Roxby cum Risby parish) to Flixborough'; *Reddam, Rededm* is of uncertain etymology); *Scallethorne, Scalethorn* eHy3 (13) (perhaps 'Skalli's thorn-tree', *v.* **þorn**, with the same pers.n as in Scawby); *sike* eHy3 (13) (*v.* **sík** 'a ditch'); *de Bosco* 132 (p), "the wood of" *Coningesby* 1431; *Suthdaile* eHy3 (13) (*v.* **sūð, deill**, cf. *Nortdaile supra*); *þu.ittecroft* Hy3 (13) (the third letter is uncertain owing to a fold in the vellum).

Flixborough

FLIXBOROUGH

> *Flichesburg* 1086 DB, *-burc* c1115 LS
> *Flickesburc* 1201 Ass, *-burg'* c1279 RRGr, *-burgh'* 1332 *SR*, *Flikesburgh(')* 1242–43 Fees, 1293 *Ass*, 1322 YD iv, 1328 Banco, 1316 FA, 1317 Ipm, 1334 (1341) Pat, *-burch* 1314 Ch, *-burg* 1248 RRG, 1291 Pap, *Flykesborw* 1303 FA

Fliccheburc 1163, 1164, 1166, 1167 P, *Flicheburc* 1165 ib
Flikeburc' 1202 Ass, *-burg* 1221, 1226 Welles, 1247 RRG, 1265
   Misc, *Flykebrugh* (sic) 1243 Pat, *Flickeburc* 1201 Ass, 1203
   Abbr, 1254 Pat
Flixeburch 1275 RH, *-burgh* 1291 Tax, (~ *alias Flikesburgh*) 1299
   Ipm, 1328 Banco, 1351 Pat
Flixburg 1295 Bodl, *-burgh(')* 1299 Pat, 1304 *FF*, 1327 Ch, 1327,
   1332 *SR*, 1333 Cl, 1343 NI, 1350 Fine *et freq* to 1697 *Terrier*,
   -burghe 1440 Visit, 1564 *Shef*, 1668, 1674, 1700 *Terrier*, *-borow*
   1589, 1598 *Shef*, *-borowe als Flixeburghe* 1600 *ib*, *-brughe* 1589,
   1591 *ib*, *Flyxburgh* 1372 Ipm, 1405 RRep, 1428, 1431 FA, 1535
   VE iv, 1556 Pat, *-borrough* 1537 *AOMB 200*, 1538 LP xiii,
   -borough 1824 O

'Flik's fortified place', *v.* **burh**. This is a hybrid p.n. with the first el.
the ON byname *Flík*, the second OE **burh**. It is highly likely that in a
p.n. with **burh** as second el. the ON first el. has replaced an earlier OE
word or pers.n. A very important AS site has recently been excavated
here.

ANDERSON'S HOLT, cf. *Anderson Close* 1840 O, named from the
Anderson family, cf. Sir Edmund *Anderson* 1600 *Shef*. ASH WOOD,
1840 *TA*. BLACK GRAVEL PLANTATION. FERRY (local), *Flixburghe
ferye* 1576 Saxton, *Flixburgh ferye* 1610 Speed, *Flixborough Ferry*
1828 Bry, referring to the same place as Flixborough Stather *infra*. FIR
BED. FLIXBOROUGH GRANGE. This must be an example of the late use
of **grange**, for which *v. Santon Grange* in Appleby parish *supra*.
FLIXBOROUGH HILL, 1828 Bry. FLIXBOROUGH PARKINGS, *the
parkyngs* 1602, ~ *park Ings* 1668, 1674, ~ *Park Ings* 1690, 1822, ~ ~
ings 1788 all *Terrier*, cf. *the Park Ings meadow* 1679 *ib*, 1840 *TA*, *v.*
park, eng 'meadow, pasture', as elsewhere in this parish. Cf. *Flyxburgh
Parke* 1431 FA, *the Park* 1668 *Terrier*. PARKINGS FM, ~ *F^m* 1828 Bry.
FLIXBOROUGH STATHER, *Flikesburgh Stather* 1299 Ipm,
Flixburgh'stather 1414 *FF*, *Flixbrough stather* 1583 *MiscDon 344*, ~
Stather 1797 *Shef*, for *Stather v.* Burton upon Stather *supra*.
FLIXBOROUGH WARREN FM, *All thatt the Warren of Conys called
Flixburgh warren* 1634 *Shef*, *the Warren* 1797, 1807 *ib*, self-
explanatory. GRANGE BECK HOLT, cf. *Grange Beck* 1840 *TA*, named
from Flixborough Grange *supra*. HALL (lost), *Site of Old Hall* 1824 O,
atte Hall' de Flixburgh 1396 Peace (p), cf. *the . . . Mannor of White Hall*

1564 *Shef.* LODGE PLANTATION. NEAP HO, 1822 *Terrier,* 1824 O, *Knephouse* 1625 *Inv, Knepe House* 1715 *ib, the Nep-house Farm* 1768 *Shef,* obscure. OLD CHURCH (lost), *Flixborough Old Church* 1824 O, *Old Church* 1828 Bry, the site of All Saints Church. OLD COMMON WOOD, cf. *Old Common* 1840 *TA,* cf. *Flixborough Common* 1840 *ib.* PARK CLOSE PLANTATION, cf. *Park Close* 1840 *ib,* cf. *Part of the Park* 1839 *Shef* and Flixborough Parkings *supra.* RECTORY, *parsonage howse* 1602, *the parsonage house* 1674, *ye Rectory or Parsonage house* 1679, *the Rectory or Parsonage Fm* 1784, 1788, *a Rectory House* 1822 all *Terrier, Rectory House* 1840 *TA.* SHARP'S HOLT, from the surn. *Sharp* and **holt** 'a holt, a thicket, a wood'. SHEFFIELD PLANTATION, cf. *Sheffield Close, ~ Hill* 1840 *TA,* named from the *Sheffield* family, prominent landowners in the parish, cf. *The Right Honourable John Sheffelde knight lorde Sheffeilde* 1564 *Shef.* WILLOW HOLT (lost), 1814 O.

FIELD-NAMES

Principal forms in (a) are 1840 *TA,* which includes Normanby in Burton upon Stather parish. Spellings dated 1304, 1414 are *FF;* 1314 Ch; 1327, 1332 *SR;* 1334 (1341), 1341 Pat; 1449 Cl; 1564, 1634, 1653, 1797, 1807, 1839, 1850 *Shef;* 1583 *MiscDon 344;* 1602, 1668, 1674, 1679, 1686, 1690, 1697, 1700, 1784, 1788, 1822 *Terrier.*

(a) Backside 1839, 1840; Baildom Cl (sic) (named from the *Baildon* family, cf. Richard *Baldon* 1674); Birk Cl (*v.* **birki** 'a birch, a birch copse'); Bottoms (*v.* **botm**); the Bratts Mdw 1784, 1822, the Brats 1784, Great, Little Bratts 1840 (*the brats medow* 1602, *Brats medow* 1679, *the Bratts* 1668, 1690, *y^e ~* 1686, *~ Brats* 1697, *~ bratts* 1700, *the Middle Bratts* 1674, 1686, *the middle ~* 1690, *ye middle Brats* 1706, *the North Bratts dike* 1674, from the pl. of ON **brot** 'a small piece of land', common in north L); Brickgarth (*v.* **garðr** 'an enclosure', clearly a late example of this word, common in north L); High Bristol Cl W, *~ ~ ~* E, Low Bristol Cl N, *~ ~ ~* S (named from the *Bristow, Bristol* family, cf. Thomas *Bristow* 1652 *Shef*); Broom cl 1839, *~* Cl 1840; Buckles Cl (named from the *Buckle* family, cf. *Mr William Buckle* 1722 *Shef*); Car (*the Carre* 1674, *Carr Closes* 1697, *v.* **kjarr** 'brushwood', 'a marsh, especially one overgrown with brushwood', as elsewhere in this parish); Castle-well Hill Top 1797, Castlewell-Hill Top 1807 (the field lay at the southern edge of Burton Wood); Chapel Fd; Church Fd 1839, 1840; Close; Cocklane Garth (*v.* **garðr**); Cow pasture 1839, *~* Pasture 1840; Croft (*v.* **croft**); Dam Leys, Damleys (cf. *atte Dame* 1332 (p), *v.* **dammr** 'a dam', 'a pond', **lea** (OE **lēah**) 'meadow, pasture' in the pl.); Drinkall Cl (presumably from the surn. *Drinkall,* found in other parishes in the area); East Croft; East Fd 1839, 1840; Far Cl; Fawn Slack Hill (sic); Fern Cl W; Five Acres; Fourteen Acres; the Glebe Cl 1788; Gravel pit cl 1788, *~* Pit Cl 1840; Grove 1839, 1840; Hare Park; Home Cl; Lr, Upr Intake (*v.* **inntak** 'land taken in or enclosed'); Lime Kiln or Saintfoin cl 1839 (*v.* **sainfoin**), Lime Kiln Cl 1840; Little Cl; Lodge Cl; Long Cl; the Long-field 1797, ~ ~ Field 1807, Long Fd 1840; Mare Walk (*v.* **walk**); Pingle 1839, 1840 (*v.* **pingel** 'a small enclosure'); Puslet Cl 1788 (probably to be identified with *the Preslet field* (sic) 1686, *y^e* ~ ~ 1697, *Pressel field* (sic) 1700); the Queen's Street 1784 (*the queen's street* 1674, *ye Queens* ~ 1679, *ye Street* 1686, *the* ~ ~ 1690, 1697); Red Ings (*v.* **eng**); Ripers Cl; Rye Garth 1839, 1840 (*v.* **garðr**); the Rye Grass Cl 1788; Great, Little Sand Cl; Sheep Dike Cl; Sheep Walk (*v.* **shepe-walk** 'a range of pasture for sheep'); Shoulder of Mutton (named from the shape of the field); Slater's Trent Cl (named from the *Slater* family, cf. Richard *Slater* 1722 *Shef* and *v.* Trent Cl *infra*); Smarrows; Smengs (sic) 1839, 1840; Sod House Cl (perhaps alluding to a dwelling roofed with turf); South Cl; Spring Head Cl; Stone Cl; Stone-Dale 1797, 1807, Stone Dale 1840; Stone Gate or Suds Cl 1839; Ten Acres' Ten Pound 1839, 1840 (the reference is a rent); Thirty Acres (*the thirty Acre Close* 1668, ~ ~ *acre close* 1674); Top Cl; Trangate 1839, 1840 (from ON **trani** 'a heron' and **gata** 'a way, a path, a road'); Trent Cl (1668, *the Trent closes* 1674, the field is close to the R. Trent, cf. *Trent Bank* in (b) *infra*); Underwoods 1839, Underwood 1840 (*the underwood* 1668, 'wood, whether growing or cut, consisting of coppice poles or young suckers, but not branches'); Walks 1839, 1840 (*v.* **walk** denoting land used for the pasture of animals, especially sheep, cf. Sheep Walk *supra*); Warp Cl 1839, 1840, ~ Land 1840, ~ land 1850 (for *warp*, *v.* Warp Fm in Bottesford parish *supra*); Wash Wells; Washingforth (*v.* **ford**); Westobys Garth (from the family name *Westoby, Westaby*, cf. *Widdow Westaby* 1722 and **garðr**); Woad Cl (*v.* **wād** 'woad'); Yowles Cliff (presumably named from the surn. *Youle, Yowle*).

(b) *the Short Lands Cald the Butts* 1668 (*v.* **butte** 'a short strip at right angles to other strips, a short strip ploughed in the angle where two furlongs meet' and cf. *the two Long Lands infra*); "the causey of" *Flikesburgh* 1334 (1341), *the Cawsey* 1674 (*v.* **caucie**); *the corn close* 1674; *Cristenges* 1449 (*v.* **eng**; the first el. may be **Crist** denoting meadow dedicated in some way to *Christ*); *the ditch* 1686, *y^e* ~ 1697, 1700 (*v.* **dīc**); *the field* 1674 (referring to the open field of the village); *the hedge* 1668; *Hestecroft* 1314, 1334 (1341), 1341 (*v.* **hestr** 'a horse, a stallion', **croft**); *Flixbrough Ingges* 1653, *the Ing close* 1686, ~ ~ *Close* 1690, *ye Ing Close* 1697, ~ ~ *close* 1700 (*v.* **eng** 'meadow, pasture'); *Ings Lane, Ingge* ~ 1668; *the two Long Lands* 1668 (*v.* **land** 'a selion' in the pl. and cf. *The Short Lands Cald the Butts supra*); *middle field* 1668, *the* ~ ~ 1686, *y^e* ~ ~ 1697, *the Middle field* 1690; *tercia vnius molendini . . . in Flixburgh'* 1304 (*v.* **myln**); *La More* 1327 (p) (*v.* **mōr**); *the north field* 1668 (cf. *middle field supra*); *ye sure called Flixbrough sewer* 1583; *Trent Bank* 1686, 1690, 1697 (self-explanatory); *Trentenges* 1449 ('the meadows, pastures beside the R. Trent', *v.* **eng** in the pl.).

Frodingham

FRODINGHAM

Frodingeham 1224 Welles, 1291 Tax

Frodingham c1128 ChronPetro, 1237 RRG, 1254 ValNor, 1281 RSu,
1519 ECB, 1556 InstBen, 1601 *Foster et passim,* ~ *otherwise*
Frothingham 1829 *Shef, Frodyngham* 1406 Pat, 1409 RRep, 1535
VE iv, 1556 Pat, *Froddingham* 1647 *Nelthorpe*

Frothengham 1190 (1301) Dugd vi, *Frothingham* 1259, 1261 RRGr,
1290, 1293 RSu, e14 RA ii, 1300 Ipm, 1301 *KR*, 1301 Cl, 1307,
1308 *KR*, 1308 Cl, 1316 FA *et freq* to 1571 Pat, *Froþingham*
c1279 RRGr, *Frothyngham* 1327 *SR*, 1356 BPR, 1360 Orig,
1360, 1378 Pat, 1379 Ipm, 1382 Misc, 1387, 1388 *Foster et freq*
to 1545–47 *MinAcct*

Forthyngham 1343 NI, *Forthingham* 1539 LP xiv

'The homestead, the estate of the Frōdingas', from the gen.pl.
Frōdinga of the OE group name *Frōdingas* 'the family, the dependents
of *Frōd(a)*' and OE **hām** 'a homestead, an estate'. Forms in *-th-* are due
to Scand influence.

SCUNTHORPE

Escumetorp (3x) 1086 DB

Scumetorp 1196 ChancR, *Scumthorp'* 1273–74 RA, 1300 Ipm, 1307
KR, 1329 *Ass*

Scumptorp 1245 FF, *-thorp* 1309, 1311 *KR, Scompthorp'* 1327, 1332
SR

Scunthorp' 1301, 1306 *KR, -thorp* 1382 Misc, *-thorpe* 1557 *KR*,
1660 *Foster et passim, Skunthorpe* 1402 FA

Scomthorp 1450, 1451 Cl

'Skúma's secondary settlement, outlying dependent farmstead or
hamlet', *v.* **þorp**. The first el. is the ON pers.n. *Skúma*. Scunthorpe was
no doubt secondary to Frodingham, in which parish it was originally
situated. Prosthetic *e* has been added before *s* + *k* in the DB forms due
to AN influence.

In the Middle Ages Scunthorpe was in the parish of Frodingham. Iron
ore was discovered in the area in 1859. As a result of the discovery of

ironstone and subsequent smelting, what were five separate settlements, Ashby, Brumby, Crosby, Frodingham and Scunthorpe, became one large town. Scunthorpe had developed as the largest of the five, and so it became an Urban District in 1894 and in 1919 was united with the other four to become the Scunthorpe, Brumby and Frodingham Urban District (sic), and in 1936 the whole of the new Municipal Borough was called after Scunthorpe.

CLAYFIELD PLANTATION, cf. *Scunthorpe Clay Field* 1834 *EnclA*. CLIFF GARDENS, cf. *the Clife* 1679 *Terrier*, *ye Cliffe* 1700 *ib*, *Frodingham Cliff* 1750, 1754 *Shef*, cf. *ye West Clife* 1677, 1697 *Terrier*, *v.* **clif**. COLES PLANTATION, presumably from the surn. *Cole(s)*. DAWES LANE, presumably from the surn. *Dawes*. FRODINGHAM GRANGE, a late example of **grange**, common in L, for which *v. Santon Grange* in Appleby parish *supra*. HIGHFIELD (Scunthorpe). REDBOURN COTTAGE. VICARAGE (Frodingham), 1822, *vicarydge howse* 1579, *the vicaridg'* 1601, *The Vicaridge Howse* 1606, *the Vicaridge houss* (sic) 1671, *the Vicaridge* 1686, *there is no Vicarage House* 1788 all *Terrier*. WESTFIELD (Scunthorpe). WINDMILL, *Wind Mill* 1834 *EnclA*.

FIELD-NAMES

Forms dated e14, 1301, 1306, 1308, 1557 are *KR*; 1327 *SR*; 1343 NI; 1356 BPR, 1518 LP ii; 1531 Wills iii; 1579, 1601, 1606, 1671[1], 1677, 1679, 1686, 1690, 1697, 1700, 1706, 1788, 1803, 1822 *Terrier*; 17, 1669, 1671[2], 1701, 1708, 1740 *LD 70*; 1616 *MiscDep 77*; 1644 LAAS ii; 1712, 1720, 1727, 1743, 1750, 1754, 1829, 1839 *Shef*; 1757, 1787, 1828 *MiscDep 77*; 1831–32 *EnclA (Plan)* 1834 *EnclA*.

(a) Bean Ridge flg 1803, ~ Rigg Flg 1828 (*beane riges* 17, cf. *Beanlands* 1616, *v.* **bēan**, **land**, **hrycg**, with two forms Scandinavianised); the Beck's Cl 1760, (the) Becke Cl 1764, Becks Close Flg 1803, Becks Cl 1828 (cf. *beckfurlong, the beck* 17, *v.* **bekkr** 'a stream'); Brigg Rd 1834 (the road to Glanford Brigg); Burringham Rd 1831–32 (the road to Burringham); Burton Rd 1834 (the road to Burton upon Stather); Calf Cl 1828, the ~ ~ 1834; the Carr Lane 1754 (*v.* **kjarr** 'brushwood' later 'a bog, marsh, especially one overgrown with brushwood'); Chivers car 1828 (from the surn. *Chivers* with **kjarr**); South, West Church Cl 1828; Church Lane 1822, 1834, the Church Rd 1822 (cf. *Church hyway* 17); Clay pitt Cl 1750, ~ Pit Cl 1754, Claypit Cl 1839 (*Clay Pitt Close* 1743, cf. *Clay pitts* 1616); the Clough Cotes 1788, Clawcotes, Clowcotes 1822 (*Cloucotes* 17, *ye clowcoats* 1677, 1697, *the Clowcotes* 1679, ~ *Clowcoats* 1690, *ye clow coats* 1700, *the furlong called the Clow coats* 1706, *Cloughcotes flg* 1803, from L dial. *clow* 'a dam for water', 'a sluice or floodgate', *v.* NED s.v. *clow* sb[1], 1a and **cot** 'a cottage, a shed' in the pl.); Cow Pasture 1757; the

Croft or Paddock 1834; Cross lands Flg 1828 (probably a furlong lying at right angles to its neighbours, as Mr. Field suggests); Dodder Lane or Pepper Lane 1754; East Common 1831–32, Frodingham East Common 1834, the East Moor 1750, Frodingham East Moor 1787 (*Frothyngham Estmour* 1318, *v.* ēast, mōr); East Ridings 1828 (*v.* ryding 'a clearing'); Eight lands 1803, ~ ~ Flg 1828 (*v.* land 'a selion' in the pl.); Fishpond Cl 1828, Fish Pond Cl 1834; Folly 1828 (probably commemorating an act of human folly, but the meaning of *folly* in p.ns. and f.ns. is uncertain); Frodingham Clay Fd 1831–32; Frodingham Ings 1754 (*Froddingham Inges* 1671, 1701, 1708, *v.* eng 'meadow, pasture'); Frodingham Moors 1754, 1828, 1839, ~ Moor 1831–32, the Moors 1834 (*le More, More meade* 1616, *one piece or parcell of moor ground called three quarters of an Oxgang of moor* 1727, *Frodingham Moors* 1740, 1743, *v.* mōr); Frodingham West Common 1828, 1831–32, 1834; Garth end Flg 1828 (*v.* garðr 'an enclosure'); Green Lane 1834 (an occupation road or access way); The Greens Close 1720, the ~ ~ 1750 (*a la grene* 1301, *de la Grene* 1302, *Atte Grene* 1327, *de Grene* 1343 all (p), *v.* grēne 'a village green'); Gunhouse Rd 1834 (the road to Gunness); Long, Short Hedge Flg 1828 (*A furlonge called ye Hedge* 1677, *the Hedge* 1679, *ye hedge* 1697, self-explanatory, *v.* hecg); Hell-whole flg (sic) 1803, Long, Short Hell-holes 1828 (a derogatory name for an unpleasant place); that land called a Hempland 1754, the Hempland 1839 (cf. *the Hempscroft* 1644, *Hempe Croft* 1701, *v.* hænep 'hemp', croft, land 'a selion'); high ridings 1822 (*v.* ryding); Hywates Flg 1803, High Waits 1828 (perhaps from waite 'a look-out place'); Home Cl 1828; Horse Paddock 1828; Lamdale flg 1803, Lampdale Flg, Lamp dale Wd 1828 (*Lampe deale* 17, *v.* deill 'a share or portion of land'; *Lamp-* probably refers to a church lamp, maintained by the rent of this land); Little Fd 1828, the ~ ~ 1834; Little Wood Flg 1828; the Long Ridings 1822 (*v.* ryding); Low flg 1803; the Low Ridging (sic) 1788, Low Riddens flg 1803 (*the lowrigings* 17, ~ *low ridings* 1679, ~ *Low Ridings* 1690, *v.* ryding); Middle flg 1803, ~ Flg 1828 (*the midle furlong* 17); Midmore 1754 (*the Midmore* 1712, *v.* mid 'amidst', mōr); Mill Flg 1828; Mill Lane Cls 1828, Mill Lane 1834; New Cl 1828, 1834 (1740); the North Greens 1750 (*The north Greens* 1720, *v.* grēne 'a grassy spot'); the Open Common 1822; Orchen-busk flg 1803 (*Orchen* is perhaps from urchon 'a hedgehog'; *busk* is from ODan buskr); Oxgang Carr 1828 (*v.* oxgang 'a measure of land' of 10 to 30 acres extent, kjarr); Ruff-hose Flg 1803 (*Roughowfurlong* 17, *v.* rūh, haugr 'a mound, a hill); the Sand Fd 1822, 1828, 1834, Sand garth 1828 (*v.* sand, garðr), Frodingham Sand Fd 1831–32; Scunthorpe Clay Fd 1831–32; Scunthorpe Common 1757; Scunthorpe East Moor (*Stompthorp Estmour* (*St-* = *Sc-*) 1518, *the East Moor of Scunthorpe* 1720, cf. the East Moor *supra*), Scunthorpe Moors 1828, 1834; Scunthorpe South Sand Fd 1831–32, 1834; Scunthorpe West Common 1828, 1831–32; the South Fd 1822; Sowers flg 1803, 1828, ~ Cl 1828, 1834 (*Sowers* 17); Stamp Cl 1828 (17, probably from the surn. *Stamp*); Stone Brigge Cl 1828, ~ Bridge Cl 1834, Stonebriggs flg 1803, Stone Bridge Flg 1828 (cf. *stone briges* 17, self-explanatory); Swike Cls 1750, 1754 (1743), Swikes Cl 1828; Tack Cars 1828 (*v.* tacca 'a teg, a young sheep', kjarr); Three Stong Flg 1803, 1828 (*v.* stong 'a pole'); Town End Flg 1828; Townside Flg 1803; Trace Hill Cl 1828, Tracehill cl 1834; Trason Fd 1803 (cf. perhaps *trasorside* (sic) 17); Upper Flg 1803, 1828 (*the uper furlong* 17); Upper Ridding 1788 (*uper*

Readings 1677, *the Upper Ridings* 1690, cf. *nether Readings* 1677, *the nether Reddings* 1679, *nether readings* 1697, *yᵉ Nether Reddings* 1706 (*v.* **ryding**); Vicarage Cl 1788 (cf. Vicarage *supra*); Warren Rd 1834 (*v.* **wareine**); the West Common (and Moors) 1834, the West Moor 1750 (*yᵉ west common* 1677, 1697); the West Fd 1788; West Ridings 1828 (*v.* **ryding**); Whate lands 1803, Waitlands Flg 1828 (*Whatlands* 17, *v.* **hwǣte** 'wheat', **land** 'a selion'); Wind Mill 1834; Winterton Rd 1834 (the road to Winterton, a few miles north); Wood Side 1828.

(b) *backside* 17; *Church Warlets* 1677, *church Warlets* 1697, *Three Lands called Warletts in the furlong called the Clow coats* 1706 (*v.* the Clough Cotes in (a) *supra*; for **warlet**, *v.* the discussion s.n. Waterhill Wood, PN L **2**, 67–68, where it is suggested that "a *warlot* would seem to have been a piece of land assessed to a specifically defined payment of geld". This el. has so far only been recorded from L in the English Place-Name Survey, where now a number of examples have been identified. Note the appellative use of the word in Frodingham in *one war-Loth* 1690); *cobb crofte* 1831, *unum toftum et croftum vocatum Cob* 1616 (from the surn. *Cob(b)* with **croft** and **toft**); *a comon* 1601, *the comons* 1606, *~ Common* 1679, 1712; *le common Drean* 1708; *comon lane* 1579; *dowcottes* e14 (*v.* **douve-cote** in the pl.); *In campis communibus, le fielde meere* 1616, *Frodingham field* 1677, 1697 (*v.* **feld** denoting the open field of the village, (**ge)mǣre** 'a boundary'); *In palustro* 1616, *Froddingham Marsh* 1669; *Fossam vocat Indyke* 1669, 1671² (the inner dike); *Lee* (for *Le*) *inge furlonge* 1557 (*v.* **eng**, cf. Frodingham Ings *supra*); *marey noble garth* 17 (from the pers.n. with **garðr**; *Mary Noble* has not been identified); *le meadowe* 1616; *Nether Land mewdewe* (sic) 1579, *nether land* 1601 (*v.* **neoðera**, **land** 'a selion'); *de Northintoun* 1308 (p) (literally 'north in the village', *v.* **norð, in, tūn**, denoting X who lives in the north of the village, a common Scand formation in L which occurs as *Northiby*, of which *Northintūn* is an anglicisation. This anglicised form, however, is rare); *north ridings* 17 (*v.* **ryding**); *Robert parkinson headland* 1697 (from the pers.n. with **hēafodland**); *Reddayle* e14 (perhaps 'the share of land where reeds grow', *v.* **hrēod, deill**); *Scunthorpe field* 1677, 1697, *Scunthorp field* 1690; *Scunthorpe Inges* 1671² (*v.* **eng**); *Scunthorpe Marsh* 1669; *Short furlong* 17; *Smithbecke, Smeethbeck* 1616 (*v.* **bekkr**); *South ridings* 17 (*v.* **ryding**); *Stanpitt* e14 (*v.* **stān, pytt**); *Stanaland furlong* (sic) 17 (probably 'the stony selion', *v.* **stān, land**); *the strete* 17, *the Quenes street* 17, *Kings street* 1690 (*v.* **strǣt**); *towne end* 17; *the West Moors of Scunthorpe* 1720; *wimspit hil* 17 (the reading is doubtful).

Gunness

GUNNESS

Gunnesse 1199, 1200 P both (p), 1201 ChancR (p), 1202 P (p), 1202 Ass (p), 1203, 1210 P both (p), 1210–12 RBE, 1218, 1219 Ass, 1245 FF (p)

Gunēs 1219 Ass (p), *Gunnes* c1300 *Shef*, 1445 Cl, (*~ beside Trent*) 1544 LP xix, 1544 *SP*

Gunneys 1280 FF (p), 1303 *KR*, (~ *iuxta Boryngham*) 1322 *FF*, 1332
  SR, 1336 Pat *et passim* to 1445 Cl, 1576 Saxton, *Gunnays* 1327
  SR, 1328 Banco, 1371 *FF et passim* to 1422 Fine
Gunnas 1391 (1544) *SP*, 1432 LNQ xii, 1459 (1544), 1480 (1544)
  SP, 1502 Ipm, 1540 WillsStow *et passim* to 1648 Hall, 1788
  Terrier, Gonnes 1510 *DCFabRents, Gonnas* 1544–47 ECP, 1564
  Shef
Gunhouse 1571 WillsStow, 1653 WillsPCC, 1668, 1686, 1690
  Terrier et freq

'Gunni's headland' *v*. **nes**, a Scand compound, the first el. being the
ON pers.n. *Gunni*. The name is topographically appropriate for there is
a marked promontory here into the R. Trent. The development to
Gunhouse is no doubt the result of popular etymology and has resulted
in a local controversy as to whether the modern form should be
Gunhouse or Gunness, *v*. for instance LNQ ix, 135–42.

CANWICK HO. GUNNESS COMMON, *Common* 1838 *TA*. GUNNESS
GRANGE, apparently a late use of **grange** for which *v. Santon Grange*
in Appleby parish *supra*. WALKS HO (lost), 1824 O, *v*. **walk** common
in north L, denoting land used for the pasture of animals, especially
sheep. A windmill marks the site of the house.

FIELD-NAMES

Principal forms in (a) are 1838 *TA*. Those dated 1306–7 are *KR*; 1391
(1544), 1459 (1544), 1480 (1544) *SP*; 1544–47 ECP; 1602, 1678, 1784,
1822 *Terrier* (Flixborough); 1772, 1800 *Shef*; 1828 *MiscDep 77*.

(a) Ashgarth Close 1800, Ash Garth 1838 (*v*. **æsc**, **garðr** 'an enclosure', as
elsewhere in the parish); Backside Cl; (Low, Second) Campbell Car (*v*. **kjarr** 'a
marsh overgrown with brushwood', as elsewhere in this parish), Campbell Cl (from
the surn. *Campbell*); Church or Chapel of Ease (cf. *atte kyrkegarthe de Gunnas* 1391
(1544), *atte kyrkgarthe* 1459 (1544), *atte Kyrkegarthe* 1480 (1544) all (p), *v*. **kirkja**,
garðr, a Scand compound); Cogdal, ~ Carrs 1800, Cogdales 1838; the Commission
dreane 1800; Corner; Croft (*v*. **croft**); Cutler Ings 1800 (from the surn. *Cutler* and
eng in the pl.); East Croft (cf. West Croft *infra*); Eight Acres Car, ~ ~ Cl (*v*. **kjarr**);
Empsons Farm (from the surn. *Empson*, cf. Joshua *Empson* 1846 White); Far Garden;
Fish Lodge; Far Groves, ~ Growes (sic), Near Groves (*v*. Trent groves *infra*); Grub
Cl 1800, Grubs Cl 1838; Gunhouse Cars, ~ Cl, ~ Moors 1828 (*v*. **kjarr**, **clos(e)**,
mōr); Gunhouse Ings 1772, 1828, Gunnas Ings 1784 (*Gunnasse Ings* 1602, *Gunnas*
~ 1679, *Gunnas Ings Meadow* 1674, *v*. **eng** 'meadow, pasture', as elsewhere in the

parish); Gunhouse Lane 1800, ~ Road 1843 *TA* (Brumby); Home Cl; Horse Cl; Kate Cl; Laughtons Cottage and Garden (from the surn. *Laughton*); Long Cl; Methodist Chapel; Narrow Car 1828; the Old Groves 1800, Old & New Groves 1838 (*v.* Trent groves *infra*); Ould Sheepfield 1800, Sheep Fd 1838; Plantation; Pond; Poors houses and Garden; Pudding Poke Cl (a fanciful name for land with sticky soil); Second Cl; Seed Cl 1800; Selby Garth (probably from the surn. *Selby* with **garðr**); Shift Ings 1800 (*v.* **eng**; *Shift* probably alludes to *shifts* in crop-rotation, cf. the discussion s.n. *a Shift Acre* in the f.ns. of South Ferriby, PN L **2**, 116 and also Shift cls in Immingham f.ns., PN L **2**, 169); Ten Acres; Three Acres; Trent Bank and Foreshore; Trent Fd 1800, 1838; Trent groves (*grove* is a dial. term for sites where digging (for turf) takes place, *v.* further PN L **2**, 155, PN L **4**, 128 and PN L **5**, 40); Twelve Acres; Twenty Acres; West Croft (cf. East Croft *supra*); West Orchard; Wheat Cl; Wilks Cl 1800 (no doubt from the surn. *Wilks*); Wyebeck Cl 1822.

(b) *campis de Guneys* 1307 (*v.* **feld**); *attegrene* 1307 (*v.* **grēne** 'a village green, a grassy spot'); *Wadnynges* (sic) 1544–57 (Dr Insley suggests that this perhaps means 'the meadow where woad grows' or 'woad-coloured meadow', from OE ***wāden**, **wǣden** and ON **eng**, but the form is late).

West Halton

WEST HALTON

> *Haltone* 1086 DB, -*ton* c1115 LS, 1158 France, 1243 RRG, 1254 ValNor, 1275 RH, 1284–85 FA, 1291 Tax, (~ *super Trentam*) 113 AD, 1322 Orig *et freq* to 1576 LER, -*tun* 1212 Fees, 1338 Pat, *Westhalton* 1397 Pat, 1423 Cl, 1428 Pat, 1434 *Yarb*, *West Halton* 1431 FA
>
> *Auton'* 1180 P, *Hauton* 1194 (Hy 4) *GCB*, 1226 FF
> *Halghton'* 1219 Fees
> *Haulton* 1263 FF, *Westhaulton* 1610 Speed

'The nook farmstead, village, estate', *v.* **halh**, **tūn**. The topograhical significance of the OE p.n. el. **halh** 'a nook' has been studied in detail by Margaret Gelling, PNITL 100–111, who points out that the village lies in "a tiny indentation of the 100' contour". Spellings in *Hau-* are due to the vocalisation of -*l*-. It is *West* to distinguish it from *East* Halton, PN L **2**, 148–49.

COLEBY

Colebi (2x) 1086 DB, 1181 P (p), 1202 Ass (p), 1212 Fees, e13
(1311) Ch (p), *-by* 1113–28 (l13), Hy2 (l13) Glouc, Hy2 (14) *VC*
(p) 1210–12 RBE, 1226 FF, 1246 Ipm (p) *et freq*, ~ *or Coulby*
1704, 1764 *Shef, Old Coleby* 1730 *Terrier*, 1794 *Shef*
Collebi 1200, 1202 P (p), *-by* 1275 RH, 1343 Ipm, ("by" *Halton*)
1415 Cl, 1428 FA
Colby 1322 YD iv, 1327 *SR*, 1328 Banco, 1332 *SR*, 1346 Fine, 1347
Pat, ("by" *Halton*) 1395 *et passim* to 1675 *Elwes, -bye* 1577
Terrier, Colbie 1650 *Yarb, Kolby* 1675 *Elwes, Ould Colby* 1583
MiscDon 344
Coulbye 1576 Saxton, *-beye* 1583 *MiscDon 344, -by* 1610 Speed,
1697, 1706 *Terrier*

'Koli's farmstead, village', *v.* **bȳ**, the first el being the ON pers.n.
Koli. This is identical in meaning with Coleby in Kesteven.

HAIRBY (lost)

Hedebi (4x) 1086 DB
Heidebi c1128 (12) ChronPetro
Haidbi 1212 Fees
Hetheby 1231 *PetLN* (p), m14 CNat
Heytheby 1246 Ipm, 1271 FF, 1297 *PetWB* (p), 1294 *Ass*, 1307 *FF*
Hayetheby 1272 FF, *Haytheby* 1304 Ipm, 1316, 1322 (m14) CNat,
1327 *SR*, 1329 *Ass et passim* to 1427 *FF, Haitheby* 1322 *ib*, 1333
(m14) CNat, *Haythby* 1577 *Terrier*
Hatheby 1289 *Ass*, 1290 Abbr, 1397 *Shef*, 1403 Inqaqd, 1474 *FF*,
1504–15 ECP
Hathby 1538, 1664 *Terrier*, (~ *alias Hareby*) 1671 1675 *Elwes*, 1697
Terrier, -bye 1690, 1786 *ib, Heathby* 1697 *ib*
Hareby Field 1730 *Terrier*, ~ *Fields* 1864 *ib*, ~ *leys* 1805–16
MiscDon 248, Great, Little Hareby 1838 *TA, Hareby* 1841 *TA*
(Alkborough), 1867 *Terrier*, ~ *Field* 1822 *ib, Hareby Leys* 1788
Shef, 1838 *TA*
Hairby Fields, ~ *Leys* 1806 *EnclA* (Burton upon Stather), ~ *Field*
1822 *Terrier*, ~ *Fields* 1867 *ib*

'The farmstead, village on the heath, on the uncultivated land', *v.*
heiðr, bȳ. This is a depopulated village, represented in the 19th century

by a series of some twenty-one contiguous fields south-west of Coleby and north of the parish boundary between West Halton and Burton upon Stather. There is a further field called *Hareby* just to the east of Fir Bed Plantation recorded in the *TA* for Alkborough. Dr Insley points out that *Hairby* is identical in origin with the name of the Viking Age emporium of Hedeby on the Schlei, for which *v.* W. Laur, *Historisches Ortsmanenlexikon von Schleswig-Holstein*, 2nd ed., Neumunster, 1992, 316.

COLEBY HALL, 1824 O, 1828 Bry, *ad Aulam de Colby* 1295 *Ass*. THE ELMS. GLEBE FM, *The Glebe Farm House* 1822, 1837, 1864 *Terrier*. HALTON DRAIN, cf. *the common drayne* 1577, 1664, ~ *dreane* 1638, *the comon dreane* 1668, 1686, 1690, *the Com(m)on Drayne* 1697, ~ *Common Drain* 1730 all *Terrier*, and cf. *y* *common sewer* in f.ns. (b) *infra*. MANOR HO. RECTORY (lost), *y* *parsonage house* 1638, 1664, *the parsonage* 1664, *The parsonage house* 1668, ~ *Parsonage house* 1686, 1690, 1730, *The Parsonage House* 1706, *the Rectory House* 1822, *The* ~ ~ 1837, 1864, 1867 all *Terrier*.

FIELD-NAMES

Forms dated 1226 are FF; 1272, 1329 *Ass*; 113 *AD*; 1327, 1332 *SR*; 1335, 1794 *Shef*; 1343 NI; 1423 Cl; 1577, 1590, 1638, 1664, 1668. 1686, 1690, 1697, 1706, 1730, 1822, 1837, 1864, 1867 *Terrier*; 1583 *MiscDon 344*; 1628 *Yarb*; 1671 *Elwes*; 1716 *Inv*; 1768 *EnclA* (Alkborough); 1774 *MiscDon 348*; a1806 *MiscDon 246*; 1806–15 *MiscDon 248*; 1806 *EnclA* (Burton upon Stather); 1835 *BH*; 1836 Andrew.

(a) Bains Garth & Pigeon Cote 1794 (probably named from the surn. *Bains* with **garðr**); Banks Ho 1794; Buckles Cl 1794, a1806 (from the surn. *Buckle*); Carr 1774 (*y* *Carr, Colby Carr* 1590, *v.* **kjarr**); Chapel Cl 1794; Church Lands 1837; Cliff 1794 (cf. *Cliff End* 1730); Coleby Catchwater Drain 1806, Catchwater Drain 1822; Coleby Fd 1806, 1822 (*Colby Field* 1590, *the Feildes of Colby* 1671, *Coleby Field* 1730, *v.* **feld**); the Commission Drain 1822; Dale 1794; Driffield Cl 1794 (from the surn. *Driffield*, cf. William *Driffill* 1846 White); Ellis Cl 1794 (from the surn. *Ellis*, cf. William *Elys* 1332 *SR*); Far Cl 1794, a1806, 1838; Far Fd a1806; Fishpond Cl 1794; the Folly 1806 (*v.* **folie**); Four Acres Car; Gally Hill 1794 (*v.* **galga** 'a gallows', **hyll**); Haverdale 1794, a1806, 1838 (*haverdayll* 1577, *haverdale* 1638, 1664, *Haverdale* 1690, *Haver Dale* 1697, *upper haverdaile* 1668, 1686, *upp' hav' Dale* 1697, *Upper Haver Dale* 1706, ~ *Haverdale* 1730, *v.* **hafri** 'oats', **deill** 'a share, a portion of land', as elsewhere in the parish, a Scand compound); Heifer Cl 1794;

Hewitsons Cl 1794, Hewitson's ~ a1806 (from the surn. *Hewitson*); Highfield 1774; Hill Top Cl 1794; Homestead, Garden and Hill Pasture; Homestead Green 1774; Horse Cl 1794; Houghton's Road 1806–15 (named from the *Houghton* family, cf. . . . *Houghton* (no forename) named in the document); Ings 1774, 1835 (*Haulton Inges* 1583, *the Inges* 1668, 1730, *~ Ings* 1697, 1730, *ye Inges* 1706, *v.* **eng** 'meadow, pasture' in the pl., as elsewhere in the parish); (Great) Intake 1794 (*v.* **inntak** 'a piece of land taken in or enclosed'); Long Cl 1794, a1806, 1838; Longland Cl 1774 (*v.* **land** 'a selion'); Low Dale; Low Hole 1794; Meadow Cl; Metcalf Cl 1794, Metcalf's ~ a1806 (from the surn. *Metcalf*); Middle Cl 1794; New Clow 1774 (*v.* **clōh**, L dial. *clow* 'a dam, a sluice-gate'); Norbeck 1794 (*Northbekke* 1423, *Norbeck* 1730, cf. *North Beck Ends* 1590, *v.* **norð**, **bekkr** 'a stream', as elsewhere in the parish); North-beck-pit 1836; Pingle 1794 (*v.* **pingel** 'a small enclosure'); Porter Garth 1794 (from the surn. *Porter* with **garðr**); Richmond Cl 1774 (from the surn. *Richmond*); Robinsons Cl 1794 (from the surn. *Robinson*, cf. *G. Robinson* 1839 *MiscDon 348*); Great, Little Sainfoin Cl 1794 (*v.* **sainfoin**); the Sand Marfew Road 1822 (*v.* **sand**, **marfur** 'a furrow marking a boundary', common in north L); (far, Near) Seven Acres 1794, 1838; South Fd 1794, a1806; S Stony Fd (sic) 1774; Ten Acres 1794; Topham Cottage 1794 (from the surn. *Topham*); Twenty Acres; Twenty Cl a1806; Wakes's Car (from the surn. *Wakes* with **kjarr**); Mr Watsons Cl 1794; Wilson's Cl a1806 (named from the *Wilson* family, cf. Thomas *Wilson* 1716); Wybeck Cl a1806, Wyby Cl 1768.

(b) *the beck* 1638, 1664, 1697, *the Becke* 1668, *~ Beck* 1686, 1697, 1730, *ye Beck* 1706 (*v.* **bekkr**); *Beenhommere* 1423; *Bracken lands* 1638, *bracken lands* 1664 (*v.* **brakni** 'bracken', **land**); *Bratbecke* 1590 (*v.* **bekkr**); *a Mear called Burton Meare* 1590 ('the boundary with Burton upon Stather', *v.* **(ge)mǣre**); *calf dayll* 1577, *calf dale* 1638, 1664, *Calfe daile Marforde* 1668 (*Marforde* is a variant spelling of **marfur** 'a boundary furrow'), *Calfe daile* 1686, *~ Dale* 1690, 1697, 1706, 1730 (*v.* **calf**, **deill**); *Colby gatt* 1577, *~ gate* 1638, 1664, *Coulbygate* 1686, *Coulby gate* 1690, 1706 (*v.* **gata**); *Colby Ings* 1590 (*v.* **eng**); *Old Colby mear* 1590 (*v.* **(ge)mǣre** 'a boundary'); *Old Coulby Marfore* 1668, *Ould Coulby Marfare* 1690, 1706, *Coulby Marfure* 1686 (*v.* **marfur**) (all named from Coleby); *the Constables Merfare* 1730 (*v.* **marfur**); *Cowlebe Common* 1628 (i.e. Coleby Common); *dowlandes* 1577, 1638, *-lands* 1664, *-land* 1668, *Douland* 1686, *Dowlands* 1690, 1697, 1706, 1730 (the first el. is perhaps ON **dauðr** 'dead' with loss of medial *-th-*; the second is **land** 'a selion'); *the east feyld(e)* 1577, *ye east field* 1638, *ye East field of Haythby* 1664, *the East Feild* 1668, *ye East feild* 1706 (cf. *the west feyld infra*); *eastgatt* 1577, *Eastgate* 1590, 1686, 1690, 1697, *East gate* 1638, 1665, 1668, 1706, *east gate* 1664, *East Gate* 1730 (self-explanatory, *v.* **ēast**, **gata**); *Estiby* 1327, *Estyby* 1332 both (p) (literally '(place) east in the village', *v.* **ēast**, **í**, **bȳ**, a common formation in L, denoting a person who lived in the east of the village, cf. *Northiby* and *Westiby infra*); *ye field* 1638, 1664, *the Feild* 1668, 1690, 1697, *~ field* 1697 (*v.* **feld**, denoting the open field of the village); *the fealdes meare* 1577, *the fields* ~ 1638, *~ fieldes meare* 1664, *~ Feild Meare* 1668, 1686, 1690, *~ Fieldes Mear* 1697, *ye feildes meare* 1706, *~ Field Meer* 1730 ('the boundary of the open fields', *v.* **feld**, **(ge)mǣre**); *the fir-Close* 1730 (*v.* **fyrs**, **clos(e)**); *la Grene* 1271–2, 113 both (p) (*v.* **grēne** 'a village green'); *Grenhill* *dike Mear* 1590 (*v.* **grēne** 'green', **hyll**, with **dīc**, **dík** and (**ge**)**mǣre**); *yᵉ hall Inges* 1583 (*v.* **hall, eng** in the pl.); *Halton Crosse* 1706; *Hawton Wathe bridge* 1683 (from Halton with **vað** 'a ford', and **brycg**); *the hedland* 1577, *yᵉ head land* 1664, ~ *Headlands* 1706 (*v.* **hēafod-land** 'the head of a strip of land left for the turning the plough'); *Hund Hill* (sic) 1577, *hand hill* 1668, 1686, *Hande Hill* 1690, *Hand Hill* 1697; *yᵉ hyghe streyt* 1577, ~ *high street* 1638, 1664, 1706, *the High Street* 1686; *Hooke House* 1716; *atte Kergarth* 1343 (p) (probably from **kjarr** and **garðr** 'the enclosure in the marsh'); *lamber dayll marford* 1577, *Lamberd dale marford* 1664, *Lamber daile Marfare* 1668, 1686, *Lamber deale* 1690, ~ *Deale* 1697, 1706, ~ *Dale* 1730 (*Lamber* is from the surn. *Lambert*, which belongs ultimately to the Frankish pers.n. *Landber(h)t, Lambert*, which was a common name in northern France and the Low Countries in the medieval period, with **deill** and **marfur**); *lamber hyll* 1577, *Lamber hill* 1638, 1690, *Lamberhill* 1668, 1706, *Lamberd hill* 1664, *Lamber Hill* 1730 (for *Lamber, v.* prec); *Little Close* 1706; *the Lordes Dayll* 1577, *yᵉ lords dale* 1664, *the Lords* ~ 1690, 1730, *yᵉ Lords Deale* 1697, ~ *Dale* 1706 (self-explanatory, *v.* **deill**); *the marfer,* ~ *marfor,* ~ *marfoure* 1577, *the mear Furrow* 1590, *yᵉ marford* 1664, *the Marfor* 1686, ~ *Marfare* 1697, *yᵉ Marfore* 1706 (all these are variant 16th–18th century spellings of **marfur**); *the Midle Field* 1730; *la Newlaund* 1271–2, *Neuland* 1332 both (p) (*v.* **nīwe, land**); *yᵉ north Ende* 1638, 1664, *Northend* 1590 (cf. *Southend infra*); *yᵉ north meareforde* 1664, *the North marfare* 1690 (further variant spellings of **marfur**); *yᵉ North Feildes mare* 1706 (*v.* (**ge**)**mǣre**); *Northiby* 1327, 1332 both (p) ((place) 'north in the village', *v.* **norð, í, bȳ** and cf. *Estiby supra*); *Orchards Close* 1690; *Park' de Haytheby* 1329, *de Parco* 1332, *del Parkes de Haytheby* 1335 all (p) (*v.* **park**); *the parsonadge garth* 1577, *yᵉ parsonage garthe* 1638, 1664, *the Parsonage garth* 1690, 1697, *yᵉ* ~ ~ 1706, *the Parsonage Garth Marfare* 1668, ~ ~ *Garth Marfure* (*v.* **garðr, marfur**); *the Parsons Nooking* 1730 (from dial. *nooking* 'a nook', common in north L, cf. Nooking Lane PN L **5**, 3); *Roxbie Close* 1583 (unless this was land held by Roxby parish, this is probably from the surn. *Roxby*); *Sand hill* 1638, 1664; *yᵉ common sewer* 1638, 1664, *The Comon Sewer* 1668, ~ ~ *Seuor* 1686, *the Common* ~ 1690, ~ ~ *Seuer* 1697, *yᵉ Common Sewer* 1706; *Snouden Closes* 1590, 1668 (from the surn. *Snowden*); *Southend* 1590 (cf. *yᵉ north Ende supra*); *Spellofield* 1590 (*v.* **feld**), *Spellow gate* 1668, 1686, 1690, 1697, *spellow* ~ 1706 (*v.* **spell** 'speech', **hōh** 'a heel, a spur of land' denoting a place where speeches were made in assemblies); *Thealby Beck alias Staple Becke* 1590, ~ ~ ~ ~ *beck* 1638, 1664, *Thileby Beck* 1668, 1686, 1706, *Theileby beck* 1690 (the beck (ON **bekkr**) is named from Thealby in Burton upon Stather parish); *yᵉ watermylne* 1583; *Welle* 1327 (p) (*v.* **wella**); *yᵉ West . . . gate* 1706 (cf. *estgatt supra*); *the west feyld* 1577, *yᵉ west field* 1638, 1664, *the West Feild* 1668, ~ ~ *Field* 1686, 1697, *yᵉ West Feildes* 1706 (cf. *the east feyld(e) supra*, the two great fields of the village); *Westiby* 1327, *westyby* 1332 both (p) ((place) 'west in the village', *v.* **west, í, bȳ**, cf. *Estiby supra*); *Winterton field* 1730 (Winterton is an adjacent village).

HIBALDSTOW

Hibaldestowa 1066–87 (12) Dugd i, 1087–88 RA i, c1115 LS, 1177,
1178, 1179 P, a1219 Welles, *-stoua* c1115 LS, 1150–60 Dane,
1163 RA i, 1191 P, *-sto* 1164, 1165, 1166, 1167 P, 1192, 1193 ib
(p), *-stov* c1170 RA iv, *-stoue* 112 CollTop, *-stowe* Hy2 (1319)
Dugd vi, 1201 FF, 1215 (m14) CNat, 1287 *Ass et freq* to 1395
Peace, *-stouwe* 1219 Ass, p1393 HPFees
Hybaldestowe 1215 *PetWB*, 1245 FF, 1254 ValNor, 1266, 1268 RA
ii, 1271 RH *et passim* to 1465 Fine, *-stouwe* 1227 Ch
Hibaldstow 1189 (1332) Ch, 1431 FA, ~ *Cornwell* 1724 *Dixon*,
-stowe 1242 RRG, 1300 Ipm, 1316 FA, 1343 NI *et passim*
Hybaldstowe 1291 Tax, 1381 RA ii, 1388 Peace, 1535 VE iv, 1536
CollTop, *-stow* 1314 Selby
Hibalstow 1276 RH, 1348 FA, *-stowe* 1428 FA, 1503 *LCCA*, 1504
Ipm *et passim* to 1553 Pat, ~ *Cornwall or Hibalstow Biron* 1671
Red
Hybalstowe 1465 Fine, 1545–47 *MinAcct*, ~ alias *Hyberstowe* 1547
Pat
Hiboldestou 1086 DB (6x), c1128 (12) ChronPetro, *-stow'* 1202 Ass
(p), *-stowe* 1226 Cur, 1375 Peace
Huboldestou 1087–88 RA i
Hubaldestowe 1356 BPR
Hib'stowe 1576 LER, *Hiberstow* 1610 Speed, 1612 *DCLB*, 1697
Pryme, 1709 *Reeve*
Hibstowe alias *Hibalstow* 1589 *DCLB*
Hylbaldstede (sic) 1503 FF, *Hylbalested* (sic) 1504 Pat, *Hibaldsted,*
Hailbalested (sic) 1504 Cl

'The burial-place, the place dedicated to St Hygebald', *v.* **stōw**.
Saints c1000 states *Đonne resteð sancte Higebold in Lindesige on þare*
stowe þe is genemnod Cecesege, neah þære ea, þe is genemnod Oncel
(i.e. R. Ancolme). The earlier name for Hibaldstow was *Cecesege* 'Cec's
island of land', *v.* **ēg** , which is topographically appropriate. The first el.
is the OE pers.n. *Cec*. The interchange between **stōw** and **stede** has only
been noted in the early 16th century.
    The manors of Hibaldstow were held respectively by the Duchy of
Cornwall and by the *Biron* family, cf. *John Biron Esq* 1671 *Red*.

GAINSTHORPE

> *Gamelstorp* 1086 DB, 1207 OblR, 1212 Fees, 1232 Ch, 1316
> CollTop, *-thorp* 1281 QW, 1316 FA, 1353 *Cor, Gamilstorp* 1275
> RH, *Gamulsthorp* 1401–2 FA
> *Gameltorp* c1115 LS, *-thorp* 1276 RH, 1382 Misc, *Gamulthorpe*
> 1401–2 FA
> *Gamelestorp*(') 1180 P (p), 1196 ChancR, 1202 Ass, 1205 Cur, 1205
> OblR, 1207 P, 1208 FF, 1338 Pat, *-thorp* 1232 Dugd vi, 1257 Ch,
> 1300 Ipm, 1311 *FF, -thorpe* 1321 RA ii, *Gamellestorp* Hy3
> CollTop (p)
> *Gainestorp* (probably *Gain-* for *Gam-*) 1156–57 (14) YCh i, R1
> (1308) Ch
> *Gaynethorpe* 1546 LP xxi
> *Gainstrop* 1697 Pryme, *-thorpe* 1824 O

'Gamal's secondary settlement, outlying farmstead or hamlet' *v.*
þorp, presumably of Hibaldstow. The first el. is the ODan pers.n.
Gamal, a name recorded independently and frequently in DB in L. The
early forms in *Gain-* are not supported by subsequent spellings (till the
16th century) and are probably misreadings of *Gam-*. The later change
to *Gainsthorpe* first noted in the 16th century does not appear to have
parallels in other p.ns. and the reason for this development is unclear.

CARR LANE, cf. *the Common Carr* 1796 *EnclA, Carr Farm* 1831 *Red,
v.* **kjarr** 'a marsh overgrown with brushwood', as elsewhere in the
parish. CASTLEFIELD HO, probably to be associated with *Castle Town
spring* 1697 Pryme. CATCHWATER DRAIN, *the ~ ~* 1796 *EnclA*, 1819
Red. CHERRY FM. CHURCH HILL, 1824 O. COUNTERDIKE DRAIN, *the
Counter Dyke Drain* 1796 *EnclA, Counter Dike* 1619 *Red, v.* NED s.v.
counterdike where it is defined as 'a second or reserve dike within or
behind the dike of a river which limits the area of floods caused by the
bursting of the river-dike', cf. *counter-drain*. CROSS CARR RD, *the ~ ~
~* 1796 *EnclA*. FIELDHOUSE FM, *Field House* 1842 White, cf. *campo de
Hibaldestowe* eHy3 CollTop, *campis de Hybaldestowe* 1316 ib, *camp'
. . . de Hibaldstowe* 1349 *LBB, campis de Hibalstowe* 1535 VE iv, *the
fields of Hibaldstow* 1650 *Red, Hibaldstow feild* 1674 *Terrier* (Manton).
GANDER HILL. HIBALDSTOW BRIDGE, cf. *Brygatte* 1321 RA ii, *v.*
brycg in a Scandinavianised form, **gata** 'a way, a path, a road'.
HIBALDSTOW CLIFF, CLIFF FM. HIBALDSTOW GRANGE, GRANGE FM,

1671 *BRA 787, the Graunge of Hibaldstowe* 1508 CollTop, "grange of"
Hybaldstowe 1537–39 LDRH, *Hibaldstow, firma grang'* 1538–39 Dugd
vi, *grangie de Hibalstowe* 1542 *AOMB 214, Hibalstowe Grange* 1569
Pat, *Hibalstow Grange* 1671 *Red*, cf. *portam Grangie* 1321 RA ii, a
grange of Newstead Priory. HIBALDSTOW MILL (lost), 1824 O, *the Mill*
1679 *Terrier*, WINDMILL, *molendinum ad uentum* 1208 FF, *molendinum
eiusdem ville* (i.e. *Hybbaldestowe*) 1215 *PetWB, molend' de Hibaldstoue*
1305 *KR, molendinum ventriticum* 1321 RA ii, self-explanatory. INGS
LANE, cf. *le ynge* 1574–75, *the inges* 1576–77, ~ *Inges* 1613–14 all
ArchJr 44, *le Inges* 1679 *Red*, *Common Ings* 1796 *EnclA, v.* **eng**
'meadow, pasture' as elsewhere in this parish. LOW BANK DRAIN (lost),
1824 O. NEWLANDS. NORTHWOOD FM, *Northwda* 1156–57 (14) YCh
i, *Nortwd'* 1208 FF, *Northewode* 1321 RA i, self-explanatory, *v.* **norð,
wudu**. OLD LEYS, *the Old Leys* 1796 *EnclA*, 1837 *CCLeases, v.* **lea, ley**
(OE **lēah**) 'meadow, pasture', in the pl. ROCK HOUSES. SLATE HO.
SOUTH CARR, 1664 *Monson, the South Car* 1843 *Stubbs*, cf. *the South
Carr Road* 1796 *EnclA*, 1837 *Red, v.* **sūð, kjarr** 'brushwood, a marsh,
especially one overgrown with brushwood', as elsewhere in the parish.
STANIWELLS, *Stainwell* (*Stain-* for *Stani-*) Hy3 CollTop, *Stanyewell'*
1321 RA ii, *Jenny-Stanny well, Julius's Stony well* 1697 Pryme,
Stanewell 1824 O, *Staniwell* 1842 White, self-explanatory, *v.* **stānig,
wella**. This is referred to by R.C. Hope, *The Legendary Lore of the Holy
Wells of England*, London 1893, p. 87, as *Julian's Stony Well*. It is also
the site of an extensive Roman settlement. TRAFFORDS COVERT,
Traffords Cover 1824 O, named from the family of John *Trafford* 1838
Red. VICARAGE (lost), *the vicarage of Hibaldstow hath not a vicarage
house, nor ever had as we have heard* 1674 *Terrier*. WEST END FM
(local), *ye west end* 1536 CollTop. WHEAT SHEAF INN, 1847 *Nelthorpe*.

FIELD-NAMES

Forms dated 1202 are Ass; 1208 FF; eHy3, Hy3, 1316, 1508, 1536
CollTop; 1257 Ch; c1270, 1321 RA ii; 1287 *Ass*; 1327, 1332 *SR*; 1343
NI; 1383, 1545, 1602 LNQ vii; p1391 HPFees; 1409, 1545, 1602, 1625
Ct; 1535 VE iv; 1545–47 *MinAcct*; 1546 LP xxi; 1561–62, 1563–64,
1566–67, 1574–75, 1575–76, 1576–77, 1613–14 ArchJ; 1647, 1650,
1656, 1658, 1664, 1672, 1673, 1678, 1679[1], 1728[1], 1737, 1738, 1739,
1768, 1801, 1819, 1831, 1837 *Red*; 1660 (1900) *LindDep 78*; 1664
Monson; 1665 *Td'E*; 1674, 1679[2], 1707 *Terrier*; 1697 Pryme; 1709
Reeve; 1738[2] *Dixon*; 1795 *Nelthorpe*; 1796 *EnclA*; 1843 *Stubbs*; 1852
Padley.

(a) Aqueduct Drain 1796; the Beck Cl, (a Lane leading to) the Beck 1796, Beck Cl 1819 (*le beke* 1383, *v.* **bekkr** 'a stream' as elsewhere in the parish; in 1383 it is described as "a certain sewer"); Cleatham Gate 1796 ('the road to Cleatham', *v.* **gata**); Durame Cottage 1768 (said in the document to be now demolished; perhaps from the surn. *Durham*); the East Carr 1768, 1796, 1837, ~ east Carr 1819 (*v.* **kjarr**); the East Fenn otherwise East Field Carr 1768 (*the East Fenn* 1656, 1658, 1739, *East Fen* 1728[1], *the East* ~ 1737, *v.* **fenn, kjarr**); the East Fd 1768 (*in Orietali* (sic) *campo* 1650, *in loco vocat orien' campu'* 1673, *the east feild* 1665, ~ *East Feild* 1739 (*v.* **east, feld**, one of the open fields of the village, cf. the North Fd *infra*); Fish Pond Cl 1819 (*Fish pond Close* 1737, 1739); The Gad Meadow 1795 (from dial. *gad* 'a rood of land', cf. *four Gads* 1768); Harrison Hill Common 1796 (from the *Harrison* family, John *Harrison*, named in the same document); Hibaldstowe Causeway 1796, Hibaldstowe Green 1796, 1819 (*v.* **causie, grēne** 'a green, a grassy place'); the High Ground 1796; the Holme 1796 (*Holm* Hy3, 1316, *Holm'* 1321, *Holme* 1679[2], cf. *Holme Flates* 1613–14, *v.* **holmr** 'an isle, higher land in marsh', **flat** 'a division in the common field'); Horse Pasture 1796 (*Horsepasture Lays* 1563–64, *the horse pasture hedge* 1613–14, self-explanatory; *v.* **lea, ley, lay** (OE **lēah**) 'meadow, pasture' in the pl.); Kirton Rd 1796, 1819 (*uiam de Kirketon'* 1208, *Kyrketungat'* 1321, *Kirton Gate* 1679[2], 'the road to Kirton in Lindsey', *v.* **gata** 'a road, a way' as elsewhere in the parish); the Lincoln Turnpike Rd 1796; Little Carr 1796 (*v.* **kjarr**); the Low Drain 1796, the low ~ 1819, 1837; the Manton Rd, Manton Gate 1796 (the road to Manton); Middle Dale, ~ dale Common 1796 (*Middledayle* 1613–14, *v.* **middel, deill** 'a share, a portion of land', as elsewhere in the parish); the new Drain 1796; the North Carr 1768, 1795, 1796 (*le North Carr* 1650, *the* ~ ~ 1658, *north-carr* 1664, *the north Carre* 1665, *North Carr* 1737, 1739, cf. *North Carre dyke* 1613–14, *v.* **norð, kjarr** and cf. *South Carre* in (b) *infra*), the North Carr Dale 1796 (*v.* **deill**), ~ North Carr Rd 1796; the North Fd 1796, 1801, ~ north fd 1819 (*in campo boriali* 1321, *the north feild* 1665, *le North field* 1678, 1679[1], 1728[2], *the North feelde* 1679[2], ~ *field* 1738, *v.* **norð, feld**, one of the open fields of the parish, cf. the South Fd *infra*), Northfield Drain 1796; Ox Pasture, the Oxpasture Ings 1796 (self-explanatory, *v.* also **eng** 'meadow, pasture', cf. *Eight Oxpasture Gates* 1738; *Gates* is the pl. of dial. *gate* (ON **gata**) 'a measure of pasture for one head of cattle'); the Pasture Rd 1796, 1852; Redbourne Bridge 1796, ~ Bridge Rd 1819, Redbourne Hedge 1796 (*Redburnhedge* 1679[2], *v* **hecg**, and cf. *Redburngat* 1316, 1409, *-gat'* 1321, *-gate* 1679[2], *v.* **gata** 'a road', and *Redburne mere* 1665, *Redburn meare* 1679[2], *v.* **(ge)mǣre** 'a boundary, land forming or on a boundary', in this case with Redbourne); the Roman Road 1796 (*super stratam* 1321, *the Streete* 1679[2], alluding to Ermine Street, *v.* **strǣt**); Scawby Gate 1796 (*Scalbygate* 1316, 1409, *Scallebigat'* 1321, 'the road to Scawby', *v.* **gata**); Seven Leys 1796 ('seven strips of pasture' from the pl. of **lea, ley** (OE **lēah**) 'meadow, pasture', as elsewhere in the parish); the South Fd 1796, 1837, ~ south fd 1819 (*in campo australi de Hibalst'* Hy3, *in campo australi* 1321, *the south feild* 1665, *le South* ~ 1678, ~ *Southfield* 1679[1], *the Southfeeld* 1679[2], *le South field* 1728[2], *the Southfield* 1737, ~ *South field* 1738, *v.* **sūð, feld**, one of the great fields of the parish, cf. the North Fd *supra*); the Stone Pit (several) 1796 (*Stainpitdail* Hy3 (*v.* **deill**), *Stanepittes* 1316, *Staynpits* 1409, cf. *Stonepithill* 1679[2], *v.* ON **steinn** (in the early forms), **pytt**); Town Street 1796; the Upper Common 1796; West Cl 1819 (*West Close* 1737, 1739); yᵉ Winterton Rd 1796.

(b) *Barndele* (sic) 1208 (perhaps 'Barni's share of land' from the ON pers.n. *Barni* and **deill**, a Scand compound); *Beurygges* (*-u-* = *-n-*) 1316, *Benrigges* 1321, *Bean Rigs* 1728[2] *v.* **bēan, hryggr** 'a ridge', 'a cultivated strip of ground'); *Blakemilde* Hy3, *-myldes* 1316, 1409, *-meldes* 1321, *Blackmiles* 1679[2] (*v.* **blæc** 'black', **mylde** 'soil, earth'); *Blackethorndic* eHy3 (*v.* **blæc-þorn** 'the black-thorn, the sloe' with **dík**); *Bosel' buttes* (sic) 1321 (*v.* **butte** 'a strip of land abutting on a boundary', the first el. is uncertain); *Brademer* 1316, 1409, *Bradmere* 1321, *le Bradmore* (sic) 1566–67 (*v.* **brād**, **(ge)mǣre**); *Brakes* 1545–47 (*v.* **bracu** 'bracken, fern'); *a furlong . . . called Bridles the Streete* 1665 (this presumably refers to a furlong which extends on both sides of *the Streete*, though Dictionaries do not record this meaning for the verb *bridle*); *Brig gate* 1679[2] *v.* **brycg** in a Scandinavianised form, **gata**); *Brocholes* 1208 ('the badger setts', *v.* **brocc-hol**); *Bushy Garth* 1656 (*v.* **garðr** 'an enclosure'); *three Carr Closes* 1707; *Cheker* 1545 (*v.* **cheker** 'ground of chequered appearance'); *Church Garth* 1697 (*v.* **garðr**); *Claydyke-daytles* (sic) 1508, *Claydykedale* 1545 (from **clæg, dík** with **deill**); *Cokegarth* 1545 (*v.* **garðr**, perhaps with the first el. the surn. *Coke*); *common field land* 1664; *Corbridge Farm* 1602, *Thomas Corbriges close* 1613–14 (from the *Corbridge* family, cf. the 1613–14 reference); *the cornefield* 1613–14; *Couplond* eHy3 ('purchased land' from ON **kaupa-land**, as opposed to *oðalsjorð* 'land acquired by customary law'); *Crechorn* (sic, *-ch-* = *-th-*) Hy3, *Gretthorn* 1316, 1321, 1409 (probably from **grēat** 'great' and **þorn** 'a thorn-tree'); *Crumbedale* 1208, *Crumdales* (checked from MS) 1321 ('the crooked share(s) of land', *v.* **crumb, deill**); *xij acras iuxta curiam Roberti Crust* 1208 ('twelve acres near Robert Crust's court'); *Doriuall'* (sic) 1321; *the est end* 1536 (*v.* **ēast, ende**); *Estholm* Hy3 (*v.* **ēast, holmr**); *Est Langes* 1316 (*v.* **ēast, lang** 'a long strip of land'); *messuage . . . called Fain house* 1737 (presumably from the surn. *Fain, Fane*); *Ferthinghill'* 1321 (the first el. may be OE **feorðung** 'a fourth part' with **hyll**, the significance of which is unclear; Dr Insley, however, thinks it is more likely to be the ON pers.n. *Farþegn*); *Fotheuedland* 1321 (the second el. is **hēafod-land** 'the head of a strip of land left for turning the plough'; the first is OE **fōt**, ON **fótr** 'a foot' used in some topographical sense); *Fourbecks* (sic) 1679[2]; *Fulbet* (*-t* = *-c*) Hy3, *-beks* 1321 ('the foul, polluted stream(s)', *v.* **fūl, bekkr**); *in campis de Gamelstorp* 1202, *in campo de Gamelsto[rp]* 1208 (*v.* **feld**), *Gainstropp Leys* 1709 (*v.* **lea, ley** (OE **lēah**), both are named from Gainsthorpe *supra*); *Giflande* 1316, 1409, *Giuelandes* 1321 (Dr Insley suggests that the first el. is connected with the ON verb *gefa* 'to give' and the name may relate to fertile land, cf. the Norwegian r.n. *Gjov* < ON **Gefr* 'the one rich in fish'; the second el. is OE **land** 'a selion'); *Glaumfordgate* 1316 ('the road to Glanford Brigg', *v.* **gata**); *campo qui uocatur Glenthamhou* 1208 (presumably from Glentham several miles to the south and **haugr** 'a mound', though the significance here is quite uncertain); *Atte Grene* 1327, *atte Grene* 1332, 1341, *at Grene* p1391 all (p) (*v.* **grēne** 'a village green'); *Haghe* 1409 (*v.* **haga** 'a hedge, an enclosure'); *Haigate* Hy3 (perhaps 'the hay road', *v.* **hēg, gata**); *Hakethon'* (sic, checked from MS) 1321 (no doubt an error for *Hakethorn'*; it is identical with Hackthorn (LWR), 'the hawthorn', *v.* **haca-þorn**, a side-form of OE **haguþorn**); *toftum Halfbarn* 1321 ('Halfbarn's messuage, curtilage', *v.* **toft**; the pers.n. *Halfbarn* is otherwise unrecorded, but is an Anglo-Scandinavian byname formation 'half-child', paralleled by the ON bynames *Hálfprestr* 'half-priest' and *Hálftroll* 'half-troll'); *Halghdyke-daytles* (sic), *Halghdyke Mills at Glomforth Bridge* 1508 (*v.* **halh** 'a nook, corner of land', **dík**); *Halmefletes* 1316, *Hialmfletes* (sic) 1409 (perhaps 'the stream(s) where thatch is obtained' from **halm** 'thatch', rare in p.ns and f.ns. and **flēot**; *in campo de Heggeing'* 1208 (*v.* **hecg** 'a hedge', **eng**); *iuxta toftum Heruei* 1208 ('Hervei's messuage, curtilage', from the OFr pers.n. *Hervieu*, *Hervi*, ultimately from Frankish **Hari-wīg*, and **toft**; *Harvey* survives in the village as a surn. till at least John *Harvie* 1575–76); *Heykenyng'* 1321 (Dr John Insley suggests that this difficult name is perhaps 'the meadow surrounded by oak-trees', *v.* **eng**, the first el. being a Scand-inavianised form of OE **ǣcen** 'a wood of oaks, oaken'); *Howslete* 1316, 1409 (*v.* **slétta** 'a level field'); *Illedeile* 1208 (*v.* **deill**; Dr Insley suggests that the first el. appears to be ME *il(le)* < ON *illr* 'poor'); *Kerfurlanges* 1316, 1409 (*v.* **kjarr**, **furlang**); *Kyrkeby feld* 1546 (presumably the first el. is a surn. since there is no place Kirkby in the vicinity; the f.n. was in Gainsthorpe); *Langbryg* 1316 ('the long bridge', *v.* **lang**, **brycg** in a Scandinavianised form); *Linland'* 1208, *Linelandes* Hy3, *Lynelandes* 1316, *le Lynlandes de Gamelesthorp*, *Lynlandes de Hib'* 1321 (*v.* **līn** 'flax', **land** 'a selion' in both sg. and pl.); *Lords Dale* 1660 (1900), *the Lords dale* 1728[1] (self-explanatory, *v.* **deill**); *Loueltoft* p1391 (from the OFr pers.n. and surn. *Louel* with **toft** 'a messuage, curtilage'); *louḷayn* 1536 (perhaps 'the low lane', *v.* **lágr**, **lane**); *Magotteland'* 1545–47 (from *Magot*, a pet-form of *Margaret* and **land**); *Marfurlanges* 1316, 1409, *Merfurlanges* 1321 (*v.* (**ge**)**mære** 'a boundary', **furlang** in the pl.); *lez marfur* 1561–62 (*v.* **marfur** 'a furrow marking a boundary', a common f.n. in north L, cf. the Gate Marfar, PN L **2**, 12); *Mikeldaile* Hy3, -*dale* 1316, *Mykelldall'* 1321 (a Scand compound from **mikill** 'big' and **deill**); *Myddelholm* 1316 (*v.* **middel**, **holmr**); *Milnercroft* c1270 (from the occupational name *Milner* or its derived surn., with **croft**); *terr' vocat Motton* 1650 (the significance of *mutton* is not clear); *the Nooking* 1679[2] (from dial. *nooking* 'a nook', *v.* PN L **3**, 144); *Northiby de Hibaldestowe* 1287 (p) ('(the place) north in the village', *v.* **norð**, **í**, **bȳ**, a common formation in L denoting X who lives in the north of the village, cf. *Westiby infra*); *Northolm'* 1321 (*v.* **norð**, **holmr**); *a place called North Woods and South Woods* 1709 (cf. Northwood Fm *supra*); *Offlet* Hy3 (*v.* **flēot**, the first el. is obscure); *Ouldeholm* Hy3 (*v.* **ald** perhaps in the sense 'long used' or even 'formerly used', **holmr**); *Pottergate* 1316, 1409 (from the occupational name *Potter* or its derived surn., with **gata**); *Rebelyn close* (sic) 1508; *croftum Ricardi filii Henrici* 1321 ('Richard son of Henry's croft'); *the Robe Closes* (sic) 1613–14; *Mara de Scalleby* Hy3, *Scalby mer'* (checked from MS) 1321 ('the boundary with Scawby', *v.* (**ge**)**mære**); *Scypstale* Hy3, *Schippēstall* (for *Schippen*-) 1316, *Schippestall* 1409 (presumably 'the site of a cow-shed', *v.* **scypen**, **stall**); *Scortedeil* 1208 (*v.* **sceort** 'short', **deill**); *vie de Scotre* 1321 ('the road to Scotter'); *Scottegaits* 1679[2] (perhaps 'the road of the Scots', *v.* **Scot(t)**, **gata** and for this name *v.* PN L **2**, 103–4, ib **4**, 138–39); *le Segges* 1321 (*v.* **secg** 'sedge' in the pl. and in a Scandinavianised form); *Shopgarth* 1545 (probably 'an enclosure with a shed', *v.* **sc(e)oppa**, **garðr**); *the short lock* 1679[2]; *ye Slade* 1316, 1409 (*v.* **slæd** 'a valley'); *terras arabiles vocat Sokelandes* 1650 (denoting land over which a right of local jurisdiction was exercised, a f.n. not noted in the survey so far, *v.* **soke**); *South Carre* 1660 (1900) (*v.* **kjarr**, and cf. the

North Carr in (a) *supra*); *Stainhille* Hy3 (a hybrid name, *v.* **steinn, hyll**, probably the same as *Stone Hill* 1665); *Staynhou* 1257 (a Scand compound, *v.* **steinn, haugr** 'a mound, a hill'); *Stockewell* 1316, *Stokewell'* 1321 ('the spring marked by a tree-trunk', *v.* **stocc, wella**); *Stodefaldes* 1316 (*v.* **stōd-fald** 'a stud-fold, a horse enclosure'); *Stowegate* Hy3 (probably 'the road to Stowe (St Mary)', *v.* **gata**); *Suineriscroft* (*Suin-* = *Sum-*) Hy3 (perhaps from the OE pers.n. **Sumor* and **croft**); *Surdeile* 1208 (*v.* **sūr** 'sour, polluted', **deill**); *Swaithes* 1728[1] (*v.* **swæð** in the sense 'a strip of grassland' (probably from the extent of the sweep of the scythe) and cf. *Swathes pratis* 1650 'swathes of meadow'); *Sweinesbrig'* 1208 ('Sveinn's bridge', *v.* **brycg** in a Scandinavianised form; the first el. is the ON pers.n. *Sveinn*); *the towens end, the townside* 1679[2] (both self-explanatory); *Turmeargate* 1678[2], *Turmill gates* 1728[2]; *a certaine place called Warreson* 1728[1] (*v.* **warison** NED sb 2 'a gift bestowed by a superior, a reward'); *Waterfures* Hy3, *-fur'* 1321, *water furbanke* 1613–14, *waterfurlong* 1665, *Waterfur* 1679[2], cf. *-beck* 1679[2] ('the water-furrow(s)' *v.* **wæter-furh**, with **bekkr**); *yᵉ watery plott* 1664; *Wellestig'* Hy3 ('the path to the spring', *v.* **wella, stīg**); *le West becks* 1679[1] (*v.* **bekkr**); *Westcarr* 1656 (*v.* **kjarr**); *Westiby* 1208, *Westyby* 1332 both (p) ('(the place) west in the village', *v.* **west, vestr, í, bȳ**, and for the significance *v. Northiby supra*); *Westlanges* Hy3, 1316, *le ~* 1321, *Westlands* 1679[2] (*v.* **west, lang** 'a long strip of land', replaced by **land** in 1679, cf. *Estlanges supra*); *Wisdomdeile* 1208 (from the ME surn. *Wisdom* and **deill**); *Wymerkdyg'* 1321 (from the ME surn. *Wimarc*, from OBret *Wiuhomarch* (*v.* Feilitzen 415), and **dīc** 'a ditch, a drainage channel'); *Yondayll'* 1321 (*v.* **deill**; the first el. is uncertain); *Yeueling* Hy3, *Yueling'* 1321 (obscure).

Holme

HOLME

> *Holme* 1067–69 (m12) HC, c1128 (12) ChronPetro, 1303, 1316 FA, 1327 SR, (~ *iuxta Botisford'*) 1329 Ass, (~ "by" *Messyngham*) 1331 Ch, (~ "by" *Botelsford*) 1335 Pat *et passim*
> *Holm* 1086 DB, c1115 LS, c1140 AD, 1212 Fees, c1216 (m14) CNat, 1241–42 Fees, 1252 FF, (~ *iuxta Messingham*) 1296 Ass, (~ *iuxta Massyngham*) (sic) 1297 FF, 1314 Ch *et passim* to 1607 DCLB
> *Hulm'* 1203 (p)

'The island of raised, firm land in the marsh', *v.* **holmr**. The present Holme Hall lies on a distinct island of land above the 75' contour. Holme is described as near Bottesford and Messingham.

RAVENTHORPE

> *Ragnaldtorp* 1067 (12) RRAN, c1128 (12) ChronPetro, Hy2 (1314) Ch

Raganaldethorp 1066–87 (m12) Dugd i
Rachenildetorp 1067–69 (m12) HC
Ragenaltorp, Rageneltorp 1086 DB
Ragheniltorp c1115 LS, *-thorp* c1216 (m14) CNat
Ragnildtorp 1212 Fees, *Ragenildthorp, -thorpe* 1228 Welles
Rahnaltorp c1160 Semp
Raghenthorp, Ragenthorp' 1272 Ass
Ragnilthorp' 1274, 1275 *FF*, 1314 Ch
Rainelestorp c1115 LS
Rayenelthorp 1242–43 Fees
Ranildethorp' Hy2 (m14) *PetML, Ranildthorp, Ranilthorp* 1249 Ipm
    both (p)
Ravenildethorp 1252 FF
Raventhorp 1232 Pat, 1291 Tax, 1312 Ch, 1316 FA, 1343 NI *et
    passim, -thorpe* 1347 Pat *et passim*
Raynthorpe 1535 VE iv, 1615 Admin
Ranthorpe 1605 WillsA, 1615 *Inv*, 1616, 1681 *BT*, (~ *als
    Raventhorpe*) 1698 *Inv*, 1662, 1679, 1686, 1700 *Terrier, -thorp*
    1606, 1662, 1686, 1700 *ib*, (~ *alias Raven-thorp*) 1693 *ib, -throp*
    1697 *ib*, 1701 *BT, Rantrop . . . I find that it's true name is
    Ravensthorpe* 1969 Pryme

'Ragnald's secondary settlement, outlying dependent farmstead or
hamlet', *v*. **þorp**. The first el. is the ODan pers.n. *Ragn(v)aldr*, forms in
-il(d)- showing confusion with *Ragnhildr*. It is not clear which place it
was "secondary" to, but it may well have been Manby in Broughton
supra.

TWIGMOOR HALL, *Twiggemore* 1202 Ass, 1593 *Inv, Twigemor'* 1202
Ass, *Twiggemor* e13 (m14) *PetML, Twygmore* 1385 Peace, 1453 Pat,
Twygmor 1387 Pat, *Twigmore* 1602 ArchJ xlviii, 1611 *Nelthorpe*, 1671
Red, 1710 *Nelthorpe, Twigmoor* 1722 *Red*, probably 'Twicga's marshy
land', *v*. **mōr**. The first el. would then be the OE pers. *Twicga*, which
occurs in Twigworth, PN Gl **2**, 157. Alternatively, as Dr Insley suggests,
the first el. might be OE **twigu**, ME **twig, twig(g)e** 'a small branch, a
twig', perhaps in some topographical sense.

ASPEN FM. BARN PLANTATION. BECK HO, cf. *holme becke* 1606
Terrier, v. **bekkr** 'a stream, a beck' as elsewhere in this parish. BLACK
HEAD PONDS, said to be named from black-headed gulls which nest

here. BLACK HOE PLANTATION. BOG PLANTATION. BOW AND ARROW
WOOD, so named from its distinctive shape. BOWERS WOOD,
presumably from the surn. *Bower*. CLARK'S FM, *Clark House* 1876
Nelthorpe, no doubt from the surn. *Clark*. GRAY YARD, from the surn.
Gray. HOLME HALL, 1824 O, 1828 Bry. HOLME WOOD, c1810 *Yarb*.
LOW WOOD, c1810 *ib*, 1824 O. MIDDLETON WOOD, from the surn.
Middleton. NEW FOREST PLANTATION. NORTH HIGH WOOD, cf. *High
Wood* 1710 *Nelthorpe*. PRIMROSE HILL WOOD. SAND PIT. SCOTCH
WOOD. SKEGS PLANTATION. SWEETING THORNS. TOP LARCHES.
TWIGMOOR GRANGE, *Grangia de Twygmore* e14 *Asw*, *grangiam de
Twyggemores* (sic) 1329 *Ass*; it was a **grange** of Louth Park Abbey.
TWIGMOOR TOP FM. TWIGMOOR WOODS is *Twigmoor Warren* 1824
O. WARREN HO, *Warren* c1810, *Holme Common or Warren* 1819 *BM*,
Holme Warren 1824 O, *Holme Common* 1828 Bry. WILLOW
PLANTATION. YARBOROUGH WOOD, named from the Earls of
Yarborough, prominent landowners here. YELLOW RABBIT HILLS.

FIELD-NAMES

Forms dated Hy2 (1314), 1314 are Ch; c1216 (m14) CNat; 1313 *KR*;
1327, 1332 *SR*; 1329 *Ass*; 1600 *Inv*; 1601, 1606 *Terrier*; 1696 Pryme;
1710, 1875 *Nelthorpe*; 1773 *Red*; c1810 *Yarb*; 1819 *BM*; 1841 *TA*
(Holme); 1851 *ib* (Twigmoor, in Manton Award).

(a) Baker Cl 1876, Baker's Hill (from the surn. *Baker*); Bank cl 1841, ~ Cl 1876;
Bassack Cl 1841; Belton's cl 1841, ~ Cl 1876 (from the *Belton* family, cf. George
Belton 1842 White); Birch Cl 1876; Bow & Arrow Cl 1876 (from its distinctive
shape); Brick Kiln cl 1851, Brick-Kiln Cl 1876; Calf cl 1841; Carrot garth 1841 (*v.*
garðr 'an enclosure', as elsewhere in this parish); Chapman's cl 1841 (from the
Chapman family, cf. Edward *Chapman* 1841); Cinquefoin cl 1841 (*v.* **sainfoin**);
Clegg cl, 1841, Cleg Cl 1851 (from the surname *Clegg*); Cocker hills c1810;
Common 1841, Holme Common 1876; Common cl, ~ fd 1841; Coulson's cl 1841
(from the surn. *Coulson*); Cow cl 1841; Cox cl 1841 (from the surn. *Cox*); Crook
Yard c1810; Croucham cl 1841; Dawson's cl 1841 (from the surn. *Dawson*); Dove
Cote Cl c1810; Edlington Car 1876 (from the surn. *Edlington* and **kjarr** 'brushwood,
a marsh overgrown with brushwood', as elsewhere in the parish); Eight Acres c1810,
1841; Everatts cl 1841 (from the surn. *Everatt*); Fiddle cl 1841 (probably referring
to its shape); Field (cl) 1841 (cf. *in campo de Holm* c1216 (m14), *in campis de Holm'*
1313, *v.* **feld**); Four acres 1841; Grass Yard 1841; Holme Hale 1819 (*v.* **halh** 'a nook,
a corner of land'); Hassock cl 1841 (*v.* **hassuc** 'a clump of coarse grass'); Herse Cl,
Herse Hanson Cottage (sic) c1810 (presumably from OE **herse** 'a top, a hill-top');
Great, Little Hill cl 1841; Hill Side Cl c1810; Hilly Cl 1876; Holland's cl 1841 (from
the surn. *Holland*); Home cl 1841, ~ Cl 1876; Horse cl 1841; Far House Cl 1851,

1876; Ling-beds 1876 (*v.* **lyng** 'heather'); Low cl 1841; Low Common 1841; Manby dale Cl c1810 (*v.* **deill** 'a share, a portion of land', the reference is to Manby in Broughton parish); Marshall's Car 1876 (*v.* **kjarr**), Marshalls cl 1841 (from the surn. *Marshall*); High, Low Moor 1841 (*v.* **mōr**); Morley cl 1841 (from the *Morley* family, cf. Elizabeth *Morley* 1636 *Foster*); Nathan's cl 1841; Nine acres 1841; First, Great Pea cl 1841; Pepper cl 1841; Plantation 1841; Raventhorpe cl 1841 (cf. *in campis de Ragnaldthorp* Hy2 (1314), ~ ~ *de Ragenilthorp* c1216 (m14) (*v.* **feld**), *in toftis de Ragenildthorp* c1216 (m14) (*v.* **toft** 'a messuage, a curtilage'); Raventhorpe Common c1810, ~ Warren 1773 (*v.* **wareine**); Roodley Car 1876 (*v.* **kjarr**); Rough Car 1876 (*v.* **rūh** 'rough', **kjarr**); Rough ling 1841 (*v.* **rūh**, **lyng** 'ling, heather'); Rowley cl 1841 (from the surn. *Rowley*); Rye cl 1841, ~ Cl 1876; Scroggs & Bushes c1810 (from **scrogge** 'a bush, brushwood'); Seaton Croft c1810 (presumably from the surn. *Seaton* and **croft**); Seed Car 1876 (*v.* **kjarr**), Seed cl 1841; Sharp cl 1841 (named from the *Sharp* family, cf. Richard *Sharp* 1642 LPR); Silver hill 1841; Six acres 1841; Stone Fd c1810; Twigmore drain & banks 1841; Well Cl c1810 (*v.* **wella**); Wood cl, ~ fd 1841; Yard bottom 1841.

(b) *Assedalehil* c1216 (m14) (perhaps from **askr** 'an ash-tree', **deill** with **hyll**); "the bridge of" *Holme* 1314; *Burton Lane* 1710 (the lane leading to Burton upon Stather); *Chappel cloase* 1696 (self-explanatory); *Croftes, Croftis* c1216 (m14) (*v.* **croft**); *Engcroft* c1216 (m14) (*v.* **eng** 'meadow, pasture', **croft**); *Eskedayle* 1314 (*v.* **eski** 'a place growing with ash-trees', **deill**); *ad collem iuxta diuisam de Manneby* c1216 (m14) ('at the hill near the boundary with Manby' (in Broughton)); *Greue* 1317, *Graue* 1332 both (p) (*v.* **græfe** 'a grove, a thicket'); *Hie wood in Twigmore* 1600, *High Wood* 1710; *Holme Becke* 1601, 1606 (*v.* **bekkr**); *Martine-, Martynwell* c1216 (m14), cf. *Martynwellsyke* c1216 (14) (from the ME pers.n. or derived surn. *Martin* and **wella**, with **sīc** 'small stream' or **sík** 'a trench, a ditch'); *Suthon* (sic, probably for *-thorn*) c1216 (m14) (*v.* **sūð** 'south', **þorn** 'a thorn-tree'); *Tuygmorecotes* 1329 (from Twigmoor and **cot** 'a cottage, a hut' in the pl.).

Manton

MANTON

Malmetun 1061–66 (m12) KCD 819 (S 1059), 1066–87 (m12) Dugd i, 1067 (12) RRAN, c1128 (12) ChronPetro, c1140 *AD*, 1212 Fees, *-tune* 1086 DB, *-tuna* c1115 LS, *-tona* c1145 Dane (p), *-ton(')* 1208 FF, c1216 (m14) CNat, 1220 Cur, 1225 Welles, 1242–43 Fees, 1265 Cl, 1275 RH, 1281 QW, 1290 Pat *et freq* to 1428 FA, *et passim* to 1695 Morden, *-tone* 1310 *FF, Malmton* 1276 RH

Mameltune (sic) 1086 DB

Maunton 1246 Ipm, 1431 FA, 1501 Ipm, 1526 Sub, *Mawnton* 1493–1500 EPC, 1535 VE iv, *Mawneton* 1536–37, *Mawnton otherwise*

called Manton or Malmeton 1671 *BRA* 787, *Mawnton als Manton*
1671 *Red*
Maulmton 1675 Ogilby
Mannton 1501 Ipm, *Manton* 1555 Pat, 1576 LER, 1584 *AD et passim*

'The farmstead, village on sandy soil', *v.* **malm, tūn**, topographically appropriate; cf. *The Sand Close* in f.ns. (b) *infra*. Forms in *Mau-*, *Maw-* are due to vocalisation of *-l-*.

AMERICA WOOD is west of the village towards the parish boundary. ASH HOLT, 1864 *Terrier*, *Plantation or Ash Holt* 1867 *TA*. BLACK WALK NOOK. GREETWELL HALL. MANTON COMMON (lost), 1824 O, *Common* 1829 *EnclA*. It was part of Manton Warren. MANTON WARREN, *warannum de novo in Malmeton* 1275 RH. MIDDLE MANTON is Manton Warren Ho 1842 O, *Warren House* 1700 LNQ xix. SAND LANE. SOUTH FM. WHITE HO.

FIELD-NAMES

Forms dated 1327, 1332 are *SR*; m14, 1417 *Asw*; 1577, 1601, 1564, 1697,1700, 1708, 1822, 1864 *Terrier*; 1583 *MiscDon 344*; 1829 *EnclA*; 1857 *TA*.

(a) Brigg Rd 1829 (cf. *briggate* 1601, 'the road to Brigg', *v.* **gata**); the "Church" Cl (sic) 1864; the Cliff 1822, 1829 (cf. *M' Pelhams Cliffe* 1671, *Manton Cliffe* 1674, *Manton's ~* (sic) 1697, *the Cliffe* 1700, *Manton Cliff* 1708, *v.* **clif**); Kirton Rod 1829, 1864 (cf. *Kirton gate* 1674, 1700, *~ Gate* 1697, 1708, 'the road to Kirton', *v.* **gata**); the Messingham and Scawby Rd 1829; the Moor 1829 (*v.* **mōr**); Paddock 1857; Rectory 1857; Sheep Lane 1864; the Town Street 1829; the Water Lane 1864.

(b) *Braken hill* 1708 (*v.* **brakni, hyll**); *Brame Furlong* 1577, *lower, upper brame furlong* 1601; *brode mearfurre ende* 1601 (*v.* **brād, marfur** 'a boundary furrow'); *the bull medowe* 1601; *Burnt house* 1577, *burnthouse meares* 1601 (*v.* (**ge)mǣre** 'a boundary', 'land on a boundary', as elsewhere in this parish); *Carpool hole* 1577, *carpooldicke* 1601; *y' church meare* 1601 (*v.* (**ge)mǣre**); *clay hole* 1601; *Cletham meere* 1671 ('the boundary with Cleatham (an adjoining place)', *v.* (**ge)mǣre**); *Cloven howes* 1577, *clouenhouse furlong* 1601 ('the cloven, split mounds', *v.* (**ge)clofen, haugr** in the pl.); *Copstow beck, ~ furlonge* 1601; *the Cottagers Close* 1671, *Cotchers close* 1674, *Cotcher's Close Lane* 1697, *Cotchers Close Hedge* 1700, *y' Cotagers close* 1708 (*cotcher* is a common dial. form of *cottager* in L); *Enderbygarth* 1417, *Enderbie hill* 1577, 1601 (named from the *Enderby* family, cf. Robert *de Enderby* 1332, with **garðr** 'an enclosure', as elsewhere in this parish, and **hyll**); *the Fallowes* 1601 (*v.* **falh** 'land broken up for cultivation', later 'ploughed land left uncultivated for a year, fallow land'); *campis de Malmetun* Hy2 (1314) Ch, *campos de Malmeton* c1216 (m14) CNat (*v.* **feld**); *the gallow meare* 1601 (*v.* **galga**, **(ge)mǣre**); *grangiē suā* m14 (it was a **grange** of Barlings Abbey); *graue dicke suer* 1583; *farre hamara* (sic) 1601 (obscure); *Henginge Neraes* (sic) 1577, *yᵉ hinging meares* 1601 ('the steeply sloping boundary lands', *v.* **hangende, (ge)mǣre** in the pl.); *yᵉ hie streete* 1601 (*v.* **strǣt**); *del Hyll'* 1327, *del Hille* 1332 both (p), *yᵉ hilledge, the hillsyde* 1601 (*v.* **hyll**); *the Inges* 1601 (*v.* **eng** 'meadow, pasture'); *lambe'becke* 1601 (*v.* **lamb, bekkr** 'a stream'); *in The Lane* 1327 (p) (self-explanatory); *yᵉ lingmore* 1601 ('the ling, heather moor', *v.* **lyng, mōr**); *Ling Ridge furlonge* 1577, *Linge Rigge* 1601 (*v.* **lyng, hrycg**); *yᵉ North Low Fielde* 1601; *lytlmoregaile* 1601 (from **lytel, mōr**, with ON **geil** 'a narrow lane'); *Mawntonshawe* 1614 WillsStow, *Manton Shawe* 1642 LPR (from the parish name and **sceaga** 'a small wood, a copse'); *yᵉ meare* 1601 (*v.* **(ge)mǣre**); *Mill furlonge* 1577, *the milne Furlonge* 1601, *yᵉ Mill Close* 1708 (*v.* **myln**); *The Mote Close* 1671, *the ~ ~* 1674, *~ Moat Close* 1697, *yᵉ Mote Close* 1700, *~ Mote close* 1708 (obscure); *yᵉ north feilde* 1601 (one of the open fields of the village); *NortLow field* (sic) 1577, *yᵉ North Low Feilde* 1601; *Pimperton dayles* 1671, *~ dales* 1674, *~ Dale* 1697, *~ North dale* 1700, *the South Dale of Pimperton's* 1700, *yᵉ Pimperton dales* 1708 (from the surn. *Pimperton* and **deill** 'a share, a portion of land' in the pl. as elsewhere in the parish); *Pinfold* 1577, *yᵉ pynfolde* 1601 (*v.* **pynd-fald** 'a pinfold'); *Puddingmire* 1577, *puddingmire-dicke* 1601 (*v.* **mýrr** 'a mire, a bog'; Mr Field points out that *pudding* occurs fairly frequently elsewhere in the country, often in the form *Pudding Poke, ~ Close, ~ Field* etc. with the sense 'land with soft, sticky soil'); *Redburnegat* 1577, *Redburne gate* 1601 ('the road to Redbourne', *v.* **gata**); *Riham* 1601 (*v.* **ryge** and probably **holmr** 'raised land in marsh'; **holmr** frequently appears as *ham* in 16th and 17th documents in L); *The Sand Close* 1671, *the ~ ~* 1674, 1697, *~ ~ Closes* 1700, *yᵉ Sand close* 1708 (self-explanatory); *Seaven Acars dayle* 1601 (*v.* **deill**); *Skippingdale* 1577, *yᵉ furlonge called Skippingdale* 1601 (*v.* **deill**; the first el. may well be a Scandinavianised form of OE **scypen** 'a cow-shed', cf. Skippingdale Plantation in Crosby *supra*); *the South Cliffe* 1671 (cf. the Cliff in f.ns. (a) *supra*); *Southgath meare* (sic) 1601; *the south Mare* 1601 (*v.* **sūð, (ge)mǣre**); *Spittlehille* 1577, *Spittlehouse greene* 1601 (*v.* **spitel** 'a hospital'; no evidence has been found in the local documents searched throwing light on the nature of the *hospital*); *Spoothill* 1601 (obscure); *(the) stony furlong* 1601 (*v.* **stānig, furlang**); *Westiby* 1327, *Westyby* 1332, *Vestiby* m14, *de Westby de Malmetun'* 1360 Peace all (p) (literally '(the place) west in the village', *v.* **vestr, í, bȳ**, a common formation in L, indicating X who lives in the west of the village); *le Westgarth* 1417 (*v.* **west, garðr**); *Whitecros Headland* 1577, *Whitecrosse headland* 1601 (*v.* **hwīt, cros**, no doubt alluding to a stone cross, and **hēafod-land**).

Messingham

MESSINGHAM

Mæssingaham 1066–68 (12) ASWills
Messingahame 1067–69 (c1150) HC, *Messingeham* (3x) 1086 DB,

1181, 1182 P both (p), 1188 ib, 1193, 1194, 1195 ib all (p), 1196
ChancR (p), 1197, 1198 P both (p), 1209–35 LAHW, 1219 Ass,
1220, 1221 Cur, 1236 Cl (p)

Massingeham c1115 LS, 1166 RBE, 1220 Cur

Massingham c1115 LS (2x), 1189–95 RA iv, 1206 Ass, 1265 Ch,
1293 Abbr, 1298 Ass

Messingham 1066–87 (m12) Dugd i, 1067 (12) RRAN, 1166–74
YCh vi (p), c1140 *AD*, Hy2 ((1314) Ch, 1184–89, lHy2 RA iv,
1199, 1200, 1201, 1202 P all (p), 1202, 1206 Ass, 1210, 1211 P
both (p), 1212 Fees, 1214 Cur, 1226 FF, 1228, 1229 Cur, 1229
Cl, 1242 FF *et freq*, *Messincham* 1212 Fees, *Meshingham* 1275
RH, *Messyngham* c1216 (m14), 1250–84 (m14) CNat, 1291 Tax,
1303 FA, 1327 Pat, 1327 Banco, 1332 *SR*, 1340 Ipm, 1343 NI,
1346 FA, 1347 Pat, 1354 Ipm *et freq* to 1573 Hall

'The homestead, the estate of the people of Mæssa', from the gen.pl.
Mæssinga of the OE group name *Mæssingas* 'the family, the dependents
of *Mæssa*', identical in etymology with Massingham Nf, and OE **hām**
'a homestead, an estate'. The OE pers.n. **Mæssa* is a hypocoristic form
of OE *Mǣrsige*, **Mǣrstān* or the like.

BARKWITH HO (local), commemorates a long-standing family in the
parish, cf. *Johannes de Barcworthe* 1295 ChronPetro, a tenant of the
Abbot of Peterborough Abbey, and John *Barkwyth* 1591 *Inv*. BILLIM
LANE (local), 1686, 1697, *byllam lane* 1577–80, *Billam lane* 1634,
Billine Lane end 1706, *Billam Lane* ~ 1718, 1745, *Billim-lane* 1775 all
Terrier, presumably from the surn. *Billam*. BELLE VUE FM (sic). BLACK
BANK FM. BLEACH YARD, 1825 Mess, self-explanatory. BLIND LANE
(local), 1811 *MiscDon 140*; a common name for a cul-de-sac. BRIGGATE
FM, cf. *Briggate* 1634, 1686, 1745, 1755, *brygge gate* 1577–80, *Brig-
gate* 1679, *Brig gate* 1697, *Brigg gate* 1706, 1718 all *Terrier*, cf. *Crosse
Brigg Gate* 1706 *ib*, 'the road to the bridge', *v*. **brycg** in a
Scandinavianised form, **gata**, as elsewhere in the parish. BROOM
PLANTATION. CARCAR FM, *Carker* 1825 Mess, *v*. **kjarr** 'brushwood',
'a bog, marsh overgrown with brushwood' as elsewhere in the parish;
the first el. is obscure. CHURCH LANE (local), *viam vulgo' vocat Le
Church Lane* 1667 *Dixon*. CROSS DRAIN. CROSS TREE LANE (local),
cf. *the Cross-tree* 1825 Mess, said in Mess to be where the village cross
had stood. GELDERS BECK (local), *Gelder beck* 1825 Mess, from the
surn. *Gelder*, cf. Richard *Gelder* 1642 LPR and **bekkr** 'a stream' as

elsewhere in this parish. HARSLEY'S PLANTATION, named from the surn. *Harsley, cf.* Robert *Harsley* 1842 White. HIGH ST., *high street* 1686, *y* *High street* 1697, *~ high street* 1706, *high Street* 1718, *the high Street* 1755 all *Terrier*. HOLLYWOOD FM, *Holland Woods* 1825 Mess. According to Mackinnon "I found that the true name was Holly Woods, and is so-called on account of the vast quantity of Holly that grew there" Mess p.17, and "The people here invariably call Holly, Prick Holland, and for that reason the natives called this part of the lordship Holland Woods" Mess p. 18. HOLME PLANTATION, cf. *holme hedge* 1577–80, 1634, *holm parke nook* 1686, *~ Park Nooke* 1697, *Holm park nook* 1706, *~ ~ nooke* 1718, *Holm Park Nook* 1755 all *Terrier*, presumably named from the adjacent parish of Holme. KEEL SIKE, *Kele Syke* 1577–80, *Keelesike* 1634, *Keelsyke* 1686, *-sike* 1697, *Keel Syke* 1706, 1718, *-sicke* 1745, *~ syke* 1755 all *Terrier*, from the surn. *Keel*, cf. William *Keele* 1642 LPR, with OE **sīc** 'a small stream' or ON **sík** 'a ditch, a trench' as elsewhere in the parish. LANDMOOR FM, *lammere* 1577–80, *landmeare* 1634, *Landmor(e)* 1686, 1745, 1755 all *Terrier*, *v.* **land-(ge)mære** 'a boundary'; the farm lies close to the parish boundary. MELLS FM, cf. *Mell close* 1679, *Mel close* 1686, *Mell Close* 1697, *Mel Close* 1706, *Mell Close nooke* 1718, *Mellclose* 1755 all *Terrier*, from the family of Robert *Mell* 1642 LPR. MESSINGHAM COMMON, 1797 *EnclA* (Bottesford), *the commons* 1577–60, *y* *Comman* 1634 both *Terrier*, *the Commons or wastes of Messingham* 1621 *Dixon*. MESSINGHAM INGS, *Le Inges* 1595 Hall, *the Ings* 1647 *CCLeases*, cf. *le Engeker* 1334 *Foster* (*v.* **kjarr**), *v.* **eng** 'meadow, pasture' as elsewhere in the parish. MESSINGHAM WATER MILL, cf. *Watermill Hows* 1825 Mess, *v.* **haugr** 'a mound, a hill' in the pl., as elsewhere in this parish. MILL (disused), *Messingham Mill* 1824 O, cf. *myll forlong* 1577–80, *Mill furlong* 1686, 1755, *y* *Mill furlong*, *~ ~ Furlong* 1706, 1718 and *mylne wythes* 1577–80, *y* *milln withes* 1634 (*v.* **wiðig** in the pl.) all *Terrier*. MOUNT PLEASANT, presumably a complimentary nickname. MUSGRAVE'S FM, from the surn. *Musgrave*. NORTH FIELD FM, *North Field* 1842 White. PRIESTHOWS. SANDHILLS. SANDHOWES, *Sand Hows* 1825 Mess, *v.* **sand**, **haugr** in the pl. SCALLOW GROVE, cf. *over scallowes*, 1577–80, *Skallowes* 1634, *Scallowes* 1679, *y* *Scallows* 1686, 1697, 1718, 1755, *Scallows* 1706 all *Terrier*. This name has been noted four times already in north L, *v.* PN L **4**, xiv, where the interpretation of The Scallows Hall, PN L **3**, 4, is corrected. Further examples occur in PN L **4**, 13–4, 102 and 111–12, as well as *Scalehau* in Scawby f.ns. *infra*. All mean 'the hill, mound with a shieling, a temporary hut', *v.* **skáli**, **haugr**. ON **skáli** is common in the north-west of the country, but is rare in the East Midlands. SCOTTER RD, *vie de Scotree* 1334 *Foster, scotter gate* 1577–90, *Scotter gate* 1634, *~ gat* 1679, *Scottergate* 1697, *Scotter Gate end* 1706, 1755, *Scottergate end* 1718, *~ gate end* 1745, all *Terrier*, 'the road to Scotter', *v.* **gata**. SOUTH GATE. TRIPPLING HOWS, 1825 Mess, *v.* **haugr** in the pl. VICARAGE, *one vicarage house* 1634, *The Vicarage house* 1686, 1697, *The Vicarage House* 1706, 1718, 1745, *-house* 1755 all *Terrier, the parsonage of Messingham* 1654 WillsPCC. WARP FM, for the meaning *v.* Warp Fm in Bottesford *supra*. WEST COMMON NORTH DRAIN, WEST COMMON SOUTH ~, 1824 O. WEST GRANGE, cf. *uiam quae venit de . . . grangiam eorum* (Louth Park Abbey) *Eikescoh* (sic) c1140 *AD* ('the oak wood', a Scand compound of ON **eik** and **skógr**), *grang' suis de Messyngham* 1535 VE iv (Thornholme Priory), *Grangie de Messinghame* 1559 *BPRentals, the graunge* 1577–80 *Terrier, Messingham Grange* 1647 *CCLeases, v.* **grange**; there were several monastic granges in Messingham. WHOPLATE FM (local), named from the family of Richard *Whaplate* 1825 Mess. WIGLOW (local), 1686 *Terrier, Wyggel howe dale* 1577–80 *ib, wiggle howe* 1583 *MiscDon 344, Wigglehowe* 1595 Hall, *Wigglehow* 1634, 1634 *Terrier, v.* **haugr**; Dr Insley suggests that the first el. might be the ON pers.n. *Vígúlfr*, though the forms are too late for any certainty. WILLOW FM, cf. *the wyllowes* 1577–80, *Willowrow* 1686, *~ Row* 1706, 1718 all *Terrier*. WOOD FM, cf. *the wodd* 1577–80, *the wude* 1634, *ye Wood* 1686, *the ~* 1745, 1755 and *ye wudgate* 1634 all *Terrier*.

FIELD-NAMES

Forms dated c1140 are *AD*; Hy2 (1314) Ch; c1216 (m14) CNat; 1275 RH; 1314[1] Ch; 1314[2] Selby; 1327, 1332 *SR*; 1334 *Foster*; 1389 Misc; 1457, 1776 *Shef*; 1535 VE iv; 1535–46, 1576–77, 1613–15 *MinAcct*; 1553 Pat; 1577–80, 1634, 1679, 1686, 1697, 1701, 1718, 1745, 1755[1] *Terrier*; 1583 *MiscDon 344*; 1600, 1643, 1670 Hall; 1614, 1640, 1660, 1661, 1667, 1678, 1755[2] *Dixon*; 1647 *CCLeases*; 1675, 1719 *Nel(thorpe)*; 1724 *BRA 833*; 1825 Mess.

(a) Aberthorn Pits 1625; Armitage Mear 1755[1] (*the armytage mere* 1577–80, *ye Armitage mear* 1634, *Hermitage Mear* 1686, *Armitage mear* 1697, 1706, 1718, *~ Mear* 1745, cf. *Armitage* 1634, *Hermitage* 1679, *v.* **ermitage, (ge)mǣre** 'a boundary', as elsewhere in this parish; no evidence has been found in the sources searched for the nature of the *hermitage*); Asks flg 1755[1] (*apud Aske* 1334, *aske holme* 1577–80 (*v.* **holmr** 'higher ground amidst marshes', as elsewhere in this parish), *Aske* 1634, *a furlong called Ask* 1679, *Ask furlong* 1686, 1718, 1745, *Aske* ~ 1697, *Ash Furlong* 1706, 1718, *v.* ON **askr** 'an ash-tree', with **furlong**); ye Beck 1755[1] (y^e *becke* 1577–80, ~ *beck* 1634, *the* ~ 1679, y^e *Beck* 1686, 1706, 1718, *the Beck* 1745, *v.* **bekkr** 'stream' as elsewhere in the parish); ye Beckfurlong 1755[1] (y^e *Beck furlong* 1686, *Beck furlong* 1697, y^e *Beck Furllong* 1706, ~ ~ *Furlong* 1718, *the* ~ ~ 1746 (*v.* prec. and **furlong**); low Beck hill, upper beck hill 1755[1], The Beck Hill 1825 (*becke hyll* 1577–80, *beckhill* 1577–80, *nether beckhill, uper beck hill* 1634, *Beckehill* 1643, *nether beck-hill* 1679, *Long, Low Beckhill, upper Beck Hill* 1686, *Beckhil* 1697, *Long, Low Beck hill* 1706, *long, low Beck Hill, upper Beck Hill* 1728, *long Beckhill, Low beck hill, Upper Beckhill* 1745, self-explanatory); Beck hill rows 1755[1] (*Beckhill Rowend* 1634, ~ *Rowes* 1686, ~ *rowes* 1697, *Beck hill Rows* 1706, ~ *Hill Rows* 1718, ~ *hill rows* 1745, *v.* prec. and **rāw** in the pl.); Beggar Hill 1825; Beggars bush (furlong) 1755[1], Beggar's Bush 1825 (*Beggars-bush* 1679, *Beggars bush (Furlong)* 1686, 1706, ~ *Bush (Furlong)* 1718, ~ *Bush* 1745, ~ *bush (furlong)* 1697, 1745, a common derogatory name for unproductive land); Besom Carr 1825 (*v.* **besma** 'a broom, a brush', **kjarr**, the exact sense of which is uncertain); Black Hows 1825 (*v.* **blæc**, **haugr** in the pl.); Braylands 1825 (*Braithelandes* 1334, *bray lande(s)* 1577–80, *Bralandes* 1634, *bray lands* 1679, *Braylands* 1697, *Bray Lands* 1706, ~ *lands* 1745, 'the broad selions', *v.* ON **breiðr** 'broad', **land** 'a selion' in the pl, as elsewhere in the parish); the Second Bull Cl 1825; Bull mdw 1755[1], ~ Mdw 1825 (*the bull middow* 1634, *Bull meadow* 1679, y^e *Bull* ~ 1686, ·~ ~ *Medow* 1706, *Bulmeadow* 1697, *Bullmeadow* 1745); long, short Butler Creams (sic) 1755[1] (*longe, short) butteranes* (sic) 1577–80, *Buttercrames* 1679, *long Butter Creames, short Butter creames* 1686, *Long, Short Butler Creames* (sic) 1706, *Long butter Creams, short Butter Creams* 1718, *long, short Butter Creames* 1745, a complimentary nickname for rich land); Butt furlong 1755[1] (cf. *the buttes* 1777–80, y^e *Buttes* 1634, *Butt furlong* 1686, 1697, ~ *Furlong* 1706, *But* ~ 1745, *v.* **butte** 'a strip of land abutting a boundary', 'a short strip or ridge at right angles to other ridges', **furlang**); Caino Hill (sic) 1825; Car dike 1775[1] (*the carre dyke* 1577–80, y^e *Car dike* 1634, *Cardike* 1686, *-dyke* 1706, *Carr-* 1718, *v.* **kjarr**, **dík**, as elsewhere in the parish); The Carrs 1825 (*v.* **kjarr**); the Church Leas 1755[2] (*v.* **lea**, **ley** (OE **lēah**) 'meadow, pasture' in the pl.); Clean Wells 1825 (self-explanatory); Closes 1755[1] (1745, y^e *Closes* 1634, 1697, 1706, 1718); Clover Hows 1825 (*v.* **haugr** in the pl.); Cow-dike 1755[1] (*Cow dike* 1686, ~ *Dyke* 1697, 1718, ~ *Dike* 1706, 1745 (*v.* **dík**); Cow Gate side 1755[1] (*Cow-gate* 1679, *Cowgate side* 1686, *Cowgate* 1697, *Cow Gate Side* 1706, ~ *gate Side* 1718, *Cow Gate* 1745, from dial. *cowgate* (ON **gata**) '(right of) pasturage for a cow'); Cracra 1755[1] (1706, 1745, *Crakeray* 1334, *Crocrow* 1634, *Craycrow* 1679, *Cracro* (sic) 1686, *cracra* 1697 (obscure); New Crane Hill 1825 (perhaps to be identified with *cromhyll* 1577–80, *v.* **cran**, **cron** 'a crane, probably also a heron or similar bird', **hyll**); Cream Poke 1825 (a complimentary term for rich pasture, as elsewhere in the county); Drake Acres 1755[1] (1686, 1745, *drake akers* 1577–80, ~ *acres* 1679, *Drake* ~ 1697, ~ ~ *Head* 1706, from the surn. *Drake*, cf. Richard *Drakes* 1640 with **æcer** and **hēafod**); Duck Hill Moor 1825; Dunker 1825; Easter woods 1755[1] (*Aisterwod* 1334, *easterwoodes aske* 1577–80 (*v.* **askr**), *Easter woodes* 1634, ~ *Woods* 1686, 1706, 1718, *Easterwoods* 1697 ('the more easterly wood(s)', *v.* **eystri**, **wudu**); the Eastfield 1755[1] (*The east fylde* 1577–80, ~ *East Feeld*

1634, *the east field* 1643, *y* *East field* 1679, ~ ~ *Field* 1686, 1697, 1706, 1718, *the East* ~ 1745, *v*. **ēast, feld**, one of the great fields of the village, cf. the South fd, *y* West fd *infra*); Fursdale 1755[1] (1686, *Fur(r)s dale* 1745, *v*. **fyrs** 'furze', **deill** 'a share of land' as elsewhere in the parish); Gee Close (nook) 1755[1] (*Gee close* 1679, *Jee close (nooke)* 1686, *Gee Close* 1697, 1745, ~ *close* 1706, from the surn. *Gee*, cf. *Anthonie Gee* 1607 *Inv* and **clos(e)**)); Goss Acres 1755[1], Gossacres 1825 (1706, *Goss acre* 1334, *go sacres* (sic) 1577–80, *Gosacres* 1643, *Gosse-acres* 1679, *Gosseacres* 1686, *Goss acres* 1697, *Gosse Closes* 1745, probably from the surn. *Goss* and **æcer**); Green Cl 1755[1], 1825 (1697, 1718, 1745, ~ *close* 1686, 1706); Gu-a Marow (sic) 1825 (obscure); high gate flg 1755[1] (1697, *y* *hie gate* 1634, *high gate* 1679, *highgate furlong* 1686, *high Gate Furlong* 1706 ('the important road', *v*. **hēah, gata**); Little Hill 1825; Holbeck Furrs 1755[1] (*Holbecke* 1577–80, *houlbeck* 1634, *Houle-* 1643, *Hol-* 1706, *Holbeck-Furlong* 1686, *Holbeck Furrs* 1718, *Howlbeck furrs* 1745, 'the stream lying in a hollow', *v*. **hol**[2], **bekkr**, probably with **furh** 'a furrow' in the pl.); The Hows 1825 (*y* *Howes* 1686, ~ *Hows* 1706, 1718 (*v*. **haugr** in the pl., cf. Black Hows *supra*); Joan Hows 1825 (cf. prec.); Kirk Cl 1755[1] (1745, *Kirk close side* 1686, -*close*, ~ *Close side* 1706, 1718); Kirk hill 1755[1] (*kyrke hyll* 1577–80, *Kirkhill* 1634, 1679, 1745, *Kirk hill* 1697, ~ *Hill* 1706, *y* *Kirk Hil* 1718, *the Kirkhill* 1724), Kirk holm 1755[1] (*kyrke holme* 1577–80, *kirk houlm* 1634, *Kirk holme* 1679, -*holm* 1686, ~ *holm* 1697, 1706, ~ *holme* 1545, *v*. **kirkja, hyll** and **holmr**); Kirton high Mear 1755[1] (*Kyrton hye mere* 1577–80, *kirton hie meare* 1634, *Kirton high mear* 1686, *Kirton mear* 1697, 1718, 1745 (probably 'the important boundary with Kirton Lindsey', *v*. **hēah, (ge)mǣre**); Lands ends 1755[1] (1686, 1697, ~ *ende* 1718, 1745 (*v*. **land, ende**)); Little Carr dike 1825 (*v*. **kjarr, dík**); Lowman Mear 1755[1], Lawman Mare 1825 (*lawman mare* 1634, *Low man Mear* 1686, ~ ~ *meer* 1697, ~ ~ *mear* 1706, *Lowman Mear* 1745 (*v*. **(ge)mǣre**; the meaning of the first el. is uncertain); Messingham beck 1755[1] (1745, ~ *Beck* 1706, *v*. **bekkr**); Messingham field 1755[1], 1776 (1745), the Field 1825 (*campo de Messingham, campis de* ~ c1140, Hy2 (1314), 1334, ~ *de Messyngham* c1216 (m14), *v*. **feld**, referring to the open fields of the village); Michlow Dump 1824 (apparently from dial. *dump* 'a deep hole in the bed of a river or pool of water' cf. Pingle Dump, Wife hill Dump *infra*), Michlow Hill, ~ dike 1825 (*Michell howe* 1583, *v*. **micel** 'big', **haugr**); Mill close nook 1755[1] (*v*. **nōk**), Mill Dale 1825 (cf. *Mill supra*); Far Owston Gate 1825 (named from Owston, an adjacent village, and **gata**); Parrot nook cl 1755[1], ~ Nook 1825 (*parrack nooke* 1634, *Parrot close nook* 1686, ~ *Close* 1697, ~ *Close nook* 1745); Pingle dike, ~ Dump 1825 (*v*. **pingel** and cf. Michlow Dump *supra*); Post wife grave 1825; Potter how Carr 1755[1], Potterhow car (*Potter how Car* 1634, 1706, *Potterhow carr* 1686, 1745, *poterhow Carr* 1718, *v*. **haugr, kjarr**; *Potter* is presumably the occupational name or the surn. derived from it); Red more hills 1755[1] (*Redemare* 1334, *Redmorhill* 1634, *Redmore hills* 1686, *Redmere hills* 1706, ~ *Hills* 1718, *Redmere* ~ 1745; the earliest form suggests that the name means 'the reedy boundary, land on a boundary', *v*. **hrēod, (ge)mǣre**, but no certainty is possible); Roaring Tub 1825; Root Thorn 1825 (*Rokethorn* 1334, *Roke thorne* 1577–80, *Rookthorn* 1634, *Rockethorne Close* 1643, 'the thorn-tree abounding with rooks', *v*. **hrōc, þorn**); Rowmells 1755[1] (*Roundemylle Hille* 1535–46, *Rowmells* 1634, 1686, 1697, 1745, -*melles* 1679, ~ *Mells* 1706, *Row meares* 1718, the forms are too diverse to suggest a convincing etymology); the Side Ings 1755² (ye side Inges 1634, 1679, Side-Ings 1634, the Side Ings 1643, Le Ing-yate in Le Side Ings 1670, Le side Ings 1678, 'the long, spacious meadows, pastures'); Slacker dyke 1755¹ (slaker dyke 1577–80, Slackerdike 1634, ~ dike 1686, Slaker dike 1697, 1706, Slacker Dyke 1745 (v. **dík**; the first el. is obscure); The Slights 1825 (magnas et paruas slettas c1216 (m14), "Great", "Little" Slegtes, "Great" Slettis 1314 'the smooth, level fields', v. **slétta**); upper Smeathorns 1755¹, Smay Thorns 1825 (nether Smathornes 1577–80, Smathornes 1634, upp smay thornes 1679, Smea Thorns 1686, Upper ~ ~ 1697, 1706, upper Smeathorns 1718, Upper ~ 1745, 'the small, little thorn-trees', v. **smá(r)** 'small', **þorn**); South End 1755¹ (ye South end 1686, self-explanatory, cf. ye North end infra); the south fd 1755¹ (The Sowthe fylde 1577–80, ye South Feeld 1634, the south field 1643, ye south field 1679, ~ South Field 1686, 1697, 1718, South field 1706, the South Field 1745, one of the great fields of the village, cf. the Eastfield supra, ye West fd infra); South mill flg 1755¹ (the South Mill 1679, Southmill Furlong 1697, South Mill ~ 1718, 1745); Stake and Gate Corner 1825; Stone Bark 1755¹, ~ Barks 1825 (stone bark 1634, Stone Barke 1686, 1697, ~ Bark 1718, 1765 (obscure); Stony flg 1755¹ (1679, ye stonie furland 1634, Stony Furlong 1686, ye stony furlong 1697, ~ Stony Furlong 1706, 1718, v. **stānig, furlang**); Three Thorns 1825; Toff Dyke (sic) 1755¹ (toft dyke 1577–80, Toft ~ 1634, Toff Dike 1686, Tofdike 1697, Toft dike 1706, ~ Dyke 1718 (v. **toft** 'a messuage, a curtilage', **dík**); Trent Hows 1825 (**haugr** in the pl.); the Trent Ings 1755² (Trent ynges 1577–80, ye Trent Ingges 1634, the Trent Inges of Messingham 1660, le Trent Inges 1661, Trent ~ 1706, 1718, 'the meadows, pastures by the R. Trent', v. **eng** in the pl.); Turky nab hill 1825 (v. **nabbi** 'a nab, a hill' with the tautological **hyll** added); Washley Moor 1825; low Waterfall 1755¹ (waterfall 1577–80, watterfall 1634, ye Waterfall 1686, Waterfall 1697, 1706, 1718, Low Waterfall 1745, v. **wæter-gefall**; Mr Field points out that besides its customary sense waterfall can also mean 'a place where a stream disappears into the ground'); Welfholme (sic) 1825 (v. **holmr**; Welf- is obscure, unless it is a mistake for Wolf-); Wellaker Dike 1825 (v. **wella, æcer**, cf. ye Well 1697); ye West fd 1755 (The west fylde 1577–80, the weste Feeld 1614, The west field 1634, the west ~ 1643, ye West ~ 1686, the West Field 1697, 1745, West ~ 1706, ye West ~ 1719, v. **west, feld**, one of the great fields of the village, cf. the Eastfield, the South fd supra); Whirlemore flg 1755¹ (Whayly more gappe 1577–80, whorlymeare, whorly mere gate 1634, Whorlimeare 1697, Whirlamore Furlong 1686, 1745, ~ furlong 1697, obscure); Wife hill Dump 1825 (Wipe Hill Dump (sic) 18, obscure; for Dump, cf. Michlow Dump supra); Little Wood 1825; Wood Bore 1825.

(b) Baland stigh 1634 (probably 'the selion where beans grow', v. **bēan, land** with **stīg** 'a path'); Barrel close Nook 1706; ye Bowcroft 1634, Bow-croft 1679 (v. **croft**; the first el. is perhaps **boga** denoting a bow-shaped piece of land); bully landes 1577–80, Bullilandes 1634, -lands 1679 (v. **land** 'a selion' in the pl; the meaning of Bully is uncertain); ye Corne feeld 1634 (v. **corn**); Crosacres 1634; Crossedale 1334, Cross Dale 1643 (v. **cros** 'a cross', **deill**); the douches, ~ dowches 1577–80 (obscure); the eye 1577–80, ye Eay 1634, Le Eah (sic) 1678, ye yea 1706, 1718 (v. **ēa** 'a river, a stream', a word rare in the West Riding, but common in the South Riding of Lindsey); Est Croftende 1457 (v. **ēast, croft**, with **ende**); the Fold or Fore garth 1729 (v. **fald** 'a fold'; the alternative name means 'the enclosure in front', v. **fore, garðr**); le Gadds 1600, Forty Gad 1686 (v. **gadd(e)** and for a discussion, v. Gads in

Appleby f.ns (a) *supra*); *gawham* (sic) 1577–80, *Gaughams* 1679 (obscure); *Glirtin* (sic) 1697; *Gunnimcar* (sic) 1643 (*v.* **kjarr**; the first el. is obscure); *the Hall garth land* 1670 (*v.* **hall, garðr** with **land**); *Le Hemp-croft* 1667, *the Hempcroft* 1724 *BRA 833*, cf. *Le hemp-yard* 1670 (*v.* **hænep** 'hemp', **croft, geard**); *Holsand* 1334; *houbankes* 1334 (probably from **haugr** and **banke**); *the hyther ynges* 1577–80 (self-explanatory, *v.* **eng**); *Kedmore hills* 1697; *Kirks-mill* 1679 (from the surn. *Kirk*, cf. Robert *Kirke* 1607 *Inv*, and **myln**); *Kirton gate* 1577–80 ('the road to Kirton Lindsey', *v.* **gata**); *the Lady Mill Hill* 1724; *lady more hyll* 1577–80; *Lairlondis* c1216 (14), *Lairelandes* 1334 (*v.* **leirr**, 'mud, clay', **land** 'a selion' in the pl.); *Lerkeholm* 1334 (*v.* **lāwerce** 'a lark', **holmr**); *John Litleas garth end* 1679 (*v.* **garðr, ende**); *ye long dike* 1643 (self-explanatory); *Lows ends* 1697; *Lushowes* 1697, *Lussows* 1686 ('the mounds infested by lice', *v.* **lūs, haugr**); *The Meddowe* 1577–80, ~ *middow* 1634, *Meadow* 1686, 1718, *ye meadow* 1886, *Meddow* 1706 (self-explanatory); *Messingham Gray banckes* 1583; *Messingham* "marsh" 1389; *the more Heade* 1577–80 (*v.* **mōr, hēafod**); *myddle forlonge* 1577–80, *ye Middle Furland* 1634 (*v.* **middel, furlang**; *furland* is a common variant form of *furlong* in L); *the myddle gate* 1577–80, *middlegate* 1634 (*v.* **middel, gata**); *ye North end* 1686 (cf. South End *supra*); *notesome gate* (sic) 1577–80, *nowsamgate* (sic) 1634 *Nowsome Gate* 1724; *ye ould milne hill* 1634 (cf. *the Lady Mill hill supra*); *the Parsonage deale* 1679 (*v.* **deill**); *ye Preest Close* 1634; *Prodom' Mese, ~ Oxganges* 1457 (from the ME surn. *Prodome, v.* Reaney s.n. *Pridham*, with ME **mese** 'a dwelling house (with adjacent outbuildings and grounds), a messuage', *v.* MED s.v. *mes* 3, and **oxgang**); *prye banke* 1577–80; *redyfures* 1577–80, *Reedifurs* 1634 (*v.* **hrēodig, furh** 'a furrow' in the pl.); *Robert Ridley Garth end* 1686 (*v.* **garðr**); *Saynt Johns dale* 1577–80, *St John* (sic) 1634, *St. John's close* 1679 (a share of land and a close dedicated to St John); *ye sand gapp* 1634, *Sand-gap* 1679 (*v.* **sand, gap**); *seavengflet barr, sevinge flet barre* 1583 ('the meadow, pasture where sedge grows', a Scand compound of **sef** 'sedge, a rush' and **eng**, to which was added **flēot** 'a stream' and **barre** 'a barrier, an obstruction'); *ye Shortfurland* 1634 (*v.* **sceort, furlang** and cf. *myddle forlonge supra*); *Sowthe becke* 1577–80 (*v.* **sūð, bekkr**); *spittle more thorne* 1577–80 (*v.* **spitel**; no references to a hospital have been noted in the sources searched); *Stacke Dyke* 1718 (the sense of ON **stakkr** 'a stack' here is not clear); *Stanpittes* 1334, *the stone pyttes* 1577–80 (self-explanatory, *v.* **stān, pytt** in the pl.); *ye stigh* 1634 (*v.* **stīg** 'a path, a narrow way'); *co'em viam sive Le Street* 1729 (*v.* **strǣt**); *Swartemildes* 1314 ('the dark, black soil, earth', *v.* **sweart, svartr, mylde**); *teynter dale* 1577–80, *Tenter dale* 1634 ('a share of land with a tenter, a frame for tenting cloth', *v.* **tentour, deill**); *the towne forlong* 1577–80, *ye Towne furland* 1634 (cf. *myddle forlonge supra*); *ye towne end* 1679, *ye Town* ~ 1686 (*v.* **ende**); *the town syde* 1577–80, *ye Towne side* 1634 (*v.* **sīde**); *Tramell sike* 1634 (perhaps from ME *trammel* 'a long, narrow fishing-net' (MED s.v. I, i) and **sīc** 'a small stream', **sík** 'a ditch, a trench'); *the tythe Dale* 1577–80 (self-explanatory); *Warannum de novo apud Meshingham* 1275 (*v.* **wareine**); *Welyngham Mese* 1457 (from the ME surn. *Welyngham* with *mese*, cf. *Prodom' Mese supra*); *Westiby* 1314, *Westhiby* 1327, *Westyby* 1332 all (p), *Westaby Gyme* (sic) 1679, 1686, 1718, ~ *Gim* (sic) (literally '(the place) west in the village', *v.* **vestr, west, í, bȳ**, denoting X who lives in the west of the village, a common formation in L; *Gyme* is obscure); *Wranglandes* 1334 ('the crooked selions', *v.* **vrangr, wrang, land** in the pl.).

Redbourne

REDBOURNE

Reburne (sic) (8x) DB, *-burn* c1230 RA ix

Radburne 1086 DB, *-burn(')* 1212 P, 1212 Fees, *borne* 1219 Welles

Ratburne 1090 RA i

Raburna (sic) 1150–60 Dane, *-burne* c1170 RA iv, lHy2 Dane (p), *-burn'* 1206, 1218 Ass

Redeburna 1154 (e14) Selby, *-burn* 1276 RH, 1281 RSu, 1285, 1287 Ipm, 1291 Tax, 1293 Abbr, 1308 Cl, 1465, 1469 Pat, *-burne* 1288 RA ii, *-born* 1300 Ipm, *-borne* 1428 FA

Redburna (4x) c1115 LS, 1150–60 Dane, 1155 (c1200) CartAnt, Hy2 (1411) Gilb, *-burnie* 1150–60 Dane, *-burn(')* eHy2 Dane, 1185 RotDom, 1196 ChancR, 1202 FF (p), 1203 Cur, 1203 Ass, 1204 ChR, 1205 Cur, 1209, 1210 P, 1219 Ass, 1221 Cur, 1229 Welles, 1231 Pat, 1254 ValNor, 1263 RA ii *et freq* to 1696 Pryme, *-burne* 1155–62 (e14) Selby, c1180 Bly, 1185–87 Dane, Hy2 (e14) Selby, Hy2 Dane, 1203 Abbr, 1219 Ass, 1262 (e14) Selby, 1305 *KR et passim* to 1535 VE iv, *-born* 1242 RRG, 1510 LP i, 1526 Sub, *-borne* 1445 AASR xxix, 1554 InstBen, 1576 LER, 1576 Saxton, ~ *alias Radbourne* 1539 LP i, 1569 Pat, *-bourn'* 1373 Peace, *-bourne* 1428 FA *et passim*

Reddeburne 1189 (m14) Selby, 1265 RRGr, 1303 Dugd vi, 1316 FA, 1379 Cl, *-burn* e13 *HarlCh*, 1275 RH, 1281 QW, 1284–85 FA, 1428 AASR xxix

'The reedy stream', *v.* **hrēod, burna**. Characteristic of stream-names in **burna**, that flowing through Redbourne has clear water in which submerged plants survive.

TUNSTALL (lost), *Tunstal* 1150–60, eHy2, (*totam insulam que dicitur*) ~ Hy2, (*proximam grangie sue de*) ~ 112 all Dane, 1338 Pat, *Tunstale* Hy2 Dane, *Tonstal* 1277 RRGr, *Tunstall* e14 *Asw*, *Tonstall* 1537–39 LDRH, *A moated area, near Redbourn, called Tunstal, is the site of a small priory of Gilbertine nuns* 1842 White. 'The site of a farm, a farmstead', *v.* **tūn-stall**. It was in fact a grange of Bullington Priory.

ACCOMODATION WOOD is *Atkinsons Cover* 1824 O, ~ *Covert* 1841 *TA*, named from the family of *George Atkinson junior* 1811 *Red*. AMERICA

PLANTATION is a nickname of remoteness, being situated on the boundary with Waddingham. BEANLANDS WOOD, *Beanland Cover* 1824 O, *Beanlands, ~ Covert* 1841 *TA*, 'the selions where beans grow', *v.* **bēan, land** in the pl. CASTLE HILLS, 1824 O, *Castle hill plantation* 1841 *TA*, cf. *le Castelcroft* 1369 Ipm, the name of earth-works north of the Hall in Redbourne Park. CLAY DYKE (lost), 1824 O, formed part of the boundary with Hibaldstow. THE CLIFF, *Cliff farm* 1839 *Red.* DUKE'S DRAIN, presumably named from the Dukes of St Albans, lords of the manor. GORTEEN. Mr Victor Watts suggests that this is a name transferred from Gorteen, Ireland. ISLAND POND PLANTATION, *Island Pond* 1824 O, *Pond Island & Plantation* 1841, self-explanatory. MANOR HO, cf. *Manor farm* 1839 *Red*. MILESTONE NURSERY, 1824 O. NAB'S WOOD, *Nabbs Wood* 1841 *TA*, cf. *Nabb-Hill* 1700 *Terrier, Nabs* 1813 *Red, Nabs Hills* 1824 O, *v.* **nabbi** 'a knoll, a hill'. OLD PARK, 1817 *Red*, 1841 *TA*. PARADISE FM, cf. *Paradise Car, ~ Plantation*, no doubt a complimentary nickname. PILFOOT FM, named from the family of *John Pilfoot farmer* 1842 White. PRIEST LANE COVERT, *Priestland Cover* (sic) 1824 O. PYEWIPE FM, *Pyewipe Hall* 1824 O, *Peewitt Farm* 1839 *Red*; both *pyewipe* and *peewit* are common dial. terms in L for the lapwing, *Vanellus vanellus*, cf. PN L **1**, 34, ib **3**, 106 and ib **5**, 39, 155. REDBOURNE GRANGE, cf. *Grange Close* 1817 *Red*, 1841 *TA*, a late example of **grange**, for which *v.* EDD s.v. 2 'a homestead, small mansion or farm-house, esp. one standing by itself remote from others', a sense quoted from L, in which it is common. REDBOURNE HALL, 1839 *Red*. REDBOURNE HAYES, *~ Hays* 1824 O, *the Heys* 1638, *pasture called the hays* 1671, *Redburne-hayes* 1674, *the Hills of Heighs* (sic) 1700 all *Terrier, Hays farm* 1817 *Red, v.* **(ge)hæg** 'an enclosure' in the pl. HAYES WOOD, *Hays Wood* 1824 O. REDBOURNE PARK, *Park* 1668 *Terrier*, 1841 *TA, Great Park* 1817 *Red*. RIVER HEAD, *Redbourne River Head* 1824 O, a stream rises here and flows east to the R. Ancholme. RYECROFT HILL (lost), 1824 O, self-explanatory. SOUTH FIELD FM (local), *in campo aust'li* e13, *in campo versus austrum* 1220–40, *The Southfield* 1577, *Suffield otherwise Southfield Common* 1773 all *Foster*. SOUTH HOLME BOTTOM (lost), 1824 O, *Great, Little Southam Bottom* 1841 *TA, v.* **holmr** 'higher ground amidst the marshes', as elsewhere in this parish. Note *ham* is frequently a reflex of *holme* in north L. SPRINGCLIFF HO, 1824 O, self-explanatory. STONEHOLMES, *Stein holm* 1150–60 Dane, *Stain-* e13 HarlCh, *Stonehams farm* 1839 *Red, Stone Holmes* 1841 *TA, v.* ON **steinn** 'stone', **holmr**, a Scand compound, with the first el. subsequently replaced by *stone*. STONEPIT PLANTATION,

Stone pit plantation 1841 *TA*. VICARAGE, *ye Vicarage* 1601, *The Vicaridge house* 1638, *A ~ ~* 1662, 1668, *a vicarage house* 1674, *The Vicarage House* 1700, 1823. WEDGE WOOD, *Wedge Wood* 1841 *TA*. WOOFHAM HILL, 1824 O, *Wlfholm* eHy2, Hy2 Dane, *Who-home* 1700 *Terrier*, 'the raised land in marsh frequented by wolves', **wulf**, **holmr**.

FIELD-NAMES

Undated forms in (a) are 1841 *TA*; forms dated 1150–60, eHy2, Hy2^1 are Dane; Hy2^2 (14) Selby; Hy2 (1409) Gilb; e13 *HarlCh*; 1202 Ass; 1220–40, 1245–64, 1270–85, 1783 *Foster*; 1221 Cur; 1301, 1311 *KR*; 1321 RA ii; 1327 *SR*; 1352 *Cor*; 1385 Peace; 1431 FA; 1577, 1601, 1638, 1662, 1668, 1700, 1776, 1823, 1865 *Terrier*; 1660 (c1900) *LinDep 78*; 1671, 1717, 1811, 1813, 1817, 1839 *Red*, 1773^2 *Stubbs*; 1841 *TA*.

(a) Alms Houses; Ancholme Bank (cf. *inter Ancolne et le Marreis* Hy2^2, the reference is to the R. Ancholme); Ash Holt Wd; Balaams (sic) 1783, Balaam Plot 1841 (the first el. is the surn. *Balaam*, v. Reaney s.n.); Bank; Beach; Bell Mount (Quarry); Best Hill; Blowthorns; South Bottom Carr (*v.* **kjarr** 'brushwood, a bog, a marsh, especially one overgrown with brushwood', as elsewhere in the parish); East, West Bottoms (*v.* **botm** 'a bottom, a valley bottom'); Bowling Green Fm 1839, Bowling Green 1841; Brick kiln Car 1817, ~ Kiln Car (*v.* **kjarr**), ~ ~ Road, ~ ~ Wd; Calf Cl; Car over the Bridge; Car 1817, A Car 1841; Carr Mdw 1776 (*v.* **kjarr**); North, South Catcher Pasture 1813 (from dial *cotcher* 'a cottager'), Cottagers Pasture 1841, The Cottagers' Pasture 1865; (South West, West of) Catherine dale (*Catherine Dale* 1668, *Katherine Dales* 1700; the first el. is the pers.n. *Catherine*, the second **deill** 'a portion, a share of land (in the common field)', as elsewhere in the parish); Church Cl 1813, the Church Lane 1823 (*ye Churchlane* 1662); Church Paddock & Buildings, Church Churchyard & Shrubbery 1841, Church Road Cl 1841; Cinquefoil Cl (*v.* **sainfoin**, for which *Cinquefoil* is a common erroneous form); Clay Walk 1817, 1841, Clay Walk Plantation 1841; Close; Coal Staith (*v.* **stæð** 'a landing-place'); Constitution Hill (probably named in imitation of the London thoroughfare, cf. PN Mx 177); Corn Cl; Cottage Pasture; Cottagers Car, ~ Mdw, ~ Plantation; Cow Cl; Cow House & Garden; Croft (*the Croftes* 1577, 1638, *y^e* ~ 1601, *v.* **croft**); a close called Crouches 1773^1 (presumably from ME **crouche** 'a cross'); North, South East Car 1813, 1841 (*v.* **kjarr**); North east Cliff (cf. The Cliff *supra*); South East fleets (*v.* **fleot** 'an inlet, a rivulet, a stream'); Evans Lake Car (presumably from the surn. *Evans*); Great, Little Fish Pond, Fish Pond Bridge; Four Acres; Garth (*v.* **garðr** 'an enclosure' as elsewhere in the parish); Gateway Cl; Gilbey Dale (from the surn. *Gilbey*, cf. Marie *Gilbey* 1691 *Inv,* and **deill**); Glebe House Garden etc.; Gordon Car (presumably from the surn. *Gordon*); Gorrington Car; Grass Paddock & shed); Green Lane; West Harewood Cliff 1813 (East, West) Harewood Cliffs 1841, Harwood Cliff Fm 1839; Hill Fields 1773^1, ~ fields 1783, a parcell of wood ground called Hill field

Spring 1772[1], 1783 (self-explanatory, *v.* **spring** 'a young plantation, a copse'); Home Cl; Middle, North Home plat (*v.* **plat** 'a plot, a small piece of ground'); Homestead Cl 1813; North, South Horse hill cl, North Horse hill pce; House Cl; Hunsley Walk (*v.* **walk**, denoting land used for the pasture of animals, especially sheep, hence the common *Sheepwalk*; the first part is no doubt the surn. *Hunsley*); Keepers House & Garden; Kelsey Cl, ~ Carrs 1817 (named from one of the Kelseys on the opposite bank of the Ancholme); Kirton Road Cl (named from Kirton in Lindsey); Land Cl 1817; Larkhills 1841, Lark Wells 1817; Lawn (*v.* **launde**); Lime Lands; Little Car; Low Car 1817, North Lower Car 1841 (*v.* **kjarr**); Low Wd; Lye Common 1773[1]; Middle Car (*v.* **kjarr**); Mill Cl (skirts) (self-explanatory; *skirts* is from ME *skirt*, from ON *skyrta* 'a skirt, a shirt', 'the edge, the outskirts'); Mill Hill Plat, North Mill Hill (*the milhill* 1577, y[e] *ould myln hill* 1601, cf. *molendini abbatis Selebi* 1150–60, *unius molendini* 1202, *v.* **myln. hyll**); Nineteen Acres; North Cliff (cf. The Cliff *supra*); North Cow Car; North Wood Fm 1839; Nursery; Occupation Road; Old Car 1817, 1841 (*v.* **kjarr**); Old Cow Pasture; Orchard(s), Orchard Platt (*v.* **plat**); East, West Orders 1813 (obscure); Ox Cl, ~ Pasture; Paddock 1817, 1841; Pinfold (*v.* **pynd-fald** 'a pinfold'); Pingle Wd (*v.* **pingel** 'a small enclosure', **wudu**); Preston's Cl, ~ Skirts (named from the surn. *Preston* and **skirt**, cf. Mill Cl *supra*); Pudding Poke Cl (a fanciful name for soft, sticky land); Quarry, Quarry Plantation; Rape Stubble; Redbourne Common 1773[1], 1783; Redburn Carrs 1773[2] (*v.* **kjarr**); Road between Plantation; Road Cl; Robinson's plat North, ~ ~ South 1813, (North, South) Robinson Platt 1841 (from the family name *Robinson* and **plat**); Rough Car (*v.* **kjarr**); Salt Marsh; Sand Cl; Middle, North Sand hill (*v.* **sand, hyll**); School House Yard & Garden; Scotland Cl (a nickname of remoteness, the field lies on the parish boundary); Scrubbs (*v.* **scrubb** 'a place overgrown with brushwood'); Seventeen Acres; Shrubbery & Walks (*v.* **walk**); South Cliff (cf. The Cliff *supra*); South Plantation; South Pond; East, West Southards 1813 (cf. perhaps *Southers* 1700); East, West South Woods; Spring Cl; Springlands Hill; Stables Coach Houses etc.; Stackyard piece; Stone Quarry; Thirteen Acres; Tid Willows; Todds Holt (presumably named from the *Todd* family and **holt**); Trefoil Cl; East of Turnpike; Twenty Six Acres; North, South Upper Car (*v.* **kjarr**); the Vicarage Garth 1823, The Vicarage Garth of Church Paddock 1865 (*v.* **garðr** and cf. Vicarage *supra*); East, West Waddingham Close Cliff 1813, East, West Waddingham Cl 1841, East, West Waddingham Cliffs 1841 (cf. *Waddinghams gate* 1638, *v.* **gata** 'a road' and Waddingham *infra*); Waterhouse Car (from the surn. *Waterhouse*, cf. *Jhn Waterhous the younger* 1607 *Inv*, and **kjarr**); Wells Platt 1817, 1841 (*ad Fontem* 1270–85, *Attewelle* 1327 both (p), *v.* **wella**); Middle, North, South West Car 1813, 1841 (*v.* **kjarr**); Middle, North west Cliff (cf. The Cliff *supra*); West fleets (*v.* **flēot**); the White House 1811 (1717, *the Whitehouse* 1671); Wood & Keepers House; Wood & Walk (*v.* **walk**); Wood (many); Wood Car (*v.* **kjarr**); Wood End 1817.

(b) *Iohannes seruiens Rogeri at ye Abotes de Redburne* 1385 (p) (*v.* **abbat** 'an abbot', the reference being probably to the *Abbot* of Selby); *Babcrofte* 1577, *bab croft* 1601 (probably from the ME surn. *Babbe* and **croft**); *the becke* 1577 (*v.* **bekkr**); *a place there called betweene the streets upon the Hiller-tree-furlonge* 1638 (*v.* **betwēonan, strǣt** and *v.* **Hillertre** *infra*. It is not clear to which *the streets* refer, though one is Ermine Street); *Bosedaile* e13 (from the ME surn. *Bose*, cf. Matilda

Bos 1245–64, and **deill**); *Braccons* 1634 (*v*. **brakni** in the pl., denoting places where bracken grows); *Bramehilla* Hy2 (1409) (*v*. **brōm, hyll**); *the Bunnockes* 1638 (obscure); *Buttes* e13, *tres Buttes* 1270–85 (*v*. **butte** 'the three butts', probably an assart consolidating three odd pieces of a furlong); *Dawburne hill* 1638; *Engcroft* 1221 (*v*. **eng, croft**); *Estlandes* Hy2² (14) (*v*. **ēast, land** 'a selion' in the pl.); *Farmerie-Carr* 1700 ('the infirmary carr', *v*. **farmery, kjarr**, no doubt originally an endowment supporting the infirmary of a monastery; there is no indication which it was. Three, Bullington, Drax and Selby, held land in Redbourne); *in campis de Redburne* Hy2¹, ~ ~ *de Reddeburn'* 1270–85 (*v*. **feld**); *Fherefures* (sic) 1150–60 (*v*. **furh** in the pl.); *la grene* 1301 (p) (*v*. **grēne** 'a village green, a grassy spot); *insula Hadhe*, ~ *Hade* 1150–60, ~ *Hadhe* Hy2¹, *in superiori Hathee* Hy2 (the first el. is doubtful; the second is OE **ēa** 'a stream, a river'); *Hatton welles* Hy2 (1409), *Hattunbech, -hil* 1245–64 (presumably from the surn. *Hatton* with **wella, bekkr** and **hyll**); *Hestfen* eHy2 ('the marsh where horses are found', *v*. **hestr, fenn**); *vie que ducit ad hibaldstoue* e13, *viam de Hibaldestou* 1245–64 ('the road to Hibaldstow (an adjoining parish)'); *Hillertre* Hy2 (14), *-tree* 1577 ('the elder tree', *v*. **hyldre, trēow**); *Hirst* 1150–60, *hirst* e13 (*v*. **hyrst** 'a hillock, a copse'); *vie puplice versus Lincoln'* Hy2 (1409) (self-explanatory); *the Locke* 1577, *lock* 1601, *Longe Lock* 1638 (*v*. **loca** 'an enclosure'); *le lowgh Riges* 1601 (*v*. **lágr** 'low', **hryggr** 'a ridge'); *manifaldikes* e13 ('the ditch(es) with many folds', *v*. **manig-fald, dīc, dík**, cf. the R. Manifold (St)); *le Marreis* Hy2² (14) (*v*. **mareis** 'the marsh'); *Martin ou* 1150–60, *Martinhoubech* 1245–64 ('Martin's mound, hill', *v*. **haugr**. The first el. is the OE, ME pers.n. *Martin*); *Midelkirne* e13 (obscure); *Neudeil* 1150–60 (*v*. **nīwe, deill**); *Norhe graue il* (sic) 1150–60, *Norgrauehil* e13 ('the north copse', *v*. **norð, grāf**, with **hyll**); *Norhegrapdal'* 1245–64; *in Campo Aquilonali* e13, *in campo versus boreā* 1220–40, *The Northfield* 1577, *the* ~ 1638 (*v*. **norð, feld**, one of the open fields of the village); *Northiby* 1301 (p) (literally '(the place) north in the village', *v*. **norð, í, bȳ**, denoting X who lives in the north of the village, a common formation in L, cf. *Westiby infra*); *Northlanges* e13 (*v*. **norð, lang²** 'a long strip of land', cf. *Westlanges infra*); *Oustiby* 1301 (p) (literally '(the place) east in the village', *v*. **austr, í, bȳ**, a Scand compound, and for the significance, *v*. *Northiby supra*); *Presteholme* 13, *Priestholme* 1700 (*v*. **prēost, holmr**); *Redburndik* 1352, *Redbourne Dike* 1600 (c1900) (*v*. **dīc, dík**); *via de Redburn'* 1321; *Salburn* 1150–60, *saleburna* e13, *Saleburnebech* 1245–64, *Sawborne* 1577, 1601 ('the willow stream', *v*. **salh, burna**, forms in *Saw-* are due to the vocalisation of [l]); *alde Scala deile* 1150–60 ('the share of land at the old temporary hut', *v*. **skáli** 'a temporary hut or shed', a word chiefly found in north-west England, but which has been noted several times in north L, **deill**, a Scand compound); *Slundale* 1638; *iuxta viam de stainton* e13 ('the road to *Stainton* (in Waddingham)'); *strett hill* 1601 (*v*. **strǣt, hyll**, the reference being to Ermine Street); *Suthdik'* Hy2² (14), *-dic* 1220–40, *Suddyk* 1245–64 (*v*. **sūð, dík**); *Sudflet* 1150–60 (*v*. **sūð, flēot** 'an inlet, a rivulet, a stream'); *Suthi irst* (sic) Hy2, *Suthirst* Hy2² (14), *suthyst* (sic) e13 (*v*. **sūð, hyrst** 'a hillock, a copse'); *Swynesty deyle* Hy2 (1409) ('the swine sty, pen', *v*. **swīn, stigu**, with **deill**); *thorne tree* 1638 (self-explanatory); *the towne end* 1577 (self-explanatory); *attunbec* 1220–40 (literally 'at the village beck', *v*. **atte, tūn, bekkr**); *Uerches holm* 1150–60 (*v*. **holmr**; the first el. is a pers.n., probably Anglo-Scand **Yrki*, a nomen agentis formation derived from

ON *yrkja* 'to work, to cultivate, to till', as suggested by Dr Insley); *westiby* 1270–85, *Westiby* 1301, 1327, ~ *de Reddeburne* 1311 all (p) (literally '(the place) west in the village', *v.* **west, vestr, í, bȳ**, and for the significance, *v. Northiby supra*); *Westlanges* 1245–64 (*v.* **west, lang**², cf. *Norhlanges supra*); *uper Wrang* 1220–40 ('the crooked, twisted place', *v.* **vrangr**).

Roxby cum Risby

ROXBY

> *Roscebi* 1086 DB
>
> *Roxebi* (2x) DB, 1201 Cur, 1210 Abbr, -*by* 1224 Welles, 1237, 1242 RRG, 1252 FF (p), 1263 ib, 1275 RH, (*iuxta Ryseby*) 1285 *FF*, 1286 Abbr, 1287 Ipm, 1291 Cl, 1293, 1313 Pat *et passim* to 1556 ib, -*be* 1314 Inqaqd
>
> *Rochesberia* 1090–1100 (1402) YCh vi, 1100–08 (17) France, 1147–53 YCh vi
>
> *Rokesbia* 1100–08 (Ed3) YCh vi, -*bye* 1186 Dugd vi, -*bi* 1188 P (p), R1 (1311) Ch, 1190, 1191, 1192, 1193 P all (p), 1199 FF, 112 Dane (p), 1201 Cur, 1202 Ass, 1210 Abbr, 1210 P (p), 1212 Fees, 1219 Ass, -*by* 1219 FF, 1220 Cur, 1223 FF, 1227 Cur, 1249 FF, 1311 Pat, 1365 Misc, 1413 Fine
>
> *Rochesbi* (2x) c1115 LS, 1162, 1163, 1168, 1194 P all (p), 1197 FF, 1206 P, -*by* 1136–40 (1464) Pat, 1166–79 (1401) YCh vi, 1206 OblR
>
> *Rokebi* 1180 P (p). 1218 Ass, -*by* 1201, 1203 Cur
>
> *Roxby* 1130–39 (1311) YCh vi, 1150–58 (m14), 1189 (m14), a1197 (m14) *Drax*, 1285 AD (p), 1290 Cl, 1291 Tax, 1292 Abbr, 1316 FA, 1319, 1322 Pat, 1327 *SR*, 1328 Banco, 1330 Pat, 1332 Orig, 1333 Pat, 1333 Cl, 1339 Pat *et freq*, -*bye* 1547, 1563 Pat, 1576 Saxton, 1610 Speed, -*bie* 1576 LER, *Rocksby* 1661 VisitN

'Hrók's farmstead, village', from the ON pers.n. *Hrókr* and **bȳ**, identical with Roxby House PN YN 225. The modern name is derived from the strong form of the pers.n., *Hrókr*; those without medial -*es*- are presumably from the weak form *Hróki*. In accordance with early AN usage OE and ON *c*/*k* is represented by -*ch*- before -*e*-. Forms in -*beria* are also recorded for Scawby and Tealby in the same documents as for Roxby. They are not however supported by similar spellings elsewhere and are no doubt to be regarded as "sports".

RISBY, HIGH & LOW

> *Risebi* (4x) 1086 DB, c1128 (12) ChronPetro, c1115 LS, 1192 P,
> 1196 ChancR, 1197, 1198, 1199 P, 1199 CurR, 1200, 1201, 1202
> 1203, 1204, 1206 P, *-by* c1200 BS, 1202 FF, 1209–35 LAHW,
> 1242–43 Fees, 1246 Ipm, 1272 *Ass*, 1279 Ch *et passim* to 1343
> Roche, 1526 Sub, *-bie* LER, *Ryseby* 1237 RRG, 1291 Tax, 1302
> Pat, 1304 Ipm, 1305 Cl, 1312 Ch, 1374 Peace, 1383 Ch, *-bye*
> 1576 Saxton
>
> *Risabi* c1115 LS
>
> *Risbi* 1212 Fees, *-by* 1254 ValNor, 1330 Pat, 1333 Cl, 1346 Orig,
> 1371 Ipm, 1372 Fine *et passim*, *Rysby* c1279 RRGr, 1333 Pat,
> 1343 NI, 1347 Pat *et passim* to *-bye* 1610 Speed
>
> *Risseby* 1275 RH, 1402 FA, *Rysseby* 1351 Pat, 1396 Peace
>
> *Reseby* R1 (1232) Ch, *Reysbye* 1535–46 *MinAcct*, 1536–37 Dugd vi,
> 1551 Pat, *-by* 1537–38 Dugd vi, 1562 *Yarb*, *Reisbye* 1551 Pat,
> 1600, 1603 *Elwes*, *-bie* 1657 *ib*
>
> *Magna Riseby* 1316 FA, ~ *Risby* 1327 *SR*, ~ *Rysby* 1328 Banco,
> 1332 *SR*, *magna Reseby* 1526 *Elw*
>
> *Parva Riseby* 1316 FA, ~ *Rysby* 1317 *FF*, 1431 FA, ~ *Risby* 1327
> *SR*, "Little" *Rysby* 1434 Cl
>
> *Overrisseby* 1451 Cl, *Vpper Resbye* 1589 *AddCh*, *Upper Reasby*
> 1696 Pryme, *High Risby* 1824 O
>
> *Netherrysby*, *Nethyr Rysby* 1428 FA, *Nether Resby* 1589 AddCh, ~
> *Risbye* 1622 *Elwes*, *Low Risby* 1675 *ib*, 1824 O

'The farmstead, village among brushwood', from ON **hrís**
'brushwood, shrubs' and **bȳ**, identical with Risby PN L **3**, 173 and Risby
Sf and YE, as well as Rejsby and Risby in Denmark. It is possible that
Risby, found four times as a settlement-name in England, is in fact a
name transferred from Denmark. If this were so, it was presumably as
topographically appropriate for the English names as for the Danish.

SAWCLIFFE FM

> *Saleclif* (3x) 1086 DB, 1212 Fees, *-clive* 1242–43 Fees, 1265 Misc,
> *-cliue* 1230 P, 1272 *Ass*, *-clife* 1250 Ipm
>
> *Salcliua* 112 (l13) Blyth, *-clifa* John (l13) ib, *-clif*(') Hy3 (l13) Blyth,
> 1275, 1276 RH, 1303 FA, 1327 *SR*, 1329 *Ass*, 1347, 1362 Pat,
> 1365 IpmR, 1365 Pat, *-clyf* 1300 Orig, 1300 Fine, 1308 Cl, 1332
> *SR*, 1358 Pat, 1368 Ipm, 1391 Fine, 1481 Pat, *-clyff'* 1332 *SR*,
> 1451 Cl, *-cliff* 1350 Ipm, *-klif* 1398 Pat

Sawclyffe 1431 FA, 1579 NCWills i, 1619 *Elw, -clyff* 1526 *ib*, 1535
   VE iv, 1553 Pat, 1559 NCWills i, 1610 Speed, *-clyve* 1536–37
   Dugd vi, *-clyf* 1576 Saxton, *-cliff* 1824 O
Saltcliue 1272 *Ass, -cliff* 1346 FA, 1428 FA, *-clyf* 1374 Peace, 1428
   FA, *-cliffe* 1488 Cl, *Salteclyff'* 1396 Peace

'The steep slope where willows grow', *v.* **salh, clif**. The farm is
situated on the steep slope on the top of which runs Ermine Street. The
development of *Sal-* to *Saw-* is due to the vocalisation of [l] to [w]. The
sporadic forms in *Salt-* appear to belong to Sawcliff and presumably are
due to popular etymology.

DRAGONBY. A geological feature now known locally as The Dragon,
was described by Pryme, 1696, as *a place . . . called the Sunken Church,
the tradition concerning which says that there was a church here
formerly, but that it sunk in the ground with all the people in it, in the
times of popery. But I found it to be false, for that which they shew to be
the walls therof, yet standing, is most manifestly nothing but a natural
rock, which lifts itself out of the ground about two yards high, in a
continuous line, like the walls of church.* It is also *Sunken Church* 1798
Elw, 1892 White, Directory. *Dragonby*, first noted 1913 Kelly,
Directory, is described by Jeffrey May, *Dragonby*, 2 vols, Oxbow
Monograph 61, i, 7, as "an unusual elongated mass of tufa which forms
a prominent rock ridge some 30m long and up to 3m high and which
appears as a snake-like feature running down the scarp slope", *v.* plate
2, for a photograph. May comments further that steel-making developed
rapidly in Scunthorpe and in about 1910 a fresh influx of workers came
from other parts of Britain and Ireland. Among them were Roman
Catholic workers who by 1912 were housed just outside the Scunthorpe
boundary in a new village on land belonging to the Elwes estate. A
single street of houses was built and was named Dragonby by Lady
Winifride Elwes.

BRACKENHOLMES, 1798 *Elw*, 1841 *TA, Bracconhoumes* 1647 *Elw,
Breckenholmes* 1659 *ib*, cf. *brakenhoulme close* 1606 *Terrier*, 'the
pieces of higher dry ground amidst the marshes where bracken grows',
v. **brakni, holmr,** in the pl., a Scand compound. For the form in
-houmes, cf. Sawcliffe Fm *supra*. THE BUTTONHOOK, a plantation, so-
named from its shape. CRINGLEBECK FM, *Cringelbeck* c1200 (c1250)

MaltCart, -bec e13 (1311) Ch, *Crinkelbek'* Hy3 (14) *Drax, cringelbek'* 113 (14) *ib, Kryngylbeck* 1577, *Cringkle beck* 1601, *Cringle beck* 1601, 1606, 1690 all *Terrier,* ~ *becke* 1668, *crindle beck* 1647 *Elw, Cringle Beck* 1798 *ib*, from ON **kringla** 'a circle', used of the circular sweep of a stream, and **bekkr** 'a beck, a stream', as elsewhere in the parish, a Scand compound. DUDLEY COVERT, no doubt from the surn. *Dudley.* HALL FM (local), cf. *atte Halle de Roxby* 1389 *FF, atte Hall' de Roxby* 1396 Peace, *atte Hall* "of" *Roxby* 1416 Fine, *at Hall de Roxby* 1428 FA all (p), self-explanatory. HIGHFIELD FM. JEFFRIES COVERT, presumably from the surn. *Jeffries.* MAUD'S COVERT. RISBY GRANGE (lost), *Reysbye,* ~ *Firma grang'* 1536–37 Dugd vi, "grange of" *Reysby* 1537–39 LDRH, *Reisby grange* 1544 LP xiii, *Reysbie Grange* 1551 Pat, *Reysbie Graunge* 1554–55 *MinAcct, le grange de Risbye* 1622 *Elw, the Grange or Farme of Reisby* 1659 *ib, the Graunge of Reisbie* 1657 *Elw;* it was a **grange** of Thornholme Priory. RISBY WARREN, 1824 O, *Warren* 1798 *Elw, v.* **wareine**. RISBY WARREN FM, ~ ~ *House* 1824 O. ROOKERY PLANTATION. ROXBY CARRS, 1824 O, *the Care* 1577, *the Carre* 1668, 1686, *the Carr* 1674, 1693, *ye Carr* 1706 all *Terrier, Roxby Carr* 1659 *Elw,* ~ *Cars* 1803 *Terrier, v.* **kjarr** 'brushwood', 'a bog, marsh over-grown with brushwood', as elsewhere in the parish. ROXBY CAUSEWAY, 1824 O, ~ *Causey* 1768 (1791) *LindDep (Plans), v.* **causie**. ROXBY GRANGE, 1824 O, *grangiam de Rokesby* R1 (1232) Ch, 1343 Roche; it was a **grange** of Roche Abbey. SCABCROFT, 1661, 1665 *Monson,* cf. *Scabcroft drean* 1700 *Terrier,* from ME *scabbe* 'a scab' and **croft**, but the significance of the first el. is uncertain, unless it is used with a derogatory sense, or as a surn., recorded in MED from 1264. SCOTNEY, 1659 *Elw, Scotney(e)* 1545 *AOMB 216, Scotteney* 1659, 1662 *Elw,* cf. *Scoteny croft* 1287 Ipm, *Far, Great Scotney* 1767 *Stubbs, Scotney Hill* 1768 (1791) *LindDep (Plans),* 1824 O; named from the *de Scotney* family, which held land in Roxby, certainly from the middle of the 12th century. SHEFFIELD'S HILL, *Sheffield Hill* 1824 O, cf. *Sheffeild close* 1647 *Elw,* named from the Lords *Sheffield,* who held land here certainly from the early 17th century, cf. *lord Sheffield* 1601 *Terrier.* SMALETHORPE (lost), *Smalethorp'* 112 (14), e14 (14) *Drax, -thorp* e13 (1311) Ch, *-torp* 1311 Pat, 'the small secondary settlement, dependent outlying farmstead or hamlet', *v.* **smal(r), þorp**, a Scand compound; there is no indication of its situation. THORNE HOLT. VICARAGE, *the vicaredge house* 1606, *The Vicaridge House* 1668, ~ ~ *house* 1674, 1693, *the Vicarage house* 1686, *the vicaridge of Rocksby* 1693, *ye Vicaridge house* 1706, *ye Vicaridge* 1712, *the Vicarage-house* 1803 all

Terrier, Vicarage House and Buildings 1841 *TA, the Old Vicarage House now used as a Farm House* 1864 *Terrier*. WALK HO, 1798 *Elw*, *v*. **walk**, denoting land used for the pasture of animals, especially sheep, hence the common *Sheepwalk*. WESTFIELD HOLT, cf. *West Field* 1803 *Terrier*.

FIELD-NAMES

Undated forms in (a) are 1841 *TA*; those dated 112 (m14), e13 (m14), 13 (m14), Hy3 (m14) are *Drax*; e13 (1311) Ch; 1272 Ass; 1275 RH; 1311, 1547, 1551 Pat; 1287 Ipm; 1327, 1332 *SR*; 1343 NI; 1360 Peace; 1395 Works; 1389–91, 1535–46, 1554–55, 1613–15, 1618 *MinAcct*; 1541, 1545 *AOMB 214*; 1544¹, 1546 LP; 1544² *Nelthorpe*; 1577, 1601, 1606, 1638, 1668, 1671, 1674, 1686, 1693, 1700, 1706, 1712, 1803, 1822, 1858, 1864 *Terrier*; 1622, 1647, 1655, 1657, 1658, 1659, 1662, 1667, 1671, 1759, 1769, 1793, 1798, 1799, c1807, 1813 *Elwes*; 1649 *Yarb*; 1660 (c1900) *LindDep 78*; 1767 *Stubbs*.

(a) Acridge Cl, ~ Fd 1798, 1841 (yᵉ *acar hedge* 1577, *the Acarydge* (*banck*) 1601, the original form of the name is indicated by the 1577 form); Appleby Lane 1798 ('the lane to Appleby'); Ball Hills 1858; Blockhouse Marfur Plat 1759, ~ Marfur 1813 (*v*. **marfur** 'a boundary furrow', as elsewhere in this parish); Bottom Car 1803 (*v*. **kjarr**); Near Bottom Dales (*v*. **deill** in the pl.); Bracken Cl 1798; Brackenhills Cl (*v*. **brakni, hyll**); Brigg Rd 1798 ('the road to Brigg'); Far, Near Bull Hills 1798, 1841 (*Bulhils* 1601, 1606, -*hills* 1647, self-explanatory, *v*. **bula, hyll** in the pl.); Bullards Cl 1798, 1822, 1841, 1864, Bullard's ~ 1803 (*Bullard Close* 1668, *Bullardes close* 1674, *Bullards* ~ 1686, 1706, 1712, *a Close called Ballards* 1693, probably from the surn. *Bullard* and **clos(e)**); Far, Near Burton Dale 1798 (*Burton dale* 1601, ~ *Dale* 1659, named from the *Burton* family, cf. John *Burton* 1798, with **deill** 'a share, portion of land' as elsewhere in the parish); Calf Cl 1798 (*the calfe close* 1606, *the caulfe* ~ 1647, *Calfe Close* 1659); Carr 1767, 1798, 1841, the Carrs 1864 (cf. *the Carmarforde* 1601 (*v*. **marfur**), *the Carre* 1659, *v*. **kjarr**); Carr Leys 1798, the ~ ~ 1803 (yᵉ *carlees, carrles* 1577, *the Carr Leaze* 1659, ~ ~ *lees* 1700, *v*. **kjarr, lea** (OE **lēah**), in the pl., 'meadow, pasture'); Church Fd 1798, the Church fd 1822, ~ ~ Fd 1864 (*the Church feild* 1647, ~ *Churchfeild* 1659, ~ *Church field* 1668, 1674, 1686, 1693, ~ ~ *Field* 1700, yᵉ *Church field* 1706, ~ ~ *Field* 1712); Church Yd; Cliff 1841, 1858, the Cliff 1864 (*the Cliffe* 1668, 1674, 1686, ~ *Clifs* 1693, yᵉ *Cliff* 1706, 1712), Cliff Btm 1798, 1841 (*v*. **botm**), Roxby Cliff Cls 1769, 1793, Cliff Cls 1798 (*the nether, the upper Cliffe Close* 1655, *the Cliff closes* 1700), Cliff Hedge 1822 (*the Cliffe hedge* 1668, 1674, 1686, ~ *Cliff hedge* 1693, yᵉ ~ 1706, *v*. **clif**); Colt Lands 1841, ~ lands 1858; Common Carr 1767 (*v*. **kjarr**); Great, Little Constable Fd 1798 (probably a field held by the village *constable*); East, West Corps 1798, East and West ~; Cottagers Mdw, ~ pasture; Cow Cl 1798, 1841 (*Cowclose* 1657, 1658), Cow Pasture 1798, 1841; Dents Carr 1767 (from the surn. *Dent*, cf. William *Dent*

1642 LPR, with **kjarr**); Far, Near Dodmoor 1798, Far Dodmoor, Near Dodmore 1841, Dodmoor Lane 1798, Dodmore ~ 1803 (cf. *Doddmor close* 1601, *Dodmore* 1659, *dodmoor-lane* 1700); Dove Cote c1807; East Cl, ~ Fd 1798, 1841; Far Cliffe 1798, Far Cliff Cl; far field 1822, the Far Fd 1864 (*the Farrfeild(s)* 1659, *the farre field* 1668, *the far* ~ 1686, *the Far* ~ 1693, ~ *Farr Field* 1700, *y* far field* 1706, *Far Field* 1712); Fenwick Cl 1798, c1807, 1841 (from the *Fenwick* family, cf. Richard *Fenwicke* 1642 LPR, and **close**); Folly 1798, 1841; Furze Walk 1798, 1841 (*v.* **fyrs, walk**); Great Cliff Cl ((*the) great Cliff Closes* 1671, *y* Great Cliff close* 1700, cf. Roxby Cliff Cls *supra*); Great Lands; Greens Carr 1767 (probably named from the family of John *Green* 1858 *Elwes*, and cf. Alan *atte Grene* 1327 *SR*); East Hall Cl 1822, Gt, Lt Hall Cl 1798, 1841 (*the Hall Close* 1668, 1700, cf. *atte Hall* 1322, 1343, *ad Aulam* 1327 all (p), *the Hall garth close*, ~ *hallgarth*, ~ *Hall garth gates* 1601, ~ *hallgarth dale*, ~ *hall garth balk* 1606, ~ *Hallgarth* 1659, *v.* **hall, garðr**, with **clos**(e), **gata, deill** and **balca** 'a ridge, a bank'); High Cliff Cl (*v.* **clif**); Holme Cls 1798, (the) Holmes Cls 1803, 1822, 1841 (cf. *Holmes* 1287, *Roxby Holmes* 1544[1], ~ *holmes* 1544[2], *Roxbie holmes* 1613–15, *Homes* (sic) 1659, *the Holmes* 1662, *the Holme closes* 1668, ~ *holme Closes* 1674, *the Holme Closes* 1686, *Holmes Closes* 1700, 1712, *y* Holm closes* 1706, *v.* **holmr**); Holt 1798, 1841 (*v.* **holt**); Holy Well 1799, Holy-well Dales 1803, Holywell Dale Cl (*Haliwelle (Daile)* e13 (1311), *Haliwell* 13 (m14), from **hālig** 'holy', **wella** 'a well, a spring', with **deill**); Home Cl 1798, 1841; Horse Cl 1798, 1841; House, Pleasure Grounds, Buildings, Yard and Garden; the Inges 1767, Roxby Ings 1798, 1803 (1658), Ings 1798, 1841, the Ings 1822, 1864, Inggs 1858 (cf. *the long ynges* 1601, ~ *longe ynges* 1606, ~ ~ *Inggs* 1657, 1700, *the Ings* 1659, 1693, *the Ingge* 1662, ~ *Inges* 1674, 1686, *y* Ings* 1706, 1712, *the ynge dyke* 1606, *v.* **eng** 'meadow, pasture'); Far Intack 1798, 1841, Intake (*v.* **inntak** 'a piece of land taken in or enclosed'); Kettle Sties (Cl) 1798, 1841 (*Kettle sties, Ketlesties* 1601, *Kettle sties close* 1606, *Ketlestye* 1659, *Kettlestiles Close* (sic) 1700, from the ON pers.n. *Ketill*, or the derived surn., and **stīg, stígr** 'a path, a narrow road'); Lane; Limekiln Cl 1798, Lime Kiln Cl 1841; Little Carr 1798 (*v.* **kjarr**); Long Cliff Cl (*v.* **clif**); Long Cl 1798; The Low Cliff 1803 (*v.* **clif**); Meadow Cl 1798; Midd Carr 1798, Middle Carr (*the Middle Carr* 1659, *v.* **kjarr**); Middle Cliffe 1798, Far, Near Middle Cliff (*v.* **clif**); Middle Fd 1798, c1807, 1841, 1864 (*the middle feild* 1647, *the Middle* ~ 1659, ~ *Middle-field* 1668, ~ *middle field* 1686, ~ ~ *Field* 1693, *the Middle* ~ 1700, *y* Midle field* 1706, *Midle Field* 1712); Mill Cliffe 1798 (*the myll clyffe* 1606, ~ *Mill Cliff* 1657, *Millcliffe* 1659, *the Mill clife* 1674), Mill cliff lane 1822 (*Milne Cliff lane* 1668, *the Mill Cliff* ~ 1686, *Mil clifs* ~ 1693, *Millcliff* ~ 1706, *Mill Cliff lane* 1712, *v.* **myln, clif, lane**); Mill Fd 1798, Mill and Paddock (*situm molendini* 13 (m14), *molendinum de Roxby* 1360, *v.* **myln**); Moat; Moor 1798; Muckmiddin 1798, -midding (*v.* **midding** 'a dung-heap'); Narrow Walk 1798 (*v.* **walk**); Near Cliff(e) 1798, 1842 (*v.* **clif**); New Cl 1798, 1841; New Pce 1767, 1798, 1841 (*Newpeece* 1659); Nooking 1767, 1798, 1841, The ~ 1803 (from dial. **nōking** 'a nook', common in north L); North Cliff Cl (cf. *the northe cliffe* 1577, *North Cliff* 1658, ~ *Cliffe* 1659, *the North cliffe* 1667, *v.* **clif**); North Lands (*v.* **land**); Ox Cl 1798, 1841 (*Ox Close* 1655, 1658, *Oxclose* 1659 and cf. *the oxecrofte* 1647, self-explanatory); Ozier Holt 1798 (*v.* **holt**); Paddock 1798, 1841; Great, Little Pepper Fd 1798, Pepper Fd 1822, Pepper-Dale 1803 (*v.* **deill**) (*Pepperfield* 1668, 1686, *peper*

~ 1674, *pepper* ~ 1893, *peperfield* 1706, *Pepper Field* 1712, probably from the surn. *Pepper* and **feld**); Pingle 1798, 1841 (*v.* **pingel** 'a small enclosure'); Plantation; Pond Cl 1798; Risby Walk 1822 (*Risbie walke* 1668, *Risby* ~ 1674, ~ *walk* 1686, 1693, 1706, *low Risby Walk* 1700, *Rysby walk* 1712, *v.* **walk** 'a sheep-walk'); Prudence Robinsons Cl 1799; Great, Little Roxdales 1798 (*v.* **deill**); Far, Near Rye Cliffe 1798, 1841 (*the Ryecliff* 1601, *Rye cliffe* 1606, *Rycliffe* 1647, *the Rye Cliffe* 1659, *v.* **ryge, clif**); Sainfoin Cl 1798, Sanfoin Cl, Old Sainfoin Cl 1798 (*v.* **sainfoin**); North, South Sands 1798, Sands 1841, 1858 (*Sablones* e13 (1311), Hy3 (14), 13 (m14), *Sandes* e13 (m14), 13 (m14), 1606, *Long sands* 1659, self-explanatory), Sands Cl 1798 (*the long sand close* 1647, *Sandclose* 1657, *Sands close* 1659 (cf. prec.); Great Seeds, Seeds Cl 1798, Seed ~; Bottom Side Lands (*v.* **sīd** 'large, spacious, extensive', **land** 'a selion' in the pl.); South Holmes 1798 (*the Southolmes* 1679, *v.* **sūð, holmr**); Sparrow Croft 1798, 1841 (probably from the surn. *Sparrow* and **croft**); Stone Pit Cl 1798, 1841, ~ ~ Walk 1798; Thealby Carr 1803, 1822 (*thelby carr* 1577, *Theilbie Carr* 1668, *Thealby Carr* 1674, 1686, 1693, 1712, ~ *car* 1706, named from Thealby in Burton upon Stather parish *supra*); The Top Cliff 1803; Turpit(t) Hill Carr 1798, Turpit Hill (*Turpetts Hills* 1659, *v.* **turf, pytt** with **hyll**); Twenty Acre Carr 1798, ~ Acres Carr (*v.* **kjarr**); (the) Vicarage Cl 1803, 1822, 1864 (cf. *the personage lande* 1601, *vikrige dale* 1647 (*v.* **deill**), *the Vicaridge Close* 1668, 1674, ~ ~ *close* 1693, *Vicaridge* ~ 1706, cf. Vicarage *supra*); Far, Near Walk 1798, 1841, The Walk (*v.* **walk**); West Croft 1798, 1841 (self-explanatory); Wheat Cl 1798, 1841 (*Wheate Close* 1657); Willow Garth 1798 (*willoughgarthe close* 1601, *willough garth close* 1606, *the willow garth* 1638, *Willogarth* 1658, *the willowgarthes* 1668, ~ *Willow garthes* 1674, *wilow garth* 1686, *the Willow garths* 1693, *Willow garth* 1712, self-explanatory, *v.* **wilig, garðr** in both the sg. and pl.); Winterton Meer 1759, 1822 (*winteron meare*, ~ *mare* 1577, *Winterton mear* 1601, ~ *meare* 1647, 1674, ~ *Meere* 1668, ~ *Meer* 1693, 1712, ~ *meer* 1706 'the boundary with Winterton', *v.* **(ge)mǣre**); *Wynterton mearbalk* 1601, *v.* **(ge)mǣre, balca** 'a strip of ground left unploughed to mark the boundary between adjacent strips of the common field', *Winterton mearforde* 1601, *v.* **marfur** 'a boundary furrow'); Winterton Lane 1798 (the last four named from the adjoining parish of Winterton).

(b) *Andersons Close* 1667 (from the surn. *Anderson*, cf Henry *anderson* 1577, with **clos(e)**); *Bidall Marford* 1601, 1606 (cf. *Grafurthe Bydale* in Waltham parish, PN L **4**, 189, where it is suggested that **bydale** probably means 'the share of land belonging to the village', from **bȳ** 'a village' and **deill** 'a share of land' a Scand compound; *Marford* is a variant form of *marfur*); *Birepit'* 112 (m14), e13 (1311), *Birpit* e13 (1311) (*v.* **pytt**); *Blindewelle* e13 (1311), *-well'* e13 (m14) ('the concealed, overgrown spring', *v.* **blind, wella**); *Brak'ndale* 1601 (*v.* **brakni, deill**); *Burnewell Dale* 1659 (*v.* **wella, deill**; the first el. is uncertain); *Butt'croft* 112 (m14), *Butercroft* e13 (1311), *Buttercroft* e13 (m14), *Butcroft dale* 1601, *Butcroftedale* 1606 ('the croft which produces good butter', *v.* **butere, croft** with **deill** added. The 17th century forms seem to be corrupt); *the Careside* 1647, *Carnooke* 1659 (*v.* **kjarr, sīde, nōk**); y^e *Causey* 1700 (*v.* **caucie**); y^e *commons* 1601, *the* ~ 1606; *the Cony ynges* 1601 (*v.* **coni** 'a rabbit', **eng** 'meadow, pasture'); *criftinge beck* 1577 (*v.* **bekkr** and *v.* following f.n.); *Criftins* 1601, *Chriften* (sic) 1606, *the chriftings, Criftinges* 1647 (*v.* **cryfting** 'a small croft'); *the crowgarth* 1657 (*v.* **crāwe, garðr**); *fossatum iuxta*

publicam stratam 13 (m14); *Roxbydyke* 1395 (*v.* **dīc, dík,** cf. *Diclande* e13 (1311)
(*v.* **land**) and *Diclanges* Hy3 (m14) (*v.* **lang** 'a long strip of land')); *Dicken hole*
1659; *dowhill hill* 1601, *Dowhill* 1606 (*v.* **hyll**; the first el. may be ME *dawe* 'a
jackdaw'); *Dudman Hill* 1601, *Dodman close* 160 (no doubt from the surn. *Dodman*,
Dudman with **hyll** and **clos(e)**); *Edwards Close* 1659 (from the surn. *Edwards*, cf.
Christopher *Edwardes* 1616 *Inv*); *Far Close* 1658, *Nether farr Close* 1679 (self-
explanatory); *campo de Roxby* 13 (m14), *the feilds of Roxbie* 1606, *the feildes of
Roxby* 1668, ~ ~ *of Roxbye* 1671 (*v.* **feld,** referring to the open fields of the village);
Fladkebec e13 (1311), *-bek'* e13 (m14), *Flaggbeck* 1577, *Flagbek* 1601, *flaghebecke*
1606, *Flagg Beck* 1700 (the first el. of the earliest forms is uncertain; the later ones
suggest ME **flagge** 'a marsh plant such as the iris'; the second el. is **bekkr**); *the
widow Fowlers Close* 1659; *Foxdale* 1606 ('fox valley', *v.* **fox, dalr**); *Gildale* 1601;
Grayston Hill 1659; *Hellecroft* 1287 (perhaps a derogatory nickname, *v.* **hell, croft**;
Helli-, Hellybriggs 1659; *Hille* 1322 (p); *Holewelle* e13 (1311), *-wele* e13 (m14) (*v.*
hol 'a hollow', **wella**); *Hugge dich* e13 (1311) (*v.* **dīc,** the first el. obscure); *Karlhow*
1272 (p) (*v.* **karl** 'a freeman of the lower class', **haugr** 'a hill, a mound'); *Kirkbanck*
1659 (*v.* **kirkja, banke**); *terra Lamberti* 13 (m14) ('Lambert's land', from the
ContGerm pers.n. *Lambert*, which was common in the medieval Low Countries); *the
landdike* 1601 (*v.* **land, dík**); *the land drean* 1700; *Langedich* e13 (1311) (*v.* **lang,
dīc**); *Laydyke* 1647; *the lordes dale* 1601, 1606 (*v.* **hlāford, deill**); *Lowfields Close*
1659; *the lowe streeate* (sic) 1647; *the lynges* 1647 (*v.* **lyng** 'heather'); *Marforead*
(sic) 1647 (*v.* **marfur**); *ad mariscum* 13 (m14); *merchauntte Howse* 1535–46; *Medail*
e13 (1311) (*v.* **deill**); *Musedail* e13 (1311), *-dailes* e13 (m14), *-daill'* Hy3 (m14) (*v.*
mūs 'a mouse', **deill**); *Neudail* 112 (m14), e13 (m14), *Neuedale* e13 (1311) (*v.* **nīwe,
deill**); *the Nine acres* 1659; *Norhiby* (sic) 1272 (p) (literally '(the place) north in the
village', *v.* **norð, í, bȳ,** denoting X who lives in the north of the village, a common
formation in L); *normandye commones* (sic) 1577 (named from Normanby in the
adjacent parish of Burton upon Stather); *Normires, -myres* 1659 (*v.* **norð, mýrr**); *the
north Inges* 1647 (*v.* **eng**); *Northpicheshers, -pikesers* e13 (1311), *Pikesdail* e13
(l31), *Pikesholes* 13 (m14) (the first el. is probably the ME surn. *Pike,* with **ears**
'buttock' in the transferred topographical sense 'a rounded hill', **deill** 'a share of
land' and **hol** 'a hole, a hollow'); *Outlandes* e13 (*v.* **ūt, land,** presumably denoting
selions lying on the outskirts of the village); *clausa vocat Padmore* 1622 (*v.* **padde**
'a toad', **mōr** 'a marsh'); *Places close corner* 1647 (from the surn. *Place* with
clos(e)); *le Priors garthe* 1545, *Priour Garth* 1546, *the Pryor Garth* 1647 (named
from the *Prior* of Drax Priory with **garðr**); *Pytenge* 1589–91 (*v.* **pytt, eng**); *Pywell
dale* 1647 ('the spring where magpies are found', *v.* **pie, wella** with **deill**); *Reddinge*
1649 (probably 'the clearing', *v.* **rydding**); *Reysbye beck* 1577, *risbie becke* 1606 (*v.*
bekkr), *reysbye Dale* 1577 (*v.* **deill**), *Reysby mare* 1577 (*v.* **(ge)mære** 'a boundary,
land on or forming a boundary', all named from Risby *supra*); *Roscalbecke* 1577
(from the ON pers.n. *Hrosskell* or the derived surn. *Roskell* and **bekkr**); *Rosewelbek'*
e13 (m14) (the first el. may be ON **hross** 'a horse', with **wella** and **bekkr**); *Ryseby
Felde* 1541, *Risebye feild* 1647 (*v.* **feld,** referring to the open field of Risby *supra*);
Scorbrouges headland 1601 (named from the *Scorbrough* family, cf. William
Scorburgh 1413 Fine, and **hēafod-land** 'the head of a strip of land left for turning the
plough'); *duor' toft' in Risbie voc' Skipwithinge* 1618–20 (from the surn. *Skipwith*

and **þing** 'property, premises'); *Smith headland* 1601, *Peter Smythe close* 1606 (named from the *Smith* family, cf. Thomas *Smyth* 1594 *Inv*, Peter *Smyth* 1601, 1606, with **hēafod-land** and **clos**(e)); *the South clyffe* 1601, ~ *south cliffe* 1606 (*v.* **clif**); *the south feild* 1647 (one of the open fields of the village); *southolme close* 1667 (*v.* **sūð, holmr**); *Southlanges* 14 (m14) (*v.* **sūð, lang** 'a long strip of land'); *Stanhill'* 112 (m14), e13 (1311), *stanghyll gate* 1577, *Stannell gate* 1601 (*v.* **gata**), *high stannell* 1601, 1606, ~ *Stanell* 1647 ('the stony hill', *v.* **stān, hyll**; the 1577 form is clearly corrupt); *regiam stratam* e13 (1311), *publicam stratam* 13 (m14), *the Queens street* 1601 (self-explanatory); *Sutherdail* e13 (1311) ('the southern share of land', *v.* **sūðer, deill**); *Swanneland* 1547 (the first el. is uncertain, but is likely to be the surn. *Swan*(n)); *Thealby Common* 1647 (from Thealby in the neighbouring parish of Burton upon Stather); *Thedgate* e13 (1311) (probably 'the peoples' road, the public road', *v.* **þēod, gata**); *Thornedale* 1601 (*v.* **þorn, deill**); *the thorne tree* 1647 (self-explanatory); *the Towneside* 1606, ~ *towneside* 1647; *Wansland* 1545 (the first el. is obscure); *warannum apud Salclif* 1275 ('Sawcliffe warren', *v.* **wareine**); *warlotes* 1601 (this name is discussed in detail in PN L **2**, 67–68, where it is pointed out that etymologically *warlott* (OE ***warhlot**) seems to refer to a lot, a share or an allotment of land subject to some form of defence or protection. A *warlot* would seem to have been a piece of land assessed to a specifically defined payment of geld. This f.n. had not been noted at all in the EPNS survey prior to the example in PN L **2**. Now we have at least eight instances of the term); *Wrangelande* e13 (1311) ('the crooked selion', *v.* **vrangr, land**).

Scawby

SCAWBY

> *Scaleby* (3x) 1086 DB, Hy2 (c1330) *R* (p), 1194 CurR, 1229 FF, 1282 Cl, 1286 Abbr
>
> *Scaleberia* 1090–1100 (1401) YCh vi, 1100–08 (17) ib, 1147–53 ib
>
> *Scallebi* (5x) 1086 DB, (2) c1115 LS, c1128 (12) ChronPetro, 1136–40 (1464) Pat, 1150–60 Dane, 1163 RA i, 1166, 1167 P, 1185 Templar, 1188, 1190 P (p) *et freq* to c1275 RA ix (p), *-bya* 1146 RA i, *-by* 1220 Welles, 1232–33 Fees, 1232 Cur, 1242–43 Fees, 1243–50 RA iv, p1250 *Nelthorpe*, 1254 ValNor, 1267 Ch, 1272 *Ass*, 1273 Ipm, 1275 ib *et freq* to 1428 FA, *Skallebi* Hy2 (1464) Pat, *-by* 1202 Ass, 1274 Cl, 1281 QW, 1321 Ipm, 1325 FA, 1327 Ipm, *Schallebi* 112 Fulstow (p), 1273 Ipm, 1275, 1276 RH
>
> *Scallabi* (2x) c1115 LS *Scallbi* c1115 LS, 1610 Speed
>
> *Scalby* c1279 RRGr, 1316 *Nelthorpe*, 1321 RA ii, 1325 Pat, 1331 Ipm, 1332 *SR*, 1338 Ipm, 1341 Pat, 1345 Pap, 1346 FA, 1347 Pat,

1350 Orig *et freq* to 1752 LAAS iii, (~ *alias Scawby*) 1608, 1663, 1679 *Nelthorpe,* (~ *otherwise Scawby*) 1796 *ib, -bi* c1300 RA iii, *-bye* 1537 *AOMB 209,* 1544 LP xix, *Skalby* 1327 *SR,* 1383 Ipm, 1383, 1388 Peace, 1393 Cl, 1402 FA, 1477 Cl, 1519 DV, 1545 LP xx, *Schalby* 1347 Pap

Scawbie 1535 VE iv, 1577, 1581, 1595, 1601 *Nelthorpe,* (~ *als Scalbie*) 1598, 1603, 1614, 1534 *ib, Skawby* 1539 *AD, Scawby* 1546 *ib,* 1552 Pat, 1584, 1593, 1613 *Nelthorpe,* 1616 Hall *et freq,* (~ *alias Skaulbye*) 1563 *Nelthorpe,* (~ *als' Scalby*) 1623, 1664, 1675, 1682, 1710 *ib,* (~ *otherwise Scalby*) 1755 *Yarb, -bye* 1551 Pat, 1555, 1691 *Nelthorpe*

'Skalli's farmstead, village', *v.* **bȳ**, the first el. being the Scand pers.n and byname *Skalli,* a name belonging to ON *skalli* masc. 'a bald head, a bald-headed person'. Dr Insley points out that as a pers.n., *Skalli* is known from ON and OSw, and is quite frequent as a byname in both Iceland and Norway. In Denmark it does not seem to be independently attested, but it forms the first el. of p.ns. in **-ruth** and **-thorp**, *v.* B. Jorgensen, *Stednavne ordbog,* 2. udgave (Copenhagen, 1994), s.nn. *Skallebolle, Skallerup.* Note that the early forms of Scawby show the ODan genitive in *-a-.* The three forms in *-beria* are paralleled in the same documents by similar forms for Roxby and Tealby. They are not supported elsewhere and must be considered "sports". In the neighbouring parish of Broughton we have the forms *Scalehou* a1176 Goke and *Scallehou* 1205–23 ib, 'Skalli's mound', *v.* **haugr**, the first el. being the same ODan pers.n./byname as in Scawby. No doubt the *Skalli* of *Skal(l)ehou* was the same person as the *Skalli* of Scawby.

STURTON

Straitone 1086 DB

Stratone (5x) 1086 DB, *Stratton* 1203 Ass, (~ *iuxta Scalby*), 1373 Peace, (~ *on the Streate*) 1535–43 Leland, *Straton'* 1225 Cur

Strettun 1212 Fees, *-ton* 1240 RRG, 1275 Ipm, 1281 QW, 1287 *Ass,* (~ *iuxta Scalleby*) 1316–20 *Nelthorpe,* 1325 Pat, (~ *"by" Skalleby*) 1327 Ipm, 1327 *SR et passim* to 1536–37 Dugd vi, *Stretun'* 1226 Cur

Stirton' (~ *iuxta Scalby*) 1388 Peace, (~ *juxta Scalbye*) 1538–39 Dugd vi, *Stirton* 1552 Pat

Sturton 1552 Pat, (~ *Iuxta Scaweby*) 1597, 1669 *Nelthorpe et passim Stourton* 1619, 1623, 1661 *Nelthorpe*

'The farmstead, village near the Roman road', v. strǣt, tūn. The hamlet is situated a little to the east of Ermine Street. There are two other Sturtons in L — Great Sturton (LSR) and Sturton by Stow (LWR) — each on a Roman road.

ALDHAM PLANTATION. BEAULAH WOOD, named from the family of John *Bewley* 1669 *Nelthorpe* and Mary *Belah* c1692 *ib*. ELM CROFT. GATE HO. GILLIATE GRAVE, cf. *Thomas Gilliat stackgarth* 1689 *Nelthorpe* (v. ME **stak-garth** (ON **stakkr**, **garðr**) 'a stack-yard). Thomas *Gillyatt* is also named in a document of 1657 *Nelthorpe*. HIGHLAND DRAIN. HIGH WOOD. LIDYETT'S GAP (local). LINCOLN HILL, 1824 O. MILL PLACE, WINDMILL (disused), cf. *molendino de Scallebi* 1185 Templar, *Wyndmiln* 1593, *the Wynd Mylle* both *Nelthorpe*, *Milnfurland* 1577, *the milne Furlonge* 1601, *Millfurlong* 1662 all *Terrier, Millfurlong* 1669, 1685, *millfurlong* 1687 all *Nelthorpe*, 1697, 1700 *Terrier* (v. **furlang**), *Mill-gate* 1675 *Nelthorpe* (v. **gata**), *the Milne hill* 1636, ~ *mill hill* 1671 both *Nelthorpe* (v. **hyll**). MOOR FM, *Moor Fs.* 1824 O, cf. *the more* 1601 *Terrier*, ~ *Moore* 1691 *Nelthorpe, more banke* 1662 *ib* (v. **banke**), *morfurlandes* 1577 *Terrier* (v. **furlang**). NEW FM. THE NUTSHELL. RAILWAY PLANTATION, self-explanatory. RED WELL (local), *Near the vicarage farm is Red Well, a strong chalybeate spring* 1842 White. SCAWBY BROOK, 1824 O, *Scawby brook* 1826 White, *Scawbie becke* 1601 *Terrier, a beck called Scawbie beck* 1602 *Nelthorpe, Scaubie becke* 1611 *Terrier, Scalby becke, Scawby beck* 1611 *Nelthorpe*, v. **bekkr**. SCAWBY GRANGE, cf. *the grange house* 1674, ~ *Grange Close* 1671, *Grange Dale* 1710 (v. **deill**) all *Nelthorpe*. This is a late example of the use of **grange** for which v. *Santon Grange* in Appleby parish *supra*. SCAWBY HALL, *Scawby hall* 1826 White, *Hall Farm* 1838 *Nelthorpe*, cf. *athall' de Scalby* 1416 *ib* (p), *le Northallestede, le Southallestede* 1321 Ipm, *le Norhalle, le Southalle* 1331 ib, *Northalle, Southalle* 1347 ib, "the manor of" *Southall* 1350 Fine, *maneria mea de Southalle & Northalle in Scalleby* 1354 *Nelthorpe, Northall, Southall* 1377 *FF, the mannors of Southall and Westhall in Scauby* 1563 *Nelthorpe, Northall* "Manor", *Southall* "Manor" 1579–80 Lanc, self-explanatory; *stede* in the 1321 forms is OE **stede** 'the site of a building'. SCAWBY PARK. SHORT'S COVERT, presumably from the surn. *Short*. SILVERSIDES, 1674, 1687, 1695 *Nelthorpe, locum vocat' silversides close* 1671 *ib*, perhaps 'the hill side where silver plants grow', v. **seolfor**, **sīde**. STONEPIT WOOD, cf. *the stone pittes* 1669, ~ ~ *pitts* 1687, *stone pitt Close* 1684, *Stone Pitts Lane*

1676 all *Nelthorpe*, self-explanatory. STURTON GRANGE (lost), *Stirton juxta Scalbye, firma grang'* 1538–39 Dugd vi, *grainge de Stirton iuxta Scalbye* 1542 *AOMB 214*, *Sturton Grange* 1588, ~ *grainge* 1589, ~ *Grange* 1593, 1601 all Nelthorpe, it was a **grange** of Newstead Priory. SWAN'S HO, presumably from the surn. *Swan*. TOP FM. VICARAGE, *the Vicarage of Scawbie als Scalbie* 1598 *Nelthorpe, the Vicaridge house* 1606 *Terrier, the viccaridge of Scawbie als Scalbie* 1634 *Nelthorpe, The Viccaridg house* 1662, *one Vicarage house* 1697, *The Vicarage House* 1700, 1784, *A Vicarage house* 1706, *the Vicarage House* 1822 all *Terrier*. WALNUT HO. WELBURN PLANTATION.

FIELD-NAMES

Undated forms in (a) are 1838 *Nelthorpe*; those dated 1240–50 are RA iv; 1275 RH; 1287, 1328 *Ass*; 1332 *SR*; 1343 NI; 1377 *FF*; 1545 LP xxii; 1578–79 Lanc; 1577, 1601, 1606, 1662, 1697, 1700, 1706, 1822, 1888 *Terrier*; 1651 DCLeases; 1660 (c1690) *LindDep*; 1659, 1667, 1672, 1690 *Yarb*; 1661 *Featley*; 1683 Yarb; 1695 Pryme; all the rest are *Nelthorpe*.

(a) Back Cl (cf. *le backside* 1601); Bracken Hill (cf. *Bracken Garth* 1710, *v.* **brakni, garðr** 'an enclosure', as elsewhere in the parish); Branan Nooking; Brick yard Carr (*v.* **kjarr** 'brushwood', 'a bog, marsh overgrown with brushwood', as elsewhere in the parish); Broughton Cl (from the neighbouring parish of Broughton); Bull Pce 1888; Calf Garth (*v.* **garðr**); Carr, Carr Heads (*v.* **hēafod**), *Carrs* 1888 (*Le Ker* 1240–50, *the comon Carre* 1597, *yᵉ common carre* 1601, *the Carres* 1621, *Scalby Carr* 1623, *the Carr* 1630, 1681, *Scawbie Carrs* 1632, *the Carre* 1661, ~ *Carr of Scawby* 1670, ~ *Carrs of Scalby*, *Scalby Carr, the great carr* 1671, *Scawby Carr* 1674, *the Carrs* 1677, *Scawby great Carr* 1680 (*v.* **kjarr**); Causeway Carr 1786 (*v.* **caucie, kjarr**); Cottagers Carr 1774, Cottager's Carr 1822 (*the Cotchers Carre* 1624, 1660 (c1900), *Cottagers Carr* 1629, 1692, *Cotagers Carr* 1631, 1651, *le Cotgers Carre* (sic) 1669, *the Cotagers Carr* 1674, *a place there formerly called Haleham Carr & now or late knowne by the name of Cotagers Carr* 1681, *Cotgers or Cotagers Carr* 1710, *v.* **kjarr**; the first el. is self-explanatory, with the variant dial. *cotcher*, which is common in north L); Court house Plot; Top Cow Carr; Dike Cl (*v.* **dík**); Dolly Platts 1818, the ~ ~ 1821, Dolly Plot (the first el. is uncertain; the second shows variation between **plot** and **plat** 'a plot, a small piece of ground'); the East Fd 1822 (*est felde* 1577, *yᵉ Easte Feild* 1601, *the east feild* 1606, *the East-field* 1661, 1700, *the East Field* 1662, 1710, *oriental' Campo de Scawlby* (sic) 1671, ~ *campo de Scalby* 1673, *the East field* 1676, ~ ~ *feild* 1678, 1687, *the east fieldes, Orientali Campo de Scalby* 1680, *the east fieldes de Scalby or Scawby* 1684, *the east Feild* 1695, *yᵉ east Field* 1706, one of the great fields of the parish, cf. the West Fd *infra*, *v.* **ēast, feld**); 50 Acres (area 50a.0r.0p.); First, Second, Third Cl; Folly Lane 1822,

~ Cl (*v.* **folie**); Gunnells Carr 1833 (*Gunnell's Carr* 1710, named from the *Gunnell* family, cf. Anthony *Gunnill* 1662, and **kjarr**); Heads (cf. *the Headings* 1662, *Le Headings* 1701, *v.* **heveding**, which is discussed in PNL **2**, 14, where it is suggested that **heveding** is a derivative of **hēafod**, and which like **heved-land**, denotes places at the end of a ploughed field where the plough is turned); Hibaldstow Fd (cf. *Hybaldestoue Mare* 1240–5, *Hebelstow mere* 1577, *hibaldstowe mearfure* 1601, *Hibaldstowe Meare* 1662, *Hibaldstow meere* 1685, *Hybalstoe meare* 1697, *Hybaldstow meare* 1706, named from the neighbouring village of Hibaldstow, with (**ge**)**mǣre** 'a boundary', alternating once with **marfur** 'a boundary furrow'); Home Cl; Holme Hill Carr (*Holme Hill Carr* 1710, cf. *Holme Hill* 1623, 1676, 1698, 1709, *holme hill* 1672, *v* **holmr**, **hyll** with **kjarr**); Horse Fd 1888; Huntsman Moor; the Ings (Cl) 1761, the Ings (Lane) 1822, Ings 1888 (*Scawbie Inges* 1601, *le Comon Inges* 1620, *The Ings in Scawby* 1651, *the Ings* 1661, 1692, 1697, 1699, 1710, *the Inges* 1662, *le Inges de Scawlby* (sic) 1671, ~ ~ *de Scalby* 1677, *le Ings de Scalby* 1680, *Scawby Ings* 1698, *le Ingg Close* 1630, *the Ing Close* 1633, 1690, *the Ing Close* 1667, ~ *Ings Close* 1710 (*v.* **eng**); Lane Cl 1822; the Leys 1821 (*v.* **ley** (OE **lēah**) 'meadow, pasture'); Little Cl; Long Btm (*v.* **botm**); Long Cl (*ye long-close* 1700); Low Carr (*v.* **kjarr**); West Mill Fd; Moore Cl 1818, the Moor Cls 1821, Moor (Cl) (cf. *le Moreheads* 1646, *the more heades* 1662, *in ripe vocat more banke* 1673, (*v.* **mōr**, **hēafod**, **banke**); Moor Fm; Nine acres 1888; Nooken Hill, Nooking 1838 (*v.* **nōking**); Nun poke; Paddock; Pikerlys Cottage (*Betty Pikerley* is named in the document); Race Course; the Old Sankfoil Cl 1757, the Saintfoil Cl 1783 (*New, Old St Foyne Close* 1710, *Sankfoil, Saintfoil* and *St Foyne* are all variant forms of **sainfoin**); School Cl 1822, ~ Land 1838; Home, Middle, Top Scrubs 1888 (*the weste* ('waste') *Ground called Scalby Scrobbes* 1561–2, *Scauby Scrubbes* 1663, *Scawby Scrubbs* 1578–79, 1687, 1695, *pasturam vocat' the Shrubbs* 1661, *ye Scrubbes* 1669, *le Scrubs* 1704, *v.* **scrubb** 'a shrub, brushwood, a place overgrown with brushwood'); Seven acres 1888; Skarthe Lane (*v.* **skarð** 'an opening, a gap'); Spridlington Cl (*Sperlingker bek'* 1260–76, *le Spridlinge Carrbeck close* 1601, *Spridlingcarrbeck Close* 1629, *Spridlingcarrebeck Close, Spridleington becke* 1671. The earliest form suggests that the first el. is probably an OE pers.n. *Sperling* compounded with **kjarr** and **bekkr**. *Sperling* occurs on a coin of Eadwig (955–959), *v.* Veronica Smart, *Sylloge of Coins of the British Isles 28, Cumulative Index of Volumes 1–20*, London 1981, p. 68a, and a number of times in London, from the late 11th century, *v.* E. Ekwall, *Early London Personal Names*, Lund 1947, 62–64. The name has subsequently been associated with Spridlington in Aslacoe Wapentake LWR. Dr Insley, however, notes the absence of a genitive -*es* in the form of 1260–76 and points out that this would speak against the pers.n. as first el. He thinks it would be preferable to suggest that we are rather concerned with ME *sperling* < AN *espelanke, esperlinge* 'a smelt, a sparling' (*Osmerus eperlanus*). The second el. is a compound of **kjarr** and **bekkr**, denoting a stream in an area of marshland. Hence, he thinks the meaning of this name is 'the stream in an area of marshland where smelt were found'); Top Staven; Stone Hills (*Stone Hill'* 1601, *Stone-hill* 1661, 1700, 1706, *Stonehill* 1669, 1685, *Ston-hil* 1697, self-explanatory, *v.* **stān**, **hyll**); Sturton Cl (cf. *Campum de Sturton* 1618, *campum de* ~ 1619, *Sturton Hedge* 1577, 1597, ~ *hedge* 1601, 1661, 1669, 1685, 1692, 1706, *Sturton Long close* 1710, *Sturton mere* 1669, all named from Sturton *supra*, and *v.* **hecg**, **(ge)mǣre**); the Sucker Cl 1822 (*Sucker's close* 1710, presumably *Sucker* is a surn. here); Swannah Cl; Ten Acres 1888; Vinyard Cl 1888 (self-explanatory); Wash Dike Carr; West Cl (*west close* 1560); the West Fd 1822, 1838 (*in occidentali campo* p1250, *the west fealdes* 1577, *ociden' campum* 1578, *Campu' occidental' de Scawby, the weste feild* 1606, *occident' Campo de Scalby* 1660, *the West Feild* 1669, 1695, ~ *West field of Scawby als Scawlby* (sic) 1676, ~ *west field* 1681, 1700, ~ *West Field of Scawby* 1698, *y^e weste field* 1706, one of the great fields of the parish, cf. the East Fd *supra*, *v.* **west**, **feld**); Willow Garth (*v.* **garðr** and cf. *in the Wylewes de Stretton'* 1286, *in The Wiles* (sic) 1327, *in the Wyllues de Stretton* 1329, *in salnibus* 1332, *in the Wilnes* (-*n*- = -*u*-) 1343 all (p), *v.* **wilig**); Wood Side Cl.

    (b) *Alston Pit* 1240–50 (from the OE pers.n. *Alstān* and **pytt**); *cespites vocat' Bagges* 1646; *Barnards Leas* 1684 (from the surn. *Barnard*, cf. *Rychard Barnard* 1558 *Inv*, and **lea** (OE **lēah**) 'meadow, pasture'); *Ro: Barnes his Carre* c1670 (*v.* **kjarr**); *le beck* 1672 1673 (*v.* **bekkr**); *Bernards lane* 1669 (presumably from the surn. *Bernard*); *Blakemildis* 1240–50 ('the black earth', *v.* **blæc**, **mylde**); *bonnie-gapp-land* (sic) 1700, *Bonny-gapp* 1706; *Boyer's Carr* 1710 (named from the *Boyer* family, cf. William *Boyer* 1694, with **kjarr**); *Bridge gaytt* 1601 (*v.* **gata**); *Brigg Cawsey* 1629, 1660, ~ *Cawesey* 1647, ~ *Causey* 1647, cf. *uiam versus pontem Glaunfordie* 1240–50, *viam vocat' le Calcie* 1672 ('the causeway to Glanford Brigg (a neighbouring parish)', *v.* **caucie**); *Burton Lane* 1710 (presumably the lane to Burton upon Stather); *the Butt-mear fore* (sic) 1697 (*v.* **butte**, **marfur**), *ye butt-mear* 1700, ~ *Butt-meare* 1706 (*v.* **(ge)mǣre**); *due butte* (sic) 1416 ('two butts', *v.* **butte**); *the Carrcloses* 1647, ~ *Carre Closes* 1663, ~ ~ *closes* 1665, ~ *Carr Close* 1671, ~ *Carre furlandes* 1601, *Car furlonges* 1669 (*v.* **furlang**; *furland* is a common variant of *furlang* in north L), *cargates* 1577, *Cargates* 1662, *the Carr gate* 1687, *Carr Gate* 1712, *the carre gates or carre furlong* 1680 (*v.* **gata** 'a way, a road; land by a way or road'), *the Carreleses* 1647, *Carr leas* 1685 (*v.* **kjarr**, **læs** 'pasture, meadow-land'); *marisci vocat' Carreground* 1601, *Carrgrounde* 1672 (*v.* **kjarr**, **grund**); *the Caulfe buttes* 1601, *Calfe-butts* 1661, 1700, *Calfebuts* 1685, *calf-butts* 1697 (*v.* **calf**, **butte**); *Cawber-furlong* 1661, *Cawber* 1669, 1706, *Colbar* 1697; *le Chappell garthe* 1787 (*v.* **garðr**); *le Churchlane* 1691; *Clay Pitt close* 1710, *Claypitt marfur* 1687, *Clay pitt marfur* 1695 (*v.* **marfur**); *Clinke-Daile* 1661; *comen mer balke* 1577, *le Common meare* 1597 (*v.* **(ge)mǣre**, **balke**); *the Common* 1606, 1662, 1695, *ye comon* 1655, *Scawby Common* 1701; *le Common banke* 1646; *le common marfurrs* 1660, *the Common Marrfur* 1669, *Common Marrfur* 1701 (*v.* **marfur**); *the Comon pound* 1669, 1690 (*v.* **pund** 'an enclosure into which stray cattle were put'); *the Common sewer* 1662; *the corne feild* 1597, *ye cornefeild* 1662, *the Corne feild of Scalby* 1663, *the Corne feild* 1670, 1679, 1691, 1694, *the Cornfeild* 1675; *Cowdam Sike* 1647; *the Cowdike close* 1671; *Cowgates* 1685 (dial. *gate* (ON **gata**) 'right of pasturage'); *le Cowpasture* 1646, 1673, *Cowpasture* 1661; *Cream Poak Carr* 1710 (*Cream Poak* is a complimentary name for rich pasture); *Henrey Creasye Closes* 1601, *James Cressie close* 1662 (*Henrie Cresye* is mentioned in 1601); *William Dent close* 1692; *Dinker pittes* 1671, *Ducker pitts* 1680; *dow marsh* 1662 (*dow* may be from ME *dawe* 'a jackdaw'); *Eastbuttes* 1662 (*v.* **ēast**, **butte**); *the East Carres* 1616, *Scawby east carr* 1629, *the east Carr of Sturton* 1630, *the East Carr of Scalby* 1682 (*v.* **ēast**,

kjarr); *the east Inges* 1606, ~ ~ *Ings* 1662, *the Eastings* 1669, *the Easte Ings* 1697
(*v*. ēast, eng); *eringston becke* (sic) 1601 (the first part of the name is uncertain);
estebek' 1260–76, *ye East-Becks* 1661, ~ *East beck* 1674, *le East-Becke* 1680, *ye East
beck* 1695, *the East beck* 1712 (*v*. ēast, bekkr); *est inton' de Streton* (sic) p1250 (p)
(literally '(the place) east in the village', *v*. ēast, in, tūn, denoting a person who lives
in the east of the village. This is common Danish formation in L, cf. *Estiby* in West
Halton f.ns. (b) *supra*, but here the formation has been anglicised with OE tūn
replacing ODan bӯ); *fallow feilds* 1673 (*v*. falh 'arable land left uncultivated for a
year'); *campis de Scalby* 1451, *campum* ~ ~ 1540, *the feilde of Scawby, the field of
Scawby and Sturton* 1593, *the feilde of Scawby* 1597, *campo de Sturton & Scawby*
1601, *the Fieldes of Scalby* 1615, *Scawby Feild* 1659, *Campis de Scalbie* 1669,
campum de Scawby 1701, *Campis de* ~ 1707 (*v*. feld, referring to the open fields of
the village); *five acre dale* 1674 (*v*. deill); *five & twentie acres* 1678; *Fryer's Yard*
1710; *glamfordholm'* p1250, *Glamerholm'* 1606, *Glamerholmes* 1662, *Glammerham*
1669, *Glameram* 1685, 1697, *Glammerham* 1706 (presumably 'the raised land in
marsh belonging to Glanford Brigg', *v*. holmr); *le Grainge Leaz* 1613, *the grange
land* 1630 (from Scawby Grange *supra* with lǣs 'pasture, meadow-land' and land);
Greenes close 1674, *Close antiently called by the name of beck close & now by the
name of Greene close* 1684, *Greene Close* 1689, *Green's Close* 1710 (*v*. bekkr,
clos(e), with the alternative name probably from the *Green* family, cf. John *Grene*
1601, William *Greene* 1698); *a Cawsey called Half dike Cawsey* c1625 (*v*. caucie);
ye half oxgange 1687 (*v*. oxgang 'a measure of land, of 10 to 30 acres extent'); *the
hardland* 1666 (*v*. heard 'hard to till', land); *Hardland Hollbelly, the hardland* ~,
the Lower Hollbelly close 1666, *Holl belly Carr* 1666, *halebelly carre* (sic), *Hollbely
car* c1670, *Howle Bolly Carr* (sic) 1710 (*Hollbelly*, etc. is obscure); *hempe garthe*
1581 (*v*. hænep 'hemp', garðr); *vna pecia terre vocat A Hempland* 1641, *vnam
peciam Terre vocat a Hempland* 1661, *hempeland* 1669 (cf. prec.; *hempland* is a
common appellative in north L); *le herd Close* 1672 (perhaps from the *Hurd* family,
well-evidenced in the parish, cf. William *Hurd* 1673); *the highe meare* 1606 (*v*.
(ge)mǣre 'a boundary, land forming a boundary'); *high way close* 1710; *High Wood*
1710; *the hogegaile* 1601, *Hoggdaile Furlong* 1662, *hogs-dale* 1706 (*v*. hogg 'a hog',
deill; the first el., however, may be the ME surn. *Hogg*); *Homestead Closes* 1710; *a
balke or mairefair called the inge mairfaire* 1673 (*v*. eng, marfur 'a furrow marking
a boundary'); *the Ings beck* 1669 (*v*. eng, bekkr); *le Ivinge howse* 1646, *Ivinge house*
1683, *a certaine Tenement or toft . . . commonly called by the name of Ivinge house*
1691; *le Kilnehouse yeard* 1601 (self-explanatory); *Kingsbroad Land* 1674; *the
narrow Kings house* 1669, *Kings house land* 1674, *the Kings house lands* 1685
(presumably from the surn. *King*, cf. John *Kyng* 1556 *Inv*); *Kirkegarth* 1670, *Kirke
garth* 1679 (*v*. kirkja, garðr), *le Churchyard* 1691 (*v*. cirice, geard; the alternation
between the Scand and English forms is worthy of note); *Kirton gayt(t)* 1601, ~ *gate*
1662, 1668, 1695, ~ *way* 1676, *Kirton-gate* 1697 ('the road to Kirton in Lindsey', *v*.
gata); *Lakeing Close* 1710 (perhaps a place for play, sport, the first el. being a
derivative of ON leik 'play, sport', cf. Yorkshire dial. *laking* 'a holiday'); *le lyne
landes* 1578, *Lynelands* 1581, *Line lands* 1669, 1685, *ye Line lands* 1695 ('the selions
where flax grows, *v*. līn 'flax', land in the pl.); *Lop laine dike* 1597; *the Lords
marfar* 1697, *ye Lords marfurr* 1700, ~ ~ *Marfur* 1706 (*v*. marfur); *Luddingtons*

close 1687, *~ Close* 1695, *Lodington-close* 1697, *Ludington close* 1706 (named from the *Luddington* family, cf. Stephen *Luddyngton* 1543 *Nelthorpe*, William *Lodington* 1597 *ib*); *Manton Moore* 1687, *~ moore* 1687, *~ Dowils* (sic) 1669 (named from *Manton*, a neighbouring parish; *Dowils* is obscure); *Marfurrs* 1647, *metas* ('boundary') *vocat' mearfurrs* 1667, *quondam metam vocat' a marfurr* 1671, *the Marke fairs* (sic) 1685 (*v.* **marfur**); *John Mawmell garth ende* 1676 (*v.* **garðr**); *Meare-furland* 1661, *Mearfurlong* 1662, *mearefurlong* 1669, *the mear furlong* 1697 (*v.* **(ge)mǣre** 'a boundary', **furlang**, perhaps identical with the land called *Marfurrs supra*); *meddell dayle* 1577, *Middledail* 1662 (*v.* **meðal**, **middel**, **deill**, the English form apparently replacing the Scand); *meddlesse* 1577; *the mere heades* 1662 (*v.* **(ge)mǣre**, **hēafod** in the pl.); *the mile-tree* 1700, *y^e ~* 1706 (there is no indication of its situation); *milne furlong* 1764 (*v.* **myln**, **furlang**); *Nelthorpes Hollybally Carr* 1666 (Edward *Nelthorpe* is named in the document; cf. *Hardland Hollybelly supra*); *the New close* 1672, *Newclose* 1685; *Newstead Causey* 1660 (c 1900) ('the causeway to Newstead Priory (in Cadney, PN L **2**, 76–77)', *v.* **caucie**); *the North becke* 1674, *North Beck Closes* 1710 (*v.* **norð**, **bekkr**); *the North Closse* 1615, *~ ~ Close* 1618, 1669, *North Close* 1681 (self-explanatory); *ye northe croftes* 1577, *the north croftes* 1601, *North-Crofts* 1662, *a furlong called Northcroftes* 1662, *Norcroftes* 1669, *North Crofts* 1680, 1695 (self-explanatory, *v.* **norð**, **croft** in the pl.); *ye northe feald croftes* 1577 (the only reference to a North Field noted); *the north hedge* 1669, *ye North ~* 1695 (*v.* **hecg**); *north Inges* 1606, *North-Ings* 1661, *the North Inges* 1662, *~ ~ Ings* 1669, 1672, *~ ~ Inge* 1689 (*v.* **norð**, **eng**); *le Opening Close* 1671, 1680, *the open Ynge close* 1673, *Open Ings close* 1710 (*v.* **eng**; the sense of *Open* here is uncertain); *the parsonage Barne* 1603, *~ ~ barne* 1623, 1634; *the peas feild* 1679 (*v.* **pise**, **feld**); *the Pingle lying betweene the two Rivers of Ancholme* 1666 (*v.* **pingel** 'a small enclosure'); *pynson oxgan'* (sic) 1505 (from the surn. *Pinson* and **oxgang**); *Queens ferme medow* 1671, 1672; *rate pitt way* 1676 (perhaps 'the rat pit', *v.* **ræt**, **pytt**, with **weg** 'a way, a path'); *rouuelbec* p1250 (the first el. may well be an early form of the next name for *rouuel* is paralleled by four forms for Rothwell PN L **4**, 154–55, *v.* also **bekkr**); *ad fontes voc' Rothwelles* 1416, *Rodwellgate* 1606, *Rothwell gate* 1662, 1668 (this is perhaps to be compared with Rothwell, PN L **3**, 154–55, for which the meaning 'the spring by or in a clearing', *v.* **rōð**, **wella** has been suggested. The later forms have **gata** added signifying 'the way, path, road to *Rothwell*', *v.* **gata**.The surn. *Rothwell* has been noted in the parish, cf. William *Rowell* 1677 *Nelthorpe*); *the Round Close* 1710; *Rysshinge* 1545 (*v.* **risc** 'a rush', **eng** 'meadow, pasture'); *the Rush Close* 1666; *Rusling Carre* 1668 (from the surn. *Rusling*, cf. Thomas *Ruslyne* 1592 *Nelthorpe*, and **kjarr**); *Scawby wood* 1695; *Scoreway gate* 1690; *Scriviner's Carr* 1710 (named from the *Scrivener* family, cf. *widdow Scrivoner* 1657, Thomas *Scrivener* 1671, with **kjarr**); *Segbeck close, Sedge beck close* 1674, *Segg Beck Close* 1684, *Sedgebeckclose* 1684–97, *Segg Beck Close* 1691, *Segbeck* 1710 (*v.* **secg** 'sedge, reed, rush', in a Scandinavianised form *segg*, **bekkr**, with **clos(e)**); *ye shawside* 1700 (*v.* **sceaga** 'a small wood, a copse', rare in north L); *Sheepe dicke* 1601 (presumably a ditch for dipping sheep); *the shorte buttes* 1601 (*v.* **sceort**, **butte** 'a strip of land abutting a boundary, a short strip or ridge at right angles to other ridges, etc.'); *Short-stinting* 1661 (*v.* **stinting** 'an individual share of the common meadow'); *Smalbek'* 1416 (*v.* **smæl** 'narrow', **bekkr**); *Smale Dayle* 1577, *Small-Daile* 1661, *smalldale*

1669, *Small daile* 1685 (*v.* **smæl, deill**); *the south furlange* 1601; *Southermerland* 1577 (from **sūðerra** 'more southerly', **(ge)mǣre, land**); *Standing Close* 1681 (the meaning of *Standing* here is uncertain); *Start-brook* 1697; *Stanry-furlong* 1661, *Stanerow furlong* 1662, *Stafferah* (sic) 1669, *Staverow* 1676, *Staverah furlong* 1687, 1695, *Staverow* 1697, *Staverah* 1706 (the variant spellings all refer to one name, which is however obscure); *the Stigh* 1662 (*v.* **stīg** 'a narrow path'); *Stone-acres-Carr* 1606 (*v.* **kjarr**); *the stone pitts* 1687; *Cōēm viam vocat Le Streete* 1597, *the Streete* 1663, 1677 (*v.* **strǣt**, the reference being to Ermine Street); *the stuble feild* 1655, 1677; *Sturton Becke* 1601, *~ Beeck* 1662, *~ becke* 1669, *~ beck* 1695, 1700, *~ Beck* 1706 (*v.* **bekkr**), *Sturton gaytt* (*v.* **gata**), *Sturton mere* 1669 (*v.* **(ge)mǣre**; all three names refer to Sturton *supra*); *Suthecroft'* 1240–50, p1250, *Southcrofte* 1416, *south croftes* 1577, *the south-croftes* 1606, *South croftes* 1662, *le South Crofts* 1668, *South crofte* 1697, *South-crofts* 1700 (self-explanatory, *v.* **sūð, croft**); *Synderuelle Both* 1240–50 (apparently from ODan **bōth** 'a temporary shelter'), *Sinderwell thorne* 1597 (*v.* **sundor, synder** 'detached, apart', **wella**); *The Tangarth* 1621 ('the tanyard', *v.* **garðr**; *William Andrews of Scawby . . .Tanner* is named in the document); *Theakers oxgan* (sic) 1669 (*v.* **oxgang**; the first el. is *theaker*, Northern dial. for *thatcher*, used here as a surn., cf. Stephen *Theker* 1332 SR); *Thornesforde* 1240–50 (*v.* **þorn** in the gen.sg., **ford**); *Threescore Acres* 1710; *too dykes* 1577, *le two dykes* 1601, *quodam loco vocat towe dike Close* 1671, *the two dickes* 1697, *two-dikes* 1706 (self-explanatory, *v.* **twegen, dík**); *tursfeild Crosse* 1669, *Turuill crosse close* 1673, *Turvile Cross ~*1674, *Turvill Cross Beck Close* 1720 (perhaps 'the field haunted by goblins', *v.* **þurs** 'a giant, a goblin, a demon', with **cros**); *Twenty Acres Carr* 1710 (*v.* **kjarr**); *Urys Carre* 1666 (named from the *Urye* family, cf. Francis *Urye* 1647, with **kjarr**); *vicar pitt land* 1577, *Viccarpitt mearfurr* 1662, *Vicars-pitt Marfor* 1697, *vicar-pitt markfarrs* (sic) 1700, *yᵉ vicar-pitt marfur* 1706 (self-explanatory, *v.* **pytt marfur**); *Waller Close* 1695, 1710 (from the surn. *Waller* and **clos(e)**); *Warannum apud Schalleby* 1275 (*v.* **wareine** 'a game preserve, a rabbit warren'); *le west house* 1597; *west inges* 1577, *the west Ings* 1672, *~ West Inges* 1669 (*v.* **eng**); *Whitwater layne* 1608; *Wood-furlong* 1661, *Wodfurlonges* 1669, *Woodfurlongs* 1685 (cf. *Scawby Wood supra*); *Wykelane* 1505, 1601.

Waddingham

WADDINGHAM

Wadingeham (2x) 1086 DB, 1168, 1169, 1170, 1191, 1192, 1193, 1194 P all (p), 1177 ib, 1202 Ass (p), *Wadingeh'* 1250 Fees (p), *Waddingeham* 1200 FF

Wadingheheim c1115 LS

Waldingeham 1218 Ass, *Waudingeham* 1219 ib, 1225 Cur, 1226 FF (p), 1226 Cur (p)

Wadingham (2x) 1086 DB, (2x) c1115 LS, c1180 Bly, 1185 Templar, 1200 P (p), 1202 Ass (p), 1203 ib, 1203 Cur, 1203 Abbr, 1211 Cur, 1212 FF, 1212 P (p), 1242–43 Fees *et freq* to 1542 *AOMB 214*

Wadincham c1180 Bly, 1212 Fees, 1338 Pat

Wadigham 1203 FF, 1239 RRG

Wadyngham 1303 FA, 1305 Pat, 1316 FA, 1322 Cl, 1332 *SR*, 1328 Banco, 1334 Ipm, 1335 Pat, 1338 Cl, 1342 Fine, 1369 Ipm, 1380 Pat *et passim* to 1551 ib

Waddingham 1526 Sub, 1551 Pat, 1533 LP xix, 1576 Saxton, ~ (*als Staynton Waddingham*) 1601 *BRA 843*, *Waddingham* 1610 Speed *et passim*

Steynton' Wadingham 1293 Ass, *Staynton Wadyngham* 1327 *SR*, 1329 *Ass*, 1316 Orig, 1327 Banco, 1331 Pat *et passim* to 1497 *LWB*

Stainton Waddingham 1531, 1549, 1567, 1648, 1624 WillsStow, 1614, 1632, 1639 Admin

Stanton Waddingham 1593, 1605, 1661 *DCLB*

'The homestead, the estate of the Wadingas' from the gen.pl. *Wadinga* of the OE group name *Wadingas* 'the family, the dependents of *Wada*' and OE **hām** 'a homestead, an estate'. The form in *-heim* is from the cognate ON **heim**, while those in *Walde-*, *Waude-* are presumably errors. The same pers.n. is found in Waddington (Kest) and Waddingworth (LSR). The affix *Stainton* is from the lost village of that name in Waddingham parish.

STAINTON (lost)

Stantone (2x) 1086 DB, *-ton'* 1226 ChR (p), *-ton* 1535 VE iv

Staintone (2x) 1086 DB, *-ton* 1086 ib, *-tona* Hy2 RPD, *-ton'* 1180 P, 1185 Templar, 1202 Ass, eHy3 (14) Selby, *-ton* 1254 ValNor, 1272 *Ass*, 1300 Ipm, 1558 WillsStow, 1559 Pat, *-tun* 1223 *Foster*

Staynton 1281 QW, (~ *iuxta Wadyngham*) 1295 *Ass*, 1303 FA, 1303 Ipm, 1306, 1311 *KR*, 1316 FA, 1328 Banco, 1337 Abbr, 1346 FA, 1348 Pat *et passim* to 1551 ib

Steintuna c1115 LS, *-ton'* 1183, 1184, 1185, 1186, 1187, 1188 P, 1196 ChancR, John RPD, 1211 Cur, 1287 Ipm

Steynton' 1242–43 Fees, 1339 *HarlCh*

Stainton Hall Farm 1914 *Waite*

From OE **stān** 'a stone' and OE **tūn** 'a farmstead, a village', with stān replaced by the cognate ON **steinn** and identical in etymology with Stainton by Langworth (LSR), Stainton le Vale (LNR) and Market Stainton (LSR). Arthur Owen, "Roads and Romans in South-East Lindsey: the Place-Name Evidence" in *Names, Places and People*, Stamford 1997, p. 265, draws attention to the fact that these three places adjoin a Roman road or a prehistoric trackway, and the same is true of the lost Stainton here. It is likely that the "stone" in all four names refers to Romano-British remains rather than to the nature of the ground, which in any case is topographically inappropriate for *Stainton* in Waddingham.

ASH HOLT. BLACK DIKE, 1768 (1791) *LindDep Plans*, 1770 *Red*, 1824 O, ~ *Dyke* 1808, 1822 *Monson*. BRANDY WHARF, 1824 O. CLAY LANE, 1837 *TA*, *clay layne end* 1602 *Terrier*, cf. *claygate* 1399 *DC*, *Clay gates* 1638, 1662, *clay gaits* 1679, *claygate* 1700 all *Terrier*, self-explanatory, *v.* **gata**. CLIFF HO, cf. *Cliff* p1770 *Waite*, *The Cliff* 1837 *TA*, *Cliffe Farm* 1851 *Padley*. CLIFF LANE, 1837 *TA*. CLOCK HO, so named from the clock on the front wall of the house. THE COMMON (local), *the comons* 1602 *Terrier*, *the Common* 1625 *ib*, *Great Common* 1702 *MiscDon 275*, *Great, Little Common* p1770 *Waite*, *New, Old Common* 1837 *TA*. COMMONRIGHT DRAIN, *Common Right drains* 1837 *TA*; for commonright, *v.* NED s.v. *common* 5c 'the right of every citizen'. EAST FIELD, 1638, 1700 *Terrier*, 1702 *MiscDon 275*, *the East field* 1625, *the East feilde* 1679 both *Terrier*, *East fields* p1770 *Waite*, one of the great fields of the parish, *v.* **ēast**, **feld** and cf. *North field and Westfield Thornes* in f.ns. (b) *infra*. FURZE CLOSES, p1770 *Waite*, 1824 O, ~ *Close* 1767 *Stubbs*, *v.* **fyrs**, **clos(e)**. GREEN DIKE, 1767 (1791) *LindDep Plans*, *Greene dike* 1625, *Greene Dicke* 1662, ~ *dicke* 1668 all *Terrier*, *Green Dyke* 1824 O. IVY COTTAGE. KELK'S FM, 1851 Padley, named from the *Kelk* family, cf. Charles *Kelk* p1770 *Waite*. MARQUIS OF GRANBY, *Marquis of Granby Inn and Garden* 1837 *TA*. MOUNT PLEASANT, a complimentary nickname, but sometimes given ironically. NORTH RAMPER, *North, South Rampart* 1837 *TA*; *rampart* is a variant of *ramper*, a dial. word found in L for 'a raised road or way, the highway', *v. The Rampart*, PN L **1**, 92. OLD MILL, 1824 O, cf. *Molendino aquatico* 1510, 1520, *molendino aquatico* 1529, 1561, 1571, *vno molendino* 1601, 1627 all *DCAcct*, *Water Mylne platt* 1600 *BRA 843* (*v.* **plat**), ~ ~ *Close* 1638 *Terrier*, *Watermill close* 1678 *ib*, *Water Miln close* 1700 *ib*, *Water Mill Close* p1770 *Waite*, 1837 *TA* and *molendinum*

Thome filii Willelmi, Milnecroft 1212 FF, self-explanatory. OLD STONE PIT(S), *Stone Pits* p1770 *Waite,* cf. *Stonepit Cliff* 1837 *TA,* cf. *quareram* 1223 *Foster.* PARADISE FM, a common complimentary nickname, though sometimes it is used ironically. PARSONAGE, *the* ~ 1625, *parsonage* 1638, *One Parsonage house* 1662, *The Parsonage house* 1678, 1700 all *Terrier, Parsonage House and Garden* 1837 *TA, the South parsonage* 1678, *north parsonage* 1662, 1668, *A close where the North Parsonage was* 1706, *personage Peter* 1662, *Parsonage peter* 1679, *parsonage Mary* 1700, *parsonage Mary* 1700 all *Terrier;* there were two churches here. PEPPERDALE FM. SALLOWROW DRAIN, *Sallow Row Bank drain* 1837 *TA.* SOUTH CARR, 1638 *Terrier,* 1696 *Red,* 1706 *Terrier,* 1743, 1760 *Red,* 1767 *Stubbs,* 1770 *Red,* 1784 *Monson,* 1795 *Red,* 1837 *TA, Waddingham South Carr* 1653 LNQ x, *v.* **sūð, kjarr** and cf. north carr in f.ns. (a) *infra.* TOLLGATE FM, cf. *Toll Bar Cliff* 1837 *TA.* WADDINGHAM BECK, 1770 *EnclA, Attebeck' de Wadyngham* 1295 *Ass, Atte Beke* 1327 *SR, atte Beck'* 1332 *ib, atte Bek* 1343 NI all (p), *the Becke* 1638 *Terrier,* ~ *Beck* 1678 *ib, v.* **bekkr.** WADDINGHAM CARRS, 1824 O, *le Wadyngham carre* 1428 AASR xxix, *Waddyngham Carre* 1538 *AOMB 409 the Carrs* 1602, 1678 *Terrier, yᵉ Carr* 1709 *Foster, (the) Carrs,* 1770 *EnclA,* 1776 *Red, The Carr Farm* 1861 *Padley, v.* **kjarr,** in both the sg. and pl. WADDINGHAM GRANGE, *one close called the Grange* 1600 *BRA 843, the Grange* 1638, 1700 *Terrier, Grange* 1824 O. This is apparently a late example of the use of **grange,** common in north L, for which *v. Santon Grange* in Appleby parish *supra.* WADDINGHAM HAYS, *terra super Micle* ('big') *haas* Hy2 *DC, super haas* 1223 *Foster, Middle Hase Close, Top Hase Barn* 1837 *TA, a close formerly called . . . Fir Close . . . but now called the Hase* 1838 *MiscDon 275.* This is a difficult name for which no plausible etymology can be suggested. WADDINGHAM HOLMES, *Hlom* (sic) 1212 FF, *holme* 1223, *the Holmes* 1625 *Terrier,* ~ *holmes* 1662 *ib, Waddingham Holmes* 1824 O, *v.* **holmr** 'an island, higher ground amidst the marshes' chiefly in the pl. WINDMILL, *yᵉ Wynmillne* 1602 *Terrier,* cf. *Millhill* 1678 *ib.* WOOD'S HOUSES, from the surn. *Wood,* cf. Thomas *Wood* 1642 LPR.

FIELD-NAMES

Undated forms in (a) are 1837[2] *TA.* Forms dated Hy2, 1380, 1399 are *DC;* 1212 FF; 1223, 1306[1], 1336 *Foster;* 1306[2] Selby; 1327 *SR;* 1343 NI; 1384, 1551 Pat; 1395 Peace; 1525–46 *MinAcct;* 1542 *AOMB 214;* 1568, 1624 LNQ x; 1593, 1605 *DCLB;* 1600 *BRA 843;* e17, 1764,

1784[1], 1808, 1822 *Monson*; 1602, 1625, 1638, 1645, 1662, 1668, 1678, 1679, 1695, 1700, 1706, 1784[2] *Terrier*; 1683 *Nelthorpe*; 1696, 1736, 1743, 1760, 1767, 1770[2], 1775, 1776, 1777, 1795 *Red*; 1702[1], 1704, 1838 *MiscDon 275*, 1702[2] *Cragg*; 1715, p1770, 1797, 1825, 1829 *Waite*; 1774, 1786, 1797, 1811 Red; 1768 (1791) *LindDep Plans*; 1770[1], 1848 *EnclA*; 1828 Bry; 1833 *Ballett*; 1837[1] *MiscDep 74*; 1851, 1860 *Padley*.

(a) Abey's Cliff (from the surn. *Abey* and **clif**); the Ace Fd 1770, Ace Cl p1770 (*the great, the litle Ace* 1625, perhaps to be identified with Waddingham Hays *supra*, cf. *the South Ace* in (b) *infra*); America (a nickname of remoteness, the field being near the parish boundary); Banks (*v.* **banke**); Barn and Car (*v.* **kjarr** 'brushwood, marsh, bog overgrown with brushwood', as elsewhere in this parish); Barn and Crew Yd (Modern English dialect *crew* 'a pen, hut, hovel'); Barn Carr 1860 (*v.* **kjarr**); Far, Near Berridge Cl (named from the *Berridge* family, cf. Thomas *Berrigg* 1674 *Terrier*); Blacksmith's Shop Cl; Boorham Yd p1770 (presumably from a surn.); Bottom Cl; First, Second Brigg lane Cl; Brown Carrs p1770 (cf. *Broynhevedland* (sic) 1339, *Browns headland* 1625, *the Browne head land* 1662, 1668, *Brown Headland* 1679, from the surn. *Brown* with **hēafod-land** 'the head of a strip of land left for turning the plough'); Butcher Kirk Acre (from the surn. or occupational name *Butcher* and *v.* Kirkacres *infra*); The Butts (probably *v.* **butt** 'an archery butt'); Bottom, Top Captains Common; the Carr Cl 1770[1], the Carr Side 1784[2] (*v.* Waddington Carrs *supra*); the Cart Way 1760 (1704, 1743, *le Cart way* 1696); River Cess (sic); Chambers Bottom, ~ Cliff, Chambers' Top Cl (from the surn, *Chambers*); Churchyard Garth 1797 (*v.* **garðr** 'an enclosure'); Clark's Carr 1860 (from the occupational name *clerk* or the surn. *Clark* with **kjarr**); (Top, Upper) Clay Cl; the Old Street called the Cliff Road 1770[1] (no doubt a reference to Ermine Street); Cockpit Cl p1770, Cock Pit Cl ('a place where cock-fights were held'); Colleywell Cl p1770, Collywells (*Koliwell'* 1212, *Colliwells Furlonge* 1602, perhaps 'the charcoal spring' *v.* **cōlig** 'pertaining to charcoal', **wella**); Constable Ings (*v.* **eng** 'meadow, pasture', as elsewhere in this parish; the first el. may refer to the village *constable*, or be the derived surn. *Constable*); Cottage and Common; Cow Cl; the Cow Fold 1770[1], 1784, Cow Fold 1768 (1791), 1848, Cowfold; Far, Near Dawson's Cl (named from the *Dawson* family, cf. . . . . *Dawson* (no forename) p1770); Far Bottom denting, Near bottom ~, Far top ~, Mear top ~; Dove Croft Cl p1770, Dove Cote Cl, ~ ~ Yd; The eight acres; Far Cl; Feeding Cl; the Ferry Boat 1786; Fir Cl (cf. Waddingham Hays *supra*); Fish Pond; Fitt Lane (*v.* **fit** 'grassland on the bank of a river'); the Five Acres 1838; Fosters Cl p1770 (no doubt from the surn. *Foster*); Four Swaiths 1760 (*v.* **swǣð**, ME **swathe** 'a strip of grassland'); Fourteen feet drain; Fowler Cls p1770, West Fowlers Bottom (no doubt from the surn. *Fowler*); Green Yd; a certain place called Groundless Wells 1760, Ground Wells (*Groundless Wells* 1696, *place called Groundless Wells* 1743 (presumably 'the bottomless springs'); Hall Cl p1770, 1837[2] (*hall close* 1602, *Hall Close* 1638, 1678, 1700); Hanson Bottom, ~ Hill (from the surn. *Hanson*); Hill Cl p1770, 1837[2], First Hills Cl 1837[2], Second hill side cl; Hoggatt Hill; Holcroft; Near, South Hollands Cliff (named from the *Holland* family, cf. *Mr Holland* 1797 *Red* with **clif**); Holmes Carr close 1774 (*Holmcar* 1339, *Holme Carre* 1625, *holme carre* 1679, *v.* **holmr**, **kjarr**); North,

South Holme Cliff; North, South Holmes Cl (*the Holme Close* 1625); The Holmes Farm 1851 (for the f.ns. in Holme(s), *v.* Waddingham Holmes *supra*); home carr 1811, Home Car; Home Cl p1770, 1860, (Far, Second, Third, Fourth) Home Cl, Home Close Bottom 1837[2], North, South Home Cl 1851 (*home Close* 1706, and *v.* Upper Cl *infra*); Home Paddock; Hop Croft, ~ Yd; Hornsby Cl p1770 (from the surn. *Hornsby*, cf. . . . . *Hornsby* p1770 *Waite* (no forename)); Horse Btm (*v.* **botm**); Inn Car 1770[2] (*Ingge Carre* e17, *v.* **eng, kjarr**); Intake (*v.* **inntak**); North, South Isaac Walk (from the surn. *Isaac*, with **walk** denoting land used for the pasture of animals, especially sheep, hence the common *Sheepwalk*); Jackhill Cl; Joshua Cl (named from the *Joshua* family, cf. . . . *Joshuas* (sic) p1770 *Waite* (no forename)); Kelah Cl (presumably from the surn. *Kelah*); Kelsey Ferry Rd 1770[1], 1837[2], 1848 (from South Kelsey PN L **3**, 34); Kirkacres p1770, Great, Little Kirk Acres (*Kirkeacra* 1212, *kirkacre* 1223, *Kirk Acres* 1678, *v.* **kirkja, æcer**); Kirton Lane (*viam de Kirketon'* 1212, *uiam q' extendit uersus Kyrketon'* 1223, *Kyrton gate* 1602, *Kirton* ~ 1625, 1662, ~ *gaite* 1679, 'the road to Kirton in Lindsey', *v.* **gata**); Lime Kiln Cliff p1770, Limekiln ~, Lime Kiln Cl 1829; Little Car (Btm) (*v.* **botm** 'a bottom, a valley bottom'), Little Car first Hill side (*lytle carre* 1602, *little Carr furlong* 1678, 1700, *v.* **kjarr**); Little Cliff; Little Lane; Lock Carr p1700, 1822, ~ Car 1808 (a reference to a Lock on the New R. Ancholme); Long close Top, ~ ~ Bottom; Long, Short Holmes (*the longe holmes* 1602, *v.* **holmr**); Long Walk (*v.* **walk**); South Low Cl 1775; Far , Near Malt Cross (*ad crucem Matillidis* 1212, *Maud Crosse* 1638, *the maud* ~1662, *Maud Cross* 1678, ~ *Crose* 1679, *mead Crosse* 1700 (from the ME fem pers.n. *Mahald, Mahalt, Maud*, a name of ContGerm origin (MLatin *Matilda*, West Frankish *Maht-hildis*) and **cros**); Meadow Btm (*v.* **botm**); Magginson's Cl 1829, Megginsons Cow Cl, Megginsons Hill, Meggitson Cliff (named from the *Meggison* family, cf. Clement *Moggison* (sic) 1702 *MiscDon 275*, Clement *Meggison* 1706 *Cragg*); Middle Carr 1808, 1822; Middle Cl 1837[1], 1838, Middle Cl (Btm), Far, Middle Cl; Miss Belton's Cl; Monks House Cl p1700, Monks House Spring Cl (*munkhouse* 1399, *Munks house* 1602, *Monks House* 1625, *the Monke hous* 1638, *the monx* ~ 1662, *Monke* ~ 1678, *Monk* ~1700, perhaps from the monks of Selby Abbey, which held land in Waddingham); Monson Cl 1770[1], p1770 (John Lord *Monson* was a landowner in 1770[1]); Top Moody Common (from the *Moody* family, cf. Joseph *Moody* named in the same document); Moors Cl p1770, 1837[2], Bottom, Far, Near, North East, North West, South East, South West, Top Moor, North Moore 1770[1], (Far, First) Moors, Moore Cl 1837[1] (*more* 1602, *the Moore* 1638, cf. *ly mor' furlang* (sic) 1380, *the moore furlong* 1625, *the moor furlong* 1700, *Moore Cawsey* 1702[1] (*v.* **caucie**), *the Common Moore* 1625, *the Moor Common* 1702[1], *the Moreheades* 1602); Nabcroft p1770 (*v.* **croft**), The Nabbs (*v.* **nabbi** 'a knoll, a hill'); Far, Near Naylor's Cl (cf. *nailor nooke* 1662, *Nalor Nooke* 1697, named from the *Naylor* family, cf. W[m] *Naylor* 1837[2] *TA*); New drain; The Nine Acres 1838; North Bank 1760 (*North bancke* 1696, *the North Bank* 1743, *v.* **banke**); the North Carr 1770[1], 1784[2], North Carr p1770, 1795, 1833, 1851, *the north carr* 1797, North Car 1837[1], North Car dyke (*le Northker* 1384, *mariscum in le North car* 1399, *Waddingham North Carr* 1558, *North Carre* e17, *the north Carr* 1602, ~ *north Carre* 1605, *the North* ~ 1625, *North Carr* 1638, *the North Carrs* 1706, *v.* **norð, kjarr** and cf. South Carr *supra*); Far, First, Middle North Cliff (*v.* **clif**); North Cl 1767; North Hills p1770, Far, Little, Near North Hill (*Northil, Northille* 1399, *the North Hill* 1638, ~ *north hill* 1662, 1700,

North Hill 1678, *v.* **norð, hyll**); (Top) Nursery Cl; Occupation Rd; Old Mdw 1760, Oadmeadow (sic) 1811 (*Odd Meadow* (sic) 1696, 1743, *Old Meadow* 1743); Orchard; Osier Holt 1837², 1851 (*v.* **holt**); Owerby Bridge Rd (from Owersby PN L 3, 78); Owstons New Ho 1828 (presumably from the surn. *Owston*); Paddock; Penny Bar House and Garden; Pinfold (*v.* **pyndfald**); Pingles p1770, 1777, Pingle (East, West) (*v.* **pingel** 'a small enclosure'); Plantation; Poor Cl; Primitive chapel; Race Course; Raisin Rd 1770¹, Rasen Rd ('the road to Market Rasen'); (The) Rakes, Part of Rakes' Coal Wharf; Rate Dikes p1770, Bottom, Top Rate Syke; Redbourne Lane (cf. *Redborne gate* 1602, *Redburn* ~ 1625, 1678, *Red born* ~ 1638, *Redburne* ~ 1662, 1668, *Redbourne Gate* 1700, 'the road to Redbourne', *v.* **gata**); Bottom, Middle, Top Robinson Cl (named from the *Robinsom* family, cf. John *Robinson* 1702¹); Bottom, East, Far, First, Little, North, Second, South, West Sand Cl; Little Sandace, Sandace Bottom, Sand Hase Cl 1837², Sand-Hayes Fd 1860 (for *ace, hase, Hayes, v.* Waddington Hays *supra*); Bottom, Middle, Top Scarborough Car (named from the Earls of *Scarborough*, cf. Richard, Earl of *Scarborough* 1770¹, with **kjarr**); School Carr p1700 (*v.* **kjarr**); School and Yard, First School Cl; Sergent Cliff p1770, Sergents Cliff; Side piece (cf. *side* 1223, *v.* **sīd** 'a side, a hill-side'); The Six Acres 1838; Skin Houses 1828; Far, First South Cliff (*the South Cliffe* 1702¹, *v.* **clif**); South Cl 1767, 1775; Southcotes land 1811 (*v.* **land**; *Southcotes* may well be a surn. here); South Sand Cl 1851; Stackyard and Paddock, Stack Yard Cl, ~ ~ pce; Steam Bone Mill 1828; Stocks Hill; Straight's Car 1808, 1822 (*Straight* may well be a surn. here); Tack Hill Cl p1770; Tandram Hill 1760 (1696, 1743); Tetterham Lane (cf. *Totorham Hill* 1602); thatch Carr 1770¹, North Thack Carr p1770 (*thacke Carre, the thacke carr* e17, *Thack Carr Closes* 1702¹, *v.* **þak** 'thatch, thatching materials', **kjarr**, a Scand compound); Third Cl; 30 acre Carr 1825; Thistle Hill Plot; Thorn Cl p1770; the toftstead now under the plough 1797 ('the site of a toft', *v.* **toft, stede**), Toft Cl (*v.* **toft** 'a messuage, a curtilage'); Top Cl; Far, First, Near Top Moor; Town-end Cl 1860; Town Street; Tuckey Cl p1770, 1784², North Tuckey Cl 1777, Turkey Cl (sic) (perhaps from the surn. *Tuckey*); Home Close now called Upper Close, Upper Cl 1837², A close formerly called the Home Close . . . but now the Upper Close 1838; Waddingham Furze Cl 1770 (*v.* **fyrs**); Waddingham lane End 1770¹; Walnut tree cl; Warehouse; Warlots p1770 (for a discussion of this name, *v. warlotes* in Roxby cum Risby f.ns. (b) *supra*); Waste; West Hill Cl; North, South Wharton's Btm, Whartons Common (from the surn. *Wharton*); Wiberdikes p1770, Wyberd Dykes 1837² (*Wyberdikes* 1702², probably from the surn. *Wyberd* and **dík**); Wigelsworth Cliff, Wiglesworth ~ 1837², Wigellworth's Cliffe 1851 (named from the *Wigglesworth* family, cf. Robert *Wiglesworth* 1642 LPR, with **clif**); Wilkinson Carr 1808, 1822 (from the surn. *Wilkinson* with **kjarr**); Wrights Btm, Wrights Top Common (named from the *Wright* family, cf. Thomas *Wright* 1642 LPR); Young Yd (from the surn. Young).

(b) *Akerdich* 1212, *acerdig* 1223, *the Acredike* 1625, ~ *acre dyck* 1678, *Acredike gate* 1625, *the acre dike hedge* 1662, ~ *Acre dike hedge* 1668, ~ *acredike hedge* 1678, *v.* **æcer-dík** 'the ditch in the field' and for details, *v.* *yᵉ acredikes* PN L 2, 13); *Aldecroft* 1212, *alcroft* 1380 (*v.* **ald** 'old' perhaps in the sense 'long used'); *Ancolme Marsh* 1685 (the reference being to the R. Ancholme); *Annet dale* 1602, *Annat dale* 1625, *a place called Annadaile Thornes* 1668 (from the ME pers.n. *Annot*, a diminutive of *Ann*, a pet-form of *Annes* (*Agnes*), with **deill** 'a share of land' and **þorn** 'a thorn-tree'); *Athelbaldeswat* 1212, *hadhelbaldewat* 1223 ('Æðelbald's ford' from the OE pers.n. *Æðelbald* and ON **vað** 'a ford'); *Atterbie ball swathes* 1625 (from Atterby, an adjacent village, with the obscure *ball* and **swæð** 'a strip of grassland'); *Atterby Mellows* 1645 (*Mellows* is obscure); *Bare daile furlong* 1662 (*v.* **bere** 'barley', **deill**, with **furlang**); *Bernardesbridge* 1212, *Borna brigghill* (sic) 1602, *Bornabrigg Hill* (sic) 1700 (the earliest form means 'Bernard's bridge', from the ME pers.n. *Bernard* and **brycg**; the later forms may belong here but the development is unusual); *Bernell thornes* 1602 (from the surn. *Bernell* and **þorn**); *Blakemildes* 1212 ('the black soil, earth' *v.* **blæc, mylde**); *Black landes* 1602, ~ *lands* 1625, 1668, *the Blacke* ~ 1662, *Blacklands* 1678, *Blake lands* 1679, *Blackland* 1700 ('the black selions', *v.* **blæc, land**, varying between sg. and pl, presumably the name refers to the colour of the soil); *Boihau* 1212 (presumably from **boi(a)** 'a boy' and OE **haugr** 'a hill, a mound', but the exact sense of *boy* in p.ns. is uncertain); *Bracken furlong* 1679 (*v.* **brakni, furlang**); *Bramigwanke* 1223 (apparently 'the garden, in-field overgrown with broom' *v.* **brōmig, vangr**); *Braunewat* 1212 (*v.* **vað**); *Brayston* (sic) 1625 (perhaps 'the broad stone', *v.* **breiðr, stān**); *super crofta Brod'* 1212; *the broad peice* 1662 (self-explanatory); *(the) Carr Close* 1662, 1668, *Carr Common* 1702[2], *the Carre furlong* 1625, *Little Carr furlong* 1638, *little* ~ ~ 1678, *Carr meddow* 1716 (*v.* **kjarr** and cf. Waddingham Carrs *supra*); *Chalkelandes* 1212, *calkeland* 1380 ('the chalky selion(s)', *v.* **calc, land**); *Chaluethethering'* (checked from document) 1212, *calf tetheringes* 1602, *Calf tethering* 1678, *the Calfe Tetherings* 1700 ('the place(s) where calves are tethered', *v.* **calf, tethering**. ME *tethering* is recorded here over 450 years earlier than the earliest reference (1671) in NED; *clay Furlay* 1602, *clay pitts* 1602, *Clay gates* 1625 (*v.* **clæg, furlang, pytt, gata**); *Conke landes* 1602; *Cor leas* 1662; *Craynhow* 1602, 1678, *Crane howe* 1638 (*v.* **cran** 'a crane, a heron, **haugr** 'a hill, a mound'); *duo lez dales* 1542 (*v.* **deill**); *two landes called by the name of Damme and daughter* 1625 (no doubt adjacent selions, one considerably larger than the other, and cf. *one headland and a fellow* 1662); *daw garres* 1625 (*v.* **gāra**); *devours land* 1602; *Durram lande* 1600, *Durrams land* 1602 (perhaps from the surn. *Durham* with **land**); *the East acre dicke* 1662, *East Acca-dike hedge* 1706 (*v.* Akerdich in f.ns. (b) *supra*, and cf. *Westakedicke* (sic) *infra*); *the eight called little eight* [i.e. swaths] 1679; *Engheflet* 1306[1], *Enghefleth, -flet'* 1336 (*v.* **eng** 'meadow, pasture', **flēot** 'a river, stream'); *Engheuedes* 1306[1], *-hewdes* 1336 (*v.* **eng, hēafod** in the pl.); *fawfeld rigs* 1662, *fafeild Riggs* 1668 (perhaps 'the fallow field', *v.* **falh, feld** with ON **hryggr** 'a ridge, a cultivated strip of ground'); *the feildes of Stanton Waddingham* 1605 (*v.* **feld**); *Fitz Carr Common* 1702[1] (the first el. is probably the pl. of ON **fit**, cf. Fitt Lane in f.ns. (a) *supra*); *flatstone thorne* 1602, *the furlong called Flaxstone thornes* 1625, *flaxton thorns* 1638; *Flete de Staynton* 1343 (p) (*v.* **flēot**); *Fornwath, -wat* 1212, *fornwath* 1399, *formouth* 1625, *formoth Brig* 1662, *formoth* 1668, *formouth* 1679 (perhaps originally 'the old ford', *v.* **forn, vað**, a Scand compound corresponding to OE *Aldford*); *the fur gappe* 1662, *the furr gap* 1668, *furr gapp* 1679 (*v.* **fyrs, gap**); *furr leases* 1679 (*v.* **fyrs, læs** 'pasture, meadow-land' in the pl.); *Le Gaires* 1212 (*v.* ON **geiri** 'a triangular piece of ground'); *Gorlandis* 1399, *the Gore leas* 1625 (*v.* **gāra, land, lea** (OE **lēah**) 'meadow, pasture'); *grene meare* 1602, *the greene* ~ 1638, *Greene* ~ 1662, *the green meer* 1678, *green meare* 1700 (*v.* **grēne** 'green', (**ge**)**mǣre** 'a boundary, land on or forming a boundary'); *greene Moore* 1679 (self-explanatory); *haldedikes* 1223 ('the old ditches, dikes', *v.* **ald, dík** in the pl.); *Hilsends* 1602, *the hills end* 1662, *hills End* 1668, *the Hills end* 1678 (self-explanatory, *v.* **hyll, ende**); *hinham* 1223, *ye ould Inoms* 1602, *Old Inams* 1678 (*v.* **innām** 'a piece of land taken in or enclosed'); *Hurlynstones* 1602, *hurling stones* 1678; *the Incroft* 1625, *the incrofts side* 1662, *Incroft* 1668, *the incrofts* 1679, *Incroffts* 1704 ('the inner croft(s)', *v.* **in, croft**); *the intax Close side* 1662, 1668, ~ *Intax close* 1679 (*v.* ON **inntak** 'a piece of land taken in or enclosed'); *Kelsey Willows* 1679 (named from South Kelsey, an adjacent parish to the east); *Kirkeacre* 1223 (*v.* **kirkja, ǣcer**); *a place called Kirues, the grounds called the Kirues* e17 (obscure); *Kyrkelees* 1602 (*v.* **kirkja, lea** (OE **lēah**) 'meadow, pasture' in the pl.); *Landefleth* 1336 (*v.* **land, flēot**); *Langelandes* 1212, *longelandes* 1339, *Long landes* 1602, ~ *Landes* 1638, *long landes* 1678, 1700 ('the long selions', *v.* **lang, land**); *Lescas* 1212 (obscure); *lincolndayle* 1399 (*v.* **deill**), *Lyncolne bottome* 1602, *Lincoln* ~ 1638, *Lincolne bottom* 1678, *Lincoln bottom* 1700 (*v.* **botm**; the significance of *Lincoln* in these two names is unclear, unless it is a surn.); *Lincolngate* 1306[2] ('the road to Lincoln', *v.* **gata**); *littel leas* 1339 (*v.* **lytel, lea** (OE **lēah**) 'meadow, pasture'); *the long dale* 1625, *the long daile headland* 1662 (*v.* **lang, deill, hēafod-land**); *the long furlong* 1625; *Manningeho* 1212 (additional forms are needed to be able to suggest an etymology); *the meare hedge* 1678 (*v.* (**ge**)**mǣre, hecg**); *mellowbecke* 1602, *Mellows Beck* 1638, 1645 (*v.* **bekkr**; *mellow(s)* is obscure, but note *Atterby Mellows* in f.ns. (b) *supra*); *Mikeldayl* 1336 (*v.* **mikell** 'big', **deill** 'a share of land'); *mole* (sic) 1602; *muddy wath* 1602, *the* ~ ~1638 (self-explanatory, *v.* **vað**); *Nevell Dale* e17 (the first el. is probably a surn., the second is **deill**); *New Brigge* 1625, *the new Brig* 1662, *a place called New Brigg* 1668, *new brigg* 1679 (self-explanatory); *New Close* 1702[2]; *North field* 1638, *North Field* 1700 (one of the open fields of the village); *the North west field* 1625; *Ospit de Wadyngham* 1343, *othe Spitell' de Wadyngham* 1395 both (p) (*v.* **spitel** 'a hospital'; unfortunately nothing appears to be known about the nature of the hospital); *the ould streete* (*leaye*) 1602 (the reference is to Ermine Street, *v.* also **lea** (OE **lēah**) 'meadow, pasture'); *person dicke* 1662, *Parsn dicke* (sic) 1668 (*v.* **persone, dík**); *the North parsonage Cliffe Side* 1638; *the parsonag Close* (sic) 1602, *the parsonage Close* 1678; *Parsonage Close* 1702[1], *the North Parsonage Close* 1625, ~ *north Personage close* 1662, ~ ~ *parsonage* ~ 1678, 1700, *land called the South Parsonage dale* 1625 (*v.* **deill**) (cf. Parsonage *supra*); *Parson Sike* 1625 (*v.* **sík**); *Poole headland* 1668; *prior garthe . . . vasto voc' le prior Halle* 1535–46 (*v.* **garðr**; the reference is to the Prior of Thornholme Priory); *Pynecroft* 1551, *Pincroft* 1600, *Pyncroft* 1624; *rat pittes* 1602 (presumably self-explanatory, *v.* **ræt, pytt**); *Readborne Banke Head land* 1679, *Redburn Bank* 1706, *Redburne Carr* 1662, *Readborne carr* 1679, *Redburn Carrs* 1706 (*v.* **kjarr**), *Redburn Dike* 1625 (*v.* **dík**); *Redburn field* 1678, *Readborne feilde meare* 1679 (*v.* **feld**, (**ge**)**mǣre**), *Redburn meere* 1625 (*v.* (**ge**)**mǣre**) (all this group of f.ns. are named from Redbourne *supra*); *the Rye close* 1662, ~ ~ *Close* 1668, *Rye close* 1700 (self-explanatory); *saw hall Rigges* 1625; *the Seath Aice* 1602, *the South Ace* 1625 (for *Aice, Ace*, cf. Ace in f.ns. (a) and Waddingham Hays *supra*); *Seaven Acredale* 1625; *Sheepe Waters* 1625; *Short Ace* 1700 (cf. Waddingham Hays *supra*); *the short care*

1668 (*v.* **kjarr**); *Short daile* 1678 (*v.* **deill**); *Short Inges* 1625 (*v.* **eng**); *Sich* 1212, *the sicke, sicke furlong* 1602, *Sikes furlong* 1638 (*v.* **sīc, sík**); *Skrorekant* 1212 (obscure); *the Slightes* 1625 (*v.* **slétta** 'a smooth, level field' in the pl.); *Snitterby garres* 1678 (perhaps identical with the following), *Snitterby Garthes* 1700 (*v.* **garðr** in the pl.), *Snitterby meare* 1638, ~ *mear* 1678, *Sniterbymear* 1700 (*v.* **(ge)mǣre**), *Snitterby* (*South*) *Ace* 1645, *the South Aice* 1602, *the Sough Ace* 1625 (cf. Ace in f.ns. (a) and Waddingham Hays *supra*; all named from Snitterby, an adjacent parish, to the south); *Southall closende* 1602 (*v.* **sūð, hall**); *the south feild* 1602, *the South Field* 1625 (one of the great fields of the village); *the South furres* 1625 (*v.* **sūð, fyrs**); *the nether, the upper South lands* 1625 (*v.* **sūð, land** 'a selion' in the pl.); *southgrete* 1399, *the South Greetes* 1602 (*v.* **sūð, grēote** 'a gravelly place'); *South west feild* 1638, *South west field* 1700 (one of the large fields of the village); *Stahelbusk* (sic) 1336 (*v.* **busk** 'a bush'); *stic Thorne* 1679; *Stone hill* 1662, *stone hill* 1668; *stonie leas* 1625 (*v.* **stānig, lea (lēah)** 'meadow, pasture'); *Stretefurlangges* 1399, *the Street furlong* 1638, 1678, *the street furlong* 1700 (*v.* **strǣt, furlang**, the reference being to Ermine Street); *Swinstie thorne* 1625, *Swinsty thorne* 1662, ~ *thorn* 1668, 1679 (*v.* **swīn** 'a pig, a swine', **stigu** 'a sty', with **þorn** 'a thorn-tree'); *Torneholm* 1223 (*v.* **þorn, holmr**); *Traneho* 1212 (probably 'the hill-spur where cranes are found' from ON **trani** 'a crane' and OE **hōh** 'a spur of land', but note that ON **trani** is also used as a byname); *Turstaneswell'* 1212 (from the Scand pers.n. *Þorsteinn*, in an anglicised form *Turstan*, *v.* SPNN 425–30); *the viper dickes* 1662; *the upper furlonges* 1602 (self-explanatory); *Welbek* 1399 ('the stream rising from the spring', *v.* **wella, bekkr**, identical with Wellbeck Spring, PN L **4**, 55); *the water layne end* 1602, *the watery Lane* 1625, *the Waterlane* 1678; *Well Coate furlong* 1668 ʾ(*v.* **wella, cot**); *Wenningdayle* 1399; *Westakedicke* (sic) 1602 (cf. *the east acre dicke supra*); *West bridge* 1625; *the Westend* 1662; *West field Thornes* 1638, *west field* (*thorne*) 1662, *West field* 1700 (one of the great fields of the village); *the west Sicke* 1602, *West Syke* 1700 (*v.* **west, sīc, sík**); *west willows* 1602; *Wiggan Close* 1638, *Wigans Close* 1645 (named from the *Wiggan* family, cf. Thomas *Wiggan* 1625 *Terrier*); *Winterwelle* 1212 (*v.* **winter, wella**, denoting a spring which flowed in winter as well as at other times of the year); *Woue* 1327 (p).

Whitton

WHITTON

> *Witenai* 1086 DB, 1130 P
> *Witena* c1115 LS, -*ene* 1178 , 1191, 1193, 1194 P all (p), 1202 FF, 1257 Ch, *Wytene* 1242–43 Fees
> *Witen* 1212 Fees' 1275 RH, *Wyten* 1250 Ipm, 1264 RRGr, 1272 *Ass*, 1279 RRGr, 1303 *FF*, 1308 YD viii, *Wytyn* 1416 Pat, *Wytten'* 1254 ValNor
> *Whyten* HY3 YD ix (p), 1291 Tax, 1323 FF, 1401–2, 1428, 1431 FA,

-ten' 1329 Ass, *Whiten* 1276 RH, 1316, 1330 FA, 1363, 1368
Ipm, 1373, 1374 Peace, 1374, 1405 Pat, 1405 Cl, 1428 FA, 1431
Fine, *Whityn* 1291 Ch, 1373 Peace, *Whitene* 1303 FA, 1327 Ipm,
1342 Cl, *Whytten'* 1332 *SR*, *Whitten* 1432 LNQ xii,1439 Cl, 1444
WillsPCC, 1697 Pryme
Wyton' 1242–43 Fees, *-ton* 1360 Peace, *Wytton'* 1294 *Ass*, *-ton* 1521
Wills iii, 1535 VE iv, 1587 LNQ v, *Witton'* 1375 Peace *Whiton'*
1373 Peace, *Whiton* 1406 Inqaqd, *Whitton* 1402 FA, 1526 Sub,
1547 Pat, 1562 *Surv*, 1576 Saxton, 1610 Speed, 1652 WillsPCC
et passim, *Whytton* 1402 FA, 1547 Pat, *Whittone* 1577 *Terrier*

'Hwīta's island of land' from the OE pers.n. *Hwīta* and **ēg** 'island of
land'. Ekwall's alternative suggestion 'white island' can be ruled out on
topographical grounds since the ground is not chalky here. On the other
hand the church is situated on a distinct island of land, an excellent **ēg**-
site.

BISHOPTHORPE, 1824 O, 1842 White. CLIFF HO (local), cf. *the common
pastur called the clyffe* 1577, *the cliffe* 1606, *the Cliff* 1662, *the cliff
field* 1702, *the Cliff Field* 1709, *Cliff Land field* 1767 all *Terrier*, self-
explanatory, *v.* **clif**. DEVIL'S CAUSEWAY. THE GRANGE, an example of
the late used of **grange**, common in L, for which *v. Santon Grange* in
Appleby parish *supra*. LOW PLANTATION. MANOR HO. NESS SAND, cf.
Whitton Ness *infra*. VICARAGE, *vicaredge* 1577, *the viccaridg house*
1601, ~ *Viccaridge house* 1606, ~ *Vickaridge howse* 1635, ~ *Viceridge
howse* 1638, *yᵉ Vicarage house* 1697, *the vicarage house* 1702, *the
Vicarage* 1822 all *Terrier*, *the Vicarage Homested* 1775 *EnclA*.
WHITTON ASHES. WHITTON CHANNEL, 1824 O. WHITTON NESS,
Whitton nesse 1607 Camden, ~ *Nesse* 1610 Speed, *Ness* 1775 *EnclA*,
self-explanatory, *v.* ON **nes**. WHITTON SAND, 1824 O. WHITTON
SCALP, from *scalp*, *v.* EDD *scalp* 5, 'a bank of sand or mud left
uncovered by the sea at low tide, esp. an oyster or mussel-bed',
topographically appropriate. Cf. The Scalp (Fishtoft, Holland), *the
muschell skelp* 1477 LNQ iv, *Scelp Hurn* 1580 Thompson, *The Scaulp*
1732 ib, *the Scalp* 1794 *BNL*, *The* ~ 1824 O. WILLWICK HILL
PLANTATION.

FIELD-NAMES

Undated forms in (a) are 1775 *EnclA*. Those dated Hy3 (14), 1301 (14),
14 are *Welb*; Hy3 (c1331) *Spald ii*; 1308 YD viii; 1343 NI; 1562 *Surv*;

1567–68 Lanc; 1577, 1601, 1606, 1635, 1662, 1693, 1697, 1702, 1706, 1709, 1822 *Terrier*; 1583 *MiscDon 344*; 1587 LNQ v; 1609 *DuLaMB*; 1652, 1653 WillsPCC; 1724 Stukeley.

(a) Alkborough Rd (leading to Alkborough, a neighbouring parish); the Argons, ~ Argons road 1775, one Inclosure called the Argons 1822; the Banks; Booth Dike (*v.* **bōth** 'a booth, a temporary shelter', **dík** and cf. *bouthewro* 14, *v.* **vrá** 'a nook, a corner of land'); the Carr of Whitton, the Carr Drain (*v.* **kjarr** 'brushwood, a marsh overgrown with brushwood', as elsewhere in this parish); the Church lane 1822; the Common of Whitton (*Whitton Common* 1567–68); the Gravel Plot; Hall Btms (cf. *ad aulam* 1308, 1343 both (p), *Hall Park* 1567–68, *Hall dale* 1609, *the Hall oxgange* 1653, *v.* **hall, botm, park, deill, oxgang**); Halton Pond 1822; Halton Road (leading to West Halton, a neighbouring parish); the Haven of Whitton; the Ings of Whitton, the Ings Road 1776, the Ings 1822 (*Great Inges, Great Inge* 1567–68, *the great Inges, the Inges* 1577, *the great Ings* 1609, *v.* **eng** 'meadow, pasture', as elsewhere in the parish, cf. *Whitton Ing Dicke infra*); Lammer fd 1767, the Lammer Fd (*one land... called a lamar* 1577, *the Lammer field* 1606, *the Lammers* 1635, *yᵉ Lammers* 1693, *Lamber field* 1702, *the Lambers* 1706, 1709, cf. *Landemarehil* Hy3 (14), *Langemarehull'* 1301 (14), *Langemarhil* 14, *v.* **land-gemǣre** 'a boundary', **hyll**, with **lang** for **land** in two early forms); the Longland Fd 1775, Long lands 1822 (*the longe landes* 1577, *v.* **lang, land** 'a selion'); the Common Marsh of Whitton (*the common marsh* 1577, *the Common Marsh* 1606), the Marsh Bank (*v.* **banke**), the Marsh Drain, the Marsh Road (*yᵉ Marsh Laine* 1697, *Marsh Lane* 1706); the North End; Rob Croft otherwise Robert's Croft; Whatams (*Wheteholm* 14, *fower dayles ... one ... called Whatham* 1562, *Whetham Dale* 1567–68, *the wheatome Deale* 1577, *Waithams Dale* 1609, *v.* **hwǣte** 'wheat', **holmr** with **deill**); Winteringham Foot Way (leading to Winteringham an adjacent parish).

(b) *the Abbat close* 1606, *Abbot Close* 1635, *Abbatt* ~ 1652 (*v.* **abbat**, referring to the abbot of Thornton Abbey); *parcel of land called Bacon flyke* 1587 (i.e. *Bacon flitch*, alluding to the shape of the piece of land); *the Backsides* 1709; *baukwell leane* 1577 (*v.* **wella**; the first el. is OE **balc(a)** 'a bank, a ridge'); *the bounegate dale* 1653; *the byrkedeale* 1577 (*v.* **birki** 'a birch copse, a birch', **deill** a Scand compound); *the common feild* 1601; *the common marfour* 1577 (*v.* **marfur** 'a boundary furrow'); *the common pasture* 1601, *The Common Pasture* 1662, *yᵉ Pasture* 1693; *yᵉ Cow Pasture* 1693; *the easte feild* 1577 (one of the great fields of the parish, cf. *the south feild, West Feild infra*); *campum de Witen* Hy3 (c1331), *the feldes of Whitton* 1562, *Whitton ffeylde* 1587, *the feildes* 1606 (the open field of the village, *v.* **feld**); *the fish garth* 1652 ('the fishery', *v.* **fisc, garðr**); *fower dayles ... one ... called Haylye* 1562, *Hally Dale* 1567–68, *one deale called the Halay, the Halay marfour* 1577 (*v.* **deill, marfur**; *Halay* is obscure); *haringhou* Hy3 (14), *Haringhou* 14, *Harrigoal dale merfor, harrigod dayle marfor* 1635, *yᵉ Henry Gold daile* 1697, *Harry gold dales* 1702, *the Herry Hould dale* (sic) 1706, *the Herry Gold dales* 1709 (the first el. of *haringhou* is the ON pers.n. *Hæringr*, the second is **haugr**, and the later development of the name reflects the influence(s) of popular etymology); *the Hye meare, the common Hye mear* 1577 (*v.* **(ge)mǣre**); *the kemp close* 1601, ~ *Kemp close* 1606, *Kemp Close* 1635, 1662 (no doubt from the surn. *Kemp*); *fower dayles ... one ...*

called Kirkdale 1562, *Church Dale* 1567–68, *Kyrke dale* 1609 (*v.* **kirkja, cirice, deill**; the interchange of *kirk* and *church* is noteworthy); *ye Midlebecks* 1693 (*v.* **middel, bekkr**); *molendino aquatico* Hy3 (14) (*v.* **myln**); *the norlande(s), norlandfeild* 1577, ~ *norland Feild* 1606 (*v.* **norð, land**, with **feld**); *the oule care* 1577 (*v.* **ūle** 'an owl', **kjarr**); *the oxmarshe* 1577 (self-explanatory); *Palme Close* 1662 (named from the *Palme(s)* family, cf. James *Palmes* 1601 *Terrier*); *Plaster pytts* 1609 (*Plaster* may well be from **pleg-stōw** 'a place where people gather for play'); *the Quenes strete* 1601, *the Kinges streete* 1606 ('the main street, the high road', *v.* **strǣt**, referring to *Elizabeth 1* and *James 1* respectively); *Shilton hye Mear* 1606 (cf. *the Hye meare supra*; no doubt *Shilton* is a surn.); *Smyth Garth* 1662 (from the surn. *Smith*, cf. Henry *Smyth* 1647 *PR,* and **garðr**); *the south feild* 1577 (one of the great fields of the parish, cf. *the easte feild supra* and *West Feild infra*); *Sowtar garthe* 1577 (from the family name *Sowter,* cf. William *Sutore* 1332 *SR*, with **garðr**); *fower dayles . . . one . . . called ten Acre dale* 1562, *one deale called the x acres* 1577, *the ten acre dale* 1609 (*v.* **deill**); *3 Mar fure gaittes for Cattle within the Commons* 1606 (*v.* **marfur, gata**); *The Tomneste headland* 1562; *the Under-Willocks* 1635, 1638, *ye under-Willock* 1697, *the Under-Wilock(e)s* 1702, 1706 (obscure); *the vicar headland* 1577, *Vicaridge* ~ (*v.* **hēafod-land**); *Wareholm* Hy3 (14) (*v.* **holmr**); *West Feild* 1609, *the west feild* 1662 (one of the great fields of the parish, cf. *the easte feild, the south feild supra*); *the wheate garthe* 1577 (*v.* **garðr**); *Whitton brook* 1724 (*v.* **brōc**); *ye Ditch cauled Whitton Ing Dicke* 1583 (*v.* **eng, dík**); *the nether wirninges* 1577; *Wranghenges* Hy3 (14), 14 (*v.* **vrangr** 'crooked', **eng**).

Winteringham

WINTERINGHAM

Wintringeham (2x) 1086 DB, c1115 LS, p1131 (e13) LibEl, 1202
Ass, 1244 Pap, *Wyntringeham* 1269 Cl

Wintringham c1115 LS, 1202 Ass, 1203 Cur, 1204 P (p), 1240 FF,
1241 Cl, 1242–43 Fees, 1266 Pat, 1275 RH, 1291 Pap, 1292 Cl
et passim to 1723 SDL, *Wyntryngham* m13 (15) FountainC, 1292
Tax, 1303 FA, 1317 Ch, 1317 Cl, 1322 Ipm, 1327 Banco *et
passim* to 1550 Pat, *Wyntringham* 1254 ValNor, 1267 Cl, 1276
RH, 1292 Ch, 1294 BS, 1304 Ipm, 1305 RA ii, 1309 Inqaqd *et
passim* to 1559 Pat

Uuintrigham (sic) eHy2 Dane, *Wintrincham* 1212 Fees, *Wintrinkham*
1265 Misc

Winteringham 1270 Pat, 1554 Pat *et passim, Wynteringham* 1297
Ass, 1559 Pat, *Wynteryngham* 1298 Ipm, 1327 *SR*, 1386 Peace,
1446 Fine, 1546 *WinteringhamPD*

'The homestead, estate of the Wint(e)ringas' from the gen.pl.
Wint(e)ringa of the OE group-name *Wint(e)ringas* 'the family, the
dependents of *Winter* or *Wintra*' and OE **hām**. Winteringham is close to
Winterton *infra*, itself derived from the same group-name; both are
presumably named from the same group of settlers.

BAY HORSE, 1842 White. BEACON HILL (local), *Beacon-hill* 1836
Andrew. BOOTH NOOKING LANE. HIGH BURGAGE, *one messuage or
burgage in the upp Burgage* 1658 *WinteringhamPD, Upper Burgage*
1679 *ib, the High Burgage* 1734, 1754, 1798 *MiscDon 34*, 1741 *Stubbs,
the Upper Burgage* 1779 *ib*; LOW BURGAGE, 1741, 1765, 1768 *Stubbs,
in inferiori burgagio* 1605, *in inferior Burgagio* 1631, *Le nether
Burgage* 1633, *the Low burgage* 1658, *in inferiore Burgagio* 1698, 1700
WinteringhamPD, the Lower Burgage 1772 *MiscDon 34*, from ME
burgage (*v.* MED) 'real estate held directly from the king or a lord,
usually with no feudal obligation other than a fixed annual rent in
money; a house or land lying within a borough', cf. Burgage
(Southwell), PN Nt 175 and Burgage (Prestbury), PN Gl **2**, 110. CLIFF
RD (local), cf. *the west clyfe* 1577 *Terrier, the Cliffs* 1771, 1778 *ib, v.*
clif. COCKHOLME LANE. EASTFIELD, *the east . . . feildes* 1625 *Terrier,*
~ *East Field* 1771, 1778 *ib*, one of the open fields of the parish.
EASTGATE FM (local). FERRY LANE, *the fery lane* 1741 *Stubbs, Ferry
Road* 1798 *EnclA*. FLASHMIRE, 1824 O, perhaps 'the mire, bog with a
pool', *v.* **flasshe, mýrr**; the land is boggy here, though no pool survives.
GATE END, *atte Gatend* 1327 *Banco, Attegatend* 1327 *SR, atte gathend*
1332 *ib, atte Gatehend* 1341 NI all (p), *v.* **gata** 'a way, a road', **ende**
'end'. LOW FM. MARKET PLACE, *our Markett* 1656 *PR, the Market
place* 1758, ~ ~ *Place* 1775 both *Stubbs*. MARSH FM, cf. *Le Marsh* 1718
MiscDep 191, y^e ~ 1733 *ib, the ~* 1734, 1736 *ib*, 1742, 1758 *Stubbs et
freq* to 1818 *MiscDep 191, Winteringham Marsh* 1798 *EnclA*, self-
explanatory, *v.* **mersc**. OLD STREET HEDGE (lost), 1824 O, cf. *ye strete*
1577 *Terrier*, the reference being to Ermine Street. RECTORY, *the
Parsonage House* 1625 *Terrier, ~ ~ house* 1693 *ib, the Rectory house*
1822 *ib*. REED'S ISLAND, *v.* PN L **2**, 111. ROTTEN SYKES, 1718
MiscDep 191, 1772 *MiscDon 34*, 1778 *Terrier*, 1798 *EnclA, ~ Sikes*
1683 *Nelthorpe*, 1733 *MiscDep 191*, 1741, 1758 *Stubbs et freq* to 1783
MiscDep 191, Rottensikes 1693 *Terrier, v.* **sík** 'a trench, a ditch'.
SILVER ST., 1741 *Stubbs*, 1818 *Dep 191, the ~* 1750, 1761 *Stubbs*; the
sense of *silver* is uncertain. SLUICE FM (local), *Sluice* 1842 White.
SLUICE LANE, 1824 O. WEST END, *the Westend* 1771 *Terrier*.

WINTERINGHAM GRANGE. According to P&H "late 18th century", so apparently a late use of **grange**, common in north L, for which *v. Santon Grange* in Appleby parish *supra*. WINTERINGHAM HAVEN, 1824 O, *in portum Wintringeham* p1131 (e13) LibEl, *Winteringham hauen* 1583 *MiscDon 344*, *the Haven of Winteringham* 1677 *Cragg*, *the Haven* 1748, 1751 *Stubbs*, 1798 *EnclA*, self-explanatory; note *the new Bridge new erected across the Haven* 1798 *EnclA*. WINTERINGHAM INGS, 1824 O, *the Ings* 1677 *Cragg*, 1693, 1771, 1778 *Terrier*, cf. *ye eng gate* 1577 *Terrier*, *ye Ingate* 1625 *ib* (*v*. **gata**), *the Ings Nooks* 1683 *Nelthorpe*, *Great Ings* 1822 *Terrier*, *v*. **eng** 'meadow, pasture', as elsewhere in the parish.

FIELD-NAMES

Forms dated 1327, 1332 are *SR*; 1341 NI; 1527 Wills ii; 1549, 1552 Pat; 1577, 1625, 1693, 1697, 1771, 1778[1], 1822 *Terrier*; 1583 *MiscDon 344*; 1677 *Cragg*; 1696 Pryme; 1700 *WinteringhamPD*; 1718, 1719[1], 1733, 1736, 1741[2], 1755[1], 1762, 1770, 1783, 1805, 1820, 1840 *MiscDep 191*; 1719[2] *Plan*; 1725 SDL; 1734, 1752, 1754, 1773, 1792 *MiscDon 34*; 1741[1], 1742, 1747, 1748, 1750, 1751, 1752, 1755[2], 1756, 1758, 1760, 1761, 1765, 1766, 1768, 1774, 1775, 1778[2], 1779 *Stubbs*; 1794 *MiscDon 251*; 1798 *EnclA*; 1864 *TA*.

(a) Ankholm Marsh 1771, Ankholme ~ 1778 (*ancome marshe* 1577, *Ancom marsh* 1625, *the Ancolne Marsh* 1693, *Ankam Marsh* 1719[2], named from the R. Ancholme and **mersc**); the Barton Rd 1798 ('the road to Barton upon Humber'); the Butt marfor 1754, ~ Butmarfur 1766, ~ Butt Marrfur 1779 (*Butt Marfurr* 1743, *Buttmear furr* 1748, *v*. **butte** 'a strip of land abutting on a boundary', **marfur** 'a boundary furrow, a furrow forming a boundary'); Church Rd 1798; Claviris's Cl (sic) 1822 (named from the *Clarvis* family, cf. William *Claruice* 1616 *PR*, Edward *Clarvis* 1798); the Cliffs 1771 (*Cliffes* 1693, *Far, Near Cliff* 1719[2], *v*. **clif**); Lower, Upper Cock thorn 1822 (cf. *kokethorne* 1577, *v*. **cocc** 'a (wild) cock', **þorn**, probably 'a thorn-bush frequented by cocks'); the Commission drain 1822; the Common Lane 1840; the Meadow Grounds call'd the Composition 1778; the Compositions 1798 (cf. *Composition Side* 1719[2]); Corn Windmill 1754, ~ Wind Mill 1775; the Cow Pasture or Marsh 1771, ~ Cow Pasture 1771, 1798 (cf. *Winteringham Cow gange* 1583, *Les Cowgates* 1700, *v*. **gang** 'a way, a path, a track', **gata** 'a way, a path'); the East End 1774 (1747, *in oriental' fine de Wintringham* 1718); the sign of the Ferry Boat House 1765, 1780 (*the Sign of the Ferry boat* 1743, said to be today Bay Horse Inn); the Flatts 1778, ~ Flats 1798, 1822 (*v*. **flat** 'a piece of flat level ground, a larger division of the common field'); the Foldings 1771, the Fold Ings 1778 (*Foldings* 1719[2], cf. *Fawding becke* 1577, *v*. **falod** a fold', **eng** 'meadow, pasture'); the Green 1774 (*v*.

grēne 'a village green, a grassy spot'); Low Groves 1750, 1751, 1755 *et freq* to 1840, Low groves 1752, 1756 *et passim* to 1768, Low Grooes 1766, low Groves 1805, the Groves 1771, 1778, 1864, The Near, the Far Groves 1822 (*Low groves* 1700, 1731, 1741[1], ~ *Groves* 1718, 1734, *Lowgroves* 1741[2], *Far, Near Groves* 1719[2], from dial. *grove* (of which *greave* is a variant form) denoting sites where digging (for turf) takes place, *v.* PN L **2**, 155, ib **4**, 128, ib **5**, 40, 163); Hall Cl 1771, Hall-Close 1778, Hall Cls 1798 (*Hall Close* 1719[2], cf. *Winteringham hallgarths* 1583, *Hall Garth* 1693, *v.* **hall**, **garðr** 'an enclosure'); the Homestead 1822; Hood lane 1750, -lane 1751, ~ Lane 1760, Hood lane Cl (*Hood lane* 1748, named from the *Hood* family, cf. *Agn' Hode* 1332, John *Hood* 1658 *PR*, William *Hood* 1772); the Hopgarth 1771, the Hop-Garth 1778, the Hop Yard 1822 (*v.* **hoppe**, **garðr**, **geard**; the variation between *garth* and *yard* is noteworthy); Ketle bottom (sic) 1822; the Kinges Street 1755; Malt Kiln 1794; the Middle Fd 1771, 1778; the Mill Cl 1754; a drain called the Out dike 1822; Parson's Cross 1822 (cf. *Parson Cross Hill* 1719[2], *v.* **cros**); Plantatiom Cl 1864; Roach Ings 1798 (*v.* **eng**); The Long Seeds 1822, Seeds Cl 1864; Sparrow Hall 1754, 1778[2] (1748); the Street 1778[2] (the reference is to Ermine Street); the Stumber (sic) 1771; a Certain Cotage called Tinkel House 1751 (*Tinkel(l) House* 1748, presumably from a surn.); the Town Street 1750, 1751, 1761, 1798 (1742); Warehouse Rd 1798; the West Fd 1771, 1778[1] (*west feildes* 1625, *v. the east, middle ... infra*); Western green 1750, ~ Green 1751, 1755 *et freq* to 1820 (1718 *et freq* to 1741[2], *v.* **grēne** 'a village green, a grassy spot'); Whitton (Corner) Rd 1798; Wintringham Fd 1798.

(b) *agman scowre* (sic) 1577, *Long, Short Nagman Stones* (sic) 1719[2]; *Back Hard* 1719[2]; *Backside furlong* 1719[2]; *beanumes* 1625 (*v.* **bēan** 'a bean', **holmr** 'an isle, higher ground amidst the marsh' in the pl.; *um, ham* etc. are common reflexes of **holmr** in L); *beckedale* 1577 (*v.* **bekkr** 'a stream', **deill** 'a share of land'); *Bramdale* 1719[2] (*v.* **brōm** 'broom', **deill**); *brod landes* 1677, *Broodlands* 1719 (*v.* **land** 'a selion'); *the Buttes* 1577 (*v.* **butte** 'a strip of land abutting on a boundary, etc.'); *Cappe Feld* 1552 (perhaps named from the shape of the field); *the carres* 1577, *Winteringham Carr* 1697 (*v.* **kjarr** 'brushwood, a bog, marsh, overgrown with brushwood'); *Chappell Garthe* 1549, *chappel garth* 1696, *Chapel-garth, where it is said that a Chauntry anciently stood* 1723 (*v.* **garðr**); *cony garthe* 1577 (*v.* **coni**, **garðr**); *Common Lane* 1748; *the comon meare* 1577 (*v.* **(ge)mære** 'a boundary'); *Cottage Cliff* 1719[2]; *Croft Ends* 1719[2] (*v.* **croft**, **ende**); *the Crose* 1577, *East, West Cross* 1719[2] (*v.* **cros**); *Dove Coat Garth* 1719[2] (*v.* **garðr**); *dyke forlonges* 1577 (*v.* **dík**, **furlang**); *the east, middle & west feildes* 1625 (three of the great fields of the parish); *Fourteen Acres* 1719[2]; *Foxhooles* 1552 (self-explanatory); *gallow hill* 1577 (self-explanatory); *godsley grene* 1577 (presumably from the surn. *Godsley* and **grēne** 'a grassy spot'); *Great Yard* 1719[2]; *Hagg thorn Cliff* 1719[2]; *del Hille* 1341 (p)); *houlesikes* 1577, *howle sikes* 1615; *how becke hill* 1577 (*v.* **hol**, **bekkr** with **hyll**); *Kirkgate* 1577, *Kirk Gates* 1719[2] ('the way, road to the church', *v.* **kirkja**, **gata**); *Lynedale* 1577, *Line Dale* 1719[2] (*v.* **līn** 'flax', **deill** 'a share of land'); *Long Close* 1719[2]; *long middle dayle* 1577, *East, Far, Short Middle Dale* (*v.* **deill**); *Low, uppr Close, Low Closes* 1719[2]; *Mill Cliff* 1719[2]; *the mores* 1577 (*v.* **mōr**); *the Nookes* 1693, *Nooks* 1719[2] (*v.* **nōk** 'a nook of land, a triangular plot of ground'); *Overflow Land* 1719[2]; *Plank Close* 1719[2]; *Pond Close* 1742; *Ryall heades, yᵉ Ryalles* 1577 (*v.* **ryge** 'rye', **halh** 'a nook, a corner of land'); *Stone hill* 1577; *the toftes* 1577 (*v.* **toft** 'a messuage, a curtilage'); *tranmer hiles* (sic) 1577 (*v.* **trani** 'a crane', **mere** 'a pool'); *Tryppe howse* 1527 (presumably from the surn. *Tripp*); *Two Furlongs* 1719[2]; *the Tyth Dayles* 1693 (self-explanatory, *v.* **deill**); *well hill* 1577; *ye west car* 1625, *West Carr* 1693, 1719[2] (*v.* **west, kjarr**); *the west clyfe* 1577 (*v.* **west, clif**); *Wintringham Fishgarth* 1653 *PR* ('the fishery', *v.* **fisc, garðr**).

Winterton

WINTERTON

æt Wintringatune 1066–68 (c1200) ASWills, *Wintringeton* 1228 Welles

Wintrintune 1086 DB, *-tone* (4x) 1086 ib, *Wintrinton'* 1182 P, 1196 ChancR, 1199 P (p), 1201 Cur, 1201 FF, 1242–43 Fees, 1343 Roche

Wintritone (2x) 1086 DB

Wintretune 1086 DB, *Wyntreton* 1338, 1395 Pat, 1399 Orig

Wintringtune (2x) c1115 LS, 1155–60 Dane, 1156–57 (14) YCh i, R1 (1308) Ch, *-tona* 1186 Dugd vi, *-ton'* 1185 Templar, 112 RA ii, 1201, 1219 Ass, 1231 FF, 1232 Welles, 1245–46 RRG, *Wyntrington* 1256 FF, 1300 Ipm, 1303 FA, 1305 Cl, 1316 Inqaqd, 1316 FA, 1334 Ch, 1346 FA, 1610 Speed, *Wyntryngton* 1281 QW, 1291 Tax, 1318 Pat, 1328 Banco *et passim* to 1428 FA, *Wintrinctun* 1212 Fees

Winterington' 1207 FF, p1220 WellesLA, *Wynterington'* 1292 RSu, 1343 NI, *Wynteryngton* 1299 Ipm, 1344 Orig

Wynterthon' 1253 ValNor, *Wynterton(')* 1298 Ass, 1313 Pat, 1318 Cl, 1319, 1326 Pat, 1327 Ch, 1328 Banco, 1332 Pat, 1333, 1350 Cl, 1351 Orig, 1351 Fine *et freq* to 1556 Pat, *Wyntirton'* 1416 WintertonPD, *Winterton* 1275 RH, 1318, 1350 Ipm, 1504 Cl, 1512 *Foster et passim*

'The farmstead, the village, the estate of the Wint(e)ringas' from the gen.pl. *Wint(e)ringa* of the OE group-name *Wint(e)ringas* 'the family, the dependants of *Winter* or *Wintra'* and OE **tūn**. Winterton is situated to the south of Winteringham *supra*, itself derived from the same group-name. Presumably both are named from the same group of people.

BLEAK HO. BOOTH HOUSE FM. BREAKWATER FM, perhaps to be indentified with *Bra Water* 1456 (1703) ArchJ xl, *Brewater meadows* (sic) 1660 (c1900) *LindDep 78, Bray Waters* 1767 *Stubbs, the Braywaters* 1772 *EnclA*, probably 'the broad waters', *v*. **breiðr, wæter**. CHAPEL LANE is *Beggargate* 1452 *MiscDon 614, Beggar Lane* 1551 *Wills, the streete called Begger lane* 1654 *MiscDon 613, v*. **begger** 'a beggar', **gata, lane**. CLIFF FM, NEW & OLD, cf. *le Clyffe* 1452 *MiscDon 614, Winterton Cliff* 1699 Pryme, *Cliff* 1748 ArchJ xl, *Winterton Cliff Ho.* 1824 O, *the Cliff farm* 1836 Andrew, *v*. **clif**. CROSS KEYS HOTEL, *Cross Keys* 1842 White. EARLSGATE RD, *Herlesgate* c1200 (c1250) *MaltCart, Yerlesgate* c.1250 *ib, yarlesgate* 1452 *MiscDon 614, yarles gate* 1577 *Terrier* (Winteringham), *Yearlesgate* 1614 *ib, Earls Gate* 1770 *MiscDon 614, Earlsgate* 1772 *EnclA*, 'the nobleman's road', *v*. **eorl, jarl, gata**, cf. SMETT s.n. *Erlesgate*. EAST FIELD FM, cf. *East Field* 1614 *Terrier, the Eastfield* 1770 *MiscDon 614*, ~ *East field* 1772 *EnclA*, one of the great fields of the parish. EASTLANDS. GEORGE HOTEL, *George Inn* 1842 White. HART LANE. HIGH ST. HOLY WELL (local), 1842 White, *Haliuel* c1200 (c1250) *MaltCart, Hallewell dales* (sic) 1633 WillsPCC, *Holiwell Dales* 1772 *EnclA*. "There is a spring at Holy Well Dale, near Winterton . . . formerly celebrated for it healing properties; and bushes around used to be hung with rags", R.C. Hope, *The Legendary Lore of the Holy Wells of England*, p. 87. *v*. **hālig, wella**. LEAP LANE. LEYS LANE, cf. *Lease gate* 1661 *WintertonPD, the leas gates* 1673 *Yarb*, ~ *Leys road* 1772 *EnclA, the Lease* 1614 *Terrier*, ~ *Leese* 1661 *WintertonPD, a parcell of ground called the Leise* 1665 *Monson, the Leazes* 1770 *MiscDon 614*, ~ *Leys* 1772 *EnclA*, from the pl. of OE **lǣs** 'pasture, meadow-land'. LOW ST. MARKET ST. MERE LANE, *Winterton meer* 1606 *Terrier*, ~ *mear* 1647 Elwes, ~ *Meer* 1679 *ib*, 'the boundary', *v*. **(ge)mǣre**. MILL FIELD HO, cf. *molendino suo apud Winterton'* 1311 *KR, vnum molendinum Ventritic'* 1616 *MiscDep 77*. NEWPORT. NORTHLANDS, 1824 O, *Norlandes* 1614 *Terrier, Norlands* 1758, 1788 *ib, v*. **norð, land** 'a selion'. NORTHLANDS RD, ~ *Lane* 1842 *MiscDon 82*, cf. *via del north* c1200 (c1250) *MaltCart*. OLD HALL FM, WINTERTON HALL (local), cf. *þa Westhealle* 1066–68 (c1200) ASWills, *aulam Hugonis Bardolf* 112 RA iv, *Atte Halle* 1327 *SR, Halle daylle* 1452 *MiscDon 614, Hallings* 1614 *Terrier, Hall Ings* 1772 *EnclA*, 1841 *TA, Hallgarth* 1637 *Wills, v*. **hall, deill, eng, garðr**. THE PARK. ROSS LANE. ROXBY RD,1772 *EnclA*. SAND HALL. SEDGEWORTH HO (local), *Segesworth heades* 1614 *Terrier, Seggsworth* 1665 *Monson, Segsworth* 1772 *EnclA, One inclosed piece of Ground called Segsworth* 1788 *Terrier, One close called the Segsworth* 1822 *ib, A close of arable Land called the Segesworth* 1864 *ib*, perhaps 'Secg's enclosure', *v*. **worð**. The

first el. would then be the OE pers.n. *Secg*, in a Scandinavianised form.
SEWERS LANE. VICARAGE, *the vicaridge house* 1606, *the Vicarege*
1668, *ye vicaridge of Winterton* 1693, *the Viccaradge of Winterton* 1700,
the Site of the Vicarage 1788, *the Vicarage* 1822, 1864 all *Terrier*.
WATER LANE, 1788, 1864 *Terrier*, *Water-lane leading to Roxby* 1836
Andrew, *the Water lane* 1844 *MiscDon 82, Watery Lane* 1772 *EnclA*.
WEIR HILL (local), *Wire hill* 1537 *Wills*, 1793 *MiscDon 82*. WEST ST.,
cf. *Westgate* 1574 *WintertonPD*, *West Gate* 1772 *EnclA* (the name of a
street), *v*. **west**, **gata**. WINTERINGHAM RD, 1772 *EnclA*, *Winteringham
gate* 1614 *Terrier*. WINTERTON BECK, cf. *Wyntertondyke* 1394 Works,
Winterton dike 1606 *Terrier*, *v*. **dík** and **bekkr**. WINTERTON CARRS,
CARR FM, CARR HO, *Winterton Carre* 1665 *Monson*, *the Carr(e)* 1666
ib, *the Carr* 1822 *Terrier*, *Winterton Carrs* 1824 O, cf. *Westcher* (sic)
c1200 (c.1250) *MaltCart*, *West carre* 1452 *MiscDon 614*, *the West kar*
1614 *Terrier*, *Common Carr* 1768 (1791) *LindDep* (Plans 2/1), 1770
MiscDon 614, 1772 *EnclA*, 1788 *Terrier*, *Carre bridge* 1614 *Terrier*, *the
Carre ditche* 1654 *MiscDon 614*, *v*. **kjarr** 'brushwood, a bog, a marsh
overgrown with brushwood'. WINTERTON GRANGE is *Gal-*,
Gallestaynes c1220 (c1250) *MaltCart*, *Gaustons* 1824 O, the first el. is
uncertain, the second of the pl. of ON **steinn** 'a stone'. The present day
name is a late example of **grange**, for which *v*. *Santon Grange* in
Appleby parish *supra*. WINTERTON HOLMES, 1668 *Terrier*, ~ *Holme*
1824 O, *Holm* c1200 (c1250) *MaltCart*, *le Holm* 1231 FF, *the Holmes*
1665, 1666 *Monson*, 1770 *MiscDon 614*, 1772 *EnclA*, 1772 *Foster*, 1778
Terrier, cf. *Holme Gate* 1614 *Terrier*, *-gate* 1624 *Wills*, *Holmes Lane*
1864 *Terrier*, *v*. **holmr** 'an island of land, higher ground amidst the
marshes', with **gata** 'a road'. The late Mr J.F. Fowler commented
"grounds rising out of the level, formerly islands when flooded all
round". WINTERTON INGS, 1652 *Yarb*, 1697 *Terrier*, 1824 O, ~ *Inges*
1456 (1703) *ArchJ* xl, ~ *Inggs* 1651 *MiscDon 614*, ~ *Yngs* 1690 *BRA
1171*, *the Ings* 1666 *Monson*, 1690 *Terrier*, *ye Ings* 1693 *ib*, *the Ings of
Winterton* 1668, 1671, 1788 *ib*, 1772 *EnclA*, cf. *the Long Ings* 1600
Wills, ~ *long Ings* 1614 *Terrier*, *the Ings ditche* 1654 *MiscDon 614*, *y^e
Ing dike* 1690 *Terrier*, *v*. **eng** 'meadow, pasture'. INGS LANE, 1864
Terrier, *the Ings Road* 1772 *EnclA*, 1844 *MiscDon 82*.

FIELD-NAMES

Forms dated c1200 (c1250), c1220 (c1250), c1250 are *MaltCart* (forms
supplied by the late Mr J.T. Fowler of Winterton); 13 (14) *Drax*; 1201,

1231 FF; 1307 *KR*; 1327 *SR*; 1375 Peace; 1452, 1597, 1651, 1654, 1770, 1772[1], 1827 *MiscDon 614*; 1456 (1703), 1748 ArchJ xl; 1503, 1537, 1572, 1575, 1583, 1587, 1594, 1600, 1603, 1613, 1620, 1626, 1628, 1633, 1634, 1637, 1642, 1645, 1647, 1694 *Wills* (forms supplied by the late Mr J.T. Fowler of Winterton); 1544, 1574, 1599, 1601, 1661 *WintertonPD*; 1552, 1555 Pat; 1606, 1614, 1619, 1668, 1671, 1681, 1690, 1693, 1700, 1788, 1822, 1864 *Terrier*; 1614 *Terrier* (forms supplied by the late Mr J.T. Fowler of Winterton); 1616 *MiscDep 77*; 1640 Imb; 1655 *BRR 833*; 1665, 1666 *Monson*; 1747 *StukM*; 1767 *Stubbs*; 1772[2] *EnclA*; 1773 *MiscDon 193*.

(a) Ailes Cl 1770 (cf. *Hales croft* 1642, perhaps from the surn. *Hales*); the Appleby Rd 1772[2] (from the adjacent parish of Appleby); Bracken Dales 1772[2] (*Brackendale* c1250, 1231, *Brakendale* 1452, *v.* **brakni, deill** 'a share, a portion of land', as elsewhere in the parish); Bricklayers Arms Inn 1841; Bull Hill 1767, 1772[2]; Burton Briggs 1772[2] (cf. *Burtonbrywes* (sic) 1452, named from the adjacent parish of Burton upon Stather); Calf Cl 1767, 1772[2] (*Calfclose* 1456 (1703)); the Calf Croft 1863; the Car Pingle 1772[2] (*v.* **kjarr** 'a marsh, especially one overgrown with brushwood', as elsewhere in the parish, **pingel** 'a small enclosure'); Cattle Garths 1863 (*Cattle garthes* 1637, *v.* **garðr** 'an enclosure', as elsewhere in the parish); Chatcroft 1863 (Mr Field suggests that the first el. may be dial. *chat* 'a small piece'); Clerk Hole 1767; Coleby Dale 1772[2] (*Colby dalle* 1614, *v.* **deill**), Coleby Rd 1772[2] (named from Coleby in West Halton parish); Cottagers' Carrs 1863 (*v.* **kjarr**); Crake Dale 1772[2], ~ dale 1841, ~ Deal 1863 (*v.* **deill**; the first el. may be ON **kráka** 'a crow, a raven'); Cringle Beck Lane 1772[2] (leading to Cringlebeck (Fm) in Roxby cum Risby parish); Decoy Carr 1767 (from *decoy* 'a trap for wildfowl' with **kjarr**); Doctor's Cl 1842; Eleven Acres 1767; Fishpond 1841; Forman Cl 1770 (named from the surn. *Forman*); Fryar Croft 1767, Fryer Croft 1772[2] (*Frier Crofts* 1456 (1703), *frearcroft neuke* 1614 (*v.* **nōk**), *Friercroft* 1642, *Fryercroft* 1645, *v.* **frere**, but no reference to *friars* has been noted in the sources searched, **croft**); Gentle men's Carrs (sic) 1788, Gentleman's Carrs 1822, Gentlemans Carrs 1841; Goose hill Lane 1772[2], the Goose hills 1822 (self-explanatory); Halton Lane 1772[2] (*Haltongate* 1452, 'the road to West Halton', *v.* **gata**); Holme Dale 1772[2] (cf. *Holme Close, ~ gate, ~ hill* 1665, *a hill called Holmes hill* 1665, *v.* **holmr** 'an island of raised, firm land in marsh', as elsewhere in the parish); Home Cl 1841, the ~ ~ 1864; the Home Gate 1772[2]; Horkstow rd 1772[2], Rd 1788 (leading to Horkstow, PN L **2**, 158); the Horn-croft 1822 (*Horncroft* 1452, *Hornecroft dale* 1594 (*v.* **deill**), *Horncroft* 1613, *v.* **horn**, perhaps referring to some horn-shaped feature', **croft**); Horne cl 1864, Horne Dale 1841 (*v.* **deill**); Lawn (cl) 1841 (*v.* **launde** 'an open space in woodland'); Line Garth 1772[2] (*v.* **līn** 'flax', **garðr**); Long Garth 1841 (*v.* **garðr**); Malt Kiln 1841; Mamwell Cl 1772[2], the Mamwells 1841, Mamwells Beck 1863 (*v.* **bekkr**), Mamwell Lane 1772[2] (*v.* **wella**; the first el. is uncertain); the Middle Hil (sic) 1770; The Minns Arms 1841; Mount Cl 1863; Near Cl 1841; the New Cl 1772[2], New Cl 1841; Nineteen Acres 1767; the North Cliffe 1772[2] (*v.* **cliff**, cf. *North Bank* 1614); the Northfield 1772[2], ~ North Fd 1830 (*v.* **norð, feld**, one of the open fields of the parish, cf. the Southfield *infra*); Old Cooper Garths 1841 (*v.* **garðr**; the first el. is presumably the surn. *Cooper*); Paddock 1841; Pan Flash Carr 1767 (*v.* **kjarr**; the late Mr Field suggests that Pan may mean 'a rounded hollow or valley', *v.* **panne**, which might therefore be susceptible to flooding, *v.* **flasshe** 'flooded grassland, a sheet of shallow water'); Pinfold 1841 (*v.* **pynd-fald** 'a pinfold'); Pool Hole 1863; Old Prudy 1863; Publick Stone Pit 1772²; Rate dikes 1863; Ratton Row 1770 ('the rat infested row,' *v.* **raton, rāw** 'a row of houses'); the great & small tithes of all the Gardens Orchards within what is called the ring of the town 1822; the Roches 1770 (*terra monachorum de Rupe* c1250, *land called roche* 1614, *Rose alias Rochland* 1620, *Roachland* 1642, *that Oxgang and one half Oxgang of Land . . . called the Roach* 1661, named from Roche Abbey which held land in Winterton); Sand Drain; Scraves Hole 1863 (*Scraues* 1231, c1250, *Scraves hole* 1640, *v.* **scræf** 'a cavern, a hole' in the pl. with explanatory *hole* from the 17th century); Shackhole 1863 (according to the late Mr F.T. Fowler this is today called Clerk's Hole); Sixteen Acres 1767; the South Cliffe 1770; the Southfield 1770, 1772² (one of the open fields of the parish, cf. the Northfield *supra*); the Sowers 1770, the Sawers 1772² (*Soures* 1614, *v.* **sūr** 'sour, coarse (pieces of land)'); the old Street Road 1772² (*Old Street* 1614 = Ermine Street, cf. *the Kings street* 1606, *yᵉ Kings street* 1690, *v.* **strǣt**); Sukon Land 1770, ~ Mdw 1771² (*Sugan, Sukan, Suken* 1614, obscure); Ten Acres 1767; Three Tree Cl 1863 (self-explanatory); Tippitts 1767, Tippets 1863 (*Typpet* 1456 (1703), *the Typett* 1606, *Tippitt* 1626, *a peece of ground cald Tippit* 1690, a shape-name for a long, narrow piece of land, alluding to a scarf-like garment formerly worn, usually as an extension to a sleeve or hood. Cf. *hood & typpett* PN L **2**, 289); Top Cl 1841; Town Drain 1863; Town End Earth 1841; the Town Side Rd 1788 (*Townside* 1614); the Town Street 177²; Tranny moor Spring 1863 (the first el. is probably ON **trani** 'a crane'); Twenty Acres 1767; The Vicarage Cl 1788, the Vicarage cl 1822 (*the vicaridge close* 1606); the long Warlots 1770 (*Warlotes* c1200 (c1250), *Warlotes* 1614, *Warlots* 1641, cf. *the shorte Warlotts* 1654, *v.* **warlot** for a discussion of which *v.* PN L **2**, 67–68, s.n. Waterhill Wood); Watebeck House 1844 (*v.* **bekkr**); the West End 1772²; Western Slack 1772² (*v.* **slakki** 'a small shallow valley, a hollow in the ground'; a word common in north-west England, but rare in the East Midlands); Whitwell 1863 (*Whitewell garth* 1534, perhaps 'the white spring', *v.* **hwīt, wella**);

   (b) *Baranrie land* 1537, *Baronry land* 1587 (*v.* **baronie** 'a barony'); *Benedale* c1250, *Bendale* 1452, *Bendall* 1614, *a parcel of ground called Bendall* 1665 (*v.* **bēan, deill**); *Bournt hales* 1614 (*v.* **brende** 'burnt', **halh** 'a nook of land'); *Braye gate* 1614, *Braygate* 1647 (*v.* **breiðr** 'broad', **gata** 'a road'); *Bulla tres* 1614, *Bullay trees* 1633 (*v.* **balace** 'a bullace or wild plum'); *terra quae vocatur Burdinhall* c1200 (c1250) (probably from the surn. *Burdin* and **hall**); *Burtongate* 1452, *viam vocat Burton gate* 1574, *Burton gate* 1606, 1690 ('the road to Burton upon Stather', *v.* **gata**); *Casterfletes* 1452, *-fleetes* 1654, *Caisterstoces* 1600 (*v.* **flēot** 'an inlet, creek' and **stocc** 'a stump, a stock'; the first element is OE **cæster** 'an old fortification', with a variety of references from a Roman station to an ancient fortification. Ermine Street runs just to the west of Winterton and terminates at the Humber at Winteringham where there was an extensive Romano-British settlement. At Winterton itself a large Romano-British villa has been excavated but unfortunately the situations of the two f.ns. are unknown); *the Cawsey ditche* 1654 (*v.* **caucie, dīc**); *Chauntrye landes* 1599 (*v.* **chaunterie, land**, no doubt named from the *Chantry called Winterton Chantry*, *v.* AASR 36, 158–9); *the beck that runs at the bottom of* *the said Cliff* 1748 (*v.* **clif**); *Clossedaile* 1613 (*v.* **clos(e)**, **deill**); *Colebihill* 1231, *Cholebyhill* c1250 (referring to the nearby Coleby and **hyll**); *Cowbridge* 1614; *Cow pastures* 1616; *Crossegates* 1614 (*v.* **cros**, **gata**); *Cutt close* 1613, *the long Cut* 1614 (*v.* **cut** 'a water channel'); *exterior dayle* c1250 (*Utterdal.* in margin) (*v.* **deill**); *fons de depwelle* c1200 (c1250) (*v.* **dēop** 'deep', **wella**); *Dock furlong* 1619 (*v.* **docce** 'a dock (the plant)', **furlang**); *duckhole* 1654; *Duuewelle* c1200 (c1250), *Duwell* 1231 (*v.* **dūfe** 'a dove', **wella**); *Dykefurlangys* 1452, *Dic furlong* 1614 (*v.* **dík**, **furlang**); *East Garth* 1614 (*v.* **garðr**); *Easterflet* c1200 (c1250) (*v.* **ēasterra** 'more eastern', **flēot** 'an inlet, a creek'); *Estiby* 1327 (p) ('(place) east in the village', *v.* **ēast**, **í**, **bȳ** (p), denoting X who lives in the east of the village, a common formation in L); *Estraner hempland* 1572; *campum de Wyntrington* 13 (m14), *in camp' de Winterton* 1307, *in Campis* 1616, *Winterton field* 1747 (*v.* **feld**); *Forby land* 1537 ('land cultivated separately from the common field in which it lay', *v.* **forbyland** and for a full discussion *v.* PN L **2**, 306–7); *Foxley landes* 1544, 1597, *Foxeley lande* 1654 (probably from the surn. *Foxley* and **land**); *Foxwelldale* 1452 (*v.* **fox**, **wella**, with **deill**); *Goyckwell' landes* 1599, *Gockwell* 1614, *Goquell* 1614 (land belonging to Gokewell Priory); *Groysse croft* 1694; *Hemplands* 1572, *Toftum et canabarium vocatum S' Rogers* 1616 (*v.* **hænep**, **land**); *Hofland* c1200 (c1250) (Dr Insley draws attention to the fact that this f.n. is formally identical with the common Norwegian p.n. *Hovland*, used to denote land near a heathen temple or holy place, a compound of ON **hof** 'heathen temple, holy place' and **land**. Whether we are concerned with a genuine heathen relic or popular superstition is unclear, but the appearance of ON **hof** in a medieval f.n. in L is remarkable); *Houedland* c1200 (c1250), *the Headland* 1614 (*v.* **hēafod-land**); *Hopyard* 1600 (*v.* **hoppe** 'the hop plant', **geard**); *the horse Pingle* 1665 (*v.* **pingel** 'a small enclosure'); *Jennyson landes* 1599 (from the surn. *Jennyson* and **land**); *the spring called Jopwell* 1665; *atte Kirke de Wynterton* 1375 (p) (*v.* **kirkja**); *lamlelle* (sic) 1452 (obscure); *the lyme pitt close* 1654; *Maine hole* 1614; *The widest of the Carre called Mastercrike* 1655, *Master Crike* 1666 (*v.* **kriki**, for *Master*, *v.* NED s.v. *master* sb[1], 15 'main, principal', EDD s.v. 1, master drain 'a principal drain'); *Michehil* (sic) c1200 (c1250), *Mikelhill* 1231 (*v.* **micel**, **mikill**, **hyll**); *Middlebecke* 1665 (self-explanatory); *Mulewelldale* c1200 (c1250), *Muluelledayle* c1250 (from **mūl** 'a mule' and **wella** with **deill**); *Mydyng* 1614 (*v.* **midding** 'a midden, a dung-heap'); *Neatherdales* 1614 (*v.* **neoðera** 'lower', **deill**); *North long* 1307, *Northlangys* 1452 (*v.* **norðr**, **lang**[2] 'a long strip of land'); *Oddercroft* c1220 (c1250) (*v.* **ōðer** 'other, second', **croft**); *Outs close* 1655 (self-explanatory); *Overdailes* 1600, *-dalles* 1614 (*v.* **ofer** 'over, above', **deill**); *Ouerfurdales* 1452 (*v.* **fyrs**, **deill**, with **uffera** prefixed); *Pighill Nooke* 1642 (*v.* **pightel** 'a small enclosure' rare in L, the usual form being *pingle*); *Pilegingate* (sic) c1250 (perhaps for *pilegrim* 'pilgrim', with **gata**); *the Pingle* 1620, 1665 (*v.* **pingel** 'a small enclosure'); *Pyehouse* 1575 (*v.* **hūs**; formally the first el. is ME **pī(e)** 'a magpie', but we could be concerned with a tavern name similar to *Pye Corner* in London (LnStN 204), or the name could have more disreputable connotation, 'thieves' den' (*v.* MED s.v. *pī(e)*, in which case it would be a compound of the same type as American English *cathouse* 'a brothel', as Dr Insley points out); *le Redes* c1200 (c1250), *le Redys* 1452 (*v.* **hrēod** 'a reed, a reed-bed'); *Reniterwelledale* (sic) 1231; *Riehil* c1200 (c1250), *Rihill* 1231, *Ryhil* c1250 (*v.* **ryge** 'rye', **hyll**); *Rosevaldale*, *Roswelldal'*, *Rossewelledale* c1200 (c1250), (obscure); *Roudale* 1452 ('the rough portion, share of land', v. **rūh, deill**); *Rowargate* 1452 (v. **gata**); *Roxbycrosse* 1452, *Roxby Hedge* 1748 (from the nearby Roxby); *le Saferene Garthe* 1555 (v. **saffroun, garðr**); *the Salt Ings* 1606 (v. **salt** 'salty', **eng**), *Pratum salsum* c1200 (c1250); *Saughe feild* 1614 (v. **salh** 'a willow, a sallow'); *Scenkesdayle* c1250 v. **deill**; the first el. is the ME byname or surn. *Schencke* derived from ME *schenche, shenke*, etc., primarily 'a drink, a draught', but here in the sense 'a cupbearer', as suggested by Dr Insley); *Scotgate* 1614 ('the road of the Scots', v. **Scot(t), gata**); y^e *Soake* 1681 (v. **soc** 'a drain'); *the South Clough* 1665 (v. **clōh**); *Southdale* 1634; *the south feild* 1601 (one of the large fields of the parish); *Spinke land* 1600 (probably 'land frequented by finches' from ME *spink(e)* 'a finch, esp. the chaffinch (*fringilla coelebs*)' rather than a compound of the etymologically identical surn. *Spink* and **land**); *Stuard lane* 1503, *steward lane* 1606, *Steward's lane* 1654, *Steward Lane* 1671 (from either the official title or the derived surn. *Steward*); *Stinkesdail* 1231, *Styngesdayle* 1452 (the first el. is obscure, the second in **deill**); *Stykeswold* 1452 (this is apparently identical with Stixwould in LSR, the meaning of which is 'Stig's wold', from the ODan pers.n. *Stíg* and OE *wald*); *sudbec* c1200 (c1250), c1250 (v. **sūð, bekkr**); *via del Suth* c1200 (c1250) (v. **sūð, gata**); *Thackhole* 1456 (1703), *thackhole* 1626 ('the hole, the hollow where material for thatching was obtained', from ON **þak** 'thatch', **hol** 'a hole, a hollow'); *Thorneholme* 1614 ('higher ground amidst the marshes where thorn-trees grow'); *Threakholme* 1665 (v. **holmr**); *Toftes waste* 1613 (v. **toft** 'a messuage, a curtilage', **waste**); *Twayorn* c1200 (c1250) (*y = th*), *Twathorn* 1231 ('two thorn-trees' v. **twegen, þorn**); *Uppdailes* 1654 (v. **upp, deill**); *Vtterfuldayles* c1200 (c1250) ('the foul, dirty shares of land', v. **fūl, deill**, prefixed by **ūttera** 'outer, more remote'); *Warnede Lande* 1616; *Warth brige* 1614 (v. **waroð** 'flat piece of land along a stream', **brycg** in a Scandinavianised form); *Atte Well'* 1327 (p) (v. **wella**); *West Close* 1634; *Westhedelande* 1452 (v. **west, hēafod-land**); *Winterton piddlebeck* 1640 ('the marshland stream', v. **pidele, bekkr**); *diuisas de Wynterington* 13 (m14), *Wyntryngham mere* 1452, *Winteringham mear* 1614 (the boundary between Winteringham and Winterton, v. **(ge)mǣre** 'a boundary'); *Wyver hill* 1606; *Yedmondale* 1583, *Yeadmerdale* 1614, *Yadmeredeil* 1647 (from the OE pers.n. *Ēadmǣr* and **deill** 'a share of land').

Aslacoe Wapentake

Aslaches hou (2x) 1086 DB
Aslocahou (sic) c1115 LS
Aslachou 1130 P
Aslacheho 1166 P
Oselakeshow 1153, 1170, *-hou* 1178 all P, 1179 ChancR, 1180, *-ho*
    1176, 1177, 1182, 1183 all P, *Oselachesho* 1169 ib
Oselacheho 1168 P
Aselachisho 1175 P, *Aslacheshou* 1175 ChancR, *-ho* 1190 P,
    Aslakesho 1177, 1178 ChancR, 1179, 1183, 1184, 1185, 1186,
    1188, 1191, 1192, 1193 P
Aselakeho 1183 ChancR, 1191, 1202, 1205, 1209 P, 1202 Ass,
    Aselachou 1265 Misc, 1316 FA
Aslacho 1200 P, *-hou* 1254 ValNor, 1275 RH, 1300 Ipm, 1304
    DCAcct, *-how HarlCh*, 1292 RSu, 1305 Ass, *-howe* 1298 ib, 1327
    SR, 1386 Peace, *-hoe* 1627 SP, *-o* 1653 *ParlSurv*, *Aslakhowe*
    1287 Ipm, 1329 *Ass*, 1332 *SR*, 1343 NI, 1347 Pat *et passim* to
    1465 ib, *-how* 1291 Tax, 1381 Ipm, 1535 de l'Isle, *-hou* 1342 Pat,
    -hoo 1519 DV i, 1526 Sub, 1535 VE iv, *Aslackhou* 1295 RSu, *-ho*
    1576 LER, *-oe* 1695 Morden
Aslakeho 1203 P, *-how* 1281 QW, 1298 Ass

The forms are preceded or followed by some form of Wapentake or
Deanery, usually in Latin.

'Aslak's mound' from the Scand pers.n. ON *Áslákr*, ODan *Aslak*, for
which *v.* SPNNf 62ff, and **haugr** 'a mound'. The same pers.n. is the first
el. of Aslackby, Kest. The forms in *Ose-* are anglicisations of the ODan
pers.n., possibly as a result of the influence of the cognate OE *Ōslác*.
The site of the meeting-place of the wapentake (ON **vápnatak**, late OE
wæpengetæc 'a subdivision of a shire') is not known.

Blyborough

BLYBOROUGH

> *Blitheburc'* 112 *DuDCCh*, *-burgh'* 1286 *FF*, *Blytheburhg* (sic)
> 1232–33 Fees, Hy3 RBE, *Blyburghe alias Blytheburgh* 1563 Pat,
> *Blithbury* 1293 Abbr
> *Bliburg* (4x) 1086 DB, 1181 Bly, Hy2, John RPD, 112 *AD*, c1200
> Dane, 1212 Fees, 1213 Abbr, 1218 Bly, 1218 FF *et freq* to 1293
> RSu, *Blyburg'* 1213 Cur, 1234 FF, 1254 ValNor, 1281 QW
> *Bliburc* (4x) c1115 LS, 1148, 1177, c1180 Bly, 1200 P (p), 1202
> Ass *et passim* to 1266 Pat, *-burch* c1160, c1180 Bly, 1185
> Templar, *Blyburch* 1263 FF, 1340 Misc
> *Bliburgh* c1180 Bly, 1198 (1328) Ch, 1253 FF, 1297 CoramR, 1292
> Ipm *et freq* to *-burghe* 1576 LER, *-borough* 1539 *AD*, *Blyburgh*
> 1256 FF, 1291 Tax, 1312 Ipm, 1314, 1327 Pat, 1332 *SR*, 1341
> Pat, 1351 Ipm *et freq* to 1610 Speed, *Blyborough'* 1542 *AOMB*
> *214 et passim*
> *Blibur* c1180 Bly, c1180 *DuDCCh*
> *Blieburc* 1181, 1182 P, 1195 (1335) Ch, 1203 Cur, 1203 Abbr, 1203
> Ass, 1206, 1207 P

There are springs at Blyborough and a stream rises here so perhaps
the first el. is the OE river-name *Blīðē* 'the gentle, merry stream' with
burh 'a fortified place'. Alternatively, the first el. may be the
unrecorded OE pers.n. **Blīða*, hence 'Blīða's fortified place', *v.* **burh**.
Most of the forms show loss of medial *-th-* due to AN influence.

BLYBOROUGH COVERT. BLYBOROUGH GRANGE, 1830 Gre, *Grange F^m*
1828 Gre. *Grange* is here a late example of **grange**, common in L, for
which *v.* EDD s.v. 2 'a homestead, a small mansion or farm-house, esp.
one standing by itself remote from others', a sense quoted there from L.
BLYBOROUGH HALL, *Hall* 1824 O, *Blyborough Hall* 1842 White, cf.
Hall Farm 1855 *Padley* . BLYBOROUGH MILL (lost), 1824 O, 1830 Gre,
and is *Heath Mill* 1828 Bry, cf. *le milnhill* 1475 Anc, *Mill Field* 1838
TA. CHURCH FM (lost), 1856 White. COLD HARBOUR (lost), *Cold
Harbor* 1828 Bry, referring to a sheltered place in the open. DOWBERS
FM (lost), *Dowbers F^m* 1828 ib, no doubt from the surn. *Dowber,
Dawber*, cf. Daniel *Dawber* 1842 White. FOSS FM (lost), *Foss F^m* 1828
Bry. FOX COVERT FM, *Fox Cover Farm* 1855 *Padley*, cf. *Fox Cover*
1828 Bry. HORNSBECK, *Horns Beck* 1838 *TA*, 1855 *Padley*, cf.
Hornesbeck Medowe 1542 *AOMB 214*, 1545 *Pat*. This may well be
identified with *Ormesbek* 1238 FF, 'Orm's stream', from the ODan

pers.n. *Orm* and **bekkr**. THE ISLANDS, self-explanatory; these are islands in the stream here. IVY COTTAGE FM, 1855 *Padley*. MIDLAND FM (local), 1855 *ib*. PROSPECT HO, *Prospect Ho*. 1828 Bry, *Prospect* 1830 Gre, usually a nickname for a place commanding an excellent view. RECTORY, *ye parsonage* 1671, 1674, 1793 *Terrier, The Parsonage House* 1690 *ib*. RED HOUSE FM, cf. White House Fm *infra*. SCOTLAND FM, *Scotland Ho*. 1828 Bry, a nickname of remoteness, the farm being situated close to the parish boundary with Northorpe. TEMPLE FM, 1855 *Padley*, cf. *Temple Ings* 1690 *Terrier*, 1838 *TA*, commemorating the holdings of the Templars who held land here in 1185. WARREN FM (lost), *Warren F^m* 1828 Bry, *The Warren Farm* 1855 *Padley*. WESTBECK LANE, cf. *Westbecfurlong* 1238 FF, *West Beck* 1828 Bry, 1838 *TA*, self-explanatory, *v*. **west, bekkr** 'a stream'. WHITE HOUSE FM, cf. Red House Fm *supra*.

FIELD-NAMES

Forms dated 1206 are Ass; 1218[1] Bly; 1218[2], 1238 FF; m13 *Yarb*; 1290, 1375 Ipm; 1327[1], 1332 *SR*, 1327[2], 1545 Pat; 1343 NI; 1389 Misc; 1542 *AOMB 214*; 1547, 1548 *Anc*, 1690, 1693, 1707 *Terrier*, 1838 *TA*, 1855 *Padley*.

(a) Andrews Cl 1838, ~ cl 1855 (from the surn. *Andrews*); Ash Holt Plantn 1855 (*v*. **æsc, holt** 'a wood, a thicket'); Avenues and Spaw (sic) 1838 (*v*. **spa**); Bean Cl 1838, 1855; Bell dyke 1838 (*v*. **dík**); Bottoms 1838, 1855 (*v*. **botm** 'a bottom, a valley bottom') Brick Kiln Cls 1838; Butcher Cl 1838, Butcher's cl 1855 (from the surn. *Butcher*); Calf Cl 1838, ~ cl 1855; Carter's Cl 1838, Carters Cl 1855 (probably from the surn. *Carter*); Cliff Cl 1838, 1855 (cf. *Tuaclives* m13, *v*. **twā** 'two', **clif**); Clover Cl 1838, 1855; Coney Green 1838 (*v*. **coni** 'a rabbit', **grēne** 'a grassy place'); Far, Near Cottage Cl 1838; Dam Cl 1838, ~ cl 1855 (*v*. **damme** (ON **dammr**) 'a dam, a pond'); Dog dale 1838; Dove Cote 1838, Dove Cote Cl 1855; Far Cl 1838; ~ cl 1855; Farm cl 1855; Furze cl 1855; Near Furze and Osier Holt 1855 (*v*. **fyrs, holt**); Garth 1838 (*v*. **garðr**); Great Bottoms 1838, 1855 (cf. Bottoms *supra*); Green Leys 1838, 1855 (*v*. **grēne, ley** (OE **lēah**) 'a meadow, open pasture'); Far, Little, Near Grimsdale 1838, 1855 (*Grimes dale* 1707, probably from the surn. *Grime* (from ODan *Grim*) and **deill** 'a share of land'); Harden Hill 1838, 1855 (cf. *Harding furlang* 1238, *Hardynges* 1389, *blyber Herdynges* 1542, *blybhardinges* (sic) 1545 (*v*. **heard** 'hard', probably in the sense 'hard to till', **eng** 'meadow, pasture'); Hay Syke 1838, 1858 (*v*. **sík** 'a ditch, a trench', as elsewhere in the parish); Heaton's Cl 1838, Heatons cl 1855 (named from the *Heaton* family, cf. John *Heaton* 1672 *BT*); Hemswell Syke 1838, 1855 (from Hemswell a neighbouring parish and **sík**); High Fd 1838, 1855; Hill Cl, ~ cl 1855; Home Cl 1838, ~ cl 1855; Home Yard Cl 1855; Horse Cl 1838, ~ cl 1855; House Cl, House Pingle 1838 (*v*. **pingel** 'a small enclosure', as elsewhere in the parish); Hutchinson's Cl, Hutchinsons Cl 1855 (named from the surn. *Hutchinson*); Intake 1838, 1855 (*v*. **inntak** 'a piece of land taken in or enclosed); Kenneck Syke (sic) 1838, Kenwick Syke 1855 (probably from the surn. *Kenwick* and **sík**); Lane Cl 1838, ~ cl 1855; Leys 1855 (cf. Green Leys *supra*); Ling Fuz (sic) 1838, Ling Furze 1855 (*v.* **lyng, fyrs**); Long Cl 1838, Long cl and Plantation 1855; Low Cl 1838, 1855; Marsh Beck 1838, 1855 (*v.* **bekkr**), Marsh Ings 1838, 1855 (cf. *in magno marisco* 1218, *blyber Mershe* 1742, *Blybmershe* (sic) 1545, *v.* **mersc, eng**); Middle Cl 1838; Mill Cl 1838, 1855, Mill Fd 1855; Moor Furze 1838 (*v.* **mōr, fyrs**); New Cl 1838, 185; New Home Cl 1855; Noddle 1838, 1855; Nordales 1838, 1855 (*v.* **norð, deill** 'a share, a portion of land', as elsewhere in the parish); North Carr 1855 (*v.* **kjarr** 'brushwood' later 'marsh, especially one overgrown with brushwood'); Norton Bottom 1838, 1855; Obadiah's Cl 1838, Obadiahs Cl 1855; Old Lands 1838, 1855 (*le old lands* 1547, *v.* **ald** 'old' in the sense long used or formerly used, **land** 'a selion'); Old Leys 1838, 1855 (*v.* **ley** and prec.); Old Park 1838 (cf. Old Leys *supra*); Oven Cl 1855; Ox cl 1838, 1855 (cf. *le oxe pastur'* 1547, *le oxepastur* 1548, self-explanatory); Osier Holt 1855 (cf. Near Furze *supra*); Pasture Leys 1838 (*v.* **ley** and cf. Green Leys *supra*); Pearson Cl 1838 (from the surn. *Pearson*); Pingle 1838, 1855 (*v.* **pingel**); Red Earth 1838, 1855 (self-explanatory); Sandals 1838, Sandales 1855 (*v.* **sand, deill**); Saunderson's Cl 1838 (*Sandersons Close* 1707, named from the *Sanderson* family, cf. *Mr Sanderson* 1690 *Terrier*); Shepherds house 1838 (perhaps from the surn. *Shepherd*, cf. *Jo. Shepheard* 1642 LPR); Shorts Cl 1838 (presumably from the surn. *Short*); Great Simpson's Cl 1838, Great Simpsons cl 1855, Little Simpson Cl 1838 (no doubt from the surn. *Simpson*); Far Sleights 1838, (Far) Slights 1855 (*yᵉ Sleights* 1707, *v.* **slétta** 'a smooth, level field'); Smith Cl 1838, Smiths cl 1855 (named from the *Smith* famiiy, cf. Thomas *Smith* 1614 *BT*); Smoot Hall (sic) 1838, Smoothill 1855; Snowdale Btm, ~ Cl 1838, Snow Dale Btm, ~ ~ Cl 1855 (named from the *Snow* family, cf. Robert *Snow* 1817 *BT*, with **deill** and **botm**); Sokes Cl 1838, 1855; South Cl 1838; Lr South Town 1838, South Town 1855; Spa Plantn 1855 (cf. Avenues and Spaw *supra*); Stone house Cl 1838; Stone pit cl 1838, ~ Pit Cl 1855; Stows Cl 1838 (probably from the surn. *Stow*, cf. Richard *Stow* 1642 LPR); Sykes 1838, Sykes Cl 1855 (*v.* **sík**); 20 acres 1838, Twenty Acres 1855; Weather Walk 1838 (*v.* **walk** 'a range of pasture for an animal', hence the common *Sheepwalk*; in this case it was for a wether 'a castrated ram'. This is the first time *Wetherwalk* has been noted in the L survey); West Cl 1838, 1855; West Pingle 1838 (*v.* **pingel**); Wheat Cl 1838, Wheat cl (and Ash Holt) 1855 (cf. Ash Holt Plantn *supra*); Wilmore Cl 1838, 1855; Woolerton Cl 1838, Willoughton cl 1855 (from the adjacent parish of Willoughton, cf. *ad diuisam de Wylcheton'* m13).

(b) *Bliburgh Wode* 1375 (*v.* **wudu**); *bondesdail* m13 (probably from the ODan pers.n. *Bondi*, or the derived surn. and **deill**); *Bradegate* m13 ('the broad road', *v.* **brād, gata**); *Est broddeyle, Westbroddeylle* 1238 'the broad share of land', *v.* **brād, deill**, prefixed by **ēast** and **west**); *le Comon* 1548; *quoddam fossatum in Blieburc* 1206, *Dikfurlang* 1238 (*v.* **dík, furlang**); *Eldelandes* m13 (*v.* **land**); *campo de Blyburg* 1238 (*v.* **feld**, a reference to the open field of the village); *Geyre, in prato quod vocatur Gayre* 1218[1], *Gayre* 1218[2] *v.* **geiri** 'a triangular plot of ground'); *Grayngham merebank* 1547 ('Grayingham (an adjacent parish) boundary bank', *v.* **(ge)mære, banke**); *atte Grene* 1332, 1343 both (p) (*v.* **grēne** 'a village green, a grassy place'); *heuedlandes* m13, *le hedlandes* 1547 (*v.* **hēafod-land** 'the head of a strip of land left for turning the plough'); *the Homestall* 1707 (i.e. of the Parsonage); *atte Kyrke* "of" *Blyburgh* 1327[2] (p); *super collem a parte boriali de Bl'gh* m13 (*v.* **norð, hyll**); *Niddinghes* (sic) m13 (*v.* **eng** 'meadow, pasture'; the first el. is uncertain); *Nortiby* (sic) 1327[1], *Northiby* 1332 both (p) (literally 'north in the village', *v.* **norð, í, bȳ**, denoting X who lives in the north of the village, a common Danish formation in L); *Parsonage Garth* 1693 (*v.* **garð** 'an enclosure');

Somerdebywode 1290 (named from Somerby in Corringham Wapentake);
Spachowegate (sic) m13 (probably '(the road to) Spak's mound', *v.* **haugr**, the first
el. being the Scand byname ON *Spakr*, ODan *Spak*, for which *v.* SPNNf 339); *ad
paruam stratam* m13; *le Tolland* 1389 (perhaps land on which some toll is levied, *v.*
toln, land); *Trentgate* 1238 (apparently 'the road to the R. Trent', *v.* **gata**); *Westiby*
1327[1], *Westyby* 1332 both (p) (literally 'west in the village', *v.* **vestr, west, í, bȳ** and
for the significance, *v. Nortiby supra*); *Westsandholm* 1238 (*v.* **sand, holmr**, prefixed
by **west**).

Caenby

CAENBY

> *Couenebi* 1086 DB
> *Cafnabi* c1115 LS (corrected reading), *Kafnebi* l13 *Foster Kauelebi*
>   1191, 1192, 1193 P, *Kauelbi* 1194 ib
> *Cauenesbi* 1202, 1203 P (p)
> *Cauenebi* 1191, 1192, 1193, 1194, 1195 P all (p), 1196 ChancR (p),
>   1200, 1201 P both (p), 1219 Ass, *-by* 1208 FF, c1220 *HarlCh*,
>   1244 Pat, 1257 FF, 1275 Ipm, 1280 *FF*, *Caveneby* 1225 Pat, 1225
>   FineR, 1229 Ch, 1266 Pat, 1281 QW, *Kauenebi* 1203 Ass (p),
>   1203 Cur, *-by* 1215–20, c1230 RA iv, 1245 FF, 1275 RRGr,
>   *Kaveneby* 1236 ib, 1253 Ch, 1280 Cl
> *Kauenbi* 1202 Ass, *-by* c1220 RA iv, 1265 Misc, 1424 *Foster,
>   Cavenby* 1245 RRG, 1254 ValNor, 1275 RH, 1292 RSu, 1309
>   YearBk, 1322 Cl *et freq* to *Cavenbie* 1591 Brasses, *Cavenbi* 1312
>   Pap, *Cauenbi* 1271 RRGr, *-by* 1279 ib, 1316 FA, 1327, 1332 *SR*,
>   1366 *Foster et passim* to 1634–42 Holles
> *Caneby* 1370 Pat, 1404 *Foster* 1428 AASR xxix, 1431 FA, 1453 Pat,
>   1458 Cl *et passim* to 1652 WillsPCC
> *Canby* 1445 AASR xxix, *Canbi* 1467 Pap
> *Caynby* 1519 DV i, 1535 VE iv, 1537–38 Dugd vi, 1539 LP xiv,
>   1575 LER, *Caynebye* 1539 LP xiv, 1590 SC, *Cainbie* 1585 ib,
>   1603 WillsA, *Cainby* 1580 ib, 1604 *Stubbs*, 1723 SDL *et passim*
>   to 1837 *CCLeases*, *Kaynby* 1548 CA, *Caynbe* 1539 *Foster, -bie*
>   1621 AASR xxix
> *Caenby* 1833 Noble (Gazetteer), 1842, 1856 White, 1855 *Terrier*

'Kafni's farmstead, village' from the unrecorded Scand byname
Kafni and ODan **bȳ**, as tentatively suggested by Fellows Jensen,
SSNEM 40, SPNLY 159. The same pers.n. but with the gen.sg *-es* is
apparently the first el. of *Kauenesholm* in West Rasen f.ns., PN L **3**, 121.
The interchange between *-n-* and *-l-* in some late 12th century forms is
due to AN influence.

BARF FM, *Barf F^m* 1828 Bry, cf. *the barff* 1577 *Terrier*, *ye Barfe* 1679, 1697, 1700, 1709, 1734 *ib*, from **beorg** 'a hill, a mound', dial. *barf*, common in L. CAENBY CLIFF, 1820 *BT*, cf. *Cliff F^m* 1828 Bry, *Cliff* 1844 *TA*. CAENBY CORNER, 1842 White, cf. *Monks Arms or Caenby Corner Inn* 1828 Bry. CAENBY HALL, 1824 O, 1828 Bry, cf. *atte halle* 1332 *SR*, *atte Halle* 1343 NI both (p) and *ye Hall Walles* 1700 *Terrier*, *the* ~ ~ 1734 *ib*. DANBY'S FM and PLACE, *cf. Danby's Plantation* 1871 *Padley*, named from the *Danby* family, cf. Joseph *Danby* 1856 White. FEN WOOD, 1844 *TA*, 1871 *Padley*, cf. *the fenne* 1577 *Terrier, ye Fen* 1679, 1697, 1700, 1734 *ib* and is *Caenby Wood* 1824 O, 1830 Gre. LOW WALK WOOD (lost), 1824 O, 1830 Gre, *v.* **walk**, denoting land used for the pasture of animals, hence the common *Sheepwalk*. MANOR FM, *Manor House* 1842 White and is *Caenby Old Hall* 1824 O, 1830 Gre. MIDDLE STREET is *the old Street* 1720 *Monson*, cf. *Middle Street Flat* 1848 *ib*. MOAT FM, *Moat Ho* 1828 Bry, cf. *Moat* 1871 *Padley,* a medieval moated site. MONKS ARMS HOTEL, *Monck's Arms* 1842 White, *Moncks Arms Inn* 1844 *TA* and *v.* Caenby Corner *supra*. The inn was named from the *Monck* family, cf. Sir Charles Miles Lambert *Monck*, landowner 1844 *TA*. PARSONAGE, *the* ~ 1577, 1734 *Terrier*, *the Vicarage* 1601 *ib*, *ye Rectory* 1709 *ib*. PAUNCH BECK, cf. *the panche* 1577 *ib*, *Paunche* 1601 *Terrier*, *ye Paunch* 1697, 1734 ib, *Paunch* 1700 *ib*, 1844 *TA*. This appears to be ME *paunch(e)*, also *panche* (*v.* MED s.v.) 'the human stomach, paunch', used in some transferred topographical sense. THE SCREED, from *screed* 'a narrow strip of land', *v.* NED sb I, 1b and cf. The Screed PN L **3**, 169.

FIELD-NAMES

Forms dated 1285 (Ed1) are *Barl*, 1327 *SR*, 1445 AASR xxix, 1537–38 Dugd vi, 1564, 1612, 1661, 1669, 1760 *DCLB*, 1577, 1601, 1679, 1690, 1697, 1700, 1709, 1734 *Terrier*, 1657, 1658 LNQ vii, 1844 *TA*, 1871 *Padley*, 1872 *TA* (Altered Apportionment).

(a) Barn Cl 1871, 1872; Blacksmith's Shop 1871; Bottom Cl 1872; Bracken Cl 1844 (*v.* **brakni**); Brick Cl 1844; (Top) Brick Kiln Cl 1844, 1871, 1872; Brown's Cl 1871, Browns ~ 1872 (from the surn. *Brown*); Caenby Cl 1844, ~ Hill 1844, 1871, 1872; Cainby Beck 1760 (*Caynby becke* 1564, *Cainbie* ~ 1612, *Cainbie Becke* 1661, *ye Beck* 1679, 1607, 1700, 1709, 1734, cf. *beck furlong* 1577, *v.* **bekkr** 'a stream', as elsewhere in the parish); Calf Cl 1844, 1871, 1872, ~ Garth 1844 (*v.* **garðr** 'an enclosure', as elsewhere in the parish); Chapel Cl 1844, 1871, 1872; Clay Hill 1844, 1871, 1872; Common Houses 1844; Corn Cl 1844; Cottage Cl 1844, 1871, 1872; Cow Cl 1844, 1871, 1872 (*the cow closse* 1577, *the Cow Close* 1601, *Cowclose* 1697, *Cow close* 1700, 1709); Middle, North, South Crackthorn 1841 (although the form is late, this is probably 'the thorn bush where crows are found', *v.* **kráka** 'a crow, a raven', **þorn**); Cream Poke Cl 1871 (a complimentary term for rich pasture or fertile arable, cf. Pudding Poke *infra*); Day's Cl 1871, Days ~1872 (named from the *Day* family, cf. William *Day* 1782 *BT*); Dove Cot Cl 1844; East Field of Caneby 1760 *LCS*, East Fd 1844 (*Cainby est feild* 1577, *the east feild* 1601, *y* *East field* 1679, 1701, *the East field* 1690, *y* *east feild* 1697, *the East Field* 1734, one of the great fields of the parish, cf. West Fd of Caneby *infra*); The Eight Acres 1871, The 8 acres 1872; The Eighteen Acres 1871, The 18 Acres 1872; Fallow Cl 1844 (cf. *y* *Fallow field* 1709, *v.* **falh**); The Fifteen Acres 1871, The fifteen acres 1872; Five Acres 1844; Furze Cl 1844 (cf. *y* *comon furrs* 1697, *Furses* 1679 (*v.* **fyrs** 'furze'); Gygarthe 1844, 1872 (*v.* **garðr**; the first el. is obscure unless it is the surn. *Guy, Gye*); Hallis Btm 1844, Hallis's ~ 1871 (probably from the surn. *Hallis* and **botm**); Hill Cl 1844, 1871, 1872; Home Cl 1844, 1871, 1872; Home Paddock & Shed 1872; Horse Cl 1844, 1871, 1872; Kitchen Cl & Garden 1844; Lilly lane Cl 1844, ~ Lane Cl 1872; Little Beck Cl 1844, 1871 (cf. Cainby Beck *supra*); Long Cl 1844; Long Plantation 1871, 1872; Meadow Btm 1844 (*v.* **botm**), Meadow Fd 1872 (cf. *in le mede* 1285 (p), *v.* OE (Angl) **mēd**, ME **mēde** 'a meadow, clearing, open field'; also 'meadowland, a tract of grassland'); Middle Cl 1844; (Top) Middle Pasture 1844; Mill Seeds 1844, 1871; Moor 1844, The Moor 1872 (*Cainbye more, the More* 1601, *y* *Moore* 1697, ~ *Moor* 1700, 1709, 1734, *v.* **mōr**); Mowed Acres 1844; The First, The Second 19 acres 1872; Normanby Btm 1844 (from the adjacent parish of Normanby and **botm**); Normer Headings 1871, 1872 (Normer is probably from **norð** and (**ge)mǣre** 'a boundary, boundary land'; for *headings v. y* *headings* PN L **2**, 14); North Cl 1844, 1871, 1872; Oak Cl 1844; Paddock 1871; The Park 1871; Pingle 1844 (*v.* **pingel** 'a small enclosure'); Plantation 1844, ~ Cl 1871, 1872; Pond Cl 1844, 1871; Pudding Poke 1844, 1871, 1872 (a fanciful complimentary name for rich pasture or fertile arable, cf. Cream Poke Cl *supra*); Ranshaw's Cl 1871, Ranshaws ~ 1872 (named from the *Ranshaw, Renshaw* family, cf. John *Renshaw* 1765 *BT*); Red Car 1844, 1871 (*y* *read carr* 1577, *the Red Carr* 1601, *red Carr* 1679, *Red carr* 1700, *Redcer* 1734, *v.* **rēad** 'red', presumably referring to clayey soil, **kjarr** 'brushwood', 'a bog, a marsh, especially one overgrown with brushwood'); Road-side Cl 1871; Rough Cl 1844, Ruff ~ (denoting rough land); Sallow Holt 1871, 1872 (*v.* **salh** 'a willow, a sallow', **holt** 'a wood, a thicket'); North, South Sands 1844, 1872, Three-cornered Sands 1872; Sandy Cl 1871, 1872; Seed Cl 1844, New, Old Seeds; Seven Acres 1844; Sheep Walk 1844, 1871, 1872 (*v.* **shepe-walk**); The 6 Acres 1844, 1872; Spittle Cl 1844 (presumably a piece of land held by Spital in the Street in Hemswell parish); Stack yard Cl 1844, 1872; Stone Pit Cl 1844, 1871, 1872 (cf. *Stone pite* (sic) 1679, *Stonepit furlong* 1697, *y* *stone pit furlong* 1709, *v.* **stān, pytt**); Low, Upr Ten Acres 1844; the Thirteen Acres 1871, The 13 acres 1872; The Thirty-five Acres 1871; Thorn Cl 1844, 1871; Top Cl 1872; Top Fd 1871, 1872; The Twenty-one Acres 1871; The Twenty-two Acres 1871; (Little, Top) Walk 1844 (*v.* **walk** and cf. Sheep Walk *supra*); Wash Dyke Cl 1844, 1871, 1872 (*v.* **wæsce, dīk**, a dyke for washing sheep); Well Cl 1844, 1871, 1872; West Field of Caneby 1760 *LCS* (*y* *west feld* 1577, *the west fyld* 1601, *Westfield* 1679, *y* *westfield* 1700, 1709, 1734, *v.* **west, feld**, one of the great fields of the parish, cf. East Field of Caneby *supra*) Wheat Cl 1844; Willow Holt 1844 (*v.* **holt**, and cf. Sallow Holt *supra*); Willows 1844; Wood Cl (and Lawn Fd); Wood Pasture 1844.

(b) *Abraham Close* 1697, *Abram close* 1700, 1709, *Abraham Close* 1734 (named from the *Abraham* family, cf. John *Abraham* 1620 *BT); Robert Bell's Close* 1734; *Bowbeck landes* 1601 (*v.* **bekkr**); *braswell syke* (sic) 1577; *the brod stone* 1577, *broad stone* 1601 (*v.* **brād** 'broad, large', **stān**); *Broke furlong* 1601; *Bromit Lane* 1658 (named from the *Brummet* family, cf. Alexander *Brummet* 1642 LPR); *y* *brother land, Brother side* 1601 (the meaning of *brother* here is uncertain; it could refer to a religious brother, a monk, or be from ON **bróðor** 'a brother', more specifically 'a younger brother'; *side* denotes land alongside a river, the edge of a wood or village); *the close* 1445 (*v.* **clos(e)** 'an enclosure'); *cogle furlong, the coggle* 1577, *Coggle* 1679, 1734, *ye Coggle* 1697, *ye Cogle* 1700, 1709, *Cogole* 1709 (*coggle* is defined in MED, s.v. *cogel*, as 'a round stone, cobblestone', and in NED, s.v. *coggle*, as 'a rounded water-worn stone, esp. of the size suitable for paving, a cobble'. Presumably the f.n. denotes a place where such stones were obtained); *Coney Close* 1657 (*v.* **coni** 'a rabbit'); *Cowdike* 1679, ~ *furlong* 1697, 1709, *Cow dike Furlong* 1734 (*v.* **cū, dík** 'a ditch'); *ye Cow-gate* 1709 ('the right of pasturage for a cow', *v.* **cou-gate** and cf. the common **shepe-gate**); *ye cow pasture* 1700, *ye Cow pastur* 1709; *Le croft* 1327 (p), *v.* **croft** 'a small enclosed field'); *ye Curt close* 1601 (perhaps from ME **court, curt** (OFr *court, cort*) 'short'); *Cutlowe hill* 1601; *the Dove Hills* 1601, *Dove hills* 1679, *Dovehills* 1697, 1709, *ye Dovehills* 1700 (self-explanatory); *drean stockes* 1577 (from ME **dreine** 'a drainage canal, a drain' and ME **stok**, here probably denoting a channel); *the East More* 1690 (cf. Moor in (a) *supra*); *Eastwell hill* 1601 (self-explanatory); *Elderston hole* 1601; *ye fearnie ground* 1601 ('the ground growing with ferns', *v.* **fearnig, grund** 'a stretch of land'); *fields meer* 1697, *fields meer* 1700 ('the boundary of the open field', *v.* **feld, (ge)mǣre**); *the Fenne Leaze* 1601, *ye Fen Leys Furze* 1734 (cf. Fen Wood *supra* and *v.* **ley** (OE **lēah**) 'meadow, pasture', with **fyrs**); *Fullpitt* 1601 ('the foul pool or pit', *v.* **fūl, pytt**); *ye furlong* 1709, *ye Furlong* 1734 (*v.* **furlang**); *ye Gate* 1697, 1700, *ye gate* 1709, *the Gate* 1734 (*v.* **gata** 'a way, a path, a road'); *Glentham Beck* 1679, 1700, 1709, 1734 (*v.* **bekkr**), *Glentham feild* 1697, ~ *field* 1700, 1709, 1734, *Glentham field meare* 1679, *Glentham mear* 1601, *Glentham Meer* 1734 (*v.* **(ge)mǣre**) (all named from the neighbouring parish of Glentham); *Gorbrod* 1601 ('the triangular breadth of land', *v.* **gara, brǣdu**); *the greene meare* 1601, *Green meer end* 1697, 1709, *Green Meer end* 1734 ('the green boundary', probably from **grēne** 'a village green, a grassy place', **(ge)mǣre**); *the hole gate end* 1577, *the Houle gate* 1601; *the Howsse Hill* (sic) 1577, *the howe house* (sic) 1601, *ye how hill* 1679, *How Hill* 1697, 1700, 1709, *How Hill* 1734 (the first el. is apparently **haugr** 'a hill, a (burial) mound'); *ye Kylnehowse* 1445 (self-explanatory); *Langsound* (sic) 1601; *Longdalls, Longe daylle* 1577, *Long dailes, Longe Dales* 1601 (*v.* **lang, deill** 'a share of land'); *longlane furlong* 1601; *ye Long rode* 1601 (*v.* **lang, rōd** 'a rood of land'); *ye meer* 1697, 1700, 1709, *(y^e) Meer* 1734 (*v.* **(ge)mǣre**); *ye Meley* (sic) 1577; *the midle furlonge* 1601; *Modde carrs* (sic), *Moddicars Syke* 1700, *Modecars* 1709, *Moddecars Close* 1734 (obscure); *Morekersyke* 1577, *Murrakers close* 1601 (*v.* **mōr, kjarr** with **sík**); *Mydle fyld* 1601 (one of the open fields of the village); *Mydelleues* (sic) 1577 (*v.* **middel, efes** 'eaves, an edge or border'); *New banke* 1679, *ye new banck* 1700, 1709, ~ *New Bank* 1734; *the new close* 1601, *new close* 1679, *ye New close* 1697, 1700, *the New Close* 1735; *normeby meare* (sic) 1577, *Normanby meare* 1601, *Normandie meare* (sic) 1679, *Normanby Meer* 1697, *Normanby meer furlong* 1700, 1709, *Normanby's feild Meer* 1697, *Normanby field Meer* 1700, *Normanby's field Meer* 1734 ('the boundary with Normanby (an adjacent parish)', 'the boundary with Normanby Field', *v.* **(ge)mǣre**); *the north more* 1601, *ye North Moor furlong* 1697, 1700, 1709 (cf. Moor in f.ns. (a) *supra*, *the east More* in f.ns. (b) *supra*); *Caynby, firma molendin'* 1537–38, *the ould miln furlong* 1577, *Old mill stegh* 1679, *ye Old Miln stee* 1697, *Old Mill Stee* 1734 (*v.* **stīg** 'a path, a narrow road'); *the oxpasture* 1690, *ye ox pasture* 1700, *Ox Pasture* 1734; *ye pales* 1679 (*v.* **pāl** 'a stake, a pole' in the pl.); *ye Pasture* 1709, *The Pasture* 1734; *Pilet hole* 1679, *Pickel hole* 1700, *Pikel hole* 1709, *Picket*

Hole 1734 (the forms are too varied to suggest an etymology for the first el.); *William Post Sike* 1734; *the pound horne* 1577, *the pound hurne* 1601, *yᵉ Pound Hourne* 1697, *yᵉ Pound Horn* 1700, *Pound Hurn* 1700, 1734, *pound hurn* 1709 (the forms are late, but it may be from **pund** 'a pound for stray animals' with **hyrne** 'an angle, a corner' in some topographical sense); *Pushbush* 1679; *Rysebushe* 1577, *rishe bushe* 1601 ('the brushwood thicket', *v.* **hrīs, busc**); *Sande pitt hill* 1601; *Shortbuts* 1679, *Short Butts* 1697, *short Butts* 1700 (*v.* **butte** 'a strip of land abutting on a boundary, a short strip or ridge at right angles to other ridges, etc.'); *short ryland* 1601 ('a selion where rye grows', *v.* **rȳge, land**); *Sinnomes* 1601, *Sinholme* 1697, *Sinholm* 1700, *sinholm* 1709, *Synholm* 1734 (the first el. is uncertain; the second is **holmr** 'higher dry ground amidst the marshes'); *Long small path* 1601 ('the narrow path', *v.* **smæl, pæð**, prefixed by **lang**); *South hills* 1700, *South Hills* 1709, 1734; *the stone wathe* 1601, *yᵉ Stone wathe* 1697, *~ stone wath* 1700, *~ Stone Wathe* 1734 ('the stone ford', *v.* **stān, vað**); *Stone gate, Stonie gate* 1679 ('the paved road', *v.* **stān(ig), gata**); *Stone more* 1697 (cf. Moor in f.ns. (a) *supra*); *Stone Wall* 1700; *stongall* 1577 (the second el. is presumably **galla** 'a sore', probably in the sense of 'a barren or a wet spot in a field'); *yᵉ Syke* 1697, 1700, 1709, *Sike* 1734 (*v.* **sík**); *yᵉ Tethering ground* 1700; *Tom Tird's Garth* 1657 (*v.* **garðr**; this is no doubt a derogatory nickname not previously noted in the survey); *the tithe dall* 1577, *the tythe dayle* 1601 (self-explanatory, *v.* **deill**); *Trencher* 1679, *yᵉ Trencurs* (sic) 1700, *yᵉ Trenchers* 1700, 1709, *yᵉ Trencher* 1734 (perhaps a fanciful f.n. for a round piece of land resembling a trencher or wooden platter); *Wafin* (sic) 1601, *Waifin* (sic) 1679 (obscure); *yᵉ wath* 1679 (*v.* **vað** 'a ford' and cf. *yᵉ Stone wathe supra*); *Waugh Hole* 1734; *Wrangle hole* 1700, 1709 (perhaps from the surn. *Wrangle*).

Cammeringham

CAMMERINGHAM

Cameslingeham (sic) 1086 DB
Camelingeham 1086 DB, *-hame* 1219 Welles i
Camringham (2x) c1115 LS
Cambrigeham 1126, 1184–88 France *Cambringeham* Hy2 (1317)
  Ch, c1175, 1192 France
Kameringeham 1219 WellesLA, 1220 LAHW
Cameringham 1202 Ass, Ed1 *HarlCh*, 1292 RSu, 1296 Pat, 1298
  Ass, 1317 Pat, 1317 ChancW, 1327 Pat, 1343 NI, *-ingam* 1563
  InstBen, 1610 Speed, *-yngham* 1291 Tax, 1303, 1316, 1325 FA,
  1325 Pat, 1327 Cl, 1332 *SR*, 1335 Cl, 1342 Fine, 1345 Cl *et freq*
  to 1535 VE iv, *Kameringham* 1232 Welles, 1289 *Ass*, *-yngham*
  1373 Peace, *Camryngham* 1327 *SR*, 1382 Pat, *Camringham* 1657
  SP
Cammeringham 1576 LER *et passim Cambryngham* 1316 Pat, 1519
  DV i, 1535 VE iii, 1545 LP xx, *-ingham* 1575 WillsCal
Caneryngham (sic) 1337 Fine, 1337, 1341, 1347 Cl, *-ingham* 1356
  Pat

This is an OE group-name formation in -**ingahām**, comparable with Fillingham *infra*. The etymology of the first el. is difficult, but we may tentatively suggest an OE unrecorded pers.n. **Cantmǣr* as first el. Dr Insley comments that this would be an extremely early borrowing into OE, in which the -*i*- of British **Canti*- had been syncopated before OE *i*-mutation, cf. by contrast the OE pers.ns. *Centwold* and *Centwine*. A parallel formation is the name of the men of Kent, OE *Cantware*, which also shows early syncope of -*i*-. Hence, the name would denote 'the homestead, the estate of the family, the dependants of Cantmǣr', from the gen.pl. *Cantmǣringa* of the group name **Cantmǣringas* 'the family, the dependants of *Cantmǣr*'. The interchange between -*r*- and -*l*- in the early forms is apparently due to AN influence.

ASHBY COTTAGE (local). BACK LANE (local). BLACKTHORN HILL, 1824 O, 1828 Bry, *Blackthorne Hill* 1830 Gre. CAMMERINGHAM HALL (lost), *Cameringham Hall* 1674, 1724 *Terrier, Camringham Hall* 1700 *ib, The Hall* 1785 *Brown*, cf. *the halle daile* 1601 *Terrier, ~ Hall Dale* 1606 *ib* (*v.* **deill** 'a share, a portion of land') and *the West Hall* 1690, 1699 *Monson, that New built Messuage . . . in Cameringham called the West Hall* 1715 *ib, West hall* 1720 *ib.* CAMMERINGHAM HILL (local), *the hill* 1606 *Terrier.* CAMMERINGHAM LOW COVERT, ~ *Low Cover* 1824 O, *Low Cover* 1828 Bry, *Lower Cover* 1830 Gre. CAMMERINGHAM TOP COVERT, *Cammeringham Cover* 1824 O. CHURCH COTTAGE (local), cf. *The Churche daille* 1601 *Terrier* (*v.* **deill**). CLIFF FM (lost), 1828 Bry, cf. *the Cliff* 1690, 1720 *Monson, the Clift* (sic) 1715 *ib, Cliff* 1844 *TA*, and *the northe cliffe, yᵉ southe clyffe* 1577 *Terrier, Northe clyf, South cliff* 1601 *ib, the Southe Clyffe* 1606 *ib.* COLD HARBOUR, 1824 ib, 1828 Bry, ~ *Harbor* 1830 Gre, a common name referring to a sheltered place in the open. EAST LANE (lost), 1828 Bry. FISH POND, 1847 *TA, Fishpond* 1848 *Monson.* FURZE HILL, 1824 O, 1842 White, *furhill* 1695 *Cragg, Furhill* 1703 *Inv*, 1822 *Terrier, v.* **fyrs** 'furze'. THE GRANGE, a late example of **grange**, common in L, for which *v.* EDD s.v. 2 'a homestead, a small mansion or farm-house, esp. one standing by itself remote from others', a sense quoted from L. LONG COVERT. MANOR HO, *Mannor house* 1715 *Monson.* MEADOW LANE (lost), 1828 Bry. MIDDLE STREET, 1785 *Brown*, 1847 *TAMap*, 1848 *Monson* and is probably *yᵉ ould streat* 1577 *Terrier, the olde Street* 1601 *ib, the old Street* 1690, 1715 *Monson.* It ran at least from North Carlton through Cammeringham to Fillingham. MOAT, a medieval moated site. MONSON HO (local), commemorating the estate in the village of the *Monson* family. PASTURE LANE (lost), 1828 Bry. RED BUILDINGS. SQUIRE'S BRIDGE, 1824 O, ~ *Br.* 1830 Gre, named from the family of John *Squire* 1725 *BT.* VICARAGE, *the vicareg* (sic) 1577, *the Vicarage* 1601, *Vicaridge of Camringham* 1668, *the Vicarage*

House 1606, 1709, 1724, *Vicarage* 1744 all *Terrier*, cf. *the Vicarage home close* 1744 *ib.*

FIELD-NAMES

Forms dated m13 (14) are *Welb*; Ed1 *HarlCh*; 1327, 1332 *SR*; 1543 LP i; 1545 *Pat*; 1577, 1601, 1606, 1634, 1668, 1674, 1700, 1709, 1724, 1744, 1762, 1822 *Terrier*; 1690, 1695, 1715, 1720, 1829, 1848² *Monson*; 1785 *Brown*; 1847 *TA*; 1848¹ *TAMap*.

(a) Ash Holt 1847, 1848² (*v.* **æsc, holt**); Atkinson's Cl 1829 (named from the *Atkinson* family, cf. Margaret *Atkinson* 1700 *BT*); Barn Cl 1847, Barn Sheds and Crew 1847 (*v.* **crew** 'a pen, a hut, a shed'); Brotlesby, Little, Lower, Great Barth 1829 (cf. *the barge* 1601, *the Barfes* 1695, *v.* **beorg**, dial. **barf** 'a hill, a mound'); The Beck 1785, Great, Little, Thistle Becks 1847 (cf. *Attebek'* 1327, *atte Beck'* 1332 both (p), *yᵉ becke* 1577, *the becke* 1601, ~ *Becke* 1606, ~ *Becks* 1690, 1715, *v.* **bekkr** 'a stream, a beck', as elsewhere in the parish); Bemrose Beck, ~ Walk 1785, Middle Bemrose Walk 1829 (named from the *Bemrose* family, cf. William *Bemrose* 1602 *Inv*, with **bekkr** and **walk** 'a sheep-walk'); Besant Cl 1847 (probably from the surn. *Besant*); Black Courners Cl (sic) 1829; Blackburn's Beck 1785 (named from the *Blackburn* family, cf. William *Backbourn* 1715 *BT*, with **bekkr**); Bottom Cl 1847 (*the bottome close* 1668, *Bottome Close* 1690, *yᵉ Bottome Closes* 1709, (*The*) *bottom close* 1715, *bottom* ~ 1720, *Bottom Close* 1724, cf. *longe lands* in (b) *infra*); The Bottoms 1847 (*v.* **botm**); Brattleby Cl 1847 (referring to Brattleby, the adjacent parish to the south); Brick Kiln Cl 1847 (*Brickin Close* (sic) 1690, ~ *close* 1715); Bridge Cl 1847; Bullock Cl 1847 (from **bulloc** 'a bull calf' or the derived surn.); Cabbage Garden 1848²; Church Yard 1847; (East, West) Cliff Cl 1829 (cf. *Cliff Fm supra*; Cottager's Cl 1785, the Cottagers Pasture 1822, Cottages Cl (sic) 1829, Cottage Lands 1847 (cf. *Cameringham Cottage Pasture* 1709); Cover Cl, Below Covers 1847 (*v.* **covert**); Cow Cl 1829, 1847; Cowpasture 1822 (*the common cow pastur* 1577, *the Cowe-pasture* 1606, *the Cowpasture or Common pasture* 1634, *the Common pasture(s)* 1690, *the Common pasture* 1715, 1720, *Cameringham Cow Pasture* 1724, *Cow-pasture* 1744); Crew Yard (*v.* **crew**); Great, Little Croft 1847 (*v.* **croft**); Dimbelby's Beck 1785 (*v.* **bekkr**), Dembleby's Cl 1829, Dimbleby ~ 1847 (*Dimblebys Close* 1690, *Dymblebeys close* 1715, *Dimblebyes* (sic) 1720, named from the *Dimbleby* family, cf. William *Dimbleby* 1722 *BT*); (Far, Near) Drain Cl 1847; Drain Five Acres 1847, ~ Four Acres, ~ Nine Acres 1847; Earland Cl (sic) 1829; Eight Acres 1847; Ermine Street 1848¹ (cf. *lincoln' yeat* in (b) *infra*); Five Acres 1847; Foal Paddock 1847; Foggy Cl 1829 (*foggy* is a derivative of **fogga** 'rough grass'); Four Acres 1847; Fox Cover 1829, New Fox Cover 1848²; Far Garden 1847; The Gorse 1847; Great Holt 1785 (*v.* **holt** 'a wood, a thicket'); the Greens 1762, The ~ 1829, 1847, Lower, Middle Greens 1829 (*yᵉ grenes* 1577, *the greens* 1601, *the greenes* 1606, *a close called the Greenes* 1634, *the Greens* 1690, *the Green's* (sic) 1715, *Greenes* 1720, *a close or pasture Comonly called the Greenes, Greenes Close* 1744 (*v.* **grēne** 'a village green, a grassy place'); (East) Heath Cl, Heath Fd 1829, Far, Great, Little, Middle Heath 1847, Twenty Five Acre Heath 1847 (*v.* **hǣð**); Hillside (otherwise Little Cl) 1785, Long Hill Side Cl 1847 (cf. *the hill* 1601 and North Hills *infra*); Great Holt 1785 (*v.* **holt**); Home Cl 1829, 1848² (*Holme Close* (sic), *one Cottage House with the home Close* 1690, *yᵉ Home Closes* 1700, ~ ~ *closes* 1709,

Homeclose 1720, *the Home Close* 1724); the homestead 1785 (cf. *Homestead Close* 1674, 1700); Horse Cl 1847; Ingham Hill Top 1785, 1829, 1847 (*ye toppe of ye hill* 1577, from Ingham, an adjacent parish to the north); Lower, Middle Ings 1829, (Far, Middle, Near) Ings 1847 (*the Ings* 1695, *v.* **eng** 'meadow, pasture'); John's Cl 1785; Jollands Moor Cl 1822 (named from the *Jolland* family, cf. John *Jolland* 1711 *BT*); East Land Cl 1847 (*v.* **land** 'a selion'); Little Cl 1785, 1829 (cf. Hillside *supra*); Long Cl 1847; Low Btm 1847 (*v.* **botm** 'a bottom, a valley bottom'); The Meadow, Meadow Cl 1847 (*the medow* 1577); (Far, Near) Middle Cl 1848^2; Old Mill Yd 1847; Moor Cl 1829 (cf. *cameringhammore* m13 (14), *super moram de Cameringh'* 1244 (14), *midyll more becke* 1577, *the mydle moor* 1601, *Moore-becke* 1744 and Jollands Moor Cl *supra*); Narrow Cover 1847; Nine Acres 1847; North Cl 1829, 1847; North Dams 1785, 1829, 1848^2 (*Nordams* 1690, 1715, 1720, cf. *the south damme* 1601, *v.* **damme** (ON **dammr**) 'a dam, a pond'); North Hills 1829, Far, Near North Hills 1847 (*ye furlonge called northhill* 1577, *north hill* 1601, *North Hills* 1690, *the North Hill side* 1715, *North Hillside* 1720); North Long Hill 1785; North Moor 1829, Far, Near North Moor 1847 (*ye north more, the north mour* (sic) 1577, *North more* 1601, *Closes called Normoores* 1695, *v.* **norð, mōr**); North Pingle 1847 (*v.* **pingel** 'a small enclosure', cf. Pingles *infra*); North Plot 1785; Nunnock Cl 1847; Osgodby Cl 1829 (probably from the surn. *Osgodby*); Outheath 1785, Cover, North, South, Top Out Heath 1847 ('the outer heath', *v.* **ūt, hǣð**); Far Middle Pasture 1829, First, Second, Third, Fourth, Fifth Pasture 1847; Piece Cl 1829 (probably to be identified with *the pease close* 1606, *Peas Closes* 1690, *the pease closes* 1715, *Pease ~* 1720, the first el. is *pise* 'pease'); Pingles and Little Walk 1829 (*the Pingles* 1690, 1720, *the pingles* 1715, *v.* **pingel** and cf. North Pingle *supra* and South Pingle *infra* and *v.* also **walk**); New Ploughed Cl 1847; Great Redmoules, Little Redmoules cottage 1829, Great, Little Red Mould 1847 (*the readmyles* 1577, *The Redmyles* 1601, *two Read mylles* 1606, *the red mils* (sic) 1690, *the Red Hills* (sic), *the Red Mills* 1715, *v.* **rēad** 'red', **mylde** 'soil, earth', with reference to the soil there); Great, Little Seed Cl 1847; Far Seven Acres 1847; Six Acres 1847; South Cl 1829, 1847; South Pingle 1847, *v.* **pingel** and cf. North Pingle and Pingles *supra*); Spring Garth Cl 1829, Spring Garth 1847 (*Spring garthes* 1690, *~ Garths* 1717, *~ Garthe* 1720, and cf. *Spring* 1690, *v.* **spring** 'a spring, a copse' and **garðr** 'an enclosure'); Stack Yard & Orchard, Stack Yd 1847; Steels Cl 1847 (named from the *Steel* family, cf. John *Steel* 1776 *BT*); Stone Pit 1847, Stone Pit Cl 1785, 1829, 1847 (self-explanatory); East, West Swan Hill 1829, Top Swan Hills 1847 (*Swan hill* 1577, *Swanhill* 1601, 1606, *Swanhills* 1695); Old Syke 1847 (*Houldsikes* 1690, *v.* **sík** 'a ditch, a trench'); Near Till Cl 1847 (named from the R. Till); Top Cl 1848^2; Town Row 1785; Tup Cl 1829, 1847 (*Tup Close* 1690, 1715, *Tupclose* 1720 (*v.* **tup** 'a ram, a tup'); Twelve Acres 1847; Twenty Acres 1847; Vinyard Cl & Holt 1829 (cf. Winyard's Cl *infra*); Middle Walk, The Two Walks 1785, the Far Walks 1822, Far, Great Walk 1829, 1847, First Walk 1847 (cf. *the Sheep walkes* 1690, (*the*) *Sheep Walks* 1715, *v.* **walk, shepe-walk**); Walker's Cottage 1785 (named from the *Walker* family, cf. Nicholas *Walker* 1682 *Inv*); Watkinson's Beck 1785, *~* Btm 1785, 1829, *~* btm 1848^2 (named from the *Watkinson* family, cf. John *Watkinson* 1729 *BT*, with **bekkr** and **botm**); the West Lane 1822 (*the West lane* 1606, *a street or lane Commonly called West-lane* 1744); 1st, 2nd, 3rd, fourth Whole Syke 1829 (*heorlsykes* (sic) 1577, *hole ~, hool syke, houl sycke* 1601, *Hole syke* 1606, *Hould sikes* 1690, *Houlsikes* 1715, 1720, *v.* **sík**; the first el. is uncertain); Wilkinson Btm 1847 (named from the *Wilkinson* family, cf. Christopher *Wilkinson* 1642 *LPR*, with **botm**); Willow Cl, *~* Holt 1847 (*v.* **holt**); Wind Mill standing on the top of the Hill, not now standing (sic) 1822 (cf. "a windmill" 1543);

Winyard's Cl 1785 (cf. Vinyard Cl *supra*); (Far, First) Wood Cl 1847.

(b) *Bettewelle* Ed1 (Dr Insley suggests that the first el. is the ME pers.n. *Bette*, which can be either masc. or fem. and is of various origins, *v.* Reaney-Wilson, s.n. *Bett*; the second el. is **wella** 'a spring'); *blake landes* 1577, *blacklandes* 1601 ('the black selions', *v.* **blæc, land**, no doubt referring to the colour of the soil); *ye bowstones* 1601 (perhaps from OE **būgstān** 'a rocking-stone' in the pl., the site of which is not known); *the hye waye called Brodgat* 1577, *broodgate* 1601 ('the broad way, road', *v.* **brād, gata**); *brodsyke* 1577, *Braidsycke, bradsicke* 1601 ('the broad ditch', *v.* **brād, breiðr, sík**; the first el. shows a variation between ON breiðr and the cognate OE **brād** 'broad'); *brattelby clifte* (sic) 1601 (*v.* **clif**), *Brattleby common* 1668, *Bratleby feild* 1668, *Brackleby Feild* 1690, 1715, *Brattleby feild* 1695, *Brackleby* ~ 1720, *Brattelby Gate* 1601, *Brattleby gate* 1606 (*v.* **gata** 'a road), *Brotlbys meare* 1577, *Bratleby mear* 1601, *Brattleby meare* 1606 (*v.* **(ge)mære** 'a boundary'), ~ *mearfurre* 1606 (*v.* **marfur** 'a boundary furrow'), ~ *Pasture* 1709 (alluding to the adjacent parish of Brattleby); *ye brough* 1577 (*v.* **burh** 'a fortified place'; the site is unknown); *the buske mear, Bushe meare* 1606 (*v.* **buskr, busc** 'a bush', **(ge)mære**; the first el. shows a variation between ON **buskr** and the cognate OE **busc**, as with *Braidsyke* and *bradsicke supra*); *The spryng called Caudwell* 1601 (*v.* **cald** 'cold', **wella**); *Clover Close* 1712; *Coates hedge*, ~ *lane* 1606, ~ *Laine* 1695 (named from the adjacent parish of Coates); *the Common* 1668; *ye comon cowgat* 1577 (*v.* **cow-gate** 'right of pasturage for a cow', cf. the common **shepe-gate**); *The Corne Close* 1724; *Cows dyke* 1601; *the east hedge* 1601; *the Easter becke* 1634 (*v.* **bekkr**); *le Est garden* 1545 (*v.* **ēast** and cf. *le West garden infra*); *the firr close* 1668 (*firr* is probably from **fyrs** 'furze'); *the fre land* 1577; *Grenedycke* 1601, *the greene dyke meare* 1606 (*v.* **grēne** 'green', **dík**); *ye grownes* 1588 (perhaps 'the grounds', *v.* **grund**); *Home Croft* 1715 (a **croft** adjacent to a house); *the hyewaye between Ingham and camerringham* 1577; *Ingham Feild* 1690, 1715, ~ *field* 1690, 1715, 1720, ~ *fieldes* 1695, ~ *gate* 1606 (*v.* **gata**), ~ *marrfure* 1577 (*v.* **marfur**), ~ *meare* 1601, 1606 (*v.* **(ge)mære**), ~ *Sycke* 1601 (*v.* **sík**) (referring to Ingham, an adjacent parish); *Kealls close* 1577, *Keale closse* 1601 (named from the *Keal* family, cf. Ann *Keal* 1678 *BT*); *Lane Close* 1715; *lincoln' yeat* 1577, *Lincolne yate*, ~ *gatt* 1601, *the gate commonly called Lincoln gate* 1606 ('the road to Lincoln' *v.* **gata**, in spite of the *yeat, yate* spellings; the reference is to Ermine Street); *littell leye* 1601 (*v.* **lea, leye** (OE **lēah**) 'a meadow, pasture'); *the littel strete* 1601, ~ *lyttle street* 1606 (there is no indication of its situation); *longe landes* 1601, *Longlands* 1634, *Longlands or bottom Closes* 1674, *Long lands or bottom closes* 1674, *Long lands or bottom closes* 1700, *Long-lands Close* 1744 (*v.* **lang, land** 'a selion' and cf. Bottom Cl in f.ns. (a) *supra*); *ye lordes dalle* 1577, *the lordes dailes* 1601, *the Lordes Dales* 1606 (*v.* **deill** 'a share, a portion of land'); *ye lordes north closses* 1577; *lyttel syke* 1577, *the Lyttle Sycke* 1601, *lyttle syke* 1606 (*v.* **sík**); *ye marefurr* 1577, *the marfer, the Lyttle mearfur* 1601 (*v.* **marfur**); *the mearfur called milnmarr* 1577, *the mylne mear* 1601, *the Myll meare* 1606 (*v.* **myln, (ge)mære** 'a boundary'; the appellative use of **marfur** is noteworthy); *ye northe feld* 1577, *the North field* 1601, ~ ~ *feild* 1606 (one of the open fields of the village, *v.* **feld** and cf. *the South feilde* and *Weste feilde infra*); *the ould swarthes* 1577, ~ *olde Swarthes* 1601 (*v.* **swæð**, ME **swathe** 'a strip of grassland'); *ye oxe pastur* 1577, *Ox Pasture* 1724; *certaine small landes called peckes* 1577, *two selions called peckes* 1601 (perhaps from the surn. *Peck*); *nether Row Close* 1601; *letill Ryngell* 1601 (*v.* **lȳtel** 'little', **hringel** 'a small ring', perhaps in the sense 'a tethering ring'); *St James brow* 1577 (obscure); *Scadmans swath* 1577, *Skadmans s.ath* 1601 (from the surn. *Scadman*, with **swæð**; the reading of the 1601 form is uncertain); *a* *close called the Sheepe walke or Southmere heades* 1634, *a close called the South mere close* 1634 (*v.* **shepe-walk** and cf. Middle Walk in (a) *supra*; the alternative name is 'the south boundary', *v.* **sūð, (ge)mǣre**); *yᵉ common shep' pastur* 1577; *short landes* 1577, 1601 (*v.* **land**); *the Closse called Smithe layts now the Bricke close* 1601; *the South feilde* 1606 (one of the open fields of the village, cf. *yᵉ northe feld supra* and *Weste feilde infra*); *the southe hill* 1577, *the south ~* 1601, *the Southe hill hedge* 1606, *South hill Sides* 1715, *South Hill* 1720; *South knowels* 1601 (*v.* **cnoll** 'a knoll, a hillock'); *Southe milnes* 1577 (*v.* **myln**); *the South more* 1577, *South Moore* 1601, *Southmoor Close* 1695, *Southmoore ~* 1724, *South-moore ~* 1744; *Stochill* 1577, *The Stockehills* 1601, *the hyther Stocke hylles* 1606; *the summer pasture* 1700, *~ Sumer Pasture* 1724 (self-explanatory); *Suthiby, Suthitune* Ed1 both (p) (literally 'south in the village', *v.* **sūð, í, bȳ**, denoting X who lives in the south of the village, a common Scand formation in L; *Suthitune* is a rare anglicised form in which OE **tūn** has replaced ODan **bȳ**, with the same meaning); *Thorpe Closes* 1695 (named from Thorpe le Fallows, a neighbouring village); *le Townesend* 1606; *the Vicars Close* 1690, *the Viccars close* 1715, *Vicars Close* 1720; *watter furs* 1577, *Water furzes* 1601 ('the wet furrows', *v.* **wæter, furh**; the form *furzes* is apparently an error); *the Water Railes* 1601; *weste feilde* 1601, *West feild* 1606 (one of the open fields of the village, *v.* **feld**, and cf. *yᵉ northe feld* and *the South feilde supra*); *le Weste garden* 1545 (*v.* **west** and cf. *le est garden supra*); *le West Lands Close* 1690, *West Land close* 1715, *Westland close* 1720 (*v.* **west, land**).

Coates

COATES

> *Cotes* (5x) 1086 DB, c1115 LS, 1157 (1407) Gilb, 1166 RBE (p), 1195 P (p), 112 Dane, 1201 P (p), 1203 Abbr, 1203 Cur, 1203 Ass, 1207 P (p), 1220 Welles, 1221–29 RA iv, 1223 Cur, c1225 (14) *Queen's*, 1227 ClR, 1227 Cur, 1242–43 Fees, *~ Abbas* 1254 ValNor, 1256 FF, 1271 *Ass*, 1291 Tax, 1291 Ch, *~ juxta Stowam* 1292 RSu, 1303 FA *et freq* to *~ juxta Stowe* 1602 Brasses, *Cotes* 1822 *Terrier*
> *Cotis* c1115 LS
> *Chotes* c1160, 1250, 1268, 1275 all (14) *Welb*, *~ iuxta Stowe* 1331 *ib*
> *Kotes* 1212 Fees
> *Coytes* 1495 IBL
> *Cottes* 1526 Sub
> *Cootys* 1535 VE iv, *Coots* 1535 ib, *Cootts* 1536–37 Dugd vi
> *Coats* 1634, 1662 *Terrier*, *Coates iuxta Stowe* 1662 *ib*, *Coates* 1703 *ib et passim*

'The cottages, the huts, the shelters', *v.* **cot**. OE neuter *cot* has the regular plural *cotu* of the short syllable neuters of the *a*-declension, but here the final *-u* of the regular form has been replaced by *-es* < *-as* from the masculine *a*-declension, no doubt as a result of the breakdown of the old inflectional system in late OE and early ME. It is *Abbas* from Welbeck Abbey which held land in Coates. It is near Stowe.

ASH HOLT (lost), 1828 Bry, *v.* **holt**. COATES DRAIN (lost), 1828 ib. COATES GORSE. FIR HOLT (lost) 1828 Bry, *v.* **fyrs**. FOX COVERT. LOW FM (lost), 1828 Bry. MOAT, a medieval moated site. NEW PLANTATION. OLD HALL (lost), 1828 Bry. PARSONAGE (lost), *we finde neither Parsonage nor Vicar-age House* 1663, *There is neither Parsonage nor Vicaridge house* 1663, *There is neither Parsonage nor Vicarage House* 1712, *~ ~ ~ ~ or Vicarage-house* 1721, *The Parsonage here is impropriated* 1724, *The Vicarage* 1822, *There is neither Parsonage House or any Glebe* 1825 all *Terrier*.

FIELD-NAMES

Forms dated 1156–57 (1407), 1157 (1407) are Gilb; 1209–35 LAHW; 1244 (14), m13 (14), eEd1 (14), 1331 (14), 14 *Welb*; 1271, 1329 *Ass*; 1337, 1332 *SR*; 1663 *Terrier*.

(b) *le Clayfurlanges* 1331 (14) (*v.* **clǣg, furlang**); *Cokacres* 1331 (14) (*v.* **cocc**[2] 'a cock, a woodcock or other wild bird', **æcer** 'a plot of arable or cultivated land'); *Depho.* 14 (possibly '*the deep hollow'*, from **dēop** 'deep' and **hōh**, dat.sg. **hō**, the latter being used in a secondary sense 'a (spur-shaped) cleft' or the like); *dicfurlonges* Edl (14) (*v.* **dīc, dík** 'a ditch', **furlang**); *Dryfurlanges* m13 (14) (*v.* **drȳge** 'dry', **furlang**); *engdic* eEd1 (14) (*v.* **eng** 'meadow, pasture', **dīc, dík**); *Estyntonne* m13 (14) (p) (literally '(place) east in the village', *v.* **ēast, in, tūn**, denoting X who lives in the east of the village; *Estyntonne* is a comparatively rare anglicised formation of the common ODan *Estiby*, cf. *Suthiby* and *Suthitune* in Blyborough *supra*); *in campo de Chotes* (sic) m13 (14), eEd1 (14) (*v.* **feld**); *super Filigham mare* (sic) m13 (14) ('the boundary with Fillingham', *v.* **(ge)mǣre**, an adjacent village); *le Gaire, le gore* m13 (14) (the first is from ON **geiri**, the second from OE **gāra** cognate words meaning 'a triangular plot of ground'); *Goselingeheuedland* m13 (14) (the first el. is ME *goslyng* 'a gosling' or the derived surn. with **hēafod-land** 'the head of a strip of land left for turning the plough'); *le Gote del Northsik* m13 (14), *super le Gote* 1244 (14) (*v.* **gotu**, ME **gote** in L 'a sluice'); *le Grange hewedelande Daile* m13 (14) (*v.* **hēafod-land, deill** 'a share or portion of land'), *iuxta grangiam suam* eEd1 (14), *grangiam Abb'is de Wellebek' apud Cotes* 1329 (as indicated in the text, it was a **grange** of Welbeck Abbey); *grenetoftedal* m13 (14) (*v.* **grēne** 'green', **toft** 'a messuage, a curtilage', **dāl** 'a share, a portion of land', here in its Northern ME form and cognate with **deill** *supra*); *halddam, -hil* m13 (14) (perhaps 'the old dam or pond', *v.* **ald, damme** (ON **dammr**)); *Hundlane* 1327 (p) (perhaps from **hund** 'a dog' and **lanu** 'a lane'); *Kirkedaile* m13 (14) ('the share or portion of land belonging to the church', *v.* **kirkja, deill**); *Lechebek, Lekbek* 1157 (1407), *Laikebek, -hil* m13 (14), *Leikebekhull'* eEd1 (14), *Laicebeck'* 14, cf. *in loco dicitur laikis* m13 (14) (*v.* **bekkr** 'a stream, a beck', with **hyll**; the first el. probably denotes a place where festivities were held from ON **leikr** 'play, sport, a game'. The same name is also found in documents for the neighbouring parish of Ingham *infra* and though its location is unknown presumably it was situated close to the boundary between the two parishes); *Langelandes* m13 (14) (*v.* **lang, land** 'a selion' in the pl.); *Linebuttes* 1244, 14 (*v.* **līn** 'flax', **butte** 'a strip of land abutting on a boundary'); *de Marisco* 1209–35, 1271, *de Marays* 1327 all (p), *terram Alan' de marisco* 1244 (14) (*v.* **mersc** 'watery land, a marsh', but note that we are here concerned with MedLatin *mariscus* and OFr *marais*, respectively); *milnedale* Ed1 (14) (*v.* **myln, deill**); *Newton holme* 1663 (probably from the surn. *Newton* with **holmr** 'an island of land, a water-meadow, higher dry land amidst the marshes'); *Northille* 1156–57 (1407), *Nordhull'* m13 (14), *Northel* (sic) eEd1 (14), *Northil* Ed1 (14), *Northil* 14 (self-explanatory, cf. *Southil infra*); *Northsik* m13 (14) (*v.* **norð, sík** 'a ditch, a trench', cf. *Soutsik infra*); *the parsonage holme* 1663 (*v.* **holmr**); *Rodewale* 1156–57 (1407) (Dr Insley suggests that this means 'the bank, the ridge at a clearing', *v.* **rodu, walu**); *Southflat* 14 (the reading is uncertain); *Southil* m13 (14) (self-explanatory, cf. *Northille supra*); *Soutsik, -sike* m13 (14) (*v.* **sūð, sík**, cf. *Northsik supra*); *Stokhille* m13 (14) (*v.* **stocc** 'a tree-trunk, a stump', **hyll**); *super Stowmare* m13 (14) ('the boundary with Stow (an adjacent village)', *v.* **(ge)mǣre**, and cf. *Filigham mare supra*); *inter stratam Reg' que ducit de Linc'* m13 (14), *a via Linc'* eEd1 (14) (*v.* **strǣt**, referring to a road west of Ermine Street).

Fillingham

FILLINGHAM

Figelingeham 1086 DB, *Figlingaham* c1115 LS
Figlingheim (2) c1115 LS
Filingeham (3x) 1086 DB, 1170, 1171, 1172 P, 1188 ib (p), 1219 Ass, 1198 (1328) Ch, 1226–35 RA ii, *Philingeham* 1173 P, 1235–38 RA iv
Fillingeham 177, 1211 P (p), 1218, 1219 Ass, 1248 RRG, 1589 NCWills, *Phillingeham* 1254 (1380) Pat
Felingeham 1086 DB, 1126 France, 1226–35 RA ii, *Felingheham* 1103 France, *Feligeham* 1123 ib
Fellingeham 1177 P
Filingham c1180 Bly, p1160 Dane, 1172 (1407) Gilb, a1183 Dane, Hy2 ib (p), c1190 RA iv, 1198 (1328) Ch, c1200 (1407) Gilb, 1202 FF, 1210–20, c1220 RA iv *et freq* to 1445 AASR xxix, *Philingham* 1220–30, *Filyngham* 1291 Tax, 1296 *Ass*, 1303 FA, 1306 Cl, 1316 FA, 1324 Ipm, 1325 Pat, 1327 Banco *et freq* to 1503 Ipm, *Fylyngham* 1303, 1325 FA, 1327 *SR*, 1330 FA, 1335 Cl, 1339 Pat *et freq* to 1538 LP xiii, *Fylingham* 1307 Pat, 1327 Ipm, 1361 Cl, c1414 AASR xxix

Fillingham 1222 Cur, 1231 Ch, 1231 FF, 1232 Cur, 1240–50 RA iv,
    1242 FF, 1244 Fees, 1250 (1446) Pat, 1254 ValNor, 1283 Dugd
    vi, 1303 Ch *et passim*, *Fyllyngham* 1324 Cl, 1401–2, 1428 FA,
    1513 LP i, 1559 Pat, *Fillyngham* 1331 Ipm, 1343 Cl, c1347
    Works, 1375 Peace, 1385 Pat, 1386 Cl *et passim* to 1436 Pat,
    Phillyngham 1535 VE i, *Fyllingham* 1553 Pat, *Phyllingham*
    1536–37 Dugd vi
Felingham 1235 FF, 1558–79 ChancP, *Felyngham* 1373, 1373 Peace

'The homestead, estate of the Fyglingas' from OE **Fyglinga,* the
gen.pl. of OE **Fyglingas,* a group-name meaning 'the family, the
dependents of *Fygla* or *Fygel*', and OE **hām**, a formation comparable
with Cammering-ham *supra.* The pers.ns. **Fygla, *Fygel* are regular *i*-
mutated hypocoristic derivatives of OE *Fugol* formed with the strong -
ila-suffix and the weak -*illan*-suffix respectively. Of these two suffixes,
the strong variant is the more frequent in OE personal nomenclature, as
Dr Insley points out. The form in -*heim* is from ON **heim** cognate with
OE **hām**.

ANCHOLME HEAD, 1824 O, 1828 Bry, self-explanatory. ANCHOLME
POND, 1828 Bry. BECK WOOD, cf. *Litelbec* 1220–30, 1221–29 RA iv,
little beck 1671 *Terrier*, ~ *Beck* 1700 *ib*, *Little beck* 1724 *ib*, *Far ~, First
Little Beck pasture* 1786 *LCS*, *inter beckes* 1220–30 ib, *Fullebech'*
1240–50 ib (*v.* **fūl** 'foul'), *v.* **bekkr** 'a stream', as elsewhere in the
parish. BEECH WOOD. BLACKLAND (lost), 1828 Bry. BROADBENTS
(lost), 1828 ib. CHURCH FM, cf. *the Church headland* 1671 *Terrier, the
Church Pasture* 1789 *LCS*. THE COTTAGE. DEER PARK (lost), 1828 Bry,
1830 Gre. FILLINGHAM CASTLE, *Summer Castle* 1763 LCS, 1819 Stark,
1824 O, 1828 Bry, 1830 Gre, *Fillingham, or Summer Castle* 1842
White, described there as *a large Gothic castellated mansion, with a
circular bastion tower at each corner erected in 1760.* FILLINGHAM
GRANGE, 1824 O, 1830 Gre, *Grange* 1828 Bry, *grangiam Abb'is de
Reuesby apud Felyngham* 1329 *Ass, usque grangeam abbatis de
Revesby* 1347 Works, *Fylyngham graung'* 1385 Peace, *the Grandge*
1671 *Terrier*, cf. *Home Grange* 1786 *LCS,* self- explanatory; it was a
grange of Revesby Abbey. FILLINGHAM LOW WOOD. FILLINGHAM
MOORS (lost), 1828 Bry, cf. *super moram* 1221–29 RA iv, *moram de
Filingh'* m13 (14), *mora in filingham* 1274 (14), *the more* 1638 *Terrier,
the moor* 1759 *LCS*, cf. *morefurlonges* m13 (14), *Morefurlanges*
1235–48, 14, *Morhille* 1221–29 RA iv, *le morewelle* m13 (14) *Welb, Le
morewell'* 1306 (14) *ib, morwell* 14 ib. FILLINGHAM PARK, 1830 Gre, cf.
Park Fm 1824 *Dixon*. FOX WOOD, *Fox W^d* 1828 ib. GIPSEY LANE,
GIPSEY LANE BRIDGE. GLEBE FM, cf. *the glebe* 1760 *EnclA*. HARE'S

WOOD, *Hare's W^d* 1828 Bry. LADY'S WOOD, *Ladys W^d* 1828 ib. THE
LAKE, LAKE HO, *Lake* 1824 O. LANE END (lost) 1828 Bry. LARCH
PLANTATION (2), *Larch Plant^n* 1828 ib. LINCOLN WOOD, cf.
Lincolnecroft c1240 RA ii, no doubt land owned by the Dean and
Chapter of Lincoln. LONG WOOD (lost), *Long W^d* 1828 Bry, cf.
Longwood croft 1638 *Terrier*. LOW WOOD. MANOR HO, 1828 Bry,
p1649 *CCLeases*, *The Estate and Manor of Fillingham with the Hall or
Manor House since pulled down by myself* [Cecil Wray] 1786 *ib*, *Manor
Farm* 1832 *ib*, cf. *Tirwitts Mannor, Paradise Mannor* 1620 LCS and
manor lane 1760 *EnclA*. The Tirwitts were lords of the manor. *Paradise*
has been noted twice as a f.n. in the parish — *Paradise* 1727 *Terrier* and
Lower Paradise 1773 *LCS*. MIDDLE STREET, *the Street* 1671 *Terrier* and
was earlier no doubt *Aldstrete* 1235–48, *Aldestret* a1236 both RA iv.
NORTH FM. OAK WALK. OLD RECTORY (local), *the Vicarage* 1649
CCLeases, *The Parsonage House* 1724 *Terrier*, *the ~ ~* 1773 *LCS*,
Rectory 1760 *EnclA*. OLD WOOD (lost), *Old W^d* 1828 Bry. PALE WOOD.
RECTORY FM, 1824 O, *~ F^m* 1828 Bry, 1830 Gre, cf. Old Rectory *supra*.
ROUND PLANTATION. SHEEPWASH (lost), 1828 Bry, self-explanatory.
SIDE FM. TURPIN FM & WOOD, cf. *Turpin* 1824 O, 1830 Gre, *Fillingham
Turpin* 1828 Bry.

FIELD-NAMES

Forms dated 112, 1210–20, c1220, 1220–30, 1221–29, 1235–48, a1236,
c1240, 1240–50, c1250 are RA iv; 1235–40, 1235–45, a1250, c1300,
e14, 1307–27, 1317, 1327^1, 1351 *DC*; m13 (14), 1274 (14), 14 *Welb*;
1275, 1276 RH; 1327^2, 1332 *SR*; 1343 NI; 1356 Cl; 1371 *Foster*; 1373,
1384 Peace; 1428 AASR xxix; 1536–37 *MiscDep 10*; 1558–79 ChancP;
1649, 1759, 1798, 1804, 1832, 1853, 1860 *CCLeases*; 1638, 1671, 1693,
1700, 1724, 1762 *Terrier*; 1707, 1759, 1764, 1768, 1783, 1786, 1789
LCS; 1760 *EnclA*; 1862 *MCD*; 1868 *Nelthorpe*.

(a) Biscuithole 1782, Biscuit Hole 1786; Bradford Cl 1768 (from the surn.
Bradford), Calf Cl 1868; Bottom, Middle, Top Car 1868 (*v.* **kjarr** 'brushwood', 'a
marsh, a bog overgrown with brushwood', as elsewhere in the parish); Caudle Btm
1782 (*Caldewell'* 1220–30, 1221–29, c1250, -*welle* m13 (14), *Cawdall bottome*
1671, from **cald** 'cold', **wella** 'a spring' with **botm**); Chalmer's Cl 1832, 1860 (from
the family of *J^o Chalmer* 1756 *BT*); North Cliff 1759 (*the Cliffe next Glentworth*
1638), South Cliff 1759 (*the South Cliffe* 1638, *v.* **clif**); the Cotchers Mdw 1783
(from dial. *cotcher* 'a cottager', common in L); Cottage Cl 1762; Cow Lane 1760;
The Cow Pasture 1759, Cow pasture 1760 (*the Cow pasture* 1671); Dog Boy Cl
1762; Eleven Acres 1860; the Farr Cl 1768; Gainsborough Lane 1768 (self-
explanatory); the Glebe Lands 1768; Glentham Hedge 1762 (*Glentham Hedge* 1700,
from Glentham, a neighbouring parish); Glentworth Gate 1760, 1804, 1853 (*via de
Glenteworth* m13 (14), 'the road to Glentworth, the adjacent parish to the north', *v.*

gata); Glentworth Hedge 1760, 1798, 1811, 1862 (*v.* **hecg**); Great Cl 1832; The High Close Nooking 1760; Hill Foot Cl 1762; Hill Side Cl 1760, ~ ~ Cls 1832, Hill side cls 1862, Middle Hillside 1832, North ~ 1759, North Hill side 1798, 1832, ~ Hill Side 1862 (*super collem* c1300, *the hils* (sic) 1638, *the hill syde* 1671, *Hill Side* 1724); Hill Top Rd (the road from Lincoln to Kirton); the Home Cl 1768, 1773, 1860; The Great and Little Hungerhill 1782 (*Hungerhyl* 1235–48, a1250, *-hyll* c1240, *Hyngrile* e14, *short hungrill* 1638, *hung' hill* 1671, a common derogatory name for infertile land, *v.* **hungor, hyll**); Ingham Rd 1760 (self-explanatory); The Ings 1759 (*the Ings* 1638, *y^e* ~ 1700, *Ings* 1724, cf. *Esteng* 112, c1220 (*v.* OE **ēast** 'east'), *Southeng* 1235–45, *Sutheng* 1235–48, c1240 and *platea prati vocatur Ousteheynge* 1307–27 (*v.* ON **austr** 'east'); *v.* **eng** 'meadow, pasture', as elsewhere in the parish. It is worthy of note that the cognate OE and ON words for 'east' occur in the same name); North Knowles Furlong 1759, North Knowles 1760, 1804, 1832, 1853, the North Knowles 1759, South Knowles 1759 (*le knoule* 1235–45, *le Knouse* (sic) 1235–48, *the Knowles* 1638, ~ *knowls* 1671, *the Crosse knowles* 1638, *South Knowles* 1700, 1724 (Dr Insley suggests that the form *le Knouse* reveals that we are concerned with a Scand loan-word corresponding to Norwegian *knaus* 'a hill-top', the *-l-* form of 1235–45 being the result of scribal error and later forms representing conflation with OE **cnoll**); Lincoln Rd 1762; Long Cl 1762; North low Fd 1762; Lyons Cl 1764, the Lion Cl 1768 (named from the *Lion* family, cf. John *Lion* 1600 *BT*); Marshdale Gate 1760, 1832, 1853, Marshdale ~ 1798; Miles Cl 1762 (perhaps from the surn. *Miles*); East, West Mill Flg 1759, 1760, Mill Cl 1832, 1860 (cf. *the east milne furlonge* 1638, *milne furlong* 1671, *West Mill furlong* 1724, *v.* **myln**); Top Moor 1868 (cf. *Fillingham Moors supra*); new Lane 1760, ~ lane 1798, 1804, the New Lane 1862 (the road to Glentworth, cf. *via de Glenteworthe* m13 (14)); North Fd 1760, 1762, 1789 (*in campo . . . aquilonari* 1220–30, *in campo aquilonari* 1235–48, *in campo uero aquilonali* c1240, *the north feild* 1638, *The North Fielde* 1649, *the North feild* 1671, *ye North Field* 1700, one of the great fields of the parish, cf. South Fd *infra* and *Westfeld de Fillingham* in (b) *infra*); Old Mill Hill 1760; Oulstone Leys 1760, Oulston Leas 1798, 1832, 1862 (probably to be identified with *owston Leis* 1649); The Far, The First Out Cl 1782 (cf. *the out acres* 1638, *Outacres* 1724, *v.* **ūt** 'outside, on the outskirts'); a close called Out Manors 1764; The Oxpasture 1759, Oxpastures Gate 1760 (*ye Ox Pasture side* 1700, *Ox-pasture* 1724); lower Paradise 1773 (*Paradise* 1724, usually a complimentary name, but occasionally used ironically of undesirable places); the Pickles 1768 (*v.* **pightel** 'a small enclosure, a croft', comparatively rare in north L, the usual form being *pingle*, a nasalised form of **pightel**); Red Earth 1759, 1804, 1832, red earth 1798, the Red Earth 1862 (*super Rubeam Terram* c1240, *Rederthe* 1235–48, c1240, *Readearth* 1638, *Red earth* 1671, *Red Earth Forlong* 1724, alluding to the colour of the soil, *v.* **rēad, eorðe**); Richardson's Barn 1760 (named from the *Richardson* family, cf. William *Richardson* 1727 *BT*); upper Rustell Bottom 1773 (cf. *Rushdale furlonge* 1638, *rich dale furlong* (sic) 1671, *Rush Dale Furlong* 1700, *Rushdale Forlong* 1724, from **risc** 'a rush', **dalr** 'a valley', with **botm**); Rye Cl 1832, 1860 (*v.* **rȳge** 'rye'); Lord Scarborough's Lands 1762 (from a landowner in the village); the second Cl 1773; The seed cl 1782, Low Seed Cl 1832, 1860; Showston 1760, The ~ 1782, 1786 (*Shoulsting* (sic) 1638, *Show stone* 1671, *Shoustone* 1700, *Shouston* 1724, obscure, earlier forms are needed to suggest an etymology); North Syke 1759, ~ Sike 1798, South Syke, the Sike 1804, 1862 (*the syke* 1671, *v.* **sík** 'a ditch, a trench'); South Fd 1760 (1724, *in campo australi* 1220–30, 1235–45, 1235–48, c1240, m13 (14), *in australi campo de Filingham* 1235–40, *in australi campo* 1235–48, *in austral' campo de Fil'* 14, *y^e*

South feild 1638, 1693, *The South feilde* 1671, *ye South Field* 1700, one of the great fields of the parish, cf. North Fd *supra* and *Westfeld de Fillingham* in (b) *infra*); Stow Lane 1760 (the lane to Stow); Thacker 1759, Thacker btm 1760 (*v.* **botm**), Great Thacker Hill 1786 (*Thacker* 1638, *thack Carr* 1671, *Thacker Furlong* 1700, *Thacker* 1724, *v.* **þak** 'material for thatching', **kjarr**); the third Cl 1773; Town Street 1760, 1804, 183, 1862; Walk Side 1860 (*v.* **walk** 'a sheep pasture'); West Barn 1760; White Leys 1759, ~ Leas 1760, 1798, 1811, 1853, *v.* **hwīt** 'white', presumably with reference to the soil, **lea, ley** (OE **lēah**) 'a meadow, an open pasture'); Wooferdal 1764, The Woofedel (sic) 1783 (*Wlfardale* 1235–48, *Wlfaredale*, *Wlframdale* c1240, *Wlfradale* m13 (14), *Wouerdale* 1638, *Short Woverdale* 1700, *Woofendale* 1671, the first el. is probably an anglicised form of the ON pers.n. *Úlfarr*, the second **deill**, as Dr Insley suggests); Mr Cecil Wray's Lands 1762.

(b) *Acteacres*, *super octo acras* 1235–48, *Achtacres, Acteacres* c1240, *le furlang qui vocatur Actacres* 1317 ('the eight acres', *v.* **æhta** 'eight', **æcer**); *toftum Andree Scott'* e14 (*v.* **toft** 'a messuage, a curtilage', as elsewhere in the parish); *Bakhawe de Felyngham* 1373 (p) (obscure); *le Buscophull* 1317 (the reading is uncertain, but the first el. is **biscop** 'bishop' with **hyll**); *bossedale, -daile, bossidaile* m13 (14) (the first el. is the ON byname *Bussi* rather than the ON pers.n. *Bósi*; the second is **deill**); "Bright Farm" 1558–79 (from the surn. *Bright*); *brodebec* m13 (14) (*v.* **brād** 'broad', **bekkr**); *bromhil* 14 (*v.* **brōm** 'broom', **hyll**); *brottelandes, brot land* m13 (14) (*v.* **brot** 'a small piece', **land** 'a selion'); *Brunhill', le brunhill'* 13 ('the brown hill', *v.* **brūn, hyll**; the appearance of Alan *Brun* named in the same document is probably fortuitous); *Bull Lane* 1724; *Buttlane Furlong* 1700 (perhaps 'the lane to the archery butts', *v.* **butt** 'an archery butt'); *City Gate Furlong* 1700, *City Gate* 1724; *the Cliff* 1649, *Clift* (sic) 1724 (*v.* **clif**); *the comon mere* 1649 (*v.* **(ge)mǣre** 'a boundary'); *Cotis mare* m13 (14) ('the boundary with Coates', cf. prec.); *Crook* 1638; *Dalefurlonges* 1219–20, m13 (14), *Daleforlonges* c1240, *the Dale furlongs* 1638, *North Dale furlong, the South Dale* ~ 1671, *North, South Dale* 1724, *v.* **dalr** 'a valley', **furlang**); *Dovehouse* 1707; *camp' de Fillingham* 1307–27, *campo de Fylingham* 1351, *campis de Fillinghan* 1536–37, *the Comon feelde* 1649 (denoting the common open field of the village, *v.* **feld**); *the fields meare* 1671, *ye Fields Meir* 1700 ('the boundary of the common fields', *v.* **feld**, **(ge)mǣre**); *14 Oxgangs* 1649 (*v.* **oxgang**); *Goswelswarthes* e14 (perhaps **gōs** 'a goose', **wella** 'a spring', with **swæð** 'a strip of grassland'); *Grendigate* 1235–45, *Grendicgate* c1240, *Grijndigate* (sic) e14 (apparently 'the green ditch' *v.* **grēne, dík**, with **gata**); *Haverdale Hills* 1638, *Haverdale* 1700, 1724 (*v.* **hafri** 'oats', **deill**, a Scand compound); *heuedland Roberti filii Alueredi* 1221–29, *heuedland' Will'i Bardolf* m13 (14), *ab heuedlande monachorum de Reuesby* m13 (14) (of the monks of Revesby Abbey), *the headlands* 1638, *the head lands* 1671, *Headlands* 1700, *Head Lands* 1724 (*v.* **hēafod-land** 'the head of a strip of land left for turning the plough'); *the horse pasture* 1649; *the hows close* 1649 (no doubt *hows* is for *howse*); *Hundred acres* 1638; *divisam de Ingham* e14 ('the Ingham boundary'), *Ingham hedge* 1671 (referring to Ingham, the adjoining village to the south); *Jollands (Hill) Cl* 1724 (named from the *Jollands* family, cf. Robert *Jollandes* 1642 LPR); *Lincoln Mear* 1724 ('the Lincoln boundary', *v.* **(ge)mǣre**, presumably named from land owned by the Dean and Chapter); *Linges* 1220–30, c1250 (*v.* **lyng** 'ling, heather'); *Litelstret* 1220–30, *Littilstrete* m13 (14), *de parva strata* e14, *ye little street* 1671, *Little Street* 1700 (*v.* **lȳtel, strǣt**; unfortunately there is no indication of its situation); *Long furland, the long furlong* 1671 (*furland* is a fairly common variant of *furlong* in L); *ye longhedge* 1638, *the long hedge* 1671, *Long Hedge* 1724; *merlewell'* 1274; *Mikeldaile* 1221–29, *mikeldaile* 1235–40,

Mickeldayle c1240 (*v.* **mikill** 'big', **deill**); *Nordmore Wro, Northmorewra* m13 (14), *Nortmore* 14 (*v.* **norð, mōr**, with **vrá** 'a nook, a corner of land', and cf. *Fillingham Moors supra*); *Northcroft* c1240; *Old Stone Layes* 1724 (*v.* **lea, ley** (OE **lēah**)); *super montem propinquiorum vie de Ouenby* 1236, *Ownby gate* 1671 ('the road to Owmby by Spital'); *oxclose furlonge* 1638, *Ox Close Furlong* 1700; *iuxta stratam quod vocatur Poke Eng* 1317 (the sense of *Poke* here is uncertain); *potterhil* 1235–45, *Potterhill* 1235–48, *Potterhyl* c1240 (from the occupational name or derived surn. *Potter*, with **hyll**); *Purwellhill* 1638, *Purly Hill* 1724 (the forms are too late for any certainty); *Quenethorn* c1250 ('Cwen's thorn-bush', from the OE fem. pers.n. *Cwēn* and **þorn**); *Sandigate side* 1638, *Sandy Gate* 1700 (self-explanatory); *Sayhdaile* (sic) 1210–20, *Saylidale* c1240; *Scawdells* 1638, *Scaldalls dales* (sic) 1671, *Skaw dale* 1724 (early forms are needed to suggest a convincing etymology); *Schortwestlandes* 1235–48 (*v.* **sceort** 'short'; -*westlandes* may be for -*westlanges*, cf. *West longes infra*); *Scortbuttes* 1221–29 (*v.* **sceort, butte**); *Sittingate side* 1638; *Slecteng* a1236, *Sleightings* 1638 (*v.* **slēttr** 'smooth, level', **eng**); *Sodhigate heuede, Sodhygatheude* m13 (14) (obscure); *Soustanc* 1220–30; *Steinhow* 1221–29, *Stheynhou* (sic) 1235–48, c1240, *Stanehowe* 1317 (a Scand compound of **steinn** 'a stone', **haugr** 'a hill, a mound'); *Staynbriggdayl* 1317 (*v.* **steinn, brycg** 'a bridge' in a Scand form, with **deill**); *the street way* 1649 (probably a reference to Ermine Street); *the sty* 1671 (*v.* **stīg** 'a path, a narrow road'); *Suddicgate, Suddicgate* 1221–29, *Suddikegate* c1250 ('the south ditch', *v.* **sūð, dīc, dík**, with **gata**); *Swaddale* 1700; *þorndeile, Thornidaile, -deile* m13 (14), *Thornidal, þorndal'* 14 ('the thorn(y) share of land', *v.* **þorn(ig), deill**); *Thorpesti* 1235–48, *Thorpsty* c1240 (presumably 'the path to Thorpe le Fallows', *v.* **stīg**); *de Toft de Felyngham* 1373 (p) (*v.* **toft** 'a curtilage, a messuage'); *Towns End* 1700; *two Acres* 1707; *Wakefin* (sic) 1700; *war' in Filingham* 1275, *Warenn' in Filingham* 1276 (*v.* **wareine** 'a rabbit warren'); *the water furs* 1638, *Water furrs* 1671, *Waterfurs* 1724 ('the wet furrows', *v.* **wæter, furh** in the pl.); *ad fontem* 1332 (p) (*v.* **wella**); *Weneker* 1221–29 (*v.* **kjarr**; the first el. is obscure); *locam qui dicitur Weruelmare* m13 (14), *weruelmar'* 1306 (14) (the first el. is OE **hwerfel** 'a circle, something circular', the second (**ge)mære** 'a boundary, land forming a boundary'); *Westerflet* 1235–48 (*v.* **wester** 'west, western', **flēot** 'a stream'); *Westerleghe* 1274 (14), *pratum de Westerlegh'* 1306 (14) (*v.* **wester, lēah** 'a clearing, a glade'); *West'slecht* 1317 (the abbreviation is probably for *Wester-*, as above, the second el. is **slētta** 'a smooth, level field'); *in campo occidentali* 1220–30, *de Westfeld de Fillingham* 1317, *de Westfeld* 1327[1], *de Westfelde* 1327[2], *of the Westfeld* 1332, *de Westfeld de Fylyngham* 1356, *de Westefeld'* 1383, *de Westfelde* 1384 all (p) (one of the great fields of the parish, *v.* **west, feld**, cf. North Fd, south Fd in (a) *supra*); *West longes* m13 (14), *Langwest Longis* a1236 (*v.* **west, lang** 'a long strip of land', with **lang** 'long' prefixed in the second form); *Westwod* 1343 (p) (*v.* **west, wudu**); *Willowdale* 1638, 1700, 1724; *viam de wyuelingh'* m13 (14) ('the road to Willingham by Stow'); *Wyleslande* 1428 (probably from the surn. *Wyles* with **land** 'a selion').

West Firsby

WEST FIRSBY

Frisebi (2x) 1086 DB, 1185 Templar, lHy2, 112 Dane, 1200 Cur,
1212 Fees, 1218 Ass, -by c1190 RA ix (p), 1210–12 RBE,
1232–34 RA ix, 1246 Ipm, 1254 ValNor, 1265 Misc, (~ *iuxta*
Hakethorn) 1272 *Ass*, 1316 FA, 1316 YD iv, 1332 *SR, Fryseby*
1251 RRG, 1252 Ch, 1291 Tax, 1295 Ipm, 1297 Cl, 1368 *AD*,
1397 Cl
Frisabi c1115 LS
Frisbeia 1137–39 YCh iii, -*by* 1272 RRGr, 1275, 1276 RH, (~ "by"
Spridlyngton), 1327 *SR*, 1343 NI *et freq* to 1401–2 FA, *Frysby*
1329 *Ass*, 1349 Ipm, (~ "by" *Sprydlington'*) 1404 ChancCert *et*
passim to 1451 Fine
Frisseby ("by" *Spridlyngton)* 1382 Cl, 1504 Ipm
Freseby 1213 Cur, -*bi* 1219 Ass
Firsbie 1585 SC
West Firsby 1824 O, 1830 Gre, ~ ~ *House* 1828 Bry

"The farmstead, village of the Frisians', from OE **Frīsa, Frēsa** and
ODan **bȳ**, identical with Firsby (LSR). This was no doubt an isolated
group of Frisians who accompanied the Danish settlers in L. Cf.
Friesthorpe which has the same first el. Firsby is described as being near
Hackthorn and Spridlington. West Firsby is a "lost" village.

ASH HOLT, 1824 O. EAST FIRSBY, 1824 O, 1830 Gre. FIRSBY CLIFF FM
(lost) 1828 Bry. FIRSBY LOW HO (lost), 1828 ib, *Low Firsby* 1830 Gre.
FIRSBY GRANGE, for the late use of **grange**, *v.* The Grange in
Cammeringham parish *supra*. MANOR HO. MIDDLE FM. WEST FIRSBY
GORSE. WEST FIRSBY PLANTATION. WEST SKREE, on the boundary with
Toft Newton, *v.* PN L **3**, 66.

FIELD-NAMES

Forms dated 1275, 1276 are RH; 1324 Ipm, 1327, 1332 *SR*; 1329 *Ass*;
1343 NI; 1737, c1751 *Dixon*; 1839 (East Firsby), 1840 (West Firsby)
TA.

(a) North, South Bracken Hills 1839 (*v.* **brakni**); Clover Cl 1840; Cow Cl 1840;
East Fd 1839 (one of the open fields of the village); East Hills 1839 (cf. West Hills
infra); Ewe Cl 1840; Farm Yard 1840; Fold Yard 1840; Great, Little Furze Cl 1839
(*v.* **fyrs**); North, South Giles Cl 1839 (from the surn. *Giles*); The Green Cl c1751;
Far, Near Out Heath Flatt 1840 (*v.* **flat**); Far, First Hill Cl 1840; North, South Hindley

1839 (early spellings are needed to propose an etymology for *Hindley*); Home Cl 1840; Far, Near Horse Cl 1839; the House Cl c1751; Ings c1751, Far, First Ings Mdw (*v.* **eng** 'meadow, pasture'); the New North Cl c1751 (*the North Close* 1737); The North Side Cl c1751, North Side Cl 1840 (*the Northside Close* 1737); Nursery 1840; Orchard 1839, 1840 (*ad Pomar'* 1327, *atte Appelgarth de Frysby* both (p) (*v.* **apaldr-garðr** 'an apple orchard', with OE **appel** replacing ON **apaldr**); Plantation 1839, 1840, Plantation Cl 1839, 1840; First, Second Sand Foil Cl 1840 (*v.* **sainfoin** 'the leguminous plant, *Ononbrychis viciifolia*'); Saxby Cl c1751 (from Saxby, an adjacent parish); Great Shawforth (Nook) 1839 (perhaps from the surn. *Shawforth*); The Sheep Walk upon yᵉ Heath c1751 (*The Sheep Walk, the Heath* 1737, *v.* **shepe-walk** 'a sheep pasture' and **hæð**); Great, Little Slough Cl 1840 (*v.* **slōh** 'a slough, a mire'); Stone Pit Flat 1840; The Little, The Low Stow c1751 (*the Little, the Low Stow* 1737, *v.* **stōw** perhaps in the L dial. sense 'a dam'); Turnip Cl 1840; Urns Cl 1839 (possibly from the surn. *Urn*); The Weather Shep Walk (sic) c1751, North East, North West, South East, South West Weather Walk 1840 (*the weather Sheep Walk* 1737, *v.* **weðer** 'a wether, a castrated ram' and **shepe-walk**); West Hills 1839.

(b) *the barf Close* 1737 (*v.* **beorg**, dial. **barf** 'a hill, a mound'); *ad Ecclesiam* 1327 (p) (*v.* **cirice**, **kirkja** 'a church'); *in Crofto* 1327, *In* ~ 1332 both (p) (*v.* **croft** 'a croft, a small enclosed field'); *Estitoune* 1327, *Estiton'* 1332, *Est in the Conne* (*C-* = *T-*) 1343 all (p) (literally '(the place) east in the village', *v.* **ēast**, **in**, **tūn**, denoting X who lived in the east of the village. This is a loan-translation of a common ODan formation, occurring as *Oustiby* in L); *Hestcroft* 1324 (probably from **hestr** 'a horse, a stallion' and **croft**); *the Sheperds house* 1737; *war'* *in Frisby* 1275, *warennam in* ~ 1276 (*v.* **wareine** 'a rabbit warren').

Glentham

GLENTHAM

> *Glantham* 1086 DB, *Glandham* 1086 ib
> *Glentham* 1086 DB, eHy2 (1409) Gilb (p), 1183–84 RA iv, 1188, 1190 P, c1190 RA iv, 1191, 1193, 1194 P, 1194 CurR, 1196 ChancR (p), 1197 FF, 112 RA iv (p), 112 (13) *Kirkst*, c1200 RA iv, 1203 Cur (p), 1203 Ass, 1203, 1204 Cur, 1204 OblR, 1205 P, 1205, 1206 Cur, 1206 P (p), 1210 FF, 1215 (1291) Ch, c1220, 1212 RA iv *et freq*
> *Glentheim* c1115 LS (2x), 112 Dane
> *Glentaham* 1163 *And*, *Glenteham* 1185 Templar, *Glent'ham* 1203 Cur
> *Glenham* 1195 P (p), a1201 RA iii, 1203 P
> *Glentam* 1539 *Foster*

Glentham is probably to be taken with Glentworth *infra*, some three miles away, the first el. of each having similar forms. Glentham, unlike Glentworth, has few early spellings with a medial -*e*-, though this is perhaps not surprising since a medial *-e-* would be more likely to survive before a following *-w* than before a following *-h*. Ekwall, DEPN s.n., suggests that the first el. of each is an OE ***glente** 'a look-out place', which is topographically appropriate for Glentham, situated on a hill when approached from the north and from the west. Furthermore, a f.n. *touthill* 1669 *CCLeases* and *toothill* 1721 *Terrier* 'the look-out hill', *v.* **tōt-hyll** has been noted in the parish, though unfortunately its site is unknown. Hence, Glentham might mean 'the homestead, estate at a look-out place', *v.* **hām**. Such an explanation is, however, less obvious topographically for Glentworth. Glentworth, situated as it is at the foot of the cliff, represented by Glentworth Cliff Farm, along which runs the medieval trackway Middle Street, might well be describing some feature on the ridge overlooking the village. In this case Glentworth would mean 'the enclosure at a look-out place', *v.* **worð**.

Ekwall's explanation is not without etymological problems. In DEPN s.n. *Glantlees*, he takes his OE ***glente** 'look-out hill' to be related to ME *glenten* 'to shine, look, move quickly', Norw *gletta* 'to peep, look, glimpse', German *Glanz* m. 'brilliance, brightness', *glanzen* 'to shine'. MED has *glent*, glossed as (a) 'a glance, look, glimpse'; (b) 'a beam of light; (c)? 'a glancing blow', and a verb *glenten*, which is unnecessarily assumed to be of Scand origin, as Dr Insley points out. He draws attention to relevant glosses in MED as (1c)? 'to bring (something) into sight or existence, reveal'; (3a) 'to look askance, look, glance'; (4) 'to shine, gleam, glitter; glisten, glint' and EDD glosses *glent* as (1) 'to shine', sparkle, gleam; to flash, twinkle'; (2) 'to glance, look, peep; to look askew; to squint'. In Old High German, there was an adj. *glanz* 'bright, shining' and there is a late OHG (c1000), MHG *glenzen* 'to produce brightness, to shine'. The Indo-European root seems to be **ghlend(h)-* 'to shine, to look'. Smith EPN s.v. ***glente** includes the possibility that we are concerned with a bird of prey and compares "Dan *glente*, Swed *glanta* 'hawk, kite'", but Dr Insley points out that there are etymological and semantic problems here which rule out Smith's suggestion.

On the whole, Ekwall's etymology has much to recommend it, though there still remains the problem that the primary sense of the word-group to which *glenten* belongs lies in the field of 'brightness', brilliance, shining'. Perhaps *glent is a substantival derivative of a verb OE *glentan formed with a *-ti-* suffix and denoting 'the bright place' or the like.

The three forms in *-heim* are from ON **heimr**, cognate with OE **hām**.

BISHOPBRIDGE, *Biscopbrigg* Hy3 (1291) Ch, "Bishop's Bridge" 1287–88 (1662) Imb, 1290, 1294, 1312 Pat, *de ponte Episcopi* 1313 ib, *Bishoppbrigg* 1331 ib, *Bisshopesbrigge* 1345 ib, *Bisshopbrigges* 1365 ib, *pontes qui vocantur Bisshopesbrigges* 1375 Works, *Bisshopbrigges* 1411 Pat, *Bissopbrigges* 1418 ib, *Bisshopbrigge* 1482 ib, "the bridges called" *Byshoppe Brygges* 1533 LP vi, *Bishop's Briggs House* 1778 WillsStow, self-explanatory, with all the early forms of *bridge* Scandinavianised. The significance of the pl. forms in some spellings is not apparent today. The present-day bridge is over the R. Ankholme at the point where it is joined by the R. Rase.

BARF FM, *La Bergh* 1327 SR (p), *Barffe* 1577 *Terrier, Barfe* 1669 *CCLeases, the ~* 1673 *ib, ye ~* 1681 *ib, the barf* 1721 *ib,* cf. *Norhberh'* c1190 RA iv, *Northbereg'* 1223–24 ib, *Barff Close* 1871 *Padley, v.* **beorg** 'a hill, a mound', dial. *barf,* common L, cf. Barf Fm in Caenby *supra.* BASSETT'S WIG, obscure. BELL INN, 1871 *Padley.* BRACKEN'S WOOD. BRICKYARD COTTAGES. CROSS LANE, 1828 Bry, cf. *ad Crucem* Hy3 (1291) Ch (p), *v.* **cros.** THE CROWN, *the Sign of the Crown Inn* 1805, 1812, 1818, 1833, *Crown Inn* 1842, 1850 all *BM.* FOX COVERT. GLEBE FM. GLENTHAM BECK (local), 1828 Bry, *the beck* 1669 *CCLeases,* cf. *Bechilles* Hy3 (1291) Ch, *bekfurlanges* c1331 *Foster, v.* **bekkr.** GLENTHAM BRIDGE. GLENTHAM CLIFF, *atte Kliffe* 1327 *SR* (p), *attecliff* 1348 *Foster* (p), *Cliff* 1764 *EnclA,* cf. *Cliff B*^{m} 1828 Bry, *Cliff Bottom* 1836 *Terrier.* GLENTHAM GRANGE. For the late use of **grange,** *v.* The Grange in Cammeringham parish *supra.* GLENTHAM WINDMILL, cf. Mill Hill *infra.* HALFMOON PLANTATION, named from its shape. HIGHFIELD (local). ICE HO. LONG SCREED. For *screed, v.* The Screed in Caenby parish *supra.* MANOR HO, 1649, 1801, 1815, 1830 *CCLeases, the manor house* 1711 *Nevile.* In the text of 1815 *CCLeases,* Sheriff's Tooth is said to be a common name for Manor House, though this sense is not recorded in dictionaries. Cf. *terr' in Glentham vocat le Sheffiffs Tooth* 1666 *DCAcct, Sheriff's Tooth* 1815 *CCLeases.* This is ME *shir-reve(s) toth* glossed in MED as 'a customary rent' and in NED as 'an annual impost . . . levied by the sheriff on each bovate of land within his county'. Professor Sir John Smith, however, points out that this was 'a rent paid by certain tenants who held by the tenure of providing entertainment for the sheriff when sitting in his county court'. MILL HILL, *Glentham Mill* 1824 O, *the Mill* 1844 *CCLeases,* cf. *Milnecroft* Hy3 (1291) Ch, *le Milnecroft* 1300–20 *Foster, ~ ~ Crofte* 1445 AASR xxix. NELLPITS WOOD. NEW CLOSE PLANTATION. NEW COVERT. NEWEL WELL, cf. *Neuwelhill* Hy3 (1291) Ch, *Neuweldale* c1320 *Foster* (*v.* **deill** 'a share of land'), *Nuwell hill* 1681 *CCLeases, Newell Hill* 1690, 1697 *Terrier (Bishop Norton),* self-explanatory, 'the new spring', *v.* **nīwe,**

wella. There is a spring here. RAY PLANTATION (lost), 1828 Bry, cf. *Wra* 1215–20, c1230 RA iv, *litle wraye* 1563 *LCCA*, *the litle wray* 1612 *DCLB, the little Wray* 1649 *CCLeases,* 1661 *Featley, yᵉ little Wray* 1661 *DCLB*, 1802, 1823 *CCLeases, v.* **vrá** 'a nook, a corner'. RECTOR'S CLOSE FM, cf. *Parsons Close* 1822, 1855 *Terrier* (Caenby). RED INN (lost), *the red Inn* 1718 *BM*, probably an earlier name of The Crown, *supra.* SEGGIMOOR BECK & BRIDGE, *le Segmore* m13 *MC, Segmor* Hy3 (1291) Ch, *segemore* 1673 *CCLeases, Segmore* 1681, 1721 *ib, ~ or Sedgemore* 1764 *EnclA*, 'the marsh where sedge, rushes grow', *v.* **secg**, in a Scandinavianised form, **mōr**. SEGGIMOOR FM, *Seggimoor Hall* 1828 Bry. SUTTONS CHARITY FM (lost), *~ ~ Fᵐ* 1828 Bry, named from Thomas *Sutton*, who in 1611 left by will to the mayor and aldermen of the city of Lincoln the profits arising from the parsonage of Glentham. VICARAGE, *the vicarage* 1606 *Terrier*, 1663, 1706 *CCLeases, the vicarage house* 1677 *Terrier, the vicaridge* 1690, 1700 *ib, yᵉ ~* 1696 *ib, The Vicarige* 1709 *CCLeases, the vicarige House* 1724 *ib, Parsonage* 1693 *ib, Parsonage House* 1724 *ib, the ~ ~* 1782, 1789, 1838 *ib*, 1867 *Terrier, the Rectory* 1714 *LCS, Rectory* 1769 *CCLeases, the Rectory and Parsonage* 1838, 1867 *Terrier*.

FIELD-NAMES

Forms dated c1190, 1196–1203, e13, 1210–20, 1215–20, c1220, 1220–30[1], 1223–24, c1230 are RA iv; c1200, 1220–30[2], c1225, 1260–70, 1260–80, 1270–80, 1281, 1282–86, 1290–1310, 1300–20, 1307, 1310–20, c1320, 1321, 1330, c1331, 1332, 1348, 1397, endorsed 15, 1462, 1477, 1483, 1539 *Foster*; eHy3 (1291), Hy3 (1291), Hy3 (1327) Ch; 1229, 1383 Peace; c1230 (14) *VC*; m13 *MC*; Ed1 *Barl*; 1314 *FF*; 1327[1], 1332 *SR*; 1327[2] Wills i; 1329 *Ass*; prob. 1330 (c1331) *Spald i*; c1414, 1428, 1445 AASR xxix; 1441, 1443 *DCAcct*; 1493, 1563 *LCCA*; 1564, 1612, 1661[1], 1669, 1768 *DCLB*; 1606, 1663, 1673, 1677, 1690, 1693, 1697, 1700, 1709, 1721 *Terrier*; 1649, 1669, 1681, 1706, 1724, 1789, 1797, 1800, 1802, 1816, 1818, 1823, 1825, 1836, 1837, 1844, 1868 *DCLeases*; 1661[2], 1694, 1714, 1719, 1735, 1760, 1763 *LCS*; 1661[3] *Featley*; 1749 *Brears*; 1764 *EnclA*; 1871 *Padley*.

(a) Aver Cl 1836, 1844, 1868 (*Close of pasture called the Haver Close* 1649. *v.* **hafri** 'oats', as elsewhere in this parish); Averdale 1836, 1868 (*v.* **hafri, deill** 'a share, a portion of land'); Bar Cl 1836, 1868, the ~ 1844; Car 1871 (*le Kerr* Hy3 (1291), *ker* 1307, *le Ker* c1331, *Glentham Care* 1483, *Carrs* 1681, *yᵉ ~* 1709, *the Carres* 1709, *The Carrs* 1724, *v.* **kjarr** 'brushwood' ME **ker** 'a marsh, especially one overgrown with brushwood', as elsewhere in this parish); Clay Cl 1836, 1868, the Clay ~ 1844; North common fd 1764 (*the comon Feild* 1649, *Common* 1724, 1735); Corn Cl 1871; Cow Gate Furlong 1760 (*Cowgate* 1669, from **gata** in the sense the right of pasturage for an animal, as in the common *Sheepgate*); the dams 1764 (cf. *long, short atterdam* 1673, *aten dam* 1721, *v.* ME **damme** which is now thought to be native despite ON **dammr** 'a dam, a pond', (cf. Middle Low German, Middle Dutch *dam*) with **atter, atten** 'at the' in earlier forms); Dinter Hill 1836, 1844, Dinton Hill 1868 (cf. the obscure *dintherthe* c1331); East Car (Leys) 1871 (cf. Car *supra* and for Leys, *v.* **ley** (OE **lēah**) 'a meadow, an open pasture'); Glentham East Fd 1760, (the) East Fd 1764, 1768, 1802, 1823, the East Fd or Oxpasture 1789, 1800, 1825 (*in campo horientali* 1260–70, ~ ~ *orientali* 1300–20, 1307, c1331, *yᵉ Estfeld* 1564, *the east feild* 1612, ~ *East Field* 1649, *in orientali campo de Glentham* 1661², *the East Feild* 1669, *East field* 1690, *East and & West fields of Glentham* 1694, *yᵉ East Feild* 1709, *Eastfeild* 1712, *v.* **ēast, feld**, one of the great fields of the parish, cf. West Fd *infra* and *v.* Ox Pasture *infra*); Bottom, Top Epworth Fd 1871 (presumably from the surn. *Epworth*); Gander Neck 1836, 1844, Gander Cl 1868 (the 1836 and 1844 forms suggest that this is descriptive of shape 'resembling a gander's or goose's neck'); First Hallis Btm 1871 (probably from the surn. *Hallis*); the Haul or eight Acres 1764 (cf. *Hacthaccres* in (b) *infra*); North Holmes 1764 (cf. *Holm* 1210–20, e13, "the" *holm* 1229, *holme, littelholme* 1307 (*v.* **holmr** 'a small island, a water-meadow', later 'higher ground amidst the marsh', as elsewhere in the parish); Home Cl 1836, 1844 (cf. *the lower home close* 1649; there is often a building in fields so named); Inggs 1764 (cf. *comon Ings* 1669, ~ *Ingg* 1724, *v.* **eng** 'meadow, pasture', as elsewhere in the parish); Kettle Btm 1836, 1868 (*v.* **botm**; *Kettle* may be a surn. here or descriptive of the shape of the field); Middle Street 1764 (this is probably to be identified with *Mikelgate* c1200, *Mikkilgate* Hy3 (1291), *mikelgate* 1307 and with *ad altam viam* c1230 (14), *super magnam stratam* 1260–70, *the heghgate* Hy3 (1291), *the high Streete* 1649, *hyegate* 1669, *v.* **mikill** 'great', **hēah** 'important', **gata** 'a road'); Mills Croft 1764; the East Moore, the West ~ 1768, East, West Moor Cl 1871 (*Estmore, Westmor* Hy3 (1291), *Estmor, Westmore* c1220, *Estmora, Westmora* 1223–14, *Estmore, Westmore* c1331, *yᵉ estemore, yᵉ westmore* 1564, *the East moore*, ~ *West moore* 1649, *yᵉ East More, yᵉ West-More* 1661, cf. *de La More* 1327¹ (p), *en la more* 1332 (p), *the more* 1669, *the Moor* 1714, *v.* **mōr**, distinguished in early forms as **ēast** and **west**); Far, First, Middle Needham's Cl (from the surn. *Needham*); Northcroft 1764 (*Northcroft* Hy3 (1291), 1220–30², *-croftes* Hy3 (1327), *North croft dyk* 1290–1310, *north croft, le Northcroft dike* c1331, *Norcroft* 1661², *Norcrofts* 1669, 1681, *Northcrofts* 1719, 1735, *v.* **norð, croft**, with **dík** 'a ditch' in two forms); the North End of Glentham 1802, 1816 (*yᵉ North End of Glentham* 1661³); The Orchard 1836; Ox Pasture 1764, the Ox or East Pasture 1802, 1823 (*Ox pasture* 1709, cf. East Fd or Oxpasture *supra*); The Packet Inn 1871; Paddock 1871; pinfold 1764 (cf. *le Pound de Glentham* 1477, *v.* **pyndfald** 'a pinfold', **pund** 'a pound, an enclosure into which stray cattle were put'); Rampart btm 1871 (*Rampart* is a variant of *ramper*, a dial. word found in L for 'a raised road or way, the highway', *v.* NED s.v. *rampire, -pier*, EDD s.v. *ramper*); Sakely Dale 1768 (*Saker lyndall'* 1563, *Sakerlyn dale* 1564, *Sakerley dale* (*a dale of land*) 1669, *v.* **līn** 'flax', **deill**; the first part of the name is ME *saker* 'a sack-maker'); Sand Close 1836 (*Sand Close* 1649, cf. *Sandas* (sic) c1190, *le Sandes* m13, ~ *sandes* 1260–80, *Sandis* 1270–80, *the sandes* 1229, 1721); the Seven Acres 1871; G. South Carr 1763 (*Glentham South Carr* 1661², *South Carr* 1673, *North & South Carrs* 1681 (there is no separate documentation extant for *North Carr*), *South Carr* 1735, *v.* **kjarr**); Stockyard Fd 1871; Taylor's Cl 1844 (from the surn. *Taylor*); the Ten Acres 1871 (*Ten Acer-dail* 1669, *v.* **deill**); West Car 1871 (*v.* **kjarr** and cf. G. South Carr *supra*); West Fd 1764, 1837, The West Fd 1768, 1797, 1802, 1825 (*in campo occidentali* 1270–80, 1307, c1320, 1330, *in campo west* c1331, *ye westfeld* 1564, *the Westfeilde* 1649, *in occcidentali campo* 1661², *the West Feild* 1669, *the west feild* 1697, 1721, *ye West feild* 1709, *v.* **west**, **feld**, one of the great fields of the village, cf. Glentham East Fd *supra*); Wrangle Hole (Furlong) (perhaps from **wrangel** 'a crooked place or stream' or a surn. from Wrangle (L. Hol)); the little Wray 1816 (*ye lyttell wrey* 1564, *v.* **vrá** 'a nook or corner of land').

(b) *Adeldayles* Hy3 (1291) (*v.* **deill**; the first el. is a pers.n. rather than **adela** 'filth, a sewer', perhaps OE *Ēadhild* fem. or ContGerm *Adela* fem.); *Adherdal'* c1190, *atherdelmor* c1331 (the first el. is perhaps the OE pers.n *Ēadhere*); *the Aker dail* 1669 (*v.* **akr** 'a plot of arable land', **deill**); *Aldescales* 1307, *Haldscales* 1310–20 (*v.* **ald** 'old, long used, disused', **skáli** 'a temporary hut, a shed', the latter being an OWScand word, associated with Norwegian rather than Danish settlement. Occasional examples have been found in L, including five in Yarborough Wapentake, one in Walshcroft and four in Haverstoe); *Auker lane* 1673, *acker lane* 1721; *benland* c1225, *benholme* 1307 (*v.* **bēan** 'a bean', **land** 'a selion', **holmr**); *Blackwell* 1307 (*v.* **blæc**, **wella** 'a spring'); *unam bouatam de borne land* 1445 (from the surn. *Bo(u)rne*, *v. bovatam terre vocatam Martyne Lytherwyte infra*); *Brailesbek* Hy3 (1291) (presumably from the ME byname Brail belonging to ME *brail* (from OFr *braiel*) 'a belt for breeches, girdle', with **bekkr** 'a stream, a beck'); *Braithebetmore* (*-bet-* = *-bec-*) Hy3 (1327), *Braidebecmore* 1220–30², *braybek mor* c1331 (*v.* **breiðr** 'broad', **bekkr**, a Scand compound, with **mōr** 'a moor, a marsh'); *le Brakenhalle quod fuit capitali manm* prob 1330 (c1331) ('Bracken Hall which used to be a capital manor'. Mr John Field suggests that Bracken Hall was a deserted building surrounded by ferny scrub); *Brandesbrige* 1220–30² 'Brand's bridge', from the ODan pers.n. *Brand* and **brycg** in a Scandinavianised form); *Breclandes* (*-c-* = *-t-*) Hy3 (1291), *Bredlaundes* 1210–20, *North, Suthbretlandes* 1307, *Suth Brettelandes* c1331 (the first el. is uncertain, the second being **land** 'a selion' in the pl.); *brighilles* c1331 (*v.* **brycg** in a Scandinavianised form and **hyll**); *brynnand heued lande* 1307 'the burning headland', *v.* **brennandi**, **hēafod-land**); *three stongs called by dale* 1649 (*by dale* has been noted in the f.ns. (b) of Waithe, PN L **4**, 181, and in Waltham f.ns. (b), PN L **4**, 189, where it is suggested that it means 'the share of land belonging to the village' from **bȳ** 'a village' and **deill** 'a share of land', a Scand compound; *de Camera de Glentham* Ed1, *de la Chaumbre de Glentham* 1314 both (p); *Cauenby beck 1307, Canebie Beck* 1649, *Canebicrithe* (sic) c1190, *Kauenbicroft* 1196–1203, *Canebycroft* Hy3 (1291), *Cauenby croft* c1220, *Kafnebi croft* 1220–30², *Cauenby crofte* c1331, *Cainby feild* 1677, *Cainby feeld* 1721 (alluding to the neighbouring parish of Caenby, with **bekkr**, **croft**, **feld** and **stig** 'a path, a narrow road'); *Cauilc-Beck* (sic) 1661³ (obscure); *Cawkin furland* 1669 (from the surn. *Calkin, Cawkin* with **furlang**); *Cirsty Gate* (sic) 1669 (*v.* **gata**; *Cirsty* is uncertain); *ye Clows pasture* 1677 (perhaps named from the *Clough* family, cf. William *Clough* 1721); *Colismanhil* Hy3 (1291), *Colemanhill* 1669, *Cowleman hill* 1681, *coulman hill* 1721 (from the pers.n. or surn. *Col(e)man* and **hyll**); *Y^e Common Pasture* 1709; *Couls close* 1669, *Coles Close* 1721 (from the surn. *Cole* and **clos(e)**); *cow close* 1669; *Cowdikes* 1663, *the old Cowdikes* 1690, *Cowedike* 1693 (*v.* **dík**); *the Cowpasture* 1700, *cowpasture* 1706, *Cowpasture* 1724; *long creues* 1669 (perhaps from dial. **crew** 'a pen, a hut, a shed' in the pl.); *in le Croftes* 1327¹ (p) (*v.* **croft** 'a small enclosed field', dial. 'a small enclosure of arable or pasture land'); *Crolles lathe* c1414 (named from the *Crolles* or *Croylles* family, cf. *Will' Croylles* named in the document, with **hlaða** 'a barn'); *ad crucem de Glentham* 1281 (p) (*v.* **cros**); *Crosholmbeck* 1307 (*v.* **bekkr**, named from Crossholme Ho in Bishop Norton parish *infra*); *Crow Close Nooking* 1669 (*Nooking* is dial *nooking* cf. The Nookings PN L **3**, 144); *douecote garthe* 1445 (*v*. **garðr** 'an enclosure'); *Dunstanhull* Hy3 (1291), *-hille* 1307, *-hill* c1331, *dunstall hill* (sic) 1669 (Mr Field suggests that this is from **tūn-stall** 'the site of a farm', with the not uncommon development to *Dunstan*, and **hyll**); *le Est Croft* m13, *le Este Crofte* 1445 (*v*. **ēast, croft**); *the even lane* 1669 (*v*. **efen** 'level', **lane**); *ye fallow feild or Common* 1677, *ye fallow feild* 1700, *the fallow Feild* 1724 (*v*. **falh** 'fallow'); *feldes of glentam* 1539, *the feild* 1697 (*v*. **feld**, denoting the open fields of the village); *the flower daile* 1669 (*v*. **deill**; the first el. is uncertain; *Foxhow* c1230 (14), *fox how* 1330, *Foxehow* 1332, *fox whols* (sic) 1721 (*v*. **haugr** 'a mound, a hill', the second el. being 'normalised' to *hole* in the 1721 spelling, as pointed out by Mr Field); *fulcherdam* 1307 (*v*. **damme**, 'a dam, a pond', the first el. being the OFr pers.n. *Foucher*, from West Frankish *Fulcher*); *Gauntgarth* 1443, *Gaunt garth* 1462 (presumably from the surn. *Gaunt* and **garðr** 'an enclosure'); *Ginesgate* Hy3 (1291) (*v*. **gata**, the first el. being obscure, though Dr Insley suggests that the first el. is probably an unrecorded EScand pers.n. **Ginni*, a hypocoristic form of OSwed *Ginniut* or the like); *de Grene* c1331, *de la Grene* 1332 both (p) (*v*. **grēne** 'a village green'); *Grimesgate* Hy3 (1291) (presumably from the Scand pers.n. *Grímr* or a surn. derived from it, and **gata**); *Grisewell* Hy3 (1291), *Gryswells* c1320, *Griswelles* c1331 ('the spring(s) frequented by young pigs', *v*. **gríss, wella**); *Hacthacres* 1196–1203, *Hactacre* (checked from MS) e13, *Actacres* c1220, 1223–24, *Aghtacres, Estre aghetacres* 1307 (*v*. **ēasterra** 'more eastern'), *eightacres* 1691, *eightecors* 1721 (sic) ('the eight acres', *v*. **eahta** (Angl **æhta**), **acer**, and cf. the Haul in f.ns. (a) *supra*); *Haidecrofte* 1441 (*v*. **croft**; the first el. is ON **heiðr** 'a heath'); *Hakedailes* Hy3 (1327) (*v*. **deill**; the first el. is uncertain); *Hakelholme more* Hy3 (1327) (*v*. **holmr, mōr**; the first el. is uncertain); *at Hall* 1428 (p) (*v*. **hall**); *Halletrehing, Westerehalle Trehing* eHy3 (1291) (*Trehing* is from ME *thrīthing* 'a third part' but the semantic context is unclear); *The headland* 1669, *the headland* 1690 (*v*. **hēafod-land** 'the head of a strip of land left for turning the plough'); *le hethegate* 1310–20 ('the road to the heath', *v*. **hǣð, gata**); *Hill Side* 1694; *hillsike* 1663, *Hillsike* 1714 (*v*. **hyll, sík**); *Holmesdic* e13, *Holmesdihic* (sic) 1210–20 (*v*. **holmr, dík**); *Houmstie more* 1690, *houmstye Moore* 1693 (*v*. **holmr, stígr** 'a path, a narrow road'); *Holmer(e), Litteholmor* (sic in transcript) Hy3 (1291), *litle howemere* c1331 ('the boundary lying in a hollow', *v*. **hol, (ge)mǣre**); *the Homestall* 1706 (*v*. **hām-stall** in the later sense 'an enclosure around a homestead'); *kirkstyghes* 1307 (*v*. **kirkja, stīg, stígr**); *be ye Kyrk* 1428 (p), *Glentham kyrke* 1493 (*v*. **kirkja**); *Lagdale* (for *Lang-* c1190, *le lange dayles* c1331 (*v*. **lang** 'long', **deill** in the pl.); *Langelandes* Hy3 (1291), *langlandes* 1207, c1331, *longlands* 1721 (*v*. **lang, land** 'a selion' in the pl.); *Lawenabbe* 1321 (*v*. **lágr** 'low', **nabbi** 'a hill-top'); *sika* "of" *Lesewelles* Hy3 (1291) (*Lese-* is ME *lēse* 'pasture land'); *The Leyes* 1735 (*v*. **leye** (OE **lēah**); *leyregravis* 1260–70 ('the clay pits', *v*. **leirr, græf** in the pl.); *lime kilne* 1669; *Linges* Hy3 (1291 ('(places where) ling, heather grows', *v*. **lyng** in the pl.); *longhedlande* 1445 (*v*. **lang** 'long', **hēafod-land**); *le lounde* 1477, *~ lownde* 1477 *v*. **launde** 'an open space in woodland, woodland pasture'); *bovatam terrae vocatam Martyne Lytherwyte* 1445, *to* (i.e two) *oxe-gangs cawlyd lederwyte & burne* 1539 (the 1539 form appears to allude to a consolidation of Lytherwyte's holding with another oxgang apparently that referred to as *unam bouatam de borne land supra*, as Mr Field suggests); *machunsik* 1307 ('Macun's ditch, trench', from the Old Northern French *Machun* 'a mason' and **sík**; *in marisco* e13, "the marsh of" *Glentham* Hy3 (1327); *matuynghow* 1307 (*v*. **haugr**; the first part of the name is obscure); "the common of" *marescal* Hy3 (1291) (*Marescal* is probably from **marescal** 'a marshal' or the derived surn.); *mastals* 1721;

Medeliemelnes Hy3 (1291) (obscure); *Melfield Bancke* 1694; *midelcrewe* 1721 (*v.*
middel, crew 'a pen, a shed'); *Mor Crofts* 1721 (self-explanatory); *Musholm*
1196–1203, *Museholm* c1220, *-holm'* 1223–24, *Musholme* 1307, *mussams* 1669,
Mussams 1694, 1714 ('the raised land amidst the marshes frequented by mice', *v.*
mūs, mús, holmr, though the first el. may alternatively be the OE pers.n. *Mūsa* or
more likely ON *Músi*); *newe Close* 1649, *Nue Close* (*v.* **nīwe, clos(e)**); *Newhill Sike*
1693 (*v.* **sík**), *newell hill* 1721; *newlands* 1669 (*v.* **nīwe, land** 'a selion' in the pl.);
Newton beck 1669 (probably from the surn. *Newton* with **bekkr**); *le northdale*
1290–1310, *le northdal* 1300–20, *le North dal'* c1331 (*v.* **norð, deill**); *Northill* 1307,
le North hul 1331, *Northhills* 1669, *North hills* 1673, 1681 (*v.* **norð, hyll**); *North lane*
c1331; *Northlangfoure* 1290–1310, *le northlangfour* 1300–10, *North langfours*
c1331 (*v.* **lang, furh** 'a furrow'); *Northmor* eHy3 (1291), *la North more* 1282–86 (*v.*
norð, mōr, cf. The East Moore, the West Moore in (a) *supra*); *Nortiby* 1327[1],
Northiby "of" *Glentham* 1327[2], *Northiby* c1331, 1332 all (p) ((the place) north in the
village', *v.* **norð, í, bȳ,** denoting X who lives in the north of the village, a common
Danish formation in L); *Nortune dik* Hy3 (1291) (presumably from the adjacent
parish of Bishop Norton and **dík**); *little oxclose* 1606; *ox piece* 1669; *Oxgates* 1724
('pasture(s) for oxen' from dial. **gate** (ON **gata**) in the sense 'pasture for an animal'
as in the common *Sheepgate*); *the road called Packhorse Bottom* 1749; *pease holmes*
1673, *Pease holmes* 1681 (*v.* **pise, holmr**); *Person Drax land* c1414 (named from the
surn. *Drax,* cf. Peter *Drax* in the same Rental); *pesewange* 1307, *-wangs* 1445, *pese
whong* 1721 (*v.* **pise** 'pease', **vangr** 'a garden, an in-field'); *lez pyngiles* 1441 (*v.*
pingel 'a small enclosure'); *Ravenestache* (*-stache* = *-stathe*) Hy3 (1291), *Ravenstath*
1307, *Rauenstigh* 1669, 1673, *Ravenstigh* 1681, *rauenstigh* 1721 'the raven place,
site', from ON **hrafn** and ON **staðr,** the second el. having been presumably replaced
by **stíg**); *Rawesicbek* (sic) 1270–80 (perhaps from **rauðr** 'red', **sík,** with **bekkr**);
Redholmor Hy3 (1291) (presumably 'the red hollow', *v.* **rēad, hol** with **mōr**); *Rischeʃ*
c1190 ('(the place) where rushes grow', *v.* **risc**); *Royleseng* Hy3 (1291) (a difficult
name which may be from the surn. *Royle* and **eng**); *Rundle* 1669 (*v.* **rynel** 'a small
stream, a runnel'); *Sandegate* 1270–80, *Sandy Gate* 1669 (*v.* **sand, sandig, gata**);
Sesonyehil (sic) 1260–80 (obscure); *Settecuppe* Hy3 (1291) (from **set-copp** probably
'a set-shaped hill', i.e. 'a flat-topped hill', as in Sedge Copse, PN L 3, 116); *ye
Shepcot* c1414 (*v.* **scēap, cot**); *les sikes* 1307, *Sikes* 1721, *little sike* (*v.* **sík**);
Smidheseng c1220, *Smidesheng* 1220–30[1], *Smithesheng'* 1223–24 (the first element
is the occupational name *Smith* or the derived surn.; the second is **eng**);
Sneerbreclandes Hy3 (1291) (obscure); *snipe dayle* c1331 ('the portion of land
frequented by snipe', *v.* **deill,** the first el. being ME **snīpe** 'a snipe, especially the
common snipe (*gallinago gallinago*)); *the south furlong* 1690, (*v.* **furlang**);
Spittlegate 1669, *spittlegate* 1673, *Spittle Gate* 1681, *Spitel gate gate* (sic) 1721 ('the
road to Spital in the Street, in Hemswell parish *infra'*, *v.* **gata**); *Staingate* c1190,
Stanegate Hy3 (1291), *Stayngate* 1307 (*v.* **steinn, gata,** the reference probably being
to Ermine Street); *Stamphowe* 1673; *Stone hills* 1669, 1681, *Stonehills* 1673 (*v.* **stān,
hyll**); *the Strets* 1663, *the streete* 1690, *The Streets* 1693, *the street* 1700 (*v.* **strǣt,**
presumably this, like *Staingate,* refers to Ermine Street); *Sudale* c1190, *Sedal'*
1196–1203, *Suthdale* c1220, 1220–30[2], 1223–24, 1307, *Southe dailes* 1669,
Southdales 1669, *-dayles* 1673, *-daylles* 1681 (*v.* **sūð, deill,** in all the late forms in the
pl.); *Suthhill'* c1220, *Sudhil* 1220–30[1] *Suth hill'* 1223–24, *South hills* 1669, 1681,
Southill 1673, *South hill* 1681, 1721 (*v.* **sūð, hyll**); *Swynstidikes* 1307, *le swynstidik*
1300–20, *Swynstidik* c1331 (*v.* **swīn, stíg** 'a path, a narrow road', with **dík**); *little
thorns furland* 1669 (*furland* is a variant of **furlang** in L); *Thorland* 1673, *Thurland*

1681, *Thurlong* (sic) 1694, *thurlands* 1721 (the forms are too late for a certain etymology); *þreacre* c1225, *threaker* c1331 ('three acres', *v.* **þrēo, æcer, akr**); *Thirsewell* 1220–30², 1307, *Thyrswelles, Thriswelnabbe* 1307, *Thorsay Nab* 1669, 1673, 1681, *thorsey nab* 1721 ('the spring frequented by giants, demons', *v.* **þyrs, wella**, with **nabbi** 'a knoll, a hill'); *Toftsyke* c1320, *-sik* c1331, *toft sike* 1669 (*v.* **toft** 'a messuage, a curtilage', **sík**); *touthill* 1669, *toot hill* 1721 ('the look-out hill', *v.* **tōt-hyll** and Glentham *supra*); *tweem gate* 1669, *Tween gates* 1681 (*v.* **betwēonan** 'between', **gata**); *Vernuncroft* 1397 (from the surn. *Vernon* (from *Vernon*, Eure) and **croft**); *the watirfour* 1300–20, *le Waterfours* c1331, 1348 ('the wet furrow(s)', *v.* **wæter, furh**); *well sik* 1445 (*v.* **wella, sík**); *ye west furh* 1677, *v.* **west, furh**); *Westlanges, Westlangfure* Hy3 (1291), *Westlanges* c1331, *west lands* (sic) 1669 (*v.* **west, lang** 'a long piece of land', replaced by **land** in the 1669 form, with **furh**); *de Whyn' de eadem* (i.e. Glentham) 1383 (p) (*v.* **hvin** 'gorse'); *Willow close Nouking* 1669 (from dial. *nooking* 'a nook', *v.* **nōk**); *Winter side* 1669; *Withe gate* c1200, *wythgatgren* 1307 (*v.* **grēne** 'a grassy spot'; *Withe gate* is perhaps 'the road to the wood', *v.* **viðr, gata**); *Winter Side* 1669; *le Wrangelandes* Hy3 (1291), *Wranglandes* 1307, c1331 ('the crooked selions', *v.* **vrangr, land**); *Wyome Place* endorsed 15 (named from the *Vyome* family, cf. *Robert' Vyome* 1462, and **place** 'a residence'); *ybrevedland* (*v.* **hēafod-land**), *ybre pit* c1331 (*v.* **pytt**; *ybre* is obscure).

Glentworth

GLENTWORTH

Glentewrde (2x), *-uurde, -urde* (2x) 1086 DB, *-worda* (2x) c1115 LS, *-worde* 1160–66 Dane, *-word* c1190 RA iv, *-wurde* a1150 Dane, *-wurd'* 1196 ChancR, *-wyrda* 1153–54 (Ed1) *Newh, -wurða* 1166, 1167 P, *-wurð* 1205 ChancR, *-wurth* 1209–25 LAHW, 1236 RRG, 1251 Ipm, 1276 RH, *-wurthe* 1218 Ass, *-worthe* 1155–60 Dane, 1212–17 RBE, 1244 Fees, 1305 Pat, 1589 NCWills, *-worth(')* Hy2 (1318) Ch, 1202 Ass, 1250 Fees, 1271 FF *et passim* to 1376 Pat, *-wrda* 1190–95 Dane, 1230 ChancR, c1263 HarlCh, *-wrth'* 1203 Ass, 1205 P, 1205 OblR, 1206 1222 Cur, 1243 Cl, 1250 Fees, 1254 ValNor

Gleintaworda c1115 LS

Glentworth 1154–72, 1172, 112 (1407) Gilb, R1 (1318) Ch, 1202 Ass, 1272 *Ass*, 1291 Tax, 1298 Ass, 1300 Ipm, 1314 Orig, 1322 HarlCh, 1322 Ipm, 1323 Pat, 1324 Cl, 1325 Orig, 1325 FA *et freq, -worthe* 1281 QW, 1312 Inqaqd, 1331 Ipm, 1445 AASR xxix, *-wrth* 1198 (1328) Ch, 1203 P, 1276 RH, *-wurth* 1203 ChR, 1212, 1242–43 Fees, *-word'* 1272 *Ass, -wrd* 1275 RH, *-wort* 1576 Saxton

The second el. is **worð** 'an enclosure'; for the first *v.* the discussion of Glentham *supra*.

ASH HOLT, 1842 *TA*, cf. *Ash W*ᵈ 1828 Bry. BIG WOOD. BLYTHE CLOSE, 1842 *TA*, *Blyth Close* 1824 O, 1830 Gre, no doubt from the surn. *Blyth(e)*. CHURCH FM (local). COACHROAD HILL PLANTATIONS. DOG KENNEL FM, *Glentworth Dog Kennel* 1824 O, *Glentworth Kennel* 1830 Gre, *Kennels* 1842 White. FOX COVER (lost), 1828 Bry. GIPSEY LANE. GLENTWORTH CLIFF FM, cf. *clifstrete* Hy3, lHy3 (Ed1) *Newh, the cliff* 1760 *LCS*, *Cliff* 1842 *TA*, *v.* **clif**. GLENTWORTH CLOSES (lost), 1828 Bry. GLENTWORTH GORSE, 1824 O, 1830 Gre. GLENTWORTH GRANGE, 1830 ib, *aquam que currit inter Thorp & grangiam* Hy3 (Ed1) *Newh*; it was a grange of Newsham Abbey, *v.* **grange**. GLENTWORTH HALL, 1726 Which, *Glentworthe hall* 1828 Bry, 1830 NCWills, *Hall* 1828 Bry, 1830 Gre. GLENTWORTH HEATH FM (lost), *Glentorth Heath F*ᵐ 1828 Bry, cf. *The Heath* 1842 *TA*. GLENTWORTH THORPE (lost), *Thorp* Hy3 (Ed1) *Newh*, ~ *iuxta Glentwrd* 1295 (Ed1) *ib*, ~ *de Glentworth* 1297 CoramR (p), *Glentworthorp'* 1383 Peace, *Glentworth'thorp* 1388 ib, *Glentworthe Thorpe* 1523 Wills ii, 1525, 1544 WillsStow, *-thorpe* 1534 CA, *Glenteworthethorpe* 1540 LP xv, *Glentworthe thorpe* 1566 *LCS*, 'the secondary settlement, the dependent, outlying farmstead or hamlet (of Glentworth)', *v.* **þorp**. HANOVERHILL PLANTATION, cf. *Hanover Lane* 1842 *TA*. HILLTOP PLANTATION, cf. *super collem* c1234 (Ed1) *Newh, super montem* c1234 (Ed1) *ib, onthe hill'* 1327 *SR*, *othe hill'* 1332 *ib* all (p). HOMEYARD FM. KEXBY RD (local), the road to Kexby in Upton parish, Well Wapentake. LARCH PLANTATION. LOW COVER (lost), 1830 Gre. LOWFIELD FM. MIDDLE STREET is to be identified with *Aldestrete* c1234 (Ed1), *le* ~ Hy3 (Ed1) both *Newh*, cf. *stret buts* Hy3 (Ed1), *stretebuttes* lHy3 (Ed1) both ib (*v.* **butte** 'a strip of land abutting on a boundary') , *the Street* 1780 *Terrier*, *v.* **ald**, **stræt**, the name of the medieval trackway running along the clif above the village. MILL FM, cf. *Glentworth Mill* 1824 O, *Mill* 1828 Bry, *Mill House* 1842 *TA*, *Milnecroft* 1154–72 *DC*, *vno molendino Ventritico* 1566 *LCS*. MOAT, a medieval moated site. MOOR PLANTATION (lost), *Moor Plant*ⁿ 1828 Bry, *Moor Furze Plantation* 1842 *TA*, cf. *More beck furlong* 1693 *Terrier*, *Moor Beck* 1745 *ib*, 1842 *TA*, *v.* **bekkr** 'a stream'. NEW GORSE. NORTHLANDS FM. NURSERY PLANTATION. OAK WOOD, *Oak W*ᵈ 1828 Bry. OLD VICARAGE (local), *the Vicaridge* 1602, *with in the foresaid bounds (of the newe vicaridge house) is the olde Vicaridge house* 1612, *the Viccaridge* 1606, *y*ᵉ *Vicarage* 1700, 1745, *the* ~ 1762, 1780, 1858 all *Terrier, Pars.* 1828 Bry, *Vicarage House* 1842 *TA*. PARK LANE, 1828 Bry, *the Park Lane* 1658 *Terrier*, ~ *-lane* 1822 *ib*, cf. *my parke at Glenteworthe* 1589 NCWills, *Glentworth Parke* 1624 *Inv*, *Parke of*

Glentworth 1651 *LCS, yᵉ Park* 1745 *Terrier, v.* **park.** PASTURE FM (local). PILKINGTON FM, no doubt from the surn. *Pilkington.* SAW PIT (lost), 1828 Bry, *v.* NED s.*v. saw-pit* "An excavation in the ground, over the mouth of which a framework is erected on which timber is placed to be sawn with a long two-handled saw by two men, the one standing in the pit and the other on a raised platform". SOUTHEND PLANTATION. STONEY LANE. WESTLANDS FM.

FIELD-NAMES

Undated forms in (a) are 1842 *TA;* those dated 1149–62 (Ed1), Hy3 (Ed1), c1234 (Ed1), lHy3 (Ed1), 1295 (Ed1) are *Newh;* c1156, c1263 *HarlCh;* 1172 (1407), 112 (1407 Gilb; 1272, 1329 *Ass;* 1313, 1365, 1367 *Foster;* 1314 Ch; 1317–18 *KR;* 1322 Banco; 1348 *DC;* 1602, 1606, 1612, 1671, 1674, 1690, 1693, 1700, 1709, 1724, 1745, 1768, 1780, 1822, 1858 *Terrier;* 1760, 1795 *LCS.*

(a) Ash Holt (*v.* **æsc, holt** 'a wood, a holt'); Avenue Cliff, ~ ~ Plantn; Low, Near Badmoor; Bank; Great, Little Bell Moor; Bellamy Cl (named from the *Bellamy* family, cf. Nicholas *Bellamy* 1735 *Inv*); Bennett Cl (from the surn. *Bennett*); Brick Garth Plantn (*v.* **garðr** 'an enclosure'); Church Yard; Clue Hill Cl; Coal-pit Cl 1768, Coal-pit cl 1822, Coal Pit-Cl 1858 (self-explanatory); Cottage Pasture, Plantation in Cottage Pasture 1842; Cow Cl; Great, Little Crab tree Cl; Crawforth Cl (probably from the surn. *Crawforth*); Crow Cl; Drawthorn; (Upper) East Lands (*v.* **land** 'a selion'); East, West Far Cl; 40 acres; Fillingham South Pasture (named from the adjacent parish of Fillingham); (Middle, North) South Furry Cl; Garden Cl; Garth (*v.* **garðr**); Glentworth hedge, ~ upper gate 1760; Great Cl; Hill side Cl; Home Cl; Horse Cl; House, Garden and Hugh Cl, Hugh Little Cl; Intack (*v.* **inntak** 'a piece of land taken in or enclosed'); Little Jacklin Cl (named from the surn. *Jacklin*); Jackson Cl (named from the *Jackson* family, cf. John *Jackson* 1688 *Inv*); Jenny Winton (sic); The Lake; The Lawn (*v.* **launde** 'an open space in woodland, woodland pasture'); Ling Moor (*v.* **lyng** 'ling, heather', **mōr**); Little-Beck 1762, Little Beck 1841 (*Littlebeck furlong* 1693, *Little Beck* 1745, *v.* **bekkr** 'a beck, a stream'); Lobley Cl (probably from the surn. *Lobley*); The Manor House; Mansion House and Court; Mashdale Gate (sic) 1760, Marshdale Nooking, Marsh Dale (*Marsh Dale* 1724, *v.* **mersc, deill** 'a share of land', with **nōking**); Meadow Cl; Mean Long Moor (*v.* **(ge)mǣne** 'common'), Long Moor Cl; Middleton part Cl (no doubt from the surn. *Middleton*); North Fd (*in aquilonali campo* Hy3 (Ed1), *in campo boriali* 1313, *v.* **norð, feld**, one of the great fields of the village, cf. *in australi campo* in (b) *infra*); Oat Cl; Orchard; Parsons Cl; Preesyke Plantn (*v.* **sík** 'a ditch, a trench'); the first el. is obscure); Reckley Dale; Sands; Sheep Close Pingle (*v.* **pingel** 'a small enclosure'); Upper Sheep Fd; Sill Park (the first el. is perhaps from **syle** 'a bog, a miry place', as Mr Field suggests); Glentworth S. Pasture 1760, South Pasture; Stack Yard; Stow-Hill 1762, 1822, 1858, Stow Hill Cl 1768, Stow Hill (Cl), ~ ~ Plantn (*Stowe hill* 1602, 1612, *Stow hill* 1674, 1690, 1693, 1745, *Stowhill* 1724, *v.* **stōw** 'a place (of assembly), a holy place'. Mr Field points out that the importance of this place is perhaps indicated by a record of its transfer, in a Terrier of 1745: "This Close was given by yᵉ Honᵇˡᵉ Sʳ Thoˢ Saunderson . . . (now Earl of Scarbrough) to yᵉ Vicarage in lieu of 5 Beast Gates"); Sugar Cl (no doubt a complimentary name for sweet land); 3 Almshouses; Waste (freq); Water House Plantn; West Pingle (*v.* **pingel**); Willow Holt (*v.* **holt**); Wood Cl.

(b) *viam que vocatur Akergate* Hy3 (Ed1), *viam que vocatam le Akergath* 1313 ('the road to the arable land', *v.* **akr, gata**, a Scand compound); *Aumude Croft* (sic) c1234 (Ed1) (probably for *Aumunde Croft* with omission of the second nasalising stroke over the second -*u*-. Perhaps from the Scand pers.n. *Auðmundr* and **croft**); *bennescroft* Hy3 (Ed1), *Bene Croft, bennecroft, benescroft* c1234 (Ed1) (the first el. is probably **bēan** 'a bean' with **croft**); *Briggedeile* c1156 (*v.* **brycg** in a Scand form and **deill** 'a share, a portion of land'); *Brunes heuedland, Bruneshedland* Hy3 (Ed1) (the first el. is either the OE pers.n. *Brūn* or the corresponding Scand pers.n. *Brúnn*, with **hēafod-land** 'the head of a strip of land left for turning the plough'); *Bunteletorp, Buntelthorp* 1314 (probably from the ME pers.n. *Buntel* with **þorp** 'a secondary settlement, an outlying farmstead'); *the common* 1671; *estdayil* (sic), -*dayle* Hy3 (Ed1), -*dayl* c1234 (Ed1) (*v.* **ēast, deill**); *in campis de Glentwrde* 1149–62 (Ed1), *in campis de glentworth* 1172, 112 both (1407), *in camp' de Glent'* Hy3 (Ed1), *in campis de Glentworth'* 1329 (*v.* **feld**, denoting the open field of the village); *Goldhawe* 1272 (perhaps *v.* **golde** 'a marigold or some gold-coloured plant', **haga** 'an enclosure'); *on the grene* 1327, *atte Grene* 1332, *oye Grene* 1367 all (p) (*v.* **grēne** 'a village green'); *Grete* Hy3 (Ed1), *Gret* lHy3 (Ed1) (*v.* **grēot** 'gravel', in the sense 'the gravelly place'); *half leifhus, halueleifhus'* c1234 (perhaps as Dr Insley suggests 'half an inherited house' from **half** plus ON *leif* f. 'inheritence' with OE **hūs** or ON **hús** 'a house', an unusual name); *the hempe yarde* 1612 (*v.* **hænep** 'hemp', **geard** 'an enclosure'); *Kirkehil* c1156 (*v.* **kirkja** 'a church', **hyll**); *le mikelgate* 1348 (a Scand compound, *v.* **mikill, gata**); *Lowth park garthe* 1610 (*v.* **garðr**; it was held by Louth Park Abbey); *Northcroftdale* 1348 (*v.* **norð, croft** with **deill**); *Padmoregat* 1365 'the marsh infested with toads', *v.* **padde, mōr**, with **gata**); *Pottertoft* c1263 (*v.* **toft** 'a messuage, a curtilage', the first el, being **pottere** 'a potter' or the derived surn.); *Prillydayle* 1365 (*v.* **deill**, the first el. being obscure); *Ruholm* c1156, *Ruchholm* 1179 (Ed1) (*v.* **rūh** 'rough', **holmr** 'raised land amidst the marsh'); *prato quod dicitur sainte marie halfe acre, sainte marie half acre* Hy3 (Ed1) ('(meadow which is called) St Mary half-acre', an endowment for a chapel or altar of the dedication); *le Southdale* 1348 (*v.* **sūð, deill**); *in australi campo* c1234 (Ed1), Hy3 (Ed1), *per medium austral' campo* c1234 (Ed1), *in campo australi* lHy3 (Ed1) (*v.* **sūð, feld**, one of the great fields of the village); *quoddam toftum quod vocatur takmantofte* 1317–18 (*v.* **toft**) (alluding to land held as perquisite of the feudal officer responsible for collecting *tak* 'a fee paid to a lord or the king for the right to let swine feed in a forest or on a piece of land; a customary fee for the right to keep swine', *v.* MED s.v. *tak*. Under (d) MED quotes *Bate le Tackman* 1322. There are numerous references to the tackman of individual villages in *KR*. A late reference has been noted to the Tackman of Spittle (i.e. Spital in the Street in Hemswell parish) paying a year's rent to John Julius Angerstein 1799 *LCS 6/7/17/1*); *the towne streate* 1612; *Wandayl* Hy3 (Ed1), c1234 (Ed1, *Wanddaile* c1234 (Ed1) (*v.* **wandale** 'a share of the common arable land of a township'); *Waterfures* Hy3 (Ed1) (*v.* **water** 'wet', **furh** 'a furrow'); *West dayl* Hy3 (Ed1), *Westerdayl* c1234 (Ed1) (*v.* **west, westerra** 'more westerly', **deill**); *the west feild upon Stowe Hill* 1602 (one of the open fields of the village, not noted in medieval forms).

Hackthorn

HACKTHORN

Haggethorn 968 (l13) RamsChron, 1193, 1194 P, *Hagetorne* 1086
   DB (3x), *-torn* 1086 ib, *-thorn* 1202 Ass, 1203 P, 1203 Cur
Agetorne 1086 DB
Hacatorn(a) c1115 LS, *Hacæthor* (sic) c1150 Dane, *Haccatorn* lHy2
   ib (p), *Haccetorn* 1202 Ass
Hachetorna c1115 LS (2x), 1130 P (p), 1175–81, lHy2 Dane, *-torn*
   1194 CurP, l12 RA iv, l12 Hy2 Dane, *Hachethorna* c1115 ib,
   c1155 (1411) Gilb, *Hacheþorn* e13 HarlCh, *Hacchetorn* 1185–87
   Dane
Haketorn(') 1156–85 (p1269) *Bard*, c1160 Semp, c1160 Dane, 1185
   RotDom, Hy2 (e13) *NCot*, lHy2 Dane, 1194 CurP, l12, c1200 RA
   iv, 1200, 1203 Cur *et freq* to 1255 Pap, *-thorn(')* l12 Dane, John
   HarlCh, 1202 Ass, 1208 FF, 1208 Cur, 1210 Ass, c1220, c1230,
   1238 RA iv, 1242–43 Fees *et freq* to *-thorne* 1553 Pat *Hacthorna*
   l12 Dane, *-thorn* lHy2 ib, 1242–43 Fees, 1254 ValNor *et passim*
   to 1444 LCStatutes, *Hakthorn(')* 1293 RSu, 1317 Pat, 1332 *SR*,
   1374 Pat *et passim* to *Hakthorne* 1539 *AD*
Hacktorn 1187 Dane, l12 *HarlCh*, 1294 Pat, *-thorn* 1233 Welles,
   1284 Abbr, 1312 Ipm, 1576 Saxton *et passim*, *-thorne* 1317
   Inqaqd, 1535 VE iv, 1575 LER
Haughthorn 1209–35 LAHW, *Haghthorn* 1281 QW, *Haghethorn*
   1299 Pat

Ekwall is no doubt correct, Studies[2], 119, when he says "The name
means 'the hawthorn', but the Old English form of that word is
haguþorn (or *hægþorn*), whence *hawthorn* by normal development.
HACKTHORN seems to presuppose an Old English sideform *hæggþorn*
or the like".

BLACKTHORN HILLS (lost), 1828 Bry. BOAT HO. BRATTONS FM (lost),
Brattons F^m 1828 Bry, named from the *Bratton* family, cf. John *Bratton*
1798 *Inv*. BRICK KILN PLANTATION. FISH POND. FOX COVERT. GLEBE
FM. GORSE COVER (lost), 1824 O, 1830 Gre. GROTAS PIT (local), cf.
Groty c1240 RA iv, *super Grot'* m13 *HarlCh*, grotigate Hy3 ib, *le Groti*,
le Grotty 1308 ib, *east Grottes, west grottes* 1556 *CCLeases, Grawtus*
(sic) 1675 ib, *East Groatasses* (sic) 1745 *Andr, North, West, East Gretas*
(*-e-* = *-o-*) 1772 LNQ iv. *At the present day a stone pit in Hackthorn is
called "Grotas pit"* 1896 LNQ iv. Obscure, but perhaps an *-ig* derivitive
of OE **grēot** 'gravel', denoting a gravelly place. HACKTHORN CLIFF,

CLIFF HO, *Clif* 112 Dane, *le* ~ 1238 RA iv, *super Cliuum* Hy3 *HarlCh*, *ye Cliffe* 1675 *CCLeases, ye Clift* (sic) 1705 *Terrier, Cliff* 1745 *Andr*, cf. *Cliff hole, ~ furlong* 1772 LNQ iv, *v*. **clif**. HACKTHORN GRANGE, 1824 O, 1830 Gre, *grangia* 1226 *DC, ex aquilonali parte Grangie* Hy3 *HarlCh, Grangie de Hacthorn* Ed1 *ib, ad portam Grangie de Hach'thorn* 1308 *ib*, "grange in" *Hakthorne* 1537–39 LDRH, "the Grange of" *Hackthorne* 1569 Pat, *Hackthorne Graunge* 1674 *LCS, ye Grange* 1705 *Terrier, Grange Farm* 1745 *Andr*. It was a **grange** of Bullington Priory. HACKTHORN HALL, *ye Hall* 1705 *Terrier, Hall* 1824 O, *atte Hall'* 1421 *DCAcct* (p), cf. *ex opposite curie Petri de Hungaria* c1200 RA iv and *ye Hall Farme* 1705 *Terrier, the hall farm* 1771 *ib, ye Farme opposite to ye Hall* 1715 *Terrier*. HACKTHORN LODGE, 1830 Gre, *Hackthorn Lo*. 1828 Bry, *Lodge and Garden* 1853 *CCLeases*. HACKTHORN LOW GORSE (lost), 1830 Gre. HACKTHORN PARK. HACKTHORN WINDMILL (local), *molendinum de Haketorn* 1148–54 (1642) *Dods 95, juxta molendinum* Hy2 Dugd vi, *The Mill* 1745 *Andr, Hackthorn Mill* 1824 O, *Mill* 1828 Bry, cf. *le myln hyll* 1574 *Anc, Mill hill* 1675 *CCLeases*. HALFWAY HO (lost), 1828 Bry. HOME FM. HONEYHOLES (local), 1824 O, 1830 Gre, *honey holes* 1675 *CCLeases*, 1705 *Terrier, Honey Hole* 1722 *Survey*, 1745 *Andr*, ~ *hole* 1772 LNQ iv, probably a complimentary nickname for good land. LOW FM. MAWKINS LANE (local), *Mawkin's Lane Close* 1867 *CCLeases*, cf. *Muchinges* c1220 RA iv, *Muchingis* 1238 *ib, Mokynges* c1240 *ib, Mukinges* Hy3 *HarlCh, le Mokinggate* 1308 *ib (v*. **gata** 'a way, a path, a road'), *Long, Short Mawkins* 1675 CCLeases, ~ *Maukins* 1772 LNQ iv, obscure. NORTH PLANTATION. OLD COVER (lost), 1828 Bry. SWALLOW HEATH FM (lost), 1828 Bry, 1830 Gre. VICARAGE (lost), *the Vicarage* 1822 *Terrier*, cf. *Vicarage Land* 1745 *Andr*.

FIELD-NAMES

Forms dated lHy2, 112, c1200 are Dane; e13 (13) *Kirkst*; e13, m13, Hy3, 13, 1308 *HarlCh*, 1203, 1243 FF; 1200–15, 1210–20, 1215–20, c1220, 1237, 1238, c1240, 1241, 1244 RA iv; 1226 *DC*; c1240 (Ed1) *Barl*; 1296 *Ass*; 1327 *SR*; 1334 *LBB*, 1383 Peace; 1389, 1417 Cl; 1530–31 Wills iii; 1556, 1675, 1798, 1800, 1822, 1835, 1867 *CCLeases*; 1568–70, 1605–7 *MinAcct*; 1602, 1668, 1671, 1690, 1697, 1705, 1715, 1771, 1822, 1827 *Terrier*; 1607 *Rental*; 1655, 1656 *LindDep 57*; 1745 *Andr*; 1772 LNQ iv; 1779 *EnclA*; all the rest are *Anc*.

(a) the Ashing 1772, The Ash Ings 1779 (*Assh ynges* 1548, *le Esshyng* 1569 (*v*. **eski** 'ashen'), *ye Ashin, Ashen* 1675, *Ashing* 1705, *The Ashing* 1715, *Ash Ing* 1745, *v*. **æsc, eng** 'meadow, pasture', as elsewhere in this parish); Barn Cl 1653; Beck 1771 (*ye Becke* 1655, *Beck* 1715 (*v*. **bekkr** 'a stream, a beck'); Burfill (sic) 1772 (probably to be identified with *Burghil* 112, 1210–20, 1238, *burchil* e13, *Burchil'* 1210–20, *Burghil* 1238, *-hill'* c1240, *Burfell* 1705, 1715, *Burfield next Risehill* 1745, 'the hill with a fortified place', *v.* **burh, hyll**, and *v.* Risehill *infra*); Chiswell gate 1772 (*Chissabell gate* 1675, *Cheslip Gate* (sic), perhaps 'the gravel road', *v.* **cisel, gata**); Clay Dale 1771, Cladales 1772 (*Cleideile* 112, *Cleydale* 1241, *Cleydale* 1602, *Claydales* 1671, *Clay Dales* 1675, 1697, 1705, ~ *dales* 1706, 1715, *v.* **clæg, deill** 'a share, a portion of land', as elsewhere in the parish); The Cow Pasture 1779 (*le Cow pasture* 1562, *le Cowpasture* 1564, *y* *Cow pasture* 1715); Crawthorn hill 1771 (*Cracathorne hul* lHy2 (*v.* **kráka** 'a crow, a raven'), *Crouthornehul* 112, *Crawethornhil* 1210–20, Hy3, *Craupornhill'* m13, *Crauthornhil* 1238, *Craghthornhill'* 1308, *Crawthornhill* 1675, *Crawthorn hill* 1705, 1715, from **cräwe** 'a crow', **þorn** 'a thorn bush', with **hyll**; note the first el. of the lHy2 form is from the ON word with the same meaning as OE **cräwe**); Daw furlong 1772 (*east, west Daw furlongs* 1675, *daw-furlong* 1705; the first el. is probably ME **daue** 'a jackdaw'); Dovecoat dale 1772 (*Dovecoat Dale* 1675, 1705, *Dove coat Dale* 1745); Lower, upper green gates 1772 (cf. *Green Gate* 1675, 1705, *Upper green gate* 1705, *v.* **gréne, gata**); Greenhill 1772 (1675, 1705, *Grenhulslake* 112 (*v.* **slakki** 'a small, shallow valley, a hollow', an East Scand word, common in north-west England, but rare in the East Midlands), *Grenhul* 112, *Grenehil, Grene Hil* 1210–20, *Greenhill Syke Furlong* 1745 (self-explanatory, *v.* **gréne, hyll**)); the Harding 1772, The Hard Ings 1770 (*Hartheng* 112, *in duris pratis de Hakethoren* Hy3, *in duro prato* c1240, m13, *le Hardyn* 1558, *le Hardyng* 1568. *le hardyng* 1569, *ye Harding bottom* 1675 (*v.* **botm**), *the Harding* 1705, 1715, *Hard Ing* 1745, 'the hard meadow', *v.* **heard, eng**, probably in the sense 'hard to till'); Haverlands 1772 (*Hauerlandsic* lHy2, *Hauerlantsike* 112, *Hauerlandesyke* c1240 (*v.* **sík** 'a ditch'), *Hauerlande* 1238, *Hauerland'* c1240, *Haverlands* 1675, *Haverland Gutter* 1705, *Haverland Gallow* (sic) 1715, *Haverlands* 1745, 'the selions on which oats are grown', *v.* **hafri, land**. Cf. *le Hauerdayle* 13, *Hauerdaile* 1308, *v.* **hafri, deill**); The North, the South Heath 1779, the Heath 1798, 1800, 1835 (*le Heth* 1558, self-explanatory, *v.* **hǣð**); Hing furlong 1772 (the first el. is probably from **eng**); Lane side Fd 1853 (cf. *en la Venele de Hackethorn* 1296 (p)); Leesdales 1772 (*Lecedale* c1220, *-dail* Hy3, *Lees dales* 1675, 1705, ~ *Dales* 1745 (perhaps the first el. is **lǣs** 'pasture, meadowland', the second is **deill**); Lincoln dale 1772 (*in ualle Lincoln, in valle Lincolnie* 1210–20, *in valle Lincoln'* c1220, *Lincolnedale* 1308, *Lincoln Dale* 1556, 1745, *Lincolne Dale* 1668, *Lyncolne dale* 1705, *v.* **dalr**); Lincoln Rd 1800 (*ad viam linc'* e13, self-explanatory; the reference is to Ermine Street); Lodge Cl 1867; the long Furlong 1771, Long furlong 1772 (*Langfurlang* 1226, *Langefurlanges* 1210–20, *Langfurlanges* c1240, 1241, Hy3, *Langfurland'* c1240, *Langfurlang'* m13, *Long furland* 1602, *long furlongs* 1671, ~ *Furlands* 1675, *y* *long Furlong* 1697, 1715, *Long Furlong* 1745, self-explanatory; *furland* is a common variant of *furlang* in north L); Nordales 1772 (*Nordailefurlang* 1226, *North Dales* 1675, *Nordales* 1705, *v.* **norð, deill** in the pl., cf. Souredales *infra*); the North fd 1771, ~ Fd 1772, The North field 1779 (*in campo aquilonali* c1240, Hy3, *in campo uero aquilonali* 1241, *in campo boriali* Hy3, *the Northfeild* 1602, *y* *northe fielde* 1671, *y* *North field* 1697, 1715, *North field* 1705, *v.* **norð, feld**, one of the great fields of the parish); Old Homestead Cl 1853, 1867; The Ox Pasture 1779 (*le oxpasture* 1565, 1566); Gt, Little Pickwell 1772; Polpils 1772 (probably for Potpits and to be identified with *Pot(t)egraues* 112, c1240, m13, *pot pitts* 1705, *Pott Pitts* 1745; Mr John Field suggests that this may well be 'the pits from which pots had been excavated', *v.* **pot(t), græf, pytt**); Top Rampart Cl 1853, 1867 (*Rampart* is a variant of *ramper*, a dial. word found in L for 'a raised road or way, the highway', v. NED s.v. *rampire*, *-pier*, EDD s.v. *ramper*); Risehill 1772 (*Rieshil* c1200, *Rissehil* e13, 1210–20, *Ryssehil'*, *Rishil* 1210–20, c1220, *Rissille* Hy3, *Risil* 1238, *Ryshill, Rysil'hill'* c1240, *Rishill'* c1240, 1308, *Rise hill* 1705, *Risehill* 1715, v. **hrīs** 'shrubs, brushwood', **hyll**); Rogers' farm 1772 (named from the *Rogers* family, cf. Samuel *Rogers* 1745 *Andr*); Souredales 1772 (*Sowdale* 1705, *Sour Dale* 1745. Mr Field suggests that despite the 1772 form the meaning is probably 'the south shares of land', v. **sūð**, **deill**, in contrast to Nordales *supra*); the South fd 1772, 1798, ~ South Fd 1779, 1800, 1835 (*in australi campo, in campo australi* Hy3, *in campo meridionali* c1241, *the Southfield* 1602, 1668, y^e *South feild* 1671, ~ *field* 1697, 1705, 1706, v. **sūð**, **feld**, one of the great fields of the parish, cf. the North fd *supra*); Spring head 1772 (*Springhead* 1705, 1715, *Spring head furlong* 1745, v. **spring**, **hēafod**, cf. *Spring Road* 1675); Stanna furlong 1772 (*Stanhou* c1220, *stanehouwe*, *stanhow* m13, *Stannah* 1675, *Stanna* 1705, *Stannay Furlong* 1745, 'the stone(y) hill or mound', v. **stān**, **haugr**); Stannal syke 1772 (cf. *Stanhille* 1226, *Stanrill Sike* (sic) 1675, *Standwell sike* 1705, v. **stān**, **hyll**); Studdy holes 1772 (cf. *Stodfaldes, Stoddefaldes* 1210–20, *Studdy folds* 1675, 1715, *Stoddy folds* 1715, *Studdy Fold* 1745, v. **stōd-fald** 'a horse enclosure'); Thirkland 1779 (*Thorkelhil, Torkelhil* l12, 1210–20, *Torkel Hil* 1210–20, *Þorkelhil* 1237, *Thorkylhill'* c1240, *Thorkhill* 1568, *Thurkland* 1745; the same name occurs in the f.ns. (b) of the neighbouring parish of Cold Hanworth no doubt referring to the same physical feature. It means 'Thorkil's hill', v. **hyll**, the first el. being the ODan pers.n. *Thorkil*, ON *Þorke(ti)ll*); Thirty Acres 1853, 1867; Townend 1772; North town side furlong, South Townside furlong 1772 (cf. *the town side* 1675, y^e *Townside* 1705, *Townside Furlong* 1745, self-explanatory); Lower, Upper Tween gates 1772 (*Nether tween(e) gate, uper tweene gate* 1675, *Nether tween Gates, Upper tween gate* 1705, self-explanatory, v. **betwēonan**, **gata**); Twenty Seven Acres 1853, 1867; Watermoresyke 1772 (*Water Moore Sike* 1675, *Waterman Syke* 1745, named from the *Waterman* family, cf. Thomas *Waterman* 1642 LPR, with **sík**); Wheat landleys 1772 (*Wetelont* lHy2, *Wetelant* l12, *in campo frumenti* 1226, *Watelant* Hy3, c1240, *Wheat Land Leys* 1745; the Latin form suggests that the name means 'the selion where wheat grows', v. **hwǣte**, **land**); Welton Moore 1771 (cf. *diuisas de Wellet'* e13, *Welten Meare* 1675, *Welton Field Meare* 1690, *Welton Meer* 1706, ~ *meare* 1715, 'the boundary land(s) of Welton (a neighbouring parish)', v. **(ge)mǣre**. *Moore* in the 1771 form is no doubt a misreading of earlier spellings in *Meer(e)*, as Mr Field points out); Woolane 1772.

(b) *Agewelles* c1240, (v. **wella**; the first el. is doubtful); *Alledaile* e13 (v. **deill**; the first el. is uncertain); *Beitesike* l12, *Baytesike* 1210–20, *-syche* c1220, *-sick* m13 (the first el. is ON **beit** 'pasture', the second **sík** 'a ditch, a trench'); y^e *Beaumont* 1675, *Beaumount pit* 1705, 1715 (perhaps from the surn. *Beaumont*); *Bennelandes* 1210–20, *beneland* e13 (13) (v. **bēan**, **land** in the pl.); *le Berg* 1226 (v. **be(o)rg** 'a hill, a mound'); *les Braches* 1226 (from ME *brache* 'land broken up for cultivation', in the pl.); *Bracklebee Dale* 1705, *Brackleby dale* 1715 (no doubt from a surn. from *Brocklesby* (PN L **2**, 61–63)); *Broneshurst* 1243 (v. **hyrst** 'a hillock, a copse'; the first el. is uncertain, but may be the ME surn. *Brun*); Bull Meadow, ~ *Mear* 1745; *Burgthorn'* 1210–20, *Burethorn'* c1240, *Burthorn* 1241 ('the thorn-tree at the fortified place', v. **burh**, **þorn**); y^e *burnt house Farme* 1705, 1715 (self-explanatory); *Burnt House Close Nook or Garth Ends* 1745 (v. **nōk**, **garðr**); *Burrs flintings* 1675; *buterwellegote* e13, *buttirwelgote* Hy3 (v. **gotu** 'a sluice'), *Butterwelles* 1238, *Butterwell'* Hy3, *Butterwells* 1675, 1705, 1715 (v. **butere**, **welle**; Mr Field points out that this name alludes to the use of wells as storage places for butter); *Church Gate*

(v. *Kirkgate infra*); *Cliff Hole* 1745 (v. **clif, hol** 'a hollow'); *Common Field and Meadow* 1556, *the Common Field* 1656; *Cotom howse, Cottome howse* 1530–31 (probably from a surn. *Cottom* and *house*); *Craw Nooking* 1745; *Crewekergarth* 1308 (from the ME surn. *Creweker with* **garðr**); *Cutts* 1745; *apud vallem* e13, *le Dale* 1308 (v. **dalr** 'a valley'), *Dalefurlanges* l12, c1240 (v. **furlang**); *West Dame furlong* 1705, *Low, Up^r Dam Furlong* 1745 (v. **damme** 'a dam, a pond'); *t're Will'i de Dene* 1308 (v. **denu** 'a valley'); *Eastfield* 1675 ('the east field', v. **ēast, feld**; the infrequency of references to this and to its western counterpart (cf. *the West field infra*) suggests that these two fields were of less significace than North Field and South Field); *Estsic* 1226 (v. **ēast, sīk**); *in campo de Hactorn* lHy2, ~ ~ *de Hacthorna* l12, ~ ~ *de Hakthorn'* 1203, ~ ~ *de Haketorn'* 1237, ~ ~ *de Hakthorne* 1308, *in camp' de Hakthorn* 1548 (v. **feld**, referring to the open field of the village); *Flaxlandes* 1226 ('the selions where flax grows', v. **fleax, land** in the pl. and cf. *les line landes* 1563, 'the selions where flax grows', v. **līn, land** in the pl.); *Flintes* 1210–20, Hy3, *Flyntes* 1210–20, *Flints* 1210–20, 1215–20, 1675, 1745, *the flints* 1705, 1715 (v. **flint**, denoting a place where flints are found); *in oriente del Fosse* 1244 (v. **foss** 'a ditch'); *Fourall* 1705; *foxpitte* m13 (v. **fox, pytt**); *frisbigate, ad occidentem uie Friseby* l12, *vie de friseby* e13, m13, *Frisbigate* 1308 ('the road to Firsby', v. **gata**) *Furehil* e13, *Furhill'* c1240, *furehil* m13 (the first el. is apparently **furh** 'a furrow, a trench', with **hyll**); *Gategraines* l12, *Gate greines* e13, *gategreynes* c1240 (Edl) ('the road forks', v. **gata, grein**); *Gosacres* l12, c1240, *Gos acres* c1240 (v. **gōs** 'a goose', **æcer**); *grindpesholm'* 1226; *Grisegarthe* c1240 (v. **grīss** 'a young pig', **garðr**); *Hagwelles* l12 (v. **wella**; the first el. is uncertain); *Hackthorne Farme* 1556; *Hakethorn hil* 1210–20, *Hakethornehill'* c1240, *hilles* (sic) 1226, *super Montem* 1327 (p), *del Hill' de Hakethorn'* 1334 (p) (v. **hyll**); *ye Farme opposite to ye Hall* 1715; *Halistouehil* l12, *Halistouhill'* c1240, *Halistowhill'* 1308, *Hally stow-hill* 1705 ('the holy place', v. **hālig, stōw**, with **hyll**; the site is unfortuately unknown); *hantege* 1226; *the Heading* 1715; *heggedic* 1226; *le Comon hedg* 1565, 1569, *le comon hedg* 1568 (v. **hecg**); *hemp landes* 1565, *Hemp land* 1656 ('the selion(s) where hemp grows', v. **hænep, land**); *pratum . . . quod dicitur Horsegang* m13, *Horsgank* Hy3, *Le Horsegang* 13 ('the horse path, track', v. **hors, gang**); *Hungerdaleslac* c1240 (from **hungor, deill**, denoting unproductive land, with **slakki** 'a shallow valley', cf. *Grenhulslake* in f.ns. (a) *supra*); *Jesabels, Jezebels* 1745 (a derogatory f.n. for unproductive land, from *Jezebel*, the name of the infamous wife of Ahab, king of Israel); *kirkaker* 1226 (v. **akr**), *Kirkedayle* 1226 (v. **deill**), *le kirkeland* 1308, *Church land* 1705 (v. **land**), *Church Gate* 1705 (v. **gata**), *ye Church lane* 1715 (the variation beween English *church* and Scand *kirk* is noteworthy); *ye Kirk hole* 1715 (this is named from the surn. *Kirk* and **hol** 'a hollow, a hole', Robert *Kirk* is named in the document in association with the f.n.); *le knowle lane* 1565 (v. **cnoll** 'a knoll, a hillock'); *le kyln house* 1563 (self-explanatory); *Laghille* (sic) 1226 (probably for *Langhille*, v. **lang, hyll**); *viam de Langwad* 1226 (partly illegible due to fading, but the reference is no doubt to Langworth in Barlings parish LWR, v. Langworth (DLPN 78): *Leys* 1705, 1745 (v. **ley** (OE **lēah**) 'a meadow, an open pasture'); *Littelhyl* 1238, *Littelhil* m13, *little hill* 1675, *Little ~* 1705 (self-explanatory); *Losletthes* l12, *Losslectes* e13, *Losleites, Losleytes* 1210–20 (the second el. is **slétta** 'a smooth, level field', the first is uncertain, but may be **hlōse** 'a pig-sty', 'a shed, a shelter'); *Lowdales* 1705 (v. **deill**); *Lutel Linges* lHy2 (v. **lȳtel, lyng**, denoting places where heather grows); *les line landes* (v. *Flaxlandes supra* in f.ns. (b)); *de la Mare* "of" *Hackthorn* 1417 (p) (v. **(ge)mǣre** 'a boundary', 'land forming a boundary'); *marestall'* m13 (this is apparently a fourth example of an OE *mar(e)stall, the likely source of *Mill Mastall butts* (PN L **2**, 133) *le marstal'* (ib, **2**, 209) and *Mastal* (ib **4**, 13). The meaning suggested for it is 'a pool of stagnant water, a pool'); *iuxta crucem Matilde* 1226 ('near Matilda's cross'); *Middlefurlanges, Midfurlanges* 1210–20, *Midilfurlang* 1226, *middelfurlanges* m13, *ye Middle furlong* 1705 (self-explanatory, *v.* **mid, middel, furlang**); *milnegate* 1226 (*v.* **myln, gata**); *la more* Hy3 (*v.* **mōr**, and cf. *west mor infra*); *namanesland* 1226 ('no man's land', probably denoting deserted land); *Neatheard Land* 1745 ('the selion held by the cattle-herd', *v.* **land**, the first el. being the ME occupational surn. *Nethirde*); *the needlehouse* 1675; *nepelandes* 1226 ('the selions where turnips grow', *v.* **nēp, land**); *viam de Neubele* ('the road to Newball (in Stainton by Langworth, LSR'); *Newdales* 1705 ('the new shares of land', *v.* **nīwe, deill**); *the new botham* 1675 (*v.* **nīwe, boðm** 'a valley bottom, a bottom', presumably denoting land in a valley bottom newly brought into cultivation); *nord mare* lHy2 (*v.* **norð, (ge)mǣre** 'a boundary, a piece of land marking a boundary'); *Northbergsik* 1210–20 (from **norð, be(o)rg** with **sík**); *ye North Gate* 1705 (*v.* **norð, gata**); *North Lands* 1745 (*v.* **norð, land**); *North Welles, Northwelles* 1210–20, c1240 (*v.* **norð, wella**); *Nothinghol* (sic) 1226; *super novem acras* e13, *super nouam* (sic) *acras* 1238, *super Nighen acre* 1308 (*v.* **nigon** 'nine', **æcer**); *ye pasture* 1705; *iuxta pomfret noke* 1563 (from the surn. *Pomfret*, with **nōk**); *in campo avena* 1226 ('the field where oats grow', *v.* **āte**); *Priestley* 1675 (perhaps 'the priest's pasture-land', *v.* **prēost, ley** (OE **lēah**) 'a meadow, an open pasture'); *Red Bottom* 1705, 1745 (*v.* **rēad, botm**); *Redailes* l12, *Rededail'* Hy3, *Reddaile* e13 (13) (perhaps 'the portion, share of land where reeds grow', *v.* **hrēod, deill**); *Rotdic* 1226 (*v.* **dík**); *ruttelpittes* 1226 ('the ruddle-pits', from ME **ruddle** red ochre for sheep-marking and **pytt**); *ye Rye Feld* 1571, 1573 (self-explanatory); *Ryland'* 1327 (p) (*v.* **ryge, land**); *usque ad Crucem sancti Andree* c1240 ('St Andrew's cross'); *super foreram sancti Egidii* c1240 ('St Giles headland'); *Sand Ends* 1745; *Sandrell* (sic) 1705; *sealfheuedlande* 1226 (*v.* **hēafod-land**; the first el. is obscure); *le Syeke Furlong* (sic) 1574, *Sike furland* 1675, *Sikefull Lands* (sic) 1705 (*v.* **sík, furlang**); *Smithistedes, Smitistedes* 1238 ('the sites of the smithies', *v.* **smiðða, stede**, cf. Smithy Steads PN YW **3**, 167); *South Ends* 1745; *Sperlingtunsike* e13 ('the Spridlington drainage ditch', *v.* **sík**, alluding to a neighbouring parish); *ye Stable* "of" *Hackthorn* 1389 (p); *Stangrauesyc* 1210–20, *-sike, Stanegrauesyke* c1240, *Staynegrauesick* m13 (*v.* **stān, steinn, græf** 'a pit', with **sík**); *at Stighle* "of" *Hackthorn* 1383 (p) (*v.* **stigel** 'a stile', perhaps also 'a steep ascent'); *Stocdeil* l12 *HarlCh* (*v.* **stocc** 'a tree-stump', **deill**); *Stocedene* 1200–15 (obscure); *Stone pit Dale* 1745 (self-explanatory); *Storiheuedland* m13 (*v.* **hēafod-land**; *Stori-* is obscure); *Stretfurlonges* l12, *Stretefurlanges* c1200, 1210–20, c1240, *Stretefurlanges* e13, *the Street* 1556 (*v.* **strǣt**, the reference being to Ermine Street); *le Stuble feld* 1571, 1573 (self-explanatory); *uia de stuppelhil, Stubelhilgate* e13, *stubelhil* e13, m13, *Stuppel hil* 1210–20, *stuppelhil* m13, *Stupil hill'* c1240, *Stupelhil* 1241, *Stopilhill'* 1308 ('the stubble hill' from ME **stuble, stubil(l)** and **hyll**); *Sudderhil* l12, *sutherhil* e13, *Sutterhil* c1220, *sudþerhil* m13 (from **suðerra** 'more southerly', **hyll**); *Swanesback* 1243 (perhaps denoting a convex piece of land, resembling the back of a swan); *Swineherd Lands* 1745 (selions held by a swineherd); *Swyncotes* 1563 (*v.* **swīn, cot** in the pl.); *Swynstye* 1564 (*v.* **swīn, stigu** 'a sty, a pen'); *Thursteindeile* c1200, *Thurstaindale* e13, *Thorstayndail* 1238, *Thorstendayle* c1240 ('Þorsteinn's share of land', from the ON pers.n. *Þorsteinn*, ODan *Thorstēn*, with **deill**); *Tug Garth* 1705 (*v.* **garðr**; earlier forms are required to suggest an etymology for the first el.); *Underneath Furs* 1745 (*v.* **fyrs**); *Uphall' House* 1668–70, *uphalhouse* 1607 ('the upper hall', *v.* **upp, hall**); *terram Thome Wdecok'* c1240; *via de Welletone* c1220, *vie de Welletona* c1240, *Welletongate* Hy3 ('the road to Welton (a neighbouring parish)', *v.* **gata**); *Midelwendinge* c1240, *Midilwendinges* Hy3 (*v.* **middel**), *suthwendinges* c1240, Hy3 (*v.* **sūð, wending** 'a turning, a bend in a road'); *Werel pit* 1308 (the first el is probably an error for *Weruel*, from **hwerfel** 'a circle, something circular', hence 'a circular pit'); *West Clife* 1558 (cf. Hackthorn Cliff *supra*); *West Close End Furlong* 1745 (cf. *West Close* 1558); *the West Field* 1690, *West Field or North Heath*, ~ ~ *or South Heath* 1745 (*v.* **west, feld** and the note on *Eastfield supra*); *West Firres* 1556, *les West furres* 1562 *Anc, le West Fyr(e)s* 1564, 1565, 1566, 1569, *campis voc' le West Furres* 1573, 1574, *West Furrs* 1675, *y* *west Furrs* 1705 (*v.* **west, fyrs** 'furze'); *Westgarthes* 1561 (*v.* **west, garðr**); *west mor* lHy2, *West mor* l12, *Westmor* 1210–20, m13, *Westmora* c1220, *Westmor'* c1240 (*v.* **west, mōr**); *Wheat Dales* 1705 (self-explanatory, *v.* **deill**); *Wheydales* 1675 (*v.* **deill**); *Wlfhacres* l12, *Wlfacres* c1240, m13, *Wlfe acres* m13, *Wool Acres* 1745 (*v.* **æcer**; the first el. is either **wulf** 'a wolf', indicating land haunted by wolves, or the OE pers.n. *Wulf*, as suggested by Mr Field); *wykesbusc* 1226 (the first el. appears to be the ME surn. *Wyke(s)*, the second is **busc** 'a bush, a shrub').

Cold Hanworth

COLD HANWORTH

> *Haneurde* (2x) 1086 DB, *-wrde* 1185–87 Dane, *-wrda* l12 ib, *-wrd* 1275 RH
>
> *Haneworde* 1086 DB, *-worda* (2) c1115 LS, 1160, Hy2 Dane, *Hanoworda (no = ne)* 1166 RBE
>
> *Hanewort* c1155 (1411) Gilb
>
> *Hanewurth'* 1185 RotDom, 1189–95 (14) *VC* (p), *-wurthe* 1208 FF, 1250–60 *HarlCh*, *-wurth* 1276 RH, 1291 Tax
>
> *Hanewrth'* 1205 Cur, 1225 Pat
>
> *Haneworth'* c1215 RA iv, 1285 RSu, 1332 *SR*, 1375 Peace, *-worth* 1281 QW, 1303 FA *et passim* to 1428 ib
>
> *Hanewurthe* c1240 RA iv, *-wurth'* 1242–43 Fees, *-uurth'* 1252 Cl
>
> *Hanneworth* 1281 QW, 1374 Peace
>
> *Hanworth* 1327 *SR*, 1374, 1387 Peace, 1402 FA, (*juxta Hacthorne*) 1411 IBL, 1428 FA *et passim*
>
> *Calthaneworth* 1322 Ipm, 1322 Cl
>
> *Caldehaneworth* 1328 Banco, 1329 *Ass*, 1331 Ipm, 1331 Cl, *Calde Haneworth* 1325 FA
>
> *Caldhameworth* 1284 Abbr, *Calde Hameworth* 1325 *DC*
>
> *Coldehanworth'* 1379 *FF*, 1405 RRep, *Coldhanworth* 1526 Sub, (*beside Donham*) LP xx i, *Cold Hanworth* 1656 *Yarb*, 1690, 1693 *Terrier et passim*

This is identical in origin with Potter Hanworth, Kest, and means 'Hana's enclosure' from the OE pers.n. *Hana* and OE **worð** 'an enclosure'. It is presumably *Cold* from its exposed situation. It is described as near Hackthorn and near Dunholme.

CHURCH FM, cf. *ad Ecclesiam* 1327 *SR*, *Bithe Kirk'* 1332 *ib*, *atte Kirk* 1343 NI all (p), *Church Yard* 1847 *TA*; the variation between the English and the Danish forms is noteworthy. GRANGE (lost), 1828 Bry, cf. Blyborough Grange *supra*. GREEN LANE FM. HANWORTH HOLT, 1824 O, 1830 Gre 1847 *TA*, *v*. **holt** 'a wood. a thicket'. This is a different place from the modern Cold Hanworth Holt. HANWORTH RUDDINGS (lost), 1828 Bry, *v*. **ryding** 'a clearing', in the pl. This el. is rare in north L. MIDDLE FM, *the Middle farme* 1606 *Terrier*. MOAT, a medieval moated site. NEW COVER (lost), 1828 Bry. OAK HOLT, 1828 Bry, *v*. **holt**. RECTORY (lost), *the parsonage* 1601, 1690, *Pars^e* 1828 Bry, *the Rectory* 1606, 1709, 1715, 1822, *ye Rectorie* 1693, *the ~* 1700 all *Terrier*. ROOKERY FM. SOUTH FM, cf. Middle Fm *supra*. THIRLANDS (lost), 1828 Bry. TOP FM.

FIELD-NAMES

The undated forms in (a) are 1847 *TA*; those dated e13 are *HarlCh*; c1215, 1215–20, 1219–39 RA iv; 1325 FA; 1327, 1332 *SR*; 1329 *Ass*; 1343 NI; 1552 Pat; 1601, 1606, 1690, 1693, 1700, 1709, 1715 *Terrier*; 1656 *Yarb*; 1665 *Sib*; 1735, 1738, 1769, 1775, 1821, 1825, 1829, 1833, 1838 *TLE*.

(a) Barn Cl; East, Far, First, Great, Rough, West Bottom (*v*. **botm** 'a bottom, a valley bottom'); Blow Cl (1690, 1693, 1700, 1709, 1715, perhaps a close open to the winds); Bratches (*v*. **brēc** 'land broken up for cultivation' in the pl.); Bush Cl (*the Little Bush close* 1656); Clay end; Clodd's Closes 1769, 1775, 1821, 1825, 1833; Cow Cl (*the cowe close* 1606); Decoy Cl; Drain Cl; Far Cl; Far Garths (*v*. **garðr** 'an enclosure'); Feeding Cl (*the feeding close* 1601, 1606, *~ Feeding Close* 1690, *ye feeding Close* 1700, 1709, *the Feeding close* 1715); Four Acres; Garden piece; Gilby Cl (*Gilber Close* (sic) 1693, 1700); Hanworth Cl; Bottom, Far, First High Cl (*the highe close* 1601, *the great High close* 1656, *the high Close* 1690); Far, First Hill Cl 1847 (*the Hill Close* 1693, *ye hill Close* 1700, *the Hill Close* 1715); Holt Cl; Home Cl; Homestead; Far, First, Little Joiner Cl (*the Joyner Closes* 1690, *the Two Joyner Closes* 1693, 1700, *ye two Joyner Closes* 1709, *ye 2 Joyner Closes* 1715, presumably from the surn. *Joiner*, *Joyner*); Keys Cl (probably from the surn. *Keys*); East, Middle, West Leys Cl (*the 2 Lea Closes* 1690, *ye two Lea Closes* 1700, 1709, *ye great Lea Close* 1693, *the Leas Closes* 1715 (*v*. **lea** (OE **lēah**) 'a meadow, an open pasture'); Lock and Key; Orchard; Ox Cl; (Little) Pingle (*v*. **pingel** 'a small enclosure'); Plantation; Pot Garths (*v*. **garðr**); land lying in a Ring Fence 1838; Stack Yard; Stamp Leys; the ten Acres; Thorn Cl; Far, First Thoroughfare (*the thorrow farr Close* 1690, *ye thorrogw fare Close* 1709, *ye thorowe farre close* 1715, self-explanatory); First Top Cl; The Urn, Urn Bottom (perhaps from the shape of the field); Far, First Walkers Cl (from the surn. *Walker*); The Yard.

(b) *Chambers close* 1656 (no doubt from the surn. *Chambers*); *the East, the West Corn Close* 1601; *Dalefurlanghes* 1219–39 (probably from **dalr** 'a valley' and **furlang**); *the East Close* 1601, *the east close* 1606; *the East farme* 1606; *ye East Furrs* 1700, 1715, *ye East Furrs growing at ye south End of Thorkhill* 1709 (*v.* **ēast, fyrs** 'furze'); *Faldingworth Feild* 1690, *~ field* 1693, *~ pasture* 1700, 1709, 1715 (named from the adjacent parish of Faldingworth); *the fallow close* 1606; *campum de Haneworth'* c1215, *campum de Haneworthe* e13, *campo de Haneword'* 1215–20 (the open fields of the village); *the Flintes* 1601, *~ flintes* 1606, *~ Flints* 1690, *~ flints* 1693, *ye flints* 1700 (literally 'the flints', *v.* **flint**, denoting places where flints abound); *the fogg close* 1606 (*v.* **fogga** 'aftermath, the long grass left standing during the winter'); *ye great Close* 1700, *~ great Close* 1709, *~ great close* 1715; *Hackthorne Cow Pasture* 1690, 1693, 1715, *Hackthorn Cow pasture* 1709; *ad aulum* 1327, *atte Hall'* 1332 both (p) (self-explanatory); *the Hardinge* 1601, *Hardings* 1606, *the harding(s)* 1690, *the Harding* 1693, *ye Hardings* 1700 ('the meadow, pasture hard to till', *v.* **heard, eng**); *Harperland* 1325 (presumably from the surn. *Harper* and **land**); *Herthewyke* 1327, *Herthwyk* 1343 both (p) (from **heorde-wīc** 'a herd farm', thought to be that part of a manor devoted to livestock); *Houton's close* 1690 (self-explanatory); *John Huggards Lane* 1715 (*John Huggard* is mentioned in the document); *the Hurn* 1690, 1693, *ye Hurn* 1700, 1709 (*v.* **hyrne** 'a nook, a corner of land'); *in the Lane* 1327, *atte Lane de Caldehaneworth'* 1329, *atte Lane* 1332 (self-explanatory); *ye little Close* 1700, 1709; *Middle Rowe* 1700, *ye middle Row* 1709, 1715 (cf. *ye north Rowe* and *ye South Rowe infra*); *Nordbereg* e13, *Northbergesike* 1215–20 (*v.* **sík**) (*v.* **norð, berg** 'a hill, a mound'); *ye north Rowe* 1700, *~ North Row* 1709, 1715 (cf. *Middle Rowe supra* and *ye South Rowe infra*); *close of meadow or pasture . . . called or knowne by the name of Pickwell* 1656, *Great Pickwell* 1665; *le Sowtheforlong* 1552 (self-explanatory); *ye South Rowe* 1700, *ye South Row* 1709, *the South Row* 1715 (cf. *Middle Rowe* and *ye north Rowe supra*); *Spridlington Field* 1693 (from Spridlington, an adjacent parish); *Thorkelhill'* 1219–39, *Thoek hill* (sic) 1601, *Thorkhill* 1606, *ye Thorkhill* 1693, *Thorkhill* 1700, *an arable Furlong usually called Thorkhill* 1715 ('Thorkil's hill', *v.* **hyll**, the first el. being the ON pers.n. *Þorke(ti)ll*, ODan *Thorkil*); *ye West Close* 1601, *the west close* 1606, *the West close* 1690; *the West farme* 1606 (cf. *the Easte farme supra*).

Harpswell

HARPSWELL

> *Herpeswelle* (5x) DB, 1312 Inqaqd, 1315 Pat, 1373 Cl, 1374 *AD*,
> 1388 Misc, 1398 Pat, *-well(')* 1180–90 RA x (p), 1234 FF,
> 1242–43 Fees, 1291 Tax, 1254 ValNor, 1295 RSu, 1300 Ipm *et*
> *freq* to 1431 FA, *Herpiswelle* 1379, 1388 Cl, *-well* 1389 ib
> *Herpewelle* 1252 FF
> *Harpeswella* (2x) c1115 LS, 1185–87 Dane, *-well(')* 1203 Ass, 1203
> Abbr, 1203 Cur, 1204 OblR, 1212 Fees, 1226 FF *et passim* to
> 1610 Speed, *Harpiswelle* 1285 Ipm, *-welle* 1388 Cl, *Harpyswell*
> 1455 Pat, *Harpswell* 1428 ASSR xxix *et passim*
> *Harpewell'* 1186 ChancR, 1202 Ass, 1204 P, 1219 Ass, *-well* 1240 FF

This is a difficult name. Ekwall (DEPN s.n. Harpenden) suggests that the first el. is OE **hearpere** 'a harper', the second *-r-* being lost through dissimilation. The name would then mean 'the harper's spring', *v.* **wella**. Smith (EPNE s.v. **hearpe** and **here-pæð**), however, argues that some p.ns. with ME forms in *Harp(s)-* may well be contracted forms of OE **here-pæð** 'a military road, a highway', hence literally 'the spring of the military road or highway'. This formation would then be paralleled, for example, by *Harpsford* (PN Sr 121), both with original OE gen.sg. *-es.* The latter is perhaps the more likely explanation philologically.

BILLYARDS FM, probably from the surn. *Billyard.* BRICK KILN HOLT. CREAM POKE LANE (lost), cf. *Cream Poke close* 1795 *LCS, Clean Poke Nook* 1828 Bry, *Clean* is an error for *Cream*; *Cream Poke* is a common complimentary name for fertile land or rich pasturage. FORTY FEET PLANTATION, *40 feet Plant.* 1828 Bry. FOX COVER (lost), 1828 Bry. GREAT MOORS (lost), 1828 Bry. HALL FM, cf. *Hall* 1830 Gre and *le Uppehall* 1389 Misc, 'the higher hall', *v.* **upp, hall**. HALLOWED LANDS, *One Plat of Ground Called Holylands* 1690 *Terrier, Holy Land Pl^m* 1828 Bry. HARPSWELL GRANGE, *Grange F^m* 1828 Bry, a late example of **grange**, for which *v.* Blyborough Grange *supra.* HARPSWELL LANE, 1824 O. HARPSWELL LOW WOOD. HARPSWELL WOOD, 1824 O, 1830 Gre, *bosco de Harpewell'* 1219 Ass. THE HERMITAGE. MOAT, cf. *The Close within the Moat* 1605 *Asw*, a medieval moated site. PASTURE LEYS (lost), 1828 Bry, *v.* **lea, ley** (OE **lēah**) 'a meadow, a pasture'. PETER'S WOOD, 1824 O, *Peters Wood* 1830 Gre, *Peter or Low W^d* 1828 Bry, presumably from the pers.n. or surn. *Peter.* THE SERPENTINE, the name of a lake, presumably named from the famous lake in Hyde Park. THOROUGHFARE WOOD (lost), *Thorofare W^d* 1828 Bry, cf. *Low Thorofare* 1828 ib, and *Thoroughfare Close* 1723 *Asw*, 1754 *BRA 1596, Thorough fare Close* 1734 *Asw.* VICARAGE, *there is noe gleabe Land in Harpswell ... neither is there any vicarage that we know or ever heard of* 1668 *Terrier.* THE VILLA. THE WILDERNESS.

FIELD-NAMES

The principal forms in (a) are 1754 *BRA 1597*; those dated 1389 are *Foster*; 1327, 1332 *SR*; 1605, 1629, 1655, 1658, 1674, 1678, 1680, 1683, 1699, 1701, 1723, 1732, 1733, 1734 *Asw*; 1690 *Terrier.*

(a) Archent Cl (*the Argent Closes or Joyners Closes* 1678, *Argent Closes* 1699, 1734, cf. Joiner Cl in the adjacent parish of Cold Hanworth; perhaps the reference is to some *silver* foliaged plant); two Beckering Closes (*Beckering Close* 1723, *the Bekering Closes* 1734, named from the *Beckering* family, cf. Robert *Beckering* 1680); Black heath Pingle (*Blackheath Pingle* 1723, 1734, *Far, House, ploughed Blackheath*

1732, *Cottagers Black Heath* 1732, self-explanatory, *v.* **blæc, hǣð**); the Bottom Cl (*Bottom Close* 1734, *v.* **botm** 'a bottom, a valley bottom'); great, little Buckwell (*Buckwell close* 1683, *great, little Buckwell* 1734, probably from **bucc** 'a buck', **wella** 'a spring'); the Button Cl (perhaps from the size of the field); Carp Pond Cl (self-explanatory); Two Closes called Cattacker & Pasture; Codd Closes (*Little Codd Cl* 1683, *Great, Little Codd Close* 1723, 1732, named from the family of Robert *Cod* 1642 LPR); Condy Garths (*v.* **garðr** 'an enclosure'); Corn Cl (*the Corne Close* 1674, 1699, *Corn Close* 1723, *Corn Closes* 1734); the Cow Cl (*Cow Close* 1723), the Lower, the Upper Cow Cl (*lower, Upper Cow Close* 1734); Cow Lanes (cf. *the Cowlans close* (sic) 1685, *Cowlanes* (sic) 1734); Crooking Dykes (*The crokindike close* 1605, *Crooking dikes* 1678, ~ *Dikes* 1723, *Crooking* is perhaps from **krókr** and **eng** denoting meadow, pasture in a bend); the Furr Cl (*Furr Close* 1723, 1734 *v.* **fyrs**); Gallowes Cl (*Gallowes Close* 1674, 1699, 1734); one Close called Holbeck or Bottom Cl (*Holbeck or bottom Close* 1734, cf. the Bottom Cl *supra* and *The lower, the upper Holbecke close* 1605, *Holbeck Tongs* 1674, 1699, *Two closes called Holbecke* 1699, 'the stream flowing in a hollow', *v.* **hol, bekkr**); Home Cl (1723, *Home Close and Garden* 1734); the East, Little Horse Cl (cf. (*the*) *Horse Close* 1674, 1699, 1734, *the horse Close* 1678); the Intac (sic) (*Intack* 1723, 1734, *v.* **inntak** 'a piece of land taken in or enclosed'); Joyner Leas (1678, 1734, cf. *Joyners Closes* 1674, 1699, probably from the surn. *Joyner* with **lea, ley** (OE **lēah**) 'a meadow, an open pasture' and cf. Far Joiner Cl in Cold Hanworth f.ns. (a)); the Lea Cl (*Lea Close* 1674, 1699, 1734); Long Thorn, Little Long Thorne (*little Longthorne* 1683, cf. *Longthorns* 1723, *Long Thorn* 1734); the two Low Closes (*the Low Closes* 1723, *two low Closses* 1734, self-explanatory); Middle Moor (*Midle moore* 1674, *Midele Moore* 1699, *the Middle Moor* 1734, cf. *moregarth* 1389 (*v.* **garðr**), *onthemore* 1327, *de la more* 1332 both (p), self-explanatory); North Moor (*the North Moore* 1674, 1699, *North Moor* 1734, cf. *the South more close* 1605); Oakdam; the Pasture Cl (*Pasture Close* 1723); the Upper Peas Cl (cf. *the Pease Close* 1674, 1699, *Pease Close* 1678, *Lower, Upper Peas Close* 1734, *v.* **pise** 'pease'); great, Little Sike (cf. *The higher, The lower sicke close* 1605, *Great Syke Close* 1674, *great Syke* 1699, *Little Sike* 1723, 1734, *v.* **sík** 'a ditch, a trench'); the South Close (1658, *the Sowth Close* 1629, *South Close* 1678, 1734, *the sowth Close* 1680); Sowerlands (1734, *Sower Lands* 1674, 1699, *v.* **sūr** 'sour, damp, coarse (of land)', **land**); Stack Cl (1723, 1734, *the Stacke Close* 1658, *the Stack Close* 1680, 1699, self-explanatory); the White Moor (*White Moor(s)* 1723, *White Moor* 1734, cf. Middle Moor *supra*).

(b) *The Black-earth* 1605, *Bishoppe Black Earth* 1674, *Bullcocks Black Earth* 1674, 1699, *the Westerne Black Earthes* 1674, *the Westerne Blacke Earths* 1699 (self-explanatory, *v.* **blæc, eorðe**, a reference to the colour of the soil; *Bishop amd Bullcock* are the names of landholders here, cf. Edward *Bishop* and Hamond *Bulcocke* both 1642 LPR); *Bowdales* 1674, 1699, 1732 (the second el. is the pl. of **deill** 'a share of land', the first may be **boga** which sometimes denotes something curved or bent in p.ns.); *the Calfe Close* 1683; *the two Cliffes* 1629, *the Clyffe, the Cliffes* 1674, *the cliffe* 1699, *The Cliffe* 1723 (*v.* **clif**, the prominent topographical feature here; cf. *Wood Cliffe Close* 1734); *the Cony close* 1629 (*v.* **coni** 'a rabbit'); *the Cony garths* 1678, ~ *Cony Garth* 1699, *Two Coney Garths* 1723, *Coney garths* 1734 (*v.* **garðr** and cf. prec.); *Connison's Close* 1732 (from the surn. *Connison*); *Cottagers Closes* 1655, 1658, 1678, 1680; *Cottagers Pasture* 1723; *the Cowdike close* 1629, *Cowdikes* 1678 (*v.* **cū, dík** 'a ditch'); *The Elme close* 1605, *the Elme Close* 1683, *Elme Close* 1732, self-explanatory); *the fulbecke close* 1605 (*v.* **fūl** 'foul', **bekkr**); *atte Gathend* 1389 (p) ('the end of the road', *v.* **gata, ende**); *the garth* 1674, *the long garthes* 1658 (*v.*

garðr 'an enclosure'); *Attegotes* 1327 (p) (*v.* **gotu** in L 'a sluice'); *Onthehill* 1327 (p) (*v.* **hyll**); *Hamundhous* 1389 (described in the text as 'a toft'; formally the first el. could be a surn. from the ON pers.n. *Hámundr*, as Dr Insley points out, but it is more likely to be from the OFr *Hamon*, a Romance form of the ContGerm pers.n. *Haimo*, *Heimo* here used as a baptismal name or as a surn. The second el. is ME **hous**, *v.* **hūs** 'a house'); *Heath* 1732 (self-explanatory); *the Highe close* 1605; *the Ingehome close* 1605, *Inge Holme* 1674, 1699 (*v.* **eng** 'meadow, pasture', **holmr** 'higher ground amidst the marsh'); *Johnson's Close* 1732 (named from the family of Thomas *Johnson* 1642 LPR); *Knot Close* 1732; *the ling more* 1629, *Close called Lingmore* 1658, *the Lingmore* 1680, *Ling Moore* 1699, *Two Lingmoors* 1723 (*v.* **lyng** 'ling, heather', **mōr**); *the little closes* 1605, *Little Close* 1723, *Little Closes* 1734; *The little tofte* 1605, *the Little Tofts* 1674, 1699 (*v.* **toft** 'a messuage, a curtilage'); *Long Furlongs* 1674, 1699; *Lower Farm* 1733; *Mansion House* 1732; *the middle close* 1629, *Middle Close* 1723, 1734; *the Milne feild* 1629, *the Milne feild* 1658, *the milnfeilds* 1680, *Millfield* 1723 (self-explanatory, *v.* **myln**, **feld**); *the north Close* 1605; *The Oke close* 1605, *Oak-close ende* 1629, *the Oake Close* 1683; *the new parke* 1683, *two Parks* 1734; *Readheads Farme* 1678 (named from the family of William *Redhead* 1642 LPR); *Ruff Close* 1733 (no doubt *ruff = rough*); *Sheepcoate Lees Close* 1674, *Sheepe Coate Leas* 1699 (*v.* **shep-cote**, **lea**, **ley** (OE **lēah**) 'a meadow, an open pasture'); *Thistle borrough hill* 1629; *The Tupp Close* 1683, *Tupp Closes* 1733 (*v.* **tup** 'a ram, a tup'); *the twelve pound Close* 1683, *Twelve pound Close* 1732 (presumably named from the rent of the close).

Hemswell

HEMSWELL

> *Helmeswelle* 1086 DB (4x), 1185–87 Dane, 1281 QW, 1316 Pat, 1382 Peace, 1386, 1426 Cl, *-wella* c1115 LS, c1145 Dane, *-well(e)* 1185 Templar, 1196 ChancR, 1202 Ass (p), 1204, 1205 P (p), 1211 ib, 1226 FF, 1230–9 RA x, 1234 FF, 1235 Cl, 1254 ValNor, c1259 RA ix, 1272 *Ass*, 1275 RH, 1281, 1287 Ipm, 1293 *Ass*, 1295 Ipm, 1299 RA ix, 1300 Ipm *et freq* to 1529 *Asw*, 1545–47 *MinAcct*, *Helmswell* 1576 LNQ iii, 1856 *Asw*
> *Elmeswella* 112 (1407) Gilb, *-well'* 1202 Ass *Hemmeswell* 1401, 1505 Pat, 1519 DV i, *Hemmyswell* 1565 HMRep xiv
> *Hemeswell* 1445 AASR xxix, 1498 *Asw*, 1501 Ipm, 1513 LP i, 1526 Sub, 1576 LER, *Hemyswell* 1486–93 ECP, 1535 VE iv, 1546 LRCh
> *Hemswell* 1532 LP v, 1576 Saxton, 1610 Speed *et passim*, *-welle* 1592 *Asw*
> *Hembeswell* (sic) 1713 *Asw*

'Helm's well, spring', *v.* **wella**. The first el. is the OE pers.n. *Helm*. There are numerous springs in the parish, cf. Aisthorpe Springs and Spring Hills *infra*.

SPITAL IN THE STREET

> *Hospitali* 1158, 1167, 1166 P, c1190 RA iv, 1337 Ch, ~ *super stratam* 1294, 1313 *Foster*, 1329 *Ass*, 1333 (14) *LOC*, *Hospitale* 112 RA ii, c1230 (14) *VC*, ~ *super Stratam* 1281 QW, 1300, 1354 Ipm, 1316 FA, 1383 Peace, 1390 Works, 1431 FA, *Hospital super Stratam* 1316 FA, 1329 (14) *LOC*, 1383 Peace, *Hospialem super Stratam* 1360, 1374, 1394 *Foster*, *Hospialie de Spittle on the Strete* 1400 *LCCA*
>
> *le Spitel oþþe stret* 1282 *FF*, ~ ~ *othestret* 1309 *ib*, ~ ~ *onthestrete* 1316 *ib*, 1322 *HarlCh*, ~ ~ *in ye stret* 1322 (14) *LOC*, ~ ~ *in the strete* 1383 Pat, ~ ~ *othestrete* 1419 *FF*
>
> *Spytelothestrete* 1295 *Ass*, 1399 Cl, *Spytell othe Strete* 1414 *LCCA*, *le Spytell over ye Strete* 1428 FA, ~ ~ *othe Strete* 1549 CA
>
> *Spitle on the streete* 1323 Inqaqd, 1560 *LCCA*, ~ *inle Strete* 1334 Orig, ~ *super Stretham*
>
> *Spitle on ye Strete* 1576 Saxton, ~ *in the Stret* 1610 Speed *Spitell* c1460 Gough, 1402 FA, 1526 Sub, 1569 SP i, 1589 NCWills, ~ *othe Strete* 1395 Pat, ~ *othestret* 1400 Pap, ~ *in le Stret* 1433 Pat, ~ *othestrete* 1467 *FF*, ~ *super le Strete* 1502 Ipm
>
> *Spetyll othe Strete* 1385 Misc, *Spetillofthestrete* 1499 *FF*, *Spetell of the Strete* 1501 ECP, *Spetell* c1414 AASR xxix *Hospitali de Herthewyk* 1301 *KR*, *Spytelothestrete alias Herwyk* 1395 Pap

'The hospital on the Roman road (i.e. Ermine Street)', *v.* **spitel**, **strǣt**. Little seems to be known about the early history of the medieval hospital, but the Chapel here is dedicated to St Edmund, King and Martyr. The name has twice been noted alternatively as the "Hospital of Hardwick", 'the herd farm', *v.* **heorde-wīc**, though no other references to this name have been found in the area.

AISTHORPE SPRINGS, *Aystrop Springs* 1785 *Asw*, from the family of John *Aistropp*, and cf. *loc' Roberto Astrop* 1587 *Asw*. BECK LANE, cf. *le Bec* e14 *DC*, *le Bek'* e14 (14) *LOC*, *Attebek'* 1327 *SR*, *atte Beck'* 1332 *ib* both (p), *Comon Suer called Beck* 1692 *Asw*, *a Comon Sewer called the Beck* 1735 *ib*, *a furlong called Becks* 1762 *ib*, *v.* **bekkr** 'a stream, a beck'. BUNKER'S HILL, a transferred name commemorating the battle in Massachusetts in 1775. BRICKYARD HO. CARR SPRING (lost), 1828 Bry, 1830 Gre, *v.* **kjarr** 'brushwood' later 'a marsh overgrown with brushwood', as elsewhere in the parish. DOWNHILL LANE (local). THE FORGE (local), HARPSWELL LANE (local), 1824 O, leading to the adjacent parish of Harpswell. HEMSWELL CLIFF, *the Cliff* 1824 *Padley*, cf. *the north cliffe* 1598 *Asw*, *ye North Cliffe* 1697, 1700, *the North Cliff* 1697, 1703, 1708 all *Terrier*, *the North Cliffe* 1730 *Asw*, *North Cliff* 1856 *BS*, *the south cliffe* 1598 *Asw*, *le Southe Cliffe* 1657 *Asw*, *ye South Cliffe* 1679 *Terrier*, *South Cliffe* 1681 *Asw*, *South Cliffe* 1689 *ib*, *the South Cliff* 1697, 1703, 1708, *ye South Clife* 1700 all *Terrier*, *South Cliff* 1856 *BS*, self-explanatory. HEMSWELL GRANGE, a late example of **grange**, for which *v*. Blyborough Grange *supra*. HEMSWELL HALL (lost), *aulam de Helmeswell'* 1294 *Ass*, *ad aulam* 1327 *SR*, *atte hall* 1332 *ib*, *atte halle* 1341 *Foster*, *athall' de Helmeswell'* 1461 *Asw*, *att Hall'* 1466 *ib*, *toftum Johaniis at Hawell* (sic) *ib* all (p), *Hall* 1828 Bry. HEMSWELL HILL (local), cf. *Hill farme* 1670 *Asw*. HEMSWELL VALE (lost), 1828 Bry, 1830 Gre. HEMSWELL WINDMILL, *windemill* 1670 *Asw*, *milne* 1689 *ib*, *Wind Mill* 1702 *ib*, *Hemswell Mill* 1824 O, 1830 Gre, *The Mill* 1828 Bry, cf. *le Milnedam* e14 (14) (*v*. **myln**, **damme** (ON **dammr**) 'a dam, a pond); *the Mylne howse* 1577 *LCS*. IVY HO. MANOR HO, 1842 White, *the Manner house* 1717 *Asw*, cf. *the Mannor Farm* 1763 *ib*. MAYPOLE LANE (local), a tall Maypole stands at the end of the lane. MIDDLE STREET. MILLERS GARTH (local) presumably from the surn. or occupational name *Miller* with **garðr** 'an enclosure', as elsewhere in the parish. NELLPITS WOOD. NORTH FIELD (local), 1828 Bry, *in campo borialli de Helmeswell'* 1322 *Foster*, *in campo borial'* e14 (14) *LOC*, *in boreali campo* 1598 *Asw*, *northfield* 1681 *ib*, *campo vocat North field* 1692 *ib*, *the North Field* 1727, 1762 *ib*, one of the great fields of the village, *v*. **feld**. OLD STREET FM, cf. *Streete furlong* 1590 *Asw*. PARSONAGE (lost), *ye Rectory* 1641 LPR, *ye vicarrage house* 1679, *ye Vicaridge* 1697, *ye Vicoridge* (sic) 1703 all *Terrier*, *the Parsonage* 1730 *Asw*, *Rectory and Parsonage* 1776 *EnclA*, *Pars^e* 1828 Bry, cf. *ye parsonage land* 1598 *Asw*, *a furlong called the Parsonage* 1785 *ib*. POPLAR HO (local). QUARRY HO (local). RAT HALL, no doubt a derogatory nickname. SAND PIT. SPITAL SPA. SPITAL PLANTATION, 1824 O, 1830 Gre. SPRING HILLS.

FIELD-NAMES

Forms dated 1259 are RA ix; 1270–80, 1294, 1322, 1341, 1381, 1384, 1393 *Foster*; 1275 RH; 1293, 1294 *Ass*; e14 *DC*; 1327, 1332 *SR*; Ed1, e14, 1329, c1329, 1333 all (14) *LOC*; 1384, 1395 Pat; 1385 Misc; 1545–47 *MinAcct*; 1557 *KR*; 1574 *DCLB*, 1576 LNQ iii; 1577, 1598, 1795 *LCS*; 1679, 1697, 1700, 1703, 1708 *Terrier*; 1723 *Which*; 1776 *EnclA*; 1827 *Padley*; 1856 *BS*; all the rest are *Asw*.

(a) a furlong called Burgall Stile 1762 (*Burgall Stile* 1730, obscure); Bramer 1762 (*Bramar* 1730); Bishops Hedge 1762 (*Bishopp hedge* 1730, cf. *Roger Bishopppe close* 1609, *Bishops Inges* 1618 (*v.* **eng**), *Richard Bishoppe Farme* 1662, self-explanatory); Barad-gate (sic) 1762 (*Broadgate* 1730, self-explanatory); Thomas Whichcot's Seigniory . . . commonly called the Barony 1759, the Barony 1769 (*that Seignorie . . . commonly called and known by the name of the Barronye of hemswell* 1609, *one of our Seigniory in Hemswell aforesaid now and heretofore commonly called the Barony in Hemswell* 1717; *Barony* is defined in NED as 'the domain of a baron'); a furlong called Caukland 1762 (*Cauklands* 1730, *v.* **calc** 'chalk', **land**); the Chancell dike 1762 (*Chancelldike* 1730, perhaps the rent of the dike went towards the upkeep of the chancel); Cliffe Field Road 1776; Cream Poke close 1795 (cf. *Creampot nooke* 1689, a complimentary nickname for good land; note the variant forms of this f.n.); Crow Hill 1785 (1730); Dawlin Lane 1765 (cf. *Dawlyn'thyng* 1492, *Dawlyngarthe* 1597, *Dawling Close* 1646, *Dawlin Lane* 1699, 1729, named from the family of John *Dawlyn* 1378); Dolwin Cl 1759 (perhaps an error for the prec.); close called the Elms 1795 (*Elme Close* 1702, 1706); the Furrs 1762 (1730, *v.* **fyrs** 'furze'); Furrleys 1762 (*fur le* 1598, *the Furr Leys* 1730, *v.* **ley** (OE lēah) 'a meadow, an open pasture'); the Greens 1762 (*Greens* 1730, cf. *attegrene* 1294 (p), *v.* **grēne** 'a village green, a grassy spot'); the Gainsborough Road 1856; the Hill Side 1762, Hillside 1776 (*the Hill side* 1730); the Home Cl 1795; the Holmes 1762 (*the Homes* (sic) 1689, *Holmes* 1730, *v.* **holmr** 'higher ground amidst the marshes'); Kirton Road 1776 (the road to Kirton in Lindsey); Kirk(e) Cl 1761, 1775 (cf. *atte Kyrke* 1378 (p), *atte Kyrk*' 1383 (p), *v.* **kirkja**); Lincoln Gate 1762 (*Lincolne gate* 1689, 1730, self-explanatory); Little Cl 1766, 1769, 1773; Long Cl 1761, 1775; Long Furlong 1762 (*Long furlong* 1675, 1681); Moor 1776, the Moor 1785 (*le commen moore* 1587, *the Moore* 1598, ~ *moore* 1689, ~ *moor* 1730, cf. *mor'hows* 1464); Moor Lands Cl 1785 (*Moor Lands Close* 1730); Moreland Furlong 1762 (cf. *More furlong* 1675); North Cliff 1776, 1856 *the north cliffe* 1598, *north Cliffe* 1689, cf. South Cliffe *infra*); Old Street Road 1776; Padman Gate 1762 (*padman gaite* 1730, cf. *padman dayle* 1270–80, from the ME surn. *Padman*, from *pad(e)* 'a path' and *man*); Sandum 1762 (1730); Smalthern 1762 (sic), Smalham 1785 (*Smalham Syke* 1657, *Smatham furlong* 1689 (sic), *a furlong called Smatham* 1730 (obscure); South Cliffe 1776, ~ Cliff 1856 (*the south cliffe* 1598, cf. North Cliff *supra*); the South Feild 1762 (*in australi campo* e14, 1596, *austral' campo de Helmeswell'* 1341, *South feild* 1675, 1681, 1689, 1730, one of the open fields of the village); Spital Rd 1776; Stone Pit 1776; Stony Gate 1785 (cf. *Stony furlong gate* 1681, *Stoney Furlong* 1730); Summer gangs 1762, (*Summergang* 1598, *Sumerganges* 1689, *Sumergange* 1700, *Sumergangs* 1730, 'the tracks, ways which could be used only in summer', *v.* **sumor**, **gang**, cf. Summergangs PN YE 215); Summer Green 1776; Summerings 1856 (*Summer'ging* (sic) 1681, *Summer ings* 1708, *v.* **sumor**, **eng** and cf. prec.); Twingates 1762 (cf. *betweene the gates* 1598, *the gate between gates* 1689, *Twingait* 1730, self-explanatory, *v.* **gata**); Town St 1765, 1776 (1699, 1729); the Ward Thorn 1785 (*Ward Thorns* 1689, *Ward Thorn* 1730, perhaps from the surn. *Ward* and **þorn**); Wattam Cl 1769 (*Wattam close* 1728, 1735, named from the family of John *Wattam of Blyborough* 1728); the West Feild 1762, the West Fd 1776, 1827, 1856 (*Westfeild* 1675, *-field* 1681, ~ *Feild* 1689, *the West Feild* 1697, ~ ~ *feild* 1703, 1730, one of the open fields of the village); W(h)eldale Cl 1756, a Pasture called Welldale 1785 (*Welldell pasture* 1690, *Welldale Close* 1706, 1717, *v.* **wella**, **dalr**); Whichcot Gate 1785 (named from the family of John and Edward *Whichcot* 1658); Willerton Hedge 1762 (cf. *Willeston Meare furlong* (sic) 1679, *Willerton meare* 1681, ~ *Mear* 1730, *v.* (**ge**)**mǣre** and Willoughton, an adjoining parish).

(b) *le Akergate* e14 (14), e14 (*v.* **akr** 'a plot of arable land', **gata**); *Asere lands* 1730; *le Berhe* 1294 (*v.* **be(o)rg**); *Bowdalls furlong* 1675, *Bowdall gate* 1681 the first el. is probably a surn. *Bowdall*); *John Bradley headlands* 1689 (*v.* **hēafod-land** 'the head of a strip of land left for turning the plough'); *Bradmoore* 1598 (*v.* **brād** 'broad, spacious'); *the Brewhouse Pond* 1723; *chapell' Dayll'* 1577 (*v.* **chapel(e)**, **deill**); *Stephen Codd's Oxgangs* 1662 (self-explanatory, for **oxgang**, *v. the Oxganges infra*); *y' common layne* 1577; *the common Sewer* 1658; *ye Comons of Hemswell* 1718; *Cottagers Pasture* 1710; *the Crosse* 1664, 1669; *Cuntland* 1384 (the elements are **cunt** 'the female genitals' and **land**, but the sense is unclear); *le dykes hend* 1332 (self-explanatory); "a toft called" *escheat royal* "which the king gave . . . for the enlargement of the said house (i.e. Spital in the Street)" 1395 (NED defines *escheat* by commenting that a fief reverts to the lord when the tenant dies without leaving a successor qualified to inherit under the original grant. Presumably the toft granted by the King was property that had lapsed to the Crown as indicated above); *Farmed Closes* 1717; *the Fields Meare* 1708 (*v.* (**ge**)**mǣre** and cf. *in campo de Helmeswell'* 1322, *campis de Helmewell* 1381, *campo de Helmeswell'* 1401, *campis de Helmswell'* 1529, *the feilde de Hemswell* 1574, *campo de Hemswell* 1639, *campis de Hemswell* 1657, the open fields of the village); *gallas' Close yate* 1689 (*gallas'* is perhaps for *gallows*); *One wasted Messuage or farm house . . . comonly called Graygarth Messuage* 1717, *Gray Garth* 1717 (self-explanatory, *v.* **garðr**); *Walter Hall's furlong* 1675 (self-explanatory); *Harpswell Hedge* 1681 (the hedge with the neighbouring parish of *Harpswell*); *Harry' Lane* 1723); *Haven crofts* 1670; *Hengdayles* 1385 (*v.* **eng**, **deill**); *Hillertree furlonge* 1657 (*v.* ME **hildertre** 'an elder tree'); *Homwel* (sic) e14 (14) (obscure); *Hoodhowse* 1577 (presumably a house named after a family called *Hood*); *Houlbeck* 1689 (*v.* **hol**, **bekkr**, fairly common in north L for a stream, 'the brook flowing in a hollow'); *Heryewyk* (*y = th*) Ed1 (14) (from **heorde-wīc** literally 'a herd farm', thought to be the part of a manor devoted to livestock; cf. Spital in the Street supra); *Jollan fee* 1384, 1393 (from the surn. *Jollan*); *Kyngesmeade* 1545–47 (*v.* **cyning**, **mǣd**); *Kilnehowse close* 1670 (self-explanatory); *in via regia in Helmeswell* 1275, *the kynges streyte* 1577 (probably to be identified with Ermine Street); *ye low field* 1679; *Mandall's* (sic) 1681 (probably from the surn. *Mandall*); *Marke' mome buskes furlong* (sic) 1681 (obscure); *Meergate* 1657 (*v.* (**ge**)**mǣre** 'a boundary', **gata**); *le midelfurlanges* 1322 (self-explanatory); *Mikilgatehend* c1329 (14) (*v.* **mikill**, **gata**, **ende**); *the Moore* 1598, *more Close* 1689, *More furlong* 1675; *mor'hows* 1464 (*v.* **mōr**, **hūs**, described in the text as *una placea*); *Nort(h)dale* e14, *le Nortdale* c1329 (14) (*v.* **norð**, **dalr**); *northlandes* 1689 (*v.* **norð**, **land**); *Outefeldes* 1384 ('the out fields', *v.* **ūt**, **feld**); *the Oxganges* 1587, *oxgangs* 1728, 1731, *Oxgang close* 1681 (*v.* **oxgang** 'a measure of land' of 10–30 acres' extent, an eighth of a ploughland); *Patchet Dale* 1690, 1696 (from the surn. *Patchet* and **deill**); *Pawmer Crosse Gate* 1657 (from the occupational name or surn. *Palmer* with **cros** and **gata**); *preste closes* 1577 (self-explanatory); *Rogers close* 1670 (from the forename or surn. *Roger(s)*); *Rankyn croft(s)* 1529, ~ *ynlande* 1529 (from the surn. *Rankin* with **croft** and **inland** 'land near a residence, land cultivated for the owner's use and not let to a tenant'); *Raven Clows, Ravens Closes* 1702, *Ravens' Close* 1706; *Ste Johne' oxgange als Crokeslande* 1609 (*v.* **oxgang**); *sande furlong* 1598; *Sandholm* 1598 (*v.* **sand**, **holmr**); *the Scrubbs* 1689 (*v.* **scrubb** 'a shrub, brushwood, a place overgrown with brushwood'); *Seuenwelles* c1329 (14), Ed1 (14) ('the seven springs', *v.* **seofon**, **wella**); *shorte furlonge* 1587, *Short furlong* 1598, 1675); *South Street* 1715; *le South town* 1557, *South Townes* 1710, *the South Town*

Close 1706, 1717 (self-explanatory); *Stanley land* 1609 (from the surn. *Stanley*); *Suhiby* (sic) 1294 (p), *Suthyton' de Helmeswell'* c1259 (this is literally '(the place) south in the village', denoting X who lives in the south of the village, *v.* **súð, í, bȳ**, a common Danish formation. The c1259 form is an anglicised version of the Danish formation with *Suthyton'* being from **sūð, in, tūn**); *the Swan* 1576, *The Ine called y' swane in y' spetill* 1577; *Swine Dikes furlong* 1689 (*v.* **swīn, dík**); *Tethering Grounds* 1717; *Thorngate* 1657 (*v.* **þorn, gata**); *the threestonge* 1598 (*v.* **stǫng** 'a pole, a stave', used as a standard measure 'a pole'); *Thuswelle closes* 1670 (perhaps *Thuswelle* stands for an AScand compound of **þurs** and **wella**, denoting a spring haunted by a goblin or a demon); *le Warlotes* e14 (14), c1329 (14), *le Warlottes* 1322 (for a discusion of **warlot**, *v.* PN L **2**, 67–68, where the suggested meaning is 'a piece of land assessed to a specifically defined payment of geld'); *le Weldyk* 1557 ('a ditch flowing from a spring', *v.* **wella, dík**); *West Close* 1618, 1689, 1715, ~ ~ *als Park Closes* 1715, cf. *parks' furlong* 1696, *the Park, the Upper Park Pond* 1723); *le Westdame* c1329 (14) (*v.* **west, damme** 'a dam, a pond'); *the Westdale* 1730 (*v.* **west**, probably with **deill**); *Whitehouse Farm* 1662, *White house* 1715.

Ingham

INGHAM

> *Ingeham* DB (12x), c1115 LS (2x), 1146 RA i, 1191 P, 1203 Ass, 1204, 1206 P (p), 1206 ChR (p), 1209, 1220 P (p), 1219 FF, 1219 Welles, 1223 Cur, 1226 FF, 1229 Ch, 1231 Welles, 1298 Ipm, 1310, 1325 Pat, *Ingaham* 1163 RA i, *Yngeham* 1180, 1192 P (p), 1202 Ass (p), 1210–12 RBE, *Hingeham* 1194, 1195 P, 1196 ChancR, 1197, 1198, 1119 P, 1224 FF
> *Ingheham* c1115 LS (5x), Hy3 Dane, eHy3 *HarlCh*
> *Ingham* Hy2 Dane, lHy2 ib, 1199 CurR (p), 112, c1200 Dane, 1203 Abbr, 1203 Ass, 1203, 1205 Cur (p), 1219 Ass, 1242 *HarlCh*, 1242–43 Fees, 1253 Pap, 1254 ValNor, 1256 (1291) Ch, 1272 *Ass*, 1281 QW, 1292 Ch, 1291 Tax, c1300 RA iii *et freq, Yngham* a1183, 1256 FF, 1501 Ipm, 1536–37 Dugd vi, *Hingham* p1169 Dane, 1185 Templar, 1191, 1193, 1194 P, 1227 ClR, 1165, 1172 *Ass*

This name has been traditionally interpreted as 'the homestead, the estate of Inga' from the OE pers.n. *Inga* and OE **hām** 'a homestead, an estate'. Dr Insley points out that an OE *Inga* is not certainly attested and the *Inga* recorded as the name of a moneyer of Æthelstan could be an anglicised form of the Scand *ingi*. Karl Inge Sandred, "Ingham in East Anglia: a New Interpretation", *Leeds Studies in English*, New Series xviii, 1987, argues cogently that Ingham in Nf (as also in L and Sf) is rather an ancient cultic p.n. OE **Ing(a)hām*, from Germanic **Ingwia-*

haima- 'the homestead, the estate of the devotees of the deity Ing'. According to Sandred the first el. of Ingham would then be a term for the Anglian king as a member of the Ingwionic dynasty, the name denoting a royal estate, *v.* further Ingham PN Nf **2**, 110. Dr Insley suggests that the Inghams could rather be estates in the possession of early cultic associations.

BESSON LANE (lost) 1828 Bry, perhaps from a surn. CHURCH HILL, CHURCH LANE (local). CLIFF HO, 1828 Bry, *v.* also Ingham Ciiff *infra*. THE CLUMPS, 1828 Bry. DISMALS (lost), presumably a derogatory p.n. FARROWS ROW (local), probably from the surn. *Farrow*. THE GRANGE, "grange in Ingham" 1537–39 LDRH, *Ingham Grange* 1570 Pat, 1613–15 *MinAcct*, ~ *Graunge* 1609 *Foster*, 1614 ChronLP, this was a **grange** of Bullington Priory. GRANGE LANE, 1770 *EnclA*. THE GREEN (local), *Green* 1828 Bry, *le Grene de Ingham* Ed1, *v.* **grēne** 'a village green, a grassy spot'. INGHAM CLIFF, *Clif de Ingham* Hy3 *HarlCh*, *Ingham Cliffe* 1830 Gre, cf. *South High Cliff Field* 1779 *LCS, the Cliff Plotts* 1795 *ib*, *Cliff Closes* 1799 *ib*. INGHAM CLIFF HO is *Ingham Heath* 1824 O, 1830 Gre. INGHAM SYKES (lost), 1828 Bry, *v.* **sík** 'a ditch, a trench'. INGHAM WINDMILL, *Ingham Wind Mill* 1770 *EnclA, molendini de Ingham* 1242 *HarlCh, duos sell' super quos molendinum uenti situm est* Hy3 *ib*, *Ingham mills* (sic) 1576 SP v, *ye Mill on little Street* 1662 *Terrier, windmill* 1663 *LCS, Ingham Mill* 1795 *ib*, 1824 O, 1830 Gre, *Mill* 1828 Bry. LINCOLN WOOD. LOW FM, cf. *North, South low field* 1779 *LCS, Ingham low fields* 1801 *ib*. MOCK BEGGAR HALL (lost), 1828 Bry. Mr Field points out that this is a derogatory name for land on which a beggar might find neither shelter nor sustenance. MONSON HO (local), 1828 Bry, named from the *Monson* family, landowners in the village. NORTH BECKS, 1828 Bry, cf. *Northbeck furlanges* 13 (c1330) *R*, *v.* **norð, bekkr** 'a stream, a beck', as elsewhere in the parish. OLD STREET LANE (local), 1828 Bry, *the Old Street Road* 1770 *EnclA*, cf. *Aldestret* 1230–50, *aldestrete* Hy3 both *HarlCh, Algatestrete* (sic) 1271 (14) *Welb, Aldstret* Ed1 *HarlCh, v.* **ald, strǣt**, the reference being to Ermine Street. THE OLD VICARAGE (local), *ye Vicarage* 1602, *Vicarrage house* 1606, *ye Vicaridge* 1662, *Vicaridge house* 1699, *the Vicarage* 1700, 1724, *ye Vicaridge, The Vicaridge House* 1762, *ye Vicarege, The Vicarage House* 1822 all *Terrier, New Built Vicarage House* 1874 *Padley*. PARK FM. PASTURE LANE (lost), 1828 Bry, *the Pastures of Ingham* 1801 *LCS*. SHERRIFF COTTAGE, presumably from the surn. *Sherriff*. SOUTH HILLS (lost), 1828 Bry.

FIELD-NAMES

Forms dated e13, 1230–50, Hy3, Ed1 are *HarlCh*; a1219, c1220 RA iv; 1226 FF; 1229 Ch; 13 (c1330) *R*; 1271 (14) *Welb*, 1332 *SR*; 1343 NI; 1373, 1382 Peace; 1532, 1558, 1579, 1610, 1657, 1663, 1779, 1791, 1795, 1798,99, 1801 *LCS*; 1545 LP xx; 1602, 1606, 1662, 1671, 1674, 1690, 1699, 1700, 1709, 1724, 1762, 1822 *Terrier*; 1609 *Foster*; 1769 *EnclA Map*; 1770 *EnclA*; 1874 *Padley*.

(a) Bottom Pasture 1874 (*v.* **botm**); the Bush Closes 1799; Calf Cl 1791, 1874; the Carr 1791 (*v.* **kjarr** 'brushwood', later 'a bog, a marsh, esp. one overgrown with brushwood); great, little Church Pasture 1770, Church Pasture 1874 (*the Church Pasture* 1663); Church Pasture Rd 1769, 1770; North, South Cliff 1769 (*ye cliffes* 1662); Clover Plots 1799; Coats Foot Rd 1769 (leading to Coates *supra*); the Cottagers pasture 1795, 1801; Cow Dale Bottom 1770; Cow pasture 1769, 1770; the Doll Cl 1791; Dunthorn Lees 1791 (obscure); the East Ox Fold 1791 (self-explanatory); Far, Near Furlong 1874; Feeding Pasture 1874; Fillingham Gate 1762, ~ ~ Cl 1874 (*filinghamgate* 1271, *fillinghamgate* Ed1, *Fillingham Gate* 1671, ~ *gate* 1690, 1699, 1700, 1709 (the road to Fillingham, an adjacent parish, *v.* **gata**); Front Lawn 1874 (*v.* **launde** 'woodland pasture, an open space in woodland, woodland'); the Gauber Lees 1791 (Gauber is almost certainly 'the gallows hill', *v.* **galga, beorg**); Glebe Lands 1770; the Hard Hill 1791 (perhaps **hard** is used in the sense 'hard to till'); North, South High Cliff Field 1770; Hill Pasture 1874, Hill peice 1770, North, South Hill Side 1795, Hill Side 1874 (*ye Hillside* 1662), Hill Top 1874 (cf. *Hilles* a1219, *ye Hill* 1602, 1671, 1674, 1709, *the Hill* 1724); *y^e* Home Closes 1762; Home Cl 1799, 1874; Homestead 1770; Ingham Low Fields, the low Fields 1801; the Ings 1770 (*v.* **eng** 'meadow, pasture', cf. *Engdic* e13, *v.* **eng, dík**, *Westeng'*, e13, Hy3, *Westheng* Hy3); *y^e* knolls 1762, North, South Knowles 1795 (*ye Knowles* 1602, 1662, *the knowles* 1606, *ye knolls* 1674, *the Knowlls* 1724, *the knolls furlong* 1690, 1700, *the knowles furlong* 1724, *v.* **cnoll** 'a knoll, a hillock'); the Lake Beck Cl 1798 (*Leichebec* a1219, *Leikebec* 1230–50, *Laikebec* e13, *laykebech* Hy3, *laykebekfurlonges* 1271, the same name, no doubt referring to the same physical feature, has been noted in Coates f.ns. (b), where it is suggested that the first el. probably denotes a place where festivities were held, from **leikr** 'play, sport, a game'); Little Street 1769 (*little Street* 1606, 1662, 1671, 1699, *Little Street* 1724, this probably refers to the trackway known in some parishes as Middle Street); the Long Cl 1791; North, South Low Fields 1770, Ingham Low Fields 1801 (*low field Lands* 1662); Low Ings 1798 (cf. the Ings in (a) *supra*); Far, Low Pasture 1874; Lyne Dykes 1799 (probably *v.* **lín** 'flax', **dík**); the Meadows of Ingham 1770; *y^e* Middle Becks 1762 (*Midle becks* 1602, *Middle beck* 1606, ~ *beckes* 1662, 1690, *ye middle Becks* 1699, *the middle Beckes* 1700, 1724, self-explanatory); the new Dyke Road, a pond called new Dyke 1770; North Cl 1874; *y^e* North Fd 1762, North Fd 1770, (*ye north feldes* 1602, *the North feild* 1657, ~ ~ *Feild* 1663, 1671, *North Feild* 1699, *the North Field* 1700, 1724, self-explanatory); *y^e* North Lands furlong 1762 (*north landes* 1602, *Northlands headland* 1662 (*v.* **norð, land** 'a selion', **hēafod-land**); Out Heath Cl 1874 (self-explanatory); Oxpasture 1770, ~ Cl 1798, ~ Rd 1770, ~ Foot Rd 1769, ~ Drain 1770; Paddock 1874; Far, First Pasture 1874); pasture closes 1799; Pear Tree Garth 1770 (*v.* **garðr**); the Rectory Farm 1874; *y^e* Sands 1762, the Sands 1795, 1801 (*Sandes* 1230–50, *ye Sandes* 1602, 1606, 1662, *ye Sands* 1674, 1709, *the Sands* 1671, 1690, 1724); First,

Second, Third Seed Cl 1874; South Field of Ingham 1770, South Field Drain, ~ Rd 1769 (*in campo australi* Hy3, *ye south fieldes* 1602, *the south feildes* 1606, *the South feild* 1657, ~ ~ *Field* 1671, 1700, 1724, one of the open fields of the village); South Hill 1762, ~ Hills 1874 (*Suthill* 1226, *ye South hill* 1602, *the South hill* 1671, *South hill* 1690, ~ *Hill* 1699, 1709, 1724); South Ings furlong 1762 (*ye South ings* 1602, 1606, *the South Inggs* 1671, *South Ings Furlong* 1690, 1724, *South Inggs furlong* 1700, *v.* **sūð, eng**); Stack Yard 1874; the Stock Moor 1791; the Sweet hills 1791; Syke Cl 1874 (*v.* **sík**); the Thorp Cl 1791 (perhaps from the surn. Thorp(e), since no examples of the name have been found earlier than 1791); Todd Moor closes 1799; the Toft hill 1791 (cf. *Toftes* a1219, c1220 *v.* **toft** 'a messuage, a curtilage'); Town Street 1770, the Town Street 1822; the Vicarage Drain 1770; Water fen 1762 (*Wakefen* 1674, *Watre fen* 1690, *Wakefenn* 1699, *Wakefen or Waterfen* 1709, *Wake Fen or Water Fenn* 1724 (obscure); The Wall Cl 1791 (obscure); Great, little Wheatlands 1874; the West Cl 1770 (1663); Wood Ash Cl 1770 (*the Wood Ashes* 1663).

(b) *Akerdicke* 1226 (noted several times in the L survey, the exact sense being uncertain though it is derived from OE **æcer**, ON **akr** 'a plot of arable or cultivated land' and OE **dīc**, ON **dík** 'a ditch'); *Arkilrigges, arkelrighes* Hy3 (the first el. is the ON pers.n. *Arnkell*, ODan *Arnketil* with ON **hryggr** 'a ridge', a Scand compound); *Brachendale* a1219, *Brakendale* c1220, Hy3 (*v.* **brakni, deill** or **dalr**); *Bradegate* 1226, 1230–50, Hy3, Ed1, *Bradgate* Hy3, *Braidegate* e13, *Bradegatefurlang* 1226, Ed1 (*v.* **brād, gata**; the form in *Braide-* is from the cognate ON **breiðr**); *atte Brigge de Ingham* 13, 1373, *atte Brigg* 1343, *at Brig de Ingham* 1382 all (p), *de Ponte* a1219, 1332 *de ponte* Hy3, *de Ponte* Hy3 all (p) (*v.* **brycg**); *Braidesic* e13, *Braythesike, Braiþesike* Hy3 (*v.* **breiðr, sík**, a Scand compound); *Bramedayle* Hy3 (probably 'the share of land where broom grows', *v.* **brōm, deill**); *le Brothgate, Brottegate furlangs* 1217 (the first el. is perhaps **broti** 'a clearing in a wood' with **gata**); *Bullyngton dayll* 1532 (a share of land held by Bullington Priory, *v.* **deill**); *Bureslond* Hy3; *cameringhammare* 1271 ('the boundary with Cammeringham', *v.* **(ge)mære**); *Cobbin furres* 1602 (from the surn *Cobbin* and **fyrs**); *ye comon land* 1606; *the Coleby dale* 1663 (probably from the local surn. *Coleby* and **deill**); *dockdale* 1606 (*v.* **docce, deill**); *Docklands* 1662 (*v.* **docce, land**); *Duranteslond'* Hy3 ('Durant's selion' from the OFr pers.n. *Durant* and **land'**); *Estbek, Hestbec* Hy3, *le furlongs de estebec* 1271 (*v.* **ēast, bekkr**); *fulbec, fulbeck'* Hy3 'the foul beck, stream', *v.* **fūl, bekkr**); *in campis de Ing'* 1271, *in campis de Ingham* 14 (the open fields of the village, *v.* **feld**); *viam de Filingham* Hy3, *Fillingham hedge* 1662 (the road to Fillingham, the hedge with Fillingham, a neighbouring parish); *Gildedaile* e13, *Gilde deiles* 1226, *Gildedale* 1230–50 ('selion(s) owned by a guild', *v.* **gildi, deill**; Dr Insley, however, prefers to take the first el. to be from the ODan pers.n. *Gildi*, for which *v.* SPNNF 138–39) ; *Grass Lea* 1699, 1709 (*v.* **lea, ley** (OE **lēah**) 'a meadow, an open pasture'); *Hall closse* (sic) 1606; *le Hallgarthe* 1558, *the Halgarth* 1579, ~ *halgarth* 1602 (*v.* **hall, garðr**); *a house called le Herdehouse* 1545; *one lea called Hoadles* 1606; *Hou* e13 (*v.* **haugr** 'a hill, a mound); *Hungerhill* 1226, 1230–50, Hy3 (*v.* **hungor, hyll**, a common term of reproach with reference to barren land); *Hylderes busk* Hy3 (presumably from **hyldre** 'an elder-tree' and ON **buskr** 'a bush, a shrub'); *Kaldewelle* e13 ('the cold spring', *v.* **cald, wella**); *Kockelwong* Hy3 (*v.* **coccel** 'tares' and **vangr** 'a garden, an in-field', but the significance is not obvious); *Langeland'* Hy3 (*v.* **lang, land**); *the Leigh Close* 1663 (*v.* **lea, ley** (OE **lēah**) 'a meadow, an open pasture'); *Leirpit* e13 ('the clay pit', *v.* **leirr, pytt**); *Lingate* e13, Hy3, Ed1, *Linegate* 1271 (14) (*v.* **līn** 'flax', **gata**); *Littelfen* Hy3 (self-explanatory); *the longe Furlong* 1657; *the longe hedge* 1657; *the long way* 1657; *middelkeueles* Hy3, *middilkeuil* 1230–50, *le Middelkeuels* Ed1 (Dr Insley suggests that the second el. here is the ME word *kevel* possibly used to denote a thick clump of earth or a bulge in the landscape, cf. the ME sense 'a big strong person' and ON *Kefli* 'a piece of wood, a cudgel', *v.* also **middel**); *Nestbeck* 1226, *Nestebec* e13 (presumably the first el. is **nest** 'a nest', with **bekkr**, but the significance is not clear); *Northbeck furlanges* 13 (c1330) (self-explanatory); *North damme close* 1662 (*v.* **norð, damme** 'a dam, a pond'); *the north Sike* 1657 (*v.* **norð, sík**); *Northlanges* e13, 1230–50, Hy3 (*v.* **norð, lang** 'a long piece of land'); *Nortwelledeile* Ed1 (*v.* **norð, wella**, with **deill**); *Noutebecfurlonges, -heynhes* 1271 (14) ('the stream where cattle are found', *v.* **naut, bekkr**); *yᵉ parsons close* 1602; *Philiptoft* 1229 (from the ME pers.n. *Philip* amd **toft** 'a messuage, a curtilage'); *Paynotestoft* Hy3 (from the ME pers.n. *Painot* with **toft**); *Oxbec* e13 (*v.* **oxa, bekkr**); *Sandales* 1271 (14) (*v.* **sand, deill**); *Scegacres* 1226, *Skegacre* 1230–50, *Schegaker* Hy3 (the first el. is perhaps the ON pers.n. **Skeggi** with **acer** or **akr**, though Dr Insley prefers to interpret the name as 'the dagger-shaped fields', the first el. being ON **skegg** 'a beard' used in a topographical sense to denote a pointed or dagger-shaped piece of land); *le Schorngate mare* 1271 (14); *Scorttebutfurlang', -gat'* Ed1 (*v.* **sc(e)ort** 'short', **butte** 'a strip of land abutting on a boundary', 'a short strip or ridge at right-angles to other ridges', with **furlang** and **gata**); *Scotgate* e13, Hy3, *Schothgate* Hy3 (there are at least five examples of *Scotgate* in the Wapentakes of Walshcroft and Yarborough, two of which may well have been named from the surn. *Scot. Scotgate* is discussed in some detail in PN L **2**, 103–4, where in three instances it is interpreted as 'the road of the Scots', *v.* **Scot(t)**, **gata**. This may well be the meaning here, though perhaps **scot** 'a tax, a payment' could also be considered); *the Shorte Furlonge* 1657; *vie de Spridlingtomᵃ* Hy3 ('the way to Spridlington, a neighbouring parish'); *Staindale, Steindale* Hy3 (*v.* ON **steinn** 'a stone', **dalr** or **deill**, a Scand compound); *Stannyes acre* Hy3 (the first el. is obscure); *Stanpittes* e13 ('the stone pits', *v.* **stān, pytt**); *Staynumdale, Steinumgate, Stainnumgate* Hy3 ('the valley, the road at the stones', *Staynum-* etc. representing the dat.pl. *steinum* 'at the stones', of ON **steinn**, *v.* also **dalr, gata**); *Steininghes* Ed1 (*v.* **steinn, eng**, a Scand compound); *Stinting* e13 (*v.* **stinting** 'a portion of common land set apart for one man's use' as in ModE dial. This is the earliest example so far noted in this survey); *Stone Wall* 1606; *sty, sti* Hy3 (*v.* **stigu** 'a sty, a pen'); *Suth Daile* a1219, *Suthdale* 1230–50 (*v.* **sūð, deill**); *terram Rob'suthitun* Hy3, *terra Rob' Suþytune* 1271 (literally 'south in the village', *v.* **sūð, in, tūn**, denoting Robert who lives in the south of the village. This is an anglicisation of a Danish formation common in north L); *Theuegrauedeiles* 1226, *Thefgrauis* 1230–50, *þeuesgraues* Hy3 ('the thief's groves', *v.* **þeof, græfe** 'a grove, a copse'); *Tuamares, Tuuamares* Hy3 ('the two boundaries', *v.* **twā, (ge)mære**); *Westlond Furlong* 1690, *the West lands furlong* 1700 (*v.* **west, land** 'a selion'); *Le Whitehouse in Ingham* 1609, *White House* 1610; *Winse daile* e13, *Winsin(g)daile* a1219 (Dr Insley suggests that this is 'Winsi's share of land', *v.* **deill**, the first el. being the OE pers.n. *Wynsige*); *Wetlands* 1606, *yᵉ Wetlands* 1699, *Wet Lande furlong* 1671, *Wetlandsfurlong* 1674, *Wet Lands Furlong* 1724 (self-explanatory); *Wartlands* 1662 (the first el. is uncertain); *Bosci de Ingham* Hy3 (*v.* **wudu**); *Wyllyngham Ynges* 1532 (*v.* **eng**; the nearest Willingham is Willingham by Stow, five miles from Ingham and no close association between the two places has been noted).

Normanby by Spital

NORMANBY BY SPITAL

Normanestouu 1086 DB
Normanebi (2x) DB, *Normanneby* 1200 ChR, 1202 Ass (p), 1245 FF
Nordmanabi (2x) c1115 LS
Normanbi 1212 Fees, -*by* 1246 Ipm (p), 1254 ValNor, 1276 RRGr,
    1271 FF, 1291 Tax, 1314 RA ix, 1314 Pat, 1323 YearBk, 1316
    FA, 1327 *SR*, 1328 Banco, (~ *iuxta Ouneby*) 1329 *Ass*, 1332 *SR*,
    (~ *juxta Ounesby*) 1334 Orig, 1343 NI, (~ *iuxta Glentham*) 1349
    1353 FF, 1359 Wills i *et freq*, (~ *next Spyttel*) 1545 LP xx (~ *nigh
    Ownby*) 1661 *DCLB*, -*bye* 1576 Saxton, 1610 Speed, -*bie* 1576
    LER, (~ *next Ownbie*) 1601 *DCLB*, (~ *next Ownebie*) 1614 *ib*,
    1612 *ib*, 1703 *Terrier*

'The farmstead, village of the Norwegians' from the gen.pl.
Norðmanna of late OE **Norðmann** 'a Northman, a Norwegian' and **bý**,
indicating an isolated settlement of Norwegians who accompanied the
Danes in the settlement of Lincolnshire. The second el. of DB
Normanestouu is OE **stōw** 'a place, a place of assembly', a form not
supported by any later spellings. For Normanby, cf. Normanby le Wold
PN L **3**, 71–72. There are two more Normanbys in LWR, Normanby in
Burton upon Stather and Normanby by Stow. The present example is
described as near Spital on the Street, Glentham and Owmby.

BOTTLE AND GLASS, 1842 White. CHAPEL LANE (local). CROSS KEYS,
1842 ib. FIELD LANE, *in . . . campis de Normanby* 1484 *DC*, *Normanbie
feilde* 1553 *Dixon*, *Normanby Feilde* 1649 *ParlSurv*, a lane leading to
the open field of the village, *v.* **feld**. GIBBET POST HO, 1841 O, 1830
Gre, *Gibbet House* 1828 Bry, self-explanatory. THE GRANGE, "the
grange" 1545 LP xx, *Grange* 1828 Bry, 1830 Gre; it is highly likely that
the **grange** belonged to Stainfield Priory, *v. Standfield House* in f.ns. (a)
infra. HEATH FM. HIGHGATE LANE (lost), 1828 Bry, *The High gate*
1670, *yᵉ High gate* 1673, *Highgate* 1733 all *Terrier*, 'the chief, the
important road', *v.* **hēah**, **gata**. MALTKILN FM (local). MANOR FM,
manner ferme 1663 *Rental* (*CC Leases 47*), cf. *the mannor place* 1614
DCLB. MOAT FM (local), a medieval moated site. NORMANBY CLIFF,
Normanby Cliff Farms 1824 O, ~ ~ *Fᵐ* 1830 Gre, *Cliff Fᵐ* 1828 Bry.
NORMANBY HALL (lost), *Hall* 1828 Bry, cf. *le Northalle* e14 (c1330)
Spald i, *Northalle, Suthalle* 1349 *FF*, *Northalle, Suthalle* 1353 *ib*, *yᵉ
North hall*, *yᵉ South Hall* 1731 *Terrier*. NORMANBY WINDMILL, *a winde
Milne builded in Normanby feilde* 1601 *DCLB*, *a wynde Milne* 1604 *ib*,

a winde milne builded in Normanbiefeild 1612 *ib, Corn Wind Mill* 1789 *EnclA, Normanby Mill* 1824 O; there was also a Water Mill in Normanby, *molendinum aquaticum* 1443 *DCAcct, prope molend' aquaticum* 1564 *LCCA, a watter mylne* 1565 *DCLB, a water Mill* 1759 *ib*, cf. *the water mille close* 1620 *Terrier* and also *Southwest milne* a1293 *DC*. PILFORD BRIDGE, 1664 *Terrier*, 1828 Bry, 1830 Gre, *pilphre Bridge* 1670 *Terrier, Pilfer Bridge* 1789 *EnclA*, cf. *Pillesfordholm* e13, 1244 *MC, Pilfordeholm* 1337 Cl (*v.* **holmr**), cf. *Pilford brig close* 1664, *~ bridge Close* 1671–77, 1707 both *Terrier*. It is on the boundary with Toft next Newton, from which parish some of the above forms are quoted, *v.* PNL **3**, 65 and where it is suggested that the first el. is either OE **pīl** 'a stake a pole' or ON **píll** 'a willow', hence 'the ford marked by a pole or where willows grow', *v.* **ford**. POUND (lost), 1828 Bry. STONE PIT (lost), 1828 Bry, cf. *Stanpittes* a1293 *DC, v.* **stān, pytt**. VICARAGE (lost), *the vicairige of Normanbe* 1601 *Terrier, the . . . parsonage . . . of Normanbie* 1604 *DCLB, the parsonage howse* 1614 *ib, the Vicaridge House* 1671, *ye Vicaridge* 1690, 1693, 1703, *Vickeridge house* 1706, *the Personge* (sic), *the Vickridge* 1724, *ye Vickridg* 1745 all *Terrier, the Parsonage House* 1753 *Dixon, the Parsonage House* 1760 *DCLB, the parsonage house* 1771 *Dixon, the Parsonage House* 1802 *MiscDep 614, the Vicarage* 1822 *Terrier*.

FIELD-NAMES

Forms dated 1245, 1271 are FF; m13, a1291, c1291, a1293, 1484 *DC*; 1327, 1332 *SR*; 1383 Peace; 1443, 1446, 1661, 1666 *DCAcct*; 1541, 1544 CA; 1564 *LCCA*; 1601, 1604, 1612, 1614, 1661, 1663, 1759 *DCLB*; 1613, 1620, 1670, 1671, 1673, 1690, 1693, 1700, 1710, 1731, 1733, 1763 *Terrier*; 1618, 1638, 1674 *Foster*; 1649[1] *Survey*; 1649[2] *ParlSurv*; 1661 *Featley*; 1673 *CCLeases*; 1789 *EnclA*; 1800, 1852, 1854, 1856 *MiscDep 614*; 1871 *Padley*.

(a) Ancholme Cl 1852, 1854, ~ Meadow 1789, ~ Piece 1800, 1856 (named from the R. Ancholme); Barn Cl 1800, 1856; Bells Cl 1800, 1854, ~ Cottage 1800, 1854; East, North, South, West By Lands 1789 (perhaps 'selions belonging to the village' from **bȳ** 'a village' and **land** 'a selion' in the pl. cf. PN L **4**, 181 and 189, for a discussion of *by dale*); Caynby Rd 1789 (cf. *Caynby meare* 1620, *Cainby Meare* 1670, 1733, *v.* (**ge**)**mǣre** 'a boundary', with Caenby, an adjacent parish); Common Pasture 1789 (*ye common paster* 1670); Cowfold 1800, 1854 (self-explanatory), Cowfold Pasture 1856; East Field 1789 (*the East feeld* 1620, *East feild* 1649[2], *East Field* 1673, 1733, one of the open fields of the village); Farr Lands 1800 (*v.* **land**); First Cl 1800; Home Cl 1854; the Honey Dale 1800 (*Honeydales* 1670, 1673, probably a complimentary nickname referring to good land, *v.* **hunig, deill**); Far Ings 1854, First, Middle Ings 1800 (*Middle Inge* 1649[1], and cf. *Great Inge, Little Ingg* 1649[1], *v.* **eng** 'meadow, pasture'); Long Dyke (Close) 1800 (*Longedikes* 1620, *Long*

Dikes 1670, 1731, *Long Dykes* 1673, self-explanatory, cf. Short Dikes *infra*); Middle Rd 1789; Normanby Bottom 1871 (*v.* **botm** 'a bottom, a valley bottom'); North Ings 1789 (*common Northinges* 1620, *little Northings* 1649[2], *common Northings* 1673, *Common Northing* 1731, *v.* **norð, eng** and cf. Far Ings *supra*); the Oat Plott 1800; the Old Street or Turnpike Rd 1789 (presumably the reference is to Ermine Street); Oxfold 1800, 1852, Oxfold Cl 1789 (self-explanatory); The Park 1800, The Park Cl 1852 (*The Parke close* 1649[2]), Park Lane 1789; Quintin Cl 1789 (from the OFr pers.n. *Quentin*); Raisin Rd 1789 (the road to Market Rasen); the Rough Piece 1800; the Rye Garths 1759 (*cottage called Ryegarthe* 1544, *Rie garthes* 1601, *The Rye garthes* 1613, *Rye Garthes* 1649[2], *Rygarth* 1661, *Rygarthes* 1673, *ye Ry garthis* 1731, 'the enclosure where rye grows', *v.* **ryge, garðr**); Far Sands Cl 1854, First Sands 1800 (*the sandes* 1620, *The Sands* 1670, *Sands* 1673[1], 1733); Synholme (Rd) 1789 (*v.* **holmr**; the first el. is uncertain); Thistle wold 1800, 1854, The Thistlewold 1852 (*Thistelwelle* a1293, *-wal* m13, *Thisselwolde* 1620, *Thistlewolde* 1670, *one stinting called Thistlewould* 1673; the first el. is **þistel** 'a thistle' but there is considerable variation in the second. The 17th century spellings are from **wald** 'woodland').

(b) *alddik* m13 (*v.* **ald, dík**); *baker head land* 1620; *othe Beks* 1383 (p) (*v.* **bekkr** 'a stream, a beck'); *Berleberg* m13 (*v.* **beorg** 'a hill, a mound'; the first el. is uncertain, but Dr Insley suggests that if the name is of some antiquity it may be the OE pers.n. *Bǣrla*); *B'fartheland* m13; *Bishop Ings* 1670, 1673, *Bishopings* 1731 (perhaps from the surn. *Bishop* and **eng**); *the great bleckes* 1620, *Little Bleckes* 1673, *Blecks* 1731 (obscure); *Brakenwelsik* m13 (*v.* **brakni, wella** 'a spring', with **sík**); *Bralands* 1670, 1673, 1731 (perhaps 'the broad, wide selions', *v.* **brād, land**); *Brotherwylowes* 1443 (the elements are **broðor** and **wilig**, but the significance is unclear); *Brombie Meare Forlonge* 1673, *Brumbie Meare furlong* 1673 ('the boundary (land) with Brumby, a neighbouring parish', *v.* **(ge)mǣre**; *the brunde house* 1670; *ye burnt Mill Hill* 1670, *Burn-Mill* 1733; *Caddowhill* 1620, *Cadwell hill* 1670 (the forms are too late to suggest a plausible etymology); *Cambio Meare forlong, Cambio mear* 1673 (it is clear that *Cambio* is to be identified with Caenby, the only such form noted so far; *v.* **(ge)mǣre** 'a boundary, land forming a boundary'); *Carehills als Brotherwylowes* 1443; *the Care* 1670, *Carr* 1673, 1733, *y[e] Car* 1731, (*v.* **kjarr** 'brushwood, a marsh, esp. one overgrown with brushwood'); *Chauntrye House* 1618, *Chauntrey house* 1674 (self-explanatory); *the Cheker* 1670, *Checker* 1733 (*v.* **cheker** 'a chequer', used to denote 'ground of chequered appearance'); *Attecherech* 1271 (p) (*v.* **cirice**); *Christopher Cave[s] farme* 1666; *the common becke* 1612; *y[e] Comon Mear* 1731 (*v.* **(ge)mǣre**); *Conny hill close* 1649[2] (*v.* **coni** 'a rabbit', **hyll**); *Coquell house, the house of Coquell* 1670 (self-explanatory); *Cottam* 1670, *Cottam Hill* 1673, *Cottame* 1733 (probably from the dat.pl. *cotum* from OE **cot** 'a cottage, a shed, a shelter'); *Dinthard* (sic) m13 (obscure); *Dray landes* 1673 (perhaps from the surn. *Dray*); *The East Stocke* 1670; *ye eight foote gadde* 1670; *Eslonges* a1293 (probably **ēast** 'east', **lang** 'a long strip of land'); *Estiby* 1327 (p), *Esteby* 1332 (p) (literally '(the place) east in the village', *v.* **ēast, í, bȳ**, an Anglo-Scand formation, common in north L, denoting X who lives in the east of the village); *far-Leas* 1733 (*v.* **lea, ley** (OE **lēah**) 'meadow', 'open pasture'); *Fen* a1293, *the fen Close* 1673, 1731 (*v.* **fenn**); *Fermerland* a1293 (*v.* **land**; the first el. is ME *fermour, fermer* 'a collector of rents or taxes, a bailiff or steward in charge of a town or manor, one who leases or rents land, etc.'); *the house of Fosse* 1670 (cf. *the house of Coquell supra*; presumably *Fosse* is a surn.); *frosinbak* m13, *Frosen backe* 1620, *Frozenbacke* 1670, *Froson back(e)* 1673, *Frozing Back* 1733 (self-explanatory; the second el. is **bæc** 'a back' used in a topographical sense of something resembling a back); *Gerildholm* m13 ('Geirhild's higher dry ground amidst the marshes', *v.* **holmr**, the first el. being the ON fem. pers.n. *Geirhild*); *Godbehere* 1673 (self-explanatory); *Gosling Acars* 1670, ~ *Akers* 1673 (self-explanatory); *Goldilocks* 1620, *Gouldylox* 1670 (the name of *Ranunculus Auricomus*, a species of buttercup); *green* 1731 (*v.* **grēne** 'the village green'); *Harbinthorne* 1673, *Harby Thorne* 1733; *The high Street* 1649², *y² high street* 1661 probably referring to Ermine Street); *Howsels* 1670 (obscure); *Howshouse* 1673 (presumably from family name *How*); *Hunding dall* m13 (Dr Insley suggests that this is doubtless an ironic name, *v.* **dalr** 'a valley', the first el. being ME *hounding* 'one of a race of dog-headed men, a cynocephalus', a being of some antiquity in medieval popular wisdom, cf. the *Hundingas* of *Widsith*); *Iveteryscroft* 1443 (from the ME surn. *Ivetery* and **croft**); *Kaldwelles, Kaldewelledale* m13 ('the cold spring(s)', *v.* **cald, wella**); *King's high way* 1673; *Land dikes* 1733 (*v.* **land, dīk**); *duo le lees* 1541 (*v.* **lea** 'a meadow, an open pasture'); *leirsikes* a1293, *Lare sikes* 1670 ('the clay ditch', *v.* **leirr** 'mud, clay', **sīk**); *Litildale* m13, *Little Dales* 1613, 1670 (*v.* **lȳtel, deill** 'a share, a portion of land'); *litilhow* a1293 (*v.* **lȳtel, haugr** 'a hill, a mound'); *Long headings* 1670 (*v.* PN L **2**, 14, for a discussion of *heading*); *Long Meares* 1733 (*v.* **lang, (ge)mǣre**); *the longe moores* 1620, *the Long Mores* 1670, *Longmoores* 1773 (*v.* **lang, mōr**); *Long Scotherne* (sic) 1733 (cf. *Skothorne* 1620, 1670 obscure, note that there is a village of the same name, *Scothern*, in the West Riding, but what connexion there is between *Normanby by Spital* and *Scothern* has not appeared, cf. *a furlong called Scotter infra*); *Langthorn* m13, *Langethorn*, *lanthorn* a1293, *Longthorne* 1673, 1733 (*v.* **lang, þorn**); *The Lordshippe garthe* 1604 (self-explanatory, *v.* **garðr** 'an enclosure', *v.* **acer**); *micklholme* (sic) 1620, *Mickleholme* 1670, 1673, 1731, 1733, *Myckleholme* 1673 (*v.* **mikill, holmr**, a Scand compound); *midden ground*, *Middon ground* 1673 (*v.* **midding** 'a midden, a dung-heap'); *middelforlong* a1293, *Middle furlong* 1670, 1673, *The Midle furland* 1731, *Methelfurlanges* m13 (self-explanatory, note however the last form, which is from ON **meðal** 'middle' and *furlang*, of which *furland* is a fairly common variant in north L); *Motton meadow* 1673 (the significance of *mutton* is uncertain); *Moulandes* 1613, *Mowlams* 1670, *Moulands* 1673, *Mowlands* 1733 (the first el. may well be **mūga** 'a heap of earth, a mound', with **land**); *Norbar* 1604, 1649², 1663, *-bor* 1670, *-bore* 1673 (the second el. in not clear, cf. *Sudbore infra*); *Northbergh* a1291, *-boroughe* 1620, *Norborrow* 1673 (*v.* **norð, beorg**); *Northcroft* a1291, *Northcroftdike* m13 (self-explanatory); *Northfield* 1673; *Northkeldewellesdale* a1283 (the elements are **norð**, ON **kelda** 'a spring' to which was added OE **wella** 'a spring' with **dalr** or **deill**. The original name must have been *Northkelde* to which was added *wella* when the meaning of *kelda* was no longer understood); *Northlangstretes* m13 (*v* **lang, strǣt**, here no doubt 'a Roman road' with **norð** prefixed); *northlantaketorhorn* a1293 (the reading is quite uncertain); *Northside furlong* 1733; *the north sike* 1670 (*v.* **norð, sík**); *Northstretfurlanges* m13 (*v.* **norð, strǣt** with **furlang** added); *the Oake close* 1649²; *Odland* 1484, *odd landes* 1564 (*Od(d)* may be ON **oddi** 'a point or tongue of land); *the oke ditch* 1670; *yᵉ outside* 1731; *Owmby meare* 1620, 1670, *Ownby mear* 1731 ('the boundary with Owmby, an adjacent parish'); *Ox dike* 1733, *Oxe close* 1620, *Oxclose* 1733, *yᵉ oxepasture* 1690, 1700, 1710, *oxpasture* 1733 (all self-explanatory); *pittes* m13 (*v.* **pytt**); *preswang* m13, *presteswang* a1293, *prestwong* 1620, *priestwong*, *Priestwong* 1673 (*v.* **prēost, vangr** 'a garden, an in-field'); *yᵉ highway called preystong gate*, *yᵉ prestong gate* 1670 (*v.* **prēost, stǫng** 'a pole, a stave'. also a standard of measure 'a pole', with **gata**); *Ravensholm* a1293 (*v.* **hrafn** 'a raven', **holmr** 'raised land amongst the marshes', a Scand compound, but the first el. might alternatively be the pers.n. ON *Hrafn*, ODan *Rafn*); *Redd earth* 1670, ~ *Earth* 1733 (from the colour of the soil); *Redhill slacke* 1620 (*Redhill* is self-explanatory; *v.* **slakki** 'a small shallow valley, a hollow', an Old West Scand word common in northwest England, but rare in the east of the country); *Riglands* m13 (*v.* **hryggr** 'a ridge' a Scand word); *loco que vocatur Riskes* m13 (from a Scandinavianised form of OE **risc** 'a rush'); *Scorthwestlangs* a1293 (*v.* **west, lang** 'a long strip of land', with **sceort** 'short'); *a furlong called Scotter* 1673 (there is a place Scotter in Corringham wapentake LWR, but what the association it has with Normanby by Spital has not been discovered; cf. *Long Scotherne supra*); *Scowelle thorn* a1293 (the etymology of *Sco-* is difficult, unless it is ON **skógr** 'a wood'); *Sheepe house* 1649[2]; *Sheepwashe* 1620, *-wesh* 1670, *-wash* 1731 (self-explanatory); *Sheepswalk (forlong)* 1673 (*v.* **shepe-walk**); *Short Dikes* 1670, 1731, ~ *dikes* 1733 (self-explanatory); *Short headings* 1670, ~ *Heading* 1731 (for discussions of *heading*, *v.* PN L **2**, 14 and ib **3**, 69); *Short longlands* 1670, ~ *Longland* 1733 (*v.* **lang, land** 'a selion'); *Smalholmes* a1293 (*v.* **smæl** 'narrow', **holmr**); *Smawelle* a1293 (perhaps from **smár** 'small' and **wella**); *Southborough* 1673; *Southcroft* m13 (self-explanatory); *ye South end* 1731; *Southlanges* a1293 (*v.* **sūð, lang** 'a long strip of land'); *ye house of Spalding* 1670 (named from Spalding Priory which held land in the parish); *The East, the West stacke* 1670; *Standfield house, the house of Standfield* 1670, *Stainfield grange* 1673, *Stainfield* 1731 (named from Stainfield Priory which held land in the parish); *Stokke* m13, *stock Furlands* 1620; *y[e] street* 1671, 1700 (*v.* **strǣt**, probably denoting Ermine Street); *The Streytte furlong* 1670, *streete forlong* 1673, *the Strete furlong* 1731 (cf. prec.); *Sudbore* 1670, *-bor* 1733 (cf. *Norbar supra* and *Westbore infra*); *Sud Croft Close* 1649[2] (probably to be identified with *Southcroft supra*); *Sudrough* 1673 (cf. the Rough Piece in (a) *supra* and *West Rough* in (b) *infra*); *Suthstretforlong* a1293 (cf. *The Streytte furlong* in (b) *supra*); *ye Swarth* 1731 (*v.* **swæð** 'a track, a pathway', 'a strip of grassland'); *Swinban* m13 (the reading is quite uncertain); *Thickwolde* 1731; *toftes* a1293 ('the messuages, the curtilages', *v.* **toft**); *Tothemendailes* m13 (*v.* **deill**, the first el. being ME **tóte-man* 'a lookout, a watchman'); *Touneshend'* 1332 (p) (*v.* **tūn, ende**); *Turky sike* 1620, 1670, ~ *Sike* 1733; *twelfaces* a1293 (the reading is uncertain); *twelve acres* 1620, *Twelve acarrs*, ~ *akers* 1673 (self-explanatory); *Twerlandes* a1293 ('land lying athwart', *v.* **land**, the first el. being ME *þvert* 'athwart, crosswise, transverse'); *well* 1649 (*v.* **wella**); *Westbek* a1293 (*v.* **west, bekkr**); *Westberg* m13 (*v.* **west, beorg**); *West bore* 1670, *-bore* 1673, 1731, *Wesbor* 1673 (cf. *Northbar* and *Sudbore supra*); *Westboroughe* 1620, *Wesbrough* 1673; *West Furres* 1620 (*v.* **west, fyrs**); *West house* 1661, ~ *house* 1673 DCLB, the *West house* 1733; *Wharbor greene* 1670, 1673, ~ *green* 1673, *Wharbore Green* 1733; *Wharlandes* 1620, *-lands* 1670, 1673, *-land* 1733 (the first el. of this and prec. appear to be the same, but earlier spellings are needed to be able to suggest an etymology); *Wherleberghdaile* a1291 (*v.* **beorg, berg, deill**; the first el. is uncertain, but may be ON **hvirfill** 'a hill-top'); *Witegate* a1293; *vuam domum vocat' Withedhowse* 1443 (presumably named from the *Whitehead* family); *le wra* m13 (*v.* **vrá** 'a nook or corner of land'); *Wraylands furlong* 1673 (the first el. is no doubt the local surn. *Wray*, common in north L, with **furlong**).

Bishop Norton

BISHOP NORTON

Nortune 1086 DB, *-tuna* 1146 (e13) *LincCart*, 1149, 1163 RA i,
1167, 1168, 1169 P, *-tun'* R1 (1318) Ch, 1221 *DC* (p), *Nortonam*
1126, 1139 RA i, *-tona* 1163 ib, *-ton(')* 1150–60 RA iv, 1166,
1182 P, 112 RA ii, 1201, 1202 P, 1202 Ass (p), 1205 Cur,
1210–20 RA iv, 1225 Pat, 1232, 1234, 1247, 1250 FF, 1254
ValNor, c1263 RA ii, (~ *super Ancolnam*) 1272 *Ass*, (~ *in
Lindeseye*) 1275 RH *et freq*, (~ "by Glentham") 1328 Banco, (~
by le Spitule o the Stret) 1338 Ipm
Nordtuna c1115 LS, *Northton'* 1282 RA ii, 1327 *SR*
Byschop Norton' 1346 *Foster*, 1431 FA, *Bisshopnorton(')* 1347 *FF*,
1384 *Foster*, 1384 Misc, 1394 *Foster*, *Bisshopesnorton* 1380 Pat,
1382 Fine, *Buscoppe Norton'* 1383 Peace, *Bischop Norton'* 1397
Foster, ~ *norton* 1402 FA, *Bysschopnorton'* 1378 *DC*,
Bisshopnorton 1441 *Foster*, *Bysshop Norton* 1455 *LCCA,
Bysshopysnorton* 1490 Ipm, *Busshop' Norton'* 1499 *FF*,
Bushoppnorton' 1531 Wills iii, *Bishop Norton* 1397 *Foster*, 1576
DCAcct et passim
Norton' episcop 1442 LCStatutes, ~ *Episcopi* 1510 *BP*, 1526 Sub,
1527, 1548 CA, 1554 PrState, 1712 *Foster*

'The farmstead, village, estate to the north', *v.* **norð, tūn**. It is not
clear which setlement it is named from, perhaps Glentham. It is named
in relation to the R. Ancholme, Glentham, Spital in the Street and
Lindsey. The manor of Norton was held by the Cathedral Church of
Lincoln, hence *Bishop*.

ATTERBY

Adredeb' 1185 Templar, 1210 P (p)
Atheradeby 1202 Ass (p), *Atheredeby* c1230 (14) *VC* (p),
Hatheradebi 112 RA ii (p)
Adrathebi 1204 P (p)
Athereby c1225 (14) *Queen's*, *Atherby* 1299 *DC* (p), 1301, 1303,
1303 *KR*, 1316 FA, 1327, 1332 *SR*, 1334 *Foster*, 1334 Ipm, 1339
Pat *et passim* to 1539 *Asw*, *Athirby* 1383, 1387 Peace, 1397
Foster
Aderby 1300 Ipm, 1310–20 *Foster*, 1465, 1469 Pat, *Adhherby* 1303
RA ix, *Adirby* 1385 Peace (p)
Adthreby 1300–20 *Foster*, *Adtherby* 1315 *DC* (p)

Atterby 1574 WillsA *et passim, -bie* 1616 ib

'Ēadrēd's farmstead, village' *v.* **bȳ**, a hybrid Anglo-Danish p.n. from the OE pers.n. *Ēadrēd* and ODan **bȳ**. There are no traces of the OE gen.sg. *-es* in the forms for Atterby and we have examples of *-th-* indicating Scand influence. It is, therefore, likely that the name was given by Scand settlers. For comparable names *v.* Audleby (PN L **2**, 88), Autby (ib **4**, 168) and Barnetby le Wold (ib **2**, 9).

CROSSHOLME HO

> *Crosholm(')* 1185 RotDom, 1197 FF (p), 112 RA ii (p), 1202 Ass,
> c1230 RA iv, 1232 FF, c1240 (14) *VC*, 1250 FF (p), 1250 (p)
> Fees, c1263 RA ii, 1272 *Ass* (p) *et freq*
> *Crosseholm'* 1220–30 RA iv (p), 1306 *KR* (p), 1311 *DC, -holme*
> 1510 *BP, Cross Holme* 1828 Bry
> *Croxholm* c1225 *Queen's*, 1210–20 RA iv (p), p1240 (14) (p)
> *Crossam* 1614 *Monson*

'The raised land in marsh marked with a cross', from ON **kross**, late OE **cros** and **holmr**, probably a Scand compound. The OIrish form **cros**, itself a loan-word from Latin *crux*, spread widely and was borrowed as ON **kross**. This word was introduced into north-west England by Norwegian Vikings from Ireland and became the common term for 'a cross' in England.

ARCHER HO, named from the *Archer* family, cf. John *Archer* 1733 WillsStow, William *Archer* 1736 *Foster*. ATTERBY BECK, 1822, *the beck* 1663, *y*ᵉ *Beck* 1668, ~ *becke* 1697 all *Terrier, the beck called Atterby Beck* 1708 *LD 15, v.* **bekkr** 'a stream, a beck'. ATTERBY CARR, 1767 *Stubbs, the Carre* 1614 *Monson, v.* **kjarr** 'brushwood', later 'a marsh, especially one overgrown with brushwood'. ATTERBY CLIFF, 1770 EnclA, ~ *Cliffe* 1788 *Terrier*. ATTERBY LANE, *Atterbury Lane* (sic) 1828 Bry. ATTERBY MILL, 1824 O, 1830 Gre, *Watermill* 1770 *EnclA, Water Mill* 1828 Bry, cf. *Mylnebeck* 1577 *Terrier*, and *water milne furlong* 1614 *Monson, y*ᵉ *water mill Furlong* 1663, *watermill Furlong* 1668, *Water mill furlong* 1673 all *Terrier*. There was also a windmill in Bishop Norton parish, *vnum molendinum ventriiticum* 1569 *Monson, wyndemylne furlong* 1614 *ib*. BOTTOM WALK, *v.* **walk** denoting a stretch of land used for pasturing animals, hence the commom *Sheepwalk*. BRACKEN'S LANE, cf. *the Brackens* 1770 *EnclA, v.* **brakni** 'bracken, fern'. CARR LANE, ~ WOOD, ~ Wd. 1828 Bry. CROSS LANE, probably to be identified with *Crossgate* 1614 *Monson*, 'the way, the road to the

cross', v. **cros**, **gata**. DEER PARK (local), 1828 Bry. EAST DRAIN.
ERMINE STREET is *the old Street* 1614 *Monson*, ~ ~ *streete* 1663, ~ ~
Streete 1668, *y^e* *oldstreet* 1673, *y^e* *street* 1697 all *Terrier*, *Old Street*
1770 *EnclA*, *old Street road* 1788 *Terrier*, v. **ald**, **stræt**. FISHPOND. FOX
DALE. THE GRANGE, a late example of **grange**, common in L, cf. The
Grange in Cammeringham parish *supra*. INGS BRIDGE (lost), 1828 Bry,
v. **eng** 'meadow, pasture'. THE LAWN, 1799 Young. LOW FM. LOW
PLACE. LOW PLANTATION. MANOR HO, 1828 Bry. MELLOW'S BECK,
1706 *Terrier*, *mellowes beck* 1614 *Monson*, *Mellowes Beck* 1668,
Mellows Beck c1650, *Mellowes beck* 1663, *Mellowes beck* 1673,
Mallowes Beck 1700, *Mellows Beck* 1745, cf. *the mellowes* 1614
Monson, *Atterbie Mellas* (sic) 1679, *Atterby Mellows* 1706, 1745 all
Terrier. NORTON BECK, 1828 Bry, cf. *Atte Beke* 1327 *SR* (p), v. **bekkr**
'a stream, a beck'. NORTON LANE. NORTON PLACE, 1799 Young, 1801,
1829 *BRA 641*, 1819 *Red*. NORTON SANDHAYS, cf. Snitterby Sandhays
infra. PARK HO, cf. *de Parco de Norton'* 1280–90 *Foster*, *de parco de
Northon* Ed1 *Barl*, *del Park' de Norton'* c1324 *Extent*, *de Parco* 1327
SR, *othe Park* 1343 NI all (p). PINGLE LANE, cf. *the Pingle* 1614
Monson, *Pingle Close* 1770 *EnclA*, v. **pingel** 'a small enclosure'. TOP
WALK, cf. Bottom Walk *supra*. VICARAGE, *y^e* *vicaridge* c1650, 1663,
1677, *y^e* *Vicridg* 1673, *the Vicarage* 1706, 1822, *Vicarage House* 1788
all *Terrier*, cf. *Pars^e* *Fm* 1828 Bry. WATERLOO PLANTATION,
commemorating the Battle of Waterloo.

FIELD-NAMES

Forms dated c1150 are *HarlCh*; R1 (1318) Ch; 1210–20 RA iv;
1248–53. 1254–58 RA ii; c1230 (14), p1240 (14) *VC*; c1230 (c1350) *R*;
c1225, 1348–49 *Queen's*; 1280–90, 1281, 1292, 1310–20, 1335, 1483,
1712, 1736 *Foster*; 1282 *FF*; 1292 Cl; 1297 CoramR; 1301, 1303 *KR*;
1327, 1332 *SR*; 1343 NI; 1378 *DC*; 1383 Peace; 1547 Pat; 1568, 1614
Monson; 1647 WillsPCC; 1660 *LindDep 78*; c1650, 1663, 1668, 1673,
1677, 1678, 1690, 1696, 1697, 1706, 1788, 1822 *Terrier*; 1643, 1667,
1669, 1670 *MiscDep 61*; 1776 *LD 15*; 1770 *EnclA*; 1823 *WG;* 1838 *Red*;
1861, 1871 *Padley*; all the rest are *CCLeases*.

(a) Ace Fld 1770 (*le graunde Ace* 1568, *little Ace* 1614, *litle Ace* 1673, *North
Little Ace* 1668, *South* ~ ~ 1706); Atterby East Fld 1788 (*Atterbie East Feild* 1668,
ye East field of Atterbie 1697, one of the open fields of the village); Atterby West
feild 1788 (*ye west field of Atterbie* 1690, 1697, one of the open fields of the village);
Avern Cl 1856, 1864; Bainten Cl 1770 (from the surn. *Bainton*, cf. John *Bainton*
1798 *CCLeases*); Barn Cl 1856; two Bennygarths 1823 (v. **garðr**, the first el. is
obscure); Bishop Norton Carrs 1767, the Carrs of Bishop Norton 1791, 1800, the
Carr 1824, The Carrs 1830, 1849, 1856, Norton Carr 1871 (*Norton Carr* 1547, 1706,
~ *carr* 1696, v. **kjarr**); Black Dike 1770, 1788 (self-explanatory); Blacksmith's Shop

1856, 1890; bottom cow pasture 1849; Bullen Lane 1809, Bulling Lane 1850 (*Bullen lane end* 1614, cf. *Bulling beck* 1614, *Bullen sike* 1614, ~ *Sike* 1668, *Bullen Sike furlong* 1677, *Bulling sike* 1690, ~ *Syke fourlong* 1706, *bullon furlonge* c1650, *bullen Furlong* 1663, *the North Bullins* 1668, v. also Thorn Cl in (a) *infra*; the forms are too late to suggest a convincing etymology, though the first part of the name may well be the surn. *Bullen*); Chambers Cl 1890 (cf. *Chamber dale* 1614, named from the family of *Allyn Chamber* 1614 *Monson*); a piece of old inclosure called the Chapel yard 1788, Chappell yard 1822 (perhaps the site of *capella Sancti Jacobi* R1 (1318)); Clay Cl 1856, 1864, ~ Closes 1822 (perhaps named from the family of John *Clay*, named in the 1864 document); the Common 1767, ~ ~ Cl 1811, 1823; Common Lane 1864 (*le Common Lane* 1547); Copyhold Cottage 1852; Copyhold Lands 1849; Cottagers Lane 1825; Crook Cl 1770; Cow Cl 1825, 1864; Cow Fold 1770 (*the Cow fold* 1614, 1706, *ye Cow Fold* 1663, 1673, *ye cowfold* 1697); Cowgate Rd 1789, 1825, 1851, 1864 (cf. *Cowgate* 1614, *ye Cowgates* 1663, 1673, a *cowgate*, a common term in L, was the right of pasturage for a single animal. in f.ns. and p.ns., being usually found in the pl.); Dales Cl 1770 (*dale close* 1667, *Dales close* 1669); Dovecoat Cl 1804; East Fld 1770, 1854, Late East Fld 1789, 1830 (*ye East Field* 1673, *ye Eastfield* 1677, 1690, *the East Field* 1706, one of the open fields of the parish); Feeding Cl 1825, 1849; first middle common 1849; Fit Furze 1770; the Highlands 1770; the High road 1860, High way 1850; home Cl 1821, 1841, Home Cl 1823, 1851; Homestead Cl 1770; Common Horse Cl 1770, the horse Cl 1825, Horse Cl 1866; Job's Cl 1825, 1860; Kerves 1770; Kiln House 1832 (*Kylne howse end* 1614); little hays 1825; the little Pingle 1811, Second Bottom Pingle 1856 (v. **pingel** 'a little enclosure'); Low Carr Cl 1856 (cf. Bishop Norton Carrs *supra*); the middle Field 1822; Miln Cl 1812 (cf. *milne wong* c1230, *mulnedeille*, *Mulnerugge* 1347–48, v. **myln**, **vangr** and **hryggr**); Monson's Cl 1770 (named from the *Monson* family, prominent in the area); The Moor 1815 (*la more* 1303, *the More* 1343, *les mor'* 1348–49, v. **mōr**); Moor Leys Cl 1861 (v. **ley** (OE lēah) 'a meadow, an open pasture'); North Cl 1829, 1835 (*the North Close* 1643); the Oxpasture Close 1823 (*ye oxpasture* 1697); Railes Cl 1770; Robinsons Cl 1789, 1850, 1890 (named from the family of John *Robinson* 1832 *CCLeases*); Sand Acre 1838; Sand Heath 1856; the Sands Close 1811; The Seeds or Middle field close 1823; the South by lands 1788 (for by lands, v. East, North, South, West By Lands in Normanby by Spital f.ns. *supra*); South Carr 1770 (cf. *Northker* in (b) *infra*); South Cliff 1838; Spittle Cl 1812 (probably land held by the Hospital at Spital); stonacres 1825, 1860, Stone acres or Stoneham close 1849 (*stone acres* 1614, v. **stān**, **æcer**, self-explanatory); Stoneham Cl 1766, 1849, 1864 (*stonham dale* 1614, *stoneham close* 1712, the forms are too late to suggest an etymology); the Straw 1857, 1860 (obscure); Thorn Close or Bulling Lane Close 1798, 1850, 1863 (cf. Bulling Lane in (a) *supra*); The Town end or Pingle (cf. the little Pingle *supra*); Town Street 1842, 1850, 1863, 1874; the West Cl 1823; West Fld 1770 (*in campo occidentali de Bishopnorton* 1568, *West Feild* 1650, *the West Field* 1668, *ye West Field* 1697, one of the open fields of the village); West Yard and Fore Yard 1830, 1856; the White House 1812.

(b) *asheyard* 1614; *Atterbery field* 1614, *Atterby Feild* 1663, ~ *Field* 1706 (the open fields of Atterby, a separate manor in the parish); *Atterbie Willoughbeck* 1614 (v. **wilig** 'a willow', **bekkr** 'a stream, a beck'); *the bank* 1673; *Robert Bets Close* 1677, *Robert Betts Close* 1690; *Bisacre, Bysacredeill* 1348–49; *Bishop dale* 1614 (probably named from the *Bishop* family, cf. Richard *Bishop* 1642 LPR, with **deill** 'a share, a portion of land'); *Bottom Close* 1614; *Bournrigges* 1348–49 (apparently from **burna** 'a stream' and **hryggr** 'a ridge', though **burna** is rare in north L); *Briggedeile* c1150, *Briggedaile* R1 (1318) (v. **brycg** (in a Scandinavianised form), deill); *Brumbyes farm* 1663, *Brumbies land* 1668, *Brunby farm* 1673 (named from the family of *Matthias Brumbie* 1663 and note *the land of James Brumbyes* 1673); *the Bull peice* 1660; *a land formerly called Mr Buntings* 1673 (*v.* **land** 'a selion'); *bygate* p1240, *Bygatenge* 1348–49 (literally 'by the road meadow, pasture', *v.* **bī**, **gata, eng**); *cauenholm* 1281 (the first el. may well be the ON pers.n. *Kafni*, as in Caenby *supra*, with **holmr** 'raised land amidst the marshes', *v.* further Caenby *supra*); *chaumbredeill'*, *Westchaumbirdeill* 1348–49 (presumably from the surn. Chambers with **deill**; note that in f.ns. (a) Chambers Cl is found only in 19th century sources with a surn. recorded in the 17th); *atte cherche de Norton* 1282, *atte Churche* 1292, *ad ecclesiam de Norton* 1292, 1327, 1332, 1335, *atte kyrke* 1327, *Atte Kyrke* 1332, *atte Kirk de Norton* 1343, *atte Kirke de Bysshopnorton* 1378 all (p) (*v.* **cirice, kyrkja**, the occurence of the English and Scand forms for 'church' is worthy of note); *ye Kirkehedland* 1614; *ye Church Headland* c1650, 1668, ~ ~ *Headlandes* 1673, ~ ~ *Headland* 1697 (*v.* **hēafod-land** 'the head of a strip of land left for turning the plough'); *Church Stockwell* c1650, 1663, 1673, *Stokwelle heued* 1348–49 (perhaps 'the spring marked by a tree-trunk', *v.* **stocc, wella**); *Colmillne* 1210–20, c1230 (*v.* **myln**); *Colemenshill'* 1210–20, c1230 (the first el. is presumably the OGerm pers.n. Col(e)man, recorded in England as early as DB, with **hyll**); *the common Mere* 1614 (*v.* **(ge)mǣre** 'a boundary'); *le comon Furr* 1568 (*v.* **furh** 'a furrow'); *ye Coniger close* 1614 (*v.* **coninger** 'a rabbit-warren'); *Cony garth* 1614 (*v.* **coni, garðr**); *Corne Close* 1614; *ye Cow Carr* 1663, 1673 (*v.* **kjarr**; *Cow Carr well furlong* 1690, 1697; *The Cowe Common* 1660, *Cow Common* 1677, 1697; *Cotedeill'* 1348–49 (*v.* **cot** 'a cottage, a hut', **deill**); *Estlanddeilles* 1348–49 (*v.* **ēast, land, deill**); *ye fallow field* 1677; *Farmery Close* 1676 (probably land dedicated to the upkeep of the infirmary of a monastery); *in campis de Norton* 1254–58, ~ ~ ~ *Nortun'* 1318 (the open fields of the village, *v.* **feld**); *Foxhow* c1230 (*v.* **fox, haugr** 'a mound, a hill'); *gallow furres* 1614 (*v.* **furh** in the pl.); *inter les Gates* 1348–49 ('between the roads', *v.* **gata**); *Glentham feild*, ~ ~ *mere* 1614 (from Glentham a neighbouring village with **(ge)mǣre**); *Godewynemulndeille* 1348–49 (from the OE pers.n. *Godwine* with **myln** and **deill**); *Godspeed hedland* 1614 (presumably a complimentary nickname, with **hēafod-land**); *la grene* 1225, *la Grene* 1248–53 both (p) (*v.* **grēne** 'a village-green'); *Grenegat* p1240 (*v.* **grēne** 'green', **gata**); *Gurrumsti* (sic) c1230 (the first el. is apparently a pers.n., perhaps ODan *Guthrum*, with **stīg** 'a path, a narrow road'); *Attehalle de Norton* 1297, *ye Hall* 1677, 1697; *Halydeille* 1348–49 (*v.* **hālig, deill**); *Hamerhow* 1348–49 (the els. are **hamor** 'a hammer' and **haugr** 'a hill, a mound', presumably a reference to the shape of the hill or mound); *haulf a hedelande* 1568 'half a headland', *v.* **hēafod-land**); *haveran, haverram* (sic) 1614 (the first el. is no doubt **hafri** 'oats', but the second is difficult to identify. It may perhaps be a reflex of **holmr**); *hempe lan* (sic) 1614 ('the selion where hemp is grown', *v.* **hænep, land**); *heuedland* c1230 (*v.* **hēafod-land**); *High Close* 1667, 1669; *hilles* 1240, *the Hill* 1614; *holm* c1230, *Holm furlong* 1348–49 (*v.* **holmr** 'raised land amongst the marshes'; *the hye more furlong* 1614; *Kekedeill'* 1348–49 (obscure); *Kirkehil* c1150, 1318 (*v.* **kirkja, hyll**); *lacheslash* (sic) 1348–49 (obscure); *langdeill'* 1348–49 (*v.* **lang, deill**); *Lichlas* (sic) p1240 (obscure); *Langholmfurlong* 1348–49 (*v.* **lang, holmr, furlang**); *Linteslassh* (sic) 1348–49 (obscure); *littel how* 1348–49 (*v.* **lȳtel, haugr**); *Long hedge dale* 1614 (*v.* **deill**); *lordship land* 1614; *lutteldeill'* 1348–49 (*v.* **lȳtel, deill**); *two landes called the mare and fole* 1614 (several examples of this f.n. have been noted in north L and it has been suggested that it is a foaling strip, *v.* PN L 3, 144); *in marisco de Norton* 1310–20 (*v.* **mersc**); *Mayden Croft* 1614, *mayden heuedland* 1348–49, *le maiden headland* 1568, *Mayden hedland* 1614 (*v.* **hēafod-land**, the first el. is **mægden**, but the significance is not clear); *the meare* 1614 (*v.* **(ge)mǣre** 'a boundary'); *in pratis de Norton* 1483 (*v.* **mǣdwe** 'meadow'); *le medel fen* 1310–20, *mydil fene* 1483 (*v.* **meðel, middel, fenn**; the interchange between the OE and ON forms is noteworthy); *meðelese* c1230 (obscure); *the middle furlong* 1614; *mikelas* c1230 (obscure); *mikelcotedeill'* 1348–49 (*v.* **micel, cot** with **deill**); *mikeldeille,* ~ *mede* 1348–49 (*v.* **micel, deill** with **mǣd** 'meadow'); *le mordyk* 1348–49, *ye More Dike* c1650, *More dike furlong* 1668, *more dike furlong* 1673, *Moor dike furlong* 1706 (*v.* **dīk** and cf. the Moor in f.ns. (a) *supra*); *More gat* 1614 (*v.* **gata**); *morwongdeille* 1348–49 (*v.* **vangr** 'a garden, an in-field', with **deill**); *Nechdelles* 1348–49 (obscure, the reading is difficult); *ye Newdike* 1690 (self-explanatory); *Newhill, New Hill Hill* (sic) 1614; *Northbeck* 1348–49 (*v.* **norð, bekkr**); *Northdeilefurlong* 1348–49 (*v.* **norð, deill**); *the north garth* 1614 (*v.* **norð, garðr**); *Northker* 1348–49 (*v.* **norð, kjarr** and cf. South Carr in (a) *supra*); *northmede* 1348–49 (*v.* **norð, mǣd**); *Northmor* 1348–49, *north more* 1614 (*v.* **norð, mōr**); *Nortondike* 1310–20 (*v.* **dík**); *parsondike* 1696 (self-explanatory); *Pibererigge* (sic) 1348–49 (the first el. is doubtful); *Rodemilne* c1150, 1318 (*Rode-* is uncertain); *Roger's oxgang* 1736 (*v.* **oxgang** 'a measure of land' of 10–30 acres extent, an eighth of a plough-land); *sheppe furres* 1614 (*v.* **scēap, furh** in the pl.); *the short furlong* 1614; *shovelinge* 1614, *shuflings* (sic) 1677, *shouelings* 1690, *Shufflings* 1697 (perhaps 'the meadow as broad as a shovel', *v.* **scofl, eng**); *Skirbek* c1230, *schyrebec* p1240, *skirbekfurlong* 1348–49 ('the clear stream', *v.* **skírr, bekkr**, a Scand compound); *Smalenges* 1348–49 (*v.* **smæl** 'narrow', **eng**); *Sondeill* 1348–49 (probably 'the sandy share of land', *v.* **sand, deill**); *Southassch* 1348–49 (*v.* **sūð, æsc** 'an ash-tree'); *viam que voc' Southgate* 1335 (*v.* **sūð, gata**); *Southlawonges* 1348–49 (the reading is uncertain); *Southmoor* 1348–49, *South more* 1614 (cf. *Northmor supra* in (b)); *le Spittlegate* 1568, *Spittle gate* 1673 ('the road to Spital in the Street', *v.* **gata**); *the stepping stones* 1614; *sterre acre* 1348–49; *stocholmdale* c1230, *Stokholmdeill'* 1348–49 (identical with Stockholm (PN YE 38) 'the raised land amidst the marsh marked by a tree-stump', *v.* **stokkr, holmr**, a Scand compound. It is pointed out that in Scand p.ns. **stokkr** had a wide variety of applications and that this compound may have denoted 'low-lying land cleared of trees'); *Standeill attestret* 1348–49 (*v.* **stān, deill**; it must have been situated on Ermine Street); *Stykwell'* 1248–49 (early forms are needed to suggest a convincing etymology); *Sudland doale* 1647 (probably 'the south selion', *v.* **sūð, land**, with **dāl** 'a share, a portion', cognate with **deill**); *Suthbeck* 1248–53 (self-explanatory, *v.* **sūð, bekkr**); *Suthlonges* 1281 (*v.* **sūð, lang** 'a long strip of land'); *Tathewellewang* c1230 (the first el. is Tathwell, a village in LSR, but the connection with Bishop Norton has not been discovered); *Thorpfeld* p1240, *In campo de thorpfeld* 1348–49, *the feild called thorpe feild* 1614, *Thorp field* 1706 (from a lost *Thorpe* 'the secondary settlement, the dependent outlying farmstead or hamlet', *v.* **þorp** with **feld**); *meadow called Two Swathes* 1547 (*v.* **swæð, swathe** 'a strip of grassland'); *the upper furlong* 1614; *Waldeille* 1348–49 (probably *v.* **wald, deill**); *Wauardeill'* 1348–49 (the first el. is uncertain); *Wayladedeill'* 1348–49; *West Headland* 1668 (*v.* **hēafod-land**); *Westiby* "of" *Norton* 1292, *Westyby* 1332 both (p) (literally '(the place) west in the village', *v.* **vestr, west, í, bȳ**, denoting X who lives in the west of the village, a common Danish formation in L); *Westlandes* 1348–49 (*v.* **west, land** 'a selion'); *Westryedeill'* 1348–49 (*v.* **ryge** 'rye', **deill** with **west** prefixed); *Westwange* 1248–53 (*v.* **west, vangr** 'a garden, an in-field'); *the Wood close* 1614; *woodcrosse hill* 1614 (self-explanatory); *Wrodayles* 1281 (*v.* **vrá** 'a nook, a corner', **deill**); *Wuldithdailles* 1348–49 (the first el. appears to be an OE pers.n. but its exact form is doubtful).

Owmby by Spital

OWMBY BY SPITAL

Ounesbi 1986 DB, *-b'* 1185 Templar, *-by* 1243 RRG, 1331, 1353 Ipm
   Ounebi 1086 (4x), c1115 LS (2x), 1166, 1167, 1180 P, 1196–1203,
   1200–10 RA iv, 1202 Ass (p), 1201 Cur, 1212 Fees, *-by* c1184
   (15) Templar, 1209 FF, 1220 Cur, 1227 Pat, 1230–40 RA iv, 1232,
   1252 FF, 1254 ValNor *et freq* to 1446 *DCAcct, Owneby* c1225 (14)
   Queen's, 1526 Sub, (~ *iuxta Normanbie*) 1661 *DCLB, Ownebie
   iuxta Normanbie* 1616 *ib, Ounabi, -bia* c1115 LS (2x), *Oumbi*
   1202 Ass (p), *Oumbye* 1576 Saxton, 1610 Speed
Aueneby 1210 FF, *Auneby* 1232 Welles, 1230–40 RA iv
Oudneby 1242–43 Fees, *Othenby* 1303 FA, *Outhunby* 1323 Foster,
   Outhenby 1428 FA
Ouenby 1383 Peace, c1414 AASR xxix
Ounby (*iuxta Normanby*) 1281 *DC*, 1373 Peace, 1383 Cl, 1402 FA,
   1535 VE iv, *Ounbie iuxta Normanbie* 1601 *DCLB, Ownby* 1445
   AASR xxix, *Ownbe* 1539 *AD*
Owmby 1661 *Featley et passim*

This is a difficult name. It is pointed out in PN L·2, 160–61 that
Owmby (Owmby cum Searby), Owmby by Spittle, Aunby (in Careby)
and Aunsby have usually been taken together, though the forms for each
do not show the same patterns. Both Ekwall (DEPN s.n.) and Fellows-
Jensen (SPNLY 41–42) take the first el. of each to be the Scand pers.n.
Auðun(n), according to the former in the shortened form *Aun*. In a recent
study, Cameron (DLPN s.n.) suggests that the first el. of Owmby (PN L
2, 261) and of Aunsby is the AScand pers.n. *Ouðen*, an anglicised
variant of the Scand ON *Auðun(n)*, cf. the L DB form *Oudon*. The first
el. of Owmby by Spital and Aunby is the contracted AScand *Oun*,
corresponding to ON *Aun*.
   It seems reasonable to suggest that Owmby by Spital means 'Aun's
farmstead, village', *v.* **bȳ**.

CHURCH LANE (local). COW PASTURE, *yᵉ Cow paster* 1695 *Terrier,
Cowpasture* 1774 *EnclA*, cf. *Cowpaster furlonge* 116, *the Cow pasture
furlong* 1662, 1671, *the Cowe pasture furlong* 1668, *yᵉ Cowpaster
forlong* 1679, *yᵉ Cowpaster furlong* 1690 all *Terrier, the Cow pasture
furlong* 1709 *LCS, the Cowpasture Drain* 1774 *EnclA*, self-explanatory.
GREEN LANE (local), cf. *the grene gate* 1323 *DC, v.* **gata** 'a way, a road'.
HILL HO, HILL LANE (both local), cf. *super collem* c1227 *Foster, le
hilles* c1287 *DC, le hille* a1290 *ib, the hille* (sic) 1323 *ib, le hil* c1330

(c1331) *Spald i, le Hille* 1337 *Foster*, *ye North-hill* 1695 *Terrier, the North hill furlong* 1709 *LCS*. MANOR HO. THE OLD RECTORY (local), *the Rectorie* 1671, *ye Rectī And parsonege* 1679, *ye Rectorie & parsonige* (sic) 1690, *the Rectory* 1695 all *Terrier, the Rectory Homestead* 1774 *EnclA*. OWMBY CLIFF, *Cliffe* 1774 *EnclA*. OWMBY CLIFF FM, *Cliff F^m* 1828 Bry, cf. *the North, the South Clyffe* 1662, *the North, the South Cliffe* 1668, *ye North, ye South Cliff* 1679, *ye north, ye south Clife* 1690 all *Terrier, North, South Cliff* 1768 *LCS, Cliff closes* 1799 *ib*. OXFOLD COTTAGE, cf. *Owmby Oxfold* 1774 *EnclA*, *Oxfold* 1791 *LCS*, self-explanatory, *v.* **oxa, fald** 'a fold for animals'.

FIELD-NAMES

Forms dated John, eHy3, 1260–90, 1281, c1287, a1290, 1291, a1291, e14, 1323, 1337 are *DC*; 1200–10, 1230–40 RA iv; 1225–41, c1227, 1230–40, 1260–80, 1270–90, 1322, 1330–50, 1337, 1339, 1347, 1348, 1357, 1382 *Foster*, 1284, 1329 *Ass*, 13 (c1350) *R*; 1327, 1332 *SR*; c1330 (c1331) *Spald i*; 1362 Ipm; 1363 BPR; 1428 AASR xxix; 116, 1662, 1666, 1671, 1679, 1690, 1695, 1697, 1818 *Terrier*; 1601, 1603, 1614, 1661 *DCLB*, 1649, 1709, 1710, 1768, 1791, 1799 *LCS*; 1774 *EnclA*.

(a) Bram ceoat Cl (sic) 1774 (cf. *subtus Bram, Culturam que vocatur bram* c1227, *super Brame* 1260–90, c1330 (c1331), *Northbram* c1330 (c1331), *Southbram* 1347, probably 'the place where broom grows', *v.* **brōm**); Bush Cl 1799; Calf Cl 1791; Carr 1774, 1791 (*The Carre* 1662, 1668, 1671, *ye Car* 1679, *~ Carre* 1690, *the Carr* 1695, *The car* 1709, *v.* **kjarr** 'brushwood', later 'a marsh, especially one overgrown with brushwood'); Causeway Cl 1774; the Common Cl 1774; Dole Cl 1791 (*v.* **dāl** 'a share, a portion'); Dunthorn Leas 1791 (cf. *Dunthorn* c1227, 1281, a1291, *-thorne* 1260–90, *Dunþorne* a1290, *Dounthornheuidland* c1330 (c1331) (*v.* **hēafod-land**) Dr Insley suggests that this is 'the thornbush on a grassy upland or in open country', *v.* ME **doun** (OE **dūn), þorn**); East Fd 1768, 1774, the East Fd 1828 (*in campo orientali* 1281, 1323, *in orientali campo de Ouneby* 1291, *in campo oriental' de Ouneby* 1330–50, *in oriental' campo* 1337, *the East field* 1709, *~ ~Field* 1710, one of the open fields of the village'); The Green 1774 (*la grene* 1260–80, *la Gren* 1270–90, *atte Gren* 1281 (p), *v.* **grēne**); the Gibbet Cl 1774; The Gauber Leas 1791, Gawber Leas, *~ Gate* 1794 (cf. *Gawberfurlong* 1710, *v.* **galga** 'gallows', **beorg** 'a hill, a mound'); Herd Hill 1791; Home Cl 1791; the Leys 1768 (*v.* **ley** (OE **lēah**) 'a meadow, an open pasture'); the Line Dykes 1799 (cf. *the Lyne Dyke Furlong* 1709, 1710, *v.* **līn** 'flax', **dík** 'a ditch'); Long Cl 1768, 1791; the Mill Cl 1828 (cf.(*The) Mylne furlong* 1662, 1668, 1674, *ye Millne furland* 1690, *The miln furlong* 1709, 1710, self-explanatory); the Moor 1774 (*la More* 13 (c1350), *The Moor* 1709, *the Moore* 1710, *estmore* c1227, *litelmore* c1287 *moreheud* 1260–90, *morehed* e14, *moreheved* 1337 (*v.* **hēafod**); Normanby Rd 1774, *~ Lane* 1828 (*Normanby Strete* a1291, leading to Normanby by Spital; the old street 1774 (this is Ermine Street, the boundary of the parish on the east); Owmby Lane 1828; Oxpasture 1828 (*The Oxpasture* 1709, 1710); the Pingle 1774 (*v.* **pingel** 'a small enclosure'; Raisen Rd 1774 (leading to Market Rasen); Sand Hills, Sand Hill Cl 1799 (*Sandhill* 116, *The*

Sande Hill 1662, *the Sand Hill* 1671, 1709); Saxby Road 1744 (*uie que ducit de Ounebi ad Saxeby* c1330 (c1331)); the South Cl 1799; South Fd 1774 (*in campo australi de Ouneby* 1270–90, *in australi campo* 1323, *in campo austral'* 1337, one of the open fields of the village, cf. East Fd *supra*); Stock Furlong, Stock Moor 1791 (cf. *super stoc* 13 (c1350), *super stock* 1337 *Estlangstok* 1284, *estlangstoc* 1291, *the East Stock* 1709, *Northlangstok* 1284, *-stock* 1287, a1291, *Stokadale* (sic) c1227, 1281, *Stockadale* 1230–40; *Stocadale* 1261, *Stokedale* 1230–40, 1270–90, 1287, *Stowke dale* 1330–50, *Stokeheuedlande* c1287, *midde stoc* 1230–40, *Middestoc* c1227, it is difficult to determine the etymology of - *stoc, stoke-* etc. which could be **stoc** 'a place' etc., or **stocc, stokkr** 'a tree-stump'; the second el. is presumably **dalr** 'a valley'); Stone Pit Plot 1774 (*Stanpettes* a1290, *Le Middel stanpyttes* a1291, *Stanpittes* 1323, self-explanatory); Sweet hills 1791; Thorp Cl 1791 (*v.* **þorp**); Todd Moor Cl 1799 (*the Tod more* 1709, *The Tod Moor* 1710) (*v.* **toft** 'a messuage, a curtilage'); The Town Fd 1768 (cf. *Towne furlong* l16, 1662, *the Towne furlonge* 1668, *ye Towne furlong* 1690, *ye Town Furlong* 1695, presumably a *furlong* belonging to the town); Wall Cl 1791; the West Close(s) 1774; West Fd 1774, 1768 (*in campo occidentali* 1281, 1291, *west campo de Ouneby* a1291, *in occidentali campo de Ounby* 1337, *the West field* 1695, 1710, one of the open fields of the village, cf. East Fd *supra*); the Wheules (sic) 1828 (cf. *Wervel* 1290, *Whervel* a1291, *Wherll'* 1337, *Wharles* l16, 1695, *Wharles furlong* 1662, 1671, 1690, *the Warles furlong* 1710, from **hwerfel** 'a circle'. The commonest meaning in p.ns. is said to be 'a round-topped hill'); the Willow Leas 1774 (cf. *the Willow Close* 1709).

(b) *aldedike* 1260–80 (*v.* **ald, dík**); *super As* c1227, *Northase* 1284, *Southase* c1227; *birtland* c1330 (c1331) (Dr Insley suggests that this is perhaps 'the shining selion', *v.* **land**, the first el. being from late OE **briht** 'bright' and cf. ON *birti* 'radiance'); *blaclandes* c1227, 1230–40, 1260–90, *blacelandes* c1330 (c1331) (*v.* **blæc, land**); *Blakestretes* c1287, 1337, *blacstretis* c1330 (c1331), *the Black-streetes* 1662, *the Black street Furlong* 1709, *ye north black stretes* 1690 (presumably the reference is to the colour of the road, *v.* **stræt**); *Bracche* 1284 (*v.* **brēc** 'land broken up for cultivation'); *Braclandes* 1230–40; *Brade stane* 1323, *atte brad stan* p1330 (*v,* **brād, stān**); *Breidemere* c1227, *Brethmergate* 1281, *Braithemergate* c1287, *Braithmergate* c1330 (c1331) ('the broad boundary, land on a boundary', *v.* ON **breiðr** 'broad', **(ge)mǣre**, with **gata** 'a road, a way'); *Braken* c1227, 1284, 1323, c1330 (c1331), *Estbraken* 1281, *Estlangbrakkyn* 1270–90, *estlangbraken* 1337 (*v.* **brakni**, the f.n. denotes a place where bracken grows); *Bretlands* 1260–90, 1281 (the reading of the form is a guess); *The Chequers* 1695, *the Chequer Furlong* 1709 (*v.* **cheker** used in f.ns. to denote 'ground of chequered appearance'); *ad ecclesiam* 1225–41, ~ ~ *de Houndeby* 1260–90 both (p); *East Church style* 1603 (*v.* **stigel** 'a stile'); *claypyttes* 1348 (*v.* **clæg, pytt**); *the Common Meare* 1662, *ye Coman Meare* 1679, ~ *Comman mear* 1690 (*v.* **(ge)mǣre** 'a boundary'); *the Cornfield* 1649; *del Croft* c1330 (c1331), *de Croft de Ouneby* 1337, *del Croft* "of" *Ouneby* 1363 all (p) (*v.* **croft** 'a small enclosed field'); *Crosse garthes* 1601, 1614, 1661 (*v.* **cros, garðr** 'a garden, an in-field'); *Dastebriggesike* c1227, *Dastbrig* 13 (c1350), *Drachtbriggesike* c1287 (the first el. is obscure); *drakehou* (sic) c1330 (c1331), *drackhole* l16, *drakeholes* 1690 (*v.* **draca** 'a dragon, **hol** 'a hollow'); *drakes clos* 1671; *le Einglandes* (sic) c1330 (c.1331) (*v.* **eng** 'meadow, pasture', **land**); *Estcroft(e)* 1287 (*v.* **ēast, croft**); *Estiby* 1322, 1327, 1332 all (p) (literally '(the place) east in the village', *v.* **ēast, í, bý**, denoting X who lived in the east of the village, a common Danish formation in L, cf. *Northiby infra*); *Estlangetoft* 1281 (*v.* **ēast, lang, toft**); *in campo de Ouneby* 1322, 1382, *in campis de Ounneby* 1347, 1357 (the open fields of the village, *v.* **feld**); *viam que vadit versus Filingham* 13 (c1350) (Fillingham is a neighbouring village); *le Gore* c1287, c1330 (c1331) (*v.* **gāra** 'a gore, a triangular plot of ground'); *le heuidland* c1330 (c1331) (*v.* **hēafod-land** 'the head of a strip of land left for turning the plough'); *the highe streete* 1603 (probably another name for Ermine Street); *lambekotes* a1227, *Lambecotes* 1281, c1287 (self-explanatory, *v.* **lamb, cot**); *ye lanes* 1661); *Langfarlages* (sic) 1284, *langeforlanges* a1290, *lange furlanges* 1291, *long Furlong* 1709, 1710 (self-explanatory); *Langtoftes* 13 (c1350), *Langetoftes* a1291, *Long toft* 1323 ('the long messuage, curtilage', *v.* **lang, toft**); *langtorinmere* c1227, *lanthornmare* a1291, *Long thorne mare* 1323 (*v.* **lang, þorn, (ge)mǣre**); *Linghil'* 13 (c1350), *Linghill'* 1337 (*v.* **lyng** 'ling, heather', **hyll**); *atte Westende de litildale* c1330 (c1331) (self-explanatory, *v.* **lȳtel, dalr**); *the lyne lands* 1662, ~ *Lyne lands* 1668, ~ *Line lands* 1679, 1695 'the selions where flax grows', *v.* **līn, land**); *Marstal* 13 (c1350), *south maristal* c1330 (c1331) (probably derived from an OE **mær(e)stall* 'a pool of stagnant water', *v.* PN L **2**, 133 and 209, ib **4**, 13); *mikeldeiles* c1227, *-dailles* 1260–80, *-dayles* c1287, *Mikeldailes* 1290 (*v.* **mikill, deill**); *le Natlandes* c1330 (c1331) (the first el. is perhaps OE **næt** 'wet, moist' with **land**); *nontoftes* c1227 (*v.* **toft**); *Normanby Furlong* 1709, 1710, *Normanby mare* a1291, ~ *meare* 116 (named from the neighbouring village of Normanby by Spital, *v.* **(ge)mǣre**); *in Northcrofto* a1291 (*v.* **norð, croft**); *in campo boriali* 1323 (one of the open fields of the village, and only found once in the numerous sources searched); *Northiby* 1260–80 (p) (literally '(the place) north in the village', *v.* **norð, í, bȳ**, (p) denoting X who lived in the north of the village, a common Danish formation in north L, cf. *Estiby supra* and *Sutheby infra*); *Northwelle* c1300 (c1331) (*v.* **norð, wella** 'a spring'); *le Oxegang lane* 1649 (*v.* **oxgang** 'a measure of land' of 10–30 acres' extent, an eighth of a ploughland); *tenementa vocata paryslande* 1428 (*v.* **land**, the first el. being ME *parish(e)* 'a parish'); *le pittes* c1287 (*v.* **pytt**); *Potter corner* 1709, 1710 (from the occupational name or surn. *Potter*); *Qitebusc* (sic) c1227 ('the white bush', *v.* **hvítr, hwīt, buskr**); *Retherhudes* 1284 (the first el. is OE **hrēðer** 'an ox, cattle', the second is obscure); *Riskacr* 1281, *Riskeacre* a1290 ('the plot of arable or cultivated land where rushes grow', from **risc** in a Scandinavianised form and **acer**); *Routheker* 1260–80, e14, *Routhker* 1281, *Routheker* a1291, *Rouker* 13 (c1350), *Roker* 1709 ('the red marsh', *v.* **rauðr** probably with **akr** 'a plot of arable land', a Scand compound); *Ryggestik* 1284, *-stygh* a1291 ('the ridge path, narrow road', *v.* **hryggr, stīg** or **stígr**, probably a Scand compound*)*; *the Sandcorner* 1709, 1710; *ye Sand-furlong* 1695, 1710; *scortebuttes* c1227, *scortbuttes* a1291 (*v.* **sceort, butte** 'a strip of land abutting on a boundary', 'a short strip or ridge at right angles to other ridges'); *scortwestlonges* c1227, *-westlanges* 1284, c1287, *-westland* 1323 (*v.* **sceort, west, lang** 'a long strip of land'); *skyppenwelles* 1260–90, *skipenwelles* c1287, *skippenwelles* 1323 (*v.* **scypen** 'a cowshed' in a Scandinavianised form, **wella**); *Southsik* c1330 (c1331), *the South Sike* 1710 (*v.* **sūð, sík**); *Stainlelhirnel* (sic) 1337; *staynwelhyrne* 1260–90, *Stanwelhirn* c1330 (c1331) (*v.* **steinn, stān, wella** with **hyrne** 'an angle, a corner'; the variation between the ON and OE forms is noteworthy); *ye stret furlonge* 116 (*v.* **strǣt**, no doubt referring to Ermine Street); *Suthlangtoftes* 1260–90, (cf. *Langtoftes supra*); *Sutheby* 1382, *Sothyby* 1357 both (p) ((literally '(the place) south in the village', *v.* **sūð, í, bȳ**, denoting X who lives in the north of the village, a common Danish formation in L, cf. *Estiby* and *Northiby supra*); *Sutheng* c1227, a 1290, 1337 (*v.* **sūð, eng** 'meadow, pasture'); *suth sike* 1323 (*v.* **sūð, sík**); *Sweles* c1227, *sweheles* 1230–40 (obscure); *Switebusc* 1230–40 (*v.* **buskr**; the first el. may well be OE, ME **swēte** 'sweet', an adj. also applied to plants); *the Syke furlong* 1695, *the Sike Furlong* 1710 (*v.* **sík**); *Tetheresike* 1323 (the first el. appears to be ME *tether* 'a cord or rope by which a horse or other animal is tied to a fixed post'; the second is **sík**); *Thorward hou* c1330 (c1331) (from the ODan pers.n. *Thorwarth* and **haugr** 'a hill, a mound'; for this pers.n. *v.* Insley SPNN, 431); *Wakewells* c1330 (c1331) (perhaps 'springs where wakes are held', *v.* **wacu, wella**); *watwelles* 13 (c1350) (the first el. is uncertain); *Wellecroft* c1287 (self-explanatory); *Wellefurlanges* a1291, *Wellfurlang* 1337, *-furlong* c1330 (c1331) (as prec.); *versus fontes* c1227, 1290, *Welles* e14, *the wells* 1337; *Westbreithmere* c1227 (cf. *Breidmere supra*); *Westereswelle* 1260–80, *Westerwelle* c1287 ('the western spring', *v.* **wester, wella**); *Westlandes* 116, *West land(s) furlong* 1709 (*v.* **west, land** 'a selion'); *Westlangstretis* c1330 (c1331) (*v.* **west, lang** 'a long strip of land', with **stræt**, probably with reference to Watling Street); *Westmer* eHy3, 1230–40 (*v.* **west, (ge)mære** 'a boundary'); *Wetelande* c1227, c1287 (*v.* **wēt** 'wet', **land**); *Wiles Close* 1710 (from the surn. *Wiles*); *Wrethewelle* c1287, *Wrethwell'* 1337 (Dr Insley suggests that the first el. is probably connected with the ODan verb *wrītha* 'to turn', cf. Danish *Vridebæk* with this first el., for which *v.* J. Kousgård Sørensen, *Danske so- og anavne* 7 (Copenhagen 1989), 252; the second el is **wella** 'a spring'); *Wysebusk* 13 (c1350), *wytbuskes* 1260–90 (the readings appear correct).

Saxby

Sassebi (2x) 1086 DB
Saxsabi, Saxsebi c1115 LS
Saxebia c1155 Dane, *-b'* 1185 Templar, 1212 Fees, *-bi* 1196 ChancR, 1202 Ass, 1205 P, *-by* Hy2 (1291) Ch, 1205 OblR, 1206 Cur, 1220 ib (p), 1236 FF, 1254 ValNor *et passim* to 1488 Cl
Saxby c1279 RRGr, 1303, 1316 FA, 1327 *SR*, 1327 Pat, 1331 Ch, 1332 *SR*, 1334 *AncPet*, 1343 NI, 1375, 1382 Peace, 1402 FA *et passim*

'Saxi's farmstead, village', *v.* **bȳ**, the first el. being the ODan pers.n. *Saxi.* Saxby is identical in meaning with Saxby All Saints (PN L **2**, 254). For full discussion of the pers.n. *Saxi, v.* Insley, SPNN 323–34.

FOLLY WOOD, *Folly Plant*[n] 1828 Bry, the sense of *folly* here is unknown. LOW FM. MANOR HO (local). SANDBECK FM (local). SAXBY CLIFF, cf. *Cliff F*[m] 1828 Bry, *y*[e] *clife close* 1689, *y*[e] *cliffe close* 1697, 1703, 1709, *Cliffe close* 1724, *y*[e] *Cliff Close* 1745 all *Terrier*. VICARAGE (lost), *Vicaridge house* 1689, *y*[e] *Vicaridge* 1703, *the Vicarage* 1724, *y*[e] *Parsonage* 1745 all *Terrier*.

FIELD-NAMES

The undated forms in (a) are 1839 *Tithe Apportionment* (Saxby Parish Records 4/1); 1689, 1697, 1703, 1709, 1724, 1745 *Terrier*.

(a) Bank; Bottoms, ~ Close (*v.* **botm** 'a bottom, a valley bottom'); Bucklands; Bull Plat (*v.* **plat** 'a plot, a small piece of ground'); Low Car(r), Upper Car, Car Lane (*v.* **kjarr** 'brushwood', 'a bog, a marsh overgrown with brushwood'); Church Cl; Common Cl; Cottagers Carr; Cow Car; Cow Pasture; Dimkin Garth (*v.* **garðr** 'an enclosure', the first el. is probably a surn.); Dog Garth; Drain Bank; Forth Car (cf. First Foth PN L **4**, 146–47, where forms in *Forth* are quoted; this is probably a variant of ME *frith* (from OE **fyhrðe**), the likely meaning of which here is 'a park, a woodland meadow', *v.* MED s.v. *frith* (2) or 'a wood, plantation, coppice', 'unused pastureland', *v.* EDD s.v. *frith*); Fox Cover; Frater (sic) (presumably from ME *frater* 'the eating or refreshment room of a monastery; a refectory'; presumably a piece of land dedicated to the upkeep of such; both Barlings Abbey and St Katherine's Priory, Lincoln, held land in Saxby); Garths (*v.* **garðr**); Gatelands (*v.* **gata** 'a way, a path, a road', **land** 'a selion'); Gorse Hill Car (*v.* **kjarr**); Hard Ings (*v.* **heard** 'hard', in the sense 'hard to till', and **eng** 'meadow, pasture'); Hill Side (*the hill side* 1724); Home Cl; Horse Car (*v.* **kjarr**); House Car; Ings (*yᵉ Ings* 1709, 1724, ~ *Ings close* 1689, 1697 (*v.* **eng**); Intake (*v.* **inntak** 'a piece of land taken in or enclosed'); Lares, Lare's Cl (*v.* **leira** 'a clayey place'); Lime Kiln Cl 1850 *TA*; Mill Garth (*v.* **garðr**); Moors, Moor Cl; Narrow Cl; Nooking (from dial. *nooking*, *v.* **nōk**, cf. The Nookings PN L **3**, 144); Nursery; Old Oval, Old Square (presumably from the shape of the fields); Old Street 1813 *Padley* (the reference is to Ermine Street); Paddock; Penny Car(r), ~ Plat (*v.* **kjarr**, **plat**, the reference presumably being to a rent); Plats (*v.* **plat**); Red Ings (*v.* **rēad**, **eng**, referring to the colour of the soil); Saint Foin Piece 1850 *TA* (*v.* **sainfoin**, the leguminous plant, *Onobrychis viciifolia*); Shift Carr, ~ Ings (probably alluding to *shifts* in crop rotation, as discussed s.n. *a shift Acre* in the f.ns. of South Ferriby PN L **2**, 116 and cf. Shift cls in Immimgham f.ns. (a) ib, 169); Sloughts (perhaps from **slōh** 'a mire', with *-t* added as in the fairly common *Clift*); South Car (*v.* **kjarr**); Stack Yard; Stones; Waddingham Plat (this is a distance from Waddingham, so may well be from a local family called *Waddingham*); Were Dyke (probably denoting a dyke with a weir, *v.* **wer**, **dík**); Wolds, ~ Bottom, Wold End, West Wold.

(b) *one close . . . called yᵉ dammes* 1689 (*v.* **damme** 'a dam, a pond'); *redd' grangie sive manerij, per grangia* 1535 VE iv, *Saxby, firma grang'* 1538–39 Dugd vi, ii (this was a **grange** of St Katherine's Priory, Lincoln); *yᵉ east calfe close* 1689; *east field* 1689, *eastfield* 1708 (one of the great fields of the village); *Frysby north side* 1689 (the name of a field bordering on the neighbouring parish of West Firsby); *yᵉ green* 1724 (*v.* **grēne** 'a village green'); *lams close* 1709 (presumably the first el. is the pl. of **lamb**); *yᵉ little Pingle* 1745 (*v.* **pingel** 'a small enclosure'); *a close called . . . little vicaridge* 1703, 1709; *Sheep field* 1709; *Soutiby* 1327 SR, *Sothiby* 1382 Peace both (p) (literally 'south in the village', *v.* **sūð**, **í**, **bȳ**, denoting X who lives in the south of the village, a common ODan formation in L).

Snitterby

SNITTERBY

Esnetrebi (2x) 1086 DB
Snetrebi 1086 DB
Snitrebi c1115 LS
Sniterby 1194 CurP, 1250 Fees, 1275 RH, 1300, 1307 Ipm, 1310 Pat,
   1338 Cl, 1361, 1506 Ipm, *-bi* 1196 ChancR, 1212 Fees, 1212 FF,
   1230–4 RA iv, *Snyterby* 1244, 1250 Fees, 1275 ChronPetro, 1275
   FF, 1276 RH, 1291 Tax, 1294 *Ass*, 1307 Pat *et freq* to 1526 Sub,
   Snytyrby 1404 *AddCh*
Sniteresbi 1219 Ass
Snitereby 1226 FF *Snytterby* 1315 Inqaqd, 1497 *LWB*, 1506 Ipm,
   1561 Pat, *-bie* 1553 ib, *Snitterby* 1506 Ipm, 1610 Speed *et passim*
Snetyrby 1265 Misc, *Sneterby* 1327 *SR*, 1465 Pat, 1490 Ipm, 1541
   Foster, 1549 Pat

Probably an Anglo-Danish formation from the OE unrecorded pers.n.
*Snytra and ODan **bȳ**, hence 'Snytra's farmstead, village', as proposed
by Ekwall (DEPN s.n.), who suggests that this pers.n. is a derivative of
OE *snotor, snytre* 'wise'. The same pers.n. has been adduced also for
Snetterton (Nf) and Snitterton (PN Db 412). The DB forms with initial
prosthetic E- are due to AN influence.

BROWN'S BRIDGE, from the surn. *Brown*. BLACK DYKE, *the* ~ ~ 1770
EnclA. HARLAM HILL, 1824 O, *Harlum hill* 1679, *Harlom Hill* 1700,
Harlem Hill 1706, 1745 all *Terrier*, 1770 *EnclA*, *Harlam Hills* 1767
Stubbs, *Harlham Hill* 1830 Gre. From its situation the second el. would
appear to be **holmr** 'higher ground amidst the marshes', but the meaning
of *Harl-* is uncertain. HILL SIDE FM (local). HOLMES BRIDGE, *super
hulmum de Sniterby* 1212 FF, cf. *the long(e) holmes* 1679, 1700 *Terrier*,
v. **holmr**. MANOR HO. PRIORY FM. SAND FM, 1828 Bry. SNITTERBY
BECK, cf. *Atte Bek'* 1327 *SR*, *atte Bek* 1332 ib both (p), cf. *Beckmore
Close* 1770 *EnclA*, *v.* **bekkr** 'a beck, a stream'. SNITTERBY CARR, *Ker*
1324 Ipm, *Snitterby Carr* 1649 *Survey* (*CC Leases 47*), 1706, 1745
Terrier, 1823 WG, ~ *carrs* 1557 *LCS*, *Carrs* 1770 *EnclA*, *the Carrs* 1843
Waite, cf. *Estcarr, the Westcarre* 1541 *Foster*, *Snitterbie West Carr*
1601 *DCLB*, ~ *West carr* 1614 *ib*, *Snitterby west Carr* 1663 *ib*, *Carr side*
1700 *Terrier*, *the Carr Close* 1770 *EnclA*, *Carr Fleets* 1770 *MiscDon
140* (*v.* **flēot** 'a stream', in the pl.), *Carr F*ᵐ 1828 Bry, *v.* **kjarr**
'brushwood', 'a marsh, especially one overgrown with brushwood'.
SNITTERBY CLIFF FM, *the Cliff* 1770 *EnclA*, *Cliff B*ⁿ 1828 Bry, *the Old*

Street called the Cliff Road 1770 *EnclA* (the reference being to Ermine Street), cf. *Snitterby North Cliff, the South Cliff* 1706 *Terrier, South Cliff* 1745 *ib.* SNITTERBY MOOR (local), cf. *Snitterby North Moors* 1770 *EnclA.* SNITTERBY SANDHAYS, *Sandhays* 1824 O, 1830 Gre. SOUTHMOOR LANE. THORNCROFT FM, *Thorncroft or Tithe F^m* 1828 Bry, *Tithe Farm* 1830 Gre, cf. *the thorne Crofte* 1679 *Terrier, Thorncroft* 1706 *ib*, self-explanatory, *v.* **þorn, croft.**

FIELD-NAMES

Forms dated 1212 are FF; 1314 *KR*; 1327, 1332 *SR*; 1404, 1453 *AddCh*; 1428 ASSR xxix; 1541, 1724, 1798 *Foster*; 1564, 1588, 1601, 1614, 1663 *DCLB*; 1679, 1700, 1706, 1745 *Terrier*; 1702 *Cragg*; 1704 *MiscDep 48*; 1715, 1825, 1843 *Waite*; 1726, 1732, 1749, 1770[1] *MiscDon 140*; 1770[2] *EnclA*; 1808 *Monson*.

(a) Ace Fd 1770[2], Snitterby South Ace 1770[1] (*the South ayse* 1679, *Snitterby Ace* 1700, 1745 *the North, the South Ace* 1706, *the South Ace* 1745; the same name occurs in Waddingham f.ns. (a)); the Cowfold 1770[2]; Crook Cl 1770[2] (1700, *the Crook Close* 1706); Fit Furze 1770[2], Fitt Furze 1798 (the first el. might be ON **fit** 'grassland on the bank of a river' with **fyrs**); Furze Cl 1770[2] (*Furr Close* 1742, cf. the prec.); Green Dyke 1770[2] (self-explanatory); Greyingham Meer 1770[1] (*Greyingham Meere* 1726, 'the boundary with Grayingham (an adjacent parish)', *v.* **(ge)mǣre**); Kelsey Ferry Road 1770[2] (from the parish of South Kelsey, PN L **2**, 36); King's Street 1770[2] (presumably another name for Ermine Street); Lock Carr 1808 (*v.* **kjarr**); the Middle Field 1770[1], 1770[2] ~ ~ field 1843 (*the Middle Field* 1726, one of the open fields of the village); Northing Bottom(s) 1770[1] (*v.* **norð, eng** 'meadow, pasture'); the Raikes 1843 (*v.* **hraca**, dial *rake* 'a rough path'); Snitterby Fd 1770[1], ~ Fields 1798 (the open field of the village); Snitterby Sand Field Road 1770[2] (self-explanatory, cf. Sand Fm *supra*); the South Furze 1798 (cf. Furze Cl *supra*); the Upper Stinting 1770[1] (*Low, the Upper Stinting* 1726, *v.* **stinting** 'a portion of common land set apart for one man's use', as in ModE dialect, cf. *ye stintings* (PN L **2**, 14)); the Stone Pit 1770[2]; Low, Upper Surlands 1770[1] (probably from **sūr** 'sour, coarse' and **land**); Thirty acre Car 1825; White Cross Moors 1770[1] (1726, cf. *ad crucem de Sniterby* 1212 (p)); Wilkinson Carr 1808 (from the surn. *Wilkinson*); Willoughton Gate 1770[1] (*Willerton gaite* 1679, *Willoughton-gate* 1700, *Willoughton Gate* 1726 ('the road to Willoughton (a neighbouring parish)', *v.* **gata**).

(b) *Atterby gate* 1700, 1706 ('the road to Atterby (in Bishop Norton parish)' *v.* **gata**); *Awcock fold* 1704 (from the surn. *Alcock, Awcock* and **fald**); *ad Pontem* 1332 (p) (*v.* **brycg**); *Branston furlong* 1700 (from the surn. *Branston*); *the Bull peece* 1679; *Burnt Arse furlong* 1679 (*v.* **ears** 'a buttock'), *arse* is perhaps used of some topographical feature resembling a buttock which had been cleared by burning); *Chappell garth* 1679 (*v.* **garðr** 'an enclosure'); *the Cerves* 1745 (obscure); *the Common* 1679, *Snitterby Common* 1745; *Cook lease furlong* 1679 (from the surn. *Cook* with **lǣs** 'pasture, meadowland'); *Fitz carr Common* 1702 (cf. Fit Furze *supra, v.* **kjarr**); *a dike called the Fleete* 1601, *the fleet* 1614, *the Fleet* 1663 (*v.* **flēot** 'a stream'; it is referred to as *a dyke* in the text); *furrs leas* 1700 (*v.* **fyrs, lǣs**); *the Gleab* 1726; *attegrene de Snyterby* 1314, *Attegrene* 1327, *atte Grene* 1332 all (p) (*v.* **grēne** 'a village green'); *atte Hall* 1428 (p), *le Haldale* 1463 (*v.* **deill** 'a share, a portion of land', *Hal-* is probably for *Hall*), *the Hall close* 1700; *ye Innecrofts* 1700 ('the inner crofts', *v.* **in**, **croft**); *Lincoln gait furrlong* (sic) 1679, *Lincoln gate* 1706 ('the road to Lincoln', *v.* **gata**); *longfurlong* 1679, *ye long furlong* 1700, *the long four-long* 1706; *the middle fourlong* 1700, *ye middle furlong* 1706; *the miln heades* 1700 (*v.* **myln, hēafod** 'a headland in the common field'); *the muddy wath* 1700 (*v.* **vað** 'a ford'); *the mynster garthe* 1564, ~ *minster garthe* 1588 (*v.* **garðr**); *Nebell hemplande* (sic) 1588 (*Nebell* is probably a surn. from Newball in Stainton by Langworth); *the neither furlong* 1679, ~ *neather furlongs* 1706, *ye Neather Furlongs* 1745; *New Close Common* 1702; *Northal Bottom Furlong* 1726 (probably *Northal* is 'the north hall', *v.* **norð, hall**); *the outgaite* 1679 ('the road leading out of the village', *v.* **ūt, gata**); *Oyllemakergarthe* 1404 (from the ME surn. *Oilmaker* 'a maker of oil', *v.* Fransson 70, with **garðr**; Henry *Candeler* is witness to the charter); *the parsonage meadow* 1715, *parsondike* 1679 (self-explanatory); *Reeds daile* 1679 (from the surn *Reed* with **deill**); *Sike furlong* 1700 (*v.* **sík** 'a ditch, a trench'); *the Sleights* 1706 (*v.* **slétta** 'a smooth, level field'); *Snetterby Dayles* 1541 (*v.* **deill**); *Snitterby South Field* 1700, 1706 (one of the open fields of the village); *South Barf Furlong* 1726, *South Barffe Furlong* 1749 (*Barf* is dial. *barf* (OE **beorg**) 'a long, low ridge or hill', common in North L); *Southiby* 1327 (p) (literally 'south in the village', denoting X who lives in the south of the village, *v.* **súð, í, bȳ**, a Danish formation common in North L); *Tanderhamhyll'* 1541 (obscure); *the upper furlong* 1679, *the upper Furlongs* 1706, *ye Uper Furlongs* 1745 (sic)); *Wandale* 1745 (*v.* **wandale** 'a share of land'); *Wigganes Close* 1700, *Wiggan's Close* 1706, *Wigans Close* 1745 (named from the family of Thomas *Wiggan* 1625); *Wyberdikes* 1702 (named from the ME surn. *Wyberd*, which goes back to the Old Northern French pers.n. *Vuibert*, a name of Germanic (Frankish) origin comparable with OHG *Wipreht*, as Dr Insley points out).

Spridlington

SPRIDLINGTON

Sperlintone 1086 DB, *-tona* 1163 RA i, *-ton'* 1200 Cur, 1202 FF, 1204, 1209 P, 1219 Ass (p)

Sperlinctone 1086 DB, *-tona* 1175–81, 112 Dane, *-ton'* 1218 Ass, 1100 Abbr, 1200 Cur, *-tone* 1210–12 RBE

Sperlingeton' 1201 Cur

Spirlintuna 1146 RA i

Spredelintone 1086 DB, *Spredelyngton'* 1297 CoramR (p), 1327 *SR*, *Spredlyngton'* 1375 Peace, 1428 FA

Spritlingtuna c1115 LS, *-yngton'* 1374 Peace

Spridlinctuna c1115 LS, *-tune* eHy2 Dugd vi, *-ton'* c1200 RA iv, *-tun* 1212 Fees, *Spridlington'* 1185 P, *-tun'* 1210–20 RA iv, *-tona* 1256 *HarlCh*, *-ton'* 1277 RRGr, 1396 Peace, 1440 Fine, 1526 Sub *et passim*, *-yngton* 1331 Ipm, 1336 *FF*, 1343 NI, 1349 Pat, 1355, 1363 BPR, 1372 Ipm *et freq* to 1502 ib, *Sprydlyngton* 1325 FA, 1411 Cl, 1431 FA, 1446 Fine, 1461, 1535 VE iv, 1559 Pat

Spridelingt' 1156 (p1269), *-tona* 1178, 1226 (p1269) *Bard,-ton* 1226 FF, 1254 ValNor, 1263 FF, 1265 Pat 1275 RH, 1288 *Ass*, 1308 Inqaqd, 1316 FA, 1353 Ipm, *Sprydelington* 1260 Cl, *Sprydelyngton* 1291 Tax, 1332 *SR*, 1428 FA, *Spridelyngton* 1303 FA, c1322 *HarlCh*, 1325, 1360, 1374 Pat, 1395 Peace, 1418 *FF Spridlinton* Hy2 Dane, 1249 RRG, *-ynton* c1414 AASR xxix *Sprillington'* 112 RA ii

Ekwall (DEPN s.n) suggests that the first el. is an unrecorded OE pers.n. **Sprytel*. The long list of forms here, however, suggests it is rather an unrecorded OE pers.n. **Sprēotel*, which would be a nickname based on OE *sprēot* 'a pole, a spike, a spear'. The meaning of Spridlington would then be 'the farmstead, the village associated with, called after Sprēotel', from the medial connective particle -**ing**- 'associated with, called after' and OE **tūn**.

ASH HOLT, 1824 O, 1830 Gre, *v.* **holt** 'a wood, a holt, a thicket'. CLIFF LANE (local), 1828 Bry, cf. *ye Cliff* 1688 *LindDep 70, the Longe, the short Cliffe* 1601, *longe clyfe, short clife* 1606, *ye Long Cliffe, ye Short cliff* 1688, *ye Long Cliff* 1706, 1724, 1752 all *Terrier, North Cliffe Drain, South Cliffe* 1774 *EnclA, North Cliffe Drain* 1822 *Terrier*, self-explanatory. FOX COVER (lost), 1822 *Terrier*, 1828 Bry. THE GRANGE (local), *ye graunge* 1688 *LindDep 70*, presumably a late example of **grange**, for which *v.* Blyborough Grange *supra*. LOWER FM, cf. *North-, South Low Field* 1774 *EnclA, Low Field Lane* 1828 ib. MANOR HO, cf. *Manor Farm* 1842 White, and cf. *ye Farm called Pickwell which was ye Mannor house to which ye Lordship has been always annexed* 1688 *LindDep 70*. MILL COTTAGE, cf. "windmill in" *Spridelington* 1263 FF, *a windmill* 1617 *Nevile, the Mill* 1822 *Terrier, Post Wind Corn Mill* 1845 *4BM11*. PADDOCK HO. RECTORY, *the mansion howse or rectorye* 1601, *ye Rectorie* 1606 both *Terrier, Rectory* 1774 *EnclA, the ~* 1822, *the Parsonage* 1662, 1690, 1724, *y^e ~* 1706 all *Terrier, ye parsonage* 1688 *LindDep 70, Parsonage* 1752, *Parsonage House* 1822 both *Terrier*. SPRIDLINGTON GORSE (lost), 1824 O, *Gorse* 1830 Gre. SPRIDLINGTON HALL (local). SPRIDLINGTON HEATH, *ye heath* 1688 *LindDep 70, the Heath* 1822 *Terrier*. SPRIDLINGTON LODGE, 1830 Gre, *~ Lo.* 1828 Bry. SPRIDLINGTON THORNS.

FIELD-NAMES

Forms dated c1200 are RA iv; Hy3 *HarlCh*; 1261 FF; 1275, 1276 RH; 1293 *R*; 1327, 1332 *SR*; 1372 Ipm; 1375, 1398 Peace; 1502 AASR xxiii; 1601, 1606, 1662, 1688, 1696, 1706, 1724, 1752, 1822 *Terrier*; 1615, 1637 *Nevile*; 1774 *EnclA*; 1778 *Lind 70*.

(a) ye Beck 1752, Beck Furlong 1752, Beck Piece 1822 (*the Becke* 1601, *the becke* 1606, *the Becke furlonge* 1662, *Beckfurlong* 1688, y^e *Becke furlong* 1706, y^e *beck furlong* 1724, *v.* **bekkr** 'a beck, a stream'); Bull Middow (sic) 1752 (*bullmedowe* 1601, *bullmedow* 1606, *the bull meadow* 1662); Capwillows 1752 (*Copwillowes* 1662, *Capwilloes* 1688, *Capwillowes* 1696, *Cap Willowes* 1706, *Capwillows* 1724, cf. *Copwilloes furlonge* 1606, probably 'the pollarded willows' *v.* **copped**, **wilig**, 17th century forms in *cop-* (**copped**) are common in names with **þorn** as second el.); Chamberlain House 1822 (named from the family of John *Chamberlain*, mentioned in the same document); Claydales 1752 (*claydales* 1601, *Claydales* 1688, *claydales* 1696, *Claydales* 1706, *Cladales* 1706, 1724, *v.* **clæg, deill** 'a share of land'); y^e *Clays* 1762 (y^e *Clay* (sic) 1688, *the Clayes* 1696, y^e *Clays* 1724, from **clæg**, denoting clayey place(s)); the Common Houses 1758 *Td'E* (this document records an annual gift *to be laid out in Bread and distributed to and among the Poor which now do and hereafter shall live in the Common Houses in Spridlington*); Coney Gate Bush 1752 (*Coney gate bush* 1724, *Coney garth bush* (sic) 1688, the earliest form being from **coni** 'a rabbit' and **garðr** 'an enclosure', the latter being replaced by **gata** 'a road'); Cottage Plot 1774; Cow Cl 1822; Cowgates 1752 (1662, 1688, 1706, *Cowgate bush* 1724, the second el. being dial. **gate** (ON **gata**) 'pasturage, or the right of pasturage for an animal' in this case cows); Dam Hill 1774 (*v.* ME **damme** 'a dam, a pond'); East Firsby Rd 1774 (self-explanatory, cf. *fursby mere* 1601, *Firsbie Meere* 1662, *Furzbey Meere* 1706, *- meer* 1724 (*v.* (**ge**)**mǣre** 'a boundary'), *Fursby hedge* 1606, *Firsbie hedge* 1662, *firsby hedge* 1688, *Firsby hedge* 1724 (*v.* **hecg** 'a hedge'), *firsby weather gate* 1688 (cf. Cowgates *supra*, in this case it is 'pasturage, or right of pasturage for wethers (OE **weðer** 'a wether, a castrated ram')); Faldingworth Rd 1774 (self-explanatory); Hackthorne Rd 1774 (self-explanatory, cf. *Hack . . orne feeld* (sic) 1601, *Hackthorne feild* 1606, *v.* **feld**); Hanworth Meer 1774 (*Hanworth mere furlong* 1601, *~ meere* 1662, *~ meer* 1688, *~ Meir* 1696, *Hanworthmeir* 1724, *v.* (**ge**)**mǣre**); high gate 1752, High Gate 1774 (*highgate* 1696, *Highgate* 1706, 1724, presumably a reference to Ermine Street); Home Cl 1822; Short Honey Holes 1752, Honey holes 1822 (*hony hole* 1601, *short hony hole* 1606, *Short honieholes* 1662, *Long, Short Honie Holes* 1688, *short Hony holes* 1706, *short honey holes* 1724, a complimentary name for good land); Horse Cl, ~ Pasture 1822; ye Long, Short House 1751, 1822 (*longe how* 1606, *The Longe Howe Furlonge, The short howe forlonge* 1601, *longe how* 1606, *longe howse* 1662, *long howes* 1706, *longe Howze* 1724, *Long, Short House* 1688; most of the forms are from the pl. of **haugr** 'a hill, a mound'); (the) Ings 1774, 1822 (*v.* **eng** 'meadow, pasture'); Kirking head 1752 (*the kirk inge* 1601, *Kirken head* 1724, 'the meadow, pasture belonging to the church', *v.* **kirkja, eng**, with **hēafod** 'a headland in the common field'. It is also recorded as *Girkin head* 1688, *Girking head* 1696); Lambcoats 1752 (*the lamcotes furlong* 1606, *North, South Lamcoats* 1662, *Lamcoates* 1706, *north Lam Cotes* 1724, 'the sheds for lambs', *v.* **lamb**. **cot**); Short Longdales 1752 (*short longe dales* 1662, *Long dales* 1688, *short Longdale* 1706, 'the long shares of land', *v.* **lang, deill**); Low Yd 1822; Middle Cl 1822 (y^e *Middle close* 1688); ye Middle Furlong 1752 (*the midlefurlonge* 1662, y^e *midle furlong* 1706, 1724); Moor Btm 1822 (*the more hedge* 1601, cf. y^e *Easter more* 1706 y^e *easter more* 1724 (*v.* **ēasterra** 'more easterly')); North Dale 1752, 1822 (*the north dale furlonge* 1606, *the North Dale* 1662, *the Northdale* 1688, y^e *north dale* 1724, *v.* **norð, deill**); North East Fd 1752 (*the north east feeld* 1601, *the north east feilde* 1606, y^e *north east field* 1688, 1724, y^e *North East field* 1706, one of the open fields of the village); Oldfield Gate 1774 (*the grange called Oudfeild* 1606, named from the family of John *Oudfeild*, mentioned in the document); Old Street Road 1774 (a reference to Ermine Street, cf. high gate *supra*); Oxpasture 1774, ~ or Cow Cl 1822 (*the oxpasture* 1662, *ye Ox pasture* 1688, *Oxpasture bushes* 1706, *ye oxe pasture* 1724, self-explanatory, cf. Cow Cl *supra*); Orchard 1822; Oxfold 1774 (self-explanatory, *v.* **fald**); Paddock 1822; Padmoor 1752 (*padmore* 1601, 1606, 1724, *Padmoore* 1662, *Padmore* 1688, 1696, 1706, 'the marsh infested by toads', *v.* **padde, mōr**); Pickwell (dale) 1752 (*Pickwell Dale* 1696, ~ *dale* 1706, *pickwell (dale)* 1724 and *v.* Manor Ho *supra*); Rye Barf 1774, 1822 (*ye Rye Barfe* 1688, *v.* **ryge**, and dial. *barf* (OE **beorg**) 'a long, low ridge or hill', cf. Short Wheat Barf *infra*); Sandgate 1752 (*ye Sand gates* 1688, *Sandgate* 1724, *v.* **sand, gata**); Sand Hill Cl 1822; the Sands 1778; Shortling Lane 1752; Smith's Farm 1752 (*Smyth Farm* 1696, *Smith Farm* 1724, named from the *Smith* family, cf. William *Smith* 1642 LPR); South Cl 1822; South Dikes 1752 (*Suthdic* c1200, *Sowth dykes furlonge* 1601, *Sowthdyckes* 1606, *Southdikes* 1662, *South Dykes* 1688, *South dikes* 1706, *South dikes* 1724, *v.* **sūð, dīk**); South East Fd 1752 (*the south east feeld* 1601, *the sowth east feild* 1606, *the South east fields* 1662, *ye South East Fielde* 1706, *ye south east field* 1724, one of the great fields of the village); South Ings 1774 (*the Southings* 1688, *v.* **sūð, eng**); Stone Pitts 1774, Stone pit Cl 1822; Sykes Cl 1822 (*the sykes* 1601, ~ *sikes* 1662, *ye Syke* 1688, ~ *Sike* 1724, *v.* **sík** 'a ditch'); Townend Cl 1822 (*ye Townend* 1688, *ye town end* 1724); Town Street 1774; Water furrows 1752 (*Water Furowes Furlonge* 1601, *Water forwes* 1606, *Water furrows* 1688, *Water Furrowes* 1706, *water furrows* 1724, 'the wet furrows', *v.* **wæter, furh** in the pl.); West Cl 1774, 1822 (*ye west close* 1688, ~ ~ ~ *end* 1706, 1724); *y^e* Westermor 1752 (*ye wester more* 1724 (*v.* **westerra** 'more westerly', **mōr**, cf. *ye easter more, supra*); West Hall 1752 (*farm called Westhall* 1615, *West Hall* 1637, 1662, 1696, 1706, 1724, self-explanatory); West Moor 1822 (cf. *y^e* Westermor *supra*); Short Wheat Barf 1752 (*the Longe Wheat barfe, short wheat barfe* 1601, *Longe, Short wheat barfe furlonge* 1606, *the long wheat barfe, short wheate barfe* 1662, *ye Longe, short wheat barfe* 1688, *the Wheat barfe* 1696, *Wheat Barf* 1724 (*v.* **hwæte** 'wheat', and dial. *barf* (OE **beorg**) 'a long, low ridge or hill', cf. Rye Barf *supra*).

(b) *Aslike acres* 1601, *aslicacres* 1606, *Aslickacres* 1688, *Asley acres* 1724 (*v.* **æcer**; Dr Insley notes that if this name is ancient, the first el. may well be the ON pers.n. *Ásleikr*); *Brunstig* c1200 (from the OE pers.n. *Brūn* or ODan *Brun* with either OE **stīg** or ON **stígr** 'a path, a narrow road'); *ye barfe* 1688 (for *barfe, v.* Rye Barf and Short Wheat Barf *supra*); *ye Bush* 1688, 1706, 1724, *ye great Bush* 1688, *the Bush Meadow* 1696, *ye Bush meadow* 1724; *furlonge called betweene the sykes* 1606, *The Furlong betweene the Sikes* 1696, *ye furlong between Sikes* 1706, ~ ~ *between sikes* 1724 (*v.* **sík**); *ye Church Leas* 1606 (*v.* **lea** (OE **lēah**) 'a meadow, an open pasture', belonging to the *church*); *The Cloase gate* 1696 (*v.* **gata**); *clouenhou* Hy3 ('the cloven mound' from OE **clofen** 'cloven, split' and **haugr** 'a mound', denoting a mound with a notch); *ye Commons* 1724; *the common streete* 1601; *the cowpasture* 1662, ~ *Cowpasture* 1688; *del Dale* (p) 1322 (*v.* **dalr** 'a valley'); *Deile* c1200 (*v.* **deill** 'a share or portion of land', an early example of a word common in L); *The Dike greene furlong* 1601, *Dike greene furlong* 1606, *Dikgreene* 1662, *ye dyke green* 1688, *Dike Greene* 1696, *Dike Green* 1706, *Dike green* 1724 (*v.* **dīk** 'a ditch', **grēne** 'a grassy place'); *the east fields* 1662 (one of the open fields of the village); *ye east firrs* 1688 (*v.* **fyrs** 'furze'); *atte Elme* 1332 (p) (*v.* **elm** 'an elm-tree'); *Endecroft* 1372 (perhaps 'the croft frequented by ducks', *v.* **ened, croft**); *ye fallow field* 1688; *Fenn Leas* 1688 (*v.* **fenn** and cf. *ye Church Leas supra*); *in campo de Spridelington* 1293, *in campis de Spridlynton* 1375 (the open fields of the village, *v.* **feld**); *Gosdales* *furlonge* 1601, *gosdale* 1606, *Goosedales* 1688 (*v.* **gōs** 'a goose', **deill**); *the great sike* 1601 (*v.* **sík**); *Haver Lands* 1688 ('the selions where oats are grown', *v.* **hafri, land**); *Haydales* 1688 (*v.* **hēg, deill**); *the hedge* 1601; *the hill* 1662, *y* *Hill* 1688, 1706, *y* *hill* 1724; *the top of the Hill* 1696, *y* *Top of y* *Hill* 1706, *y* *Hill top* 1706, *y* *hill top* 1724; *Atte Holme* 1327 (*v.* **holmr** 'raised drier land amidst the marsh'); *the knoles* 1601, (*v.* **cnoll** 'a knoll, a hillock'); *y* *Lidgate* 1688 (*v.* **hlid-geat** 'a swing-gate'); *Lyly Garths* 1688 (*v.* **garðr**); *Lingeyll* (sic) 1606, *Linge Hill* 1688 (*v.* **lyng** 'ling, heather', **hyll**); *Lin Land* c1200 (*v.* **līn** 'flax', **land** 'a selion'); *the Litle close* 1601; *the Litle more* 1601, *y* *little more* 1606; *the long more* 1601, 1606, *the longe moore* 1662, *the Long Moor* 1688, *y* *long moore* 1724 (cf. Moor Btm in (a) *supra*); *Macamathehou* (sic), *Mornmatehou* (sic) Hy3 (Dr Insley points out that the meaning of this name is 'the heathen mound', *v.* **haugr**, the first el. being a corrupt ME form of the name of the prophet Mohammed, for which *v.* MED, s.v. *Makomete*, also used to denote a pagan god or an idol); *Maws farme* 1696 (from the surn. *Maw*); *mylegaitte* 1606; *Neviles great farme* 1662, *Mr Nevills house* 1696, *Mr Nevils house* 1706 (named from the family of George *Nevile* 1642 LPR); *y* *North head land, the south headland* 1688 (*v.* **hēafod-land** 'the head of a strip of land left for turning the plough'); *the north Inges* 1606, *y* *Northings* 1688 (*v.* **norð, eng** 'meadow, pasture', cf. South Ings in (a) *supra*; *the northe west feild* 1601, *the north west fielde* 1606, *the north west fielde* 1662, *y* *North Westfield* 1688, *y* *north west field* 1706, 1724 (one of the open fields of the village); *the Old Garth* 1688 (*v.* **garðr**); *y* *parsonage headland* 1688, *y* *parsons headland* 1724 (*v.* **hēafod-land**); *pease close nooke* 1606, *the Pease Close* 1688 (*v.* **pise** 'pease'); *Plekwell* 1662 (*v.* **wella** 'a spring', the first el. being ME **plek** 'a small plot of gound'); *Pott pitte furlong* 1688 (*v.* **potte** 'a deep hole', **pytt**); *y* *ratte pittes* 1606 (self-explanatory); *Red Jerthe* c.1200 (*v.* **rēad, eorðe** 'earth, soil', a reference to the colour of the soil); *y* *sand pits* 1688; *shawe fold nooke* 1601, *Shawforth nooke* 1688; "the manor called" *South parisshe* 1372, "manor of" *Spridlyngton* "called" *Sowth Maner* 1502; *the South west feild* 1601, *the Sowth-west feilde* 1606, *the South west fields* 1662, *y* *Southwest field* 1688, *The south west field* 1724 (one of the open fields of the village); *Staingraue* c1200, *Stangraves* 1696, *Standgraves* 1724 (*v.* **stān, steinn** 'a stone', **græf** 'a digging, a pit, trench'); *y* *Stangate* 1706 (*v,* **stān, gata**, probably a reference to Ermine Street); *The stigheg* (sic) 1601, *the stigh* 1662, *y* *styghs* 1688, *the north stighes, the sowth styghtes* 1606 (*v.* **stīg** 'a path, a narrow road', in the pl.); *y* *stiles* 1706 (*v.* **stigel** 'a stile'); *stony hill* 1688 (self-explanatory); *Thorthing Lane* (sic) 1696 (the form is too late to suggest a convincing etymology); *Twifald Fure* c1200 (from OE **twifald** 'twofold, double', **furh** 'a furrow'); *the upper headlands* 1662, *The Upper headland* 1688 (*v.* **hēafod-land**); *war' in Spridelington* 1275, *warrenam in Spridelington* 1276 (*v.* **wareine** 'a rabbit warren'); *Westfeld* 1263, *the west fields* 1662, ~ *West field* 1688 (one of the great fields of the village); *Wilsons farm* 1615, 1637, *Wilson's farme* 1688, *Wilsons Farme* 1696 (named from the family of Ann *Wilson* 1688).

Willoughton

WILLOUGHTON

Wilchetone (2x) 1086, *Wilketon'*, *Wilcketum'* 1185 Templar
    Wilgatuna c1115 LS, 1317 Pat, *Wilgeton'*, *Wilegeton'* 1219 Ass
    Wyllegeton 1276 RH
Willeton' 1178 P, *-tona* 1179 ib
Wilweton' Hy2 (c1331) *Spald i*, 1254 ValNor, *Wyleweton* 1240 FF,
    Wyleweton 1294 Pat
Wiluton 1296 *Ass*, 1312 Pat
Wilghetone 1199 (1330) Ch, *-ton'* 1200 ChR, 1217–19 RA vii,
    1242–43 Fees, *Wylgheton'* 1242–43 Fees, 1272 *Ass*, *Wilegheton*
    c1221 Welles, *Wileghton* 1313 Fine, *Wylghton* 1291 Tax, 1324
    Cl, 1409, 1414 Pat, *Wilghton'* 1298 Ass, 1324 *Extent*, *-ton* 1327
    Cl, 1369 Orig, 1386 Fine, 1389 Pat
Wylgton' 1291 RSu, *-ton* 1346 ib
Wylughton 1313 Fine, 113 Cl, 1314 Pat, 1316 FA, 1322 Orig, 1322
    Fine, 1323 Inqaqd, 1324 Misc *et freq* to 1445 Pap, *Wilughton*
    1327 Pat, 1343 NI, 1362 Cl, 1407 Pat, 1415 Pap, *Willughton* 1428
    FA, 1453 Pat, 1434 Dugd vi, 1453 *Tat*, *Wiluhton'* 1322 *HarlCh*
Wiloughton 1396 Pat, 1431 FA, *Wyloughton* 1440 Pat, *Willoughton*
    1503 *LCCA*, 1530–32 *MinAcct*, 1535 VE iv, 1545 Pat *et freq*, (~
    alias Willerton) 1723 SDL, *Wylloughton* 1535 VE iv, 1548, 1562
    Pat, *Willoghton* 1440 ib
Willuton' 1477 Pap
Willowghton 1551 Pat, *Willowghtonne* 1582 *DCLB*
Wyllyton 1519 DV i, 1576 Saxton, 1610 Speed
Willerton 1526 Sub, 1542 *AOMB 214*, 1547 Ormsby, 1549 Pat,
    ("alias" *Willoughton*) 1554 ib, 1576 LNQ iii, 1594 SP iii, 1609
    WillsStow
Wilington R1, 1200 both (c1331) *Spald i*, *Willingthon* 1233 Welles,
    1442 Pap, *Willyngton* 1545, 1562 Pat, *Willington* "alias"
    Willoughton "alias" *Wallorton* (sic) 1572 ib

'The farmstead, village where willows grow', *v.* **wilig, tūn**. The
forms in *Wilington* etc. may indicate an alternative form of the name
which has given Willington (PN Bd 99 and PN Db 513), but which,
however, did not survive continuously here.

COPELANDS FM (lost), *Copelands Farmstead* 1828 Bry, from the surn.
Copeland, cf. George *Coupland* 1842 White. GLEBE FM, 1855
EstatePlan (LAO), cf. *Glebe Lands* 1769 *EnclA*. GLOVERS FM (lost),

Glovers F^m 1828 Bry, from the surn *Glover*, cf. John *Glover* 1842 White. HILLS FM, *Hills Fm* 1828 Bry, perhaps from the surn. *Hill(s)*, cf. Thomas and William *Hill* 1842 White. HOLLOWGATE HILL, 1855 *EstatePlan*. IVY HO (lost), *Ivy Ho*. 1828 Bry. KENNINGTON FM, *Kenyngton* 1515–18 ECP xxxviii, *Kenning(e)ton* 1589 NCWills, perhaps a transferred name from *Kennington* (PN Sr 23). LONG LANE (local), 1855 *EstatePlan* (LAO). LOW FM, 1855 *ib* (LAO). MOAT, 1855 *EstatePlan* (LAO), a medieval moated site. MONKS GARTH, *ye Mannor of Monk Garth* 1745, *Monk's-Garth Farm* 1762 both *Terrier*, *Monksgarth* 1769 *EnclA*, *Monk Garth* 1828 Bry. THE MOUNT, 1855 *EstatePlan* (LAO). NORTHFIELD LANE, *Northfield road* 1769 *EnclA*, *North-field Road* 1774 *Terrier*, *Northfield Lane* 1822 *ib*, *North Field Lane* 1828 Bry. OLD LEYS, *ye Old Leys* 1762 *Terrier*, *Old Leas* 1824 O, 1830 Gre, *Willoughton Old Leys* 1828 Bry, *v*. **ald** 'old', in the sense long used or formerly used, **lea**, **ley** (OE lēah) 'meadow, open pasture'. PATCHETT'S CLIFF, named from the surn. *Patchett*. RICHARDSON'S FM (lost), *Richardsons Farmstead* 1828 Bry, named from the surn. *Richardson*, cf. John *Richardson* 1842 White. SOUTHFIELD LANE, *the south field road* 1769 *EnclA*, cf. *Southfeld'* 1542 *AOMB 214*, *South Field* 1769 *EnclA*, *Bennet's South Field* 1855 *EstatePlan* (LAO). STONE PITS (lost), 1828 Bry, *Stone Pit* 1855 *EstatePlan* (LAO). TEMPLE GARTH, *ye Mannor of Temple Garth* 1745 *Terrier*, *Temple-Garth Farm* 1762 *EnclA*, cf. *claus' voc' Temple Parke* 1535 VE iv, *temple Woodes al's dict' Saynt Johns wooddes* 1542 *AOMB 214*, *Seynt Joh'ns Wood alias dict' Temples Wood* 1545 Pat, *Templewood* 1550–52 *MinAcct*, 1554 Pat, Temple Fm. 1828 Bry, *v*. **garðr** 'an enclosure', a name commemorating the holdings of the Knights Templars and Knights Hospitallers in the parish, *v*. 1185 Templar. VICARAGE (lost), *the new vicaridge house* 1635, *the Vicaridge* 1671, 1690, *Willerton Vicaridge* 1674, *the Vicaridge house* 1703, *ye vicaridge house* 1724, *Vicaridge House* 1745, *The Vicarage House* 1788, 1822 all *Terrier*. WHITE HART, 1828 Bry. WIDOW DALES (lost), 1828 Bry. WILLOUGHTON CLIFF, *the Cliff* 1769 *EnclA*, cf. *clif pasture*, *Netherclif, Southclif* 1542 *AOMB 214*, *Clyff pasture*, *Netherclyff, Southclyff* 1545 Pat. WILLOUGHTON GRANGE, 1824 O, 1830 Gre, *The Grange* 1828 Bry, a late example of **grange** common in L, cf. Blyborough Grange *supra*. WILLOUGHTON LANE (lost), 1828 Bry. WILLOUGHTON MANOR, cf. *Manor Ho*. 1828 Bry. WILLOUGHTON MILL (lost), 1824 O, 1830 Gre, *Mill, molendino de Wilcketun'* 1185 Templar, *Willoughton Wynd' Myll* 1542 *AOMB 214*, ~ *Wyndemyll* 1546 LP xxi ii.

FIELD-NAMES

Undated forms in (a) are 1855 *EstatePlan* (LAO); forms dated 1272, 1296 are *Ass*; 1327, 1332 *SR*; 1343 NI; 1530–32 *MinAcct*; 1540–42 LDRH; 1542 *AOMB 214*; 1545 LP xx, ii; 1548 *Anc*; 1554, 1566 Pat; 1576 LNQ iii; 1601, 1606, 1635, 1671, 1674, 1690, 1703, 1706, 1724, 1747, 1762, 1774, 1788, 1822, 1662 *Terrier*; 1718 *MiscDep 428*; 1757 LNQ v; 1769 *EnclA*.

(a) bainfurs Wall 1757 (probably from the local surn. *Bain*, with **fyrs** 'furze'); Barn Cl; yᵉ beck 1757 (*Atte Becke* 1327, *atte Becke* 1327, *atte Beck*' 1332 all (p), *v.* **bekkr** 'a beck, a stream'); Bird Cages; Blyburgh Hedge 1774, Blyborough Cl (named from the adjacent parish of Blyborough, *supra*); Big, Bottom Moor; Brick hills or Brickins; Big, Litle Browser; Building Cl; Bull Cl; Calf Cl 1774; Candle Lane 1822, Candles 1822; clapit yatestead 1757 (for Clapit, *v.* **clǣg, pytt**; *yatestead* is probably simply 'the site of a gate'); Clixby's Cl (from the surn. *Clixby*, cf. John *Clixby* 1842 White); Cocked Hat (named from the shape of the field); Codling Cl 1774, Big, Little Codlins (cf. *Codlyn dayll*, ~ *layne* 1601, *great Codlin-dale* 1635 (*v.* **deill** 'a share, a portion of land'), *Codling Close* 1690, *Codlin Close* 1706, perhaps from the ME surn. *Codlin(g)*); College Fd(s) (commemorating the holdings by King's College, Cambridge in the parish); Corn Cl 1822; Cowgate Cl 1774 (a *cowgate*, a common term in L, was the right of pasturage for a single animal, in p.ns. and f.ns. being usually found in the pl.); Cow Pasture (*the Cowpasture* 1718); Dickie May's Fd, Big, Far, Middle Dickie Mays; (the identity of *Dickie May* has not been discovered); Feeding Cl; Foot Pad Cl; Foster's Pasture (from the surn. *Foster*); Fourteen Acres; Fox Cover Cl; Gainsburgh Road 1769, Gainsborough Lane Cl (the road leading to Gainsborough); Garden Cl, ~ Fd; Gear Ings, Little Gear Paddock; Ginny winks or Kitty winks (in a note to the text Mrs Rudkin comments that Ginny winks is the old name, Kitty winks the modern); Green Hills; Hairy Jack's Barn; Hen house Cl; Hillfoots; Hillside Cl 1774, Far, Middle Hillsides; Home Fd; Honey Nookings (from dial. *nooking* 'a nook', *v.* **nōk** and PN Nt 288 s.v.; *honey* is likely to be used as a complimentary nickname for good land); House Cl; Ings Leys 1769, Ing Leys 1855, ye Ingleys yate 1757 (*v.* **eng, ley** (OE **lēah**) 'a meadow, an open pasture', in the pl.); Kirton Road 1769 (the road to Kirton in Lindsey, *v.* **gata**); Lincoln gate 1757 (the road to Lincoln, cf. prec.); Little-Hills 1762; Middle, Top Longmire, Longmire or Well Cl (*v.* **lang, mȳrr** 'a mire'); the low road 1864, Low Passage; Low Moor; Mangold Cl ('land on which mangel-wurzels are grown', *v.* Field 133); the Middle Fd 1769; Middleton Cl (no doubt from the surn. *Middleton*, cf. Joseph *Middleton* 1842 White); the Moor Cl; the Moor Meadow 1769; New Pasture; New Road Fd; Norbeck 1774, Norbecks (*v.* **norð, bekkr**); Nuddall (*a certain pasture called*) 1769, Lower, Top Nuddle or Church Cl (cf. *Church Close* 1576; *Nuddall* may be from **nīwe** 'new' and **deill**); Oxdale (*Oxdale* 1542, *v.* **oxa, deill**); Park (cf. *Park Lane* 1576); pingles 1769 (*v.* **pingel** 'a small enclosure'); Pump Fd; Ramper Fds (from dial. *ramper* 'a raised road or way, the highway', *v.* EDD s.v. *ramper*); Red Gate; Rose Cottage; Sain foin (*v.* **sainfoin**, the leguminous plant, *Onobrychis vicufolia*); Sallow Holt (*v.* **salh** 'a willow, a sallow', **holt** 'a holt, a wood, a thicket'); Sornthrop (sic) (the first el. is obscure, the second is **þorp**); Spring; Stackyard Fd; Stone Bridge Fd; the Street road (the reference is to Ermine Street); Strawson's Cl or Long Cl, Strawson's Hill or Stable Fd (from the surn. *Strawson*); Swarth Lands 1769 (*v.*

sweart, svartr 'black, dark', **land** 'a selion'); Town End; Vicarage Cl 1762; Little Warren or Warren Bottom (cf. *unam Cunicular' in Willerton* 1542); Wash Dyke Fd (*v.* **wæsce, dík**); Bottom, Top West Leys (for *leys v.* Inge Leys *supra*); Willow Dale; Willow Holt Fd; Wood Cl.

(b) *Cawden* 1542; *atte chrche* (sic) 1296, *ad Ecclesiam* 1327, *ad ecclesiam* 1332, 1343 (cf. Church Close *supra* in (a)); "capital messuage called" *le Comaundry* 1566 (*v.* **commandery, commandry** NED s.v. 2, 'A landed estate or manor . . . belonging to an order of Knights', in this case the Knights of St John of Jerusalem); *Attecote* 1327 (p) (*v.* **cot** 'a cottage, a shelter, a hut'); *lez Cottelles Furlong* 1548; *lez dailes* 1545 (*v.* **deill** in the pl.); *the field of Willoughton* 1718 (the open field of the village); *Furbell dale quarter* 1542 (obscure); *les Fyrres* 1546 (*v.* **fyrs** as elsewhere in the parish); *atte Grene* 1332 (p) (*v.* **grēne** 'a village green'); *Griffyng* 1542 (the first el. is perhaps **gryfja** 'a hole, a pit', dial. *griff* 'a small deep valley, the second is **eng**); *the Hall Farme* 1703; *Horsedale* 1542 (*v.* **hors, dalr** or **deill**, the situation of the field is not known); *le Intak* 1542 (a comparatively early example of **inntak** 'a piece of land taken in or enclosed'); *Will' Kitchin Cl* 1706; *lawfeld'* 1542 (almost certainly for *lowfeld*); *pasture'. . . vocat'* . . . *Madge of the More* 1542 (no similar name appears to have been noted so far in the EPNS survey); *the Mancyent house* 1601 (a reference to the Vicarage House and a spelling for *mansion* not recorded in NED); *parrocke close* 1530–32, *Parrokes* 1540–42 (*v.* **pearroc** 'a fence enclosing a piece of ground', later 'a small enclosure'); *Poke Close* 1554 (perhaps 'the goblin infested enclosure', *v.* **pūca, clos(e)**); *Samuel Robinsons Close* 1690; *le Shepcote* 1542 (*v.* **shep-cote**); *Stonebregeles* 1542 (the form is late and on its own, but the second el. may be an OE ***bærgels** 'a burial place, a tumulus', the first is **stān** 'a stone'; though substantial amounts of Romano-British and AS pottery have been dicovered in Willoughton, there does not seem to be any record of a tumulus in the parish); *ad Fontem* 1272 (p) (*v.* **wella** 'a spring'); *Westiby* 1327, *Westyby* 1332 both (p) (literally 'west in the village', *v.* **west, vestr, í, bȳ**, denoting X who lives in the west of the village, a common Danish formation).

INDEX

This index is based on the following principles:
- (a) It includes all the place-names in the body of the work.
- (b) It covers only the main reference to each place and no cross-references have been noted.
- (c) Street-names are included.
- (d) "Lost" names are printed in italics.
- (e) In grouping names no distinction has been made between those written in one word or two.
- (f) Only very few field-names (of special interest) have been included.

217

Beck Lane	179	Brandy Wharf	111
Beck Wood	149	Brank Well	23
Beech Wood	149	Brat Hill	19
Bell Inn	157	*Brattons Fm*	167
Belle Vue Fm	81	Brickhills Fm	30
Besson Lane	184	Brick Kiln Holt	176
Bidall Marford	99	Brickyard Cottages	157
Big Wood	164	Brickyard Ho	179
Billim Lane	81	Bridge Fm	30
Billyards Fm	176	Briggate Fm	81
Birdhouse Clough	14	Breakwater Fm	125
Bishopbridge	157	*Broadbents*	149
Bishop Norton	193	*Broadham Cover*	30
Bishopthorpe	119	Broomfield Plantation	30
Black Bank Fm	81	Broom Hill	14
Black Dike	111	Broom Plantation	81
Black Dyke	205	Broughton	27
Black Gravel Plantation	56	Broughton Carrs	30
Black Head Ponds	76	Broughton Common	30
Black Hoe Plantation	77	Broughton Decoy Fm	30
Black Kiln Plantation	167	Broughton Bridge	30
Blackland	149	Broughton Grange	30
Blackthorn Hill	142	Broughton School Houses	30
Blackthorn Hills	167	Broughton Vale	30
Black Walk Nook	79	*Broughton Wood*	30
Bleaching Ho	30	*Broyl, del*	55
Bleach Yard	81	Brown's Bridge	205
Blind Lane	81	Brumby	37
Blowthorne Sitwate	30	Brumby Common East	37
Bleak Ho	125	Brumby Common West	37
Blyborough	134	Brumby Grange	37
Blyborough Covert	134	Brumby Grove	37
Blyborough Grange	134	Brumby Hall	37
Blyborough Hall	134	*Brumby Lane*	38
Blyborough Mill	134	*Brumby Warren*	38
Blythe Close	164	Brumby Wood	38
Boat Ho	167	Bullwood Holt	45
Bog Plantation	77	Bunker's Hill	179
Booth House Fm	125	Burbage, High	122
Booth Nooking Lane	122	Burbage, Low	122
Bottesford	22	Burgess Hall	38
Bottesford Beck	23	Burnt Slip	14
Bottesford Moor	23	*Butterwelles*	170
Bottle and Glass	188	Butterwick, East	49
Bottom Walk	194	Butterwick Common	49
Bow and Arrow Wood	77	Butterwick Hale	49
Bowers Wood	77	Butterwick Hall	49
Bracken Hill	30	Buttonhook, The	95
Brackenholmes	95	Burringham	40
Bracken's Lane	194	*Burringham Common*	40
Bracken's Wood	157	*Burringham Ferry*	40